CISTERCIAN STUDIES SERIES: NUMBER ONE HUNDRED-SIXTY

The Joy of Learning and the Love of God

Studies in Honor of Jean Leclercq

CISTERCIAN STUDIES SERIES: NUMBER ONE HUNDRED-SIXTY

The Joy of Learning and the Love of God

Studies in Honor of Jean Leclercq

edited by E. Rozanne Elder

Cistercian Publications
Kalamazoo, Michigan – Spencer, Massachusetts

© Cistercian Publications Inc., 1995
The work of Cistercian Publications is made possible in part
by support from Western Michigan University to
The Institute of Cistercian Studies

1001077338

Library of Congress Cataloguing in Publication Data

The joy of learning and the love of God : studies in honor of Jean Leclercq / edited by E. Rozanne Elder.
p. cm. — (Cistercian studies series : no. 160)
Includes bibliographical references.
ISBN 0-87907-560-0 (alk. paper)
1. Monasticism and religious orders—History—Middle Ages, 600–1500. 2. Monasticism and religious orders—Europe—History. 3. Europe—Church history—600–1500. 4. Spirituality—Catholic Church—History. 5. Catholic Church—Doctrines—History. I. Leclercq, Jean, 1911– . II. Elder, E. Rozanne (Ellen Rozanne), 1940– . III. Series.
BX2590.J69 1995
270—dc20 95-41678
CIP

Jean Leclercq

1910–1993

. . . cum perveneris quo nos praevenis . . .
nullatenus putes quod tua dulcis memoria recedat a nostra,
etsi praesentia dolentibus subtrahatur.

Contents

Preface xi
Frequently Used Abbreviations xiii

In memoriam Jean Leclercq.
Remarks Delivered at the Twenth-Eighth International Medieval Congress, Kalamazoo, Michigan, 7 May 1994 1
by Bernard McGinn

From λόγος to *verbum*: John Cassian's Use of Greek in the Development of a Latin Monastic Vocabulary 5
by Columba Stewart OSB

Late Ninth-Century Saints: Hathumoda and Luitberga 33
by Suzanne F. Wemple

Saint Otmar, Model Benedictine 49
by Hugh Feiss OSB

Peter Damian Against the Reformers 67
by Phyllis Jestice

The Abyss of Love: The Language of Mystical Union among Medieval Women 95
by Bernard McGinn

Cistercian Nuns and the Development of the Order: The Cistercian Abbey at Saint-Antoine-des-Champs Outside Paris 121
by Constance Berman

As Above, So Below: Architecture and Archaeology at Villiers-la-Grange of Pontigny. 157
by Terryl N. Kinder

A Sixteenth century Heraldic Stained Glass Panel from La Maigrauge 179
by Helen Zakin

Affectus Confessus Sum, et non Negavi: Reflections on the Expression of Affects in the 26th Sermon on the Song of Songs of Bernard of Clairvaux 187
by Dorette Sabersky

Jean Leclercq's Attitude toward War 217
by Eoin de Bhalthraite, OCSO

Bernard of Clairvaux on the Truth Accessible Through Faith. 239
by John R. Sommerfeldt

Aelred of Rievaulx and Isaiah 253
by Thomas Renna

Aimery of Limoges, Patriarch of Antioch: Ecumenist, Scholar, and Patron of Hermits 269
by Bernard Hamilton

'In Their Mother Tongue': A Brief History of the English Translation of Works by and attributed to Saint Bernard of Clairvaux: 1496–1970 291
by David N. Bell

What We Are Not Supposed to Know 309
by G. R. Evans

The Light Imagery of Saint Bernard's Spirituality and Its Evidence in Cistercian Architecture (being revised) 327
by Emero Stiegman

Who Founded the Order of Cîteaux 389
by Brian Patrick McGuire

A Bibliography of the Works of Jean Leclercq 415
compiled by Michael Martin

List of Contributors 499

Preface

JUST AFTER Father Jean Leclercq died, on 27 October 1993, a last article by him appeared in *Studia Monastica*. Its title, 'Mourire et sourire dans la tradition monastique'[1] provides a fitting motto for the monk-scholar who reinserted monastic theology into the scholarly world through an impressive series of books and articles, who carried delight in the monastic vocation to communities around the world, and who ended his elliptical but always prompt correspondence with the single wish 'joy!'.

The affiliations and the span in professional ages of the contributors to this *Festschrift* testify to Father Jean's influence on the anglophone worlds of cloister and classroom. Had we invited papers in others languages, the debt of an entire generation of monastic scholars would be even more strikingly apparent.

Among many rich Jean Leclercq memories, we at Kalamazoo cherish the interest he took in our academic program and our annual medieval studies congress. Already a legendary figure in medieval monastic studies, Father Leclercq first attended the Congress in 1971. He 'dropped in', he explained to startled organizers, because he was in the neighborhood, travelling from Tokyo to Buenos Aires. Senior scholars already acquainted with him assured awed junior scholars of his approachability. Young scholars fortunate enough to persuade someone to introduce them or bold enough to introduce themselves, not only discovered how genuine an interest he took in their nascent studies but usually later received an offprint of some article germane to their research.

The next year Father Leclercq returned to read a paper, modestly taking a place in one the Institute of Cistercian Studies sessions. When the swelling throng made it apparent that the room would never contain the number of those eager to hear him, he affably lead a parade of medievalists through the corridors—hand raised like a tour guide—until he found an empty room capacious enough to contain the crowd. 'Be free!', he gently admonished harried organizers with furrowed brows and frantic schedules. In addition to becoming a frequent congress participant, he twice accepted invitations to Kalamazoo to be scholar-in-residence at intensive workshops on western christian spirituality. There he lived in the dormitory with students, hiked to the cafeteria for meals, and struck up countless conversations with undergraduates happily innocent of his importance in the world of medieval scholarship, or, in fact, of medieval studies or monasticism at all. The insights he brought to discussions of the various medieval writers under study illuminated their theological works and brought their personalities vividly to life. Often he remarked on how eager he was someday, soon, he already hoped, to meet Saint Bernard and ask him just a few questions on some obscure point or other.

Now we can be sure he is taking full advantage of his opportunity. With a passage, not by his beloved Bernard, but by his spiritual son, Isaac of Stella, Father Leclercq closed his article on Dying and Smiling in the Monastic Tradition. It echoes advice he gave, implicitly or explicitly, to the many monks, nuns, scholars, and students whom he met and influenced during his long and active life:

> Let God's Son grow ever greater in each of you, brothers. He has indeed been formed in you, but he must grow infinite in you if your laughter, gladness, and joy are to be so full that nobody can take it away from you.[2]

ERE

NOTES

1. *Studia Monastica* 35 (1993) 55-67.

2. Isaac of Stella, Sermon 7.16 (translation by Hugh McCaffery OCSO, CF 11:61–62).

Abbreviations

Adm	*Sugerii abbatis Sancti Dionysii liber de rebus in administratione sua gestis*
ASOC	*Analecta Sacri Ordinis Cisterciensis = Analecta Cistenciensia*
Bapt	Bernard of Clairvaux, *Epistola de baptismo*
CC	Corpus Christianorum series
CCCM	Corpus Christianorum Continuatio Medievalis
CCSL	Corpus Christianorum Series Latina
CF	Cistercian Fathers series
Cons.	Suger of Saint Denis, *Libellus alter de consecratione ecclesiae sancti Dionysii*
CS	Cistercian Studies series
CSEL	Corpus Scriptorum Ecclesiasticorum Latinorum
Csi	Bernard of Clairvaux, *De consideratione (Five Books on Consideration)*
Dil	Bernard of Clairvaux, *De diligendo Deo (On Loving God)*
DSp	*Dictionnaire de Spiritualité*. Paris: Beauchesne, 1932– .
Ep(p)	*Epistola(e)*, Letter(s)
ET	English translation
G.C.S	Griechische Christliche Schriftsteller series
GO	*Glossa Ordinaria*
Hum	Bernard of Clairvaux, *De gradibus humilitatis et superbiae (The Steps of Humility and Pride)*

MGH	Monumenta Germaniae Historica
MGH SS	Monumenta Germaniae Historica Scriptores
Miss	Bernard of Clairvaux, *Homelia super 'Missus est' in laudibus Virginis Matris (Homilies in Praise of the Blessed Virgin Mary)*
MS	Michael the Syrian, *Chronicle*
Pent	Bernard of Clairvaux, *Sermo in die pentecostes (Sermon for Pentecost)*
PG	J.P.Migne, Patrologiae cursus completus, series graeca, 162 volumes
PL	J.P. Migne, Patrologiae cursus completus, series latina, 221 volumes
QH	Bernard of Clairvaux, *Sermo super psalmum 'Qui habitat' (Lenten Sermon)*
RAM	*Revue d'Ascétique et de Mystique*
RB	*Regula Benedicti (Rule of Saint Benedict)*
SBOp	Jean Leclercq, Henri Rochais, C.H. Talbot, edd. *Sancti Bernardi Opera.* Rome: Editiones Cistercienses. 8 vols. in 9. 1957–1977.
SC	Bernard of Clairvaux: *Sermones in Cantica canticorum (Sermons on the Song of Songs)*
SCh	Sources chrétiennes
Statuta	J. M. Canivez, ed. *Statuta capitulorum generalium ordinis cistercienses ab anno 1116 ad annum 1786.* Louvain, 1933.
TLL	*Thesaurus lingue latinae.* Leipzig, 1900.
Tpl	Bernard of Clairvaux, *Ad milites Templi de laude novae militiae (In Praise of the New Knighthood)*
TU	Texte und Untersuchungen series
V Nat	Bernard of Clairvaux, *Sermo in vigilia nativiatis Domini (Sermon for Christmas Eve)*
WT	*Willelmi Tyrensis Archiepiscopi Chronicon*

Scriptural abbreviations follow the style of *The Jerusalem Bible.*

In Memoriam Jean Leclercq
Remarks Delivered at the Twenty-Eighth International Medieval Congress Kalamazoo, Michigan 7 May 1994

Bernard McGinn

JEAN LECLERCQ, of the Order of Saint Benedict and the Abbaye Saint-Maurice in Clervaux, Luxembourg, died on 27 October 1993. These brief remarks regarding his life and his contribution to medieval studies in general and to the International Congresses on Medieval Studies at Kalamazoo are a necessary but insufficient expression of the debt which all of us, as well as a community of scholars and readers around the world, owe to this remarkable man. I am privileged to speak for so many in expressing these words of appreciation. Though I knew him for almost thirty years and collaborated with him on several projects and publications, there are others who knew him longer and better. I beg their indulgence.

Jean Leclercq was born in Avesnes in northern France on 31 January 1911. His infancy was marked by the troubled times of the First World War, which left him with the kind of delicate health that often seems to produce both productivity and longevity. In 1927 he requested admission to the Abbaye Saint-Maurice, a request at first refused because he wished to be accepted as a simple monk with no desire for ordination. But he was finally received into Saint-Maurice in 1928 and submitted (if I may use the word) to ordination in 1936. From 1933 to 1937 he pursued theological studies at the College of San Anselmo in Rome, where he was influenced by Anselm Stolz, whose seminal work *Theologie der Mystik* announced a number of the themes that Jean Leclercq was to disseminate to a wide audience in scores of books and hundreds of articles.

Dom Leclercq (a title he came to view with distaste after Vatican II) completed the dissertation work he had begun in Rome at the Institut Catholique in Paris in 1940. Providential circumstances prevented him from being mobilized during the weeks of the fall of France, and he spent the war years in the motherhouse of all French monasticism at Ligugé. By 1944, just half a century ago, the young monk, who had already published his dissertation on the ecclesiology of John of Paris in 1942 as well as nineteen articles, was ready to begin his remarkable career. With the encouragement of Étienne Gilson, the undisputed master of the history of medieval scholastic thought, and no doubt also on the basis of the reading he was able to accomplish during the *vacatio* of the war years, he turned his full attention not to the scholastic thinkers who had occupied French medieval studies for almost a century, but rather to the monastic authors whose cause he was to champion in such impressive fashion throughout his life. These almost fifty years of astonishing productivity began with three books appearing in 1946 (on Peter of Celle, Peter the Venerable, and John of Fécamp), and another three in 1948 (on Bernard of Clairvaux, on monastic vocabulary, and on the life of perfection). In 1948 the Procurator General of the Cistercian Order, with singular wisdom, commissioned the still young Benedictine to undertake the preparation of a new critical edition of the works of Saint Bernard, the project that was to occupy Leclercq's efforts for many years and to constitute his most lasting contribution to medieval studies, both for the edition itself, as well as for the numerous volumes and hundreds of articles it inspired.

I realize that at this point we have brought Jean Leclercq to 1948, when, according to Louis Leloir's bibliography, he had published seven books and one hundred twenty-four articles (a lifetime's work for many). You are probably wondering if this memorial will go on to talk about the fifty or sixty more volumes he wrote after 1948, and whether it will try to survey the further articles—perhaps a thousand—that this indefatigable worker and prolific author poured out with such seeming ease down to the last months before his death. Perhaps you are thinking that such an ordeal might even be worth it if I could finally reveal the secret of how any one person could really write this much. Well, I can't, because I remain as mystified as we all are. Nor will I try to give even the briefest survey of Leclercq's later productivity. This is a task for the bibliographers—and I wish them well at it.

That Jean Leclercq was the most prolific medievalist of the past fifty years seems difficult to question. I also doubt that he was really concerned with how much he wrote and how significant his influence on medieval studies was going to be, even in those areas which mattered the most to him. This is not to say that he refrained from making judgments and taking stands, or at getting annoyed at what he thought were mistaken views and even unfair criticisms of his work. He once told me that he had largely given up reviewing books, except to encourage beginning scholars, because he felt that at his age he did not need to make any more enemies.

Although scholarship occupied much of his life, Jean Leclercq was a monk before he was a scholar. Better put, he was the kind of scholar he was precisely because he was a monk in the great tradition of learned Benedictinism. If professional medievalists incline to think of the 1950s and 1960s as the most creative era of Leclercq's scholarship, they should also be reminded that for the final thirty years of his life Jean Leclercq's greatest efforts were not devoted to purely academic pursuits, but rather to something more central to his life and thought—the renewal of christian monasticism in the wake of the Second Vatican Council and its dissemination throughout the entire world. Leclercq's global peregrinations over these decades, which led to his oft-repeated *bonmot* that he had taken a vow of *stabilitas morum et conversio loci* (see RB 58), made him a figure of international reputation—a kind of 'world-monk'. When the history of twentieth-century monasticism comes to be written, it is hard not to think that two monks will dominate the story: Thomas Merton and Jean Leclercq.

It is especially fitting that some words of homage be offered to this remarkable monk and man at this Kalamazoo Congress. Jean Leclercq was the first european medievalist to attend these Medieval Congresses, and the presence of a scholar of his already towering international reputation at the early meetings of the 1960s did much to encourage both those whose efforts built these gatherings into the largest meetings of their kind and also to attract the thousands of medievalists who found that attending these Congresses provided such a serendipitous combination of information and inspiration.

However much we grieve that Jean Leclercq is no longer with us to provide the warm and encouraging presence which matched his scholarly productivity, this is not a sad occasion. Few if any here will not have read something by Jean Leclercq. Many will remember the stimulating addresses and incisive interventions he made here over the years. Others will recall incidents of the personal kindness that he invariably displayed to all he encountered, both here at Kalamazoo and throughout the world.

I close with a personal reminiscence. In the mid–1980s Jean Leclercq, the Orthodox theologian John Meyendorff, and I collaborated in the planning and editing of the first volume of the Encyclopedia of World Spirituality, entitled *Christian Spirituality I. Origins to the Twelfth Century* (New York: Crossroad, 1985). The last time I saw Jean Leclercq was at the International Congress celebrating the nine-hundredth anniversary of the birth of Bernard of Clairvaux held at Rome in September of 1990, where he told my wife Pat and me that this was indeed his swan-song and that his failing health had convinced him it was time to give up his travelling and to retire to Saint-Maurice. We corresponded a number of times through 1991, 1992, and into 1993. One item in these exchanges remains fixed in my mind. When I learned of the early and unexpected death of our friend and collaborator John Meyendorff in July of 1992, I wrote to Jean, sending him a copy of the obituary notice from the New York *Times*. I shall never forget the reply I received, a brief card inscribed with the typical Leclercq scrawl, often unintelligible even to the initiate. It concluded:

> I envy our friend, John Meyendorff; he sees.

Jean Leclercq himself also now sees. We take this opportunity to pay our homage to someone who taught us all to see so much.

From λόγος to *verbum*: John Cassian's Use of Greek in the Development of a Latin Monastic Vocabulary

Columba Stewart OSB

ALTHOUGH HE WAS one of the greatest monastic travellers of all time, Père Jean Leclercq wore his million miles like his many hats, lightly and with panache. He once observed of the benedictine vow of stability that it must always be understood as a dynamic rather than as a static concept. He then cocked his head and added, 'of course, for some of us it is an *aero*-dynamic stability'. Jean Leclercq devoted his scholarly life to the latin monastic tradition of the Middle Ages, bringing it to life for his students and readers. His monastic namesake, John Cassian (*c.* 360-after 430), was another notable traveller, writer, and teacher. In Cassian's case, the tradition he learned and taught was Greek, for he lived at a time when the western monastic tradition embodied in Jean Leclercq was still in its theological and literary infancy. Cassian bridged the linguistic divide between greek monastic traditions and the emerging latin monasticism of southern Gaul which he nurtured in the last two decades of his life. His goal, he wrote, was to present the teaching of the monks of Egypt 'exactly as he received it', and even more, 'speaking in the latin language'.[1] But of course they actually spoke Greek, not Latin, and furthermore, Cassian did not always adhere to his promise.

One way to study Cassian's role as a transmitter of eastern monastic theology to western monks is to examine the linguistic traces of his formation in the Greek-speaking monasticism of Palestine and especially of Egypt.[2] He used well over a hundred greek words, some already domesticated in latin usage, but others still fresh. With the help of those words, he crafted a latin language of monastic experience. This article is a study of the greek vocabulary of Cassian's monastic writings, the *Institutes* and *Conferences*.[3]

It is particularly appropriate that I write this essay in memory of Jean Leclercq, for he was responsible for my first published article, also on John Cassian. When I was a junior monk, Père Jean was teaching at Collegeville, and I was appointed his 'guardian angel'. Plying me with wine and chocolate chip cookies, he encouraged me to follow my heart's lead into the field of monastic studies. We kept in touch for the rest of his life. With each year his letters grew even harder to read, but began to glow with the peace and joy that the great monastic writers foretell. I write these words as my last letter to him.

The Issue

The influence of Greek upon an evolving christian Latin has been studied in several articles by the great Christine Mohrmann.[4] The issue has also been approached through the study of latin translations of christian greek texts,[5] and there are editions of several monastic ones.[6] One also finds studies of the vocabulary or method of latin translations of particular greek monastic texts such as the *Life of Antony*,[7] or of greek words used by a certain translator or author such as Rufinus.[8] To these one can add the researches of Adalbert de Vogüé, which continue to shed light on monastic terminology.[9] Despite Cassian's importance for the development of latin monastic theology, his literary style and his vocabulary have been little studied, and the one substantial study of his Latin excludes words of greek origin.[10]

Although Cassian is in a certain way acting as a translator, he is translating, not a specific text, but a thought-world.[11] The words of greek origin in his writings can point us to that thought-world and help us to situate Cassian himself in the greek monastic tradition. Editors and commentators have noted greek terminology in his writings and provided definitions or illuminating parallels, but have not stepped back to consider the topic systematically. There has been textual assistance available for centuries, however, as a brief history of previous work on Cassian's vocabulary will indicate.

The earliest notable work on Cassian's use of greek terminology was done by Petrus Ciacconius, editor of the 1588 Rome edition of Cassian's monastic writings,[12] who augmented and improved the earlier edition by Henricus Cuychius.[13] Ciacconius' edition includes a thirty-page appendix listing greek and obscure latin words and providing a definition of each along with relevant classical and patristic witnesses.[14] He also prepared an appendix indicating those quotations from the Old Testament which seemed to be based on the Greek of the Septuagint rather than the Latin of the Vulgate.[15] Ciacconius' work was incorporated into the subsequent edition of Cassian's works by the benedictine monk Alardus Gazaeus, published at Douai in 1616,[16] and later used by Migne for his edition of Cassian in volumes 49 and 50 of the *Patrologia Latina.* Migne did not include all of Gazaeus' textual aids, but his edition does provide an index to the 'things and words' explained in Gazaeus' commentary.[17] Some of the same material can be found in the 'Onomasticon rerum et verborum difficiliorum' in the 1628 edition of Rosweyde's *Vitae patrum*, along with useful references to material in the *Vitae patrum*. This 'Onomasticon' was included in Migne's edition of the *Vitae patrum.*[18]

The standard modern edition of Cassian's works is that prepared by Michael Petschenig in the 1880s for the Vienna Corpus of Latin Christian texts.[19] Petschenig included four indices: 1) of texts cited, both patristic and biblical (with the Septuagint-based texts indicated); 2) of 'names and things'; 3) of 'words and expressions'; 4) of orthographical variants. Distributed throughout the second and third indices are the greek words used by Cassian. However, because Petschenig produced an edition but not a commentary, one must return to Ciacconius and Gazaeus for meanings and parallels, as well as consult the standard reference works.[20]

For this study I have made use of the following tools to assure a thorough retrieval of Cassian's greek terminology: a complete text of Cassian's monastic writings in electronic form,[21] from which I have produced a complete vocabulary;[22] Petschenig's indices; the index of Ciacconius; the commentary of Gazaeus; the 'Onomasticon' from the 1628 edition of Rosweyde. In addition to these, I have consulted the usual lexica, the CETEDOC electronic library of texts, and other resources as indicated in the notes.

The Results: an Overview

Cassian uses more than one hundred twenty words of greek origin (and a handful of coptic ones).[23] Some of these he must have known directly from greek texts or personal experience in Greek-speaking environments. In addition to using words of greek origin, he was able to sprinkle his writings with greek phrases and the occasional literary quotation.[24]

Some of the words he used had become part of the general Latin vocabulary: *genus* (=γένος), *grypes* (=γρύψ, griffin), *(h)ebdomas* (=ἑβδομάς, week), *mysticus* (=μυστικός, mystical), *pharus* (=φάρος, lighthouse, from the famous beacon at Alexandria). Others would have been familiar to readers of the Latin Bible, of biblical commentaries or of theological texts: for example, *auxesis* (=αὔξησις, growth), *genealogia* (=γενεαλογία, genealogy), *myrum* (=μύρον, chrism, ointment). These common words number about twenty.

There are also words associated with a particular theme, such as athletic and gladiatorial terminology used in descriptions of the spiritual life (*agon*, =ἀγών, contest; *agonotheta*, =ἀγωνοθέτης, judge of a contest; *athleta*, =ἀθλητής, athlete; *pancarpum*, =πάγκαρπον, gladiatorial contest; *scamma*, =σκάμμα, wrestling place; *schoenobata*, =σχοινοβάτης, tightrope walker; *tropaeum*, =τρόπαιον, trophy) or medical terminology (*biothanatos*, =βιοθάνατος, suicide; *caustica*, =καυστικά, burning, used with *medicamenta* to mean cauterizing remedy; *cefelargia*, =κεφαλάλγια, headache; *chiragrica*, =χειραγρικά, suffering from gout; *flegma*, =φλέγμα, phlegm; *ophthalmicus*, =ὀφθαλμικός, suffering from eye trouble; *otalgicus*, =ὠταλγικός, suffering from earache; *theriaca*, =θηριακή, antidote). Again, these fifteen or so terms would have been more or less familiar to the latin monastic reader (especially to the infirmarian!). Cassian uses them all in the transliterated and latinized forms which had become standard by his time.

Of greater interest for the purposes of this essay are the approximately eighty-five words which can be considered more directly related to monastic or spiritual vocabulary. Some of these had already become standard in latin monastic writings, but others were introduced by Cassian. These can be arranged under the headings of 'monastic taxonomy', 'everyday monastic life', and 'theological and spiritual vocabulary'. I will conclude with a brief discussion of Cassian's diplomatic omission of a certain greek word.

Monastic Taxonomy

The first category for consideration is that of monastic types or titles.[25] These are words, such as *abbas* (=ἀββᾶς, father, abbot), *anachoreta* (=ἀναχωρητής, anchorite), *cella* (=κέλλα[26]), *coenobita* (=κοινοβιώτης, cenobite), *coenobium* (=κοινόβιον, cenobium), *heremus* (=ἐρῆμος, desert, cf. hermit), *monachus* (=μοναχός), *monasterium* (=μοναστήριον), *xenodochium* (=ξενοδοχεῖον, guesthouse), which had become known to latin monks through the writings and translations of Jerome, Rufinus, and others.[27] It seems that Cassian was the first to use certain forms of these words, indicating that they were words he had known in a greek context and later introduced to his latin readers. For example, he simply transliterates the Greek ἀναχώρησις and ἀναχωρητικός, producing the noun *anachoresis* and the adjective *anachoreticus*. These forms are not found in earlier texts, which employ the form *anachoreta*.[28] While he uses *heremita*, a simple transliteration of the Greek ἐρημίτης which had already appeared in the *Dialogues* of Sulpitius Severus, Cassian creates an adjectival form, *heremiticus*.[29] When writing about monks who live in cenobitic community, Cassian refers to their dwelling place as a *coenobium*, as does Jerome. But when he describes the monks themselves, he calls them *coenobiota*, a form closer to the Greek κοινοβιώτης than is the *coenobita* which Jerome and also writers after Cassian preferred.[30] Finally, like the latin pilgrim Egeria, Cassian uses the Greek word μονάζοντες (a plural of μονάζων, one who lives alone) defining it as equivalent to *monachi*.[31] This word did not become standard latin usage, for the simpler *monachus/monachi* was found to be more convenient.

Cassian employs three other words which can be placed in this category. The first, *diaconia*, is quite familiar from other texts, but Cassian uses it in a special sense to designate a monastic office involving the administration of temporalities and the dispensing of alms.[32] There is also the official title of *oeconomus* (=οἰκονόμος), given to someone charged with the *diaconia*.[33] The third term, *syncellitas* (=συγκελλίτης) simply means 'cell-mate', though this form does not correspond exactly to the usual greek one.[34]

Everyday Monastic Life

The second category of monastic words contains those related to the everyday life of the monk. These can be divided into three groups according to topic: clothing, diet, household and work items. Cassian devotes the first book of the *Institutes* to the monastic habit, providing a theological commentary on each item of monastic dress more or less along the lines of Evagrius' *Letter to Anatolius* which introduces the *Praktikos*.[35] Many of the names for clothing are greek words which can be found in other latin monastic texts:[36] *colobium* (=κολόβιον, tunic) and *mafortes* (=μαφόρτες, cape).[37] Two words of greek origin used to describe the cloth used for monastic garments are *cilicium* (=κιλίκιον, a tough weave of goat's hair, of Cilician origin) and *linea* (=λίνεος, linen), both in common latin use.

When he is describing the 'scarves' which keep the tunic girded when working (Gk: ἀνάλαβοι, usually translated, misleadingly, as 'scapular'), Cassian is obviously at a loss as to how to find a latin equivalent for the greek name. He describes the item, gives its greek name, and then offers three latin equivalents.[38] The greek word is common in monastic texts, including Cassian's primary source for this section, Evagrius' *Letter to Anatolius*.[39] The word does not, however, occur in other latin texts. Here one is in direct contact with the greek tradition.

In the next chapter (*Institutes* 1.6) two synonyms, *byrros* and *planetica*, have puzzled both philologists and commentators. Their meaning is clear: an ample cape or cloak which Cassian thought too costly and flashy for monks. Both words have greek connections, though each presents its own mystery. The first, *byrros*, is probably a celtic word which was adopted into Latin and then passed on to Greek and other languages.[40] Cassian's use of a greek spelling may indicate that he thought it was a greek word, though he does not present it as such. *Planetica* is more difficult. Cassian's is the only occurrence I have located. It seems that *planetica* may be derived from *planeta*,[41] a word derived from the Greek πλανήτης, 'wanderer' or 'wandering'. The problems begin with the fact that the greek word is not used for a garment.[42] In the seventh century Isidore of Seville had tried to bridge the etymological gap with a pejorative definition of *planeta* based on πλανήτης that made wearing a *planeta* an indication of instability and potential error.[43] His monastic rule, probably following Cassian, forbids both *planeta* and *birros*.[44] Isidore's etymological justification for the ban seems, however, to be more ingenious than accurate. The connection with the greek πλανήτης probably has more to do with travel than with erratic behavior, and Cassian's objection appears to have more to do with expense and ostentation than with suspicious behavior. DuCange equates the Latin *planeta* with *casula* (cf. English 'chasuble'), a word used for both the liturgical vestment and the everyday cloak.[45] Blaise defines *planeta* simply as 'raincoat'.[46] J–C. Guy, editor of the *Institutes* for Sources chrétiennes, sidestepped the etymological problems by equating Cassian's *planetica* with *paenula*, a common word derived from the Greek φαινόλης, cloak (see 2 Tim 4:13).[47] As Cassian's is evidently the only extant example of the word, little more can be said about the matter of the *planeta* except to note that it does have greek roots.

There are other mysteries about monastic outfitting. Cassian concludes his survey of monastic dress with the goatskin worn on top of everything else, 'which is called *melotis* or *pera*', and the *baculus* (=βάκυλον, staff).[48] The greek original of *melotis*, μηλωτή, is found in the Septuagint and the Greek New Testament, and the transliterated form finds its way into the Vulgate of Hebrews 11:37. The word is common in greek monastic texts and is preserved both in Jerome's translation of the pachomian rules and in latin translations of the *Life of Antony*.[49] Cassian himself uses it several times. The problem comes with Cassian's synonymous use of *pera*. The common latin word of this spelling is a transliteration of the Greek πήρα, a sack or wallet used for travelling.[50] There appears to be a problem here, one recognized by Gazaeus and others: a goatskin used as a bodily garment is not the same thing as a sack or wallet.[51]

Cassian knew the standard meaning of *pera*, for he uses the word elsewhere. In *Conferences* 24.23.3, paraphrasing Matthew 10:9–10, Jesus' travelling instructions to the Twelve, Cassian includes the injunction to take no 'wallet' when on the road. Both the biblical text and Cassian's paraphrase use *pera*. Despite Jesus' ban on luggage, however, Cassian seems in Book One of the *Institutes* to include a bag of some kind among the monk's essential equipment. This was what bothered Gazaeus and later commentators. Gazaeus resolved the problem by concluding that *pera* is a misreading for *paenula* (cloak), and that Cassian is equating the goatskin not with a bag, but with a cloak. Unfortunately there is no apparent manuscript support for such a reading,[52] and Cassian does not use the word *paenula* anywhere else. DuCange is more ingenious with the suggestion that the text be rearranged to read 'the goatskin, which is called *melotis*, the wallet, and the staff', though again there seems to be no textual support for this revision.[53]

The third occurrence of *pera* in Cassian's works, in *Conferences* 11.3.1, provides the answer. There Cassian describes the anchorite-turned-bishop Archebius who began a journey by taking up his 'staff and *pera*'. Cassian notes that this is customary for all egyptian monks when they travel. The mention of *pera* in *Institutes* 1.7 also adds a reference to the monk's staff or walking stick. It is clear that the monk's goatskin also served as a kind of pouch or haversack for travelling,[54] and along with his staff would be the standard equipment for a journey. After all, egyptian monks had to eat while on a journey, but were normally forbidden to eat with seculars. They either had to rely on monastic hospitality or carry their own lunch, and their goatskin would have been just the place to tuck some bread.[55] The problem seems to require a solution along these lines, given that the lexical entries for *pera* or πήρα all give the meaning 'wallet' or 'pouch',[56] and that Cassian clearly intends *melotis* and *pera* to be understood as synonymous.[57]

The second group of greek words used for everyday purposes has to do with diet. Some are the names of foods: *labsanion* (=λαψάνιον, cherlock, a bitter green herb),[58] *maenomenia* (=μαινόμενα, sardine),[59] *myxaria* (=μυξάρια, plum), *paxamadion* (=παξαμάδιον, a loaf of bread, often dried), *trogalia* (=τρωγάλια, a kind of dessert).[60] All are common enough in greek tradition, but rare or unique in Latin. *Labsanion* and *paxamadion* are used in monastic texts to describe the staples of the egyptian monastic diet: greens and bread. *Labsanion* (with a slightly different spelling) is used in Jerome's translation of the Pachomian material[61] but is not found elsewhere in Latin before

Cassian's use of it. *Paxamadion*, later more usually *paxamas*, is a very common term in the *Apophthegmata* and other monastic texts.[62] Cassian is the first in the latin monastic tradition to use *paxamadion*; the fact that he uses what will prove to be a less common form is not surprising at this early stage in the latin transmission of the word. He uses two other words to describe alimentary regimens: *xerofagia* (=ξηροφαγία, eating only dried foods) and *omofagia* (=ὠμοφαγία, eating only uncooked foods). The first is common enough in greek texts and is also found in Tertullian's *On Fasting*;[63] the second is somewhat rarer in both greek[64] and latin texts. Cassian likely got them both directly from the greek monastic tradition.

The third group of words in this category consists of names of everyday items and implements. Many of these are common words, such as *absis* (=ἀψίς, apse), *graphium* (=γραφίς, stylus), *calamus* (=κάλαμος, lit., reed, meaning pen), *nomisma* (=νόμισμα, coin). Others are more unusual, though found in other latin sources: *entheca* (=ἐνθήκη, granary), *clibanus* (=κρίβανος, a pan for baking bread), *naphtha* (=νάφθα, the flammable spirit). Finally there are words from the greek monastic vocabulary of Egypt having to do with baskets and other woven items: *plecta* (πλεκτή) and its synonym *sira* (σειρά), monastic argot for palm bough, the raw material for much manual labor; *prochirium* (=προχείριον), a basket for carrying and storing the week's ration of bread (the *paxamadia* mentioned above); and *psiathium* (=ψιάθιον), a rush mat for sleeping.

Plecta literally means 'bent' or 'twisted', and refers to the plaiting of palm leaves in the making of baskets or rope.[65] In one of the latin versions of the *Apophthegmata*, the singular form denotes 'weaving' as an activity or as a finished product rather than the raw material itself.[66] *Sira*, which Cassian says is the name used in Egypt, can be found in various monastic texts meaning 'woven palm leaves'.[67] Neither word seems to have been used in latin texts before Cassian. Cassian himself perhaps preferred *plecta*, as he used that word twice and *sira* only once.[68] Cassian's *prochirium* is an unusual word; etymologically it is simple enough, meaning 'at/for the hand', or better, 'something handy'. It is apparently a word used in Egypt, as the other occurrences of it are in the papyri.[69] Cassian himself uses it only once, but in doing so he brings us into direct contact with the egyptian customary usage. By contrast, *psiathium* occurs frequently in greek monastic texts, and is preserved in latin translations of some of them.[70] Cassian himself uses it seven times.[71]

Two unusual words can be found in the *Institutes* when Cassian is describing the public penance required of any monk who breaks anything. He gives the example of breaking a *gillo* or *baucalis*, which is an earthenware vessel of some kind. The first word, *gillo*, is not to be found in the greek lexica, though there are some possibly related forms.[72] In Latin it is considered by the authorities to be an unusual word of uncertain derivation.[73] The synonym, *baucalis*, is the word Cassian says was used by the egyptian monks: *gillonem fictilem, quem baucalem nuncupant.*[74] The word is found in Greek monastic texts and in the papyri as βαυκάλη or βαυκάλιον, with the same meaning Cassian gives it.[75] Etymologists have inclined toward a coptic origin for the word, but admit that the original form is uncertain.[76] Some light is shed by a saying from the Systematic Collection of the *Apophthegmata* which is extant in three versions, one Greek and two Latin (one translated by Rufinus, the other by Pelagius).[77] The greek text uses βαυκάλιον. Rufinus uses *gello* (and, once, a diminutive form, *gellunculus*); Pelagius uses *suriscula*, an even rarer word which he seems to have liked,[78] and the common *vasculum*. This pattern of translation proves Cassian's point: *baucalis* was a word unfamiliar to latin monks, who knew the thing as a *gillo*. And so it is *gillo* rather than *baucalis* that Cassian uses a few chapters later.[79]

Theological and Spiritual Vocabulary

When we turn to more properly theological and spiritual vocabulary, it is not surprising to find that Cassian, like all latin theologians, used a number of words of greek origin. Many of these had become common by his time, especially words having to do with liturgical arrangements: *antiphona* (=ἀντιφώνη), *diaconus* (=διάκονος), *canon* (=κανών), *synaxis* (=σύναξις), *hymnus* (=ὕμνος). Of greater interest here, however, are the terms he employs when interpreting biblical texts. The great latin exegetes of the fourth and fifth centuries—Ambrose, Jerome, Rufinus and Augustine—had made a number of greek terms familiar both by their own works and by their translations of greek texts. Cassian, like them, used such words as *allego-*

ria/allegoricus (=ἀλληγορία, ἀλληγορικός), *anagoge* (=ἀναγωγή), *historia/historicus* (=ἱστορία, ἱστορικός), *tropologia/tropicus* (=τροπολογία, τροπικός), and *typus* (=τύπος). Cassian uses these words in the simply transliterated or the latinized forms found in other texts.

He also makes evident his own direct knowledge of greek exegetical conventions by using other greek terms. For example, in *Conferences* 17.16.2 he has Abba Joseph cautioning his listeners not to discard the parts of the Old Testament that narrate the weaknesses of patriarchs and prophets, but rather to read them with an οἰκονομία (allowance) for such human sinfulness.[80] The word appears again a few chapters later (*Conf.* 17.19.4), this time transliterated and in the plural.[81] He also uses an adverbial form, *oeconomice*, to mean 'providentially' (*Conf.* 13.11.4).[82] Similarly, when discussing biblical references to the divine wrath in *Institutes* 8.4.3, he warns his readers not to understand such passages ἀνθρωποπαθῶς ('anthropopassionately'), as if they referred to the human passion of anger. Jerome uses the word,[83] as do Greek exegetes.[84]

Cassian knew not only greek exegetical terminology, but also the Bible itself in Greek. He actually quotes the Septuagint text, in Greek, five times, and the Greek New Testament three times, always finding something in the greek text that he could not in the latin.[85] As commentators since Ciacconius have pointed out, many of his biblical quotations and allusions in Latin are clearly based on the greek text of the Septuagint rather than taken from Jerome's Vulgate version based on the Hebrew.[86] Given the fluid nature of the pre-Vulgate latin biblical tradition, it is difficult to determine in a given instance whether Cassian was quoting a written version (something in the line of what is conventionally, though artificially and imprecisely, called the *Vetus Latina* or 'Old Latin' version) or translating directly from the greek text. Doubtless he did both. To the modern reader it may seem odd that Cassian did not standardize all biblical quotations according to the Vulgate. In fact, more often than not he does quote the Vulgate, and he was well aware of that translation's fidelity to the hebrew text of the Old Testament.[87] But it is natural that the greek text of the Bible should make itself felt, because he is sharing the fruit born of living closely for many years with the Septuagint and Greek New Testament.

Ciacconius, noting that nearly all of Cassian's quotations from Proverbs and Ecclesiastes are based on the Septuagint rather than the Vulgate, suggested that he may have been translating those texts which were 'committed to his memory' in Greek.[88] Memorizing these texts particularly prized by monks would not have been unusual in Palestine or Egypt in the late fourth century. What is more surprising is that Cassian almost always cites the Psalms according to the Latin ('Gallican') version rather than according to the Septuagint.[89] Perhaps the liturgical use of the latin psalter in the monastery at Marseilles made the latin psalms come more readily to his mind than the greek. Books such as Proverbs and Ecclesiastes, however, used more in his private *meditatio* than in the liturgy, remained familiar to him in their greek form. When using those texts in the *Institutes* and *Conferences*, then, he would have translated the Greek of his memory into Latin for the written page. Like other early christian writers, he worked from both written and remembered biblical texts, and delighted in comparing different versions of the same text.

At times his interpretation of a biblical text actually depends on the greek version, as in the play on the Septuagint text of Judges 3:15, where Ehud is described as ἀμφοτεροδέξιος (ambidextrous). Cassian uses this as the basis for an extended discussion of virtue and vice.[90] His interpretation of the story of Martha and Mary (*Conf.* 1.8; Lk 10:38–42) uses a variant reading from the greek manuscript tradition unknown in the latin tradition, at least as we know it.[91] His commentary on the phrase 'give us today our daily bread' from the Lord's Prayer involves comparing the different latin translations of the Greek ἐπιούσιον.[92]

Two unusual words, *arras* and *subarratum*, belong in this category of biblically-related terms. They are derived from the Greek ἀρραβῶν (pledge), which is itself a transliterated aramaic word.[93] The word ἀρραβῶν occurs three times in the Septuagint, and is later used by Paul to mean a 'pledge' or 'guarantee' of good things to come. In the Vulgate it is translated as *arrhabon* (Gen 38:17–18) or *pignus* (Gen 38:20; 2 Cor 1:22, 5:5; Eph 1:14). Cassian cites none of these texts, never uses *arrhabon*, and uses *pignus* only once.[94] But he uses *arras* and *subarratum* in the same way Paul uses ἀρραβῶν.[95] The first word, *arras*, is a direct equivalent for ἀρραβῶν, while *subarratum* is a neuter perfect participle from a derivative verb, *subarro*. Both are unusual words, with few other witnesses for the metaphorical use made of them by Cassian;[96] *arras*, like its Greek parent ἀρραβῶν, was used by both earlier and contemporary writers with its financial meaning of a 'down-payment' or 'pledge'.[97] It may be that the Pauline use of ἀρραβῶν inspired Cassian's own application of these words to the spiritual life.

Cassian also evinces some familiarity with greek apocryphal literature, though the contact may have been through a secondary source. In *Conferences* 1.20–22 he develops an extended metaphor about discernment based on an apocryphal saying of Jesus to the effect that his followers should be *probabiles trapezitae*, good moneychangers able to distinguish good coins from bad. The apocryphon is quite a common one; among greek authors Clement, Origen, Basil, and John Chrysostom knew and quoted it, as did the authors of the Ps-Clementine *Homilies* and the *Didascalia*. Ambrose, Jerome, and Rufinus quoted it. The way Cassian uses the saying is closest to one of Origen's *Homilies on Leviticus*.[98] Usually the saying was quoted with respect to 1 Thessalonians 5:21–22: 'test everything; hold on to what is good; abstain from every kind of evil'. Cassian, however, uses it in its own right, and plays out the metaphor of money-changing at wearying length. The figure of genuine gold coins contrasted with various kinds of fakes requires him to use a number of greek or greek-inspired words like *exagium* (=ἐξάγιον, assaying) *nomismata* (=νομίσματα, coins), *obrizum* (=ὄβρυζον, pure gold), *paracharaxima/ paracharaximus* (=παραχάραγμα/παραχαράξιμος, noun and adjective meaning debased) and *trapezita* (=τραπεζίτης, money-changer).[99]

All of these monetary words can be found in other latin texts except *paracharaximus*,[100] which Cassian perhaps read in the now-lost greek original of that homily of Origen's referred to above.[101] Rufinus' latin translation of the homily preserves Origen's signal of an upcoming colloquialism (*et, ut vulgo dicitur* . . .) but then substitutes an entirely innocuous translation (*extra monetam formata*, 'made without the [proper] stamp') for the original greek word, doubtless because it would have been opaque to the Latin reader. Cassian notes that *paracharaximus* is a *verbum vulgarum* (*Conf.* 2.9); he may well be preserving for us the word Origen actually wrote.

When Cassian writes of the monk's spiritual life, he employs a number of greek words. Some of these had become familiar through earlier latin texts, and are unremarkable. Others, however, seem to indicate that he was unable to find latin equivalents and had to use the greek words themselves. Sometimes, too, he nuances a latin word by relating it to a greek one.[102] Among those in the first, unremarkable, category are: *agon/agonotheta* (noted above), *ethicus* (=ἠθικός, ethical), *zelus* (=ζῆλος, fervor or jealousy). Others are rooted in the greek spiritual tradition that Cassian communicates to his readers: the Platonic division of the soul into the three faculties called ἐπιθυμητικόν, θυμικόν, λογικόν (desiring, repelling, rational), also used by Evagrius;[103] a kind of partial perfection he calls μερική (lit., partial);[104] a distinction between two kinds of love, ἀγάπη and διάθεσις (love and special affection);[105] the Greek νοῦς used for the Latin *mens* (mind) or *ratio* (reason);[106] σκοπός/ *scopos* (goal)[107] and *telos* (end)[108] for the aims of monastic life.[109]

When Cassian gives his account of an early stage of the egyptian Origenist controversy of 399 (*Conf.* 10.1–4), he refers to those whom he accused of harboring a bodily concept of God as *anthropomorphitae* (=ἀνθρωπομορφῆται or ἀνθρωπομορφῖται, lit., 'the human form-ites') and their belief as *anthropomorphos* (ἀνθρωπόμορφος, 'in human form').[110] The controversy itself takes us far from the scope of this essay, though this section of Conference Ten is absolutely central to any understanding of Cassian's teaching on prayer.[111] For now it can be noted that Cassian uses the words only in transliteration. While other latin commentators on the controversy (Rufinus, Jerome, and Augustine) used the noun *anthropomorphitae*, the adjective *anthropomorphos* seems to be introduced into Latin by Cassian.

Cassian's own sympathies, of course, lay with the Origenist group. He himself was taught to approach the christian and monastic life through the neo-platonic mysticism that Evagrius learned from his Cappadocian teachers and then developed in the Egyptian desert. This tradition is so bound up with the greek philosophical and spiritual vocabulary that Cassian has to strain to bring it into Latin. Often he must posit a greek word as a starting-point, and then try to translate it. Often the translation requires several latin words (cf. ἀναλάβος!). This is most noticeable in two crucial areas of his teaching: his re-working of the Evagrian ascetical agenda of eight principal thoughts; and his teaching on the relationship between asceticism and contemplation (πρακτική and θεωρία). Theologically these are vast subjects, and here we can look only at the words themselves.

Cassian's teaching on the eight principal thoughts finds him to be very much the bridge between Greek east and Latin west.[112] He manages to translate the overall concept without resorting to Greek, using *vitia* (faults) for λογισμοί (*thoughts*) or πάθαι (*passions*). His choice of *vitia* stiffens the more supple (that is, ambiguous) Evagrian concept, but such is often the effect of translation. He must have ruled out possibile equivalents such as *cogitatio*, *ratio* or *passio* because of their other meanings or because he in fact wanted to pin down Evagrius' vaguer approach. For the eight λογισμοί themselves, Cassian found latin equivalents for four: *fornicatio* (=πορνεία, lust), *ira* (=ὀργή, anger), *tristitia* (=λύπη, sadness), *superbia* (=ὑπερηφανία, pride). For the other four he used the greek word, usually citing it once in greek letters and thereafter in transliteration, with an accompanying translation: *gastrimargia* (=γαστριμαργία, gluttony, more than forty times),[113] *filargyria* (=φιλαργυρία lit., 'love of money', almost fifty times), *acedia* (=ἀκηδία, listlessness, more than twenty-five uses), *cenodoxia* (=κενοδοξία, vainglory, about forty-five times). In each case he provides a latin translation but clearly prefers the greek word. Only one of these four can be found in the latin biblical tradition,[114] and none of them is common before Cassian's writings and later translations of monastic literature.[115]

Cassian echoes Evagrius in describing the spiritual life in two stages, the ascetical discipline of the πρακτική or 'practical' life,[116] and the contemplative experience of θεωρία (contemplation) or the θεωρητική (contemplative life). Cassian uses these greek words several times, either in greek letters or in transliteration. He also finds latin equivalents for them. His role in this linguistic development is of tremendous importance.

As he writes about the first stage, Cassian follows Evagrius in preferring the term πρακτική to the common monastic word ἄσκησις (ascesis).[117] He uses the word, in greek letters, six times.[118] When he writes about the πρακτική, he often uses the latin adjective *actualis*, which is a literal translation of the greek adjectival form πρακτικός. Cassian defines the πρακτική as *actualis scientia*[119] or *actualis disciplina*.[120] He also uses *actualis* with an array of latin nouns to situate them in this realm of the spiritual life; these include *vita*, *conversatio*, *opus/operatio*, *congressio*, *discretio*, *experientia*, *fructus*, *instructio*, *perfectio*, *virtus*.[121] Although one finds in his writings a number of the words used by other latin monastic writers or translators for ἄσκησις, he uses them for other purposes.[122] Finally, to describe the total renunciation of material things required of the monk as part of the *vita actualis*, he uses the greek word ἀκτημοσύνη ('being without possessions'), and then provides a definition linking it to monastic poverty.[123]

When he turns to the contemplative aspect of the monastic life, he once more stays close to Evagrius. He uses θεωρητική in both greek letters[124] and in transliteration (*theoreticus*),[125] and both transliterates θεωρία as *theoria* and translates it as *contemplatio*.[126] Despite its familiarity to modern readers, *contemplatio* was not a particularly striking word in latin christian literature before Cassian. It appears in latin versions of the Bible with a variety of meanings ranging from the quite mundane to the religious; among christian writers, only Augustine gave the word an importance comparable to what it has in Cassian's thought.[127] But although their two kinds of neo-Platonic mysticism had affinities, the lines of descent from philosophical ancestors had followed different courses. For Cassian's use of *contemplatio* we must look, not to Augustine, but to Evagrius.

A Greek Word That Does Not Appear

I end this essay with a greek word that will not be found in Cassian's monastic writings. It is the most intriguing word in the Evagrian tradition, ἀπάθεια ('passionlessness'). Cassian was aware of its controversial and potentially misleading aspects, and replaced it with the phrase, 'purity of heart' (cf. Mt. 5:8), which was both biblical and venerably monastic.[128] He also devoted an entire conference (*Conf.* 23) to combatting the suggestion that a human being could be sinless (*anamartetos*, =ἀναμάρτητος[129]). But even though the word ἀπάθεια itself does not appear, Cassian certainly teaches the basic outline of the Evagrian doctrine, and his choice of this phrase from the Beatitudes leads one back to his source. Evagrius himself was fond of the literary form of the beatitude,[130] and liked to use the word μακαριότης (blessedness, beatitude) to describe the ultimate goal of the christian life: e.g., 'the end of the human person is blessedness'.[131] He quotes Matthew 5:8 several times in his extant writings,[132] and alludes to it frequently.[133]

Perhaps the clearest example of Evagrius' linking of the beatitude to the monastic goal of *theoria* is in Evagrius' *Scholia on Proverbs.* He is commenting on the text of Proverbs 14:9, 'the dwellings of the senseless will have to be purified, while the dwellings of the righteous will be acceptable'. His scholion reads: 'so that, having become pure, they might see God: this is the blessed end which is reserved for each rational nature'.[134] To this one can compare Cassian's typically effusive summary of the monastic end in *Conference* 1.10.5:

> all people will pass from this manifold practical work (*actualis operatio*) to the love of God and the contemplation of divine things in perpetual purity of heart. Those who are eager to devote themselves to knowledge and to purifying the mind have already in this life chosen with all their effort and strength to give themselves over, even now in the corruption of the flesh, to that service (*officium*) in which they will abide after they have put off corruption and come to the Lord's promise of salvation, which says: 'Blessed are the pure of heart, for they shall see God'.

Conclusion

John Cassian was in touch with greek terminology at various levels of immediacy. Some greek words were well-worn in their latin guise by the time he used them; others are clear proof that he himself knew the Greek language and found it at times to be more helpful than the less-sophisticated Christian Latin he was helping to develop. He provides direct evidence for the greek (and occasionally coptic) monastic argot of fourth-century Egypt. He helped to create for latin monasticism a descriptive language based on what he had learned there. He knew greek biblical commentaries and theological works, and helped to bring their tools and insights into the latin west. This was most evident in his debt to the traditions of Origen and Evagrius.

Yet this overview of Cassian's use of greek terminology has perhaps been misleading. There is no doubt that at times he was a 'cultural imperialist', presenting hellenized egyptian monasticism as the model to be imitated by the monks of the west. But a broader look at his monastic writings would show that he adapted his language and thought to the latin world of southern Gaul. His success is evident in the influence his work had on western monasticism: he was never viewed as an exotic creature or as a pathetic nostalgic pining away for a long-lost monastic ideal. Nonetheless, as we read his work, the mark of the greek tradition which formed him is evident on nearly every page. To understand the man we must understand his background and his efforts to communicate what he had learned. His was the paradigmatic life of a monk, marked by fidelity to what he had received from the tradition, and by dedication to making it live in his own time and place.

NOTES

1. *Conferences*, Preface I.6.

2. To explain Cassian's facility in both Greek and Latin, it has been thought that he was born in a bilingual region, probably in the Balkans. The debates about Cassian's birthplace are notoriously intricate and in the end the evidence is very meager. This essay accepts his bilingualism as a fact; how he acquired it is not relevant here. For details, see my forthcoming study on Cassian's life and monastic writings.

3. I exclude here the treatise *On the Incarnation Against Nestorius* because the terminological issues it raises have more to do with Christological controversy than with monasticism.

4. E.g., 'Les emprunts grecs dans la latinité chrétienne', *Vigiliae Christianae* 4 (1950) 193–211, reprinted in *Études sur le latin des chrétiens*, vol. 3 (Rome, 1965) 127–45; 'La langue de saint Benoît', *Sancti Benedicti Regula Monachorum* (Maredsous, 1955), reprinted in *Études*, vol. 2 (Rome, 1961) 325–45; 'Wortform und Wortinhalt', *Münchener Theologische Zeitschrift* 7 (1956) 99–114; 'Le rôle des moines dans la transmission du patrimoine latin', *Revue de l'histoire de l'Eglise de France* 47 (1961) 185ff, reprinted in *Études*, vol. 4 (Rome, 1977) 293–307.

5. E.g., the important and fascinating work of P. Courcelle, *Les lettres grecques en Occident de Macrobe à Cassiodore*, 2nd ed. (Paris, 1948), and Mohrmann's studies, noted above. A helpful though incomplete list of latin translations can be found in J.T. Muckle, 'Greek Works Translated Directly into Latin Before 1350', *Mediaeval Studies* 4 (1942) 33–42 and 5 (1943) 102–114. For translations in the opposite direction, with helpful bibliography, see E. Dekkers, 'Les traductions grecques des écrits patristiques latins', *Sacris Erudiri* 5 (1953) 193–233, with ample bibliography.

6. E.g., A. Boon, *Pachomiana Latina*, Bibliothèque de la Revue d'Histoire Ecclésiastique 7 (Louvain, 1932); H.W.F.M. Hoppenbrouwers, *La plus ancienne version latine de la vie de saint Antoine par saint Athanase* (Utrecht/Nijmegen, 1960); K. Zelzer, *Basili Regula, CSEL* 86 (Vienna, 1986); J.G. Freire, *A versão latina por Pascásio de*

Dume dos Apophthegmata Patrum, 2 vols (Combray, 1971), and of course the texts in Migne.

7. L.T.A. Lorié, *Spiritual Terminology in the Latin Translations of the* Vita Antonii, Latinitas Christianorum Primaeva 11 (Nijmegen, 1955); H.W. Hoppenbrouwers, 'La technique de la traduction dans l'antiquité d'après la première version latine de la *Vita Antonii*', *Mélanges Christine Mohrmann: Nouveau Recueil* (Utrecht/ Antwerp, 1973) 80–95.

8. H. Hoppe, 'Griechisches bei Rufin', *Glotta: Zeitschrift für griechische und lateinische Sprache* 26 (1937) 132–44.

9. See most recently the first two volumes of his *Histoire littéraire du mouvement monastique dans l'antiquité* (Paris, 1991 and 1993); the third volume is at the press and an English translation is projected by Cistercian Publications. De Vogüé has identified the first appearance in Latin of many elements of the greek monastic vocabulary.

10. See C. von Paucker, 'Die Latinität des Joannes Cassianus', *Romanische Forschungen* 2 (1886) 391–448 for a study of Cassian's latin vocabulary; the comment about Greek is on p. 394. Paucker wrote before the critical edition of Cassian's works by M. Petschenig was available, and his observations must be complemented by Petschenig's indices in *CSEL* 17: 409–530.

11. In a few places he has translated or paraphrased either a greek biblical text or a text from Evagrius (see S. Marsili, *Giovanni Cassiano ed Evagrio Pontico*, Studia Anselmiana 5 [Rome, 1936]), but these cases are rare, and outside the scope of this article; see my forthcoming study for his handling of his sources. Cassian's works were themselves translated into Greek, at least in epitome; see Petschenig's remarks in CSEL 17: xcv–ciiii and the information in *Clavis Patrum Latinorum*, 2nd. ed. (Steenbruge, 1961) 118. In this article I resist the temptation to include light shed by the greek versions of Cassian's own writings.

12. *Ioannis Cassiani Eremitae de institutis renuntiantium Libri XII. Collationes Sanctorum Patrum XXIIII. Adiectae sunt quarundam obscurarum dictionum interpretationes ordine alphabeti dispositae: et observationes in loca ambigua et minus tuta*, etc. (Rome, 1588) [hereafter: Ciacconius].

13. *D. Joannis Cassiani Eremitae, Monasticarum Institutionum libri IV, de Vitiis capitalib. lib. VIII, Collationes SS. Patrum XXIV, de Verbi Incarnatione lib. VII. Nunc demum post varias editiones ad complurium mss. fidem a non paucis mendarum millibus incredibili labore expurgati: id quod ex subjectis ad calcem castigationibus facile cognosci poterit*, etc. (Antwerp: C. Plantin, 1578).

14. Ciacconius, 668–699.

15. Ciacconius, 699–718.

16. *Joannis Cassiani presbyteri, quem alii eremitam, alii abbatem nuncupant, Opera Omnia. Novissime recognita, repurgata et notis amplissimis illustrata*, etc. (Douai, 1616) [hereafter Gazeus].

17. The index is at the end of PL 50: cols 1309–24, and can easily be overlooked owing to the almost 1000 columns of texts by other authors which separate it from the end of Cassian's works.

18. PL 74:399–516.

19. CSEL 13 and 17.

20. The forthcoming english translation of Cassian's *Conferences* by Fr Boniface Ramsey includes a very useful commentary which often incorporates Gazaeus' most helpful suggestions. I am grateful to Fr Ramsey and to Cistercian Publications for allowing me access to the typescript of this commentary.

21. *Concordanza elettronica alle opere di Giovanni Cassiano* (Rome, 1990), developed by J. Mark Sheridan, OSB, to whom I am indebted for permission to use this very valuable product.

22. There is now also a concordance to Cassian's works in the *Corpus Christianorum* series of *Instrumenta Lexicologica Latin*, published by CETEDOC and Brepols of Turnhout.

23. This total does not distinguish different forms of a basic term (i.e., noun vs. adjective), and does not include proper names or the words found in the non-theological greek quotations (see next note). I will indicate when Cassian cites words in greek letters, and provide greek spellings when he does not. The spelling will be that of Petschenig's edition, except for the replacement of consonantal 'u' with 'v'. I will follow english alphabetical order, and will generally avoid cluttering the notes with references to precise locations in Cassian's works. The interested reader can consult Petschenig's indices, Gazaeus' or Ciacconius' editions, or my forthcoming study.

24. See *Conf.* 2.16.1, 4.6.2 and 13.5.3–4 for the non-religious examples; none of these has been identified, though he himself attributes the material in *Conf.* 13.5 to Socrates and Diogenes. Quotations related to theological or monastic texts will be discussed below.

25. For more information on key words, see Mark Sheridan, 'Monastic Terminology: Monk, Cenobite, Nun', in *RB 1980: The Rule of St. Benedict in Latin and English with Notes*, ed. Timothy Fry, et al. (Collegeville, 1981) 301–21, and also De Vogüé, *Histoire littéraire, passim.*

26. Although κέλλα is apparently derived from *cella*, itself derived from the Greek καλιά, hut, dwelling (see E.A. Sophocles, *Greek Lexicon of the Roman and Byzantine Periods*, 2nd ed. [Cambridge, Mass., 1887] 657b, and P.G.W. Glare, *Oxford Latin Dictionary* [Oxford, 1982] 295), Cassian would have known the word both in its greek form in the east and in the latin form in the west. The latin monastic use is probably derived from the greek monastic tradition rather than from the native (non-monastic) latin use of the word.

27. For information on many of these words, see de Vogüé's *Histoire littéraire.*

28. See Jerome, *Ep.* 22.34.1 (CSEL 5:196, l. 14) and Sulpitius Severus, *Dialogi* 1.15.2 (CSEL 1:167 l. 16).

29. Although this looks like a transliterated greek form, there is no lexical evidence for ἐρημιτικός; the greek adjective was ἐρημικός. He also makes an adjective out of *monasterium*, producing *monasterialis*, which is a more latinized form than is *heremiticus.*

30. This point was noted by de Vogüé, *Histoire littéraire*, 1:293. Cassian also develops a latinized adjective, *coenobialis*, just as he modified *monasterium* to get *monasterialis* and *heremita* to get *heremiticus.*

31. *Conferences* 18.5.4. Both Egeria and Cassian also use *monachus*. For a discussion of the two words, see de Vogüé, *Histoire littéraire*, 1:82,n.5.

32. See *Conf.* 21.1.2, 21.8.1, 21.9.7, 21.10.3. Although this *diaconia* includes almsgiving, it is a broader responsibility. In *Conf.* 18.7.7 the word is used in a narrower sense as 'alms'. See A. Blaise, *Dictionnaire Latin-Français des auteurs chrétiens* (Strasbourg, 1954) 268a, and T. Sternberg, 'Der vermeintliche Ursprung der westlichen Diakonien in Ägypten und die Collationes des Johannes Cassian', *Jahrbuch für Antike und Christentum* 31 (1988) 173–209, esp. 185ff.

33. *Inst.* 4.6, 4.18, 4.20, 5.40. See G.W.H. Lampe, *Patristic Greek Lexicon* (Oxford, 1961) 943b–944a for greek examples, and *Thesaurus Linguae Latinae* (Leipzig,

1900) 9/2:478–79 for Latin uses. Jerome uses *oeconomus* in *Ep.* 22.35.6 (CSEL 54:199, ll. 13–14).

34. *Conf.* 20.2.1. Cassian is the only source I have found for this form of the word, and Sophocles' entry for συγκελλίτης cites only Cassian. Both Sophocles and Lampe, however, list several references for a similar word, σύγκελλος, used for a patriarch's or abbot's aide, and later as an ecclesiastical title; see Sophocles, *Greek Lexicon*, 1020a and Lampe, *Patristic Greek Lexicon*, 1270b.

35. For a close study of Cassian's text, see A. de Vogüé, 'Les sources des premiers quatre livres des *Institutions* de Jean Cassien', *Studia Monastica* 27 (1985) 247–67.

36. Another term, *cucullus* (hood), is a latin word which in a greek form, κουκούλλιον, became a common monastic term in greek texts. Cassian would have heard it in the east, but he uses it in its original latin form. See A. Guillaumont's commentary on Evagrius' text in SCh 171:485, and R. Draguet, 'Le chapitre de l'*Histoire Lausiaque* sur les Tabennésiotes dérive-t-il d'une source copte?', part one, *Le Muséon* 57 (1944) 103–08.

37. Also found in the form μαφόριον, commonly used both for the monk's cowl and for the veil worn by women in Egypt. Both Ambrose and Jerome use the word *mafortes* before Cassian does. See TLL 8:49–50.

38. *Gestant etiam resticulas duplices laneo plexas subtemine, quas Graeci* ἀναλάβους *vocant, nos vero subcinctoria seu redimicula vel proprie rebracchiatoria possumus appellare* (*Inst.* 1.5).

39. Sch 171:488, l. 29, with Guillaumont's commentary. See also R. Draguet, 'Le chapitre', part one, 98.

40. See H. Frisk, *Griechisches Etymologisches Wörterbuch*, 2nd ed (rpt Heidelberg, 1973) 239. TLL describes it as a '*vocabulum peregrinum*' (2:2005–06). In any case, it occurs fairly commonly in its usual greek form βίρρος and its common latin form *birros*. Cassian's spelling seems to be based on the Greek variant βυρρός (which Liddell and Scott find in the papyri, *Greek-English Lexicon*, rev. ed. [Oxford, 1940] 333b); Sulpitius spells it the same way (*Dial.* 1.21.4; CSEL 1:174, l. 4). See the 'Onomasticon' in PL 74:413–16 for a review of latin monastic texts using the word.

41. So suggests Blaise, *Dictionnaire*, 628a.

42. See, e.g., H. l'Estienne, *Thesaurus Graecae Linguae*, rev. C.B. Hase *et al.* (Paris, 1831–65) 6:1151, who offers only 'erro, homo erraticus s. erroneus, i.q. πλάνης et πλάνος'. No lexicon has any meaning approaching 'garment', except for a reference in Lampe's *Lexicon* to a passage in the *Stromateis* where Clement uses it to describe a priestly robe decorated with planets and stars (*Stromateis* 5.6, as in Lampe, 1089a).

43. Isidore, *Etymologiae* 19.24.17–18 (PL 82:691B).

44. *Regula monachorum* 12.1 (PL 83:882A).

45. Du Cange, *Glossarium ad Scriptores Mediae et Infimae Latinitatis* (Paris, 1733–36) 5:539–40.

46. Blaise, *Dictionnaire*, 628a.

47. Guy, Sch 109:47. On *paenula*, see TLL 10/1:68–70, suggesting that the Latin *paenula* is derived from a Dorian form, φαινόλα. Liddell and Scott, however, consider φαινόλης to be derived from *paenula* (*Greek-English Lexicon*, 1912a). A. Walde suggests that *paenula* comes from ὁ φαινόλης and later by back-formation is the source for the Greek τὸ φαινόλιον/φαιλόνιον (*Lateinisches Etymologisches Wörterbuch*, 4th ed. [Heidelberg, 1965] 2:235). Let the reader decide.

48. *Inst.* 1.7. The latin text reads: *Ultimum est habitus eorum pellis caprina, quae*

melotis vel pera appellatur, et baculus, quae gestant ad imitationem eorum qui professionis huius praefiguravere lineas iam in veteri testamento.

49. See, e.g., Jerome, *Praefatio* 4 [to his translation of the pachomian texts] (Boon, p. 6, l. 11); Jerome usually translates it as *pellicula* or *pellis*. For Antony, see *Vita Antonii* 91 (PG 26:971–72).

50. It occurs several times in the Vulgate: 1 Sam 17:40, 49; 2 Kgs 4:42; Mt 10:10, Mk 6:8, Lk 9:3, 10:4, 22:35–36.

51. Gazaeus, PL 49:74D–75B, though Ciacconius seems unconcerned; see also the comments of E.C.S. Gibson, the nineteenth-century translator of most of Cassian's works into English (in the Nicene and Post-Nicene Fathers, *Second Series* 11:203, n.12), who offers several solutions.

52. At least not from what one gleans from Petschenig's apparatus (CSEL 17:13, l. 7).

53. Du Cange, *Glossarium*, 5:367.

54. Liddell and Scott define πήρα as '*leathern* pouch' (*Greek-English Lexicon*, 1401B).

55. Suidas' definition of πήρα as 'container for breads' becomes intriguing in this context (*Suidae Lexicon Graece et Latine*, ed. T. Gaisford and G. Bernhardy [Halle and Brunswick, 1853] 2:265).

56. If they offer a second definition as *melotis*, it is based solely on the text of *Inst.* 1.7, as in Blaise, *Dictionnaire*, 607a.

57. After writing this I found my solution both anticipated and confirmed by R. Draguet, who provides examples from *Historia Lausiaca* and *Apophthegmata* for the μηλωτή used to carry food for a journey ('Le chapitre', part one, 99).

58. The greek original is spelled variously in the papyri and in other texts: normally λαψάνιον or λαψάνη, but also λαμψάνη (especially in the papyri, and also as a variant in manuscripts of literary texts, e.g. *Historia Lausiaca* 32 [ed. C. Butler, *The Lausiac History of Palladius*, Texts and Studies 6, vol. 2:95, l. 9]). The variant could account for Cassian's *labsanion*, with the μπσ being heard as bs as in modern (and Byzantine) Greek; the papyri often follow pronunciation rather than orthographical convention. Jerome's *lapsania*, used in the translation of a written document, is more faithful to the normative spelling of the word. Draguet mentions the coexistence of the two forms in the egyptian Greek of the period ('Le chapitre', part two, in *Le Muséon* 58 [1945] 69–70).

59. *Maenomenia* is somewhat unusual, being a derivation of the word μαίνη, 'sardine'. See the entry in the 'Onomasticon' in PL 74:465–66.

60. Derived from τρώγω, 'to eat vegetables or fruit'. Another word, τραγήματα, derives from the aorist form of the same verb and is more common in the papyri; it is thought to be the older of the two, and occurs in *Hist. Laus.* 25 (p. 79, l. 13) and in Jerome's translation of the Pachomian *Praecepta* 37 (p. 22, l. 6). See Suidas, *Lexicon*, 2:1228; Frisk, *Griechisches Etymologisches Wörterbuch*, 2:938–39; Liddell and Scott, *Greek-English Lexicon*, 1831b; F. Preisigke, *Wörterbuch der griechischen Papyrusurkunden* (Berlin, 1927) 2:613.

61. *Praecepta* 53, with explanation: *quod genus herbarum est viliorum* (p. 29, l. 2).

62. There are two forms in Greek, παξαμᾶς and παξαμάδιον, with the first being more particular and the second more generic; they are both used in *Hist. Laus.* 22 (παξαμᾶς: p. 72, ll. 4, 11, 13–14; παξαμάδιον: p. 72, l. 12). For latin occurrences based on greek originals, see e.g. *Vitae Patrum* 5.4.64 (PL 73:872D), 5.10.65 (923C), 6.3.2 (1005B), 6.3.12 (1010C). There is a useful summary in the 'Onomasticon', PL 74:480D–482D.

63. *De jejunio* 1.4, 2.4, 9.1–9 (CCSL 2:1257, 1258, 1265–67).

64. Though see *Hist. Laus.* 11 (p. 34 l. 4) on Ammonius. Palladius' chapter on Evagrius describes his omophagic diet (which he eventually had to abandon); see *Hist. Laus.* 38.

65. Lampe, *Patristic Greek Lexicon*, 1415a. The word seems to have been used in various ways; for the plural form, Lampe gives the definition 'mats' (1415a); for πλέκω, Sophocles gives 'to braid' (*Greek Lexicon*, 895a).

66. *Vitae Patrum* 6.3.2 : *Quid operabimur hic? Dico eis: Plectam de palmis; et sumens folia palmarum de palude, ostendi eis initium plectae, et quomodo consuere deberent* (PL 73:1005a).

67. See, e.g., *Apophthegmata* Antony 1, his vision of an angel in the form of a monk who sat τὴν σειρὰν πλέκοντα (PG 65:76B), and *Hist. Laus.* 2, διὰ πάσης νυκτὸς καθήμενος ἔπλεκε σεῖραν τὴν ἐκ θαλλῶν φοινίκων (p. 17, ll. 10–11).

68. *Plecta*: *Conf.* 18.15.3 and 18.15.4; *sira*: *Conf.* 18.15.5.

69. See Preisigke, *Wörterbuch*, 2:428 for προχείριον. Neither L'Estienne nor Lampe has an entry for the word; Sophocles (*Greek Lexicon*, 956a) for the Greek and Blaise for the Latin (*Dictionnaire*, 666b) cite only Cassian; Liddell and Scott (*Greek-English Lexicon*, 1541a) note the papyri and an adjectival form in Plutarch.

70. See, e.g., Jerome's translation of Pachomian material, *Praec.* 88 and 95 (Boon, p. 39, l. 4, and p. 40, l. 2).

71. *Inst.* 4.13 and 5.35; *Conf.* 1.23.4, 4.21.2, 15.1.1, 17.3, 18.11.2.

72. There are entries in L'Estienne's *Thesaurus* for γύλειον, 'a persian vessel'; γύλιον, 'a container woven from palm-branches'; γυλιός, 'container for travelling, used by soldiers to keep essential items' (2:805). Liddell and Scott have γυλιός, γύλιος, γύλλιον: 'long-shaped wallet' (*Greek-English Lexicon*, 362a), while Preisigke has γυάλας, 'flask' (*Wörterbuch*, 1.313a).

73. TLL 6/2:1730 and Blaise, *Dictionnaire*, 376b.

74. *Institutes* 4.16.1.

75. See the references in Sophocles, *Greek Lexicon*, 303b. For the papyri, see the references in Preisigke's *Wörterbuch*, 261 and H.-A. Rupprecht's *Supplement 2 (1967–76)* (Wiesbaden, 1991) 31.

76. See Frisk, *Griechisches Etymologisches Wörterbuch*, 1.228 and G. Nencioni, "Βαύκαλις -αλιον e καυκάλιον", *Rivista degli Studi Orientali* 19 (1941) 98–104.

77. Greek: Nau 176, as in *Revue de l'Orient Chrétien* 13 (1908) 268–69; Rufinus: *Vit. Patrum* 3.14, *PL* 73:746C; Pelagius: *Vit. Patrum* 5.5.24, *PL* 73:879D.

78. He used it several times; see the "Onomasticon" in *PL* 74:508–09 for examples.

79. *Institutes* 4.20. One might compare here a text from the seventh-century spanish *Vitae sanctorum patrum emeretensium*, which reads: *vasa vinaria, que husitato nomine gillones aeut flascones appellantur* (ch. 2, ll. 45–46 in CCSL 116:16–17).

80. Cassian then translates οἰκονομία in this passage as *dispensatio*. See Sternberg, 'Der vermeintliche Ursprung', 185, on Cassian's use of *dispensatio*, and also Lampe, *Patristic Greek Lexicon*, 942b.

81. TLL notes that the plural is found only in this instance (9/2:477).

82. TLL cites only Cassian for this form (9/2:478).

83. E.g., *In Hieremiam* 6.48 (CSEL 74:344, 10).

84. See Lampe, *Patristic Greek Lexicon*, 140b.

85. LXX: Ex 18:21 (*Conf.* 7.5.2, a macaronic quotation in which he uses one greek word from the LXX), Ps 115:9 (*Conf.* 9.12.1), Ps 145:8b (*Conf.* 3.15.3), Si 5:3

(*Conf.* 9.12.1), Wis 9:15 (*Conf.* 7.4.2). To this list one might add his commentary on Job 1:9–10, where he elucidates the text with the greek phrase ἕως σφόδρα, although it does not actually appear in that biblical text. Greek NT: Mt 6:11 (*Conf.* 9.21.1), Phil 3:14 (*Conf.* 1.5.3), 1 Tim 6:20 (*Conf.* 14.16.4).

86. Ciaccionius listed dozens of examples (pp. 699–718) and Petschenig indicates more than a hundred. These are but a fraction of the recognizable biblical quotations or allusions, but in some cases the proportion of LXX passages becomes substantial or even preponderant, e.g., for Proverbs, Ecclesiastes, Song of Songs, Wisdom, and some of the Minor Prophets.

87. See *Inst.* 12.31, *Conf.* 8.10.1 and 23.8.2, where he compares his own latin version of the LXX to the version which 'expresses the Hebrew truth' (*Inst.* 12.31), viz., Jerome's Vulgate.

88. Ciacconius, 699. About half of his quotations from Job and Song of Songs are clearly based on the LXX, as are just under half of those from the Book of Wisdom; he also prefers to cite some of the minor prophets (Joel, Jonah, Habbakkuk, Haggai, Zachariah) in the LXX form.

89. The *Psalterium Gallicanum* was Jerome's revision of the Old Latin on the basis of the Hexapla text of the LXX. This version, rather than Jerome's later *Psalterium iuxta Hebraeos*, became the liturgical Psalter of the Roman Church. On the latin Psalters, see C. Estin, 'Les traductions du Psautier', in *Le monde latin antique et la Bible*, ed. J. Fontaine and C. Pietri, Bible de Tous les Temps 2 (Paris, 1985) 67–88.

90. *Conf.* 6.10.1. In Rufinus' version of Origen's homily on this passage one finds an extended discussion of the word *ambidexter*, a latinization of the greek word. Rufinus does not use or transliterate the greek word itself. See Origen, *In librum Iudicum homiliae* 3.5–6 (*Origenes Werke* [*G.C.S.*] 7.485–87), and Hoppe, 'Griechisches bei Rufin', 137. See also the discussion of this passage by M. Sheridan, 'Models and Images of Spiritual Progress', in *Spiritual Progress: Studies in the Spirituality of Late Antiquity and Early Monasticism*, Studia Anselmiana 115 (Rome, 1994) 102–03.

91. The greek variant of Lk 10:42 reads, 'there is need of few things, or even one' (ὀλίγων δέ ἐστιν χρεία ἢ ἑνός); the familiar text, of course, reads 'there is need of but one thing' (ἑνὸς δέ ἐστιν χρεία). For the manuscript evidence, see *Novum Testamentum Graece*, 27th ed. (Stuttgart, 1993) 194n. Cassian uses this as the basis for comparing different degrees of contemplation.

92. *Conf.* 9.21.1. *Supersubstantialem* in Vulgate Mt 6:11, *cotidianum* in Vulgate Lk 11:3. This section of *Conf.* 9 was inspired by Evagrius' commentary on the Lord's Prayer, preserved in what seems to be an epitome in Coptic (Bohairic text in P. Lagarde, *Catenae in Evangelia aegyptiacae quae supersunt* [Göttingen, 1886] 13; a misleadingly free translation by J. Simon was included by Irénée Hausherr in 'Le Traité de l'Oraison d' Évagre le Pontique', RAM 15 [1934] 88–89. For more on both Evagrius and Cassian on the Lord's Prayer (and for a new translation of the Evagrian text), see my forthcoming study. Cassian's comparison of latin versions, of course, was not inspired by Evagrius!

93. For a brief discussion of the semitic background, see my *Working the Earth of the Heart: The Messalian Controversy in History, Texts, and Language to A.D. 431* (Oxford, 1991) 200–202.

94. *Conf.* 17.25.16, quoting Ezk 33:13–16.

95. Cassian uses *arras* twice (*Conf.* 7.6.4, 10.7.3), and *subarratum* once (*Conf.* 7.6.4).

96. See Blaise, *Dictionnaire*, 780a. Sulpitius uses *subarro* in the context of betrothal (*Ep.* 2.12, CSEL 1:241, 22).

97. See TLL 2:631–33, citing Pliny, the latin version of Irenaeus, and Augustine. Tertullian and Jerome seem to have preferred *arrabo* or *arrabonem*.

98. See A. Resch, *Agrapha: Aussercanonische Evangelienfragmente*, TU 5/3 (Leipzig, 1889) 116–27. The usual greek form of the part of the text quoted by Cassian is γίνεσθε τραπεζῖται δόκιμοι. The latin versions vary, with Cassian's being closest to that found in Rufinus' translation of Origen's *Homilia in Leviticum* 3.8. Origen's homily also provides the closest parallel to Cassian's exposition; after citing the short form of the saying and also 1 Th 5:21, Origen's text continues: *Solus enim est dominus Noster Iesus Christus, qui te huiusmodi artem possit edocere, per quam scias discernere, quae sit pecunia, quae veri regis imaginem tenet, quae vero sit adulterina, et (ut vulgo dicitur) extra monetam formata, quae nomen quidem habeat regis, veritatem autem regiae figurae non teneat* (GCS 29 [=vol. 6 of Origen's works] p. 315, 6–14). The brief summary of Cassian's discussion provided in *Conf.* 2.9 strongly resembles this passage by Origen. As will be seen below, Cassian may well have known Origen's homily in its original Greek.

99. Both *paracharaximus* and *trapezita* are used again in *Conf.* 2.8–9 when Cassian recapitulates the earlier discussion.

100. The entry for *paracharaximus* in TLL 10/1:293 refers extensively to Cassian, and additionally only to a pseudonymous epistle attributed to Ignatius of Antioch. Blaise cites only Cassian (*Dictionnaire*, 592b).

101. Ciacconius suggested the link to Origen ('Annotationes', 685). Origen, in turn, may have been inspired by Clement; cf. *Stromateis* 7.15.90, τοὺς δοκίμους τραπεζίτας τὸ ἀκίβδηλον νόμισμα τοῦ κυρίου ἀπὸ τοῦ παραχαράγματος διακρίνοντας (GCS 17 [=vol. 3 of Clement's works], p. 64, ll. 17–18).

102. A phenomenon noted by Mohrmann, 'Les emprunts', 130 and 'Wortform und Wortinhalt', *passim*.

103. *Conf.* 24.15 and 24.17. Cf. Evagrius, *Praktikos* 89 (Sch 171:680–88) and *Ep. 29* (ed. W. Frankenberg, *Euagrius Ponticus*, Abhandlungen der königlichen Gesellschaft der Wissenschaften zu Göttingen, Philol.-Hist. Klasse, Neue Folge 13.2 [Berlin, 1912] 586 [Syriac MS. fol. 172 bβ] and 587 [Frankenberg's Greek retroversion].

104. *Conf.* 13.5.2 and 19.9.1; cf. Evagrius, *In Psalmum 4.*7 on ἡ μερικὴ γνῶσις, 'partial knowledge' (ed. J. B. Pitra, *Analecta Sacra*, vol. II [Frascati, 1884] 454).

105. *Conf.* 16.14.1. I have not found a source for his distinction between the two.

106. *Inst.* 8.10 (=*mens, ratio*) and *Conf.* 7.4.2 (νοῦς as ἀεικίνητος καὶ πολυκίνητος).

107. Once in Greek, *Conf.* 1.5.3, and several times in transliteration.

108. *Conf.* 1.2.1.

109. See M. Harl, 'Le guetteur et la cible: Les deux sens de *Skopos* dans la langue religieuse des chrétiens', *Revue des études grecques* 74 (1961) 450–68, esp. 458. I am indebted to Fr Boniface Ramsey for this reference. See also Terrence Kardong, 'Aiming for the Mark: Cassian's Metaphor for the Monastic Quest', *Cistercian Studies* [Quarterly] 22 (1987) 213–21, and Sheridan, 'Models and Images', 114–16.

110. See Sophocles, *Greek Lexicon*, 169b; Blaise, *Dictionnaire*, 85b; and Lampe, *Patristic Greek Lexicon*, 140a.

111. See the analysis of it in my forthcoming study.

112. See *Inst.* 5–12 and *Conf.* 5.

113. *Gastrimargia* is used only in transliteration.

114. *Acedia/ acedior* in various versions of Ecclesiasticus 6:26, 22:16, 29:6.

115. Augustine uses greek forms of φιλαργυρία (*De libero arbitrio* 3.17 [CCSL 29:303, 26] and *Enarrationes in psalmum 118 11.6* [CCSL 40:1699, l. 28]). But even if Cassian had read these texts, he was not dependent upon them here.

116. πρακτική, like θεωρητική, is a substantive use of the adjective.

117. E.g., Evagrius uses ἡ πρακτική/πρακτικός sixteen times in the *Praktikos*, but ἄσκησις only three times, and even less frequently in other works.

118. *Conf.* 14.1.3, 14.2, 14.4.1, 14.8.1, 14.8.3, 21.34.4.

119. *Conf.* 14.1.3; cf. Evagrius, *Prak.* 78 (Sch 171:666); also cf. *Conf.* 14.2 and 15.2.2.

120. *Conf.* 21.34.4; cf. *Conf.* 10.3.1, 14.3.1, 14.8.3, 14.9.2, 14.9.4.

121. The first four are used a few times each, the remainder occur once each.

122. On the Latin equivalents for ἄσκησις, see Lorié, *Spiritual Terminology*, 88–99, although Lorié's reading of Cassian is a bit misleading in this regard.

123. *Conf.* 18.7.5 and 19.9.1. See Lampe, *Patristic Greek Lexicon*, 67ab.

124. θεωρητική: *Conf.* 14.1.3, 14.2, 14.8.1.

125. *Conf.* 1.1, 14.2, 14.8.3, 14.9.2, 19.5.2, 19.9.1, 23.4.4.

126. *Inst.* 11.18; *Conf.* 1.8.2–3, 1.12, 3.1.3, 3.7.3, 6.10.2, 7.3.4, 10.8.5, 10.10.1, 10.10.14, 14.3.1, 19.4.1, 19.6.4, 22.13.2, 23.3.1, 23.5.4–5, 23.13.2. On θεωρία in monastic tradition, see Lorié, *Spiritual Terminology*, 144–50 and Lampe, *Patristic Greek Lexicon*, 648a–649b.

127. See the entries in TLL 3:647–652, and de Vogüé's remarks in *Histoire littéraire*, 2:111–12 and 146 on Augustine's reworking in *De moribus* of Jerome's monastic taxonomy in *Ep. 22*; also cf. Lorié, *Spiritual Terminology*, 157–63. On the significance of the vision of God in Augustine's thought, see B. McGinn, *The Foundations of Mysticism* (New York, 1992) 232–43.

128. See the classic treatment by J. Raasch, 'The Monastic Concept of Purity of Heart and Its Sources', *Studia Monastica* 8 (1966) 7–33, 183–213; 10 (1968) 7–55; 11 (1969) 269–314; 12 (1970) 7–41. For the monastic understanding of ἀπάθεια, see N. Groves, 'Mundicia cordis: A Study of the Theme of Purity of Heart in Hugh of Pontigny and the Fathers of the Undivided Church', in M. B. Pennington, ed., *One Yet Two: Monastic Tradition East and West*, Cistercian Studies 29 (Kalamazoo, 1976) 304–331, esp. 314–18 on Cassian, and D. N. Bell, 'Apatheia: The Convergence of Byzantine and Cistercian Spirituality', *Cîteaux* 38 (1987) 141–64, esp. 147–48 on Cassian.

129. Cassian uses this word only in transliteration, while his opponent, Jerome, used it in its greek form in *Ep. 33*, ch. 3 (CSEL 56:244–45).

130. E.g., *De oratione* 117–23 (PG 79:1193A-C); *Kephalaia Gnostica* 3.86–88, ed. A. Guillaumont, *Patrologia Orientalis* 28.132–35; *Ad monachos* 92 (cf. 21), ed. J. Driscoll, *The 'ad monachos' of Evagrius Ponticus*, Studia Anselmiana 104 (Rome, 1991) 62 and 49.

131. *Scholia in Ecclesiasten* 55 (ed. P. Géhin, Sch 397:156). Cf. *Prak.*, Prol. 8 and ch. 24 (Sch 171:492 and 556); *Ep. fidei* 7, three times (=Ps-Basil, *Ep.* 8.7, ed. M. F. Patrucco, *Basilio di Cesarea: Le lettere*, Corona Patrum [Turin, 1983] 1.98–99); *Schol. in Ps. 5.11* (ed. Pitra, *Analecta Sacra* 2:455); no. 41 of the *Parainesis* which is at least influenced by Evagrius if not actually written by him (ed. J. Muyldermans, *Evagriana Syriaca* [Louvain, 1952], 132 [Syriac] and 162 [French]).

132. *Ep. fidei* 12 (=Ps-Basil *Ep.* 8.12, ed. Patrucco, 1:110); *Ep. 56* (ed. Frankenberg, 604 [Syriac MS. fol. 182bα-β] and 605 [Greek retroversion]); *Schol. in Ps.* 68.29 (PG 12:517AB), 118.1 (PG 12:1588C).

133. E.g., *Ad mon.* 8, 131, 133 (Driscoll, *Ad monachos*, 46, 69–70); *Schol. in Proverbia* 199, 247, 291, 328 (Sch 340:294, 342, 382–84, 418).

134. *Schol. in Prov.* 136 (Sch 340:232).

Late Ninth-Century Saints Hathumoda and Liutberga

Suzanne F. Wemple

THE SEARCH for autonomy to act, freedom of choice, and perfection in spiritual matters was as much the objective of women as it was of men in the Middle Ages. In religious life, these goals were far more attainable than in secular existence. I have shown in my writings that after the sixth century, living a spiritual life devoted to God was the only mode of life open to women outside the home in the lands occupied by the Franks. At that time, the female diaconate—baptizing and teaching by women—was abolished and the status of clerical wives was degraded.[1]

In the latter half of the ninth century, churchmen became bolder and refused to accept the mandate that their wives were mere concubines. The ordination of deaconesses over forty was once again permitted. In spite of this liberalization, women in monasteries or in their recluse cells appeared only in roles thought suitable to their sex. They made no attempt to claim a share in pastoral or ministerial functions. Deaconess was a title taken by queens and princesses when they withdrew to a monastery which possessed a ruling abbess; or, it may have served the superior of a monastery.[2]

The purpose of this article is to examine the spiritual lives women religious lived as nuns/canonesses or recluses in the latter half of the ninth century as the carolingian empire began to disintegrate. How did the authors represent female saints, and how did they describe their distinguishing character traits?

Female saints were few in carolingian times, when compared to the great numbers living among the Merovingians.[3] The difference may be explained by the real enthusiasm toward religious life that marked the late sixth and seventh centuries. Men regarded women as capable of transcending their biological and sexual roles and of seeking fulfillment in religious life. Churchmen's efforts were supported by the frankish kings, who punished crimes of rape and the abduction of religious women by loss of property.

By this time, double and single female monasteries flourished. The double monastery was a community of men and women living in separate quarters, over which an abbess usually presided. She was the ruler over the everyday needs—economic, disciplinary, sacramental, scholarly, and spiritual—of her community. Some professed virgins and widows remained living in the world, devoting themselves to the poor, orphans, and widows, looking after churches as housekeepers, praying, and contemplating.[4]

In the carolingian period, anglo-saxon missionaries, instead of irish, as had been the case earlier, predominated on the continent. Whereas the irish monks had been enthusiastic about the creation of monasteries, anglo-saxon monks brought all forms of religious life under episcopal control and, in return, the bishops cooperated in the creation of a frankish *Reichskirche*. Benedictine rule or canonical life were the only acceptable forms of communal living. Earlier monasteries had followed various rules, Caesarian, Aurelian, Columban, an amalgamation of these, or none at all. As advisers to kings and educators of princes and other notables, abbots were able to mitigate the constraints placed on their communities by the benedictine rule. Abbesses could not lessen the difficulties; they were not allowed to be the advisers of bishops and they were forbidden to educate boys. The distinction between the benedictine and the canonical life for women was that canonesses could own personal property, although it had to be administered by an outsider. Canonesses had to be cloistered and were carefully guarded from all contact with men. Moreover, women who desired to be veiled had to join a community. Small nunneries were merged and double monasteries were gradually dissolved. New monasteries were introduced only in recently conquered lands.[5]

To understand the lives of women who devoted themselves to religion, I have elected to look at and compare two saints, Hathumoda[6] and Liutberga[7]. Both lived in Saxony, a land conquered by Charlemagne. The Saxons had to adopt Christianity at the beginning of the ninth century. That in less than a half a century it could produce saints of such impact as Hathumoda and Liutberga tells a great deal about the strength of Christianity. Both women practised the virtues that distinguished female saints for centuries to come, but their lives of service differed in most respects. Their hagiographers sought to produce lives which showed that intelligence, willingness to be poor, readiness to work, fast, pray, read the Scriptures, and be charitable, an affectionate disposition towards others, and above all, humble and willing readiness to accept God's demands, were essential to female saints. They differed, however, in their descriptions of the activity, character, life-style, visions, power to prophecy, and death of their heroines.

They wrote about the same time. Hathumoda's life was written in 875, a year after her death; and Liutberga's about ten years earlier, around 865. Liutberga died in the reign of Louis II, king of the Franks and Saxons, who ruled between 840–875[8]. The authors were personally acquainted with their subjects. Agius, Hathumoda's brother, wrote the *Vita sanctae Hathumodae* together with *Dialogus Agii de obitu sanctae Hathumodae abbatissae*, for the use of the nuns at Gandersheim. Agius was a monk at Lamspring, not far from Gandersheim, where Hathumoda served as first abbess from 852–874[9]. In both Agius' works, but especially in the *Dialogus*, a poem, he tells the nuns about his devotion for his sister: 'Her beloved image does not recede from my heart, whether I am sleeping or whether I am awake.'[10]

Liutberga's *Vita* was written by a monk, probably from Fulda, who visited her at her cell built beside or in the church of Saint Pusinna, a monastery in Wendhausen.[11] Although he did not write a poem about her, the author of Liutberga's *Vita*, made it clear that everybody loved her: 'and briefly, she was the beloved of all, not only of those with whom she had conversation but by all those who knew her. She thought highly of everybody and everybody thought highly of her.'[12]

Hathumoda was the daughter of Liudolf, the duke of East Saxony, and of Oda, who was descended from eminent frankish nobility.

Agius tells us of their brothers and sisters, especially of Liudberga, who was the wife of Louis the German's son, Louis II, and of Gerberga and Christiana who were abbesses of Gandersheim after Hathumoda's death. He devotes the first part of the *Vita* to the praise of their parents, Hathumoda's education at Herford, and her virtues.[13] By contrast, Liutberga's author did not know anything about her family, and gave a garbled name for the town where he claimed she was born.[14] He does tell about the family of Count Hessi, whose widowed daughter, Gisla, was Liutberga's protectress and patroness. Countess Gisla chose Liutberga from a monastery, attracted by her intelligence and sweet disposition, to be her companion in the travels she undertook to look after her estates. After Gisla's death, Liutberga served the countess' son, Bernhard as manager of his estates. Gisla had loved Liutberga as a daughter and her son and his two wives regarded her as a mother.[15]

Both saints manifested in their childhood the characteristics that made them famous as an abbess and a recluse. Hathumoda, from the time of her early childhood, seemed to be destined for her ultimate vocation. We are told that she considered sports and play a waste of time. She had no desire for gold and jewels. When she had to dress up and wear headdresses, ribbons, combs, earrings, necklaces, bracelets, wigs, and perfume, she would protest with tears and anxious sighs. None of these adornments did she ordinarily affect. Above all else, Hathumoda preferred her studies. Her sympathetic parents sent her to the famous monastery of Herford to be educated. As she grew, so did her desire to become a bride of Christ, and she took the veil while at Herford. Agius informs us that from her early days at Herford, she demonstrated the attributes that made her a loving abbess. She was remembered for her affectionate attention to the persons with whom she lived. She praised each for that person's strength *in monastic service*, charity, humility, obedience, patience, liberality, or abstinence, and extolled all for their modesty, piety, and chastity.[16]

Liutberga, as a girl, was prudent in her judgment, truthful in her words, faithful with what was entrusted to her, generous in alms, steady in works, outstanding in piety, and superior in kindness. She took medical care to the infirm. Besides her willingness to help, she

> especially persevered in divine lauds, psalms, hymns, and spiritual songs . . . evil things and attractions of the world, she declined as if they were the precipice of the abyss [hell]. In Sacred Scriptures she trained herself assiduously, and daily she meditated.'[17]

The author declared that if the imbecility of her sex did not hinder it, she would appear well informed. Apparently, he was repeating the accepted view of churchmen that the essence of all women was foolishness. Agius did not make such disparaging comments about his sister Hathumoda.

By nature Liutberga was talented, and she became skillful in the various arts which were the crafts of women, by observing and having conversation about them. She remained faithful to Countess Gisla, she was said to be the mother of the needy, and her fame spread among aristocratic ladies.[18]

The circumstances that prompted Hathumoda to become an abbess and Liutberga a recluse were connected in the case of Hathumoda with her parents, and in the case of Liutberga with her patron. Bishops consecrated both, and for Liutberga, a bishop was instrumental in her obtaining a recluse cell.

We are told that Hathumoda's parents went to Rome to pray, bring home bones of saints, and talk to the pope. They must have mentioned their desire to establish a monastery on their own property and to have their daughter serve as the first abbess, for the pope apparently gave his blessing. On their return home, the father and the mother sent for Hathumoda:

> With apostolic authority and the benediction of her bishop, she was elected and constituted to be the spiritual mother at first to a few and later to many sisters. There, afterwards she lived with her sisters in so much corporal chastity and so much mental sanctity that is not in our capacity to explain.[19]

Liutberga, after the death of Countess Gisla, travelled, usually alone, to supervise work on various parts of the estate. Whenever she had time, and that was mostly in the evening, she visited churches. If there was not a consecrated sanctuary in the neighborhood, it was her habit to go to the nearest church at night, accompanied only by a boy or a girl. She remained there until daybreak when the Mass was celebrated and she received communion. Going without sleep, frequently fasting, and working assiduously, she changed her appearance. Her body became emaciated, and the color of her face extremely pale. Count Bernhard, thinking that she was ill, upon inquiry found out that her condition was the result of the demands made upon her body by her work and her devotions. Astonished, the count told Liutberga that she was endangering her life. In the evenings, as she walked and prayed without protection, he informed her, she ought to be afraid of pagans, robbers, falsely-named Christians, savage beasts, and the bite of foxes. The determined Liutberga answered in quotations from the Bible, among them Romans 8:31: 'If God is for us, who is against us'. She quieted the count to the extent that he promised he would give her whatever she desired. She confessed that she wished to spend the rest of her days as a recluse to atone for her sins. When Bishop Theotgrim came to visit the count, Liutberga made known to him her desire. Warning her that she had to withstand the attacks of the devil and the detractions and false praises of men, he acceded to her wishes. With his entourage he travelled to Wendhausen to bless the cell which the count had built at the church of the monastery of Saint Pusinna. He led Liutberga into it and forbade others' access to it.[20]

The hagiographer tells us of Liutberga's busy reclusive life. Her existence was spartan. She ate very little, salted bread and herbs regularly. She treated herself to vegetables and once in a while a small fish on Sundays and feast days. Wild apples and berries in season offered some variety in her diet. She prayed and meditated, heard Mass daily, and gave oblations to God. When the sisters assembled for the canonical hours, she sang and prayed with them. In addition, she dyed cloth in her cell; she refreshed and consoled the poor, the widows, the children, and orphans; she healed the sick, and gave comfort to those who for their crimes were in custody. 'To all who came to her . . . she was affable, even her absence was delightful to those who departed from her, because they considered the time spent with her a great advantage.' Her influence soon expanded beyond her cell and great men and women, even prelates, sought her counsel. Ansgar, bishop of Bremen, sent her many girls to be trained in psalms and skillful handiworks. When they were educated, Liutberga gave them freedom to return home or to go wherever they wished.[21]

Gandersheim, under Hathumoda's care, became an outstanding institute of canonesses, distinguishable from a benedictine monastery in that the members could own personal property. Some members of the community, possibly Hathumoda herself, remained Benedictine. Brunshausen, where Hathumoda was a nun prior to becoming the abbess of Gandersheim, was Benedictine. She was buried next to her father, at Brunshausen which became a male Benedictine house after the foundation of Gandersheim.[22] Agius refers to a rule that says that all those that chose to lead a common life, should have the same food and vestments. All should eat, rest, work, and pray at canonical hours together at the same time. Contrary to the custom of many consecrated women, nobody should go out of the monastery to visit either parents or possessions or to speak or eat with parents or guests without permission. Nobody was to have a cell or servants. All were equal, even those who had very little property. The separation from men was absolute. Only a priest could enter the cloister and then only to heed the call of a sick sister or perform a ceremony.[23] The way the members lived was presumably the creation of Hathumoda. It differed from the *Institutio sanctimonialium*, proclaimed in 816, in that it prohibited the virgins from having servants. Hathumoda did not want servants because she wanted the community to resemble a benedictine house. In other words, she probably ran Gandersheim as a house of mixed rules, with some members being benedictine and some canonesses.[24]

Hathumoda did not only all that the sisters of Gandersheim had to do, but more. She abstained from meat, wore woolen cloth against her skin, never left the monastery, was among the first at canonical hours and the last to leave, slept in the same house with the others, went to bed last and was the first to get up. Eager to be a saint and beloved by God, she did these and similar things easily. She wanted to be loved rather than feared. She sought to teach by example rather than discipline. She shunned the ways of the world, and the sensuality of the married. The vow of virginity she observed carefully; she would not give cause to the envious for slander. Impudent speech and ugly words never issued from her lips. No one ever heard her quarrel, abuse, swear, humiliate, or lie. Nobody saw her angry, turbulent, or sneering. She either loved all according to their singular qualities or honored them with reverence.[25]

Her collective love for her sisters was shown in her correction of their faults. She manifested care for them and, in return, she was venerated with affection. 'She wept for their digression as if it were her own; whenever someone became insecure in faith or in mind, she was likewise ill; whenever someone was scandalized, she was shocked also.' She was so humble, despite her illustrious birth and the high place she occupied, that nobody was more inclined to bow to others, and be more submissive. Patience was among her many virtues.[26]

She was also very generous. She fed the hungry and provided for the destitute. With sick people, she was very charitable, not only with the sisters but also with those who were far away, to whom she sent food by messengers. Shortly before her illness, several sisters were gravely sick. She visited, fed, and nursed them, and tried to cheer them up.[27]

She read the Scriptures diligently and urged the practice on the other sisters. Her brother was of the opinion that no one could approach the Scriptures with more understanding than Hathumoda. The strength of her intellect, understanding, and energy was applied to teaching the sisters. She not only taught with words, but also with questions. Hathumoda lived her faith, and carried its message to all with whom she came into contact. She praised God and the Scriptures, and her life reflected this praise.[28]

Both Hathumoda and Liutberga had a special attachment to Saint Martin of Tours. Liutberga had a vision in which the saint advised her on the quality of food and clothing, perseverance of praying, and the use of her life.[29] Hathumoda, once when she was sick, had a dream about a beautiful field with many flowers. When she looked more closely, the flowers were the sisters she had known in her younger days. All of a sudden, the field caught fire. Hathumoda prayed to the Lord and especially to Christ, and called on Saint Martin, whom she had always treated with special reverence. Martin appeared to say that the fire was extinguished and the sisters were saved. Another time he became visible when she was awake, although the sisters, who were sitting on her bed, did not see him. She made them get up to show him that they were very glad about his presence and to make room for him.[30]

The visions of Liutberga and Hathumoda were very dissimilar. Liutberga was besieged by Satan. She heard a voice telling her that it was not pleasing to God that she should sleep in bed, and the devil appeared as a young vassal bringing her a gift. In both instances, she was quick to recover her senses and recognized the devil. He appeared on another occasion looking like a boy and when she told him that she was not afraid of him, he returned, first with a dog, then with a terrible looking goat. He was disappointed when she declared that he could have only the power God permitted. Another time, when the devil arranged for mice to cover the floor, walls, and ceiling of her cell, she dispersed them with holy water. Sometimes the devil referred to himself as one of the angels, saints, or apostles. At other times, puffed up with pride or incited by insanity, he told her that he was Christ and asked Liutberga to pray to him. When a brother inquired how she knew that she was seeing false images, Liutberga replied that her prayers were answered: 'Whenever I am in doubt, I will see a black stain on their behinds'. Hearing this, Satan appeared 'in his terrible deformity'. He talked about domestic fights, civil wars, parricides, adultery, incestuous marriages, and all kind of evil crimes, and he boasted of being the author of all this collectively. In short, now terrifying, now reproaching, now insulting, now tearing her to pieces, now insisting on pleasure, the enemy did not leave her in peace.[31]

In Hathumoda's *Vita*, we find, instead of Satan, startling visions of herself and the sisters. She saw a huge wheel with the heads of animals, to which she and several sisters were bound with chains and which revolved into a river. She feared falling into the river, but instead fell to earth, where awakened, she lay trembling. Likewise, on the days that followed, she saw herself flying between the earth and the sky, and saw a large hole in the floor of her church. When she inquired how it had occurred and how it could be filled, she heard a voice telling her that she would fill it; it would be her future mark of distinction. Then a multitude of voices began singing to a stringed instrument and she joined them saying: 'This is my rest, I will live here in eternity.' The two visions together tell a story. The wheel was God's plan, with the four evangelists. Hathumoda and the sisters of Gandersheim were tied to an important, significant place on the wheel. Instead of falling through the river into hell, she was to be buried and then celebrated in the church at Gandersheim.[32]

At times lay people played roles in Liutberga's visions and prophecy. For example, a vassal was in love with a chambermaid. One day towards evening, Liutberga, seeing the girl hurrying to meet him, called her, asking that she finish the work she had begun, making thread and wicks for candles and lamps. The chambermaid longed to go to her lover, but shame made her stay. Seeing this, the devil made such a noise that the bottom of Liutberga's cell was thought to have collapsed. The maid fainted, but she was comforted. Liutberga saw the devil take the soul of the lover, who was so shaken that he went to bed and died.[33] On another occasion, she reminded a countess to pray for her mother. Only three days later did messengers announce the death of the countess's mother. When a brother asked Liutberga whether she knew everyone's day of death and especially her own, the answer was 'no'. She added, however, that God had communicated to her that she would live in the cell for thirty years.[34] Through these stories the author wanted to convey that Liutberga was indeed God's special spokesman.

Liutberga was very mindful about the pronouncements of the papacy and the orders of the penitentials. For instance, if someone wished to fast for her, she chose Saturday because the 'Roman Bishop' stated by a decree that Christ had been buried on Saturday.[35] Or, despite the permission that she obtained from the bishop to baptize a child, when she heard that the child was dead prior to baptism and, like the couple's firstborn who had also died before baptism, had been the fruit of Sunday love, she told the desolate mother to repent, because the day of conception prevented the salvation of both babies.[36] Indeed, both of these cases served to remind the readers, the nuns of Wendhausen, to obey the church's pronouncements and commands.

Hathumoda's active mind worried about things as diverse as royal protection for her cloister,[37] and whether or not to see her brother when she became sick.[38] Hathumoda's final illness must not have been restful. Her devotions produced visions which Agius tells us must have been so illustriously divine that Hathumoda could not disclose them to any one, not to her sister Genberga, and not even to her mother. Agius describes in some detail her futile efforts to communicate them.[39]

Liutberga's death scene is short. When she began to be ill, she summoned the priests daily, making confession and accepting benedictions with prayers. When she accepted the last sacrament, she lay down before the crucifix that hung on her window, stretched out her arms in the manner of the cross and said: 'You were worthy to mount the pillory of the cross for us sinners and had compassion on the hanging thief, have compassion on me, because into your hands I command my spirit'. Surrounded by sad friends, she said psalms and gave her spirit up to God.[40]

A much more detailed discourse on Hathumoda's last days was provided by Agius. Whenever her pain permitted, she looked after her very old aunt, her father's sister, who was in the monastery. The dean, the monastery's second in command, and the guardian often visited Hathumoda with their problems. The sisters said psalms, prayed, and slept outside her cell. Her blood sisters, Gerberga and Christina, were especially anxious. They sat at her bed, helped her, made her bed, put pillows under her head, sustained her, raised her body in bed, rubbed her hands, and warmed her feet and stomach. When she was agitated, they cooled her with a fan, dried her perspiration, cooled water for washing, prepared and served her meals, and anticipated everything that had to be done. Above all, her loving mother, hiding her concern, consoled the weeping sisters. She ran between the church and Hathumoda's bed, crying on a saint's tomb in the church that she should die instead of her daughter. Agius noted that Hathumoda's mind remained sharp as her body began to fail. With Christ in her heart, she confessed her sins continuously, prayed and sang the psalms, and spoke about the salvation of her soul.

On her death bed, Bishop Marquard with his clergy gave her sacred unction, last reconciliation, and the sacrament. 'All joining together, they sang psalms, said litanies and prayers, read the Gospel, so that not one of them should omit anything that must be done before a soul leaves . . .' As the last verse of psalm forty was said, ... 'she gave her saintly soul to heaven, she breathed her last spirit'.[41]

It is apparent that the authors each exhibited a strong bias which colored their portraits of their respective subjects. Agius was driven by a desire to show the religious fervor of his entire family and their role in Hathumoda's saintly behavior. The parents' tolerance of her childhood affectations of dress, refusal of ornaments, play, and sports, their encouragement of her scholarship, the establishment of the monastery, the devotion of her siblings and her mother throughout her last illness, all demonstrated the family's contribution toward her sainthood.

Liutberga's hagiographer was very concerned with her ability to overcome her female weaknesses in a man's world. He reported on Liutberga's ability in handling secular situations. He was interested in her capacity to administer the estates of her benefactress and patroness, and continued to do so for her son. Through her talent and natural powers of observation she became famous as a dyer of cloth. He noted that her learning would have been acclaimed even had her sex not been deemed imbecilic. He portrayed her lifelong involvement with the devil in almost embarrassing detail. His point seems to have been that in spite of her female qualities, she was, by God's help, strong enough to meet these challenges and to defeat the devil. Strength of character played a big part in his work. Agius, on the other hand, emphasized the sweet, soft, and loving aspects of his sister's life.

Despite these differences, both hagiographers were conscious, as were their subjects, that a devotion to Scriptures, to the canonical hours, to the offices of the church, and to the power of bishops were instrumental in achieving sainthood. All were aware that the strength of virtues in gaining holiness was important—patience and devotion with those who were near, charity and generosity with the poor, orphans, widows, sick, and prisoners. Love of God in the person of Christ above all, and for his sake modesty in vesture, abstinence in food, chastity in thought and act.

The strong personality of Liutberga and the reliance of Hathumoda on her family were character traits we know from earlier lives. Neither of them labored in the shadow of great men. Liutberga demonstrated that a recluse could be useful both socially and spiritually. Hathumoda provided an example of feminine leadership in monasteries. Both did this in Saxony, an area recently converted. Both showed to future generations in an age of great uncertainties what it takes for a woman to achieve sainthood.

Abbreviations

MGH SS *Monumenta Germaniae Historica, Scriptorum* 4 Hannover: Impensis Bibliopolii Hahniani, 1841.

PL J. P. Migne, ed., *Patrologiae cursus completus, series latina,* 221 volumes. (Paris, 1844–54).

NOTES

1. Suzanne Fonay Wemple, *Women in Frankish Society, Marriage and the Cloister, 500–900* (Philadelphia: University of Pennsylvania Press, 1981) 128–141; and 'Female Spirituality and Mysticism in Frankish Monasticism,' *Peaceweavers*, Medieval Religious Women 2, eds. Lillian Thomas and John A. Nichols, Cistercian Studies Series, 72 (Kalamazoo MI: Cistercian Publication, 1987) 39–53.
2. Wemple, *Women*, 145–148, 173.
3. Jane Tibbets Schulenburg, 'Sexism and the Celestial Gynaeceum, 500–1200', *Journal of Medieval History* 3 (1978) 12–122.
4. Wemple, *Women*, 149–165.
5. *Ibid*, 165–172.
6. Agius, *Vita sanctae Hathumodae, primae abbatissae Gandersheimensis; PL* 137: 1169–1184; and *Dialogus Agii de obitu sanctae Hathumodae; PL* 137, 1183–1198. Another edition of the two works, is found as *Vita et obitus Hathumodae* 20–21, *MGH SS* 4, ed. G. H. Pertz, 165–175, 176–185. Translated into German, by Georg Grandeur, ed., and tr., *Leben des Abtes Eigil von Fulda and der Aebtissin Hathumoda von Gandersheim . . .*, Die Geschichtschreiber der deutscher Vorzeit, 9. Jahrhundert, Zweite Gesamtausgabe, 10 (25) (Leipzig: Dyksche Buchhandlung, 1890) pp. 37–64.
7. *Ex vita sanctae Liutbirgae; MGH SS* 4: 158–164. This is an incomplete edition, the complete one is *Das Leben der Liutbirg; Eine Quelle zur Geschichte der Sachsen in karolingischer Zeit*, ed. Ottokar Menzel, *MGH Deutsches Mittelalter* 3, Kritische Studientexte des Reichsinstituts für altere deutsche Geschichtskunde (Leipzig, Karl W. Hiersemann, 1937) pp. 10–54. German translation, *Das Leben der Liutberg*, tr. Ernst Witte, Die Geschichtschreiber der deutschen Vorzeit, Dritte Gesamtausgabe, by Karl Langosch, 97 (Leipzig, Ernst Wiegandt, 1944).
8. Witte tr., *Das Leben der Liutbirg*, pp. 18–19, had that the *Vita* was written after 865, when Archbishop Ansgar of Bremen died. Liutberga must have lived until the last decade of the reign of Louis the Younger, that is, Louis the German's reign, 840–76, because Bishop Theotgrim of Halberstad, 827–840, consecrated her and she lived about thirty years in her cell. Therefore, she must have died around 865, at the latest 869–70. Witte had put her death between 860–65. Menzel, p. 2, thought that Louis the Younger was Louis III, 876–882, king of the Franks and Saxons, and that she died around 880. G. H. Pertz, *MGH SS* 4, 158–164, thought that the *Vita* was written between 866–876; A. Reinecke, 'Das Leben der heiligen Liutbirg; Ein Beitrag zur Kritik der altesten Quellengeschichte der Christianisierung des Nordostharzes', *Zeitschrift für Harzvereins für Geschichte* 30 (1897) 1–34, wrote that the *Vita* could have been composed in the twelfth century with older pieces in it. Paul Hofer, 'Ertfelde, Michaelskirche und Liutbirgs Klause, eine Studien zur *Vita* Liutbirgae,' *Festschrift für P. Zimmermann*, Quellen und Forschungen zu braunschweigischen Geschichte 6 (Wolfenbüttel: J. S. Zwissler 1914) 159–175, revindicated the ninth century for the composition of Liutbirg's *Vita*. Ottokar Menzel, 'Das Leben der Liutbirg', *Sachsen und Anhalt* 13 (1937) 78–89, gives the essential information on her life. But he is mistaken about her death being in 880.
9. Pertz, *MGH SS* 4: 165–166.
10. Menzel 'Das Leben der Liutbirg', *Sachsen und Anhalt* 13 (1937) 78–79.
11. *Ex Vita . . . Liutbirgae*, 35–45; *MGH SS* 4: 159. Menzel, 13.
12. Agius, *Dialogus*, lines 649–650; *MGH SS* 4: 186; *PL* 137: 1195B:

    Nec de corde meo sua cara recedit imago
    Vel cum dormito, vel potius vigilo

13. Agius, *Vita*, 2–3; *MGH SS* 4: 167; *PL* 137: 1170–1171; Hrotsuith, *Carmen de primord. coenob. Gandersheimensis*, *PL* 137: 1135–1144.

14. *Ex vita . . . Liutbirgae* 3, *MGH SS* 4: 159, *Menzel*, 12.

15. *Ex vita . . . Liutbirgae* 1–8, *MGH SS* 4: 158–160, Menzel, 10–15.

16. Agius, *Vita* 2–3, *MGH SS* 4: 166–167; *PL* 137: 1170–1171.

17. *Ex vita . . . Liutbirgae*, *MGH SS* 4: 160; Menzel, 13.

18. *Ibid.*

19. Agius, *Vita* 4, *MGH SS* 4: 168; *PL* 137: 1171.

20. *Ex vita . . . Liutbirgae* 10–22, *MGH SS* 4: 160–163; Menzel, 16–26. Quoted from Menzel, 23.

21. *Ex vita . . . Liutbirgae* 23, 35–36, *MGH SS* 4: 163, 166–167; Menzel, 25–26, 43–45.

22. In *Women in Frankish Society*, p. 174, I wrote: "Hathumoda could have organized the community as an institute of canonesses. She chose instead the more rigorous Benedictine observances.' I missed in the text: 'nullus cuidam extra monasterium aut ad possessiones subjectas egressus . . . , from *PL* 137: 1171D. I corrected this statement in 'Monastic Life of Women from the Merowingian to the Ottonians', in *Hrotsvit of Gandersheim, rara avis in Saxonia?* ed. Katharina M. Wilson, Medieval and Renaissance Monograph Series 7, ed. Guy R. Mermier (Ann Arbor, Mich.: M.A.R.C., 1987) p. 43, where I said that it was possible that Hathumoda and some members of her community remained benedictine, and thus she could have run a house that was partially benedictine and partially canonical. On this see Hans Goetting, *Das Bistum Hildesheim*, 2 vols., Germania sacra N.F. 7–8 (Berlin, New York: De Gruyter, 1973–1974) vol. 2: pp. 22–27. In the tenth century, the abbesses were not as conscientious, and Gandersheim became an institute of canonesses, a *monasterium sanctimonialium* as opposed to a *monasterium monialium*, the newly founded benedictine monastery of Saint Mary of Gandersheim, on which see *ibid.*, vol. 2: pp. 102–105. Apparently Hathumoda did not rest at Gandersheim; she was transferred to Braunshousen next to her father, see below note 31.

23. Agius, *Vita* 4; *MGH SS* 4: 168; *PL* 137: 1171–1172.

24. *Conc. Aquisgranense* 20–21; MGH Concilia 1: 451–452. See also Rudolf of Fulda, *Vita Leobae* 1, MGH SS 15: 121, who spoke of Hathumoda as a *ereligiosa virgo*; and Louis the Younger who called members of Gandersheim *sanctimoniales feminae*, in MGH *Diplomatum Hlodowici III Iunioris*, 20 Jan., 877, 3–4.

25. Agius, *Vita* 8; MGH SS 4: 168; PL 137: 1172.

26. Agius, *Vita* 8; MGH SS 4: 169; PL 137: 1173D, from which I have taken the quotation.

27. Agius, *Vita* 10; MGH SS 4: 170; PL 137: 1174.

28. Agius, *Vita* 9; MGH SS 4: 169–170; PL 137: 1172–1173.

29. *Ex vita . . . Liutbirgae* 35; MGH SS 4: 164; Menzel, 43.

30. Agius, *Vita* 13–14; MGH SS 4: 171; PL 137: 1176–1177.

31. *Ex vita . . . Liutbirgae* 24–30; MGH SS 4: 163–164; Menzel, 27–37, quoted from Menzel 29, lines 23–32.

32. Agius *Vita* 11–12; MGH SS 4: 170–71; PL 137: 1175–1776, quote from 1175D. See supra note 22.

33. *Ex vita . . . Liutbirgae* 30; MGH SS 4: 163–164; Menzel, 34–37.

34. *Ex vita . . . Liutbirgae* 35; MGH SS 4: 164; Menzel, 40–41.

35. *Ex vita . . . Liutbirgae* 36; MGH SS 4: 164; Menzel, 44.

36. *Ex vita . . . Liutbirgae* 31–33; MGH SS 4: 164; Menzel 37–40. F. W. H.

Wasserschleben, *Die Bussordnungen der abendlandischen Kirche* (Graz: Akademische Druck und Verlagsanstalt, 1958), includes—from penitential of Pseudo-Theodor C2(17) p. 577, and Vallicellanum II C XXV, Seq., p. 560—prohibitions to have it occur on Saturday or Sunday.

37. Agius, *Vita* 11; MGH SS 4: 170; PL 137: 1175.

38. Agius, *Vita* 13; MGH SS 4: 171; PL 137: 1176.

39. Agius, *Vita* 16–17; MGH SS 4: 172; PL 137: 1177–1178.

40. *Ex vita . . . Liutbirgae* 37, MGH SS 4: 164; Menzel, 45–46. Quoted from Menzel, 46.

41. Agius, *Vita* 19–29; MGH SS 4: 172–175; PL 137: 1179–1184, from which I quote, 1181C–D.

Saint Otmar, Model Benedictine

Hugh Feiss OSB

AROUND 1930, Luke Eberle, then a young monk from Mount Angel Abbey in Oregon, was sent to the Abbey of Clervaux in Luxemburg for musical and monastic training. During his stay he helped Dom Jean Leclercq with his study of English. Later, the two monks became regular correspondents. In almost every letter he wrote to Father Luke during the last dozen years of his life, Father Leclercq included a compliment about some article he had read of mine. This was a mark of the breadth of his reading and of his kindness. In his last letters, Father Leclercq wrote serenely of his impending death, citing medieval anecdotes and modern scholarship in the graceful combination which was characteristic of his work. In gratitude for his kindness in remembering me, I dedicate this article to his memory.

Community of Memory

Robert Bellah and his associates, in their studies of individualism and community in American society, speak of 'communities of memory'. A community to which people commit themselves in order to bring about something greater than themselves and distinct from their individual self-interest draws sustenance from a shared tradition. The tradition inspires present-day members by recalling the stories of their predecessors. This recollection of the past binds the present-day members of the community with each other and with their forebearers in shared ideals and goals.[1] The attainments and sacrifices of past heroes are both examples and encouragements; if past heroes are saints, they are also intercessors.

It is not surprising then that a community like the monastery of Saint Gall took a keen interest in the lives and accomplishments of their founders: Saint Gall, the Irish hermit, whose isolated cell was a magnet drawing others to seek God in the monastic life; Saint Otmar, the Swiss who refounded and organized those who gathered around the cell and grave site of Saint Gall and later introduced the *Rule* of Saint Benedict as the norm of their communal lives. With these two saintly founders there would later be associated Saint Wiborada, a recluse who was murdered by the Huns in 926, and in 1047 became the first woman ever to be officially canonized by the new process which the papacy adopted at that time.[2]

Two Founders

In 612 AD, the irish monk Gall constructed a hermit's cell near a waterfall on the brook Steinach in eastern Switzerland. Gall had been a companion of the great Saint Columban, but had become too ill to travel, and Columban, rather uncharitably, had concluded that Gall was a weakling. During his first night alone at the place Gall made a bargain with a bear. If the bear would carry some wood for Gall's fire and then promise to leave the place forever, Gall would give him some fish to eat. The bargain was struck. Ever afterward Saint Gall's emblem would include a bear.

Gall's ecological sense was excellent, but he was not one for long-range institutional planning. His tiny eremetical community would have died out had it not been for the advent, a century later, of the alemannian priest Otmar, who in 719 AD began the refounding of the community. In later centuries, Otmar's emblematic attributes were an abbot's crozier, a wine flask, and sometimes a copy of the *Rule* of Benedict.[3] The writers who have recounted for us the lives of the two founders present them quite differently. Gall was an heroic irish hermit who deserved admiration; Otmar, was a fellow alemannian coenobite who could serve as a model Benedictine. In fact, as we shall see, Otmar was another Benedict, a man of God (*vir dei*). Because of him, the monastic foundation of Saint Gall became a benedictine monastery. In their accounts of his life and miracles, his biographers present Otmar as a model monk, although with some suprising twists. At the same time, to be sure, the abbey's historians and hagiographers glorify Otmar to enhance the prestige of their monastery and its credentials as a place of pilgrimage. It is Otmar the model Benedictine who is of interest here.

Early Prose Sources for the Life of Saint Otmar

Two of the three early prose sources for Otmar's life were written within a century of his death in 759: *The Life of Saint Otmar* (*c.* 834–838) and the *Miracles of Saint Gall* (833–834). The third source, the *Miracles of Saint Otmar* was written by the monk Iso before the latter's death in 871. The original redactor of the first two sources, the *Life of Otmar* and the *Miracles of Saint Gall*, was a monk of Saint Gall named Gozbert the Younger or Gozbert the Deacon, so-called to distinguish him from his contemporary, the great Abbot Gozbert (816–837) who initiated the abbey's first golden age. Neither of these two works by Gozbert the Younger survives in its original form. Of each we have only a version prepared between 834 and 838 by Walahfrid Strabo, a monk of Reichenau. Walahfrid, born in Swabia in 808–809, was educated at Reichenau, a swiss abbey which was then becoming one of the most important cultural centers in the western world. He was sent to Fulda around 826 to study under the celebrated master, Rhabanus Maurus, and about 830 summoned to the court of Louis the Pious to tutor Louis' children. In 838, when his tutoring work was finished, he was appointed abbot of Reichenau. He died in 849 AD, having achieved renown as writer of prose and verse. His works include a book on liturgy, a revised version of Einhard's *Life of Charlemagne*, and a poetic account of a vision which one of his former teachers, Wetti, had the night before his death. Significantly for what follows, Walahfrid Strabo drew on the *Dialogues* of Pope Saint Gregory the Great (+604) in writing this work of eschatology, which he completed when he was about eighteen years old. Among the later works of this gifted stylist is a versified account of horticulture. It was no mean writer who was asked to abbreviate and improve the existing life of Otmar.[4]

1. *The* Vita *of Saint Otmar by Gozbert and Walahfrid Strabo (c. 834–838* AD*)*

Although the first life of Saint Otmar, written *c.* 830 by Gozbert the Younger does not survive, we have the revision prepared by Walahfrid Strabo between 834 and 838.[5] It contains seventeen chapters; six devoted to Otmar's life, and eleven to the miracles worked by his relics at their various resting places. The following analysis of the *Vita* is framed by studies of two titles which Gozbert-Walahfrid bestows on Otmar: 'Man of God' and 'Father of the Poor.' These sections frame a discussion of Otmar's biography and virtues as these are presented in the *Vita.*

Man of God

In the title to the first chapter and often thereafter (41,21; 43,24; 48; 45,13; 46,15), Otmar is called '*vir dei*' (man of God). This is a title which the the Old Testament books of Judges, Samuel and Kings applied to prophets and patriarchs. When in his *Dialogues* Gregory conferred this title on Benedict and other italian saints of his time, he meant to show that they were filled with the same divine miracle-working power as the patriarchs and prophets of the Old Testament. In later monastic hagiography, the connections Gregory drew between Old Testament worthies and latter day monastic saints were repeated many times by writers convinced that God worked similar wonders through his saints at all stages of the history of salvation.[6] One might expect Gozbert and Walahfrid Strabo to draw parallels between Benedict's miracles and Otmar's, but they do not do so. As we shall see, there is a refreshingly matter-of-fact character to Otmar's miracles; they are neither facsimiles of biblical (or Benedict's) wonders nor totally implausible. But first let us turn to Otmar's origins.

Otmar's Origins and Monastic Foundation

Otmar, a local boy, an Alemannian by race, is not said to have been a noble. His brother took him to Chur when he was a boy, and there he took service with a Count Victor. Otmar was ordained and acquired a good reputation. A certain Waltram, having inherited the deserted area where Gall had once erected his cell (*vastitatem eremi in qua sanctus Gallus cellulam construxerat*) (42,5), asked Victor to let Otmar take over the cell. Victor granted his request, and King Pippin confirmed Otmar as abbot. Thus two facts are established, one theological, the other political. Otmar is starting in a desert. He may not have been a hermit-successor to the desert fathers in the same way Gall had been, but he did begin in a desert.[7] Moreover, Otmar owned this desert by grant of its owner Waltram, and confirmation of the king. With his monastic credentials and his title to the real estate thus confirmed, Otmar began his life as an abbot attempting to establish a community living the regular life (*regularem inibi vitam instituere*) (42,13). At this stage the community did not follow the *Rule of Benedict*.[8] Otmar zealously set about the first task of a good monastic founder (*boni mandritae studium*) (42,14): he built suitable monastic buildings everywhere and refashioned the place for divine service (*ad utilitatem divini servitii*) (42,16; cf. RB Prol 45, 65.12).[9] The number of devout monks attracted to the warfare of a holy life (*ad sacrae militiam vitae*) (42,18–19; RB 1.2; 2.20) and the extent of their possessions grew quickly. Otmar governed them with his teaching and care (*magisterio suo et cura*) (42,19; RB Prol 50; 2.8, 10, 24, 38).

The Prayerful Monk

Prayer is a primary task of the monk. By his zeal for prayer (*assiduitate orandi*) Otmar repelled spiritual evils (42,25) and he spent the last days of his life in solitary prayer (44:7). Since most of his miracles were worked at the site of his tomb in the abbey's churches, those whom he favored were those who frequented places of prayer. On one occasion, for example, a brother arrived early for the nightly vigils, and so entered the oratory near Otmar's tomb to pray. He prayed with all his heart (*totoque affectu precibus insistens*) (47,10) and was rewarded with a vision of someone in priestly vestments, facing east in deep prayer. So dazzling was the brightness of his garments that they beat back weak human gaze (*humanae infirmitatis reverberarent obtutus*) (47,14).[10]

Yet not all efficacious prayer took place within church buildings. Ten years after his death, the brethren transporting Otmar's body back to Saint Gall stopped to rest and offered praise to the Lord before they sat down to eat. When they were miraculously provided with something to drink as well, they offered due thanks with praise (45,1). When they arrived home the rest of the brothers came to meet them, praising God (45,3).

Otmar's Disgrace and Death

The great ones of the world, aided and abetted by one of Otmar's own monks, provided the abbot with his supreme test, one which recalls the several times Benedict was assaulted by his monks and neighbors.[11] Their attack on Otmar came at the instigation of the devil, who resented Otmar's good deeds and the way his example helped the lives of the others.[12] Two magnates, Warin and Ruthard, who had been put in charge of Alemannia by Pippin, forcibly gained control of some of the abbey's property. Otmar, afraid that community life would become impossible, twice appealed to King Pippin, who, the *Vita* claims, supported him. The magnates put Otmar in chains and convinced Lantpert, Otmar's confrère by profession but not by holiness of life (43,26–27), to accuse Otmar of a sin of lechery. Otmar, a man of venerable chastity and mature years, was hauled before a council and accused by Lantpert. Otmar chose not to exert himself in his own defense and spent the the short time remaining him incarcerated on an island. He died on 16 November 759, at about the age of 70. Ten years later, the *Vita* tells us, his body, which he had disciplined with fasting (42,22–24), was found incorrupt (ch. 7, 44,13–23).[13]

The Father of the Poor

The *Life of Otmar* clearly emphasizes the saint's love of neighbor. The *Rule of Benedict* says one should love one's neighbor as oneself and love the brethren with a chaste love (RB Prol 4.2; 72.8), It singles out various categories for special consideration: the poor, sick, pilgrims, visiting monks, young and old. In the *Vita* people in these categories are the object of Otmar's special care.

So great was Otmar's concern for the poor that he strove to care for them personally rather than through others. He was second to none in almsgiving. Accommodations for the poor were provided near the monastery. Not far away was a hospice for lepers, of whom Otmar zealously took care personally. Even at night he would leave the monastery and take care of them with wondrous devotion. He washed their heads and feet, wiped away the puss from their wounds, and gave them the food they needed, all the while repeating in his mind, 'What you have done to the least of my brothers, that you have done to me' (Mt 25:40). He came to be called by many 'the father of the poor'. Often he would return to the monastery half naked, because he had taken off his clothes and given them to the poor. He preferred to be stripped of earthly finery rather than of the garment of incorruptibility (ch. 2; 42,19–45). Once, after being received with great honor by King Pippin and given seventy pounds of silver for the support of the brethren, as soon as he left the king's presence, he began giving the money to the poor at the gate of the castle. The brethren who were with him managed to persuade him to keep a few *solidi*. With these he bought some land near the monastery (ch. 3; 42,46–43,7).

Two of Otmar's miracles concern children. Once a blind man arrived and was afforded the hospitality needed by the poor (ch. 13). That night he wanted to go to the church, but the boy who was supposed to lead him there refused to help him because it was too cold. A youth so crippled that he had to drag himself along by his hands was resting in the same place. This youth took pity on the blind man, got up from his bed, and guided him to the church. When they entered the church, they inadvertantly went to the tomb of Saint Otmar, who then cured the crippled boy (46,5–25). Another time, one of the monastery students stole some wax from Otmar's tomb (ch. 14), only to find that it had turned as hard as stone when he returned to his quarters (46,26–32).

This generosity toward the poor, the sick, and the needy was coupled with the conviction that for himself and his brethren poverty was better than unnecessary possessions which burden the mind. He did not worry about the morrow, knowing that a monk must be content with his food and clothing (*monachum victu et tegumento contentum esse debere*) (43,5–6). In fact, he loved voluntary poverty (*voluntariam paupertatem diligebat*) (42,26). Whenever he had to go somewhere on monastery business, he rode on the back of a humble donkey.

The authors of the *Vita* insist strongly on Otmar's kindness to those in need and his love of poverty. Perhaps they felt that these were the two lessons which the members of his monastic family most needed to hear one hundred years after Otmar's death. Otmar was a model of humility (*summae autem humilitatis gratia praecipue praeditus*) (42,25–26) in and for a monastery which had many dealings with the great ones of this world.

Models for 'The Father of Poor': A Wider Community of Memory

Here it is advisable to pause for a minute and see what models Gozbert or Walahfrid had for this depiction of Otmar as the 'Father of the Poor.' There were several written sources in the library at Saint Gall which Otmar's biographers seem to have used. The phrase itself, 'Father of the Poor,' comes from the Book of Job 29:16. There Job declares: 'I was a father to the poor (*pater eram pauperum*), and I championed the cause of the stranger'. Benedict, Gregory's quintessential 'man of God', is certainly a second model. Yet only once does Gregory show Benedict dealing with someone called poor (*pauper*),[14] though in his *Rule* Benedict manifests a high degree of concern for the poor (RB 4.14; 31.9; 53.15; 55.9; 58.24; 66.3).

It was not Benedict but another 'man of God', Boniface, bishop of Ferentis, whom Gregory presented as a special friend of the poor. Boniface's activities are described in the *Dialogues* 1.8–9. This Boniface was a third model for Gozbert and Walahfrid Strabo in portraying Otmar. Ferentis was a very poor place.[15] Once Boniface was asked for alms to save some poor people. He had no money at the time, so he gave them twelve gold pieces which his nephew had just obtained by selling his horse.[16] Even in his youth, when he lived with his mother, he often came home without some of his clothes, because he had given them away to poor people. His mother thought it inconceivable that Boniface, who was needy himself, should give his clothes away to the poor.[17] Another youthful exploit occurred after his mother had saved up a year's worth of grain in her storeroom. She discovered that young Boniface has emptied the place by giving everything away to the poor. Boniface, the 'boy of God', tried to console his mother. When that failed, he asked her to leave, then knelt in prayer. When she came back, she found the storeroom full.[18] These stories are similar enough to those in the *Life of Otmar* to suggest dependence.

A fourth source which may have influenced the composition of Otmar's Life is Jerome's *Letter* 60 to Heliodorus, a eulogy on Nepotian. There we are told that from his youth Nepotian gave what he had to the poor. He wore the same cheap tunic and outer garment day and night. His whole concern was to help the poor, visit the sick, provide hospitality; he was a staff to the blind, food to the hungry, hope for the miserable.[19]

2. *Otmar in the* Miracula sancti Galli *by Gozbert and Walahfrid (833–834)*

A second, slightly earlier, source for the life of Otmar is the account of the miracles of Saint Gall written by Gozbert about 830 and revised by Walahfrid Strabo soon after 833/834. Four chapters of this work mention Otmar.[20] They add only a little to what we know of him from the *Vita*. According to Chapter Ten, the site of Saint Gall's cell and burial was attracting enough visitors and gifts to provide the financial basis to support a larger community. So Waltram, to whose inherited patrimony belonged the vast solitude (*vastae solitudinis*, Dt 32:10; cf. Nm 14:3) where the man of God's cell had been built, petitioned Victor, Count of Chur, for Otmar. At the urging of a duke named Nebi, they to went to see Charles Martel, who personally approved the appointment and accompanying donations of land, and commanded Otmar to strive to institute regular life there. At this point if any rule was employed it was probably that of Columban; it was was not Benedict's. For later, when Carloman had tired of ruling and was seeking a quieter life in Rome, he stopped by the monastery to pray. Impressed, he wrote his brother Pippin III, asking that the book which Father Benedict had composed about the cenobitic way of life (*libellum, quem Benedictus pater de coenobitarum conversatione composuerat*) be given to Abbot Otmar along with other gifts, and he urged the abbot to strive to institute the regular life there (*ut regularem inibi vitam instituere studeret*).[21] The authors note: 'That moment marked the beginning of monastic life in the coenobium of Saint Gall; its increase and advance continue in a praiseworthy manner still today.'[22]

The other three chapters which mention Otmar (chs. 14, 25, 17) do so in connection with the opposition he met from civil and episcopal authorities. Before many years, Otmar became the father of many (*pater multorum*) (c. 14). He was imprisoned by Warin and Ruthard and then left the prison of this life.[23] Then the brothers at the monastery decided to submit to episcopal rule, lest worse befall them. The disgusting death of Bishop Sidonius (c. 17) showed how wicked it is to violate a sacred place because of greed (ch. 15).

3. Miracula sancti Otmar *by Iso (+871)*

Besides providing precious information about the chronology of Otmar's life (in Chapter Five), Iso's two books (divided into nineteen chapters) reveal more about the monastic ideals of the monks of Saint Gall during the first golden age of the abbey.[24] Gozbert/Walahfrid told of the miracles which marked the translation of Otmar's body back to Saint Gall (769 AD) and the tearing down of the old church (830 AD). Iso begins with miracles worked by Otmar in Saint Peter's basilica during the thirty-four or five years Otmar's remains rested there (1.1). He proceeds to tell of miracles which occurred on 25 October 864, when Otmar's remains were transferred from Saint Peter's chapel to the Saint Gall minster (1.4). He describes how, on 25 September 867, Otmar's body was placed in the recently completed church dedicated to him and the archangel Saint Michael (2.1–2).

The first miracle (1.1) recalls one described by Gozbert/Walahfrid (Chapter Seventeen). Now it is *many* of the brothers of the community who customarily came early for the celebration of the night vigils in order to pray in the oratory. There they *often* saw the candles spontaneously light, heard choirs of angels singing sweetly and saw them shining with dazzling brilliance, and smelled a pleasing fragrance they had not encountered before. All of this provided proof of Otmar's great merit with God. We are probably justified in detecting here some of the argumentation which led to Otmar's canonization by Bishop Salomo in 864 AD.

Otmar had been quietly working such miracles at Saint Peter's for more than thirty-four years when the community, serving Christ devoutly under his rule, began to discuss the excellence of his merits. The brothers urged each other until, by divine intervention, they were unanimous in wishing to translate Otmar's body to the church of Saint Gall. Wisely and justly a *Vita* was compiled and taken to Bishop Salomo so he could read it. All the brothers were ready to follow the bishop's will. He was much impressed, but felt that the matter of Otmar's sanctity should be discussed at a synod (1.2). After the synod, the matter was discussed still further at Saint Gall in the presence of the royal chaplain. Finally, after Abbot Grimald had reassured some fearful brothers, by the unanimous will and counsel of the community, the body was transferred. When the body was moved, offerings of bread rolls (*panis rotulae, quae vulgo oblatae dicuntur*) were found under his head and near his chest. They were completely fresh, even though the tomb had not been opened for thirty-five years (1.3). The next morning the bishop gathered the brothers together in one place and granted them permission to celebrate Otmar's feast (1.4). This narration provides a model of monastic decision-making: all are involved; the brothers talk together until they reach consensus; those who are fearful about the decision are reassured; despite their unanimity, the brethren are ready to obey whatever legitimate authority decides.

Many of the miracles recounted by Iso occurred in the context of liturgy. Candles ignite on their own, lamps burn without oil being consumed, fire fails to melt lead. The monks see these miraculous events because they are busy preparing for the liturgy or celebrating Mass and the liturgical hours (1.7–9).

In Iso's account, Otmar continues to favor the sick, children, and the poor. He cures one youth (*adolescens*) from an allergy to bread (1.10). A poor (*pauperculus*) cripple spent Christmas at Saint Gall then moved on. Saint Otmar appeared to him in the guise of an old priest and told him, in the form of a riddle, to visit his tomb. The crippled man reached the abbey, spent the night in vigil, and after the gospel had been read at the public Mass, was miraculously cured of his lifelong malady (1.11). Three weeks later a man born mute was given the gift of speech at Otmar's tomb (1.12).

A certain man took a crippled boy to Rome. He was starting back when one night he was told in a vision to seek Alemannia and the monastery of Saint Gall. After much difficulty they reached the basilica and as they first entered, they came to Otmar's tomb. The boy began to roll on the ground and howl terribly. Soon he began to recover the use of his limbs. Bishop Salomo was present and intoned the *Te Deum*. The boy joined the monastery where he remained, a qualified witness to this miracle (1.13).

Iso's second book tells of miracles connected with the translation of the body of Otmar, the man of God (*virum Dei*) (2.2; p. 53.2), to the church newly dedicated to him. In the course of the ceremony a mute man was given the gift of speech, but at first the monks did not believe him because he was poor and unknown to them.

This ceremony gave the monks of Saint Gall the chance to demonstrate hospitality toward one additional group especially recommended by Saint Benedict: monks from other monasteries. Present for the ceremony were the abbot of Aix (*Augia*) and monks from Kempten. When the day came for them to leave, they proceeded outside the precincts of the monastery amid music and praises. After conversation befitting fraternal charity and the giving of the kiss of peace, they were allowed to return home (2.2).

Not wanting to tire his readers, Iso concludes with a small selection of the miracles worked after the translation of the saint's relics to the church dedicated in his honor (2.3). The serf of a well-known land owner was cured of a wound in his foot (2.4). Another man with a crippled foot was cured when he prayed at Otmar's altar (2.5). And, finally, a nun from Basel who had been blind for four years was brought to the monastery by her sister. She stayed at the monastery for three weeks until she was finally cured on the vigil of Pentecost.

Conclusions

Otmar introduced the *Rule* of Benedict at Saint Gall after he had been abbot there for over twenty-five years. He is presented by his early biogaphers at Saint Gall not just as a model monk, but as another Benedict (*vir dei*), and so, presumably, endowed with the virtues of all the just, as Gregory the Great and the liturgical commemoration describe Benedict.[25] And yet the special character of Otmar's sanctity stands out clearly in these accounts of his life and miracles—his was a preferential option for the poor. He never worked a miracle for a rich person; he preferred to care for the poor and the sick personally; he was generous to a fault; and he tried to make sure that he and his monks lived more like poor people than like the rich. Hence, his nickname, 'Father of the Poor'.

These are very striking features, when one realizes that these lives were written during the first golden age of Saint Gall, when it was a religious and cultural center of Europe. Perhaps Gozbert, Walahfrid Strabo, and Iso were worried by the growing prosperity of the abbey, and so emphasized poverty in their accounts. Perhaps they were urging the monks to remain true to a tradition of simple living and almsgiving which was a legacy from Otmar. In any case, the most striking feature of the Otmar presented in their *vitae* and *miracula* is his commitment to poverty for himself and his monks and his personal concern and care for the poor of this world.

Of chastity one hears little in this account. The topic arises only because Lantpert, the servant of falsity, claims he knows a woman who had been raped by Otmar.[26] In fact, Otmar was 'a man of venerable chastity, integrity of life, grown old in mature morality'.[27] Otmar, knowing that this accusation was simply a pretext in the service of wider and perhaps irresistible political forces, makes no defense. He is finally coaxed into saying simply: 'I confess I have sinned without measure in many things. I call on God as my witness to investigate this accusation about a secret sin of mine'.[28] In any case, Otmar is not shown in the company of women. The only women mentioned in any of these texts are the blind nun and her sister who brought her to Otmar's tomb in the final miracle story in Iso's account.

We know from history that Otmar's final troubles stemmed from changes in the balance of power in Western Europe which favored centralized frankish rule. In contrast to the politics of power, to which (in the person of Bishop Sidonius), the monks of Saint Gall accede until the time of liberation (experienced by the authors) and divine vengeance (recounted by Ekkehard IV in the *Casus* or chronicle of the abbey),[29] we see Otmar leading by example and care. Decisions in the community are made by consensus under the guidance of the Holy Spirit,[30] whose feast concludes these accounts of Otmar's life and miracles (Iso 2,6), and who also came to be called 'Father of the Poor'.[31] The holy bishop Salomo is clearly an authority, but he, too, consults the community (Iso 1.2).

The authors of the sources for our knowlege of Saint Otmar, especially Walahfrid Strabo, were gifted writers. They wrote in a style that is both simple and convincing, subtle and reminiscent of the Bible and the early christian writers. Otmar is 'a man of God' like Benedict, and 'father of the poor' like Job and Boniface of Ferentis. Otmar is even Susannah, falsely accused of sexual immorality. Otmar works miracles; so do his mortal remains.

How credible is all this? While I would not vouch for all the details, my impression is that in what concerns Otmar's character and behavior, especially his intense concern for the poor, these accounts are historically accurate. Otmar's hagiographers are writing within a century of his death. The authors would not have stressed Otmar's love of the poor, if the memory of the abbot as a charitable man had not been widely shared.

Finally, we have in this account a tribute to monastic stability and to communal conversion. Gall, the wandering monk, settled down in an alemannian wasteland; by his presence it became a sacred place. Otmar spent forty years in that place, patiently laying the spiritual and physical foundations for a great abbey. A century later, the stories of his life and miracles were written down, not simply to glorify the abbey, but also to remind the monks of their heritage. The stability of the community, its perdurance into the future, depended on the depth and sincerity of the *conversatio* of those who read the accounts by Gozbert/Walahfrid and Iso. As a model of monastic *conversatio* they could do much worse than emulate the example of 'the father of the poor', their father, Otmar. Would they be his brothers only in profession or also in sanctity of life?[32]

NOTES

1. Robert Bellah, *et al.*, *Habits of the Heart: Individualism and Commitment in American Life* (Berkeley: University of California Press, 1985).

2. Walter Berschin, 'Latin Literature from Saint Gall,' in *The Culture of the Abbey of Saint Gall*, ed. James C. King and Werner Vogler (Stuttgart: Belser, 1991) 152–154; Gereon Gecht, 'Sprachliches in den Vitae S. Wiboradae (II),' *Mittellateinisches Jahrbuch* 24/25 (1989/90) 1–9, with the literature cited there. Wiborada's life was written about 960/70 by Ekkehart I (d. 973), and revised in connection with her canonization.

3. Johannes Duft, ed. *Sankt Otmar. Die Quellen zu seinem Leben* (Lindau: Thorbecke, 1959) pp. 7, 95–96.

As a points of reference the following dates will be helpful:

612	Saint Gall founds his hermitage on the Steinach.
719	Otmar founds a coenobium on the site of Gall's hermitage.
759	Otmar's death in prison.
769	Translation of Otmar's body to Saint Gall.
830	Demolition of the church where his relics lay and their translation to Saint Peter's chapel.
c. 830	Gozbert's *Vita* of Otmar.
833/34	Walahfrid Strabo's revision of the *Vita* and miracles of Saint Gall.
833/4–838	Walahfrid Strabo's revision of the *Vita* of Otmar, *c.* 833/834–838.
864	Translation of Otmar's relics from Saint Peter's chapel to the Saint Gall minster.
867	Translation of Otmar's relics from Saint Gall minster to the Church of Saint Otmar and Saint Michael.
c. 860/70	Iso (+871) writes the *Miracula sancti Otmari*.
c. 884	Ratpert, Iso's student, writes the *Casus monasterii sancti Galli* up to 884 AD.
c. 1050	Ekkehart IV brings the *Casus* up to his time, mid-eleventh century, and sees divine vengeance at work in the fate of the descendents of Otmar's persecutors.

4. Franz Brunhölzl, *Histoire de la littérature latine du Moyen Age*, tr. Henri Rochais (Louvain-la-Neuve: Brepols, 1991) 1/2, pp. 102–115, 287–290; J. M. Wallace-Hadrill, *The Frankish Church* (Oxford: Calendon, 1983) 322–326

5. The *Vita S. Otmari* of Walahfrid Strabo was edited by Ildephonse von Arx in *MGH Scriptores* (Hanover, 1829) 2: 41–47. Since this edition has line numbers I will cite from it, giving first the page, then the line. Duft, *Sankt Otmar*, pp. 22–39, does not print the last ten chapters, which recount Otmar's posthumous miracles.

6. The phrase is used frequently in Judges and the four books of Kings. Duft, *Sankt Otmar*, p. 24 note 1, gives the following references: Judg 13:6, 8; 1 Sm 2:27; 9:6, 7, 10; 1 Kg 12:22; 13 *passim*; 17:18, 24; 20:28; 2 Kg 4 *passim*; 5:8, 15; 6:9, 10; 7:17; 8:7, 11; 13:19; 23:16. For the literature on this phrase in Gregory's usage and in later monastic hagiography, see Gregorio Penco, 'Le Figure Bibliche de *Vir Dei* nell' Agiograpfia Monastica,' in *Medievo Monastico*, Studia Anselmiana 96 (Rome: Pontificio Ateneo S. Anselmo, 1988) 81–97 (= *Benedictina* 15 [1968] 1–13). The *Dialogues* of Gregory the Great contain four books. The first three of these are biographies of wonderworking saints and form a triptych. Book II is devoted entirely to Saint Benedict, whereas Books I and III present twelve and thirty-seven saints respectively. Saint Benedict clearly occupies the place of honor in this crowd of witnesses. To the forty-nine saints of Books I and III, Gregory adds a fiftieth, Benedict. In Gregory's number symbolism, fifty symbolizes repose (cf. *Moralia in Job* 16.55.68, ed. M. Adriaen; CCSL 143A (Turnhout: Brepols, 1979) 838:11–12: '*Iubilaei quippe requies quinquagenarii numeri mysterio continetur.*' Cf. *Homilia in Ezehielem* 2.5.15; ed. M. Adriaen, CCSL 142 (Turnhout: Brepols, 1971) 288:427; 2.7.4, 318:110–111. From Book II of the *Dialogues* is derived almost everything we know of Benedict's life. See Adalbert de Vogüé, ed., *Grégoire le Grand, Dialogues*, 3 vols., SCh 251, 260, 265 (Paris: Cerf, 1978–1980) 1: 51–55, 155–160.

7. He also ended his life as a solitary in a cell on Werd, an island in the Rhine,

where he spent his time in prayer and fasting (*orationibus ac ieiuniis vacans*), freed from human contact and worldly cares (44:7–9).

8. Otmar did not start out using the *Rule* of Benedict. Probably he began with a mixed (partly Columbanian) rule, then was forced to adopt the Benedictine Rule by Carloman in 747, after Carloman's defeat of the Alemannians at Cannstatt in 746. Thus Duft, *Sankt Otmar*, p. 74 and note 15.

9. References to the *Rule* of Benedict (RB) will be to *RB 1980: The Rule of Benedict*, ed. Timothy Fry (Collegeville: Liturgical Press, 1981).

10. *Reverberare* (to beat back) is almost a technical word, because of Gregory the Great's use of it to describe contemplative experience. The CETEDOC *Thesaurus Sancti Gregorii Magni* (Brepols) gives thirty instances of the word used in this sense; e.g. *Homiha* in *Ezeckielem* 2.2; ed. M. Adriaen, 232:276; 2.5.16, 284:316; *Moralia* in *Job* 16.8, ed. M. Adriaen, 805:33.

11. Gregory the Great, *Dialogues* 2.3.4, ed. A. de Vogüé, SCh 260 (Paris: Cerf, 1979) 2:142; 2.8.2–3, 2:160–162.

12. According to the *Rule* of Benedict, good example is a duty of the abbot; e.g., 27.8; 60.5; 61.19.

13. Otmar's lifetime coincided with the transition between Merovingian and Carolingian rule. Warin and Ruthard were Carolingian Franks, who wished to assert central control over alemannian territory, just as carolingian bishops wished to assert episcopal jurisdiction where heretofore there had been local autonomy. It seems that after Otmar's death there was effected a personal union of the abbacy of Saint Gall and the bishopric of Constance. A privilege of Louis the Pious in 818 loosened the dependency on Constance; in 833 Louis the German granted the monks the right to elect their abbot freely, and in 854 the last ties to the bishop were cut. Gozbert and Walahfrid Strabo wrote at a time the abbey was recovering its never-forgotten independence. That Otmar was honored with a *vita* at that time is probably not a coincidence.

The political setting of Otmar's life is summarized by Duft, *Sankt Otmar*, pp. 67–80. See also Ferdinand Vetter, 'Sankt Otmar, der Gründer und Vorkämpfer des Klosters Sankt Gallen', *Jahrbuch für schweizerische Geschichte* 43 (1918) 94–193; Otmar Scheiwiller, 'Zur Biographie des heiligen Abtes Otmar von Saint Gallen,' *Zeitschrift für schweizerische Kirchengeschichte* 13 (1919) 1–32.

14. *Dialogues* 2.61.2; ed. de Vogüé, 2:154–157.

15. *Dialogues* 1.8.2; Vogüé, 2:76, line 8: "gravis paupertas inerat."

16. *Dialogues* 1.9.10; Vogüé, 2:84, lines 113–126.

17. *Dialogues* 1.9.16; Vogüé, 2:90: 'ipse inops pauperibus vestimenta largiretur' (lines 185–186).

18. *Dialogues* 1.9.17; Vogüé, 2:90.

19. Jerome, *Ep.* 60 *ad Heliodorum* [*Epitaphium Nepotiani*]; ed. Daniel Ruiz Bueno, *Cartas de San Jerónimo* (Madrid: BAC, 1962) 1: 523–549.

20. I will cite these four chapters from Duft, *Sankt Otmar*, pp. 40–49.

21. As Wallace-Haddrill notes (*The Frankish Church*, 69–70) the *Rule* of Columban contained elements of the *Rule* of Benedict. Moreover, during this period—and so perhaps under Otmar after he received the copy of the *Rule* of Benedict—monasteries often followed a mixed rule, combining the legislation of Benedict, Columban, and sometimes others as well. On Carloman's predilection for the *Rule* of Benedict, see Giles Brown, 'The Carolingian Renaissace,' in *Carolingian Culture: Emulation and Innovation*; ed. Rosamond McKitterick (New York: Cambridge, 1994).

22. *Et ex illo tempore monasticae vitae in coenobio sancti Galli exordium quidem coepit; augmentum autem et profectus hodieque laudabiliter dilatari non desinit* (p. 44).

23. The topos earthly life=prison was suggested by the fact that Otmar died in prison. Similarly, that of body=sewer in ch. 17 was suggested by the disgusting disease which brought about Bishop Sidonius' demise. According to the *Vita* Otmar was an ascetic but his aim was not the destruction of his body, which in fact remained incorrupt ten years after his death.

24. Cited here by book, then chapter (e.g., 2.3) from MGH, *Scriptores* 2:47–54. Where greater precision is called for, the citiation will include page and line number (e.g., 49,10).

25. The collect prayer for the Solemnity of Saint Benedict on July 11 reads: *Deus, qui beatissimum confessorem tuum Benedictum omnium justorum spiritu replere dignatus es. . . .* The readings at the first nocturn were drawn from Sirach 45–48, which praise the great men of the Old Testament.

26. *Vita Otmari*, ch. 5 (43:32–35): *se quandam feminam nosse, quae a viro beato vim pollutionis fuisset perpessa.*

27. *Vita Otmari*, ch. 5 (43:31–32): *Vir venerabilis castitate, integer vitae, ac morum maturitate grandevus. . . .*

28. *Vita Otmari*, ch. 5 (43:36–38): *Fateor . . . me quidem supra modum in multis pecasse, de huius autem obiectione criminis secreti mei inspectorem Deum invoco testem.*

29. Duft, *Sankt Otmar*, 18, 58–61.

30. Iso 1.2 (48:53): *divino, ut credimus, nutu.*

31. See the sequence for Pentecost in the Roman Missal: *Veni, Pater Pauperum, Veni dator munerum. . . .*

32. *Vita Otmari*, ch. 4 (43:26–27): *Lantpertum quendam, qui fratribus eius professione connumeratus erat non vitae sanctitate. . . .*

Peter Damian against the Reformers

Phyllis Jestice

WHILE JEAN Leclercq is most renowned for his work in cistercian history, his interests ranged over a myriad of times and groups both before and after the twelfth century. One of the most interesting facets of his work is that which deals with the development of eremitical monasticism in the eleventh century. My own fascination with the many and often ambiguous reforms of the eleventh century has been fanned by Leclercq's many books and articles on various aspects of the subject. In this paper, I attempt to link two recurring themes of Leclercq's immense literary output: the new eremitism of the eleventh century as exemplified by Peter Damian (d. 1072) and the growing strength of the ecclesiastical reform movement in the same period. Damian was certainly a central spokesmen in his time for monastic reform as well as the more general reform of the clergy and christian laity. Less passionate than his demanding friend, the archdeacon Hildebrand, Peter Damian's values are usually accepted as those of at least the best and most thinking Christians of the period immediately preceding the Investiture Contest. Cantor goes so far as to refer to him as 'a sort of barometric indicator of eleventh-century attitudes'[1], while many historians would agree with Miccoli in describing him as the only person to attempt to make orderly sense of the monastic and eremitical fervor of the early eleventh century.[2]

But Peter Damian's simultaneous interest in two very different reform movements, the reform both of monks and of the greater *ecclesia*, led to irreconcilable conflicts and, indeed, to active attempts on his part to impede ecclesiastical reform by placing the reform of 'professional religious' first. I use such a general term for those vowed to a life of celibacy advisedly. Historians, including Leclercq, have concentrated on Damian's distinction between traditional monks and the new eremitical orders. Another, more important, division exists in his writings, though: that of the professional religious (monks and the new orders of hermits) who lived withdrawn from the world on the one hand, and on the other hand anyone who claimed to lead a religious life but left the cloister for the 'pollution' of the world. While monks and new hermits can be good or bad, the category of those who interact with the world outrages Damian's every religious sense, and he heaps all possible abuse upon so-called religious who involve themselves in secular affairs. It is, however, these venturers into the world who probably carried the ideas of the gregorian reform produced by such theorists as Peter Damian himself to the mass of the population. This is disguised by an historiography that has focussed on eremitical orders on the one hand and intellectual defenses of Church reform on the other. The two worked at cross-purposes—the new hermits avoided contact with the world and had little influence on the expansion of the Church into worldly affairs that precipitated the Investiture Contest. But Peter's correspondence shows his conflict both with more traditional individual hermits and with new groups who did not live up to his requirements for professional religious. From his letters, it is possible to see that the sorest point for Peter was the involvement of those who claimed to lead a religious life in the area of broader ecclesiastical reform. With all the emphasis that has been placed on the eremitical orders, it is easy to forget that old-fashioned, individualistic hermits continued to exist after the formation of new eremitical orders. They did, however, and are central to our story. I will refer to them as 'evangelical hermits' to avoid confusion with the orders of 'new hermits' such as the Camaldolesi. With a passion surprising in such a collected and rational man, Peter Damian hated these evangelical hermits and all religious who stuck their noses into the world. This raises a series of questions about the two reforms and Peter's own role in them: if Peter Damian was in favor of hermits, why was he so violently opposed to the simple wandering hermits of the 'golden age' of the Ottonians,[3] who had taught his own spiritual master, Romuald? And, if Peter Damian was in favor of ecclesiastical reform, why was he so desperately opposed to letting his own organized hermits or even inferior monks act in the world, and so stringent in his criticism of figures like Teuzo, the 'city hermit' of Florence, who did so? A much more ambivalent and nuanced picture of Peter Damian emerges when we examine these questions, for it appears that Damian was at times willing to speak for the cause of ecclesiastical reform, but did his best to prevent the grassroots support that eventually made it possible. An investigation into Peter Damian's own writings on good and bad hermits reveals some of the mechanisms that gave force to the high politics and theology of the Gregorian movement.

It is in the case of the hermit Teuzo of Florence that we get our best look at Damian's views of evangelical hermits. Most of our knowledge of Teuzo comes from Peter Damian's letter to the hermit, written sometime between 1055 and 1057 according to the editor of Peter's letters, after Damian had failed to reconcile Teuzo to his abbot. This is one of Damian's harshest letters, and exposes as does no other the radical break he and his followers at Fonte Avellana had made from the hermits of the previous eight centuries. It can also be used to reveal Peter Damian's understanding of the process of ecclesiastical reform. Teuzo was a monk of La Badia in Florence. After a quarrel with his abbot, Teuzo withdrew from the monastery. But he did not follow any of the steps Peter Damian would have considered proper in such a situation. He did not enter another monastery, nor did he join one of the more stringent orders of hermits. Instead, Teuzo became a recluse attached to his original monastery in the center of Florence.

It seems likely that Teuzo referred to himself as a hermit, for in his Letter 44 Peter Damian always refers to him in such terms as 'city hermit' or 'false hermit' rather than as a recluse. Elsewhere Damian does speak of recluses in cities, such as the prophetic recluse of Paderborn who burned in his cell after giving warning of a coming fire.[4] This taking the name of hermit by Teuzo and his supporters seems to have irked Damian, great popularizer that he was of Romuald of Ravenna's brand of 'rational hermits who live by a law', i.e., hermits who live in communities under strict authority.[5] The use of specific terminology should not be underrated, especially at the hands of a master of eleventh-century rhetoric. In his Letter 50, written to the *hermit* (actually recluse) Stephen *c.* 1057, Damian makes a careful distinction. Stephen is a true holy man, and a friend of Peter Damian. Peter writes him a careful and long definition of and set of rules for hermits. In it, he distinguishes between two types of hermits: the first are good, honest, Fonte Avellana-style hermits; they live in cells in a community, under the direction of a spiritual advisor; the second are anchorites, who go out to the desert to live in solitude. As Damian bluntly points out, *holy* anchorites occur rarely or never in their age.[6] That is why, rather than using the term anchorite, or its more common synonym, recluse, to describe men like Teuzo who have not proven their worth and stability by such drastic means as the Paderborn recluse, Peter usually employs such expressions as 'false hermits', 'false monks', or 'pseudo-hermits'. In this letter, Damian appears to present Stephen with the possibility of someday becoming one of the few good anchorites, in terms that make it plain he is speaking about a recluse. In both cases, the term hermit regarding Stephen and Teuzo is a statement that each is, or ought to be, living in solitude, far from the temptations of the world.

That, of course, is the problem with Teuzo, according to Peter. He has made the mistake of leading an eremitical life among the people of Florence instead of in a hermitage where weak-willed mortals belong, far from the pollution of the laity. Peter is adamant: the *proper* life of a hermit is one of silence and penitence.[7] It is worth quoting Peter's comments on Teuzo's central location at length:

> But I ask you, if you are a monk, what do you have to do with cities? If you are a hermit, what are the crowds of a city to you? What sort of cells or walls or outside rules give you protection? Indeed, what else can be thought of those who seek solitude in cities instead of under the trees, except that they are more concerned with the favor of the crowd and glory than with the perfection of the solitary life?

Peter goes on to say that in such a situation, one listens to the voice of the crowds, rather than to his own conscience. Rough, irreligious city-dwellers are also likely to see as extraordinary holiness matters that should be part of every monk's or hermit's life. For example, although it is downright 'ignoble' to drink wine in a hermitage, in the city it is considered a prodigy to abstain; a hairshirt in the hermitage is a garment, while in the city it is a spectacle.[8]

This mixture of two worlds—the silence of the hermitage and the bustle of the city—is not the only reason Peter Damian is so vitriolic against Teuzo (besides, perhaps, a level of personal antagonism between the two). Damian's major complaint (which shows him clearly as an opponent of ecclesiastical reform), concerns how Teuzo spends his time. His life is not one of quiet retreat, nor is it one of drunken dissoluteness, which Peter might have been better able to understand, since his reform work led him to deal with monks and hermits who simply did not live up to the basic tenets of their Rule. Instead, Teuzo claimed that he was living a holy life, but nevertheless became embroiled in the most burning issue of the day: the ecclesiastical struggle against simony. He had apparently left his own monastery because the abbot was a simonist and soon established himself as a master advisor against simony for others. He is noted in several other sources for his unremitting stand against simony. All the hagiographers of John Gualbert, the founder of Vallombrosa, for example, agree that John, after he left his simoniacal monastery, went to Teuzo for advice. The advice he received was so inflammatory that it led to John's public denunciation of his abbot.[9] Teuzo became very famous as a spiritual advisor; many came to ask for his prayers and for his advice on the religious issues of the day. Indeed, he was so famous that the Emperor Henry III came to him for counsel and friendship, according to one of the *vitae* of John[10], and he is listed as an intercessor in documents of both Conrad II and Henry IV. The second document dates from 1073, showing that he prospered a long time in spite of all the mud Peter Damian was able to sling at him.[11] Quilici also suggests that both Conrad II and Henry III asked for his prayers, as for those of other great holy men of the time.[12]

While all contact with the laity met with Peter's disapproval, it was the public propaganda against simony that was the focus of Letter 44. Teuzo is a hermit, but his public speech on ecclesiastical reform makes him a bad one. There are several reasons for this, according to the rules Peter holds appropriate for professional religious. Hermits in general, argues Peter, should be humble, not contentious. They should not spend their time in sermonizing. Teuzo does not even have the excuse of edifying; instead he just speaks interminably.[13] But an added disturbance was Teuzo's involvement in anti-simony campaigns—always questioning who ordained priests, and asking other awkward questions. With his interminable questions, Peter rages, Teuzo has put the world into confusion, has created a tempest on his own, and since he himself does not know peace, Teuzo will not permit others to live in tranquility. He is also arrogantly assuming the right to judge others, overstepping the proper limits of his position, whether he is viewed as a monk or a hermit or even an anchorite. This again suggests that Teuzo played a very active role, and his questions threw Damian into a passion.[14] Although Damian ends by asking for Teuzo's prayers, and even throwing himself at Teuzo's feet to try to win him back to 'proper' monastic behavior, it is impossible to believe that he saw much of sanctity in his way of life.[15]

It is clear, as Gajano states, that Peter Damian disapproved violently of teuzan religiosity. She argues that it broke out of the traditional eremitical model, uniting ascetic life with contact with the world and influence on the laity, and that this was the issue. In her opinion, what irritated Damian above all about Teuzo was his contact with the laity by itself.[16] But Teuzo is not doing anything very different from the usual job of a recluse or hermit. Throughout the tenth and eleventh centuries laity of all states came to both recluses and hermits for spiritual advice. Some of these hermits tried to run away to solitude[17], but recluses especially were restricted by their vow of stability. They had to give advice, because they were bound for life to their cells and could not just pick up and move to a new area. Advising the laity and other religious was such a common part of the life of reclusion that Grimlaicus' treatise on the solitary life from the early tenth century devotes almost as much attention to the sections of Gregory the Great's *Pastoral Rule* on how to teach various sorts of people as it does on the benedictine *Rule*.[18] Indeed, Peter himself, when considering a more active life in the affairs of the Church, went to a hermit for advice.[19]

I believe that the heart of Peter Damian's complaint lies in two areas: the traditional criticism that Teuzo was too involved in the world, against which Damian did indeed fight; and the more specific problem of unregulated preaching on such a sensitive issue as simony. He did not believe, as did the followers of John Gualbert, that it was possible to live a holy life in a large city 'for there is no place that is not remote for those who have compunction of mind,' as one of John Gualbert's followers defends his master.[20] Teuzo is guilty of too much compunction on too fragile a ground. When Damian calls Teuzo inept in his teaching, he states that such ineptness often leads to heresy and schism, a very telling comment about how Peter Damian viewed the offense.[21] He is clearly referring to Teuzo's teaching on the heresy of simony, suggesting that Teuzo had been teaching his followers that the sacrament of an improperly ordained priest was not valid. This indeed appears to have been the case with Teuzo's disciples, at least John Gualbert and his followers.[22] This was an issue into which Peter put enormous time and energy. He argued in such treatises as his *Liber Gratissimus* that it is God who gives the sacrament, no matter how flawed the instrument.[23] This stand only gradually won the approval of the ecclesiastical reform circle, mostly thanks to the persuasiveness and erudition of Peter Damian himself. He had to compete against more hot-headed reformers, such as Humbert of Silva Candida, who wished to declare the sacraments of simoniacs invalid. So for Peter, to speak without proper instruction can lead to catastrophe in the fragile world of the early reform, and Teuzo, while he argued for reform, was too inflammatory. It is also unlikely that he was a highly trained theologian, and the subtleties of simoniacal ordination were probably beyond his competence. If he had taken a less radical stand, Peter might have been more understanding. But one still cannot avoid the implication of Peter's basic conviction in all his works dealing with monks and hermits is that professional religious, the most available weapon for reform, were separate from the cares of the *ecclesia* in general. Indeed, in this as in all matters, they were dead to the world.

In Letter 44, however, we find Peter caught on the horns of his own dilemma. In the prologue to Teuzo, Peter says that he ought not speak, but that it is better to speak in censure than remain silent and let wrong actions take place uncontested.[24] This displays Peter Damian's own moral tightrope. He was a monk, indeed a reformed hermit, and yet he had been forced into a bishopric and cardinalate that involved him in all the issues of the world. He faced with particularly poignant intensity the same problem that had been faced long before by Pope Gregory I and to which Teuzo supplied his own answer: how can a contemplative help in the needs of the world? Peter comes down with a simple answer that almost completely bars professional religious from ecclesiastical reform activities; it is next to impossible to lead both the active and contemplative lives together. Peter is an anomaly, as he himself was well aware, trapped by obedience to the papacy in activity he thought improper to his profession. In the letter to Teuzo, Damian tells of a fellow monk caught in the same contradiction, who '. . . often worked for the necessities of the churches, or to make peace treaties, which I personally know very well to be detrimental, although others consider it proper to proceed in this way. . . .' This monk did well because of his holy simplicity, a skill certainly not sharpened by contact with the world, and that the arrogant Teuzo certainly lacked. In general, the various groups of religious—monks and hermits alike—are meant to enlighten others, but Peter asks of his deep weariness, 'How can a candle provide light for others, when it is itself consumed in the flame?'[25] It, like a monk, must remain separate to avoid being devoured alive by the world.

Flame and ashes, contemplation and action, involvement in the needs of the world or separation from them, improper teaching versus true doctrine provide much of the framework for Peter Damian's meditations. I believe that his distinction between hermit and monk has been overstated—to understand him, one must understand that monks and hermits exist on one side of the fence of salvation; those who do not comply with the spiritual quarantine imposed by centuries of practice and supported by contemporary interpretation of the benedictine *Rule* are on the other side. Peter Damian spent most of his life working with both monks and hermits. For example, while at Fonte Avellana he was invited to reform the religious life of several traditional monasteries,[26] and many of his most encouraging letters are to monks rather than hermits, as is his correspondence with Desiderius of Monte Cassino.[27] Damian goes so far as to compare the monastery to Noah's ark in one of his letters to Desiderius: God has chosen a few to save them from the cataclysm.[28] Indeed, although he had never been a monk himself, going directly from the world to the hermitage, Damian typically called himself *monachus peccator*, 'sinful monk,' in his correspondence, a sign that he did not see a clear distinction between good monk and new model hermit.[29]

For Damian, monks and members of eremitical communities such as his own were part of the same spectrum, differing in degree rather than in sort. Monks were inferior. Brethren who accomplished the vow of stability in a monastery must certainly be tolerated, as he says while explaining why he has taken in a monk without the abbot's permission, but hermits are better.[30] Along the same line of reasoning, a monk is better the more secluded he is, as Peter demonstrates in a letter to Abbot Bonizo of Saint Peter's, Perugia. Peter congratulates the recipient for wanting to abdicate his abbacy. He states resoundingly his belief that the abbot was divinely inspired in his decision to leave his unproductive labors in the world for the peace of the cloister, with many examples of the evils of worldly dealing incumbent on an abbot.[31] The note of stability that enters both the definition of the office of abbot and Peter's admonition to escape is telling. It is separation from the world that distinguishes a good monk or hermit from the rest of humanity, and thus stability is the defining point of monks, whether eremitical or not. Therefore Damian is able to say without contradiction that monasticism is second only to the life of the apostles. He is, of course, defining apostolicity according to Acts 2, as a community living in harmony, not as a group of men sent out to preach to the world.[32]

Peter Damian's brand of hermits is better not because they do anything fundamentally different, but because they go *further* than monks on this path of separation from the world. Peter Damian is firm in his belief that the eremitical life, that is, the organized, Camaldolese style of hermitage, is the highest possible path to God. As he says in his Letter 50 to the new hermit Stephen, there are many ways to God, and diverse orders can exist under the umbrella of certain universal laws. But no way is as right and certain as that of the hermit; it eliminates all occasions to sin, and, because of that, increases virtues.[33]

The reasons why eremitical communities are better than many of their monastic counterparts is because Peter Damian felt monasteries had given in too much to the ways and life of the 'world', that ill-defined realm of chaos that encompasses all outside the walls of the sanctuary. For example, many houses had fallen from the rigor of the *Rule*—it is highly blameworthy to take, as some monks have, the remissions allowed by the benedictine *Rule* in cases of necessity for weaker brethren, and make their own use of them.[34] Many monasteries have become rich, with the attendant business that keeps their inmates from a life of prayer.[35] Some monks (Damian never accuses Benedictines as a whole of blameworthy behavior) commit a variety of sins. With rhetorical flourish, he declares that Ananias and Saphira (Acts 5) sinned less than monks who have money. Christ and mammon will not fit together in such a small place as a monastic cell.[36] Similarly, Damian criticizes the building ambitions of some abbots, most notably in a letter in which he tells of the reforming abbot Richard of Saint Vanne of Verdun continuing his building projects in hell, since he was so preoccupied with enlarging his monastery in life.[37]

Some contemporary abbeys, the subjects of his scathing criticism, have let worldly concerns take too important a place even in the heart of the monastery. He seems to be speaking of real situations when he complains in a letter to his nephew some time between 1065 and 1071 about how ill it becomes monks to speak of secular things. Worse yet, he tells how unnamed religious are in the habit of speaking of secular things with laymen in the cloister itself, a place almost as much at the heart of the monastery as the church. What, he asks, has justice to do with iniquity, or light with darkness? (2 Cor 6:14). A monk simply should not talk about judgments and king's courts, not to mention common tavern talk and women's gossip appearing in cloisters, conversations about ships on the Adriatic or how much salt is sold. Damian describes such impropriety as turning to murky cisterns instead of to fountains of living water (Jer 2:13).[38] It is apparently for these reasons that Peter Damian defended monks who came to his hermitage without their abbot's permission. They were moving to a more stringent life, and, as the benedictine *Rule* itself said, the monastery is only a school for beginners.[39] A hermitage is better than a monastery because it offers *more* quiet, silence, and distance from all interference than does a monastery.[40] As Tabacco points out, in general there was *concordia* between monks and hermits in the eleventh century, as can be seen in Peter Damian's own works. The aim of monastic life, cenobitic or eremitic, was to strive for perfect penitence, to the point that Damian tends to equate 'monk' and 'penitent' in his writings.[41] The norms of the monastery were fundamentally those of the hermitage: silence, prayer, reading, and meditation.[42] A good monk, 'if he wishes to be intent and fervid in advancing [these] fruits of good works, should not seek at all to be outstanding among other people.' It is only the cold and arid monk who despises the simple penitential life for one of greater visibility.[43] Clearly this letter, dated to 1059/1060, is drawn up in a more general attack than upon Teuzo alone.

Clearly Damian has also decided that if a monk or hermit is a priest, the solitary life takes precedence. It seems peculiar that in the late Letter 153, written after 1067, Damian calls monks to fight fervently and manfully in their *militia*, only to tell them a few paragraphs later to seek out secret places and silence in order to reach God.[44] But, following the expectations society had of monks, a view that can be traced even before the anianian reforms of the early ninth century,[45] Damian believed that the religious were performing an invaluable gift for the world by their prayer and contemplation.

Both monastery and hermitage were, or should be, engaged in a desperate struggle to survive against the fatal charms of the world. This theme appears repeatedly in the corpus of Damian's eremitical/monastic works. Entering the monastery from the world is 'leaving Sodom'. Among the laity, love of God is benumbed by pleasures and sins.[46] Certainly he argues that : 'All our conversion and all our renunciation of the world aims for nothing else but rest.'[47] Both monks and hermits exist on earth for a very specific function: to fight as soldiers in the battle against the world. But how does one fight evil? This question is at the heart of Peter Damian's assessment of the religious life of his time, and is what makes him such an unlikely ecclesiastical reformer. Certainly for him it was the contemplative life that formed the most active part of spiritual warfare.[48] The hermit's cell is a 'spiritual arena' in which the solitary, again either monk or hermit, engages in battle.[49] To undertake the struggle, the solitary needs three things: quiet, silence, and fasting. It is for priests to celebrate Mass, and for the learned to preach. Neither is the role of the ascetic.[50]

So, for example, Peter saves some of his warmest approval for two members of the community of Fonte Avellana who set up an isolated cell away from the mother house. Peter tells in a glowing account how these hermits asked him, their prior, for permission to remain within this hermitage for life, and afterwards to be buried in their cell. This, to Peter Damian, is a proof of the sincerity of their religious life, the firm evidence that 'their life is built on rock, not sand'. He gladly gave his sanction, adding at the end of his letter to them that someone who persists in the hermitage until death, only going out in great necessity, *merits* to be buried there.[51]

Peter sums up much of his feeling of good versus evil in the religious life in his late Letter 165, written in 1069 to the hermits Albizo and Peter. It is not surprising that the old Patrologia Latina edition should have entitled this long letter '*Apologeticum de contemptu saeculi*'.[52] This letter sums up the mature Peter Damian's views on the life of professional religious. In this treatise, Peter makes it abundantly clear that it is not the business of either a monk or a hermit to have dealings with the world. Specific statements deal with the avoidance of all worldly obligations, such as that one should have no contact with relatives, and should give no heed to worldly vanities.[53] The only proper course for a monk or a hermit is to stay firmly mewed up in his cloister. For, as he says, 'Custom makes the monk's cell sweet, while wandering makes it appear horrible. For wanderers the cell is a prison, for those who remain in stability it is a delightful chamber'.[54] 'Vagabond' monks, like Isaac's son Esau in the Genesis story, lose the blessing that stay-at-homes like Jacob receive.[55] What is more, they risk a spiritual defilement, such as that prefigured by Dinah, who went out among strangers only to be raped (Gen 34).[56] One may wonder why this treatise was addressed to two hermits. The most logical answer I can find is that perhaps they, like Damian himself, were tempted by the lure of ecclesiastical reform. Certainly the letter brings up the issue of a desire to undertake salutary action in the world, since Peter apparently felt it necessary to address the issue.

The new eremitism was, according to Peter Damian, the best possible way to avoid the evils of interaction with the world and perhaps also had as a goal to discourage the ecclesiastical interference that was common in situations such as that of Teuzo described above. The basic structure of a Camaldolese hermitage, in which the spiritual experts, the hermits, are served by a system of monks and lay brothers who buffer them from the impingement of the world for practical matters of support, expresses this attitude very clearly. The language of the earliest camaldolese documents provide an added dimension about the goals of the new hermits. The oldest source on the founding of this combination monastery/hermitage, a document of Bishop Theodald of Arezzo from August 1027, outlines how the hermits were established in individual cells, '[because] those alone who are remote from the world and its cares will continue to pursue divine contemplation'. The bishop goes on to delineate clearly the necessary stability of the hermits.[57]

Similarly, in his letter number 50, from the year 1057, Peter includes the vow of stability for all hermits entering Fonte Avellana, recommending it for general adoption by all hermits. Its wording is very revealing:

> I, brother *N.*, promise obedience and perseverance all the days of my life in this hermitage which is built for the honor of God and the holy Cross, for fear of our lord Jesus Christ, and the healing of my soul. If at any time I should flee from here, or be tempted to leave, the servants of God who live here are permitted to require me to submit to their authority, and to recall me by force and violence into this service.

This written promise was then to be placed on the altar, as in a benedictine monastery.[58] Thus the new member is obligated to remain for life in a particular hermitage, although earlier hermits, including Damian's role model Romuald of Ravenna, were free to move about as they wished. What Peter Damian is describing as the 'new eremitism' is moving into much closer alignment with traditional cenobitic monasticism than the word 'hermit' would have suggested to writers of earlier generations.

By about 1055, I believe, Peter had taken a firm stand against all ascetic wanderers. Certainly according to his works after that time, hermits should bind themselves to permanent membership in a community, or, if they are strongly drawn to the solitary life, to stability in the place of hermitage they have chosen. In his Letter 39 of *c.* 1051, Damian quite simply states that monks who wander around are not monks at all but gyrovagues or sarabaites, taking the terminology of the benedictine *Rule* for the two worst sorts of monks, who wander and follow their own will instead of giving themselves up to God.[59] The statements become even stronger over time, precisely in those areas where the issue of ecclesiastical reform appear.

But it is not only monks whom Peter sees in this light. In Letter 165, the long treatise on withdrawal from the world already discussed above, he calls wandering hermits among the worst of those who fall from their vows. He tells of hermits who spend only Lent in their cells, wandering the rest of the time, 'and thus pass their lives worthlessly'. They cannot see God, since anyone who wants to attain to that inaccessible light must first cleanse his interior eyes from all mundane things.[60] Indeed, *all* clerics, not just professional religious, should flee from the oppression of dealing with the laity. The reason is simple: one must be pure to minister at the altar, and clerics are polluted by associating with evil people, who are unavoidable in contemporary society.[61] Thus the danger of dealing with excommunicates alone should be enough to keep a religious from breaking his stability.[62]

There has been some debate over whether Peter Damian believed that a life of mixed action and contemplation was possible. Bultot argued strongly that Damian saw an unbridgeable gap between the two.[63] Hamilton, on the other hand, argues that Bultot has seriously overstated the case, although without providing much evidence.[64] Ferretti points to several areas in Peter Damian's own work in which he speaks of the unity of the active and contemplative lives,[65] but without, I believe, taking into proper account the recipients of the letters in question. In general, for Peter Damian there exists at best a tension between the active and contemplative lives, as he implies in his Letter 27 to the clerics of Fano, probably written before 1059.[66] But by the end of his life, as we see in Letter 165, he thought it simply not possible for a monk to live a mixed life of contemplation and action—neither will be productive and one will corrupt the other.[67] But already in his Letter 86, dated to late 1061, Damian, in one of his more telling passages, describes a rotten world, lacking in decency or honesty, in which vice and depravity are growing.[68]

The problem with this definition of sequestration for one's own good and that of others is that it was becoming fragmented at the edges in the early eleventh century. Peter Damian himself was trapped by papal command into becoming the cardinal bishop of Ostia, and found himself on a round of legations and services to the papacy that chafed him very badly, and from which he regularly begged to be excused.[69] But, of course, Peter Damian was an exception. As prior of Fonte Avellana he did not entirely escape the mold of the abbot in service to secular or religious authorities. As a brilliant writer and theologian, his services were bound to be demanded by someone. But it is peculiar that Peter Damian started his own personal fight against simony and other abuses in the Church on his own initiative, rather than working with a group.[70] It was only chance that made him 'respectable', able to claim superior authority as a reason to conduct himself with what he himself regarded as grave impropriety in others. Whatever his misgivings, Damian's work for ecclesiastical reform came from an individual impulse, most likely a feeling that *someone* had to take a stand and that he was well-equipped by his education to do so.

From careful reading of the works of Peter Damian, it appears that the choices of religious life in eleventh-century Italy were life in a hermitage or a monastery, with an outside chance of winning salvation as a canon regular. But Damian really ranges the full force of his eloquence to support the traditional view of the contemplative life, both monks and new hermits, against the outsiders, the religious not controlled by any rule or authority in a way that surpasses simple traditionalism on his part. I believe that he was vehement in his rejection of Teuzo and an undisclosed number of people like him for several compelling reasons: Peter Damian could not conceive of a productive religious life that was not conducted in solitude. Besides this, as we have seen, he feared the dangers of unauthorized preaching in the sensitive area of reforming ecclesiastical politics. To him the telling line was not between professed religious and dangerous innovators, but between those religious who stayed at home and those, either singly or in groups, who went out voluntarily into the world. Worst of all, the evidence of Peter Damian and others suggests that the numbers who fit in this category were increasing, and caused Damian grave alarm.

There were certainly plenty of old-fashioned, non rule-oriented hermits and recluses in Italy in the eleventh century. Meerseman sees a phenomenal rush toward eremitical life from the second half of the eleventh century,[71] a view supported by Penco's excellent article on 'irregular' hermits in Italy in the eleventh century. Penco suggests that these independent holy men were part of a new search for spiritual liberty, away from the constricting rules of the cloister. It is not surprising that he has found their activities consistent with those against which Peter Damian was fighting. Penco lists their chief characteristics as an interest in popular and lay piety, a tendency to promote women, and an effort to teach a more gospel-based spirituality.[72] This turn towards the gospels, one of the reasons why I have labelled these old-fashioned hermits 'evangelicals', has an interesting side note. One of these evangelical hermits of the eleventh century, Renald, reproved cloistered monks, observing that: 'They guard the observances of the cloister, and hold the Lord's precepts in contempt'.[73] In other words, as the evangelical hermits saw themselves, they were turning from exclusive submission to monastic tradition to a more inclusive view of binding duty that included Jesus' teaching of his apostles. Many of these hermits left monasteries because of discontent or because the institute in question was out of alignment with the ecclesiastical reform movement. Some of these after a time founded monasteries that better suited their goals.[74] An interest in ecclesiastical reform in a monastery founded by an evangelical hermit was a potent, and for Peter, dangerous combination, as we will see in the case of Vallombrosa.

These evangelical hermits were following the original model of the Fathers of the egyptian and syrian deserts who, especially in the early years of the ascetic movement in the fourth century, frequently lived highly unstable lives, moving from area to area, without the support of a community. Some of these early hermits devoted much of their lives to preaching and educating the laity on the margins of whose society they lived.[75] Damian was, of course, not willing to criticize the authority of these saintly fathers of the monastic life, so he was forced to juggle veneration of ancient authority (which by definition is good) with contemporary practice (which he saw as at least misguided, and at worst evil). To do this, he turned to analyze the motivations and the propriety of different forms of life in different eras, in a manner that goes far beyond the facile use of *topoi* as straw figures against which to tilt.

All these characteristics, along with the very virulence with which Peter Damian attacks such practices, presents us with the outline of a story of both individual hermits and at least a few monastic communities going into the world to preach the cause of reform for the Church. Peter's words are too harsh and too specific to be taken as simply a *topos*, drawing a contrast to the ideal religious life. Once again, Letter 165, not addressed to any particular group working on ecclesiastical reform, alerts us to the depth of the problem. Again and again Peter warns monks to avoid snares in the form of action in the world. Mary is better than Martha, as Moses surpasses Aaron. Even religious who set out with good intentions risk shipwreck in the maelstrom of the world. As he tells his fellows, we who are on the beach have as our job, in the dark night of this life, to put up a light to guide ships, so they can see the right course and reach port, 'not, however, that we, going out to them, should be sucked up in the whirlpool of the foaming sea'.[76] If a monk wants to attain perfection, Peter repeats, he should stay in the cloister and occupy himself in spiritual things. He certainly will not do anyone any good by immersing himself in the lake of blood that constitutes the world, where he will become more polluted every day.[77]

The audience of these lessons in Letter 165 are good hermits, whom Peter addresses respectfully and indeed with affection. But the tenor of the letter suggests that even these men think they will do good by venturing into the world, and believe they can effect change by preaching reform in society. While allowing for the fact that Peter was trying to discourage this particular group in society from reform preaching, his views are so negative that it is hard to believe that he saw ecclesiastical reform as possible before the Second Coming. Preaching, he states, is no longer effective. In former times preaching was fruitful, but not now. Modern people hear crowds of preachers and are not convinced, while Nineveh was converted by one man. Now it is not even possible to convert one man away from an illicit marriage, despite two papal councils in the very year he writes. A monk can desert his religious life 'under the pretense' of saving souls, only to waste his efforts in barrenness. His words will not have an effect on simoniacs, he will not be able to restore people to their rightful inheritances, bring about peace on battlefields, or do anything else praiseworthy. 'Everything in the world is in confusion, and all rules of piety and faith are overthrown.'[78] Evangelical monks and hermits only add to the problem.

Certainly monks and hermits were going out to preach, and Peter Damian was doing his best to stop it, calling on all his formidable arsenal of biblical knowledge, centuries of monastic tradition, and rhetoric. Professional religious, interfering in the world, always act 'under the pretense' of trying to help.[79] Peter implies by his language that the problem was really itchy feet and a desire for excitement and notoriety. For a monk to preach is great audacity, as can be seen from the fact that Paul forbade it to Timothy in better circumstances than now exist (2 Tim 3).[80] He argues that it is particularly presumptuous that a monk should speak against a bishop at a synod—for which he must have had a particular case in mind, most likely the Vallombrosans speaking against the bishop of Florence. With his biting wit, Peter declares: 'But, oh new presumption! We are subject to the opinions of the dead [monks, traditionally considered dead to the world] and they are made judges over bishops, over those under whom they were legally placed'.[81]

In other words, in at least some cases this wandering rabble did not merely leave the stability of the claustral life; they did it in willful disobedience to superior authority. According to Peter, leading a holy life consists in large part of giving up one's will to a lawful superior. He denounced the disobedient and willful spirit of some of these 'pseudo-hermits', arguing that they were not truly holy men because they did not blindly follow a superior. The besetting sin Damian sees in Teuzo, as well as others of these interfering would-be reformers, is that of pride.[82] Besides obedience and stability, the other absolutely vital requirement for a man to be a good and holy religious, is humility. There are references in eleventh-century texts to lack of humility among the professional religious. Bishops complained about the *ruinosa superbia*, the 'ruinous pride' of monks,[83] while Peter Damian inveighed against any men, monastic or eremitical or falling into the cracks between the two sorts, who were guilty of the sin of pride. Was this a complaint against fat, rich monks who exuded an air of smug superiority? Or was it the assumption of some religious that they had a duty to tell the world what a mess it was in, especially in the case of simony? It is hard to imagine a bishop such as Peter Mezzabarba of Florence praising the monks of Vallombrosa for their public attacks on his simony. As Damian reminds the reader, the role of a monk, or of any ascetic, is to weep over sins rather than to teach.[84] As he complains to the Vallombrosans, they think themselves so holy that they are arrogant enough to set themselves up even against the authority of the pope.[85]

The most pernicious form this disobedience could take was for a monk or hermit to break ties with the discipline of a cloister and its abbot or prior, giving up the habit of obedience that is central to the religious life. It is plain that Peter knew cases in which hermits (or monks) had failed in obedience and abandoned their superiors to take up the life of a wandering or isolated holy man. Most common is the case when a monk left his monastery as a protest against simony. Peter was plainly worried about protesters who became disillusioned with organized religious life as a whole and opted for personal forms of unregulated eremitism, where they could be sure they would not fall under the power of other simoniacs. We know that this occurred in the case of several of Italy's leading reformers, as well as of idiosyncratic hermits like Teuzo. For example, John Gualbert, the founder of Vallombrosa, left his monastery because the abbot was a simonist. He spent considerable time wandering, then founded a hermitage that re-entered the main stream of religious life by adopting the benedictine *Rule*.[86] Even then, the Vallombrosans were included in the group of 'others' because, unlike proper monks, they continued under John Gualbert's guidance to work against simony.

Already in the *Vita Romualdi*, which was probably begun in 1042, the year before he became prior of Fonte Avellana,[87] Peter makes it clear that anyone should prefer the new hermits who followed Romuald's preaching (rather than his practice) and lived in stable communities to wanderers. But he is still able to speak admiringly of Bruno of Querfurt, who left the hermitage to become a missionary.[88] He also describes the beginnings of a missionary journey by Romuald himself, which, although Romuald had to turn back because of illness, several Camaldolesi continued to the mission field.[89] Indeed, one of the most effective scenes of this beautifully-crafted *vita* is when Damian tells how his hero Romuald was tempted by a demon to neglect the welfare of others for the sake of quiet contemplation, an evil thought that Romuald successfully resisted.[90] H. P. Laqua has described this early work as a rather triumphant statement that hermits should care for the spiritual well-being of others, and as the model for the care of souls at the heart of the reform movement.[91] This is almost certainly going too far, especially since Damian stresses above all how Romuald brought others to the life of 'rational' hermits, rather than working with people in the world, but it does highlight the greater openness of Peter Damian's early writings, and makes one regret his growing disillusionment with the world.

His attitude hardened over time as the issue of ecclesiastical reform played an ever greater role in spiritual life. The immodest and improper religious of Peter's later works are certainly preaching on the issue of simony, which doubles the offense in Damian's eyes. Peter complains that when wandering hermits appear in public they spread wrong opinions among the people, in addition to all their other faults.[92] He wants matters to flow in a smooth and hierarchically-correct order. Despite what he says about the general irredeemability of the world, he urges his audience to consider how imperial edicts, papal decrees, and synods are working to correct the wrongs of the Church. A monk should ask himself what he has to do with the kings of the earth and synods. It should suffice for him to weep for his own sins.[93] But who is going to do the work of reform, if the bishops are simonists and monks and hermits are disbarred from service? Peter the theorist never answers that question.

It was neither monks nor hermits against whom Peter Damian fought—it was anyone who broke his notions of religious propriety. One of Peter's more important tasks as papal legate was to deal with the new, reformed order of Vallombrosa, headed by the fiery anti-simonist John Gualbert. The problem in this case is that the Vallombrosans denounced the bishop of Florence, their own diocesan, for simony. The first evidence of Vallombrosa's campaign against Bishop Peter Mezzabarba is an appeal to the emperor against him in 1062; it was reported in both Italian and French sources.[94] By 1064 the monks had certainly taken the pulpit against their bishop. In that year, Pope Alexander II wrote a letter ordering an unnamed group of monks to stop preaching, a group that was almost certainly John Gualbert's followers. The pope quoted against them the authority of the Council of Chalcedon (451) that monks should not wander about in cities.[95] But papal letters had no effect, and Peter Damian was sent to Florence, probably in 1066, to mediate between the bishop and the anti-simonists. He wrote his main statement against the Vallombrosans, Letter 146, only after conciliatory efforts had failed.[96] In this treatise, addressed to the people of Florence, it is clear that Peter is speaking about monks rather than hermits, but he uses the same arsenal of complaints against them as he had against the 'city hermit' Teuzo over a decade earlier. Those who should be cut off from the world are purposely telling the laity what to do, in this case in the cause of Church reform. And, in their ignorance, the monks do not understand the issues well enough to teach them to others, even if they were allowed to do so. Peter introduces the treatise by asserting that some monks are saying that simonists cannot consecrate chrism, dedicate churches, make clerics, or celebrate Mass; in other words, they were arguing that the ordination of simonists is invalid, a claim leading back to the most disputed issue of the ecclesiastical reform.[97]

Peter's complaints against the Vallombrosans are basically the same as those of all of his statements against religious acting in the world. The monks are guilty of pride for thinking they have a right to interfere. Even the apostle Paul was content to appeal to the emperor—is the pope worse than Nero? Damian cuts at Vallombrosan pretensions in his finest rhetorical style: 'Do we believe that these monks are holier than Paul? Paul, who was found worthy to ascend before the tribunal of the third heaven, but did not disdain to appeal to the court of Nero? Who are these monks who, through the arrogance of their sanctity, think they can reject the judgment of the Apostolic See?'[98] Both here and at the synod that nearly condemned the Vallombrosans, Peter compared these trouble-makers to locusts, destroying the Church in their misguided fervor.[99] The arguments for the desperate need for separation from the world and against pride, disobedience, and improper teaching mark the letter against the Vallombrosans just as they do Peter Damian's statements about evangelical hermits. But it is questionable whether Peter would have been so vehement if the issue had not been that of ecclesiastical reform and the fragile edifice of the definition of simony he was central in building.

Peter Damian was deeply sensitive to the need for reform, and spent much of his life attempting a compromise between withdrawal and involvement, doing as much of his work as possible by letter to avoid direct contact with the outside world. It is this conviction that the world outside the cloister is fundamentally polluted and polluting that lies at the heart of Damian's dislike of this 'other stream' of the religious life, the evangelical hermits and supporters of general Church reform, and thus his monastic reform efforts cut him off from the main body of Church reformers. These unregulated hermits and overly bold monks, far from cutting themselves off from the world, actually cultivated a role as mentors of the laity.

Peter Damian's view of the world did not include the possibility that a normal human being could interact with the world and avoid corruption. But it was these very men on the fringe of acceptable ascetic life who were thus paradoxically most likely to have a direct impact on the society in which they lived. People in the eleventh century listened to hermits, and numerous complaints give ample evidence that ascetics found it very easy to draw an audience. Peter's deep suspicion of 'the world', of the normal human relations of lay life, lays the basis for his division between good monks and hermits and these active 'pseudo' monks and hermits who present at best a pretense of holiness and yet wield a pernicious influence on a world already marred by original sin.

This attitude marks Peter Damian in a fundamental sense as a reactionary against the current of ecclesiastical reform in eleventh-century Italy. For him, the world is a place of temptation. It does not even have the positive value of a testing-ground; even the best ascetic runs a grievous risk if he wantonly involves himself in the concerns of the world. Therefore it is impossible for a Peter Damian to ally himself with this rabble who, according to him, must just be pretending to a holiness that they cannot actually possess. As he complained to Teuzo, a 'city hermit' is a contradiction in terms. One cannot be a hermit, or a monk, without silence and withdrawal. Peter is simply unable to conceive of a positive relationship with the world; the best one can hope for would be to escape relatively unscathed. This, at heart, is why history books speak of a 'Gregorian Reform' rather than a 'Petrine Reform', even though the theoretical underpinning of the ecclesiastical reform is much more the work of Peter than of Hildebrand/Gregory. Gregory VII thought the world improvable and was willing to enter the fray; Peter the pessimist did his best to avoid action in the world.

Peter Damian was still trapped in a mental state that sees the world as a slimy pit into which even the forewarned and forearmed souls of monks and hermits can all too easily be lost. He said of a monk who went into the world more than necessary: '*Caritas* is diminished in him, because his mind, which is blown by the winds of action in the world, grows lukewarm from [its original] fervor of profound love.'[100] Perhaps the greatest tragedy of Peter's life is that he saw exactly the same thing happening to himself, yet could not draw back. He describes his active life for reform in almost the same terms: 'I, who daily am trapped by the business of secular cares, grow lukewarm from [my original] fervor of divine love. . . .'[101]

Part of the problem of traditional historiography has been a tendency to see the eleventh century in terms of the most major and visible movements and try to fit everything into a framework of what is well known. A few great men, such as Gregory VII and Humbert of Silva Candida, loom large in historical accounts, and their beliefs and attitudes are assumed to have been widely accepted. But by whom? Simonist bishops and married clergy? Someone had to carry the reform to the common folk, no matter how distasteful the job was to purists such as Peter Damian. That the message became simplified and flawed in transmission is the nature of popularizing, especially making sense out of profound theological theories about which even the experts did not agree. But there were men in Italy, and, one may presume, in the rest of the Empire, to spread this popular teaching and make the Investiture Contest the public issue it became. The evangelical hermits played a much greater role in ecclesiastical reform than did Peter Damian's antiseptic new hermits, and Peter admits as much in his correspondence, at the same time that he tries, with little success, to halt their course of reform.

NOTES

1. Norman F. Cantor, 'The Crisis of Western Monasticism, 1050-1130', *American Historical Review* 66 (1960) 61.

2. Giovanni Miccoli, 'Théologie de la vie monastique chez Saint Pierre Damien' *Théologie de la vie monastique* 49 (1961) 482.

3. 'O aureum Romualdi seculum, quod etsi tormenta persecutorum non noverat, spontaneo tamen martyrio non carebat! Aureum, inquam, seculum, quod inter montiu et silvarum feras tot cęlestis Hierusalem cives alebat.' Peter Damian, *Vita beati Romualdi* 64; ed. Giovanni Tabacco, Fonti per la storia d'Italia 94 (Rome: Nella sede dell'istituto palazzo Borromini, 1957) p. 105.

4. See, for example, Peter Damian Letter 44; ed. Kurt Reindel, *Die Briefe des Petrus Damiani*, 4 vols. (Munich: MGH, 1983-1993) 2: 13. There is a more detailed account in the Chronicle of Mariannus Scottus including the name and location of the recluse. MGH SS 5 [1058], p. 558.

5. 'Ut fama venit Romualdum patrem rationabilium hermitarum qui cum lege vivunt.' Bruno of Querfurt, *Vita quinque fratrum eremitarum* 2.1; ed. Jadwiga Karwasinska, Monumenta Poloniae Historica series nova (1973) 32.

6. Peter Damian, Letter 50; Reindel 2:83–84, emphasis mine. See Bernard Hamilton, 'S. Pierre Damien et les mouvements monastiques de son temps' *Studi*

Gregoriani 10 (1975) 188. Leclercq argues in his '"Eremus" et "eremita." Pour l'histoire du vocabulaire de la vie solitaire', *Collectanea ordinis Cisterciensium reformatórum* 25 (1963) 25, that the distinction between these two sorts of solitaries was rare and artificial. I make no claims for the overall popularity of this distinction, only for its presence in Peter Damian's own thought. It is interesting to note that Owen Blum in his recent translation of this letter left out the word 'holy' completely, leaving the text to read 'anchorites occur rarely or never', in other words taking Peter to mean that this form of life was extinct. Peter Damian, *Letters*; trans. Owen Blum, The Fathers of the Church, Mediaeval Continuation (Washington, D.C.: Catholic University of America Press, 1990) 2: 293 (Letter 50).

7. Peter Damian, Letter 44; 2:13.

8. *Ibid.*, 2:13–14.

9. See especially Andrew of Strumi, *Vita Iohannis Gualberti* 6 (MGH SS 30/2: 1081) and Atto, *Vita s. Joannis Gualberti* 10 (PL 146: 675). The *vitae* of John Gualbert are also careful to refer to Teuzo as a recluse, giving him the proper title for a religious solitary within a city, and placing him within the tradition of spiritual advice expected of a recluse. See Andrew, 41 (1089); Atto, 36 (683); *Vita Iohannis Gualberti auctore discipulo eius anonymo* 1 (MGH SS 30/2 1105).

10. Anonymous, *Vita Iohannis Gualberti* 1 (1105).

11. Werner Goez, 'Reformpapsttum, Adel und monastische Erneuerung in der Toscana,' in Josef Fleckenstein, ed., *Investiturstreit und Reichsverfassung* (Sigmaringen: Jan Thorbecke Verlag, 1973) p. 230, note 130. The documents are in *MGH Diplomata*, Konradi II #273 and Heinrici IV #262a.

12. Brunetto Quilici, 'Giovanni Gualberto e la sua riforma monastica', *Archivio storico italiano* 99/2 (1941) 38.

13. Peter Damian, Letter 44: 2.9

14. *Ibid.*, 2: 32.

15. *Ibid.*, 2: 33.

16. Sofia Boesch Gajano, 'Storia e tradizione Vallombrosane', *Bullettino dell'istituto storico Italiano per il medio evo* 76 (1964) 150.

17. There is a large literature on recluses. For a good overview, the best work is still Louis Gougaud, *Ermites et Reclus* (Vienne: Abbaye Saint-Martin de Ligugé. 1920). See also Eva Irblich, *Die Vitae Sanctae Wiboradae. Ein Heiligen-Leben des 10. Jahrhunderts als Zeitbild* (St. Gallen: Kommissionsverlag Fehr'sche Buchandlung, 1970), for a more specific look at the uses to which recluses were put. The articles in *L'Eremitismo in Occidente nei secoli XI e XII*, Settimana Internazionale di Studio 2, Mendola, 1962 (Milan: Società Editrice Vita e Pensiero, 1965) are also indispensable in understanding the interactions of both recluses and hermits with secular society.

18. Grimlaicus, *Regula solitariorum*; PL 103: 573–664.

19. Jean Leclercq, *Saint Pierre Damien, ermite et homme d'église* (Rome: Edizioni di storia e letteratura, 1960) p. 66.

20. Anonymous, *Vita Iohannis Gualberti*, 1 (1105): '. . . *quia nullus locus est remotus compunctae menti*. . . .'

21. Peter Damian, Letter 44; 2: 27. Already in the *Liber Gratissimus* (Letter 40), written in 1052, Peter states that one cannot go elsewhere to receive the sacraments from a priest who is free of simony (1: 466).

22. See Atto, *Vita Joannis Gualberti* 23 (680). Peter Damian accuses the Vallombrosans of belief in this more radical attitude towards the sacraments in his general

letter against the Vallombrosans, which he sent to Florence during Lent of 1067. See Letter 146. 3: 533.

23. Peter Damian, Letter 40; 1: 384–509. Peter himself named the treatise *Liber Gratissimus*, which marks it as his central statement on the sacraments. See p. 384, n. 1.

24. Peter Damian, Letter 44; 2: 8.

25. Peter Damian, Letter 44; 2: 16.

26. Giovanni Luccesi, 'Clavis S. Petri Damiani,' in *Studi su San Pier Damiano in onore del cardinale Amleto Giovanni Cicognani*, (Faenza:Venerabile Seminario vescovile Pio XII, 1961) 31.

27. See, for example, Letter 86 of late 1061, in which Peter Damian gently urges Desiderius to greater separation from the world, comparing religious to sheep who have been snatched from the jaws of a wolf. Peter Damian, Letter 86; 2: 461. H. E. J. Cowdrey, *The Age of Abbot Desiderius* (Oxford: Clarendon Press, 1983) 35–36, detects an undertone of criticism and anxiety in Peter Damian's letters to Monte Cassino. For his argument he cites especially the beginning of a letter from early 1065, Letter 119 (3:341ff.); Letter 90 (2:573–579, dated to *c.* 1062); and Letter 95 (3:41–46 from *c.* 1063).

28. Peter Damian, Letter 86; 2:461–462.

29. For some discussion, see Leclercq, *Saint Pierre Damien*, p. 41. Pietro Palazzini describes Peter Damian's transition from the world to the hermitage in 'S. Pier Damiani Eremita e Priore a Fonte Avellana,' *Studi Gregoriani* 10 (1975) 71.

30. Peter Damian, Letter 152; 4:5-12. See Hamilton, p. 178.

31. Peter Damian, Letter 105; 3:159-168 dating from early 1064. The whole treatise is permeated with Peter's ideas of monastic improvement. In the same letter he tells how a monk should be dead to the world, but an abbot is involved the whole day in worldly business, and spends nights in counsel. He can never be silent, and is like nothing so much as Etna erupting. Letter 105; 3: 160.

32. See, for example, Fridolin Dressler, *Petrus Damiani. Leben und Werk*, Studia Anselmiana 34 (Rome: Pontificium Institutum S. Anselmi, 1954), 66, cites several references. One of the works his argument rests upon has been pronounced spurious, but the other, Letter 38 of 1051 (1:347–373), deals exclusively with this issue.

33. Peter Damian, Letter 50; 2:81. Miccoli provides a useful summary of Peter Damian's views on the solitary life in his 'Théologie,' pp. 466–468. As he points out, for Damian the hermitage is the way to a mystical union of love. It is divine, a paradise, a school of heavenly doctrine. Above all it is a place to conquer demons, and become the *socius angelorum*. This last makes it possible to understand Hamilton's statement that Damian saw the eremitical life not as a tool for saving individual souls, but as a vital instrument to bring about the coming of God's kingdom (Hamilton, p. 177).

34. Peter Damian, Letter 153; 4:27–8.

35. See Jean Leclercq, 'Une lettre inedite de saint Pierre Damien sur la vie eremitique,' *Studia Benedictina*, Studia Anselmiana 18/19, p. 288.

36. Peter Damian, Letter 165; 4:175–178.

37. Jean Leclercq, 'La crise du monachisme aux XIe et XIIe siècles,' *Bullettino dell'istituto storico Italiano per il medio evo* 70 (1958) 23. For an early statement on monastic poverty, see Letter 3, from 1043 (1:105–108).

38. Peter Damian, Letter 132; 3:450.

39. Celestino Pierucci, 'La vita eremitica secondo S. Pier Damiano,' in *San Pier*

Damiano nel IX centenario della morte (1072-1972), 4 vols. (Cesena: Centro studi e ricerche sulla antica provincia ecclesiastica Ravennate, 1972) 4:76; Dressler, pp. 41–42.

40. Pierucci, p. 72.

41. For an analysis of this statement, see Miccoli, 'Théologie,' pp. 469-471; Dressler, p. 61.

42. Giovanni Tabacco, 'Eremo e cenobio,' in *Spiritualità cluniacense* . Convegni del centro di studi sulla spiritualità medievale 2. (Todi: Presso l'accademia Tudertina, 1960) 327–330.

43. Peter Damian, Letter 66; 2:274 from *c.* 1059/1060.

44. Peter Damian, Letter 153; 4:15, 17.

45. The benedictine reforms of 816 and 817, usually named after Benedict of Aniane, had as a central purpose the separation of monks from the influence of the world, so they could better pray for society.

46. Peter Damian, Letter 152; 4:8. It is small wonder that Bultot extrapolates from this that the secular order as a whole is perverted, and that the mass of people in Damian's view of the world was not only less perfect than religious, but appears to be without grace as well. Robert Bultot, *La Doctrine du mépris du monde*. Vol. 4: *Le XIe siècle*. Part 1: *Pierre Damien* (Louvain: Editions Nauwelaerts, 1963) pp. 58–65.

47. Peter Damian, Letter 153; 4:29.

48. See analysis in Hamilton, p. 177.

49. Peter Damian, Letter 50; 2:84.

50. *Ibid.*, 20; 86.

51. Leclercq, 'Un lettre inedite', p. 287.

52. Peter Damian, *opusculum* 12; PL 145: 251–292.

53. Peter Damian, Letter 165; 4:203.

54. *Ibid.*, 4:211.

55. *Ibid.*, 4:203-4.

56. *Ibid.*, 4:202.

57. Wilhelm Kurze, 'Campus Malduli. Die Frühgeschichte Camaldolis,' *Quellen und Forschungen aus Italienischen Archiven und Bibliotheken* 44 (1964) 7–8.

58. Peter Damian, Letter 50; 2:93. On the novelty of this vow for hermits, see Dressler, p. 49.

59. Peter Damian, Letter 39; 1:378.

60. Peter Damian, Letter 165; 4:210. In Letter 27 (1:244) Peter compares the food gathered in meditation to manna, tasting like honey.

61. Peter Damian, Letter 39; 1:383.

62. Peter Damian, Letter 165; 4:192.

63. Bultot, p. 13.

64. Hamilton suggests that Peter Damian was not basically a pessimist in regard to the world. He draws the conclusion that Damian was really interested not in the salvation of the individual soul, but in the work of the Church. Hamilton, p. 201.

65. Walter Ferretti, 'Il posto dei laici nella Chiesa secondo San Pier Damiani,' in *San Pier Damiano*, 1: 247, 257. Feretti also criticizes Bultot for too great a rigidity in his analysis. Ferretti, p. 250, note 13.

66. Peter Damian, Letter 27; 2:242–248. See Giovanni Miccoli, 'Pier Damiani e la vita comune del clero,' in *La vita comune del clero nei secoli XI e XII.* Settimana Mendola 3. 2 vols. (1962) 1: 187–188.

67. Peter Damian, Letter 165; 4:173–230. On this interpretation, see Miccoli, 'Théologie,' p. 477, Paulo Brezzi, 'Fuga dal mondo e conquista cristiana del mondo nella riforma gregoriana,' in *Chiesa e riforma nella spiritualità del sec. XI.*, Convegni del Centro di studi sulla spiritualità medievale 6 (Todi: Presso l'accademia Tudertina, 1968), p. 20; and more generally Leclercq, *Saint Pierre Damien*, p. 140.

68. Peter Damian, Letter 86; 2:461.

69. See for example Peter Damian's letter to Pope Nicholas II (dating from some time between December 1059–July 1061): Letter 72; 2:326–366.

70. Dressler, pp. 94–5.

71. Gérard G. Meerseman, 'Eremitismo e predicazione itinerante dei secoli XI e XII,' in *L'Eremitismo in occidente*, p. 164.

72. Gregorio Penco, 'L'Eremitismo irregolare in Italia nei secoli XI - XII', *Benedictina* 32 (1985) 206.

73. Gerd Tellenbach, 'Il monachesimo riformato ed i laici nei secoli XI e XII,' in *I laici nella 'societas Christiana' dei secoli XI e XII*. Settimana Mendola 3 (1968) 120.

74. See Penco, pp. 213–4.

75. See Peter Brown's magisterial study, 'The Rise and Function of the Holy Man in Late Antiquity,' in *Society and the Holy in Late Antiquity* (Berkeley, 1982) 103-152.

76. Peter Damian, Letter 165; 4:214.

77. *Ibid.*, 4:225.

78. *Ibid.*, 4:218–220.

79. *Ibid.*, 4:221, 223.

80. *Ibid.*, 4:222.

81. *Ibid.*, 4:224.

82. See e.g., Peter Damian Letter 44; 2:9.

83. Giovanni Tabacco, 'Vescovi e monasteri,' in *Il monachesimo e la riforma (1049–1122)*, Settimana Mendola 6 (1971) 106.

84. Leclercq, *Saint Pierre Damien*, p. 140. See Peter Damian, Letter 165 (4:223) for a very clear statement of this. The phrase comes from Jerome, *Librum contra Uigilantium*; PS 23:351. I cannot agree with Ferretti, who argues that Peter Damian perceived the proper monastic life as a balance between the active and contemplative lives, except in the most limited sense of physical activity interspersed with periods of contemplation. See Ferretti, 1:247.

85. Peter Damian, Letter 146; 3:540.

86. Both Andrew 8 (1082) and Atto 11 (675–6) tell ofJohn Gualbert's wandering phase, but insist on John's desire to lead a pure benedictine life. At first, however Vallombrosa was almost certainly eremitical, and became benedictine by 1048. See Meade, pp. 329–330.

87. See Dressler, p. 21.

88. Peter Damian, *Vita Romualdi*, 27 (56–61).

89. *Ibid.*, 39 (80).

90. *Ibid.*, 18 (43–44).

91. Hans Peter Laqua, *Traditionen und Leitbilder bei dem Ravennater Reformer Petrus Damiani 1042-1052* (Munich, 1976) 103ff. There has been a long scholarly argument about the level of Camaldolesi involvement in mission. Hamilton (p. 94) agrees with Laqua on Romuald's interest in mission. A. P. Vlasto, *The Entry of the Slavs into Christendom* (Cambridge: Cambridge University Press, 1970) 128, goes so far as to speak of Romuald's 'training center' for missionaries. The currently-held

view is that Romuald was not particularly interested in mission. See Jean Leclercq, 'Saint Romuald et le monachisme missionaire,' *Revue bénédictine* 72 (1962) 307-323; and Reinhard Wenskus, *Studien zur historisch-politischen Gedankenwelt Bruns von Querfurt*. Mitteldeutsche Forschungen 5 (Münster/Cologne: Böhlau Verlag, 1956) especially pp. 134–5. Both of these works, however, focus on the *vitae* written by Bruno of Querfurt and ignore the unwilling evidence of Peter Damian that suggests that in the earliest history of Camaldoli and especially of Romuald himself there was very considerable interest in mission.

92. Peter Damian, Letter 165; 4:210.

93. *Ibid.*, 4:223.

94. Quilici, pp. 74–75.

95. PL 146: 1406, #120; Meade, p. 333.

96. Goez, p. 233.

97. It is interesting to note that in Migne's edition of Damian's works this treatise is entitled 'Concerning the Sacraments when they are administered by unworthy persons.' Damian makes it plain in the treatise that the Vallombrosans had taken a donatist stand and had declared the sacraments of simoniacal priests invalid. See PL 145: 523–530; in the new edition this letter is Reindel, Letter 146; 531–542.

98. Peter Damian, Letter 146; 3:540.

99. Peter Damian, Letter 146; 3:542. Also in Anonymous, *Vita Iohannis Gualberti*, pp. 1106-7. See Goez, p. 233 for a discussion of Peter Damian's speech at the synod of 1067 as presented in the *vita*, which he accepts as authentic. It is very interesting to note that the archdeacon Hildebrand defended the monks against the arguments of both the pope and Peter Damian, praising them for their zeal for the faith. See Quilici, pp. 80–1 and all three *vitae* of John Gualbert.

100. Peter Damian, Letter 165; 4:188.

101. Peter Damian, Letter 72; 2:342. *a divini amoris fervore tepesco, et letiferum torpentis animae frigus incurro. . . .*

The Abyss of Love

Bernard McGinn

Abyssus abyssum invocat in voce cataractarum tuarum.
Omnia excelsa tua et fluctus tui super me transierunt.

Abyss calls out to abyss in the voice of thy cataracts.
All thy heights and thy billows have passed over me.

THESE WORDS from the Vulgate version of the Bible provide a prism that can help to focus a subject large and profound enough to threaten sinking the writer in the depths of mystical ineffability and battering the reader into insensibility in a surf of scholarly literature.[1] My topic is mystical union in the later Middle Ages, especially the contribution that women made to its expression.[2] My perspective is that of the language and terminology employed to express union, particularly the language of the *abyssus*, the depth-without-ground suggested by the Hebrew *TeHÕM 'EL TeHÕM* that lies behind the *abyssus abyssum invocat* of the Vulgate of Psalm 41:8.[3]

The word *abyssus* (from the Greek *a-byssos*, without ground) was a biblical interpolation into Latin. In Classical Greek it indicated the underworld, or the abode of the dead, a sense that it keeps in a number of New Testament passages (e.g., Lk 8:31, Rom 10:7, Apoc

9:11, 11:7, 17:8, 20:3). But *abyssos* was often employed with other meanings in the Septuagint and among those who translated this first christian Bible into Latin. The word occurs forty-two times in the Vulgate Old Testament, eleven of these being found in the Psalms. A number of such texts went beyond the netherworld identity of the classical tradition, as in Psalm 35:7 which describes God's judgments as abysses (*judicia tua abyssus multa*), and Ps 103:6 which has God clothing himself in the abyss as with a garment (*abyssus sicut vestimentum amictus eius*). Among other important, if ambiguous, uses, we should note Genesis 1:2, *et tenebrae super faciem abyssi.*

Concentration on the language of the abyss as a way to investigate christian attempts to express the inexpressible—the experience which, since the seventeenth century, has often been called mystical union (*unio mystica*)—highlights significant characteristics of christian mystical discourse. The first is the priority of the language of the Bible. It may seem an exaggeration to say that the history of the first millennium of christian mysticism can be conceived of as a chapter in the history of biblical exegesis, but down to the twelfth century what we call mystical experience almost always took place within the context of reading and praying the biblical text. Even after the thirteenth century, when many mystical writers abandoned the directly exegetical mode, the Bible retained an important role in the history of mysticism. Early christian mystics would have been convinced that it was because God revealed himself in the Psalm as 'clothed in the abyss' that the experience of the divine abyss is possible in this life, rather than that the mystic must first have had an experience of union with divine nothingness before she can search for a way to express it, such as that found in abyss language.

The priority of biblical language, however, did not mean the dominance of some kind of fundamentalist view of the meaning of the text. Modern hermeneutical theory has helped us to a better understanding of the basic intention of what the medievals called the *intelligentia spiritualis*, that is, the conviction that the meaning of the Bible was rooted in its *historia*, or literal sense, but could not be exhausted by it. The inner depth of any biblical passage would become fully meaningful to the reader only when the original author, the Holy Spirit, revealed its significance to a person already attuned to receive the message. The relationship between the biblical text and the inner text of experience, the *liber experientiae* of the twelfth-century mystics, was a fluid one whose changing contours are evident in studying the history of the interpretation of Psalm 41:8.[4] Especially when women, who *ex professo* could not be masters of the sacred text (that is, trained expositors of Scripture) began to produce signicant mystical literature, the boundaries between the Spirit's biblical and personal revelations—if I may be permitted these terms—took on new configurations.

In order to understand the development of the mystical understanding of *abyssus abyssum invocat*, we may begin by looking at two interpreters separated by almost a millennium: Augustine of Hippo writing shortly after 410, and John Tauler who wrote in the mid-fourteenth century. Augustine's *Enarrationes in Psalmos* is not only his longest work but is also a central resource for his mystical theory. Psalm 41, which begins with the image of the hart or deer (that is, the soul) thirsting for the fountains of divine grace, might be described as the mystical psalm *par excellence*.[5] It is interesting to note, then, that verse eight, where the abyss calls out to the abyss, is not given a mystical reading by Augustine. The first part of the bishop's exegesis of the psalm (*En. in Ps.* 41.2–6) speaks of the soul's longing for God and its preparation for interior illumination through overcoming vices and faithful living within the *domus Dei* of the Church. The consideration of what kind of vision of God is possible in this life, discussed in the second part of his exegesis (*En. in Ps.* 41.7–10), reaches only as far as v. 6a. The treatment of the 'abyss calling out to the abyss' comes in the third part of Augustine's sermon (*En. in Ps.* 41.11–17), where his primary concern was to emphasize the soul's constant need for repentence and confession of sin, no matter what favors she has received, as long as she remains in this life. Here Augustine defines *abyssus* as 'an impenetrable and incomprehensible depth, principally applied to a large body of water'.[6] While he notes that Psalm 35:7 describes God's judgments as abysses, it is evident from the bishop's treatment that he does not want to call God an abyss. The real abyss is the impenetrable human heart which can call out for (*invocat*) death and judgment. The 'abyss calling out to abyss', then, is read as the hearts of preachers, all of whom, like Peter and Paul, experienced their own sinfulness and now call out to other sinners to remind them of the dread judgments of God (*En. in Ps* 41.13–14). A clue as to why Augustine does not want to call God an abyss can be found in his anti-Manichaean treatise *Contra Faustum*. There he counters the misunderstanding of those who think that Christians interpret Genesis 1:2 (*tenebrae erant super abyssum*) to mean that 'God was at some time covered with darkness, . . . as though we should speak of God as an abyss'. No, Augustine says, 'God is light and there is no darkness in him' (1 Jn 1:5) even before the creation of physical light on the first day.[7]

Over nine hundred years later, in his Sermon 41 on the appropriately nautical text 'Jesus got into the boat that was Simon's' (Lk 5:3), the dominican preacher John Tauler gave a very different reading of Psalm 41:8:

> Here the word the prophet spoke in the psalter becomes true: *Abyssus abyssum invocat*, or, 'the abyss (*abgrunde*) draws the abyss into itself'. The [first] abyss is the created thing that draws the uncreated abyss into itself, and the two abysses become a single one (*ein einig ein*), a pure divine being, so that the spirit is lost in God's Spirit. It is drowned in the bottomless sea.[8]

Tauler's rich teaching on the mutual abyss cites Psalm 41:8 in several other places, notably in Sermon 61, where he employs it in reference to sinking into the abyss of our own soul, claiming, 'In this abyss alone the divine abyss belongs—*Abyssus abyssum invocat*'.[9] Surprisingly enough, here the Dominican goes on to cite the authority of Augustine himself.[10] Further, Tauler closes the sermon with an analysis of the four stages of love that effect the merging of the created and uncreated abysses. There is the 'wounding love' (*wundende minne*) that leads us into the depths, and the 'imprisoned love' (*gevangene minne*) that keeps us in the 'hidden abyss'. These are followed by 'agonizing love' (*qwelende minne*), and 'insane love' (*rasende minne*) which represent the soul's confusion and sickness in the midst of this depth experience in which love is making the soul perfectly her own. The suffering is real, even extreme: 'Such a person knows well the heat of love; it causes confusion in all the faculties. A person agonizes after such love and does not know that she possesses it. It will devour you, flesh and blood.'[11] This use of the abyss motif in relation to an analysis of the stages of violent charity is what Tauler meant when, in another context, he spoke of 'the abyss of love' (*der minnen abgrunde*).[12]

The gap that separates these two mystical authors, both male, is obvious. In seeking to explain how the meaning of *abyssus abyssum invocat* changed so radically from the fourth to the fourteenth century, however, it will be necessary to appeal to female writers. Though adumbrated by some twelfth-century male mystics, the two primary themes that characterize Tauler's teaching on the dual abyss were first advanced in explicit form, it seems, by the women mystics of the thirteenth century. These essential themes were first, the understanding of mystical union as at least a union of indistinction (*das einig ein*) between two equally incomprehensible abysses; and second, the fact that this union takes place through the power of violent and fully mutual love. These shifts were of considerable importance in the history of christian mystical traditions. They also have something to tell us about the interaction between male and female authors in the creation of the mystical discourse of the later Middle Ages.

During the early Middle Ages, the use of the term *abyssus* appears to have been fairly standard and conventional, referring sometimes to the divine judgments (with reference to Ps 35:7), but more often to the abyss of wickedness, alternately of the devil, of heretics and sinners, or of the vices they practice.[13] It could also refer to the depths of Scripture, so that one of the common readings of Psalm 41:8—found in Jerome, Cassiodorus, and many medieval expositors—interprets it as the abyss of the Old Testament calling out to the abyss of the New.[14] As in much of the language of western mysticism, however, some significant changes begin to become evident in the twelfth century. The premier mystic of that era, Bernard of Clairvaux, provides a starting point.

Bernard uses the word *abyssus* sixty-three times in his works, with most of the references signifying the depths of human sinfulness or the inscrutable divine judgments. But Bernard also speaks of the *abyssus divinae pietatis*,[15] and he refers to heaven as an *abyssus luminis* or *abyssus aeternitatis*.[16] The mystery of the divine Incarnation can also be called an abyss for the abbot.[17] Bernard uses Psalm 41:8 three times. Unlike Augustine, the Cistercian reads the abyss that calls out to the other abyss as the Abyss of divine light and wisdom calling out to the abyss of the darkness and sinfulness of the human heart. As he puts in one of these texts: ' "Abyss calls out to abyss"—the luminous abyss to the abyss of darkness, the abyss of mercy to the abyss of misery, for the human heart is deep and impenetrable.'[18] For Bernard, the text has already come to express the relation between God and the human person, but not yet a mutual relation based on love. For Bernard the two abysses have opposite polarities: light vs. darkness.

Bernard's use of Psalm 41:8 seems to have given it some popularity among the other cistercian authors of the twelfth century. With several of them we can detect another significant development: the entry of an erotic dimension into language of the abyss. In an important passage in his *Exposition on the Song of Songs* William of Saint Thierry uses the verse to help explain the image of the embrace of the left and right hands in Song 2:6:

> The embrace surrounds the person, but is above her, for the embrace is the Holy Spirit who is the communion of the Father and the Son, the charity, the friendship, the embrace. He is all these things in the love of the Groom and the Bride. . . . The embrace is begun here, but perfected there. This abyss calls out to the other abyss; this ecstasy dreams of something quite different from what it sees; this secret sighs for another secret; this joy imagines another joy; this sweetness foretells another sweetness.[19]

The embrace that is an abyss is the experience that is the Holy Spirit, but William is still intent upon emphasizing the difference between present experience of the Spirit, the embracing abyss of love at times found here on earth, and that embrace we will enjoy in heaven.

The affective nature of the abyss is also highlighted in one of the sermons on the Song of Songs of Gilbert of Hoyland, the first continuator of Bernard's commentary. Discussing Song 4:7–8, this english abbot emphasizes how the Divine Lover, enraptured by the beauty of the Bride, longs for her presence. Gilbert expresses his amazement over the divine attraction (*affectus*) for the human soul, citing Psalm 41.8: 'Attraction (*affectus*) merits attraction, and abyss calls out to like abyss in the voice of flowing cataracts. Good are the cataracts which drip down your attraction, good Jesus, and pour in your love.'[20]

Another Englishman, Aelred of Rievaulx, spoke of the purified soul as being absorbed in love (*affectus*) for Christ as in a kind of abyss;[21] and his contemporary, Isaac of Stella, used Psalm 41:8 to explain how the mortification the monk endures in this life calls out to its model and exemplar, Christ's passion.[22] John of Ford, the last of the continuators of Bernard on the Song, follows his master in using the text to indicate how the *abyssus divinae pietatis* calls out to the abyss of our tepidity through the cataracts that are the voices of the apostles and prophets.[23] Therefore, among the twelfth-century Cistercians we can already detect a shift in the use of the image of the abyss away from early medieval uses, especially the augustinian interpretation of Psalm 41:8 which eschewed any divine reference. The abyss begins to be used in terms of a personal relation between God and the human lover, though there is still no full-blown and mutual abyssal discourse, as we have seen it in Tauler.

This general pattern is also found among non-cistercian users of abyss language in the twelfth century. The most extensive treatment I have found is that in the fifth of the *Meditations* of the Carthusian prior, Guigo II, who died about 1188. Guigo's text is a personal and meditative prayer on the meaning of Genesis 1:2: *terra autem erat inanis et vacua et tenebrae super faciem abyssi*. In dependence on the Genesis commentary of the Cistercian Arnold of Bonneval,[24] Guigo interprets the *terra* of the text as indicating human nature which was created 'empty and void' because it had not yet received the fullness of blessedness, but which separated itself from God by sin, thus becoming an 'abyss covered with darkness'. Redemption signifies 'making an earth out of the abyss and a heaven from earth', that is, restoring the image of God in us and eventually leading us on to heaven. Like Bernard, Guigo here appeals to Psalm 41:8 to describe how the 'deep and dark' abyss of the mind calls out to the divine abyss on high for mercy.[25]

Tauler, as we have seen, linked the abyss to experiences of love's pain, violence, and madness—what the twelfth-century authors often called *amor vehemens*, or *caritas violenta*. Both Cistercians and Victorines appreciated the madness and suffering of love. Despite their over-arching desire to integrate every form of love into that 'ordering of charity' (*ordinatio caritatis*) proclaimed in Song of Songs 2:4, the male mystics of the era knew that love was the most powerful force in the universe and that the encounter between the created spirit and the Uncreated Spirit was a stormy and passionate one.

By way of illustration, let us look briefly at the three premier mystical authors of the century: Bernard, William, and Richard of Saint Victor. Bernard of Clairvaux was as impetuous in his mystical theory as he was in his personal life. Commenting on how it is possible that God might become one with lowly, sinful humanity, he exclaims: 'It is love, taking no thought of dignity, rich in honor, powerful in affection, potent in persuasion. What is more violent? Love triumphs over God. What is nevertheless so non-violent?. . . . What power is there, I ask, that is so violent to gain the victory, so vanquished by violence?'[26] If the abbot's reflection here seems to dwell on the metaphysical violence of human love that dares to seek out God, other passages reflect the vehemence of the human experience of loving God, as when Bernard apostrophizes, 'O headlong love, vehement, burning, impetuous, which cannot think of anything besides yourself! . . . You mix up proper order, you leave ordinary usage unnoticed, you are ignorant of due measure. . . .'[27] William of Saint Thierry had an even more powerful sense of the way in which the power of love overcomes the soul and temporarily destroys its health and good sense, as a lengthy passage discussing Song of Songs 2:4–5 shows.[28] Those who continued Bernard's exegesis of the Song also commented on love's madness.

None of the twelfth-century mystics, however, gave a larger role to the *insania amoris* than Richard of Saint Victor, especially in his short treatise entitled *The Four Degrees of Violent Charity*. Building on themes found in his teacher Hugh, but with impressive originality, Richard argues that *caritas* cannot be the paradigm of all love unless its violence and insanity surpass the most extreme forms of human love-madness, with which the twelfth century was no less familiar than the twentieth. *Amor vulnerans* pierces the soul with fever; *amor ligans* binds it to continual thought on the beloved, while *amor languens* produces a condition in which constant desire absorbs all other human concerns in a state of erotic tyranny. Finally, in the fourth degree of *amor deficiens*, 'nothing at all is able to satisfy the love of the intellectual soul on fire . . . because it can always find something more to love'.[29] This 'insatiable love' is rightfully directed only to God. If we attempt to love any creature in this way, we will wind up destroying it and ourselves. Richard's treatise on the violence and insanity of love is the major contribution of its time to a theme that was to become more and more powerful in the succeeding century,[30] but it does not emphasize the language of the abyss, and its view of mystical union does not surpass the typical twelfth-century teaching that the goal of all love is to become one spirit with the Creator—'Who adheres to God is made one spirit with him' (1 Cor 6:17).

It is clear that twelfth-century male authors had already begun to make use of the language of the abyss to describe the soul's relation to God and that they had developed a notion of the violence of the love involved in the mystical encounter. But these two linguistic trajectories were still separate. It was only in the thirteenth century, and first among the women mystics, that the two became fused into a new language about mystical union. More and more union with God came to be described, not as an *unitas spiritus* of traditional Pauline origin, but as an *unitas indistinctionis*, or *unio sine differentia* (union without difference)—the conviction that at the deepest level the soul in its origin was, and can once again become, one reality (*ein einig ein* as Tauler put it) with God through the madness of love.[31] Among the early tentative expressions of this new form of mysticism it is not surprising to find a Cistercian, but this time a female Cistercian, Beatrice of Nazareth.

Beatrice was born about 1200 not far from Leuven into a well-to-do and deeply religious family. She was given an excellent education by Beguines and entered the cistercian nunnery at Bloemendaal at an early age. Trained as a scribe, she eventually became prioress of the new cistercian house at Nazareth, where she remained until her death in 1268. We are well informed about her life because we possess an extensive Latin *Vita* in three books, put together by her confessor and based in large part on Beatrice's own spiritual journal which is lost. Fortunately, Beatrice's brief mystical treatise, the *Seven Manieren van Minne (The Seven Experiences of Love)*, the earliest surviving netherlandish prose work, remains. (A version of it, reworked by the confessor, is also found in the latin *Vita*.)[32] Although Beatrice's notion of mystical union generally conforms to basic cistercian teaching on the *unitas spiritus*, her obsession with love, especially its pain and insanity, and her use of the language of the abyss to describe her experience of God (these are the earliest autobiographical abyss texts), makes a significant addition to what we have seen thus far.

Beatrice's life is filled with accounts of her ecstasies and experiences of direct contact with God.[33] Several of the late visions recounted in Book Three utilize the language of the abyss. For example, in chapter 9, speaking of one of the persistent themes of Beatrice's mysticism, the conflict between her insatiable desire for God and the human weakness which prevents her from realizing this goal, she is rapt in ecstasy while lying on her bed after Compline. 'Peace of heart suddenly fell on her, and in this ecstasy of mind she soon found herself rapt into the most profound abyss of the judgments of her God.' Here she not only sees the inscrutable divine judgments (a traditional reference to Ps 35:7), but also has an unusual vision of the 'very causes of things' (*ipsas quoque rerum causas*), the kind of vision of the archetypes in God once given to Saint Benedict.[34] In chapter 13, in an editorial comment on the nature of Beatrice's visions, the translator once again appeals to the experience of those who have been caught up into 'the abyss of God's judgments', such as Paul and David, to confirm 'that Beatrice is not inferior in this regard'.[35]

The abyssal references are not additions by the translator, as can be seen from a brief analysis of the *Seven Experiences of Love*. This remarkable text is one of the earliest and most striking products of the new vernacular theology to which the women mystics made such great contributions.[36] *The Seven Experiences* actually seems to describe six stages in the soul's love relationship to God, with the seventh stage possibly reflecting a later interpolated summary.[37] Briefly, the first stage is characterized by active longing in which the soul desires to return to the perfection it had when it was made by its Creator. The second stage stresses the necessity for pure and disinterested love, in good cistercian fashion. The third stage marks a distinctively beatrician note—the pain and suffering attendent upon the soul's inability to love as much as she wishes. Beatrice says:

> It does what it can; it praises and thanks Love; it works and labors for Love; it desires and sighs for Love; it gives itself wholly to Love, and it perfects in Love everything it does. All this gives the soul no rest; what it ought to desire but cannot attain is a great pain to it. Therefore the soul must remain in agony of heart and dwell in grief. Thus it seems

> to the soul as if it lives while dying and dies while it feels the pains of hell.[38]

The fourth stage is that of the experience of pleasure in loving that God grants to the soul who has endured this torture. Both the latin and the flemish versions here speak of the 'abyss of love'. In the Latin:

> In this stage . . . Beatrice, because of such great abundance of spiritual sweetness, became totally celestial, as if she were absorbed into the abyss of charity. Like a little drop of water running down into the vast expanse of the sea, her whole heart's affection took on a kind of heavenly nature at the same time that she was immersed in the ocean of eternity.[39]

The language of absorption and liquefaction of the heart (another favored cistercian theme) pervades this part of the account. Beatrice's images may suggest a kind of indistinction between God and the soul, but her expressed teaching maintains the distinctions between God and the soul that Bernard and other twelfth-century mystics insisted on (see, e.g., *Vita* III.12 [239]).

Whether or not we are dealing with a clear mystical itinerary in Beatrice's work (and there is some question about this), the final two, or possibly three stages make further use of language of the abyss of love and its equivalents. Stage five represents a return to the experience of the *excessus amoris*, that is, the fire, the pain, and the insanity of love (*orewoet*), both in its spiritual and its physical manifestations. Stage six is described as a more permanent, though by no means final, form of love's delight in this world. Here the Charity that is God rules tranquilly in the heart. Beatrice is compared to a 'housewife who governs her house well', and, in the flemish text only, to 'a fish swimming in the vast sea and resting in its deeps [i.e., abysses], and like a bird, boldly mounting high in the sky, so that the soul feels its spirit freely moving through the vastness and the depth and the unutterable richnesses of love.'[40] Finally, the seventh experience of love, whether meant to be the final stage or merely a summary of the previous six,[41] stresses the distance between all experience of God enjoyed in this life and that which Beatrice still longs for in heaven. It too employs the language of abyss, speaking of how the soul is drawn into ' . . . the deep Abyss of the Godhead, which is totally present in all things and remains incomprehensibly beyond all things, which is immutable, perfect being, all-powerful, all-intelligent, almightily operating.'[42] While we do not have in Beatrice a mutuality of abysses, nor direct appeal to the text of Psalm 41:8, her linking of the insanity of love with God as the abyss of love constitutes one half—God's half, if we can be allowed such language—of the mystical complex that was gradually emerging in the thirteenth-century women mystics.

We do not have far to look to find the other, or human, half. The Beguine Hadewijch, another flemish mystic, wrote around the same time as Beatrice. Her visions, letters, and poems are among the richest documents of medieval women's mysticism. Like Beatrice, Hadewijch's evocation of love is deeply passionate, and she too employs the language of the abyss. What the Beguine adds, however, is an explicit appeal to the mutuality of the abyss, a mutuality which, I believe, also suggests a different understanding of mystical union, the *unitas indistinctionis*, which was later to be expounded in more explicit fashion by both female mystics like Marguerite Porete and male authors like Meister Eckhart. Space does not permit a lengthy description of Hadewijch's thought, but a consideration of several key passages will suggest the importance of her contribution.[43]

Like almost all the thirteenth-century woman mystics, Hadewijch was a forceful exponent of the *insania amoris*, the irresistible divine force that draws the soul to God with such power that it is often sensed as torturing her and making her insane. In her Vision Eleven, for example, which begins with a showing of the divine abyss, she experiences divine Love as a 'heavy burden and disgrace', something 'terrible and implacable, devouring and burning without regard for anything'.[44] As befits an inhabitant of the Low Countries, Hadewijch was fond of liquid images. Among these watery symbols the abyss (Middle Netherlandish *afgront*) and its equivalents (e.g., *omoedicheit/grondelooze diepte/diepheit*), expressing the immeasurable depth and overwhelming power of the mystery of divine *minne*, have a favored position. A passage from the seventh of the Poems in Stanzas is typical:

> My soul melts away
> In the madness (*oerwoede*) of Love;
> The abyss (*afgront*) into which she hurls me

Is deeper than the sea;
For Love's deep new abyss
Renews my wound:[45]

The flemish Beguine often used the language of the abyss, the whirlpool, or the flood to indicate how the utterly hidden and supremely free divine nature flows out from itself into all things: 'He is outside of all, for he rests in nothing other than the tempestuous nature of his own profusely overflowing flood (*vloyende vloededeghe vloede*), that overflows everywhere on everything.'[46] What is perhaps most significant about her appeal to these images, however, is how she used them in some texts to create a mystical, or better 'abyssal', equality between God and the soul. Perhaps the most powerful expression of this is found in her Letter 18:

> The soul is a bottomlessness (*ene grondeloesheit*) in which God suffices to himself; and his own self-sufficiency ever finds fruition to the full in this soul, as the soul, for its part, ever does in him. Soul is a way for the passage of God from his depths into liberty, that is, into his inmost depths, and God is a way for the passage of soul into its liberty, that is, into his ground that cannot be touched without contact with the soul's depth. As long as God does not belong to the soul in his totality, he does not truly satisfy it.[47]

A similar passage in Letter 12 speaks of 'those who are ready to content Love' as being as 'unfathomable' as God is, adding ' . . . even if they were loved with Eternal Love (Jer. 31:3), they also are never attained by the depths of Love'.[48] Although Hadewijch does not use the term *afgront* itself in this context, or cite Psalm 41:8, these passages seem to be the earliest surviving appearances of the mutual abyss theme later used by Tauler and others.

Hadewijch's understanding of the kind of union the soul can attain in this life deserves a more extensive investigation than can be given here. Like many of the thirteenth-century women mystics, she fluctuated between traditional formulas that speak of the loving union of wills which effects a 'oneness of spirit' between God and the soul and occasional uses of a language that seems to express something more primordial, essential, and undifferentiated. I would argue that it is important not to press the early vernacular theologians, like Hadewijch, further than they would have wished to go toward some misleading synthesis. Like all mystical theologians, they knew that mystical union constitutes an ineffable mystery. The forms of language they used to assay the impossible but essential task of expressing such union must of necessity be always tentative, varied, and even contradictory, especially when the inherited categories tended to emphasize only one aspect of what they wanted to say. The gradual and tentative emergence of the category of *unitas indistinctionis* is not at all surprising.

While it is virtually absent in Beatrice of Nazareth, some hints of this new view of union can be found in Hadewijch. For example, in Letter 30, the Beguine talks about how our imitation of Christ eventually leads to marriage with the Word by which we live in him 'with one spirit, and with one heart'. But then an enigmatic addition occurs, as the Beguine continues ' . . . one must ever know certainly, without any doubt, that one is wholly in the unity of love. In this state one *is* the Father' (*Met desen wesene es men den vader*).[49] A passage in Letter 17 helps explain this. Here Hadewijch becomes one with the Son through a kiss, a standard theme of bernardine bridal-mysticism. But what follows is more unusual: 'There the Father took the Son to himself with me and took me to himself with the Son. And in this unity (*enicheit*) into which I was taken and where I was enlightened, I understood this essence (*wesen*). . . .'[50] Similar "strong" expressions of identity with God occur—for example, in Letter 28, which speaks of being enriched in the same blessedness (*verweentheit*) that God enjoys in his Godhead;[51] and in other texts scattered through the Beguine's corpus.[52] To be sure, this may be nothing more than a new way of putting the ancient christian mystical theme of deification, but it also seems to hint at some new directions. One indication that such expressions may contain something new is the emphasis that Hadewijch places on the neoplatonic language of all things flowing out from God eventually to return to union with him through a process of flowing-back that restores the original state.[53] This theme was to become more powerful in the later thirteenth century.

Hadewijch's mysticism has been compared with that of the german Beguine, Mechthild of Magdeburg, whose life spanned most of the thirteenth century and whose collection of mystical visionary accounts, *Das fliessende Licht der Gottheit* (*The Flowing Light of Godhead*), ranks among the most powerful poetic mystical texts of the era.[54] One difference between these two Beguines, however, is that Mechthild rarely if ever uses the term abyss (MHG *abgrunt* and its equivalents), though she sometimes hints at the mutual depth-relation between God and the soul.[55] Her collection of visions also contains a significant reference to something that hints at a form of deep, or indistinct, union with God. Chapter 44 of the first book of the *Flowing Light* is an allegorical drama played out among the Soul, the five senses, the Holy Spirit, and Christ, the Divine Bridegroom. During the course of this erotic play God tells the Soul: 'Dame Soul, you belong to me by nature to such a degree that nothing at all can come between you and me.'[56] This daring expression of union was attacked. Subsequently, in the sixth book of the *Flowing Light*, Mechthild defends herself by appealing to the pre-existence of all things in the divine 'cell' or 'enclosure' (*klote*) before all creation came forth from God.[57]

The growing use of the language of the abyss to express both the divine nature in itself and also as a way to present the relation between God and the mystic is evident in two late thirteenth-century women mystics from diverse areas of the growing world of vernacular theology, Angela of Foligno in Umbrian Italy and Marguerite Porete in northern France. Angela, born in 1248, lived the life of a dedicated third-order Franciscan after the death of her husband and children about 1288. Her visionary experiences culminating in a great showing given her at Assisi in 1291 are recorded in the *Memorial* and *Instructions* that she dictated to an anonymous Brother Arnaldo. She died in 1309.[58]

Angela plunges into the divine abyss with a recklessness perhaps unrivalled among the thirteenth-century women mystics. It is in the course of describing the seventh step in her complex mystical itinerary, 'the most wonderful step of all', that she first begins to speak of God as abyss. Chapter nine of the *Memorial* puts it thus: 'I am convinced that there is no saint, angel, or creature which has anywhere near the capacity to understand these divine workings and that extremely deep abyss' (*illud profundissimum abyssum*).[59] According to Angela, in this state God gathers her totally into himself and produces so many divine workings that 'there is so deep and ineffable an abyss that this presence of God alone, without any other gifts, is that good that the saints enjoy in eternal life'.[60] In the *Instructions* that serve as a supplementary description of her experiences from

1296 to 1309 increased use of abyss language (see *Instructions* 4, 5, 19, 32, 35, and 36) creates new verbal formulae, as when she speaks of 'abyssal absorption' (*abyssalis absorptio*) into God.[61] Here Angela also has a vision of her followers swallowed up in God to such an extent that she says it is 'as if God had totally transubstantiated and abyssated (*inabyssasse*) them in himself'.[62] In another place Angela speaks of 'the abyss of human and divine realities', referring to the experience of meeting Jesus who is both God and man in the Eucharist.[63] Though Angela lacks explicit appeal to the motif of the dual abyss found in Hadewijch, her emphasis on the abyss as an appropriate term to point to the 'Unknown Nothingness' (*O nihil incognitum*) that she constantly cried out to on her death-bed is another indication of the growing use of abyss language among thirteenth-century women.[64]

The french Beguine Marguerite Porete, burned at the stake as a relapsed heretic in 1310 for continuing to circulate her mystical text, *Le mirouer des simples ames (The Mirror of Simple Souls)*, also was no stranger to the language of the abyss. Indeed, the sheer number of references to *abyssus*, *abyssale* and *abyssata* in her book (seventeen in all) indicates that she found abyssal themes essential to the presentation of her mystical message. Dame *Amour* herself, the chief character in the courtly dialogue that presents Marguerite's teaching, is addressed as 'O most sweet abyssed one, . . . at the bottom without bottom of total humility'.[65] *Amour*'s message is designed to enable the soul to become 'abyssed in humility' (*abysmé en humilité*) and poverty (*in telle abysme de pouvreté*).[66] For Marguerite this abyss of humility is more than just an appropriate metaphor for a necessary virtue. Not unlike Meister Eckhart's notion of *abegescheidenheit*, or detachment, it is the essence of the experience of annihilation by which the soul comes to God. Dame *Amour*, speaking to Holy Church the Little, that is, the Church of reason and the clergy, says of the soul that lives for love alone:

> This Soul, says Love, possesses memory, understanding and will totally abyssed in one Being, that is, in God. And such Being gives being to her, without knowing, feeling, or willing any being, except the ordination (*ordonnance/ordinatio*) of God alone. This Soul, says Love, has for many a day languished in love.[67]

This is the abyss which in one chapter is called 'the abyss of glory' (60,33–38). Because such an abyss is less than nothing, it gives the soul everything, to such an extent that she cannot even pray (51,7–11)—this is the kind of statement for which Marguerite was taken to task by her inquisitors.

The role of the abyss in the Beguine's teaching about annihilation is especially clear in chapter 118, the noted account of the seven stages of the soul's advance to God (five of the seventeen uses of the term occur here). Steps one and two, the observance of the commandments and of the evangelical counsels, constitute the mortification that brings about the first death, the death of the body of sin. Stage three, where the soul gives up all self-will is the more difficult second death, the death of the spirit. In the fourth step the soul is drawn up to 'the touch of the pure delight of Love' (118,70–71), an experience that so inebriates and dazzles her that at first it seems to mark the journey's end. But the two highest stages that result in reason's death still remain (stage seven is the glory of heaven). The all-important fifth stage (118,94–173) begins from the consideration of the absolute Goodness of God and the total wretchedness of the soul in whom the divine Goodness has placed free will. It is only by totally relinquishing this free will and placing it back in God, its source, that the soul can be transformed into love and find its true self in total self-annihilation. This is to plunge into the abyss that is the true reality of the soul:

> Now such a Soul is nothing, because she sees her nothingness from the abundance of divine Understanding, which makes her nothing and places her in nothingness. And so she is all things, for she sees by means of the depth of the understanding of her wretchedness, which is so deep and so great that she finds there neither beginning nor middle nor end, only an abyssal abyss without bottom (*abysme abysmee sans fons*). There she finds herself, without finding and without bottom.[68]

Opposites fuse at this point. The soul is nothing and everything; because it cannot see, it sees itself perfectly; because she 'is at rest in the bottomless depths', she can clearly see 'the Sun of the Highest Goodness'. 'The fall is so deep', says Marguerite, 'she is so rightly fallen, that the Soul cannot lift herself from such an abyss. And also she ought not to do it, but instead she ought always to remain there.'[69]

The fifth stage makes possible brief access to the sixth. Here 'in the abyss of humility' (*abysme d'umilité*: 118,176) the soul sees neither God nor self, 'but God sees himself in her by his divine majesty, who clarifies this soul with himself. . . .' This is the state of absolute identification, a true *unitas indistinctionis*. 'But this Soul, thus purified and clarified, sees neither God nor herself, but God sees himself of himself in her, for her, without her. God shows to her that there is nothing except him. And thus this Soul understands nothing except him, and so loves nothing except him, praises nothing except him, for there is nothing except him.'[70] Marguerite, unlike the other women mystics we have surveyed does not explicitly identify God with the abyss, but her form of mystical discourse—in which the soul reaches its goal by attaining *its* own abyss—effectively comes down to the same thing by making the *anima abyssata* the place where God sees himself. If God now sees himself in the soul, he *is* that abyss in a form of fused identity that Eckhart expressed with the noted claim, 'The eye in which I see God is the same eye in which God sees me'.[71] Put in the language of the abyss, later developed by Eckhart's disciple Tauler,[72] we might say, 'The abyss from which I call out to God is the same abyss in which he calls to me'.

To summarize. The language of the abyss first began to acquire mystical overtones among the twelfth-century mystics, especially the Cistercians. The understanding of the abyss as an abyss of love, however, and especially of *equal* love in which God and the human lover are both without bottom and therefore identically one in experiencing the abyss, was initiated by the women mystics of the thirteenth century, especially Beatrice, Hadewijch, Angela of Foligno, and Marguerite Porete. None of these women explicitly cite the text *abyssus abyssum invocat* of Psalm 41:8, but when John Tauler took up the mystical use of the abyss in the fourteenth century, he was able, as a trained scriptural scholar, to complete the circle by anchoring this new understanding of mutual and indistinct union in the supreme locus of christian mystical teaching, the Bible. For him the 'abyss that calls out to the abyss' was no longer the Old Testament calling out to the New, as had been the case in the early Middle Ages, but the abyss of the *liber experientiae* calling out to the *liber psalmorum* for confirmation and clarification.

There is no need to speculate on whether or not the dominican preacher actually read any of the women mystics we have investigated. The shift to new forms of language in thirteenth- and fourteenth-century texts dealing with union with God was part of a broad spiritual movement, one shared by both men and women in ways that the historical evidence can make only partially available to us today. Tauler's rich teaching on the mutual abyss of love, however, is scarcely conceivable without the profound and daring teaching about union with God first advanced by the women mystics of the thirteenth century.

NOTES

1. This essay is an expanded version of a paper given at a Symposium on 'Literary Dimensions of Medieval Women's Mysticism', sponsored by the College of Arts and Sciences and the Departments of Religion, French and Italian, and English of Northwestern University on 16 October 1993. I wish to thank the organizers of that Symposium, as well as the audience, not only for the opportunity to present my ideas, but also for the helpful suggestions I received.

2. For my perspective on the topic of mystical union, see B. McGinn, 'Love, Knowledge and *Unio Mystica* in the Western Christian Tradition', *Mystical Union and Monotheistic Faith*, edd. Moshe Idel and Bernard McGinn (New York: Macmillan, 1989) 59–86. The present essay is a companion piece to a previous article in which I study another of the forms of language employed to describe mystical union; see B. McGinn, 'Desert and Ocean as Symbols of Mystical Absorption in the Christian Tradition', *Journal of Religion* 74 (1994) 155–81.

3. During the past fifty years, no scholar made greater contributions to the study of the vocabulary of medieval spirituality and mysticism than Jean Leclercq. For a programmatic statement on the significance of such study, see the 'Avant-propos' of his *Études sur le vocabulaire monastique du moyen âge* (Rome: Herder, 1961. Studia Anselmiana 48) 1–6.

4. On the *liber experientiae*, see Jean Leclercq, 'Aspects spirituels de la symbolique du livre au XIIe siècle', *L'Homme devant Dieu. Mélanges offerts au Père de Lubac*, 3 vols. (Paris: Aubier, 1963) 2:63–72.

5. Augustine's *Enarratio in Psalmum* 41 (hereafter *En. in Ps.*) can be found in PL 36:466–71. Cuthbert Butler in his *Western Mysticism* (New York: Dutton, 1923) 26–36, was among the first to note its importance for the study of Augustine's mysticism. See also my treatment in *Foundations of Mysticism* (New York: Crossroad, 1991) 238–40.

6. *En. in Ps.* 41.13 (PL 36:473): *Abyssus enim est profunditas quaedam impenetrabilis, incomprehensibilis: et maxime solet dici in aquarum multitudine.*

7. *Contra Faustum* 22.8 (PL 42:404).

8. John Tauler, Sermon 41 in *Die Predigten Taulers*, ed. Ferdinand Vetter (Zürich: Weidmann, 1968) 176,6–11: *Hie wirt das wort wor das in dem salter der prophete sprach: 'abyssus abyssum invocat, das abgrúnde das inleitet das abgrúnde.' Das abgrúnde*

das geschaffen ist, das inleitet in sich das ungeschaffen abgrúnde, und werdent die zwei abgrúnde ein einig ein, ein luter götlich wesen, und do hat sich der geist verlorn in Gotz geiste; in dem grundelosen mere ist er ertrunken.

9. Sermon 61 (Vetter: 331,12–17): *In dis abgrúnde gehört allein das göttelich abgrúnde. Abyssus abysssum invocat.* For another citation, see Sermon 45 (Vetter: 201.3). On Tauler's teaching on the *grunt/abgrunt,* see Kurt Kirmsse, *Die Terminologie des Mystikers Johannes Tauler* (Engelsdorf-Leipzig, 1930) 32–38.

10. *Ibid.* (Vetter: 333,23–30). Augustine is here cited on the power of love, but in other sermons (e.g., Sermon 24 and Sermon 65 in Vetter: 101,29–102,9, and 358,5–16), Tauler appeals to him as an authority on the abyss of the soul. These claims depend on the bishop's teaching regarding the *abditum mentis,* as shown by Paul Wyser, 'Taulers Terminlogie vom Seelengrund', *Altdeutsche und Altniederländische Mystik,* ed. Kurt Ruh (Darmstadt: Wissenschaftliche Buchgesellschaft, 1964) 333–41.

11. *Ibid.* (Vetter: 334,1–3): *Der minne hitze der wirt er wol gewar; si machet in ungestüme in allen sinen kreften: er qwilt nach der minne, und das er si hat, des enweis er nút. Si verzert dir das marg und das blut.* The four forms of love discussed in this sermon are based on the four degrees of 'violent charity' of Richard of Saint Victor's *De quatuor gradibus violentae caritatis;* see Gerveis Dumeige, *Ives. Épitre à Severin sur la charité. Richard de Saint-Victor. Les quatres degrés de la violent charité* (Paris: Vrin, 1955).

12. Sermon 24 (Vetter: 102,18). For other appearances of the *abgrunde* in Tauler's sermons, see especially Sermons 9, 26, 27, 55 (Vetter: 45,33–46,9; 109,17–20; 113,32–34; 257,27–35). Altogether Tauler uses the term in no less than twenty-four sermons (## 1, 9, 11, 15, 21, 23, 24, 26, 27, 28, 32, 36, 38, 41, 45, 46, 50, 52, 55, 61, 63, 66, 67, and 81).

13. Helpful for the review of these uses are the references contained in the 'Index de allegoriis Veteris Testamenti' contained in PL 219:113–228 (s.v. *abyssus*). Most of the references there, however, are taken from the same handful of authors: Alcuin, Rabanus Maurus, Rupert of Deutz, and Garnier of Saint Victor. See also *abyssus* in the *Mittellateinisches Wörterbuch bis zum ausgehenden 13. Jahrhundert* (Munich: Bayerische Akademie der Wissenschaften, 1959-).

14. For a list of some of these uses, see Henri De Lubac, *Exégèse médiévale,* 4 vols. (Paris: Aubier, 1959–63) 1:349.

15. All references to Bernard's works indicate the edition of Jean Leclercq, *et al., Sancti Bernardi Opera,* 8 vols. (Rome: Editiones Cistercienses, 1957–77). (Reference will be according to the standard abbreviation of works used by Cistercian Publications, and will be cited according to the form SBOp with volume, page and line). The term *abyssus pietatis* appears, for example, in Humb 6 (SBOp 5:445,8), and in Ep. 458.2 (SBOp 8:435,10). A comparable term, *abyssus mansuetudinis,* appears in HM 4.8 (SBOp 5:62,11).

16. *Abyssus aeternitatis* occurs in Ep. 107.5 (SBOp 7:271,4); *abbyssus luminis* occurs in Ep. 107.6 (SBOp 7:272,5–6), SC 26.5 and 38.5 (SBOp 1:173,10 and 2:17,15). Richard of Saint Victor also uses the term *abyssus luminis,* e.g, *De quatuor gradibus violentae caritatis* 38: *Tertius itaque amoris gradus est quando mens hominis in illam rapitur divini luminis abyssum. . . .* (ed. Dumiege, 167).

17. See Ann 2.1 and Dom in Oct Ass (SBOp 5:30,12–13 and 268,13).

18. Quad 4.3 (SBOp 4:370,13–15): *ABYSSUS enim ABYSSUM INVOCAT: abyssus luminosa, abyssum tenebrosam; abyssus misericordiae, abyssum miseriae. Profundum*

namque est cor hominis et imperscrutibile. Cf. Ass 4.3 (SBOp 5:246,14–17) and Ep 107.5 (SBOp 7:271,12–16).

19. See *Guillaume de Saint-Thierry. Exposé sur le Cantique des Cantiques,* ed. J.-M. Déchanet, *Sources chrétiennes 82 [hereafter SCh]* (Paris: Du Cerf, 1962.), #132 (p. 282): *Amplexus iste circa hominem agitur, sed supra hominem est. Amplexus etenim hic Spiritus sanctus est. Qui enim Patris et Filii Dei Communio, qui Caritas, qui Amicitia, qui Amplexus est, ipse in amore Sponsi ac Sponsae ipsa omnia est. . . . Amplexus autem iste, hic initiatur; alibi perficiendus. Abyssus haec alteram abyssum invocat; extasis ista longe aliud quam quod videt somniat; secretum hoc aliud secretum suspirat; gaudium hoc aliud gaudium imaginatur; suavitas ista aliam suavitatem praeorditur.*

20. Gilbert of Hoyland, *In Cantica* 29.3 (PL 184:150D): *Affectus enim affectum meretur, et abyssus abyssum similem provocat in voce profluentium cataractarum. Bonae siquidem cataractae sunt, quae tuum, bone Jesu, distillant affectum, infundunt amorem.* Gilbert also refers to *abyssus* in more traditional terms in *In Cant.* 18.4, 24.4–5, and 38.1.

21. 'In Ypapanti Domini de diversis Moribus,' in *Sermones inediti B. Aelredi Abbatis Rievallensis,* ed. C. H. Talbot (Rome: Apud Curiam Generalem Sacri Ordinis Cisterciensis, 1952) 51.

22. Isaac of Stella, *Sermo* 15.14, as found in *Isaac de l'Étoile. Sermons I,* ed. Anselm Hoste (Paris: Du Cerf, 1967. SCh 130) 292.

23. *Ioannis de Forda. Super Extremam Partem Cantici Canticorum Sermones CXX,* edd. Edmund Mikkers and Hilary Costello, 2 vols. (Turnhout: Brepols, 1970. Corpus Christianorum Continuatio Mediaevalis 17–18 [hereafter CCCM]), Sermo 72.10 (CCCM 17:439). John uses the verse in another sense in Sermo 105.2 (CCCM 18:710). References to the *abyssus* are found in several of John's other sermons on the Song; see, e.g., Sermones 62.10, 82.7, 97.6, and 109.2.

24. See Arnold of Bonneval, *Tractatus de operibus sex dierum* (PL 189:1518C–19A). Arnold, however, does not discuss the *abyssus.*

25. See *Meditatio* V in *Guigo II. Lettre sur la vie contemplative. Douze méditations,* edd. Edmund Colledge and James Walsh (Paris: Du Cerf, 1970. SCh 163) 148–52.

26. Bernard of Clairvaux, SC 64.10 (SBOp 2:171,16–19): *Quis hoc fecit? Amor, dignitatis nescius, dignatione dives, affectu potens, suasu efficax. Quid violentius? Triumphat de Deo amor. Quid tamen non violentum? Amor est. Quae ista vis, quaeso, tam violenta ad victoriam, tam victa ad violentiam?*

27. SC 79.1 (2:272,5–8): *O amor praeceps, vehemens, flagrans, impetuose, qui praeter te aliud cogitare non sinis, fastidis cetera, contemnis omnia praeter te, te contentus! Confundis ordines, dissimulas usum, modum ignoras. . . .*

28. William, *Expositio* 117–21 (SCh 82:254–64).

29. *De quatuor gradibus* 14 (ed. Dumeige, 139,25–28): *Quartus itaque violente caritatis gradus est quando estuantis animi desiderio jam omnino nichil satisfacere potest. . . . , quia semper invenit quod adhuc concupiscere possit.*

30. See B. McGinn, 'The Language of Love in Christian and Jewish Mysticism', *Mysticism and Language,* ed. Steven T. Katz (Oxford: New York, 1992) 212–15.

31. On the difference between *unitas spiritus* and *unitas indistinctionis,* see McGinn, 'Love, Knowledge and *Unio Mystica*', 61–81.

32. Beatrice's treatise was editied by Léonce Reypens and Jozef Van Mierlo, *Beatrijs van Nazareth. Seven Manieren van Minne* (Leuven, 1926). The latin *Vita* was edited by Reypens, *Vita Beatricis. De Autobiographie van de Z. Beatrijs van Tienen O.Cist., 1200–1268* (Antwerp, 1964). For the netherlandish text I will cite from the edition of Reypens-Van Mierlo, while the Latin will be cited according to the

corrected text available in *The Life of Beatrice of Nazareth*, translated and annotated by Roger DeGanck (Kalamazoo: Cistercian Publications, 1991. Cistercian Fathers Series, 50). On Beatrice, see DeGanck's two-volume study, *Beatrice of Nazareth in her Context* and *Towards Unification with God* (Kalamazoo: Cistercian Publications, 1991. Cistercian Studies Series 121, 122).

33. See, e.g., *Vita* I.11 (para. 54–9); II.14 (145–50); II.19 (170–82), the Seraphim vision; III.2 (192–95) and III.5 (206), which are eucharistic experiences; III.7 (213–18, a vision of the Trinity); III.9 (223–25); and three concluding visions grouped in III.11–13 (234–45) (texts in DeGanck, *Life of Beatrice*, 66–74, 174–78, 200–210, 224–26, 238, 246–52, 260–62, and 274–86).

34. Beatrice, *Vita* III.9 (223) (DeGanck, 260). On the history of the vision of the archetypes, see David N. Bell, 'The Vision of the World and the Archetypes in the Spirituality of the Middle Ages', *Archives d'histoire doctrinal et littéraire du moyen âge* 44 (1977) 7–31.

35. *Vita* III.13 (244) (DeGanck, 284–86).

36. On the use of the term 'vernacular theology', see B. McGinn, 'Meister Eckhart and the Beguines in the Context of Vernacular Theology', *Meister Eckhart and the Beguine Mystics: Hadewijch of Brabant, Mechthild of Magdeburg and Marguerite Porete*, ed. Bernard McGinn (New York: Continuum, 1994) 1–14.

37. For the debate on this, see L. Reypens, 'De *Seven Manieren van Minne* Geinterpoleerd?' *Ons Geestelijk Erf* 5 (1931) 287–322; and P. Wackers, 'Het interpolatie probleem in de "Seven manieren van minne" van Beatrijs van Nazareth,' *Ons Gesstelijk Erf* 45 (1971) 215–30.

38. *Seven Manieren* III (ed. Reypens-Van Mierlo, 11.38–12.49): *Si doet al datsi mach: si danket ende louet der minnen, si werct ende arbeit om minne, si sucht ende begert die minne, si leuert har seluen al op der minnen ende al har werc wert voldaen in der minne. Al dit engheuet hare geen raste, ende dat es hare ene grote pine, datsi dat moet begeren datsi niet enmach vercrigen, ende hier omme moet si bliuen in die weelicheit van herten, ende wonen in der ongenuechten. Ende so es hare also of si al leuende steruet, ende steruende die pine van der hellen gevoelt. . . .* (see *Vita* III.252). I make use of R. De Ganck's translation, *Life of Beatrice*, 301–02. The flemish version is longer than the latin on stage three.

39. The latin and vernacular texts, while providing the same basic message, have important linguistic differences. Both, however, speak of being absorbed into the abyss of love: (1) Flemish: . . . *ende datsi so diepe es versonken ende verswolgen int afgront der minnen, ende selue al es worden minne* (ed., Reypens-Van Mierlo, 14.24–15.26); (2) Latin: . . . *velut in abissam caritatis absorpta, tota caelestis effecta fuerit* . . . (DeGanck, *Life of Beatrice*, 304).

40. *Seven Manieren* VI (ed. Reypens-Van Mierlo, 25.35–26.42): *Ende also gelijc als die visch die swimmet in die wijtheit van der vloet, ende rast in die dipheit, ende als vogel die kunlike vlieget in die gerumheit ende in die hoegheit van der locht, also gelijc geuult si haren geest vrieleke wandelende in die witheit ende in die dipheit, ende in die gerumheit ende in die hoecheit der minnen* (cf. the latin in *Vita* III.14 [#258], DeGanck, *Life of Beatrice*, 316). Here I am using the translation from the Netherlandish of Edmund Colledge, *Mediaeval Netherlands Religious Literature* (London: Heinemann, 1965) 25.

41. Several new elements in the seventh stage indicate that we might be dealing with a subsequent re-working of ideas by Beatrice. Among these are (1) the stress on the *fruitio amoris*; (2) the notion of *communis amor*; and (3) the emphasis on the refusal of consolations.

42. *Seven Manieren* VII (ed. Reypens-Van Mierlo, 29.9–14): . . . *ende in die diepe afgronde der godheit, die es al in alle dinc, ende die onbegripelec bliuet bouen alle dinc, ende die es onwandelec, al-wesende, al-mogende, al-begripende, ende al-geweldeleke werkende.* For the latin, which lacks a reference to the abyss here, see *Vita* III.14 (#259), as in DeGanck, *Life of Beatrice*, 320). I use DeGanck's translation from *ibid.*, 321.

43. There is an extensive literature on Hadewijch. For an introduction, see J.-B. Porion, 'Hadewijch', *Dictionnaire de spiritualité* (Paris: Beauchesne, 1937-) 7:13–23 [hereafter DS]. See also John Giles Milhaven, *Hadewijch and Her Sisters. Other Ways of Knowing and Loving* (Albany: Suny Press, 1993), especially Part I, 'Hadewijch and the Mutuality of Love' (1–72), which stresses the originality of Hadewijch's insistence on the mutuality and equality of love between God and human.

44. Hadewijch's visions were first edited in two volumes by Jozef Van Mierlo, *Hadewijch: Visioenen* (Louvain: Vlaamsch Boekenhalle, 1924–25). A later edition based on one of the better MSS. is *Het Visioenenboek van Hadewijch. Uitgegeven naar handschrift 941 van de Bibliotheek der Rijkuniversiteit te Gent*, ed. H. W. J. Vekeman (Nijmegen: Dekker & van de Vegt, 1980). I cite here from the translation of Vision 11, lines 121–33 (according to the Van Mierlo edition) as found in *Hadewijch. The Complete Works*, translated by Columba Hart (New York: Paulist Press, 1980) 291.

45. See *Hadewijch Strofische Gedichten*, edd. E. Rombauts and N. De Paepe (Zwolle: Tjeenk Willink, 1961) 72–74: Mi smelten mine sinne/ In minnen oer-woede;/Die afgront daer si mi in sende/ Die es dieper dan die zee;/ Want hare nuwe diepe afgronde/Die vernuwet me di wonde:. . . . Translation from *Hadewijch. The Complete Works*, 145. For other texts where the abyss is identified with the hidden Godhead, see, e.g., Letters 5,28–36, 20,36–43, and 22,362–67 (all citations are by number of letter and lines of text), in *Hadewijch. Brieven*, 2 vols., ed. Jozef Van Mierlo (Antwerp: Standaard, 1947) 1:44, 171 and 203 (trans., 56, 91, and 101). See also Vision 13,255–56 (trans. Hart, 302). On Hadewijch's use of these terms, see R. Vanneste, 'Over de betekenis van enkele abstracta in de taal van Hadewijch', *Studia Germanica* 1 (1959) 9–95, who summarizes the meaning of *afgront* with the words: ' . . . "afgront" wordt tegelijk gebruikt voor de onpeilbare diepte van Gods wezen én als plaats der unio mystica' (40).

46. Letter 22,252–55 in *Hadewijch. Brieven* (1:198): *Hi es buten al: want hine rustet in ghene dinc dan in die druusteghe nature siere vloyender vloedegher vloede, die al omme ende al oervloyen* (trans. Hart, 99).

47. Letter 18,69–79 in Van Mierlo, *Brieven* 1:154–55: . . . *daer es de ziele ene grondeloesheit daer god hem seluen ghenoech met es, Ende sine ghenoechte uan hem seluen altoes te vollen in hare heuet, Ende si weder altoes in heme. Siele es een wech vanden dore vaerne gods in sine vriheit van sinen diepsten; Ende god es een wech vanden dore vaerne der zielen in hare vriheit, Dat es in sinen gront die niet gheraect en can werden, sine gherakene met hare diepheit; Ende god si hare gheheel, hine waer hare niet ghenoech* (trans. Hart, 86, slightly altered). For another text that stresses the equality of love, this time using the term *diepheit*, see Letter 9,4–13 in Van Mierlo 1:79–80: *Daer de diepheit siere vroetheit es, daer sal hi v leren wat hi es, Ende hoe wonderleke soeteleke dat een lief in dat ander woent, Ende doe dore dat ander woent, Dat haerre en gheen hem seluen en onderkent. Mer si ghebruken onderlinghe ende elc anderen Mont in mont, ende herte in herte, Ende lichame in lichame, Ende ziele in ziele, Ende ere soete godlike nature doer hen beiden vloyende, Ende si beide een dore hen seluen, Ende als eens beide bliuen, Ja ende bliuende.*

48. Letter 12,42–52 in Van Mierlo, *Brieven* 1:103: *Mer die daer na staen der Minnen ghenoech te doene, die sijn oec ewech ende sonder gront;. . . . Ende al mindemen die oec*

met eweleker Minnen, si en worden oec nummermeer van Minnen gronde veruolghet. . . . (trans. Hart, 70–71).

49. Letter 30,142–44 in *Brieven* 1:257: *Ende dat men emmer seker wete buten allen twifele datmen gheheel es in enigher Minne. Met desen wesene es men den vader* (trans. Hart, 118).

50. Letter 17,107–11 in *Brieven* 144: *Ende in die enicheit daer ic doen in ghenomen was ende verclaert, daer verstondic dit wesen ende bekinde claerlikere dan men met sprekene ocht met redenen ocht met siene enighe sake Die soe bekinleec es in ertrike bekinnen mach* (trans. Hart, 84).

51. Letter 28,153–64 in *Brievan* 1:235–36 (trans. Hart, 111).

52. For some other texts that seem to express a deeper understanding of union, see, e.g., Letter 19,55–62 in *Brieven* 1:165 (trans. Hart, 90); Visions 7,35–37 and 64–97, as well as Vision 12,152–62 (trans. Hart, 280–82 and 296); and Poem in Couplet 12,85–96 (trans. Hart, 342).

53. See, for example, the passage in Vision 14,81–84 (trans. Hart, 303).

54. A new edition of this important text has recently appeared, *Mechthild von Magdeburg 'Das fliessende Licht der Gottheit'*, ed. Hans Neumann (Munich: Artemis, 1990). For an introduction to Mechthild, see Margot Schmidt, 'Mechthilde de Magdebourg,' in DS 10:877–85. For one comparison of Hadewijch and Mechthild, see Kurt Ruh, 'Beginenmystik. Hadewijch, Mechthild von Magdeburg, Marguerite Porete', in *Kleine Schriften II. Scholastik und Mystik im Spätmittelalter*, ed. Volker Mertens (Berlin: De Gruyter, 1984) 237–49.

55. For passages suggesting a mutual depth relation between God and the soul, see, e.g., 1.2 (Neumann 8,19–20): . . . *wenne der endlose got die grundelosen* sele *bringet in die höhin* . . . ; and 4.2 (Neumann 127,104–07): *Swa mitte ie ich mich me zu dir geselle*, ie *got grössor und wunderlichor uf mich* vellet. *O herre, ich kan dir in der tieffi der ungemischeten diemütekeit nit entsinken. . . .* An explicit reference to the *abgront der lyebden der heilger dryueldickeit* is found in Mechthild's younger contemporary, Christina of Hane (1269–92). See Franz Paul Mittelmaier, 'Lebensbeschreibung der sel. Christina, gen. von Retters,' *Archiv für Mittelrheinisches Kirchengeschichle* 18 (1966) 223.

56. *Das fliessende Licht* 1.44 (ed. Neumann, 31,82–83): *Frow sele, ir sint so sere genatúret in mich, das zwúschent úch und mir nihtes mag sin.*

57. *Das fliessende Lichte* 6.31 (ed. Neumann, 238–40), especially 239,28–29: *Rehte ze glicher wis als* ein clote *und allú ding* waren *in gotte besclossen ane sclos und ane túr.*

58. I will use the critical edition of Ludger Thier and Abele Calufetti, *Il Libro della Beata Angela da Foligno* (Grottaferrata: Collegii S. Bonaventurae ad Claras Aquas, 1985). For a study, see Paul Lachance, *The Spiritual Journey of the Blessed Angela of Foligno according to the Memorial of Frater A.* (Rome: Pontificium Athenaeum Antonianum, 1984).

59. *Il libro della Beata Angela da Foligno*, chap. 9 (380,299–301): *Et video et intelligo quod illas operationes divinas et illud profundissimum abyssum nullus angelus et nulla creatura est ita larga et capax quod posset illud comprehendere. Et omnia ista quae modo dico sunt ita male dicere et minus dicere quod est blasphemare illa.* Unless otherwise noted, I will use the translation of Paul Lachance, *Angela of Foligno. Complete Works* (Mahwah: Paulist Press, 1993) 211.

60. *Ibid.* 384,339–43 (trans. Lachance, 213): *Alio modo praesentatur magis specialiter et valde diverse a praedicto modo, et dat aliam laetitiam a praedicta, quia recolligit me totam in se. Et facit in anima multas operationes divinas cum multo maiori gratia et cum* tanto

profundo et inenarrabili abysso, quod solum illum praesentare Dei, sine *aliis donis, est illud bonum quod sancti habent* in vita aeterna.

61. This is especially true of Instruction 4 which seems to be one of the more authentic visionary accounts of the *Instructiones*, see ed. 486,24–28 and 488,38–40, where the cited phrase is found (trans. Lachance, 244–45).

62. *Ibid*. 500,179–80: . . . *ita quod istos videtur totaliter* in se *transsubstantiasse et inabyssare* (my translation). The verb *inabyssare* also occurs in 404,4 in relation to being buried in the depths of humility, and in 516,103 concerning being buried in the divine goodness. These are the earliest uses of the latin verbal form known to me.

63. Instruction 32 (668,67–72; trans. Lachance, 295). For other appearances of the term and its cognates, see Instructions 5 (590,51), and 36 (726,31–34 and 736,152–54).

64. Angela's language of the abyss may have been influenced by its appearances in her contemporary, Jacopone da Todi, though he uses it less frequently than she. One impressive text comes from his great Laude 90 on Love: *Sappi parlare, ora so fatto muto;/ vedea, mo so cieco deventato./ Si grande abisso non fo mai veduto:/ tacendo parlo, fugo e so legato,/ scendendo salgo, tengo e so tenuto,/ de for se dentro, caccio e so cacciato./ Amor esmesurato, perché me fai empazire,/ en fornace morire de sì forte calor?* See *Iacopone da Todi. Laudi*, ed. Franca Ageno (Florence: Le Monnier, 1953) 372,139–46.

65. *Marguerite Porete. Le Mirouer des Simples Ames*, edd. Romana Guarnieri and Paul Verdeyen (Turnhout: Brepols, 1986, CCCM 69), 53.3–4: *O tres doulce abysme, dit Raison, ou fons sans fons d'entiere humilité*. . . . (references are to chapter and line of the Old French text unless otherwise noted). Chap, 79.47–49 also refers to Love as the abyss. Unless otherwise noted I will use the translation of Ellen L. Babinsky, *Marguerite Porete. The Mirror of Simple Souls* (Mahwah: Paulist Press, 1993) where this passage is found on p. 130. For a study of Marguerite's language of union, see Michael E. Sells, *Mystical Languages of Unsaying* (Chicago: University of Chicago, 1993), chap. 5. See also Paul Mommaers, 'La transformation d'amour selon Marguerite Porete,' *One Geestelike Erf* 65 (1991) 89–107.

66. *Mirouer* 40.8–10 and 38.16. For other passages on the soul being 'abyssed' in humility, see, e.g., 23,53–56.

67. *Mirouer* 43.58–62: *Ceste Ame, dit Amour, a la memoire et l'entendement et la voulenté abysmé tout en ung estre, c'est en Dieu; et tel estre luy donne estre, sans savoir, ne sentir, ne vouloir nul estre, fors seulement l'ordonnance de Dieu. Ceste ame, dit Amour, a maint jour languy d'amour* (trans. Babinsky, 123, slightly altered).

68. *Mirouer* 118.130–35: *Or est telle ame nulle, car elle voit par habondance de divine cognoissance son nient, qui la fait nulle, et mectre a nient. Et si est toute, car elle voit par la profondesse de la cognoissance de la mauvaisté d'elle, qui est si parfonde et si grant, que elle n'y trouve ne commencement ne mesure ne fin, fors une abysme abysmee sans fons; la se trouve elle, sans trouver et sans fons* (trans. Babinsky, 192, slightly altered). A few lines on such a Soul is described as being . . . *abysme de mauvaistié, et gouffre de tel haberge et de telle garnison*. . . . (139–40).

69. Mirouer 118:147–49 and 160–62: *Or est ceste Ame assise ou fons de bas, la ou il n'a point de fons, et pource y fait il bas; et ce bas luy fait veoir tres cler le vray Soleil de haultiesme bonté*. . . . *Laquelle cheue est si parfont cheue, se elle est adroit cheue, que l'Ame ne se peut de telle abysme relever; et aussi faire ne le doit, ainçoys y doit elle demourer* (trans. Babinsky, 192–93).

70. Mirouer 118,186–90: *Mais ceste Ame, ainse pure et clariffiee, ne voit ne Dieu ne elle, mais Dieu se voit de luy en elle, pour elle, sans elle; lequel (c'est assavoir Dieu) luy monstre, que il n'est fors que lui. Et pource ne cognoist ceste ame sinon luy, et si n'ayme sinon luy, ne ne loue sinon luy, cal il n'est fors que luy* (trans. Babinsky, 193).

71. Meister Eckhart, Predigt 12 in *Meister Eckhart. Die deutschen und lateinischen Werke* (Stuttgart and Berlin: Kohlhammer, 1936-), *Deutsche Werke* 1:201,5–6: *Daz ouge, dâ inne ich got sihe, daz ist daz selbe ouge, dâ inne mich got sihet. . . .* There are many equivalent passages.

72. Eckhart himself, despite his frequent use of the term *grunt* and its analogues to describe both God and the soul, rarely uses *abgrunt.* See Benno Schmoldt, *Die deutsche Begriffsprache Meister Eckharts* (Heidelberg: Quelle & Meter, 1954) 58–59, who cites only two appearances.

Cistercian Nuns and the Development of the Order: The Abbey at Saint-Antoine-des-Champs outside Paris.

Constance Berman

RECENT HISTORIANS of the Cistercian Order have begun to question models of the Order which attribute its administrative innovations to a few early twelfth-century leaders.[1] Instead, we are beginning to view the Order as an institution which changed over time, developing policy (sometimes by trial and error) to meet pressing institutional needs. Such an understanding—one derived possibly from our own experiences in administering organizations—allows historians of the Cistercians not only to show the long-recognized expansion of the Order's numbers of houses, but also the increasing articulation of administrative procedures in the Order in 1215 or 1250 over that of 1115 or 1130.[2] Indeed, the cistercian attempt to hold a large congregation to more or less standard practices did not succeed overnight, but only gradually over the first century of the Order's history. This concept of a developing Order, of one transformed from oral to administrative culture and one which was different in 1120 than in 1150 and different again in 1220 and 1250, provides a way of seeing the transfer of monastic practices from an earlier informal, oral culture in which *ordo* was a status and monastic formation in the customs of Cîteaux was given by one individual to another, and thus in a diversity of ways, to one in which monastic practice was legislated by an Order which had become an administrative apparatus with a legislative body (the General Chapter), with published legislation (the Statutes). Although we can argue to some extent that the earlier silence of the documents does not necessarily make it true that these things were not there in the twelfth century, the fact that the first official collection and distribution of the Order's Statutes occurred only in 1202 under Arnold Amaury is of considerable significance in suggesting a somewhat loosely-ordered institution until that time.[3]

This viewpoint restores to the earliest Cistercians an eremitical disorganization which is not only rather appealing to the romantic, but more sensible to the historian than a picture of either gradual or precipitous administrative decline after the death of Stephen Harding or Bernard of Clairvaux. It also allows historians to reemphasize the strong concentration the early Cistercians laid on spiritual rather than worldly things—something at odds with earlier historians' conviction that the Order had had a monolithic administration from the very beginning. This model seems to avoid the judgmental trap of ranking individual cistercian abbeys and their practices according to an 'Ideals and Reality' model which, while it succeeded in opening up considerable new research on the Order, has perhaps now been pushed beyond the limits of its usefulness.[4] The developing Order model, in contrast, when it is applied to the study of both men's and women's communities within a region—as I have recently done in a study of almost eighty houses from southern France—reveals also that the relationships of men's houses to and in the Order were not always regularized much earlier than were those of women.[5]

A developing-Order model thus makes it easier to incorporate women into the picture, allowing us to understand that, although communities of cistercian nuns appeared at a relatively early date, their relationship to the Order or to individual houses of monks within it was not always clearly established until the early or mid-thirteenth century.[6] In this way of thinking, cistercian abbeys of nuns can be seen as positive, or at least neutral, rather than problematic or marginal aspects of the history of the Order as a whole. Cistercian women need no longer be seen as aberrations to be regretted and bemoaned, but appear as one of the logical developments in the Order's history.[7] The recent increased study of local administrative documents, which was made possible in part by the introduction of the 'Ideals and Reality' model, has thus provided abundant evidence, taken from papal and episcopal privileges and early charters, that from at least the second quarter of the twelfth century, houses for cistercian women began to be founded, like men's houses, in a variety of circumstances.[8] Such documents show that cistercian women, although they did not participate as members of the General Chapter, may have had their own chapter at le Tart and from a relatively early date have enjoyed many of the privileges and responsibilities of the congregation of Cîteaux—such as tithe exemption and eventually freedom from episcopal visitation.[9] This research has also shown that women's communities in the Order were not always satellites of men's houses. From as early as the second third of the twelfth century, but particularly in the early thirteenth century, many nunneries were founded by important patrons who attached their foundations directly to Cîteaux; some were founded by bishops who retained visitation rights over 'their nuns' for some time; some originated in the same eremitical growth from which emerged so many cistercian houses for men.[10]

An important chapter as yet barely recorded in the history of the Cistercian Order concerns an extremely wealthy house of cistercian nuns at Saint-Antoine-des-Champs outside the eastern gates of Paris. In the developmental model of the Order, this house appears at the moment when monasteries of nuns were beginning to be incorporated directly by the abbot of Cîteaux. According to surviving evidence, Saint-Antoine-des-Champs-lèz-Paris was founded, at the site of an existing chapel dedicated to Saint Anthony, probably in 1198 by the preacher Foulques de Neuilly. Possibly it was a refuge for prostitutes and usurers converted by his preaching.[11] Saint-Antoine soon developed into a monastery of contemplative women under the early patronage of important noble and bourgeois families of Paris and the vicinity. The community was given in 1204 by Eudes de Sully, bishop of Paris, to the Cistercian Order and to the supervision of the abbot of Cîteaux.[12] The earliest surviving document yet found in the archives dates from 1206, when it was described as a mixed community of men and women.[13]

Saint-Antoine was one of many communities of cistercian women founded in northern France between 1200 and 1250, but of these women's houses in the region I have studied, twenty percent had disappeared by the end of the Middle Ages.[14] In contrast, Saint-Antoine seems to have grown in importance along with the capital next to which it was located. Although their early properties had been largely rural, the nuns of Saint-Antoine had accumulated considerable property in the city of Paris itself by 1300 (as we shall discuss below). In later centuries, privileges from bishops and popes granting indulgence to those who visited the abbey on a number of holy days made it a convenient pilgrimage objective less than an hour's walk from the heart of the medieval city.[15] Today one can still see the remains of the abbey buildings on the Rue du Faubourg-Saint-Antoine which divides the eleventh from the twelfth arrondissement between the Place de la Nation and Place de la Republique; most had been rebuilt in the eighteenth century and were converted after the Revolution to secular use as hospitals—as they continue to be used today.[16]

Patrons of the medieval cistercian nuns of Saint-Antoine included both men and women and donors both lay and clerical, urban and rural—if the last distinction may be made between certain members of the wealthy bourgeoisie and of the lower nobility who were both rising to greater social heights at the time. Citizens of Paris and clerics associated with the university stand out as early patrons, as do certain officers of the king.[17] Saint-Antoine's early fortunes were tied to those of rising knightly families like the Montmorency, Mauvoisin, and Montfort families who had made their fortunes, in part at least, by their association with the cistercian abbots who led the crusade against the albigensian heretics in the south of France.[18] Documented royal patronage on the other hand, turns out to be relatively slight. Although the nuns received confirmation of acquisitions of land in Paris on which the king held ground-rent (*in censiva domini regis*)—and these may have been considered royal gifts—little real estate was conveyed by the royal family to Saint-Antoine.[19] Possibly, nuns were sent from Saint-Antoine at Blanche of Castile's request to found her cistercian abbey for women at Maubuisson and thence to her second foundation at Lys, but there is no evidence that Blanche lavished the attention on Saint-Antoine which she and her son showered on Royaumont, Maubuisson, or Lys.[20] Standing as it did just outside the eastern gates of the city, Saint-Antoine was the departure point for Louis IX and his

1240s Crusade. Moreover, Saint-Antoine was the first place in greater Paris at which Louis IX displayed the Crown of Thorns after bringing it back from the East.[21] Queen Blanche and the young Louis IX seem to have attended the consecration of the church of Saint-Antoine in 1233—hence its architecture may have influenced that of other cistercian foundations by this royal pair. Unfortunately, although we know that the church had a cathedral-like apse with radiating chapels, the relationship of the church of Saint-Antoine to the thirteenth-century cistercian gothic architecture of the region is difficult to gauge, and will remain so, for on the site of the church, razed soon after the French Revolution, stands an ultra-modern high-rise dormitory for the hospital's nurses—making excavation unthinkable.[22]

With regard to the internal workings of the Order, Saint-Antoine seems to have acted as the 'mother-house' for several other communities of cistercian women in the vicinity whose documents mention that they followed 'the customs of Cîteaux as practiced at Saint-Antoine'.[23] Yet Saint-Antoine is not mentioned in lists of houses associated with cistercian women's chapters at le Tart.[24] Its nuns are first mentioned in Canivez' notes published from the Order's General Chapter meetings for 1213, when monks and lay-brothers of the Order were forbidden to request food or lodging from its abbess when in Paris.[25] Such a discussion in the General Chapter must have originated in complaints from the abbess of Saint-Antoine about the burden of such visitors, for there is no indication that the issue was one of protecting the nuns' enclosure or that the decision had been taken up because of any scandal or because the abbess was under any censure from the General Chapter.[26] It suggests the importance of Saint-Antoine's location, as well as reminding us that in the first decades of the thirteenth century there was no hospice for cistercian monks in Paris.[27] Most striking is the casual acceptance that the abbey of Saint-Antoine was part of the Order, and that its abbess's complaints should be heard and answered. Later disputes about property suggest its wealth.[28]

Substantial archives for Saint-Antoine-des-Champs survive. They include two cartularies, several inventories, an atlas of plans showing holdings in the Faubourg-Saint-Antoine on the eve of the Revolution, and large numbers of loose parchment and paper 'originals' including many from the thirteenth and fourteenth centuries. These important archives for parisian history are just beginning to be exploited, but their use has exploded in the past several years: an edition of the earliest original charters has recently been completed by a student at the Ecole des Chartes, scholars are studying sermons addressed to its nuns, and efforts have begun to reconstruct its medieval library holdings.[29] In a sermon delivered to the nuns on 6 May 1273 Nicolas du Mans, a well-known Dominican who studied and preached in Paris and later became the confessor of Philip III's eldest son, mentioned the importance contemporaries attached to the prayers of this community of women: 'Surely, such donors made gifts to you not for your beautiful eyes, but in order to have a part in your prayers'.[30]

Towards the end of the thirteenth century one of the all too often enigmatic references in Canivez' *Statuta* again mentions the nuns of Saint-Antoine. This one, dated 1293, says 'That the dispersion of the nuns should be left to the judgement of the abbot of Cîteaux'.[31] Unless this was a temporary dispersion because of some kind of fire in their buildings—a very shaky inference which others seem to have drawn from the fact that the previous item in the Statutes mentions destruction by fire elsewhere—I do not know what this means. The charter record makes no suggestion of any hiatus at this point.[32] There is no precipitous falling away of numbers of contracts at this moment; the only evident pattern is a continuing shift towards more and more contracts concerning urban properties and donors.[33] Some of their most important acquisitions had been made by the nuns in the two preceding decades, and certainly the nuns were still there in 1302, less than a decade later, as I shall discuss.

Saint-Antoine was a power to be reckoned with in the last years of the Hundred Years' War, when a parisian diarist wrote in 1432:

> At the end of August the abbess of Saint-Antoine and some of her nuns were put in prison. They were accused of having agreed with a nephew of this abbess, who made himself out to be a true friend of Paris, to betray the town by the Porte Saint-Antoine. The gate-keepers were to be killed first and then everyone in the town without exception; this was generally known after their arrest.[34]

At the time Paris was held by the Burgundians supporting Charles VII, but virtually surrounded and threatened by the English. I can go no further in explaining this accusation, but by all accounts, the abbey continued generally to thrive right up to the French Revolution.[35]

This study of the abbey of Saint-Antoine, which forms part of a larger consideration of more than twenty houses of cistercian nuns in the ecclesiastical province of Sens, will demonstrate how bourgeois patrons joined those from the countryside around Paris in endowing and entering the community.[36] I shall also show how money coming from citizens of Paris was used to purchase non-parisian lands and rents and the extent to which small numbers of urban donors began to have a significant effect on both acquisitions and on the community's internal administration of property in the last quarter of the thirteenth century. In my work thus far, I have concentrated on the evidence of the abbey's two surviving cartularies or charter-books. One of them is medieval. The other was made later, but includes much of the contents of what, I believe, must have been a second medieval cartulary—now lost. The second, Paris, A.N., S*4386, is a folio-sized manuscript of one-hundred eighteen folios on paper, written in an eighteenth-century hand. It contains copies of documents dating from 1208 to the early seventeen hundreds, about two-hundred fifty of which charters date from the period before 1350. Those two-hundred fifty charters do not replicate those from the same dates in the surviving medieval cartulary, but instead record grants of non-parisian rents and income to the nuns, as well as acquisitions of land, vineyards, wine-presses, meadows and forest rights in the region around Paris. This paper volume includes on folio 75 the copy of a memorandum dated 1277, written by the abbot of Cîteaux and describing purchases made by Saint-Antoine with a large cash bequest from a single nun.

The earlier cartulary, Paris, A.N., LL1595, is a parchment quarto volume of ninety-nine folios written in a fourteenth-century hand with extensive rubrication and lists of contents. Several acts and lists were added to it *c.* 1344 and *c.* 1370, but its main contents must have been collected *c.* 1300.[37] This cartulary contains almost exclusively charters for properties acquired either within the medieval walls of the city of Paris itself or in its built-up suburbs just beyond the walls.[38] It also provides considerable evidence about the abbey's archival organization. In addition to a group of rent rolls, it contains copies of one-hundred forty charters for dates from 1208 to 1303, and refers to another one-hundred forty to fifty charters not copied. There is considerable cross-indexing to particular shelves in archival cupboards located near the church, and to sacks of original parchments on those shelves. Indeed, in some senses, this cartulary is an inventory of a part of the larger archival collection. For instance, a complicated system of numbering in the cartulary appears to correspond to endorsements which refer to shelves and bags. The volume is replete with such phrases as, 'with this is found the confirmation by the abbot and community of Saint Maur', or 'note another charter which begins', or 'eleven other charters kept in many little bags discuss the same material'.[39] I suspect that there probably was a second medieval cartulary at one time—and that the survivor was the second in a pair. *Censiers* included at the end of the medieval cartulary concern both properties in the city (for which title deeds are included earlier in the same cartulary) and properties in the countryside (for which charters are found in the later paper cartulary). Missing from the surviving medieval cartulary are the very documents often treated as the most important, those usually listed first in cartularies made at this time: royal, papal, and noble documents of confirmation, privilege, and gift.[40] Thus some of the most important noble donors are to be found in charters in the eighteenth-century paper cartulary, but not in the surviving medieval cartulary. These charters provide a picture of the patronage of this particular community, of its accumulation of properties up to *c.* 1350, and also of the nuns' property management as it is reflected in the medieval cartulary's organization.[41]

The tendency of the medieval cartulary to collapse certain sets of documents into summaries, and its organization according to what a compiler of *c.* 1300 considered the most valuable documents, are not the only interesting features of this record. As I have mentioned, its charters consist almost entirely of conveyances of urban rights to the abbey. We are at the moment in legal history, moreover, when the written charter began to replace the face-to-face transaction, and when French was beginning to replace Latin.[42] In it are what seem rather common problems in medieval contracts about legal language. One finds scribes attempting to stretch old types of contracts to cover new types of transactions—

particularly ones which deal with credit or the transformation of money into income. I will mention only one problematic type: the conveyances to the nuns of increases or augmentations of rents on houses in the city of Paris. Adam Hermandus and Sanche his wife granted the nuns an 'augmentation of rent' on a house they owned in Paris in 1216.[43] In 1228, Master William of La Tiniac, a canon of Chalons, gave a rent of ten *livres per annum* of increased rent on a certain house in Paris for the nuns to have after his death.[44] These 'augmented rents' seem to have been newly-created rents or annuities granted to the nuns on property already paying ground-rent or within the *censive* of other lords. In a few cases such increases of rent may have operated like the constituted rents or annuities which R. Génestal claimed came to replace the medieval *mort-gage* after ecclesiastical censure of the first.[45] That is, donors either borrowed money from the nuns in return for promising such perpetual annual payments, or they made a gift equivalent to a theoretical principal sum in the form of a new annuity to be paid in perpetuity by the tenant of a dwelling, who may or may not have been identical with the donor.[46] In other cases, however, it seems as if the increase in rent to the nuns may actually have been negotiated with a new tenant of property already in Saint-Antoine's hands; in such cases the new tenancy agreement or augmentation may reflect simply increasing values of urban property. In these cases the tenant got a leasehold in return for an increased (to market-value?) rent payable to the nuns. Sometimes also he or she agrees to make improvements to the property, promising to spend a specific amount of money over a term of several years; again, the nuns may have been providing that cash up front. Thus, while in some cases the nuns may have acted as lenders of money against a perpetual rent, in others they seem to have been promoting improvements to their property by granting 'home improvement loans' or 'second mortgages' to new or existing tenants in return for increased rents in future.

In addition to nearly one-hundred fifty copies of charters, the medieval volume contains several *censiers*. The two most important concern money-rents owed to the nuns in the countryside and in the city of Paris respectively.[47] The total income in cash recorded in these *censiers* dated *c.* 1300, amounted to more than 1600 *livres per annum*. Of this 1600 livres, over 1000 came from non-parisian sources while the rest—a little over 600 came from the abbey's properties in the city of Paris itself.[48] Thus the nuns had a substantial cash budget per year. And such lists of cash income do not include returns in kind deriving from the granges belonging to Saint-Antoine, or large sums of cash which might be the payments if they were 'at farm'. So in addition the produce of those granges which fed the nuns and their dependents may have contributed significantly to their total wealth. Although it is difficult to know precisely what such values mean, we do know, by comparison, that in a successful plea of poverty for tax-relief, Constance, abbess of the cistercian house of nuns la Cour-Notre-Dame near Sens, reported in 1286 a cash income of only about 320 *livres* per year for a community of more than forty.[49] What we lack for comparison is any notion of the number of nuns at Saint-Antoine. Nor have we any sense of what the nuns owed in ground-rents to others. The example of la Cour-Notre-Dame suggests, however, that cistercian nuns, like the rest of the Order, were finding it difficult by the late thirteenth century to avoid taxation.[50]

Urban rents of over six hundred *livres* were derived from more than a hundred thirty houses located in a variety of places in the medieval city, most of them near its eastern walls or in the Latin Quarter. Many of the sites still have a familiar ring: near the Petit Pont, near the Porte de la Grève, in the Marais, on the Grand Rue Saint-Denis, aux Halles (where the nuns had *notre grant maison des Halles*), at the Porte Montmartre, at the Place de Châtellet across from the King's Palace, in the Cité, on the Rue de-la-Harpe, in the Grand Rue Saint-Jacques.[51] This list makes clear that at least some houses adjoined other properties also belonging to the nuns, and that selective acquisition on particular streets or in particular quarters seems to have been underway. This process of consolidation within the medieval walls was replicated later in the Faubourg-Saint-Antoine, as we know from an atlas of Saint-Antoine's properties held there just before the Revolution which shows street upon street of houses and lots in that vicinity.[52] Unfortunately, there is no comparable eighteenth-century atlas for properties held within the walls of the city by Saint-Antoine. Whether medieval holdings were traded for suburban ones in order to consolidate land in the faubourg, or whether the atlas is incomplete (as seems more likely) I have yet to determine.

Donors to the nuns of Saint-Antoine were diverse, although it is sometimes difficult to identify with certainty the social class of individual donors.[53] Early contracts include a confirmation by one of my own favorite great feudal ladies, Isabelle, countess in her own right of Chartres.[54] Particularly important were the conveyances by newly-powerful, upwardly-mobile knights and lords of castles; these included a number of grants from those departing for the Midi to fight the heretics or returning thence, including Simon de Montfort (and his wife who was a Montmorency) and related crusading knights like Robert of Mauvoisin, Dreux de Cressonessart, and Matthew of Montmorency.[55] Some donors were particularly interested in religious benefits. For example, in 1208, in one of the earliest recorded bequests to Saint-Antoine, Lady Agnes of Cressonessart made a gift of land 'in order that anniversary Masses be said for her soul and that of her two [presumably successive] late husbands'; she retained usufruct of half of the conveyed land for her lifetime.[56] The earliest chapel to be founded at Saint-Antoine was given for her brother Robert of Mauvoisin, knight on the Albigensian Crusade, dead by 1223, who in his last testament had given a number of rents 'for the institution of a chapel for his soul'. His executors established it 'in honor of Saint Peter' at the abbey of Saint-Antoine-de-Paris.[57] Thus, in many of its earliest charters, gifts and patronage for Saint-Antoine were not very different from what would have been given to any cistercian monastic community of either men or women.[58]

In addition, it is clear that among the earliest gifts to the nuns of Saint-Antoine were a small number of bequests from city people and of city properties. In 1218, for instance, Robert le Ber and his wife Agnes gave a house in Paris to the nuns.[59] Benefactors of Saint-Antoine also included clergy, some of whom may have been associated with the cathedral or university.[60] In 1213, a cleric named Peter gave a vineyard to the nuns of Saint-Antoine who were caring for his mother—probably as a permanent boarder or corrodar—and the nuns promised to bury her when she died. This property (or any property for which it was exchanged) was perpetually to provide wine for the nuns—in the strings attached it is typical of bequests made to women's houses.[61] Similarly, in 1229, John of Paris *magister scholarum Suessonensis* made a gift to the nuns so that they would celebrate an anniversary mass for his patron, Hugh of Provins.[62]

Gradually in the course of the thirteenth century came a shift from rural to urban patronage. *Gifts* (as opposed to *sales* and other contracts) were increasingly being made by such townspeople as Peter le Ber, Baker to the Lord King and Agnes his wife in 1225, or Petronille, the Smith's wife in 1235, or Agnes la Bouchière in 1260, or Peter the Cook in 1261.[63] Moreover, many bourgeois donors were making gifts to Saint-Antoine because their daughters were becoming nuns there. Although we have no documentation for many of the gifts which accompanied entrances into the community, there are some. In 1300, for example Peter the Wool-seller or Draper (*dictus Lanierguas*) with his wife Michelle, citizens of Paris, gave rents over parisian properties to provide for their daughter Colette, a nun at Saint-Antoine.[64] A similar gift was made by Simon Denis of Saint-Benoît, draper, and Agnes his wife to Saint-Antoine because of their two daughters, nuns of that house.[65] The process of property acquisition followed closely the pattern I have shown among the monks of the Order in their communities in southern France.[66] The nuns of this unusually wealthy community of Saint-Antoine acted in land acquisition much more like the Order's houses of monks than like their poorer female counterparts.[67] The reason behind the nuns' ability to do as monks so often did was not simply Saint-Antoine's location near Paris, but also the developing ties between Saint-Antoine and the parisian bourgeoisie. The land holdings which comprised early gifts from feudal families (who continued to act as patrons) became the cores around which the nuns of Saint-Antoine created granges by the purchase and consolidation of additional lands and rights. It was urban donors far more often than the increasingly cash-hungry feudal lords who provided the cash to purchase land for granges in the countryside.[68]

The process of land purchase in the countryside was begun quite early by the nuns. A section of charters in the early-modern cartulary shows, for instance, that purchases were undertaken in the region east of Paris in 1214, when Saint-Antoine purchased an *arpent* of meadow along with a weir in the river near the port of Bry-sur-Marne from Simon de Bry, knight, and his wife Marie, for eighty-five *livres parisis*. Other meadows were willed to the nuns in 1217 by Roger, canon of Paris. Another charter promised that lordship over lands there would be confirmed to the nuns when their seller returned from fighting the albigensian heretics. The nuns further developed these holdings by purchases, such as local land bought in 1219 from Adam Carpentarius and Thibault his son, both of Bry, whose social class as wealthy artisans may be revealed in their surname.[69]

At another location a grange was developed at Beaumont-sur-Oise, northwest of Paris, with parts purchased in the 1250s and 1260s, as we will see below. More directly north of Paris, in the villages of Aulnay, Savigny, and le Blanc-Mesnil, initial gifts from Agnes of Cressonessart and Simon de Montfort were followed by purchases which eventually resulted in the creation of a great grange there as well.[70] Similar granges and wine-producing properties were created by the nuns in the forested areas east of Paris near Fontenay sur/sous Bois, and at Montreuil near Vincennes.[71]

The most startling evidence of how such purchases in the countryside by the nuns of Saint-Antoine were fueled by bourgeois money is recorded in the 1277 memorandum adverted to earlier. This concerns gifts brought to Saint-Antoine by Blanche of Paciac, a very wealthy bourgeois woman who entered the community before 1260.[72] This memo tells us that when she entered the community Blanche brought to Saint-Antoine an income which amounted to 400 *livres parisis per annum* in rents or income from her own lands in and near Paris. Moreover, she had provided the nuns with an additional 1500 *livres tournois* cash with which land had been purchased between the date of her entrance and 1277, when the memorandum detailing her gifts was written up by the abbess of Saint-Antoine and the abbot of Cîteaux. The importance of this gift is underlined by the fact that this is the first contract surviving in the cartularies for which the abbess of Saint-Antoine drew the abbot of Cîteaux into the affairs of the community. In it Abbess Agnes, who like John of Cîteaux affixed her seal, attested that with Blanche's money had been purchased major parts of eight properties at six places as well as two rents. The purchases made by Blanche, or rather by Saint-Antoine with her money, were thus part of a larger late medieval phenomenon by which urban cash and credit gradually encroached on the surrounding countryside and its land and rental market. Indeed, such purchases distorted the price-structure for rural acreage in those suburban areas.[73]

The properties listed were the following items—literally *item* in the latin text, most of which are identifiable from the rubrication of cartulary A.N. S*4386:

> The manor which had been owned by Lord Thibault of Champagne-sur Oise, knight, at Beaumont-sur-Oise, with all its appurtenances.
>
> Also, at the same place, three *arpents* of arable land next to the *culturae* belonging to Lord John of Champagne, knight.
>
> Also at Savigny-le-Temple adjoining Saint-Antoine's grange there, a quarter part of the *champart communal.*
>
> Also, another four *arpents* of arable land adjoining *la Sauveté-Saint-Antoine.*
>
> Also, in the territory of Praelles, four *arpents* of land.
>
> Also, in the same place, two *arpents* of land above the fishpond.
>
> Also, at Montreuil, a certain winepress called *Pressoir Major*, with all pertaining to it.
>
> Also, at the grange of Bordes fifteen *arpents* of arable land.
>
> Also, eight *livres* annual rent from the *péage* [passage-tolls] at Franqueville.
>
> Also, at Paris, one hundred *solidi parisis* annual rent over a house located across from the court of the Lord King in the land and lordship of Saint-Magloire.

These property acquisitions may be traced in part in the cartularies, allowing us to assert that Blanche entered the abbey before 1259.

When we turn to the charters for the grange of Beaumont, for example, we find that acquisitions for the first item listed in the 1277 memo—the manor which had been owned by count Thibault of Champagne-sur-Oise—began by November 1224.[74] In that year a dispute had been resolved over rights there between Saint-Antoine and the heirs of the late Matilda, wife of Philip of Tournasel; as a consequence, the nuns received a rent of 35 *solidi* and 6 *deniers* annually at Beaumont-sur-Oise. By 1260, properties at Beaumont owned by the nuns had come to include rights 'in the field held from the Lord King', in a vineyard called *Clos de Thoriac*, and in two arpents of meadow at Pont-de-Beaumont. In 1261 King Louis IX confirmed another sale to the nuns of Saint-Antoine, and the nuns' right to *mainmorte* on property there.[75] This was a sale of rents worth 8 *livres* by Reginald of Champagnes, knight;

he received 120 *livres parisis* as the purchase price. Probably this sum was paid to consolidate rights at this place and possibly to secure the grant of *mainmorte* came from Blanche of Paciac. Other holdings nearby—in the fief and farm of Champagnes-sur-Oise on the opposite side of the river from Beaumont—are those specified in the memorandum as having been purchased and consolidated with Blanche's money.

The most important conveyance is one dated 1264 in which Jean de Champagne, knight or armiger, and his brothers Henry and Robert, attested that, along with their mother Jeanne, they held rights from their late father, Lord Thibault, knight of Champagnes-sur-Beaumont 'in a certain manor which the late Thibault had held, that is: in a great hall or tower (*aula*), a small hall, a winepress, a grange and smaller stables for cows, all joined together in a court, as well as a *quartier* of vines behind that court'. This same purchase contract also mentions the second item in the 1277 memorandum: from their mothers' rights, three *arpents* of cultivated land adjoining the vineyards of Colardi. These rights were purchased by the nuns for 280 plus 30 *livres*.[76] Thus, in contracts dates 1261 and 1264, we can account for 440 livres spent for rights at the first two places listed in the 1277 memo.[77]

One can, of course, go on with this exercise. For Savigny, item three in the 1277 memorandum, we find purchases in 1261 for 30 *livres*, and in 1262 for 18 *livres*.[78] Item four on the memorandum—four *arpents* of land near la Sauveté-Saint-Antoine, was purchased in 1264 for 100 *livres* from Simon of Ville Evrard and his wife Lady Marie.[79] Property at Montreuil near Vincennes may well constitute the earliest purchase which can definitely be associated with Blanche of Paciac's cash gifts. The winepress mentioned in item six of the memorandum was purchased in 1259 for 46 *livres* from Peter of Buciac, citizen of Paris, and his wife and heirs. The contract tells us that they had purchased it earlier from John of Bobigny, draper, citizen of Paris, and his wife Margaret, and from Lord Thomas of Clamartis, knight, and Sedilia his wife. This contract points up the problems in talking about citizens as owning urban property and knights holding rural. In this case, both were sellers of suburban property which was then consolidated by Peter of Buciac, who immediately sold it to the nuns—incidentally making a 3 *livres* on 43 profit.[80]

Who was this Blanche of Paciac who brought an almost unimaginable dowry and gifts? There is no charter in the cartulary recording Blanche's entrance into the community. Possibly the memorandum was seen as replacing an earlier contract, or series of documents. In other documents making gifts or sales to the abbey, we do find someone who may have been a son or nephew, Raoul de Paciac. Raoul's status as wealthy bourgeois executor is clear from his appearance as executor for the rich merchant draper John of Popiac—who would endow a place for his own daughter at Saint-Antoine. This must also suggest Blanche's status.[81] It is plain that Blanche of Paciac was anxious that her gifts be remembered, for the memorandum concludes that it had been made and sealed: 'so that she be remembered perpetually and especially that after her death she be included in the prayers of the nuns, serving the Lord at this house.'

It is unusual to have information about a donor like Blanche of Paciac in such a memorandum rather than in what might be called a nun's dowry contract—in which land or a rent would have been given but without its being called a dowry.[82] But then so were the circumstances of the cash bequests after Blanche's entrance into the community. What the memorandum documents is how gifts in cash were transformed into the permanent real property of the abbey—how money became specific tangibles whose ownership by the nuns of Saint-Antoine could protect Blanche's soul through eternity. Without this memorandum, the historian would have no indication of the source of cash for the purchases mentioned.[83] Most historians would not have concluded that so much cash had come from a single individual. Disturbing is the fact that such very rare references—I have seen only four such contracts in many years of working on monastic cartularies—are all associated with rich women donors making large cash gifts. Those women's gifts would otherwise go undocumented. Possibly behind such documents as the four I have seen lies a hidden pattern of undocumented monastic patronage by women who gave cash gifts—and who gave gifts in cash because families gave cash to daughters as dowry, while land went to sons as inheritance.[84] If this is so, then the participation of women in monastic patronage may well be under-reported because cash gifts, unless they are exceedingly large, are unlikely to leave any 'parchment trail' in the records.

If we look at the recorded parisian rents for *c.* 1300, we find the sum of little over 600 *livres per annum*; thus the 400 *livres* per year which Blanche brought to the abbey of Saint-Antoine at the time of her entrance amounted to the equivalent of two thirds of the urban rents held forty years later. What is not quite clear is whether the rents she gave were permanently alienated to the abbey and thus part of the 600 *livres*.[85] In addition, purchases made with the cash Blanche of Paciac gave to Saint-Antoine provided major additions to grange holdings in the countryside surrounding Paris, holdings which would aid the nuns in maintaining a healthy income in rent and kind from that point on. We must conclude that many of its urban rents and a large portion of the mid-thirteenth century improvement of its rural properties came from the bequests of this single nun. Yet we have no indication that Blanche herself acted in any of these purchases, or that she ever held office in the abbey. Only with this memorandum is she raised to the status of virtual founder of the community—as well she should have been. But how did the incredible indebtedness of this community to a single bourgeois woman affect social relationships within an abbey where, as far as we can tell, bourgeois women were admitted, but abbesses and other office-holders seem to have remained noblewomen?[86] It is not difficult to imagine that this may have become a stressful situation. Indeed, perhaps the memorandum written not by the abbess alone but with the abbot of Cîteaux, signals an attempt to alleviate discontent which might have been felt by Blanche of Paciac. Such possible murmuring may even have been what led to the talk of dispersion mentioned earlier. Certainly it did affect how abbesses at this one monastery, *c.* 1300, administered the monastic property—a subject for which the medieval cartulary of Saint-Antoine provides possibly unique information, as we shall see.

Knowing how monastic property was administered in the twelfth and thirteenth centuries is often very difficult. The administrative records we have for this period are primarily acquisition documents. These documents are much better at showing what land was acquired and how it had previously been exploited than at indicating how land once acquired would be used.[87] With regard to Saint-Antoine, it is quite easy to show that most of the rural properties which the nuns acquired in their first century of existence had been under cultivation before being acquired by the nuns.[88] But we are often left guessing about how any property, whether rural or urban, once acquired, was exploited. Although for Saint-Antoine, we have lists of rents due at various places at various times, including the long list of rents from houses in Paris, we know nothing about produce or payments in kind and we have almost no inkling as to how cash once paid into the hands of the abbey was dispersed for its expenses. Indeed, our understanding of property administration by cistercian abbesses (or by any monastic administrators) often rests heavily on the evidence of donors' wishes that income conveyed should be used for a specific purpose—to purchase wine, to be spent for a pittance meal following the anniversary Mass for a particular donor.[89] We are left assuming that donor's wishes were carried out—and, if not careful, we may conclude that the nuns had no minds of their own on this subject. Moreover, it may be that donors to cistercian nuns were more intrusive in their directives about how property should be used than were the same donors when making gifts to cistercian monks.[90]

The medieval cartulary for Saint-Antoine, like most such surviving records for nuns, reveals bequests which were to be assigned to specific purposes: chaplaincies, anniversary Masses, pittances, wine in one case, and fur for their cloaks in another.[91] It also reveals that from a relatively early date, certain donors were making bequests of property on which those donors retained usufruct for life; in such cases the abbey was given the reversion to income.[92] In some cases, usufruct was exchanged for an annual income in cash or kind paid for the donor's lifetime; this happened in the case of the priest Yves who was to receive 50 *solidi per annum*.[93] Such gifts in some cases might be thought to establish a kind of corrody, particularly if religious confraternity or permission to live in a house belonging to the community was included.[94] Such arrangements between donors and monasteries were fairly common for both men's and women's communities and for a variety of Orders from at least the twelfth century, if not earlier.[95]

What is new to my eyes at Saint-Antoine is what happened when this type of contract was pushed one step further: that is, to the granting of a private income at the time a daughter or female relative entered the community. At Saint-Antoine, beginning in 1281, certain nuns seem to have received at least a part of their 'dowry' as private income assigned to them for life. In 1281, for example, Jehanne, daughter of Henry, lord of Trainel, received five *livres* per year for life; in 1282, Agnes of Compas and Agnes la Pydoe received life income; in 1287, Regine, daughter of a bourgeois, received 75 *sol* per year for life. The list goes on.[96] Such gifts were made only eventually to the abbey, for the income involved would come to the abbey only after the nun's death, the lifetime usufruct remained in the hands of the nun herself, 'for her necessities'.[97] This practice, seemingly instituted at first by a few bourgeois donors, did not remain confined to them alone.[98] Moreover, there is evidence that the practice continued at least into the mid to late fourteenth century.[99] This innovation immediately raises questions regarding monastic vows of personal poverty. Cistercian nuns, like cistercian monks, followed the *Rule* of Saint Benedict as interpreted by the constitutions of Cîteaux, and did not, as far as I know, normally hold private property.[100] We know about this money 'for necessities' at Saint-Antoine because of a cartulary section entitled:

> Here begin letters for rents which this church holds over houses in Paris, which are held by the Lady Nuns for life and which will come to the church after their deaths.[101]

It is obvious that the private property of some nuns soon caused a crisis in the community—a crisis solved by assigning income to even more, if not all, nuns. This cartulary section contains a series of acts by which nuns at their entrance were granted property by their families; but also included are contracts concerning other holdings which were not given as dowry for anyone, but which had been assigned to those nuns who had no private income. The cartulary rubrics show land presumably purchased specifically for the settlement of income on certain nuns:

> About the six *livres parisis* over a certain house located in Les Halles of Paris, adjoining on one side the house of Henry Marshal and on the other by the house of Peter called Cleric, located in the *censive* of the Lord King, of which [said] six *livres*, Sister Agnes de Compans, Sister Melania la Bordone, and Sister Juliana of la Roe [together] hold 40 *solidi*, which *solidi* will continue to go to whichever of them outlives the others; also in the same way another 40 *solidi* are held by Sister Agnes la Pidoe, Sister Johanna of Giroles,

> and Sister Genovespha la Pidoes, and another 40 *solidi* are held in the same way, for life by Sister Marguerite la Petite, Sister Agnes of Saint-Victor, and Sister Agnes la Petite.[102]

When I first saw some of these rubrics in a hasty glance through the Saint-Antoine cartulary in the summer of 1988, I thought perhaps these women had been beguines living near the community, but when I read through the contracts themselves, I found fathers and mothers settling income on daughters as they entered the community. What had been a common practice of establishing life income for friends of the community or corrodars had, by a simple extension of that logic, become in the 1280s the establishment of private income for nuns within the community of Saint-Antoine des Champs.

We can point to 1302 as the year when Abbess Gile came to terms with the crisis over personal income which must have been brewing for some time—in fact from at least the 1280s, when some nuns began having private income while others did not, if not back to the time of Blanche of Paciac herself. In the previous year, 1301, Abbess Gile herself received a personal gift of ten *livres* of rents in private income from her cousin, the Lady Marguerite of Beaumont, widow of John of Montfort.[103] At one and the same time we get evidence of the social rank of the abbess, of her relationship to a family of founders, and to the way in which a personal gift allowed her to provide a solution to the private income problem. Only after she had received income from her family (for she could not possibly have provided for herself by purchase of a rent from common funds without grave censure) could the abbess arrange for the nuns of her community who had not brought income with them as a family gift, to be provided with income. I should like to see Gile's cousin's gift as providing a solution rather than as effectively compounding the problem. In any case, once the abbess had an income, other nuns would want one as well, and Abbess Gile's resolution of the problem was a pragmatic one. She did not enforce individual poverty, did not outlaw private property, but instead used the abbey's funds to buy other rents which she could assign as private income to those in the community who did not already have it.

How does the historian contextualize this information on the introduction of private income into the community? How do we avoid simply jumping to the alluring conclusion that it is an index of decadence within this house of nuns? What were the 'necessities' to be purchased with such income? Food, basic clothing, books or frivolities?[104] And is it the evidence of private income at Saint-Antoine which is unusual, or the practice of having it? Indeed, was private income becoming widespread in religious communities of the late middle ages—whether for monks or nuns? I have not made a careful study of this question, but I do know of several other examples from the cistercian documents on which I have been working. Alphonse of Poitiers' alms rolls show several gifts to a single nun at la Cour-Notre-Dame of what must have been private funds.[105] Paulette Leclercq has shown similarly that the nuns of la Celle in Provence had private income by the late middle ages.[106] In some cases economic necessity may excuse the innovation, but Saint-Antoine was clearly rich and the question becomes a different one: what did private income mean in the hands of nuns of an obviously wealthy community? Does the crisis of private income have anything to do with the proposed *dispersio* of 1293, mentioned in the Statutes of the General Chapter? Did the earliest recipients of such income actually ever take it or even want to take it, or were these arrangements made by bourgeois fathers concerned about an institution willing to take their money, but dominated by nobles? Does what might be conjectured to be the discontent and insecurity of a Blanche of Paciac in 1277 lead to the institution of private income for other bourgeois women in the next few years? I do not have answers to these questions, but they remind us that although the evidence for such private income is clear, our interpretation of its meaning and its consequences will probably remain a savory puzzle.

About cistercian nuns generally we can learn many things from my thus far very abbreviated history of the early years of this house. The wealth of Saint-Antoine-des-Champs made its fortunes far more comparable than many other cistercian houses for women to those of the average cistercian house of monks. Yet in comparison to either most men's houses or many of the Order's womens' houses, Saint-Antoine was in many senses unique. By the end of the thirteenth century Saint-Antoine-des-Champs had clearly established itself as a community in which both noble women and wealthy bourgeois women could find a place. The location of the abbey near

Paris meant that its urban properties were particularly important and its nuns seem to have learned early how to increase urban rents to keep up with the inflation of the later middle ages. Such policies would eventually make its abbess have the title of *Seigneur* or Lord of the Faubourg-Saint-Antoine, and its nuns among the richer religious communities in Paris—a position they would maintain right up to the French Revolution. On the other hand, like other women's houses, Saint-Antoine had disproportionately more rents than land, and its wealth in lands was primarily achieved by the fortunate purchases made in the third quarter of the thirteenth-century and funded by Blanche of Paciac. This consolidation of great rural properties must have made the nuns virtually self-sufficient in cereal and wine production, but whether the properties were actually managed by the nuns themselves or farmed out for rents in kind is not yet known.[107] They also, like many late medieval urban women, had more access to the amenities of city-life—such as the preaching of famous mendicants—than did their sisters in rural communities. The insistence by its abbess that Saint-Antoine was not a way-station for visiting monks and lay-brothers of the Order may have been the impetus for the founding of a cistercian hospice (eventually the College of Saint Bernard) in Paris. The relationship of the members of that College to Saint-Antoine, particularly as regards provision of priests to the various chapels endowed by donors at Saint-Antoine, may have been close, and records for the College need to examined in this regard.

Most importantly, the nuns of Saint-Antoine, were the beneficiaries of gifts by members of the Paris university who did not seem to question the efficacy of their prayers. The example of Saint-Antoine should not only confirm to us the importance of women's houses in the Cistercian Order, but remind us that thirteenth-century scholars did not discount the prayers of contemplative women. Historians of religious Orders should not therefore assume that fewer nunneries than monks' houses were founded because women's prayers were less valued. Indeed, much of the argument that there were fewer religious houses for women is based on misinformation; although they tended to be smaller in numbers and were less well-endowed, there were almost as many cistercian houses for women in France as there were for men, and by the later middle ages, the smaller endowment of those women's houses was supporting nearly the same numbers of inhabitants as were men's houses.[108] That there were a number of other extremely wealthy houses of cistercian nuns like Saint-Antoine—Queen Blanche's foundations at Maubuisson and Lys, those of her cousin Isabelle of Chartres, and the abbey of Flines founded by the countesses of Flanders come to mind—also suggests that historians should not assume that all women's communities were simply poorer and less well-managed abbeys than were men's.[109] Some of these abbeys for women became extremely wealthy, and with that wealth generally came power. This acquisition of wealth and power was not necessarily correlated to that of patrons, however, but occurred sometimes as a result of adaptations to circumstances different from those chosen by other Cistercians. In this case, the willingness of Saint-Antoine to accommodate the bourgeois women who brought large sums with which to consolidate its properties was implicitly confirmed in 1277 by the Father Visitor, John Abbot of Cîteaux.

GLOSSARY

Arpent: a measure of land, probably smaller than an acre, but varying from region to region.

Censier: see Rent-books

Corrody: an end-of-life pension of a guaranteed annual amount of food, clothing, etc. along with residence in a religious house for an elderly lay-person, established either by appointment (by a bishop, king, or other patron) or by purchase for a fixed sum.

Farm, at farm: the process of leasing land at a fixed annual rent for a relatively lengthy term (perhaps twenty years) to someone who was often a middleman and who undertook the direction of its cultivation in hopes that it would produce profits for him in the form of more than the agreed-upon rent.

Mort-gage: a contract deemed usurious in the course of the twelfth century by which land or other property was transferred to the lender of cash until the cash was repaid. The fruits of the property were not deducted from the principal (as they were in th parallel *vif-gage*).

Noval tithes: tithes paid on land (called noval land) which had been brought under cultivation relatively recently.

Rent books (*censiers*): a list of rents owed on properties.

Appendix
Memorandum of John, Abbot of Citeaux, November1277.
Paris, AN. S*4386, fols. 75r-v.

M. Blanche de Pacy, religieuse de Saint-Antoine dona en prenant l'habit et même auparavant la somme de 1900 livres au moyen de quoi l'on acheta la maison de Champagnes, etc. Item a Savigny proche la grange de Saint-Anthoine la 4e partie d'un certain champart commune. Item la meme 4 arpents de terre proche de la Sauvetaye de Saint-Anthoine. Item 4 arpents de terre, etc.; item au terroir de Praelles 4 arpents de terre. Item deux arpents de Terre sur la Vivier. Item a Monstreuil un pressoir avec ses appartenances. Item a Franqueville sur le péage 8 livres de rente. Item 5 livres parisis de rente sur un maison a Paris, etc. Item a la grange des Bordes 15 arpents des terres labourables.[1]

Universis presentes litteras inspecturis frater Johannes dictus abbas Cisterciensis salutem in domino sempiternam. Noveritis quod sicut ex relationem religiosis mulieris Sororis Agnetis abbatisse monasterii Sancti Anthonii juxta Parisius et conventus ejusdem loci didiscimus Soror Blanchea de Paciaco monialis dicti monasterii Sancti Anthonii antequam ipsa habitum recepisset monachalem dederat et concesserat monasterio Sancti Anthonii predicto et conventui ejusdem quadringentas libras parisiensis super exitibus terre ejusdem Blanche necnon et post modum quando ipsa habitem assumpserat predictum mille et quingentas libras turonensis que in parte fuerunt in emptionem possessionum predicto monasterio Sancti Anthonii et conventu ibidem deo servienti implicatur que quidem possessiones tales sunt videlicet: manerium quod fuit domini Theobaldi de Campaniis militis cum suis pertinentiis situm apud Campanias juxta Bellum montem. Item ibidem trius arpenta terre arabilis ibidem juxta culturam domini Johannis de Campaniis militis. Item apud Savigniacum juxta Granchiam Sancti Anthonii dicti quartam partem cujusdam campipartis communis. [fol. 75v]: Item ibidem quatuor arpenta terre arabilis juxta salvetium Sancti Anthonii. Item

[1]Note that the rubric has collapsed the gifts of 400 *livres parisis* rent coming from Blanche's lands *super exitibus terre ejusdem* with the 1500 *livres* of cash with which lands listed were purchased.

in territorio de Praeriis quatuor arpenta terre. Item ibidem duo arpenta terre super vivarium. Item apud Monesterolium quoddam pressorium quod dicitur pressorium majorissoy cum suis pertinentiis. Item apud Francovillam super pedagio ejusdem ville octo libras annui redditus. Item apud Parisius centum solidos parisiensis annui census seu redditus super domo quadam sita ante curiam domini regis in terra et dominio Sancti Maglorii. Item apud Granchiam de Bordis quindecim arpenta terre arabilis. Et ut de predictis sic a predicta sorore Blanche donatis et de dicta pecunia acquisitis memoriam in perpetuum habeatur et specialiter de ipsius monialisa post ejus obitum in monasterio Sancti Anthonii predicti ut in orationibus predictis monialiis ibi domini de servientium commendetur, sigillum nostrum ad petitionem dictarum abbatisse et conventus una cum earumdem religiosarum sigillo presentibus litteris duximus apponendum. Datum anno domini 1277 mense novembri et scelle.

Notes

Papers on Saint-Antoine-des-Champs have been presented at the Medieval Academy of America annual meeting at the University of Wisconsin, Madison, April 1989, at a Conference on Monastic and Mendicant Life, University of Toronto, Centre for Medieval Studies, February 1992, at the annual meeting of the Western French Society for French History, at Orcas Island, Washington, fall 1992 (its proceedings have kindly granted me permission to include parts of that paper); at the Cistercian Studies Conference, Kalamazoo, Michigan, spring 1994, and for the Medieval Studies Group at Cambridge University, October 1994. Research in the French archives has been supported by the NEH, an AHA Bernadotte Schmitt Grant, a Mellon fellowship at the National Gallery of Art, Center for the Advanced Study of the Visual Arts, Washington, DC, and a University of Iowa Faculty Scholar Award. Space and accommodations were provided by a Visiting Fellowship at Clare Hall, Cambridge, England, and by the University of Iowa Center for Advanced Study.

1. See, for example, Jean-Baptiste Auberger, *L'Unanimité cistercienne primitive: mythe ou réalité?* (Achel, Belg., 1986).

2. Older views, such as that in R. W. Southern, *Western Society and the Church in the Middle Ages* (Penguin, 1970) 255, stressed the creation of an organization 'achieved at one stroke'. David Knowles, *The Monastic Order in England. A History of its development from the Times of St Dunstan to the Fourth Lateran Council: 940–1216*, 2nd ed. (Cambridge, 1966) 223, similarly, believed that 'the system of government of unrivalled excellence, . . . in a virile and unfolding society' was contemporary with Bernard of Clairvaux's earliest years.

3. See Louis J. Lekai, *The Cistercians. Ideals and Reality* (Kent, Ohio, 1977) 75–76, and *passim*; this means that the final articulation of an Order was contemporary

with trends towards the regularization of all religious Orders within the early thirteenth-century Church.

4. This view, which allowed very productive research in local archives to continue despite perceived abrogations of 'Rule' or 'Plan' was articulated by Father Louis J. Lekai in 'Ideals and Reality in Early Cistercian Life and Legislation', *Cistercian Ideals and Reality*, ed. John R. Sommerfeldt, 4–19 (Kalamazoo, 1978); see also the more economically-oriented Richard Roehl, 'Plan and Reality in a Medieval Monastic Economy, the Cistercians,' *Studies in Medieval and Renaissance History* 9 (1972) 83–113. To the extent that 'Ideals and Reality' encouraged some to see an ideal which excluded or prohibited women's houses until the late twelfth century, it did curtail some study of cistercian women. So too, however, did assumptions that unless they were referenced in the Statutes of the General Chapter, such houses of 'cistercian' nuns were not cistercian; see for instance, Sally Thompson, 'The Problem of Cistercian Nuns in the Twelfth and early Thirteenth Centuries', *Medieval Women*, ed. Derek Baker (Oxford, 1978) which assumes a complete record within the twelfth-century Statutes; but see note 6 below.

5. The tension between incorporation and annexation, as well as attempts to put limits to numbers of men's and women's houses, as played out in one region, are discussed in Constance H. Berman, *Monks and Nuns Reforming a Mediterranean World: Cistercian Expansion into Southern France, 1119–1249*, forthcoming.

6. Given how very fragmentary those statutes are for the twelfth century, their silence can hardly be used to argue that women were not there, for, if we are to do this, we must deny as well the existence of most men's houses. See the Introduction to *Statuta capitulorum generalium ordinis cistersiensis ab anno 1116 ad annum 1786*, ed. J.-M. Canivez, 8 vols. (Louvain, 1933), which sets out the manuscripts from which it was compiled and makes it clear that many of the 'Statutes' are randomly surviving notes and not a court-reporter's transcript of proceedings. Although there are additional manuscripts now available which were not included in the Canivez edition, we will still probably never know what happened in many of those early years. 'Only from 1180 onwards do we have systematic collections in which each annual series of statutes are dated', says Chrysogonus Waddell OCSO, on page 29 of 'The Cistercian Institutions and their Early Evolution: Granges, Economy, Lay Brothers', *Espace cistercien*, ed. Léon Pressouyre (Paris, 1994) 27–38; see also *idem*, 'Toward a New Provisional Edition of the Statutes of the Cistercian General Chapter *c.* 1119–1189', in *Studiosorum Speculum: Studies in Honor of Louis J. Lekai, O. Cist*, ed. Francis R. Swietek and John R. Sommerfeldt (Kalamazoo, 1993) 389–422.

7. Examples of this marginalization of women's houses and their history abound. Lekai, *Cistercians* 347–63, treats nuns apart and isolated in Part II: Cistercian Life and Culture, after Art, Economy and Lay-brotherhood. Southern, *Western Society*, p. 315, commented on the Order's accommodation of cistercian women, 'It is a remarkable example of demand creating supply'; but a careful reading of this section, in which he talks of the 'official acts of the Cistercian Order,' suggests how convoluted a view of women in the Order he has developed because of assumptions of an Order created 'in a single stroke', (see note 2 above). Cistercian nuns are treated along with all other nuns in a single paragraph in Knowles, *Monastic Order*, p. 362, 'Along with the canons, the nuns continued to multiply, and here again the increase was chiefly among those who followed the rule of one of the new orders. Of the thirty odd cistercian nunneries which were in course of time established in England almost one-half date from the period 1175–1215. . . .' This is a distortion,

for what Knowles does not say here is that most of the 'other half' of the cistercian nunneries in England had been founded earlier than 1175; see Roberta Gilchrist, *Gender and Material Culture: The Archaeology of Religious Women* (London, 1994), figure 7, page 37. As for recent studies of nuns, Penelope D. Johnson, *Equal in Monastic Profession. Religious Women in Medieval France* (Chicago, 1991), treats nuns of all orders together. While Sally Thompson, *Women Religious: The Founding of English Nunneries after the Norman Conquest* (Oxford, 1991), treats cistercian nuns separately, she assumes a lack of evidence elsewhere similar to that in England. Earlier studies by Micheline de Fontette, *Les religieuses à l'âge classique du droit canon: recherches sur les structures juridiques des branches féminines des ordres* (Paris, 1967), and Ernst G. Krenig, 'Mittelalterliche Frauenklöster nach den Konstitutionen von Cîteaux; unter besonderer Berucksichtigung frankischer Nonnenkonvente,' *Analecta Sacri Ordinis Cisterciensis* 10 (1954) 1–105, treat cistercian women as a separate group or alone, but generally limit their treatment to juridical or legislative materials.

8. See the province of Sens discussed in Constance H. Berman, 'Fashions in Monastic Patronage: the Popularity of Supporting Cistercian Abbeys for Women', *Proceedings of the Western Society for French History* 17 (1990) 36–45; perhaps more women's houses had origins in small nursing hospitals for the sick or lepers than did men's, as the leprosaria at la Cour, discussed in William C. Jordan, 'The Cistercian Nunnery of La-Cour-Notre-Dame-de-Michéry; A Community that Failed,' *Revue bénédictine* 95 (1985) 311–20.

9. Jean de la Croix Bouton, *et al.* 'L'Abbaye de Tart et ses filiales au moyen âge', *Mélanges Dimier*, ed. B. Chauvin (Arbois, 1984) 2/3: 19–61 is the most recent study on le Tart, but see also Fontette, *Religieuses*, pp. 35–42, which comments on the silence of the Chapter at Cîteaux about that at le Tart (p. 41), but notes also that after the fourteenth century most texts of the General Chapter at Cîteaux and most papal bulls were addressed to both abbesses and abbots of the Order; cf. Krenig, 'Mittelalterliche Frauenklöster', pp. 13 ff. References to the chapter at le Tart are based on old editions of documents, primarily in Migne, which are often difficult to trace to their sources; new editions and additional archival study are desperately needed. Once established as a 'daughter' (*filia*) of an exempt house of cistercian monks, the nuns too were free from episcopal visitation, but the situation of many of them was regularized only in the mid to late thirteenth century, particularly those which had been founded by bishops; see for example, the abbey of Voisins west of Paris, discussed briefly in Berman, 'Fashions', p. 39, documents for which are published in *Cartulaire de Notre-Dame de Voisins de l'Ordre de Cîteaux* ed. Jules Doinel (Orléans, 1887), especially charters 1 ff. (gifts of bishops). An exemption from noval tithes is granted by Innocent IV to Maubuisson: *Cartulaire de l'abbaye de Maubuisson (Notre-Dame-la-Royale*, ed. A. Dutilleux and J. Depoin (Pontoise, 1890), no. II (1243), p. 3.

10. Constance H. Berman, 'Men's Houses, Women's Houses: The Relationship between the Sexes in Twelfth-Century Monasticism', *The Medieval Monastery*, ed. Andrew MacLeish (St. Cloud, Minnesota, 1988) pp. 43–52, and *eadem*, 'Fashions', *passim*. Blanche of Castile petitioned the Chapter that her foundations be made subject directly to the abbot of Cîteaux: *Statuta*: 1236:60 and 63.

11. *Gallia Christiana in provincias ecclesiasticas distributa* ed. Denys de Sainte-Marthe (Paris, 1716–1865) 7: 897; Beaunier-Besse, *Archives de la France Monastique* (Paris: Poussielgue, 1905) vol. 1: pp. 85–87, and Laurent Cottineau, *Repertoire Topo-bibliographique des Abbayes et Prieurés*, (Macon, 1939) 2: 2202–03, where it is

listed under Paris; M. Garsonnin, *Histoire de l'Hôpital Saint-Antoine et de ses origines. Étude topographique, historique et statistique* (Paris: 1891) treated the nineteenth-century hospital; Hippolyte Bonnardot, *L'abbaye royale de Saint-Antoine-des-Champs de l'Ordre de Cîteaux. Étude topographique et historique* (Paris, 1882) repeats materials from published medieval chronicles and other texts which mention Saint-Antoine, including *Gallia Christiana*; he has also consulted some archival materials, but does very little with the rich archives on property acquisition other than including a section which identifies streets listed in the medieval cartulary. His materials concerning the Capetians were incorporated wholesale into Anselme Dimier, *Saint Louis et Cîteaux* (Paris, 1953); I have not been able to consult Du Breul, *Théâtre des antiquitez de Paris* (Paris, 1612), which both Bonnardot and Dimier cite as evidence for certain Capetian gifts to Saint-Antoine, nor have I yet found such documents in the archives; on Foulques, see R. Gutsch 'A Twelfth-Century Preacher—Fulk of Neuilly', in *The Crusades and other Historical Essays in honor of Dana C. Munro*, ed. L. J. Paetow (New York, 1928, 1969) 191. On the general importance of this abbey, see, *Du Faubourg Saint-Antoine au bois de Vincennes* (Paris 1983) *passim*. The only reference to this community in Lekai, *Cistercians*, p. 356, is somewhat confusing; according to Lekai, the then abbot of Savigny, Stephen of Lexington, while attempting to regulate the age of reception at houses of nuns such as Biaches and Port-Royal, which were subject to Savigny, seems to have noted that the age of reception was eight at Saint-Antoine (which was subject not to Savigny, but to Cîteaux, and hence would not have been being visited by Stephen).

12. Bonnardot, *Saint-Antoine*, p. 87–88, I-III reproduces documents which I have not found in the archives for Saint-Antoine: I (1204): *Odo divina miseratione Parisiensis episcopus: omnibus ad quos litterae istae pervenerint, in Domino salutem. Notum fieri volumus quod cum domus sancti Antonii Parisiensis de concessione et voluntate nostra ordinem Cisterciensem receperit, et facta sit domus Cistercii filia specialis, et etiam ibidem abbatissa sit auctore Domino instituta; eidem domui benigne concessimus et concedimus immunitates illas quibus gaudent caeterae Cisterciensis ordinis abbatiae. In hujus itaque nostrae concessionis testimonium praesentem paginam notari fecimus, et sigilli nostri munimine roborari. Actum anno incarnati verbi M. CC. IV. pontificatus vero nostri anno VIIII.* Ibid., no. II (1206), pp. 87–88, is the response of the abbot of Cîteaux in Chapter to the request of Eudes to incorporate both Saint-Antoine and Porrois (later Port-Royal). Ibid., III (1208), is a concession by the abbot of Cîteaux and the Chapter to Saint Antoine of Paris, and all its daughters (*et omnibus filiabus*) that the houses of the Order receive its *conversi* and priests as if they were coming from men's houses of the Order.

13. Paris, A. N., H5 3859–1, is a loose parchment original of an act not included in the cartularies; it is a charter dated 1206 recording the gift of 100 *solidi* in rents by Agnes of Cressonessart to the hospital of Saint-Antoine-de-Paris (*infirmarie sancti antonii parisiensis*) and to the brothers and sisters (*tam fratrem quam sororem*); on Agnes see below, note 57.

14. Berman, 'Fashions', pp. 36 ff. On the similar rate of disappearance of Cistercian women's communities in southern France, see Berman, *Monks and Nuns*, forthcoming.

15. Paris, A. N., S*4384, (an eighteenth-century inventory) suggests on fols. 7–8 that by the time of Louis XIV one would have received some remission from sins for visiting this church on more than half the days in any year.

16. Garsonnin, *Saint-Antoine*, passim; Bonnardot, *Saint-Antoine*, pp. 80 ff.

17. For instance, the king's baker, or *valet de chambre*: Paris, A. N., LL1595 (medieval cartulary described below), fols. 12v–13r, and 24v–25r.

18. On these families' patronage, particularly bequests for anniversaries and chapels, see Constance H. Berman, 'Dowries, Private Income, and Anniversary Masses. The Nuns of St. Antoine-des-Champs (Paris)', *Proceedings of the Western French History Society* (1993) 20:3–20.

19. Most royal gifts found in the two cartularies are confirmations, like Paris, A.N., S*4386, fol. 22v (1261). Possibly there was an early confirmation of properties, made by Philip Augustus, possibly even made at the request of Blanche of Castile after she had delivered the royal son who would be Louis IX; but Dimier, *Saint Louis et Cîteaux* (Paris, 1953) p. 155, 'Chronologie,' which reads, '1214, ap. avril 25, à la naissance de Saint Louis, son Père Louis, pour feter cet heureux événement, fait don à l'abbaye de Saint-Antoine-des-Champs de l'emplacement de l'église et alentour, pour une superficie de 14 arpents', simply follows Bonnardot, *Saint-Antoine*, p. 22, who says this 'is read in du Bruel, *Théatre des Antiquités de Paris*, p. 1240', but Bonnardot can produce no document for this purported gift, nor can I.

20. On sending nuns, see note 23 below; on Maubuisson, see note 9 above and Henri de L'épinois, 'Comptes relatifs à la fondation de l'abbaye de Maubuisson, d'après les originaux des archives de Versailles', *Bibliothèque de l'école de chartes* 19 (1858) 550–69; on Lys much less has been done, but see M. L'Hullier, 'Inventaire des titres concernant la seigneurie que les religieuses de l'abbaye royale de Notre-Dame du Lys possédaient à Malay-le-Roi', *Bulletin de la société historique de Sens* 10 (1882) 34–5, and A. Dimier and & R. H. Delabrouille, *Notre-Dame-du-Lys* (Paris, 1960), and an unpublished study by Armande Gronier-Prieur.

21. Bonnardot, *Saint-Antoine*, pp. 23–24,

22. Bonnardot, *Saint-Antoine*, p. 23; Dimier, *Recueil de plans d'églises cisterciennes*, vol. 1 (Paris, 1949) p. 156; its influence is mentioned in Terryl Kinder, 'Blanche of Castile and the Cistercians: an Architectural Reevaluation of Maubuisson Abbey', *Cîteaux* 22 (1969) 161–88. The church of Saint-Antoine had at least five private chapels endowed during the course of the thirteenth century: see Paris, A.N., LL1595 fols. 27v (1246), 33v–34r (1260), 42r–42v (1243), 47v–48v (1219), and 50v–51r (1296); and S*4386, fol. 63r (1223).

23. *Filiae* are mentioned in document II of Bonnardot, *Saint-Antoine*, as discussed above, note 12; the sending of nuns from Saint-Antoine to Maubuisson is mentioned in Elie Berger, *Histoire de Blanche de Castille, Reine de France* (Paris, 1895) 320–21, but the fact that Blanche requested that her foundations answer directly to Cîteaux (see note 10 above) suggests that Maubuisson was not treated as a daughter, and I have found no document to that effect. For la Cour-Notre-Dame and les Isle or Isle-Saint-Marie near Auxerre: *Gallia Christiana* 12: cols. 129, 480–82, inst. 153–154, 162, says, 'Insulae Beatae Mariae dicatur parthenon fundatoremque agnoscit Guillelmum de Seignelay episcopum Autissiodorensis circa anno 1219 monasterium virginum, quas ex Parisiensi S. Antonii de Campis arcessivit, uno ab urbe milliari eo in loco condidit, cui nomen olim Cellae locum donante Gerardo Baleine B. Mariae canonico illudque monasterium abbati Cisterciensi subjecit. . . .' For la Cour, see Auxerre, A.D. Yonne H787, fol. 12v: *abbatiam ad usus et consuetudines cisterciensis ordinibus prout monasterium sancti anthonii parisiensis eiusdem ordinis*. The link may have been the 'hospital' origins of all three; see note 8 above and also *L'abbaye du Pont-aux-Dames, assise en la paroisse de Couilly (1226–1790)*, ed. A. Berthaut (Meaux, 1887).

24. Bouton, 'L'Abbaye de Tart', *passim*; Fontette, *Religieuses*, p. 36, n. 52.

25. *Statuta*: 1213:4: *Prohibetur firmiter ut nullus monachus vel conversus Ordinis nostri in domo monialium Sancti-Anthonii iuxta Parisios comedat vel pernoctet.*

26. The document dated 1208 published by Bonnardot, *Saint-Antoine*, p. 88, no. III, which promises the *conversi* and priests of Saint-Antoine accommodation at houses of monks within the Order, may have created an expectation of reciprocity burdensome to Saint-Antoine given that Paris would have been visited much more than any rural house in the years before a hospice was founded there.

27. A cistercian hospice in Paris, founded *c.* 1224, had by 1244 become the college of Clairvaux; there are many scattered studies; see E. Kwanten, 'Le collège Saint-Bernard à Paris. Sa fondation et ses débuts', *Revue d'histoire ecclésiastique* 43 (1948) 443–72, which emphasizes the role of Stephen of Lexington in this foundation; Maurice Dumolin, 'La censive du collège des Bernardins', *Bulletin: Société de l'histoire de Paris et de l'Ile de France* 62 (1935) 25–58; Constance H. Berman, 'Monastic Hospices in Southern France: The Cistercian Urban Presence', forthcoming, emphasizes the stage of urban hospice which was usually the origin of such colleges. One of the properties in Paris sold by the nuns of Saint-Antoine to the Praemonstratensians, would be a site for their hospice or college there; see Bonnardot, *Saint-Antoine*, pp. 89–90, no. V.

28. *Statuta* 1236:44: *Querela abbatis de Sacracella contra abbatissam de Sancto Antonio Parisiensi de Pruliaco, de Curia Dei et de Sancti Portu abbatis committitur pace vel iudicio terminanda, et quid inde, etc. Statuta* 1243:56 *Querela abbatis Vallis Sarnaii contra abbatissam Sancti Anthonii, de Bellobecco et de Sancti Portu abbatibus committitur, etc. et quid inde, etc. Statuta*: 1240:64 which refers to Boeriis, probably has to do with the abbess of Porrois. There is a nearly entirely indecipherable reference to negotiations with the abbot of Barbeaux at the end of Paris, A.N. LL1595, fol. 98v.

29. Melle Sandrine Delaforge has just completed an edition of the early charters at the École des Chartes. I wish to thank her for information on the S*4386 cartulary; I have not yet had access to her edition of the charters. On libraries, see Anne Bondeelle-Souchier, 'Les moniales cisterciennes et leurs livres manuscrits dans la france de l'Ancien Régime,' *Cîteaux* 45 (1994) 193–338. Private communications: D. Nebbiae and N. Beriou.

30. *Certe non propter pulcros oculos vestros, sed propter habendum partem in vestris orationibus hoc fecerunt.* This single sentence comes from a much longer sermon; for sending me the text I would like to thank Nicole Beriou; she is not responsible for my extracting.

31. *Statuta*: 1293:15: *Item, dispersio monialium de Sancto Antonio prope Parisios domino Cisterciensi committitur, ut inde, per se vel per alium, faciat prout melius iudicaverit opportunum.* Other thirteenth-century references are cited in note 28 above.

32. A reference in Bonnardot, *Saint-Antoine* p. 25 from Du Bruel p. 1242—certainly misdated and misidentified—refers to an order to tear down the abbey in 1257; that it did not happen is treated as a miracle of Saint-Antoine; the reference to the dispersion comes just before any response on the part of Order or king to *Clericos laicos* and appears to have nothing to do with taxation; but see in general Daniel S. Buczek, 'Medieval Taxation: The French Crown, the Papacy and the Cistercian Order, 1190–1320', *Analecta Cisterciensia* 25 (1965) esp. 72 ff.

33. Total contracts for Saint-Antoine found in the two cartularies by decades: 1200–1209 are 3; 1210–19: 42; 1220–29: 34; 1230–39: 36; 1240–49: 42; 1250–59: 25; 1260–69: 73; 1270–70: 27; 1280–89: 24; 1290–99: 21; 1300–09: 13; such numbers probably overstate the later percentages of actual charters, since many early charters were not copied into Paris, A. N. LL1595, but still suggest no large change *c.* 1293. On the other hand, the tilt is towards charters in A.N. LL1595—hence towards more and more urban acquisitions, with all those in the

first decade rural and only 1 of thirteen in the first decade of the fourteenth century.

34. *A Parisian Journal* ed. Janet Shirley (Oxford, 1968) p. 281.

35. See references in note 11.

36. Constance H. Berman, *Sisters in Wealth and in Poverty: Endowment and Administration of Cistercian Houses for Women in the Ecclesiastical Province of Sens, 1190–1350*, in preparation.

37. We know the approximate date of A.N. LL1595, for the fourteenth-century cartulary ends with a pair of *censiers*, one dated 1300 and the other probably from 1340 (it says in the year 40), located on fols. 77v ff. and 87r ff. respectively.

38. Paris, A.N., LL1595, thus records many conveyances to the nuns of houses and rents on houses in diverse parts of the city—some were in craft areas: near the weavers, the silk-makers, the belt-makers, the gold-smiths, the furriers, or the slaughter-houses: *ibid.*, fols. 71r, 28v, 11r, 28r, 45r, 71r–72r, etc. Others were in quarters still familiar today: near le Petit Pont, in the Marais, near Saint Médard, near the place de la Grève, and in the area between the Baths and Saint Germain; *ibid.*, fols. 18v, 19r, 21v, 22r, 39r, 43r, 44r, 46r–47v, etc. In cases where the location of property is not clear, it is often possible to infer that a charter concerns urban property because of the identity of its donors—often describing themselves as citizens of Paris, although such an inference is obviously not always foolproof.; but see, *ibid.*, fols. 11v–12r, 'Petrus Coquillarius, civis parisiensis', (1261); *ibid.*, fol. 39r, 'Guillelmus Marescalli, draperius, civis parisiensis', (1268); *ibid.*, fols. 53r–53v, 'Stephanus dictus Carnifex, civis parisiensis', (1283); *ibid.*, fol. 50r, 'Johannes dictus Lechaus et Petronilla eius uxor, cives parisiensis', (1291).

39. Paris, A.N., LL1595, fol. 6r: *cum ista invenientur confirmationem abbatis et conventus sancti Mauri Fossatensis*, and *nota alia littera . . . quam sic incipiet, . . . Ibid.*, fol. 38v; *cum istis duabus litteris precedentibus insimul. . . .* or *undecim alie littere in pluribus baculis posite que locuntur de eadem materiam . . .* ; see also the lists of contents and summaries: *ibid.*, fols. 16v, 23v, 30r, 36v, 40r, 43r, 49v.

40. There are many more in Paris, A. N., S*4386, opening folios.

41. The arrangement of material in cartularies is of particular interest to historians wanting to know how nuns managed their properties, as I have discussed in two recent papers: 'The Myth of Female Bad Management: Some Accounts for Cistercian Women in Northern France', presented 1992, and 'The Care of Lepers, the Labors of Hercules, and the Cistercian Nuns of La Cour-Notre-Dame', presented 1994. They are part of my larger study of nuns in the province of Sens: *Sisters in Wealth*. On the arrangement of medieval cartularies more generally, see D. Walker, 'The Organisation of Material in Medieval Cartularies', *The Study of Medieval Records*, ed. D. A. Bullough and R. L Storey (Oxford, 1971) 132–50.

42. Most charters included are contracts registered by the archbishop's chancellery or by the clerk of the prévoté at the King's Palace at the Châtellet; a few were composed and presumably written or dictated by the abbess herself. Contracts composed by the abbess and those registered at the Prévoté tend to be in French rather than Latin.

43. Paris, A. N., LL1595, fols. 19r–20v (1216).

44. Paris, A. N., LL1595, fol. 41v (1228).

45. R. Génestal, *Le Role des monastères comme établissements de crédit, étudié en Normandie du XIe à la fin du XIIIe siècle* (Paris, 1901) 75 ff.

46. Paris, A. N., LL1595, fol. 16v (1211), the conveyance of a house sited opposite the house of Adam of Moulent *cum augmento census* which the donor had been accustomed to collect on it.

47. Paris, A. N., LL1595, fols. 77v ff. and 87r ff. respectively.

48. 'Somme conte des rentes des maisons de Paris VI/C livres X sol. et VIIII den. . . .' Paris, A. N., LL1595, fol. 90r.

49. Abbess Constance was making a plea of poverty to escape a Crusader tithe; see Auxerre, A. D. Yonne, H 787, fol. 21r ff.; Jordan, 'La Cour', *passim*, and my response in Constance H. Berman, 'The Cistercian Church of La Cour-Notre-Dame-de-Michery,' forthcoming.

50. In this case, for the Aragonese Crusade; on the general problem, see Buzcek, *Medieval French Taxation*, pp. 62 ff, and citations in previous note.

51. Paris, A. N., LL1595, fols. 89v–90r: 'EN LA GRANT RUE SAINT JAQUES:' lists sixteen houses (one described as small), a courtyard, and an empty lot on this street held from the nuns by a variety of individuals, including the priest of Montmartre; many of the streets listed in the censier are identified by Bonnardot, *Saint-Antoine*, pp. 83 ff.

52. Paris, A. N., Plans, Seine N004.

53. Ambiguity is especially apparent in this earliest charter; we cannot tell, for sure, if the 1218 gift by Hersendis, wife of Garnerius of Saint-Lazare,—a gift of vineyards at Montreuil—is that of a citizen/artisan who has accumulated rights in the gardens and vineyards of the suburbs; see Paris, A.N., S*4386, fol. 58r (1218). Similarly, when his son died in 1208, William de-Blé-Nouvelle—a resident or citizen of Paris ?—promised the nuns of Saint-Antoine one fourth of a house in that city—a gift which was executed ten years later after William's own death: Paris, A. N., LL1595, fols. 40r–40v. Similarly, Isabelle of Montesay, who in 1211 gave a house to Saint-Antoine 'in pure and perpetual alms' was obviously the owner of rights to urban property; but was she a resident or citizen of Paris? See *ibid*. fol. 16v (1211).

54. Paris, A. N., S*4386, fol. 1r; on Isabelle of Chartres, see Berman *Sisters*, forthcoming.

55. On the participation of these individuals in the Albigensian Crusade, see Monique Zerner-Chardavoine, 'L'abbaye Gui des Vaux-de-Cernay, prédicateur de croisade', *Les Cisterciens de Languedoc (XIIIe-XIVe siècle. Cahiers de Fanjeaux* 21 (Toulouse, 1986) 185–204, esp. 190; probably it was too early in the history of this community for the nuns to be lending them money against Crusading expenses.

56. Paris, A. N., S*4386, no. 171 (1208), fol. 61v; Agnes of Cressonessart, sister of Robert of Mauvoisin, married in second marriage to Dreux of Cressonessart, is identified by Bonnardot, *Saint Antoine*, pp. iii, 12, and 23 note 4 as an abbess of the community from 1233–40. This attribution is based on a reported epitaph found in the chapel she founded—but need she have been abbess to have been buried there, and if so, why not identify her as Agnes I (1214–21) which fits bitter with a gift in the widowhood following two marriages, dated 1208?

57. *Guillelmus dei gratia parisiensis episcopus omnibus presentes litteras inspecturis salutem in Domino. Notum facimus quod cum bone memorie Robertus Malusvicinus in ultima voluntate ad unum capellaniam institutendam pro remedio anime suo legasset res inferius anotatus videlicet unum modium hybernagii in campiparte de Alneto in perpetuum percipiendum, viginti solidos in censum de Corberon singulis annis percipiendos, decem arpentos nemoris in octava parte illa quam idem Robertus emit a Domina Hodeburge de Corcellis, prata qua residua erant post donationem factam de prato ecclesie Sancti Antonii*

parisiensis, prata sita sunt in loco illo qui dicitur de Pons David et super hoc et aliis que in testamento suo ordinavit fratrem Thomas Prioris Sancti Victorio et fratrem Radulfum de Templo et fratrem Haimardum constituisse executores, idem post mortem predicti Roberti res supra nominatas cuiusdam capelle quam idem Robertus fundavit in honore sancti Petri apud Sanctum Antonium Parisiensis consilio bonorum virorum assignarunt, . . . Paris, A. N., S*4386, fol. 63r (1223); Brother Haimard is probably the royal official of that name, see John Baldwin. *The Government of Philip Augustus* (California, 1986) p. 427.

58. Compare southern-French donors in Berman, *Monks and Nuns*, forthcoming.

59. Paris, A. N., LL1595, fol. 12r (1218). Also, Emelina, widow of Jobert Torti of Saint Severin, gave two 'chambers' at Saint Severin to the nuns in 1217: *ibid.*, fol. 47r (1217); by Tostennis of Chartres and Cecilia his wife, presumably residents of Paris, who gave a house in Paris to the nuns in 1218: *ibid.* fol. 38r. (1218); Roger de Camera and Jeanne his wife who gave a rent of forty-six *solidi* in the same year: *ibid.*, fol. 47v (1218); rights over half a house in the 'Autheria' given by Maria widow of Godefrey Godethaur: *ibid.*, fols. 28r–28v (1218).

60. Eudes de Sully, bishop of Paris, seems to have been involved in the original transfer of Saint-Antoine to Cîteaux. His successor, Pierre de Montreuil, in 1213 gave Saint-Antoine a house which, as he explained in the charter, he had earlier purchased for seventy *livres* out of his own private funds; this house occupied by Peter of Bray was located in the *censive* of Saint-Magloire facing the house of the Lord King and the abbot of Saint-Magloire gave up claims to it in a charter accompanying that for the bishop's gift; Paris, A. N., LL1595, fols. 38r–38v (1213). Similarly, Sagannus *matricularius* of Notre-Dame-de-Paris in 1210 gave a *post-obit* gift to Saint-Antoine for his soul and those of his ancestors of half a house in the Clos Brunel; *ibid.*, fols. 42r–42v (1210). Roger, canon of Notre-Dame in Paris gave Saint-Antoine two *arpents* of meadow at Bry; *ibid.*, fol. 19r (1217). The parisian canon, Hervé Marshall, in 1212 confirmed to the nuns of Saint-Antoine certain vineyards at Montreuil, again in a port-mortem gift: Paris, A.N., S*4386, fol. 44r (1212).

61. *Petrus presbiter de Fontaneto iuxta Sarceliam et Gazo frater eius dederunt coram nobis in puram et perpetuam elemosinam ecclesie sancti anthonii parisiensis tres partes vinearum . . . Boteraye et Geroumont apud Sarceliam et hortum situm juxta ecclesiam absolutionem anime matris sue que dum viveret in eadem ecclesia sancti anthonii sibis eligerat sepulturam ubi num ipsius corpus requiescit,* . . . ; Paris, A. N., S*4386, fol. 9r (1213).; this gift by Peter and his brother is linked in the cartulary to a property near modern Fontenay sur/sous Bois, east of Paris.

62. Paris, A. N., LL1595, fols. 28v–29r (1229).

63. Paris, A. N., LL1595, fols. 12v–13r, 32v, and 11r–11v, respectively. Slightly less clear as members of the bourgeoisie are 'Guillelmus Brico, talliator domini regis . . . Valletus de Camera, et Katherina, ejus uxor, . . .' *ibid.*, 24v–25r: [1264]; the shift in acquisitions from rural towards urban is accompanied by an even more impressive shift towards bourgeois patrons, particularly with regard to cash given; see Berman, 'Dowries', *passim*.

64. Paris, A. N., LL1595, fols. 64v–66v.

65. Paris, A. N., LL1595, fols. 66v–67r (1299).

66. Constance H. Berman, *Medieval Agriculture, the Southern-French Countryside, and the Early Cistercians. A Study of Forty-three Monasteries* (Philadelphia, 1986).

67. On this phenomenon elsewhere, see Constance H. Berman, 'The Economic Practices of Cistercian Women's Communities. A Preliminary Look', *Studiosorum*

Speculum. Studies in Honor of Father Louis J. Lekai, OCSO, ed. Francis R. Swietek and John R. Sommerfeldt (Kalamazoo, 1992), 15–32; and Catherine E. Boyd, *A Cistercian Nunnery in Medieval Italy: The Story of Rifreddo in Saluzzo, 1220–1300* (Cambridge, Mass, 1943) pp. 139 ff. which contrasts an idealized cistercian and benedictine economy, arguing that the nuns followed the benedictine.

68. See Guy Bois, *Crise de féodalisme. Economie rurale et démographie en Normandie du début du XIVe siècle au milieu du XVIe siècle* (Paris, 1981).

69. Paris, A. N., S*4386, fols. 18v–21v; on artisans getting suburban land see the register for Maubuisson, Pontoise, A.D. Val d'Oise, H 58: 4 discussed in Berman, *Sisters*, forthcoming.

70. Paris, A. N., S*4386, fols. 60r ff., esp. 61v.

71. See gift in note 62 for Fontenay; Paris, A. N., S*4386, fols. 54r ff., which concerns vines and a winepress at Montreuil.

72. Paris, A. N., S*4386, fols. 75r-v: appendix one below and note 81.

73. The quick profit made by Peter of Buciac in consolidating lands at Montreuil sold to the nuns in 1259 effectively raised land-values as well; Paris, A. N., S*4386, fol. 54r.

74. Paris, A. N., S*4386, fols. 21v. ff.

75. Paris, A. N., S*4386, fol. 22v.

76. Paris, A. N., S*4386, fols. 24v–26r including a *censier* of rents owed.

77. That *tournois* and *parisis* were not equivalent is irrelevant to the argument here.

78. Paris, A. N., S*4386, fol. 65r–67r.

79. Paris, A. N., S*4386, fol. 67r-v.

80. The earlier purchase price had been 43 *livres*, so the nuns were paying Peter of Buciac, who had consolidated, 3 *livres* more than he had paid—but he may well have done the work of collecting and consolidating many small holdings; Paris, A. N., S*4386, fol. 54r.

81. This Blanche of Paciac (Passy?) was the female relative (probably aunt) of a notary named Raoul of Paciac who appears with his wife Sedelia as donors in 1260. Paris, A. N., LL1595, fol. 33v; presumably the same Raoul appears in 1291 when identified as notary and executor for an important patron of the nuns, John of Popin, citizen of Paris and member of the powerful guild of long-distance drapers, the *marchands d'eau*; John of Popin funded a chapel and anniversary at Saint-Antoine and his daughter Petronilla was a nun there; *ibid.*, fols. 50v–51r.

82. On dowries for entrance into religious life, see Joseph Lynch, *Simoniacal Entry into Religious Life from 1000 to 1260* (Columbus, Ohio, 1976) *passim*.

83. See Berman, *Medieval Agriculture*, pp. 38 ff.

84. This is one of the main points of investigation of my study of nuns in the province of Sens. That is, can we tell from such evidence whether in fact women's inheritance or monastic dowry was smaller in value than that of their brothers, and does this help explain the economic difficulties of late medieval communities of nuns.

85. The charter (see appendix) does not indicate the source of the rents.

86. Although there is a list of abbesses in the *Gallia Christiana* and in Bonnardot, *Saint-Antoine* there documentation is scant; see Paris, A. N., LL1595, fols. 73r–75r, for one citation; Bonnardot, p. 29 identifies several fourteenth-century abbesses as bourgeois, including the election in 1324 of Marguerite le Petit, daughter of Henry Petit, bourgeois of Paris and of Marie his wife who are found in Paris, A. N. LL 1595, fol. 75v (1295); she was succeeded by a noble woman in 1330; two other

fourteenth-century abbesses, Ameline de Bourdon and Marguerite d'Allemant may have been born in Paris according to Bonnardot, *Saint-Antoine*, p. 29.

87. See Berman, *Medieval Agriculture*, pp. 61 ff.

88. Saint-Antoine may have cleared some land east of Paris, for instance, at the woods of Sariel, see Paris, A. N., S*4386, fols. 11r ff., but most other contracts in that cartulary concern lands already under cultivation.

89. Paris, A. N. LL1595, fol. 51r ff. (1291 and 1296) in which John Popin, provost and member of the long-distance merchant's guild of Paris, left money for three pittances, one each at Easter, Pentecost, and Christmas, and to build a chapel and to give an annual income to his daughter Petronilla for life.

90. One might posit a greater protectionism, even paternalism, towards communities of nuns, which is seen in gifts of flour for their bread or wine for their divine service; given that gifts in rent and in kind were so much more frequent in thirteenth than in twelfth century gifts, however, it is almost impossible to compare whether women among the Cistercians—who were given most of the endowment in the thirteenth century—got such gifts oftener than men who had received almost all their initial endowment in the twelfth century; again this notion will be tested in the larger study.

91. For instance, *Noverint etiam universi quod coram nobis constituta Petronilla relicta defuncti Johannis dicti Mathei quondam civis Parisius recognovit quod ipsa dederat et concesserat in puram et perpetuam elemosinam abbatisse et conventui sancti anthonii parisiensis octo libras parisius annui redditus expendas in proprius usus conventus pro ferraturis ad mantellos percipendas et recipiendas annuatim de cetero super viginti libris parisius annui redditus*, . . . Paris, A. N., LL1595, fols. 36v–37r.

92. Paris, A. N., LL1595, fol. 41v (1228), is an example of a post-mortem reversion contract.

93. Paris, A. N., LL1595, fol. 63r.

94. Paris, A. N., S*4386, fol. 9r (1213).

95. One might cite the example of Hodearde described as *conversa* of the abbey of Cistercian monks at Vauluissant; discussed by William Duba, '"Not Fully Conversant", Monks, Conversi and Donors at the abbey of Vauluissant,' forthcoming.

96. Paris, A. N., LL1595, fols. 63r. ff., shows one nun receiving such a gift in 1281, two for 1282, 2 in 1287, 2 in 1293, 1 in 1295, 1 in 1296, 12 in 1298, 3 in 1299, one in 1300, 4 in 1301, 1 in 1302 in addition to ten assigned by the abbess (counting two daughters getting such income in one contract as two bequests), and see text in next note.

97. In the case of Colette, daughter of Peter 'Woolseller', mentioned above, . . . *de liberatione et contemplatione Colete ipsorum coniugum filie, monasterium sancti anthonii iuxta parisius ingresse ad hiis inducti ut dicebant dederunt, concesserunt et penitus quitaverunt exiunt in perpetuum coram nobis, abbatisse et conventui monasterii eiusdem ipsarumque abbatisse et conventus heredibus et successoribus in ipso monasterio in puram et perpetuam elemosinam, retento tamen et salvo eiusdem conjugibus in bonis predictis eorumque heredibus usufructu, quam diu vixerit predicta Coleta monialis eiusdem monasterii ipsorum conjugam filia super quidem bonis iidem conjuges recognoverunt et confessi sunt coram nobis se assignasse, dedisse et concessisse predicta Coleta eorum filie quamdiu vixerit donatione facta legitime inter vivos ad usum et necessitata ipsum Colete novem libras parisiensis annui redditus volentes et expresse consentientes*, . . . Paris, A. N., LL1595, fols. 64v–66v ff.

98. Records which have survived regarding recruitment of nuns into the thirteenth-century community seem to disproportionately record gifts made for

women of bourgeois families; for example, in 1296 John of Forrenis, who called himself Imperator, citizen of Paris, gave forty *livres* in cash and three arpents of vines to the nuns of Saint-Antoine in order that his daughter Jeanette enter that community: Paris, A. N., S*4386, fol. 52r-v. Similarly in 1261 Peter Coquillarius, citizen of Paris, assigned to Saint-Antoine six *livres* per year in the name of his sister Margaret nun at that house: Paris, A. N., LL1595, fols. 11v–12r.

99. At end of Paris, A. N., LL1595, another list dated *c.* 1380 includes: Suer Johanne de Handone 120 sol.; Suer Johanne la Frisonne 210 sol.; Suer Marguerite de la Donnelle et Suer Jehanne de Hoderne 60 sol. shared; Suer Marie la Coqueterxe 341 sol.; Suer Jehanne de Rueil 100 sol.

100. On the assertion of cistercian practice, see the foundation charter in *Cartulaire de l'abbaye royale du Lieu-Notre-Dame-lez-Romorantin*, ed. Ernest Prat (Romorantin, 1892), no. 33 (1222): *Scientes dilectarum in christo monialium de loco beate Marie prope Remorentinum cum sit novella plantacio redditus tenues et exiles, et ipsas moniales subsidio indigere nos earum inopie consulere cupientes eisdem monialibus Deo et Marie sub regula et habitu cysterciensis ordinis ibidem famulantibus in puram et perpetuam elemosinam dedimus et concessimus. . . .*

101. Paris, A. N., LL1595, fols. 63r ff.

102. Paris, A. N., LL1595, no. 266 (1302), fols. 70r–71r, the rubric reads: *De sex libris parisis super quadam domus sitam in Alis parisius contiguam ex una parte domui Henrici Marescalli et ex altera domui Petri dicti Clerici in censiva Domini Regis quarum sex librarum Soror Agnes de Compans, Soror Milina la Bordone et Soror Juliana de la Roe tenent xl solidos in solidos .. et quilibet pro se que supervixerit; item eodem modo tenent alios quadraginta solidos Soror Agnes la Pidoe, Soror Johanna de Giroles et Soror Genovespha la Pidoe, et alios xl solidos tenent eodam modo ad vitam Soror Marguerite la Petite, Soror Agnes de Sancto Victore et Soror Agnes la Petite.* The contract itself is the purchase in 1302 by Saint-Antoine of an *incrementum census* of six *libri* over a house; that rent was assigned to groups of nuns in the rubric. Other such assignment is found in *ibid.*, fols. 71r–73r (for 1299 and 1301).

103. Paris, A. N., LL1595, nos. 269 and 270 (1301), fols. 73r–75r, is the gift to abbess Gila from her cousin Margaret, Lady of Beaumont-sur-Oise.

104. Jeffrey Hamburger has pointed to the fifteenth-century private ownership by nuns of books, statuettes, and other devotional objects as part of a developing practice of private devotion; private communication, 1994.

105. *Layettes du Trésor des Chartes*, ed. A. Teulet, et al., 5 vols. (Paris, 1896–1909) IV, nos. 4993 and 5267.

106. Paulette l'Hermite-LeClercq, *Le monachisme féminin dans la société de son temps. Le monastère de La Celle (Xie-début du XVIe siècle)* (Paris, 1989) pp. 205–12.

107. The *censier*, Paris, A. N., LL1595, fols. 87r ff., contains no rents in kind comparable to those found in censiers for other cistercian women's cartularies, for example that of the Abbaye-aux-Bois (Chicago, Newberry Library, MS 20.1 which I have discussed in a paper cited in note 37 above); on that abbey; see Brigitte Pipon. 'Un monastère de moniales cisterciennes: L'Abbaye-aux-Bois (1202–1906)', *Cîteaux* 45 (1994) 91–108.

108. Johnson, *Equal*, pp. 173 ff.

109. On Flines, see Erin Jordan's unpublished M.A. thesis at University of Iowa; on the others mentioned, see Berman, *Sisters*, forthcoming.

As Above, So Below
Architecture and Archaeology at Villiers-la-Grange of Pontigny

Terryl N. Kinder

IN 1956 Dom Jean Leclercq published a 'Voyage rétrospectif aux eaux de Vichy et autres lieux' in the *Bulletin de la Société d'Histoire et d'Archéologie de Vichy et des environs*.[1] It is testimony to the extraordinary breadth of Dom Jean's interests that a scholar whose primary area of study was the literary culture of monasticism should also concern himself with archaeology.

It therefore seems fitting that a volume dedicated to his memory would include an article concerning history, archaeology, and water belonging to a great burgundian abbey in the cistercian heartland. Unlike Vichy, however, the fame of this water is entirely local. It was never bottled and sold; indeed, the water itself is not cause for celebrity. It is rather the extraordinary structure built to store it—and the rural context which obliged its creation—which are the object of this study.

Just as it is a delight to the textual scholar to discover an unpublished manuscript, it is a delight to the archaeologist to find and identify material remains of past life inscribed in the landscape. Such is the case at Villiers-la-Grange, a twelfth-century grange of Pontigny, located some 35 km southeast of the abbey.[2] This property is first mentioned in connection with Pontigny in 1144/45, when Bishop Hugues of Auxerre verified that the sons of Landry of Préhy had confirmed a donation made to the monks of Pontigny by their father of all that he owned in the territory of Villiers (*Villariis*).[3] The following year, Anséric de Montréal gave all that he owned in this region—woods, cultivated and uncultivated lands and pasture rights—to Pontigny,[4] a donation which was immediately disputed by the monks of the great benedictine abbey of Saint-Germain d'Auxerre.[5] The next few years were also marked by litigation with the monks of the nearby cistercian abbey of Reigny (filiation of Clairvaux), located only 15 km to the west of Villiers. This dispute required the bishops of Auxerre and of Troyes, plus the abbot of Cîteaux, to come to an agreement over pasturing rights for sheep belonging to the two abbeys, including the penalty which would befall lay brothers who did not obey.[6]

Villiers-la-Grange is not listed in the bulls of protection accorded Pontigny in 1138 and 1142 by Pope Innocent II, although it is named as one of eleven granges belonging to Pontigny in 1156.[7] The surviving documents show the mid-1140's as a time, not only of important donations, but of conflicts of a nature which suggest the importance and prosperity of this settlement. It would thus appear that Villiers became a grange of Pontigny in the mid-1140s,[8] and that not only were the lands already being farmed (there is no mention of clearing new land at this time), but the site may already have been inhabited. Recent excavations have shown that Villiers was a merovingian settlement,[9] and its very name, *Villariae*, hints at gallo-roman origins.[10]

Located near the bottom of a small valley in the rolling burgundian countryside, Villiers seems primarily to have been a sheep farm in the twelfth century; in addition to evidence of the conflict with Reigny Abbey, a donation in 1181/82 specifies the gift of further pasture rights destined for the *oviam et animalium de Vilers*.[11] In 1263, Milon de Noyers confirmed the pasture and passage rights given by his ancestors for the Pontigny cattle (provided the monks pay any damages caused by their animals); in exchange they were to give him a colt each year.[12] But the grange probably had a somewhat diversified economy, as is suggested, for example, by the donation of a vineyard 'in the valley of Villiers' in 1266.[13] In 1374, Lady Marguerite de Vienne, of nearby Isle, declared that her sergeants had 'no right to exact twelve cheeses from the *religieux* who govern the farms of Pontigny abbey located within [her] domain',[14] which gives the reader a taste—if not of local cheese—at least of the petty extortion that the lay brothers had to bear, and hints at the type of troubles to come.

The precise date when this grange ceased to be run by lay brothers and was leased to laymen is of obvious interest for its architectural as well as its economic history. Villiers appears to have passed from direct to indirect management in 1479, when a nineteen-year lease *de la grange de Villiers les Noyers* was accorded to an inhabitant of nearby Massangis. In the ensuing years, other fields and properties were rented out to various individuals. In 1545, five named men (four with the same surname) and 'several others' (not named) rented the *metairie et finage de Villiers la Grange*, judged to be *belle et ample* and consisting of—besides *beaux maisons*—a grange building, orchards, meadow, and garden, all once enclosed within a wall that was by then in ruins, and having outside it *plusieurs bois buissons et plusieurs belle grande piece labourable* [sic].[15] A small farming community thus came to live within the walls at Villiers, and here we learn something further about the drawbacks of the site. Although the Hundred Years' War had perhaps been the cause of the ruined wall mentioned above, Villiers was in any case located on a major road where *gens d'armes* passed. In another document of the same period, the inhabitants of Villiers complained to the abbot that, because of the location of Villiers on this busy (and apparently dangerous) road, many inhabitants had been obliged to abandon the town and seek shelter elsewhere, leaving their property to fall into ruin. They therefore asked for a perpetual lease to Villiers and its lands, which was accorded.[16]

By the late seventeenth century, hard times had fallen on this town (and many others); the high taxes levied by Louis XIV to pay for his nearly continuous wars could not be met by the villagers. In 1692 they requested a reduction in taxes, stating that the population of Villiers was considerably lower than it had been twenty-two years earlier, when taxes had also been much lower. Because of lack of pasture, cattle were insufficiently fed; there were no meadows or vineyards or woods. A population of only seventeen families remained at that time: twelve ploughmen-farmers, three poor women, and two workers.[17] Whether or not their request was granted is not known. The last lease dates from 1789.

This handful of documents opens a few windows into the constitution and evolution of the economy of Villiers-la-Grange, but what about its architecture? This is a region of beautiful stone construction, using the local yellowish stone, *lave calcaire*, which has the disadvantage of freezing and therefore had to be cut and laid in thin layers. The small courses are regular, with larger stones being used for door and window jambs and for quoining; the walls are perfectly plumb, details are finely executed, and as a result even the smallest buildings are a delight.[18] A few still have their roofs of *lave*, made by overlapping slabs of stone in shingle fashion.

At least one building at Villiers-la-Grange dates, by its design and construction, from the twelfth or early thirteenth century.[19] Largely concealed behind modern farm equipment, it is the best-

1. Villiers-la-Grange, lay brothers' building from the northeast

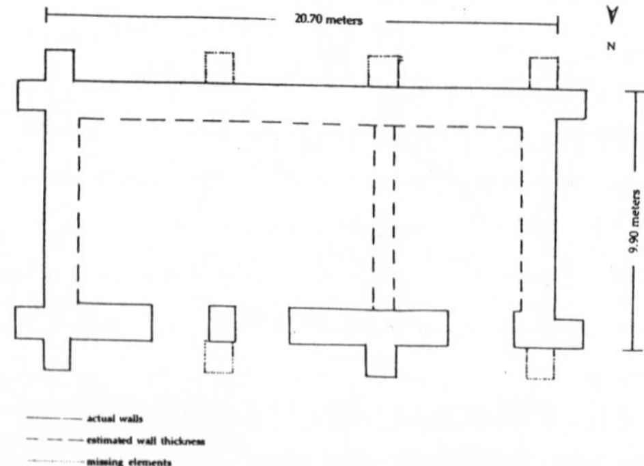

2. Villiers-la-Grange, plan of lay brothers' building

built of all Pontigny's surviving granges and is used today for grain storage (Ill. 1 & 2).[20] Rectangular in shape, two stories in height and measuring 20.7 by 9.9 meters, its volumes and wall openings have been transformed, yet the basic structure and much of the detail are original or can be ascertained from remaining traces. This structure is all the more astonishing in that the walls—inside and out—were made in uncharacteristically (for the region) high stone courses of 12 to 16 cm, with horizontal widths varying from 13 to 50 cm. The corner buttresses are of ashlar block and rival those of any church in beauty and quality of stone-cutting and detail, even down to pairs of small half-round projecting corbels to support the moulding at the top of the buttress (Ill. 3).[21] The east gable wall is slightly over 10 meters in height, pierced by a round-arched window that was framed with large ashlar blocks. There are traces near the top of the gable suggesting that the building may have had a *lave* roof.

The long side of the building faces north and has been modified a great deal. The two large openings at ground level were no doubt added at a later date; a wall buttress between them was sacrificed to make enough space.[22] The upper level once had a series of four small vertical windows; one entire window and traces of three others are visible (Ill. 4). The three that have been enlarged still have lintels in place, each with a (blind) rounded arch over the rectangular window. The presence of one hole in the center underside of the lintel may have been for a rotating shutter that could be opened for ventilation or closed for protection from inclement weather. Another identical blind-arched lintel is still in place on the ground floor, to the east (left) of the wagon entrances, although the opening has been enlarged to create a pedestrian door.

The interior has been separated into two sections, the eastern part now comprising two-thirds of the total volume. This larger eastern portion is currently a single space two stories in height with a modern timber frame supporting a tile roof. Wall thickness along the north side (1.40 meters)—together with the missing wall buttress—could have supported a vault. The interior surface of the north wall seems to curve inward at the top of the second storey, but the interior of the building is presently too encumbered to assess the upper stonework of the other walls,[23] and the cornice has disappeared. One section of a large beam remains inserted into the north wall under the four upper windows, precisely where the wall

3. Villiers-la-Grange, lay brothers' building, east gable

4. Villiers-la-Grange, lay brothers' building, north face (detail)

was reduced back evenly by 20 cm. This would suggest that a plank ceiling once divided the space into upper and lower stories. It is quite possible that the upper storey was originally vaulted, and that the building was radically transformed to serve another purpose by dismantling the vault, eliminating two central buttresses (no longer needed to support the vault) as well as the floor separating the two stories, enlarging windows, and adding two wagon entrances on the north face.

The upper floor of the western third of this building was converted into apartments at an unknown date; corner wall buttresses were eliminated, a back staircase and windows were added,[24] and the lower part was made into a cellar. The entrance to this cellar passes under a large round-arched opening made of large ashlar blocks. While the opening has been modified at least twice, the masonry suggests that this was the original wagon entrance.

If we compare this building to the grange of Reigny Abbey at Oudun (Ill.5), located 3 km to the southwest, the similarities are striking. Oudun's building measures 22 by 10 meters, is two stories in height, has walls made of *lave* with ashlar corner buttresses and voussoirs around windows and doors, and small windows along the upper storey with a blind round-headed arch in the lintel. The interior, while modified, is still spectacular. The ground floor had ten groin-vaulted bays; the transverse arches rest on four central columns with crocket capitals, plus an engaged half-column at each end and graceful corbels on the long walls (Ill. 6). The vault of the upper floor has been dismantled, but the departure of a barrel vault is clearly visible.

The original use for either of these buildings remains a mystery. One may speculate that the upper portion was a dormitory for the lay brothers, while the ground floor served various utilitarian or domestic functions. There would have needed to be a kitchen; if cheeses were extorted from the lay brothers at Villiers, they were presumably made on the premises, but we do not know what other buildings may also have served these purposes. It has been argued that elegantly constructed buildings with fine detail cannot have been used for such mundane activities, but this notion is not borne out by recent research into industrial buildings—which have carved capitals, corbels, and groined or ribbed vaults just as do churches or chapter rooms—or drains, which frequently used excellent ashlar in their construction. Until further evidence is produced, the general designation of 'lay brothers' building' is the least presumptive, and leaves the greatest latitude for imaginative research.

Whatever its original destination, the Villiers building was described as a *maison* in 1729, and it was inhabited by Jean Boucherat,

5. Oudun, lay brothers' building, west face

6. Oudun, lay brothers' building, interior

a ploughman. A plan of that date (Ill. 7) shows it as part of a group of three or four buildings surrounded by a wall which separated it from another cluster of houses in the center of town.[25] A small gatehouse marked the entrance to this sub-section of the village; neither gatehouse nor traces of the wall or towers exist today. At this time there were sixteen houses in the town, plus a barn, church

7. Villiers-la-Grange, plan of the village in 1729 (Arch. dép. Yonne, H.1555). The lay brothers' building is designated as V., located at the top just below the two towers.

and presbytery, and the surrounding wall—apparently rebuilt since 1545—had six round towers along its exterior face. The designation of the twelfth-century lay brothers' building as a house in 1729 (particularly as a different building is described as a barn) is a strong argument for its original function as a dwelling, with post-1729 transformation into a barn.

Lay brothers were to return to their abbey for Mass on Sundays and feast days, but many granges had a chapel for daily prayers. When Villiers was leased in 1479, the village which then arose would have needed a church. Interestingly enough, the modest church of modern-day Villiers has two distinct parts. The aisleless nave, measuring approximately 4.5 meters in width by 7.3 m in length, is covered with a pointed barrel vault and supported by exterior wall buttresses. The side walls are thick[26] with only one window, to the south; otherwise it is without architectural decoration of even the most rudimentary sort, and entirely whitewashed on the inside. A square belltower to the north is contiguous with the façade.

8. Villiers-la-Grange, church

9. Villiers-la-Grange, church, interior of nave looking east

The apse, on the other hand, is nearly square (5.87 x 6.16 meters interior dimensions), with angled corner buttresses to support the ribbed vault. A large window pierces the east wall behind the altar, while a smaller one allows light through the south wall. Ribs and window mouldings have a late medieval concave profile with disappearing shafts and no capitals. The tracery of the eastern window is also fifteenth or sixteenth century in design and in profile, although the glass—containing images of Saint Edmund and Saint Joan of Arc—must date after 1920, when the latter was canonised. Judging from the molding around its base, the octagonal baptismal font—now located by the entrance door—was also made in the late medieval period. A room, probably to serve as a sacristy, was added at a still later date against the south wall of this apse.

It is difficult to date small rural churches. The tie with Pontigny is clear in that the chapel was dedicated to Saint Edmund (of Abiugdon) who died in 1240, was canonised in 1246, and is buried at Pontigny.[27] Parat thought the entire church had been constructed after the Hundred Years' War,[28] but it is difficult to imagine how the inhabitants of Villiers—who had suffered significantly in the hands of the English—would erect a chapel and dedicate it to Saint Edmund, Archbishop of Canterbury. It seems more likely that at least part of the chapel dates from the time when the lay brothers ran the grange and when a relic for the altar would have been easily obtainable from the abbey church.

Analysis of the form and fabric of this chapel underline this possibility. The simplicity of the nave—its one unadorned window in the south wall, barrel vault, simple and heavy construction—leads the viewer at first glance to suggest a twelfth or thirteenth century date, with a reconstruction of the apse in the later medieval period. Yet there are troublesome details which must also be taken into account. The form of the three wall buttresses of the nave (two along the south wall, one on the north) with squared setbacks instead of drip mouldings, and the surface of the façade, western door and *campanile* suggest major rebuilding: stones are regular, mortar is hard and has not been re-pointed, tooling marks are modern, door and bell-tower openings do not have the ashlar voussoirs seen elsewhere. And rebuilding there was. A sign on the interior over the western door reads:

> Le 30 juin 1830 les eaux des cieux
> submergerent cette eglise : il y avoit
> de leau de dix pieds d'hauteur. Elle a ete
> retablie par la munificence de Louis XVIII, et de
> son august famille.

Ten feet of water would certainly have submerged the church, which is considerably downslope from the lay brothers' building to the west; the nave is a further two steps (36 cm) below ground level. The vault crest is only five meters above the floor of the church, nearly on a level with the floor of the lay brothers' building. Of the three wall buttresses, the bottom of at least one has a *lave* base, albeit nearly invisible under the mortar covering, as is the lower portion of the *campanile*; these may date from the original construction.

Taking all these anomalies into consideration, the church at Villiers appears to be an architectural echo of the history of this grange: an unadorned barrel-vaulted prayer house with bell-tower for the lay brothers, somewhat rebuilt after the 1830 flood but following the original form, with a late medieval cross-ribbed apse added to serve the secular community after 1479. Villiers was a dependency of the parish of Cours, and in 1511–1512—when the town had one hundred twenty-five inhabitants—there had been a dispute with the curé of Cours who apparently served this lay community. The bailiff of Noyers ruled in favor of the monks of Pontigny, however, who were to 'retain possession of this chapel'.[29] Even such a tiny building has survived a multitude of architectural and ecclesiastical complexities.

The term 'grange' (*grangia*) when used to describe a cistercian property may refer to one of two things, either a barn, or the ensemble of buildings and fields which make up the agricultural establishment. If we take the second meaning, the surrounding field system at Villiers-la-Grange show fascinating traces of monastic field management.

The irregularly-shaped fields lie outside the precinct wall, abutting land which belonged to neighboring lords. To avoid property conflicts, fields had to be measured and boundaries marked. The departmental archives of the Yonne now possess an extraordinary map of 1782—which once belonged to the Pontigny archives (Ill. 10)—along with a description of the process of surveying and placing boundary stones.[30] Each one was marked with a crosier between **S** and **E** (for Saint Edmund of Pontigny) on one face, and the coat-of-arms of the neighbor on the other. The document notes that they are replacing earlier markers; this process had to be renewed as

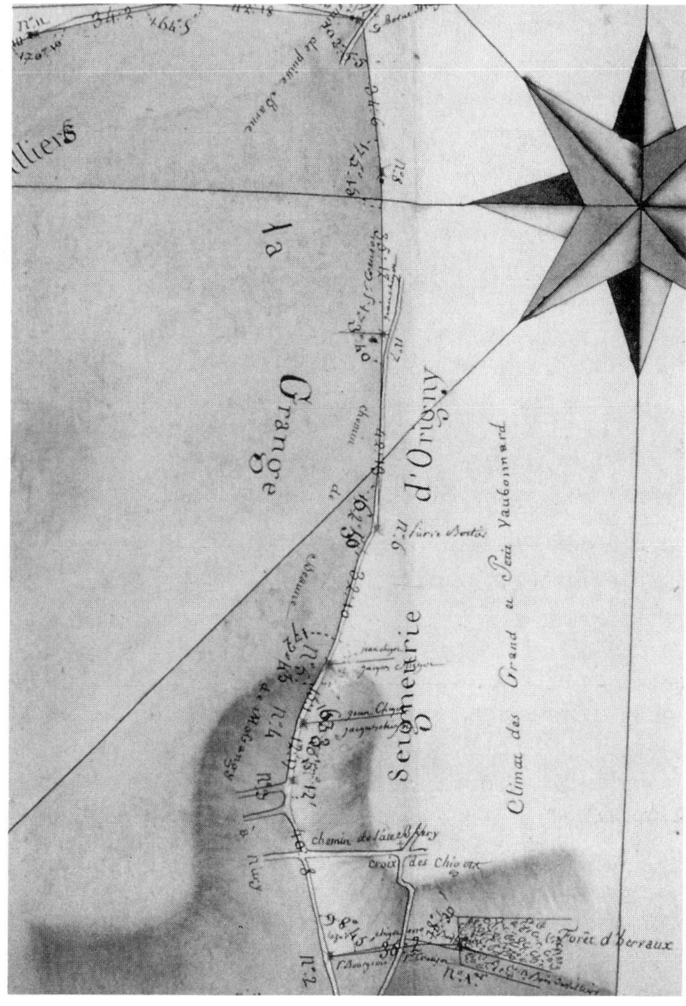

10. Villiers-la-Grange, map of field markers replaced in 1729 (Arch. dép. Yonne, H.1554)

the stones became worn and illegible, and probably refers back to medieval practice.

In addition to the beauty of the carefully engraved initials on each stone block, three elements make these property markers interesting and worthy of study. In every case but one, they prefigure the field limits of today, which shows to what extent civil boundaries simply

11. Villiers-la-Grange, property marker n° 9 in foreground, n° 10 in the distance behind it.

took over monastic property lines at the Revolution, becoming communal and cantonal limits.[31] As a result, the cistercian past is still 'registered' in the land. Secondly, it appears that while these stones frequently marked corners of fields, they were placed whenever possible on salient landscape features, probably so they could be better seen during plowing or when moving herds of animals (Ill. 11). A third element is the extraordinary survival of a map, accompanied by a description of the process of marking the boundaries and placing the stones. In addition to their historic value, these documents allow us to interpret traces in the landscape today which would otherwise be uninteresting or unintelligible.

The map was made in 1782 by a professional surveyor employing trigonometry and direct measurement; he recorded all the angles in relation to the markers, as well as the field names (Ill. 10).[32] The new stone markers are numbered from 1 to 15, and lines engraved on top of the stone indicate the boundary lines on which the markers stand. Four of the original fifteen are still in place and have legible numbers, although the crosier and initials must be seen in raking light to be deciphered.

In studying the plan and the description together with the land and the remaining stones, it is possible to go still further. The number and initials on another of the markers are no longer visible, and the stone is broken in two at ground level, the top now simply posed on the buried half. Yet the stone itself is triangular; and it is located on precisely the spot of a marker, formerly number 15, described as triangular in the accompanying text. Further along is a pile of broken stones, but when the angle and the distance from the previous markers is verified, the location corresponds on the plan to marker number 13 in the series.[33]

Needless to say, these markers are disappearing and are not now replaced. These ephemeral traces are vanishing reminders of how the monastic habitation has left its imprint in the land—in the markers, in their location, and ultimately in the way the fields were constituted centuries earlier.

Having discussed places for living, for work and for worship, and some details of field management at Villiers-la-Grange, we turn to still one more important element without which the lay brothers could not have lived. This brings us back to the inspiration for this article. A major drawback to this site is its location in a shallow valley without a source of potable water. Dramatic measures had to be taken to ensure a sufficient water supply, and so the brothers appealed to that abundant burgundian resource, rainwater.

Between the barn and the church is a stone lip 95 cm wide and projecting 68 cm above the ground, its modest appearance hardly preparing the casual observer for the architectural splendour below.[34] Less than one meter below ground level is the crest of a vaulted cistern measuring 8 by 16.12 meters and 4.15 meters in depth, with a capacity of some 525 cubic meters of water (Ills. 12–16). It consists of two parallel naves, each covered with a barrel vault, and joined over a central arcade containing ten arches which rest on nine 'capitals'; these in turn are supported by chamfered rectangular shafts on pyramidal bases.[35] The arcade comes to rest at the end walls on simple curved corbels, such as one typically finds in a cistercian church and other claustral buildings (Ill. 16). Arcade, shafts and corbels are made of ashlar; the arcade is particularly noteworthy because of the very fine joints. The vault was constructed of smaller cut stones; it and the exterior walls are now covered with pitch. The stone lip on the surface provides the only access to the cistern; the underside is worn in grooves by ropes used to lower buckets. There

12. Villiers-la-Grange, cistern, north nave looking west (overflow visible in vault crest)

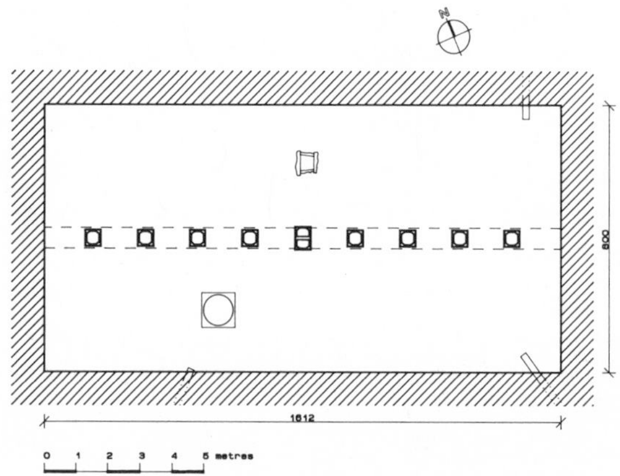

13. Villiers-la-Grange, plan of the cistern (drawing by Alain Creac'h)

is a stone floor throughout; Blin described a large square stone with a slightly concave surface directly underneath this orifice.[36]

Water enters the cistern today via three stone channels, two in the south wall, one in the north (see plan, ill. 13).[37] These ducts likely brought rainwater from the roofs of neighboring houses. To avoid an explosion of the vault in the north nave in case of flooding, an overflow was built into the crest; stones are posed—but not sealed—over a trapezoidal armature, and would be displaced by water pressure below.

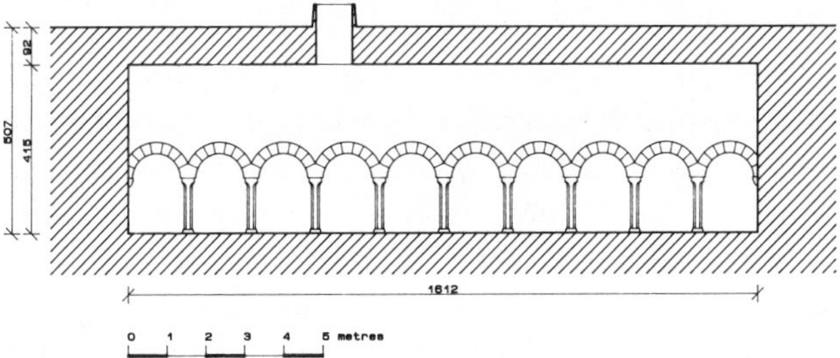

14. Villiers-la-Grange, cistern, longitudinal section (Alain Creac'h)

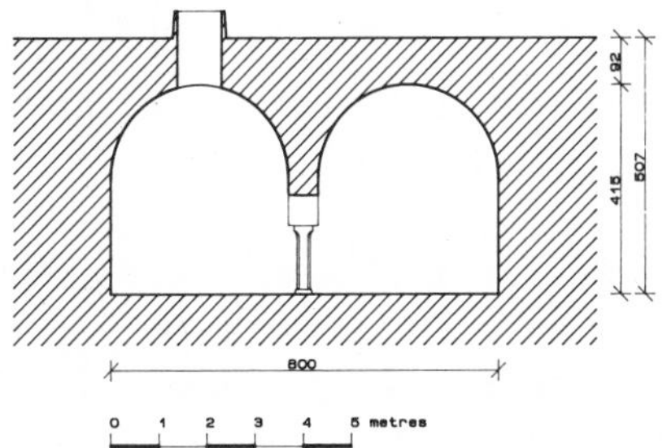

15. Villiers-la-Grange, cistern, transverse section (Alain Creac'h)

16. Villiers-la-Grange, cistern, detail of arcade and corbel

There is no known date for construction of this cistern; neither its building nor its upkeep are mentioned in any text. It is, however, inconceivable that lay brothers could have lived at Villiers without a water supply, and this method is not uncommon for collecting excess water in enclosed areas, or at hilltop sites. An excellent example is the tiny thirteenth-century burgundian priory of Vausse, where water is collected in stone gutters from the cloister roofs and channeled through hollow columns into a cistern in the cloister. Vézelay, located on a hill, also collected roof water in a magnificent two-nave cistern in the cloister next to the church which dates to the twelfth century. It measures 16.85 by 6.30 meters, with the two barrel vaults resting on nine central columns.[38] The Knights Hospitalers of Pontaubert also had a long barrel-vaulted cistern. By resemblance in conception and in function to these neighboring examples, particularly that at Vézelay, as well as by the economy of the design, excellent quality of the construction and form of the capitals and corbels, it would appear that Pontigny was responsible for construction of this cistern in the twelfth century.[39]

All of the structures discussed in this brief summary—lay brothers' building, chapel, houses, field markers and cistern—were purely utilitarian in function. They were designed and made during monastic habitation, taken over by laymen when the abbey could no longer provide the personnel to run them, sold at the Revolution, and (some are) still in use today.

Although of diverse functions, these structures are linked by the care with which they were made, quality of design and materials, and the resulting beauty, even though none of them was created with the primary intention of providing an aesthetically pleasing result. Today—when drinking water is piped from another town, fields have been grouped and are plowed as one, most of the houses are vacant, and a former dwelling narrowly survives as a barn—the beauty of proportions, of construction, of materials continue nevertheless to inform us of the monastic tradition that created them.

NOTES

1. Vol. 56, pp. 171–190.

2. *Département* of the Yonne, canton of Noyers, commune of Grimault. This grange, or portions of it, have been published by three authors: Ernest Blin, 'La citerne de Villiers-la-Grange', *Bulletin de la Société des Sciences historiques et naturelles de l'Yonne*, v. 61 (1907) 213–216; Abbé A. Parat, 'Villiers-la-Grange.

Une exploitation monastique modèle', *Bulletin de la Société des sciences historiques et naturelles de l'Yonne*, v. 72 (1918) 117–13; Jean-Baptiste Auberger ('Une grange cistercienne à Villiers-la-Grange,' *Le Paissiau*, n° 3 (1987) 13–25 and n° 4 (1987) 3–8). The present study draws on these previous works only where cited, and includes newly measured and drawn plans, descriptions and interpretations of the buildings discussed.

3. Arch. dép. Yonne, H.1554, published by Martine Garrigues, *Le cartulaire de l'abbaye de Pontigny* (Paris, 1981) 116–117, n° 43. This grange is not to be confused with lands owned and tithes received by Pontigny at Villiers-Vineux, on the Armançon River 14 km northwest of Tonnerre, 32 km to the north of the Villiers under discussion here.

4. Garrigues, *Le cartulaire*, 115–116, n° 42.

5. The dispute was resolved when both parties agreed that Pontigny would pay three *sous provinois* per year to the abbey of Saint-Germain (Garrigues, *Le cartulaire*, 117, n° 44), which suggests that the latter had some previous dominion over this land.

6. Garrigues, *Le cartulaire*, 118, n° 45. The Reigny sheep were from their grange at Oudun, three kilometers southwest of Villiers. The punishment dictated that a transgressing Pontigny lay brother from Villiers would have to spend three days at Oudun, sleeping on the floor and receiving only one bowl of soup per day; a transgressing Reigny lay brother from Oudun would receive the same treatment at the Villiers. How well this worked is hard to know; in 1209 Reigny complained that the Villiers shepherds crossed the boundaries established in the earlier agreement. In the fourteenth century there were further disaccords between the two abbeys concerning tithes and sheep; complaints from both sides were recorded on two parchment rolls, each several meters in length (Arch. dép. Yonne, H.1554).

7. Bull of confirmation from Pope Hadrian IV, published by Max Quantin, *Cartulaire général de l'Yonne*, I (Auxerre, 1854) 549–550, n° 384.

8. Parat (p. 120) believed that the 1263 document, in which Miles V of Noyers confirms donation of the grange of Villiers to Pontigny by his ancestor of the same name, referred to Milon III, and that this (original) donation—for which no document survives—was therefore made in 1120. Missing documents are always problematic, but had such an important donation been made at that early date, by such an important man, it would surely have been included into the cartulary, and the grange cited in an earlier papal bull of protection. A register made in 1721 (Arch. dép. Yonne, H.1399), into which titles to abbey properties were copied, contains a section concerning Villiers that begins with the 1144/45 confirmation (p. 751–770). While incomplete insofar as post-medieval documents (principally leases) are concerned, this register nevertheless contains all the early titles to Villiers that are now to be found in H.1554 of the departmental archives.

9. Robert Biton excavated part of what he believed to be a merovingian cemetery in a field to the west just outside the present village, where he identified at least portions of seventeen skeletons ('Les cimetières mérovingiens de Villiers-la-Grange', *Bulletin annuel de la Société et d'Histoire du Tonnerois*, n° 41 (1988) 4–9). He also mentions another merovingian cemetery to the east, much disturbed by plowing, but where surface prospecting has recovered human bones and fragments of sarcophagi. A sarcophagus lid, decorated with alternating oblique bands of a type common in this region, was recovered and deposed in the Musée de l'Avallonais in Avallon.

10. Place names evoking *villa*, a roman country dwelling, usually having farm buildings and living quarters around a courtyard, suggest gallo-roman origins. See Max Quantin, *Dictionnaire topographique du département de l'Yonne* (Paris, 1862) viii, xviii. The roman road from Auxerre to Montbard passed only six kms to the north, between Aigremont and Noyers. See Victor Petit, *Itinéraire des voies gallo-romaines qui traversent le département de l'Yonne* (Paris, 1851) 50.

11. Garrigues, *Le cartulaire*, 118 & 120, n. 46.

12. Arch. dép. Yonne, H.1554. This is an example of how seeming 'donations' were, in reality, exchanges. In this case, however, the document clearly states that Milon's descendants would not inherit the right to a yearly colt, although they would inherit the obligation to allow animal passage.

13. Arch. dép. Yonne, H.1554.

14. Arch. dép. Yonne, H.1554.

15. Arch. dép. Yonne, H.1554.

16. Arch. dép. Yonne, H.1554. For an analysis of these documents, see Parat, 128–130.

17. Arch. dép. Yonne, H.1554. Parat, 129–130.

18. This tradition of construction in local stone was practiced in the region into the twentieth century.

19. Rural buildings are very difficult to date, and it is not possible to know at what point the abbot would decide to build. Here the proportions of the building, form of the wall buttresses, ashlar voussoirs and wall thickness point to a twelfth or thirteenth-century date.

20. It is now the property of M. Joseph Poitou, for whose assistance in the study of several aspects of Villiers I am deeply grateful. Attention was first brought to this building by Parat, and it was also discussed by Auberger (see note 2).

21. Blocks in the buttresses are set 3-1-3, alternating between a full (buttress) width of 114 cm (× 33 × 36) and three blocks set short side out. Frost has taken its toll; the large blocks in the lower courses are separating into smaller segments.

22. The thin voussoirs making up the arches are unlike those anywhere else in the building, where fine ashlar blocks define the openings. The two upper windows were perhaps enlarged when these wagon entrances were created.

23. Vice massive grain bins fill the building up to the roof level; the only visible area is a small margin between the bins and the inner face of the north wall.

24. It is impossible to know if these changes were effected all at once, or in increments. The windows inserted in the upper story on the south (back) side have a concave molding late medieval date. It is worth noting that Parat's 1918 plan of this building shows only two missing buttresses; three more have been eliminated since his article was published.

25. Arch dép. Yonne, H.1555. This plan is somewhat difficult to decipher because of its deteriorating condition and its small size (with a tiny representation of the village in the midst of a large plan of the fields).

26. Façade 70 cm; north and south walls (weight-bearers for the barrel vault) are 95 cm.

27. From that time on, Pontigny was called *Notre-Dame et Saint Edme de Pontigny*, in honour of this archbishop of Canterbury. The name of Edmund or Edme (Edmée for women) became popular in this region in subsequent centuries.

28. 'Après la guerre, qui se termina en 1453, une chapelle, qui porte sa date dans la fenêtre de l'autel, du style du XVe siècle, s'éleva . . .' (p. 127).

29. Arch. dép. Yonne, H.1554.

30. *Ibid.* I published this map with a brief mention of the corresponding property markers in an article on monument protection and conservation, 'Pontigny et ses domaines: Richesse et précarité d'un patrimoine agricole' in the acts of the 1993 colloquium *L'Espace cistercien* (Paris, 1994) 441–450.

31. When this is not the case, it can almost always be traced to the *remembrement* of lands in the 1960s.

32. Arch. dép. Yonne, H. 1554. The field names are the same today.

33. In this case the base of the marker was well planted in the ground; the upper part was slightly tapered and is where the break occurred. Fragments of the rest of the marker are lying on the ground around it.

34. I would like to thank Professor David N. Bell for his varied and indispensable assistance in studying this cistern and other aspects of Villiers. A popular version of this venture in nautical archaeology first appeared as a joint article '*De profundis*: une descente archéologique dans la citerne de Villiers-la-Grange' in the *Bulletin des Amis de Pontigny*, v. 3 (1992) 25–32.

35. This cistern has long been the object of local interest. Two brief articles with spectacular photographs have appeared in the local newspaper, the *Yonne Republicaine* (29 December 1988, p. 10) and the cover of the weekend edition, *Yonne Magazine* (18–21 January 1989). The cistern was first published by Ernest Blin in 1907 ('La citerne de Villiers-la-Grange', [note 2]. He visited the cistern when it was being cleaned, and made the plan which he published in this article. The plan presented here is, however, a newly measured one, established in 1992 (Ill. 13), and it differs slightly from Blin's plan. I have used his description only for the bases of the shafts and the floor, as our inspection of the cistern took place from inflatable boats when there were approximately 1.4 m of mud under 40 cm of water.

36. p. 215.

37. The one closest to the entrance opening appears to be modern. In Blin's time, the cistern was used uniquely as a repository for surface water from the streets and courtyards of the village, and therefore had to be cleaned about every ten years, at which time 100 cubic meters of stones and mud were evacuated (p. 214). We studied the structure extensively in July 1991 on a day when it was raining consistently; all three ducts were functioning.

38. Its collectors were dismantled when Vézelay was restored in the nineteenth century, but village lore maintains that gutters, similar to those still in operation at Vausse, collected roof water and channeled it into the cistern.

39. Abbé Parat (p. 124–125) discussed an archaeological curiosity at Villiers which no longer exists, but which was perhaps linked to the cistern or to another type of water collection at this site. Already in ruined condition in his time, this underground structure, called a *citerneau*, was located in the fields 80 meters south of the village and consisted of a small rectangular *caveau* measuring 3.55 by 1 meter, and 55 cm in height. Built partly on bedrock and partly on loose soil, it was covered with 30 cm of earth. The vertical walls, 2.40 m in height, were made of large curved clay tiles piled one on top of another and lightly cemented together. To hold these clay-tile 'walls', miniature square pillars 15 cm wide were placed at 15 cm intervals the length of the long walls. The bedrock floor was covered with a thin layer of clay containing charcoal bits, which 'archaeologists from Paris' believed were filters for rainwater destined for cisterns, and gallo-roman in origin.

A Sixteenth Century Heraldic Stained Glass Panel from La Maigrauge

Helen Zakin

AT THE KALAMAZOO conferences Dom Jean Leclercq was always calm and serious, although one had the sense that there was a wonderful sense of humor lurking not far below the surface. His presence lent significance to the scholarly enterprise, and his commentaries on Saint Bernard influenced my work as well as that of many others. In a recent book, he wrote: 'Bernard's was the literature of a theologian. As such, he esteemed woman as the creature and image of God as highly as man.'[1]

In that spirit, it is appropriate to discuss here a stained glass window that was made for La Maigrauge, a swiss cistercian house of nuns. It incorporates the shield of Clairvaux; and images of Saint Bernard and Saint Benedict appear at the sides of the panel.[2] The present essay concerns the Maigrauge glass and the abbey, and the function of the heraldic stained glass panels in Switzerland in the sixteenth century.

The Maigrauge panel (figure 1; 31.6 x 22.7 cm) is now in the Cleveland Museum of Art.[3] The shield of arms in the center is blazoned as: *sable à la bande échiquetée de gueules et d'argent*. The inscription along the bottom of the panel reads: *des Wirdige gotzhus orde s bernhartz in der magere ouw zu friburg 1547*. In the spandrels above there are two putti blowing horns. The inscription at the top

Figure 1. La Maigrauge stained glass panel with the shield of Clairvaux, 1547; Cleveland Museum of Art, 54.384, J.H. Wade Fund.

and the arch itself are modern replacements. The rest of the panel is original.

1. Technique

This panel was painted with a vitreous enamel that had a relatively low melting point, and was baked onto the glass. The enamel was usually applied on the inner side of the glass, the side that one sees on the inside of the window. In this case, enamel was also applied on the outer side of the pieces that constitute the standing saints and the putti. In fact, the artist produced the gray of Saint Benedict's habit, on the left, by back painting. The painter also used silver stain: a colloidal suspension of silver, likewise fired onto the glass. Silver stain yielded yellow areas on the white glass.

Abrasion of red flashed glass produced the red and white checker pattern on the diagonal stripe (the bend) of the shield. As a rule, red glass was flashed: a layer of white glass was coated with a layer of red, because the pure red glass was too dark to be translucent. Glaziers discovered that they could scratch away bits of the red to yield both white and red on the same piece of glass. This technique was especially popular for making heraldic shields.

2. Iconography

Although the two standing saints were previously identified as Bernard and Malachy,[4] it is more likely that they are Bernard and Benedict. Bernard, on the left in the Cleveland panel, wears white, and Benedict, on the right, wears gray. Bernard and Benedict are depicted together more often than are Bernard and Malachy.[5]

Swiss works of art that show Bernard and Benedict include, among others, the stained glass windows dated about 1452 from la Fille Dieu, a cistercian nunnery near Fribourg. Here a nimbed Benedict wears a gray habit and carries a crosier with *panisellus*, as in the Cleveland panel. Bernard, also nimbed, wears a white habit and carries the same objects.[6] Saints Bernard and Benedict are also shown in stained glass in the abbey church (ca. 1330–1340) at Hauterive, Maigrauge's father immediate.[7]

In panels where he is clearly represented, Malachy's attributes correspond to his position as archbishop of Armagh. He wears a mitre and a cope, and carries a crosier with a cross at the top. He is shown in this way on the late fifteenth century panel painting that was formerly part of an altarpiece at Clairvaux, and is now in the Musée de Dijon. On another panel from the same altarpiece, Bernard is represented with the attributes of a cistercian abbot: tonsure, white habit, and crosier with a crook at the top.[8]

Malachy is depicted with the attributes of an archbishop in several other paintings. He wears a mitre and cope with morse in a painting from the abbey of Ossegg. Here he stands on the right; Bernard is on the left. Both are identified by inscription. Saint Andrew appears in the center.[9]

An inscription on a panel from the abbey of Lichtenthal (Baden-Würtemberg), dated 1534, identifies Malachy, as does the cross

Figure 2. La Maigrauge, near Fribourg, Switzerland (photo: author).

crosier and mitre.[10] In addition, the irish saint appears on the right wing of a triptych, dated 1533, from the flemish cistercian nunnery of Flines. Jean Bellegambe painted the latter, now in the Metropolitan Museum of Art.[11]

3. Architecture

Built on the east bank of the Sarine river, the abbey of La Maigrauge (figure 2) is a short distance from the center of Fribourg.[12] La Maigrauge was founded in 1255, and became cistercian in 1262 as a daughter of Hauterive.[13] The monastery was built between 1261 and 1284.[14]

The design of the abbey church was derived from that of Hauterive, where the first stage of construction took place between 1150 and 1160.[15] In addition, the designs of the present north portal capitals (the former west portal capitals), were influenced by those of the Hauterive west portal capitals, carved about 1250.[16]

La Maigrauge was rebuilt about 1350. At that time the nave was shortened by two bays, and the nave walls were heightened and covered with rib vaults. The west facade was reconstructed, and the west portal capitals were moved to the north side of the church.[17]

Some of the present cloistral buildings were erected in the last third of the seventeenth century, after a fire in 1660.[18]

4. Swiss heraldic stained glass panels

In Switzerland, small scale heraldic panels were popular from the late fifteenth through the seventeenth centuries. They were set into 'bull's eye' windows made of round pieces of clear white glass. Abbeys, guilds, cities, and cantons commissioned these heraldic panels to be given as gifts when new buildings were constructed. Installations of such presentation panels are still found in the cloisters of the abbeys of Wettingen (Cistercian)[19] and Muri (Benedictine),[20] and in the club house of the Basel shooting society.[21]

Heraldic panels were also commissioned as wedding gifts. The family shields of the bride and groom were shown either on the same panel or on two contiguous panels. Often religious or secular scenes, depictions of saints, and cityscapes were included in addition to the shields of armorial bearings.[22]

5. The function of the La Maigrauge panel

The La Maigrauge panel in Cleveland shows the shield of Clairvaux, which was used by houses in this filiation, such as La Maigrauge. The Clairvaux arms appear on the shield of Hauterive, a daughter of Clairvaux, impaled there with those of Hauterive's founder, Guillaume de Glâne.[23] The painted shield of an abbot of Hauterive, Antoine Gribolet, turns up on the vault of the church.[24] It contains Clairvaux in the second and third quarters.[25]

During the following centuries the shield on the Cleveland panel was used at La Maigrauge with certain variants. Shields painted above the granary and almonry doors show the arms of Abbess Anne Techterman (1607–1654) and those of Clairvaux.[26] In the eighteenth century the abbey began to use the arms of Kibourg quartered with those of Clairvaux.[27]

I suggest that La Maigrauge stained glass panel now in Cleveland panel was made to be installed in a different abbey. Another such presentation panel showing one angel carrying the Maigrauge

Figure 3. La Maigrauge stained glass panel with the shield of Clairvaux, 1536; Romont, Musée Suisse du Vitrail (photo: Swiss National Museum, Zürich, neg. nr. 6386)

shield, dated 1536, is attributed to Hans Funk (figure 3).[28] It is likely that both were commissioned for and given to other institutions, either religious or secular, that requested heraldic windows from the Maigrauge nuns.

NOTES

1. Jean Leclercq, *Women and Saint Bernard of Clairvaux*, Cistercian Studies Series, 104 (Kalamazoo, Mich.: Cistercian Publications, 1989) p. 158.

2. An earlier version of this paper was read at the 25th International Congress on Medieval Studies, Western Michigan University, Kalamazoo, Michigan in May, 1990, at a session honoring Saint Bernard. I thank Professor Meredith Lillich, Syracuse University, who chaired the session and excited my interest in heraldry as well as things Cistercian. I also thank Soeur Marie-Bernard Winklhofer, abbaye de la Maigrauge, and Stefan Trümpler, Centre suisse de recherche et d'information sur le vitrail.

3. The Cleveland Museum purchased it in 1964 ('Stained Glass before 1700 in American Collections: Midwestern and Western States (Corpus Vitrearum Checklist III),' *Studies in the History of Art* 28 (1989) p. 211).

It appears in a late nineteenth century auction catalogue of a private collection: J. Rudolf Rahn, 'Die schweizerischen Glasgemälde in der Vincent'schen Sammlung in Constanz,' *Mittheilungen der antiquarischen Gesellschaft in Zürich*, 22 (1890) p. 192 (14), Nr. 46. There were two other editions of this catalogue with the same text: J. Rudolf Rahn, *Catalog der Reichhaltigen Glasgemälde und Kunst-Sammlung der Herren C. and P. N. Vincent* [exhibit catalogue, Constanz, Capitelsaal, July, 1890] Constance: C. & P. N. Vincent, 1890, pp. 5–6, Nr. 41; and J. Rudolf Rahn, *Katalog des Reichhaltigen Kunstsammlung der Herren C. and P.N. Vincent in Konstanz am Bodensee* [sale catalogue, Contstance, J. M. Heberle, Sept. 10–11, 1891] Cologne: M. Du Mont-Schauberg, 1891, pp. 5–6, Nr. 41.

4. 'Stained Glass before 1700 in American Collections,' p. 211.

5. For a discussion of the iconography of Saint Bernard and examples of works of art that depict him with Saint Benedict, see Arno Paffrath with P. Gabriel Hammer, *Die Darstellung des Heiligen in der bildenden Kunst.* Vol. II of *Bernhard von Clairvaux* (Bergisch Gladbach: Heider, 1990) esp. pp. 43, 55–57, 86, 101–102, 118, 130, 142, 144, 205, and note 410; and also Pieter Batselier *et al.*, *Saint Benedict: Father of Western Civilization* (New York: Alpine, 1981), p. 72, fig. 39, and p. 119, fig. 83.

6. Bernhard Anderes, *Die spätgotische Glasmalerei in Freiburg i. Ü.* (Freiburg: Paulusdruckerei, 1963), pp. 34–36, figs. 13–15.

7. Ellen J. Beer, *Die Glasmalereien der Schweiz vom 12. bis zum Beginn des 14. Jahrhunderts.* Corpus Vitrearum Medii Aevi: Schweiz, III (Basel Birkhäuser, 1956) pp. 80, 82, 92, 93 and figs. 68–70.

8. For an illustration of the Malachy panel, see: Angelo Maria Raggi, 'Iconografia [Malachia di Armagh],' *Bibliotheca Sanctorum* (Rome: Pontificia Università Lateranense, 1967) 8 cols. 581–582. For an illustration of the Bernard panel, see: *Saint Bernard et l'art des Cisterciens* (Dijon: Musée de Dijon, 1953, p. 55, no. 139–140 and pl. XIV.

9. P. Tiburtius Hümpfner, *Ikonographia S. Bernardi: Abbatis Claravallensis* (Augsburg: Benna Filser, 1927), I: 13.

10. *Die Zisterzienser: Ordensleben zwischen Ideal und Wirklichkeit* (Cologne: Rheinland, 1981), pp. 618–619, Kat. Nr. H 8.

11. Illustrated in: *New Catholic Encyclopedia* (New York: McGraw Hill, 1967) vol. IX, 101. For an illustration and discussion of a fragmentary sixteenth century stained glass panel showing the death of St. Malachy, as well as additional bibliography regarding this saint, see: Arno Paffrath, *Bernhard von Clairvaux 2: Die Darstellung des Heiligen in der bildenden Kunst* (Bergisch Gladbach: Heider, 1990), p. 111, no. 62 and p. 205, notes 413–419.

12. The area is bi-lingual, but the monastery is usually known by the French name. The German name is Magerau.

13. Patrick Braun, 'La Maigrauge (Magerau),' in *Die Zisterzienser und Zisterzienserinnen, die Reformierten Bernhardinerinnen, die Trappisten and Trappistinnen und die Wilhelmiten in der Schweiz.* ed. Cécile Sommer-Ramer and Patrick Braun, Abteilung III, Band III, Zweiter Teil of *Helvetia Sacra: Die Orden mit Benediktinerregel* (Bern: Francke, 1982) pp. 798–799.

14. Marcel Strub, *La ville de Fribourg*, Les monuments d'art et d'histoire du canton de Fribourg, 2 (Basel: Birkhäuser, 1956) 317–318, note 9.

15. Catherine Waeber-Antiglio, *Hauterive: La construction d'une abbaye cistercienne au moyen âge*, Fribourg: Éditions Universitaires, 1976) 30, 63–64.
16. Waeber-Antiglio, *Hauterive*, 108–109, fig. 72–73 and 76-77.
17. Strub, *La ville de Fribourg*, 318–319.
18. Strub, *La ville de Fribourg*, 320–321.
19. Bernhard Anderes and Peter Hoegger, *Die Glasgemälde im Kloster Wettingen* (Baden: Baden-Verlag, 1988).
20. Bernhard Anderes, *Glasmalerei im Kreuzgang Muri: Kabinettscheiben der Renaissance* (Bern: Verlag Bern, 1974).
21. Barbara Giesicke, *Glasmalereien des 16. und 17 Jahrhunderts im Schützenhaus zu Basel* (Basel: Wiese, 1991).
22. For more information about the practice of commissioning gift panels, see Elisabeth Landolt, 'Von Scheibenrisse, Kabinettscheibe, und ihre Auftraggebern,' in *Spätrenaissance am Oberrhein: Tobias Stimmer 1539–1584* (exhibit catalogue) (Basel: Kunstmuseum, 1984) esp. pp. 395–412.
23. Anselme Dimier, 'Héraldique cistercienne,' *Cîteaux: commentarii cistercienses* 24 (1973) p. 268.
24. Waeber-Antiglio, *Hauterive*, p. 46, fig. 22 and p. 202.
25. The Clairvaux shield is also on a late fifteenth-century manuscript page from Salem (Heidelberg, Universitätsbibliothek, Cod. Sal. IXc, fol. 18v), beside the arms of the abbot (illustrated in *Die Zisterzienser*, colorplate 8, opposite p. 256).

Salem is in the filiation of Morimond, whose arms are blazoned as *d'argent à la croix ancrée de gueules, cantonnée des quatre lettres M.O.R.S. de sable*. The shield of Clairvaux frequently appears on other objects from Morimond, and objects from other abbeys in the filiation of Morimond. The explanation may be that the Clairvaux shield came to be associated with the Cistercian Order in general, rather than with houses in the filiation of Clairvaux in particular.

26. Strub, *La ville de Fribourg*, pp. 366 and 378, fig. 418; and Braun, 'La Maigrauge (Magerau),' p. 823.
27. Strub, *La ville de Fribourg*, pp. 16–17, fig. 8–5; *J. Siebmacher's grosses und allgemeines Wappenbuch in einer neuen, vollständig geordneten und reich vermehrten Auflage mit heraldischen und historisch-genealogischen Erläuterungen*, I/5, 2, *Klöster* (Nuremberg: von Bauer und Raspe, 1882), p. 81 and Taf. 96.
28. Anderes, *Spätgotische Glasmalerei*, p. 119, fig. 88, pp. 120 and 180.

'Affectum Confessus sum, et non Negavi'.[1] Reflections on the Expression of Affect in the 26th Sermon on the Song of Songs of Bernard of Clairvaux

Dorette Sabersky

MY INTEREST in Bernard's style developed very much in connection with Jean Leclercq's studies on Bernard: Leclercq's remarkable sensitivity to the literary character of Bernard's texts attracted my attention to Bernard's affective language.[2] His monumental work on Bernard's spirituality and on his texts—above all, the establishment of a critical text and his studies on the history of the manuscripts and on the development of Bernard's writings—laid the necessary foundation for further investigations of Bernard's style. Later on, Leclercq sustained my interest in Bernard by his personal encouragement and support. Furthermore, at this point, his work has become significant to me in a new way: his late attempt to examine Bernard's psychology[3] has encouraged me to focus on the exploration of Bernard's affectivity and to venture beyond the conscious model of his spirituality. In this preliminary attempt, I am following Leclercq's lead in innovating different perspectives for a fuller understanding of Bernard's writings.[4]

Bernard's spirituality is based on experience, *experientia*.[5] Since knowledge and insight are not sufficient for an understanding of oneself and of God, one must be touched, affected, and transformed by this process. The text of the Song of Songs in particular became to Bernard the 'book of the experience'.[6] It speaks the language of the affect, not of the intellect.[7] This 'affective' experience is bound by his spiritual model in the context of Bernard's faith, but it involves as well his psychology, his personal organization of affect.[8] To focus on the psychological aspect of this 'experience' by exploring Bernard's own affective experience I consider an interesting and worthwhile endeavor for the following reasons. We get many glimpses of the human dimension in Bernard's texts. These reveal a strong sense of his affective experience which were meaningful enough for him to describe with accuracy. In addition, Bernard was able to translate his experience into language. I find that his art of writing allows him to articulate the complexity of affective experiences at different levels, since the formal structures support the content and become significant in conveying additional affective meanings.[9] Bernard's style is compelling because it is grounded in his genuine feelings, which makes it psychologically true.[10]

Bernard's lament for his deceased brother Gerard in SC 26 is of special interest for the purpose of examining his distinct affective experience.[11] Grief highlights the problems around affect: Bernard had intense feelings in reaction to Gerard's death and he could not easily reconcile these with his faith. This brought about his conflict.

Peter von Moos has dedicated a large part of his monumental research on the medieval literature of consolation over death and on the christian problem of grief to Bernard's SC 26.[12]. These extensive philological studies provide a wealth of text material. They were an indispensable tool which allowed me to focus on my own perspective without ignoring the philological and theological background of this rich and complex text.[13]

By placing Bernard's sermon in the context of the tradition of the consolation literature, von Moos emphasizes the dialectic between lament and consolation which is often expressed in a dialogue between affect and reason in an attempt to rationalize away the experience of grief. Although von Moos' detailed interpretation of this text goes far beyond that model, he is somewhat bound by it. He holds the view that Bernard presents a true conflict by being equally convincing in his defense of and his prosecution of the lament, in that Bernard finds a solution that reconciles the opposites of grief and consolation.[14] There is no doubt that Bernard's thinking was influenced by this tradition or that traces of it are present in SC 26; but I suggest that his lament is integrated into the structural model of a gradual ascent to God. Bernard's articulation of grief is anchored in the search for God because Bernard associates Gerard's death with God's anger and therefore with the loss of a sense of being held by God. The experience of the loss of God's comforting presence indicates the depth of meaning Gerard's death had for Bernard. Therefore, re-establishing a state of harmony with God determined the course of Bernard's bereavement.[15] The dilemma between his faith and the force of his grief, and its impact on his bond with God, can be understood as the underlying organizing structure. The metaphor of the gradual ascent is more helpful in understanding the interplay of such stylistic elements as repetitions and variations, and the associative process that orders this text.[16]

The composition of this text is determined mainly by a continuous spiral movement.[17] This is reinforced by the transitions that link the different parts so tightly together that it is difficult to decide where to put a caesura.[18] Since these transitions are dedicated to the lament, they also serve the purpose of reiterating the centrality of the lament. In addition, we can distinguish two parts ordered around a center, which is accentuated by symmetrical structures such as repetition, contrast, reversal, and intensification.[19]

Gerard, a fellow monk at Clairvaux, had been the cellarer and active in the administration of the abbey; he died in 1138. Bernard's lament for his brother Gerard is embedded in the interpretation of the Song of Songs. After a short transition in which Bernard explains why he cannot continue his examination of the tents of Kedar (Sg 1:4),[20] the lament for Gerard is introduced with a reference to his state of mind: *Quamquam et maeror finem imperat, 'et calamitas quam patior'* (Jb 6:2).[21] This statement has two important aspects: Bernard takes his affective experience seriously enough to interrupt his sermon on the Song of Songs to express and share it with his fellow monks.[22] And, right away, he presents Job as a model for his suffering.[23]

Bernard struggles with the validity of expressing his grief: 'But up till now I have done violence to myself and kept up a pretence, lest my affection should seem stronger than my faith'.[24] He compares the disguise of his affect to a hidden fire that consumes him from within.[25] He adds: *Clausus latius serpit, saevit acrius.*[26] This sentence is typical of Bernard's use of repetition to achieve an affective intensification—here it is a repetition not of the content but of the sound. The second phrase consists of a verb and an adverb; it repeats in reversed order the phonological structure of the first: *s-e-it a-i-us.*[27]. As his introduction to the lament serves the purpose of demonstrating the force and validity of Bernard's experience of grief, I understand this repetition to be a linguistic confirmation of the intensity of his affect.

Another Job quotation associates his pain with the terrors of God: *Vis doloris abducit intentionem, et 'indignatio' Domini 'ebibit spiritum meum'* (Jb 6:4).[28] Having introduced this theme right away, he uses this mere allusion to it to make a link between his pain and God. This indicates that Bernard perceives his affect states in reference to God, as a response to God's feelings of him.

Bernard goes on to describe how he held his tears back during the funeral, while everybody else wept. Significant here is that Bernard emphasizes that 'all took pity, not so much on him who had gone as on me who had lost him. . . . Everyone had experienced the loss, but they regarded theirs as nothing in comparison with mine.'[29] The monks' compassion for his loss, their surprise at his stoic attitude, and their recognition that he had suffered the greatest loss seem to legitimize the acknowledgment and expression of his 'suppressed sorrow': 'I could control my tears but not my sadness. . . . I confess I am beaten. All that I endure within must needs issue forth.'[30] After his fellow monks had helped him validate his experience, it only made sense that he wanted to share it with them as he can be assured of their understanding: 'But let it be poured out before the eyes of my sons, who, knowing my misfortune, will look with kindness on my mourning and afford more sweet sympathy'.[31] Bernard advocates brotherly compassion and here demonstrates an appreciation of human suffering.[32] Yet this concept becomes more problematic when it involves one's own experience of a loss which, if it does not correspond with how the dead person is affected, is easily perceived as selfish or if it is seen as being in conflict with faith in God.[33] It is my view that this is the struggle which underlies this text and that it cannot be fully resolved by Bernard. Therefore, he switches back and forth between asserting the importance of his experience and disavowing it, as I will show below.

A very likely literary model for Bernard's heroic effort to suppress his pain and his growing need to express it, is Augustine's report of his mother's death.[34] There is, however, a significant difference:

although Augustine is ashamed of his tears, he does not hide them from God; he lets them flow solely in the presence of God, where no one else can hear him who in his pride might have scorned him for weeping.[35] Bernard, on the other hand, experiences his fellow monks' compassion and seeks their comfort, whereas at the outset of his lament he perceives God as a harsh judge.

After this introduction—in which Bernard asserts the dilemma between his need to express his painful affective experience and his faith, finally allowing his feelings to emerge—his actual lament for Gerard begins. At first Bernard's sense of abandonment dominates. His loss is twofold: he experiences the loss of Gerard as the loss of God's comforting presence. Bernard begins his lament by addressing his monks: 'You, my sons, know how deep my sorrow is, how galling the wound it leaves. You are aware that a loyal companion has left me alone. . . . Share my mourning with me, you who know these things.'[36] The contact with the audience goes beyond mere rhetoric: it is a prerequisite for Bernard in order to legitimize and to contain his pain.[37]

The following sentence consists of two pairs of clauses of parallel order:

> *Infirmus corpore eram, et ille portabat me;*
> *pusillus corde eram, et confortabat me;*
> *piger et negligens, et excitabat me;*
> *improvidus et obliviosus, et commonebat me.*[38]

Although the sentence is meant to praise Gerard's services, the emphasis appears to be on Bernard; every clause leads to the culminating 'me'. Consciously, his own self-abasement—seen as an expression of humility—has the purpose of elevating Gerard, which very likely facilitates the expression of his own experience. Furthermore, a biblical passage from a scene describing the Last Judgment clearly served as a structural model.[39] Gerard's love for Bernard thereby becomes his love for Christ and benefits his salvation. This connotation with Christ allows Bernard to focus on his own need and on his lament for his brother, since Gerard's death is understood as being part of the order of salvation.

Short exclamations and questions reflect the affective reasoning of the lament: 'Why has he been torn from me? Why snatched from my embraces...?'. The two pressing questions lead Bernard to introduce the antithesis of life and death, which is intertwined with the antithesis of love and separation or loss which he develops in this section: *Amavimus nos in vita: quomodo in morte sumus separati?*[40]

This whole passage is an example of Bernard's ease in carefully and convincingly developing themes by association. Although on the surface the sequence appears to be directed by logic, I think that the associations are governed by affect, and are similar to his frequent phonological associations.

The next sentence opens with *Amarissima separatio* [the bitterest separation]:[41] *Separatio* obviously refers to the last word of the previous sentence - *separati* - and moves Bernard's ideas forward. On the other hand, he associates *Amarissima* with *Amavimus*, the first word of the previous sentence. Here the link consists of the sound structure *ama-i*, the sound similarity highlighting the irony of the contrast between the warmth of love and the bitterness of separation. At the end of this passage Bernard condenses the antithesis to two phonologically similar verbs: *Cur, quaeso, aut amavimus, aut amisimus nos?*[42] With every sentence in this passage, death becomes, almost naturally more personified and in the process is attacked by Bernard:

> And how bitter the separation that only death could bring about! While you [Gerard] lived when did you ever abandon me? It is totally death's doing, so terrible a parting . . . Death indeed, so aptly named, whose rage has destroyed two lives in the spoliation of one.[43]

In death Bernard has found a safe target for his rage, deflecting from the hurt of feeling abandoned by Gerard and, even more critically, deflecting from a confrontation with God whose perceived rage he cannot challenge by his own rage. Replacing God by death allows Bernard to express his hurt directly.

The conflict with death then leads step by step to the paradoxical reversal of the experience of life and death: 'Surely this is death to me as well? Even more so to me, to whom continued life is more wretched than any form of death. I live, and I die in living: and shall I call this life?' Bernard plays here with the different meanings of the terms life and death and their reversal.[44] Finally, death is addressed directly: 'O cruel death, if you had deprived me of life itself rather than of its fruit!'.[45] Then death, who is presented as devil, is accused of being envious: 'And because you envied the works that I performed, you removed him beyond my reach. . . .' If his own works were fruitful, Bernard adds, it was because of Gerard. Bernard uses this thought to make the transition back from death to Gerard: 'How much better for me then, O Gerard, if I had lost my life rather than your company . . .'. The phrase mentioned above—*Cur, quaeso, aut amavimus, aut amisimus nos?*—leads to the idea that Gerard does not share equally in the misery caused by separation. Bernard signals the connection between the loss and his deplorable state by associating the word *miseranda*[46] with *amisimus* in the previous sentence: *Dura conditio, sed mea miseranda fortuna, non et illius!*[47] Bernard continues articulating the contrast between them, highlighting his sense of abandonment:

> And the reason, dear brother, is that though you have lost your loved ones, you have found others more lovable still. As for me, already so miserable, what consolation remains to me, and you, my only comfort, gone? . . . All that was pleasant we rejoiced to share; now sadness and mourning are mine alone.

Bernard's state of misery is again associated with God's rage, although God is not even mentioned here: 'anger has swept over me (Ps 87:17), rage is fastened on me (Ps 87:8)'.[48] Gerard, who now enjoys the presence of God, has no reason to complain about the separation, but Bernard asks a poignant, amazingly direct question about himself: 'But what do I have in your stead?' This leads him to ask whether his brother still thinks of him. The passage starts: 'I long to know what you now think about me, once so uniquely yours . . . Perhaps you still give thought to our miseries. . . .' And it ends with the dread of being forgotten: 'It is possible that . . . now you no longer know us . . . and you will be mindful of his righteousness alone, forgetful of ours'. The pounding *immemor nostri* concludes the sentence.[49]

Bernard uses a syllogism to prove that Gerard still loves him. Perhaps he hoped to be able to refute with objective arguments his dreadful doubts whether or not he still exists for his brother. The first clause is based on 1 Co 6:17: *'qui adhaeret Deo unus spiritus est', et in divinum quemdam totus mutatur affectum.*[50] The second clause is based on 1 Jn 4:8: *'Deus autem caritas est', et quanto quis coniunctior Deo, tanto plenior caritate. Porro impassibilis est Deus, sed non incompassibilis.*[51] The conclusion is addressed directly to Gerard, as if he were to prove to his brother the neccesity of remembering Bernard: *Ergo et te necesse est esse misericordem, qui inhaeres misericordi, quamvis iam minime miser sis, et qui non pateris, compateris tamen. Affectus proinde tuus non est imminutus, sed immutatus.*[52] Bernard emphasizes here the contrast between the meaning of the word *imminutus* ['diminished'] and the word *immutatus* ['changed'] by two similarly sounding words. It is almost as if he forces the too threatening word *imminutus* to change to the more hopeful *immutatus*, using the language as evidence to verify his statement. By playing with words—*impassibilis - incompassibilis, misericors - miser*, and *pati - compati*—Bernard uses affective means to make the logical structure of the syllogism tangible and therefore cogent. He concludes the passage, by affirming his point with two biblical quotations: 'And since love never comes to an end (1 Co 13:8), you will not forget me for ever' (Ps 12:1).[53] To reassure himself still further, he lets Gerard answer him with Is 49:15, a reference to the bond between God and Israel: 'It seems to me that I can almost hear my brother saying: "Can a woman forget the son of her womb? And if she should forget, yet I will not forget you" '.[54] Yet even this attempt to restore the bond does not succeed in altering his state of mind. By quoting 2 Co 12:1 he reflects his resignation: 'Not that it does any good'.[55] Although he continues, 'You know how I am situated, how dejected in spirit, how your departure has affected me; there is none to give me a helping hand', this very sentence nevertheless might indicate that something has changed somewhat: Bernard can trust that his brother knows about his situation and that therefore he can at least let him know about his misery.

In my view, this passage confirms the affective authenticity of this text. Bernard cannot be consoled by his almost desperate attempt to prove that Gerard is still connected to him, although his syllogism rests on core ideas of his spirituality.[56] A convincing explanation would be that Bernard is not yet facing God directly: as long as that bond is not in place, the content of his syllogism is only abstract knowledge without any immediate positive emotional impact, because he experiences God only as punitive and not as compassionate. And under these circumstances, the fact that Gerard is united with God highlights his sense of abandonment and the inequality between Gerard and him: Bernard is deprived of Gerard's love as well as of God's love.

From his state of deprivation Bernard looks into the future with urgent questions: 'To whom shall I turn for advice when perplexed? In whom shall I confide when fortune is against me? Who will save me when danger threatens?'. This reminds him again of the oneness experienced in the past: 'Were not my worries, O Gerard, better known to your heart than to mine...?'.[57] His ensuing praise of Gerard's services is centered around Gerard's dedication to him. Bernard reports, quoting Gerard, that before his death, Gerard had told God that he wanted a tranquil life with God: ' " . . . But fear of you, the community's will, and my own desire to obey, and above all my deep love for someone who was both my abbot and my brother kept me involved in the business of the house." ' Bernard comments on Gerard's sacrifice with a quite factual statement: 'That is how it was!' He thanks him for whatever fruits result from his own studies and adds: 'What progress I have made, what good I have done, I owe to you'.[58] Bernard appears to see Gerard's sacrifices for him as being in accordance with God's will and as signs of Gerard's humility.

Bernard pays tribute to the qualities of Gerard's inner life and to his spiritual gifts. Typically, he goes to an extreme, using contrasts and role reversal to express the affective charge behind his praise. Bernard was the one who learned from Gerard: 'I who approached to enlighten him came away enlightened instead!' Again Gerard is seen as an example of humility: 'And yet, he whom all esteemed as supremely wise was devoid of wisdom in his own estimation'. Bernard sums everything up by asserting: 'I found him helpful above all others and in every situation. . . . It was only right that I should depend entirely on him, he was all in all to me. He left me little more than the name and honor of provider; he did the work. I was saluted as abbot, but he was the one who solicitously watched over everyone'. As in the first part of his tribute, the acknowledgment of his owing everything to Gerard concludes this section: 'my preaching was more effective, my prayer more fruitful, my study more regular, my love more fervent'.[59] Gerard is presented as having dedicated his life totally to Bernard's need for him, which Bernard experienced as blissful oneness. Did all this happen at Gerard's expense? All the qualities mentioned by Bernard made Gerard indispensable to him.

Was the bond onesided in favor of Bernard and could he not accept and adjust to the reversal of it after Gerard's death? Or, is the other part of the bond left out in Bernard's report because of modesty? Gerard's dedication to Bernard is understood as his dedication to a spiritual life in the service of God, thus benefitting Gerard. This understanding of the meaning of Gerard's life makes it possible for Bernard to express the experience of his loss and his needs for his brother in a very open and direct way.

Gerard's obituary painfully reminds Bernard of having been left alone with manifold troubles. He again addresses his lament to Gerard directly: 'Alas! You have been taken away . . . O, if I could only die at once and follow you!'. Bernard refers here to David's lament for Absalom: 'If only I had died instead of you'[60] but changes *pro te* to *post te*.[61] To make sure that his correction is understood, he quickly adds: 'Certainly I would not have died in your stead, I would not deprive you of the glory that is yours'. Bernard's acute concern that his own needs might interfere with Gerard's supreme happiness shows clearly how drastically the situation had changed for Bernard. While Gerard was alive, Bernard had perceived his need for him as legitimate because it was in harmony with God's will.[62] Now, this is seen as more problematic, which adds to the severity of his experience of loss: 'But to survive you can mean only drudgery and pain' (Ps 89:10).

THE TURNING POINT

This lament-segment serves as an introduction to what I consider the turning point of the sermon: Bernard summarizes the central themes, he expands them by adding new elements and creating new links between them. This spiral process structures the text. The significance of it at this point is that the single themes are linked directly with God and thus take a different direction. The following points that refer again to the model of Job mark the sequence of Bernard's development of the text:

1. The starting point is the state of his bereavement: 'My life, if you can call it that, will be one of bitterness and mourning'(Jb 3:20). Closely associated with his sense of his own misery is God's anger as the deeper cause of it: ' "the hand of the Lord has touched

me" ' (Jb 19:21). Whereas the earlier references were vague, isolated allusions, here the connection between his grief and God's will has become the focus.

2. ' . . . it will even be my comfort to endure this painful grief. I shall not spare myself (Jb 6:10), I shall even co-operate with the hand of the Lord'. How is this statement to be understood? On the background of the tradition it can be seen as a recognition of the meaning of suffering. With Gregory the Great, consolation could be taken in the idea that suffering is granted to the just as an opportunity to do penance on earth in order to avoid punishment in eternity.[63] The context suggests to me the interplay of several meanings: Bernard appears to want to hurry God's hand in order to shorten his misery.[64] The fact that this is the first place where Bernard makes contact with God suggests that he needs to feel to be on God's side rather than being isolated by God's anger.[65] Furthermore, the process of grieving itself emerges in this passage as the hope for consolation (see below, under 4.).

3. The contrast between his own and Gerard's situation leads to the reversal of the meaning of life and death:

> It is I who am touched and stricken, not he, for [death] has but summoned him to repose; in cutting short his life it has brought me death.[66] One can scarcely speak of him as dead! Was he not rather transplanted into life?[67] At least what was for him the gateway to life is simply death to me; for by that death it is I who died, not he who has but gone to sleep in the Lord (Act 7:60).[68]

What is changed here is that Bernard attributes Gerard's death and in consequence, his own experiential death to God's doing and not to the meanness of the personified death. The reversal of life and death and Bernard's ensuing death-like state are a reflection of God's anger.

4. As in the beginning, Bernard knows that his tears need to come out and here he addresses his tears emphatically:

> Flow on, flow on, my tears, so long on the point of brimming over; flow on, . . . let my tears gush forth like fountains, that they may perchance wash away the stains of those sins[69] that drew God's anger upon me (Jb 6:2). When the

> Lord shall have been appeased in my regard, then perhaps I shall find the grace of consolation, if I had not ceased to mourn:[70] for those who mourn shall be comforted (Mt 5:5).[71]

Whereas in the beginning Bernard was overcome by his tears of grief, here they blur with the well-respected and recommended tears of penance. Grieving becomes penance: cause and consolation are one.[72] Grieving is now not only tolerated but even strongly advocated because it is elevated to a prerequisite for consolation and thereby salvation. God's anger is also explicitly brought together with its cause: man's sinful condition.

The lament has become grounded in God, in the clearly defined order of salvation. By tracing Bernard's understanding of the causal connection of the different elements, we may establish the following sequence: because of his sinful human condition that gives rise to guilt and shame,[73] Bernard deserves God's anger. In consequence, Bernard is subjected to the pain and anguish of bereavement, the tears of grief. These tears that become tears of penance, can in turn eventually appease God, and then there is hope that Bernard will deserve to be consoled by God.

Most interesting is that this link between his mourning and God's anger allows him to sustain his affective experience. It represents a powerful and ingenious attempt to reconcile the two. The idea of spiritual mourning legitimizes the mourning for his brother. This strongly suggests that Job serves not only as a model of the patient acceptance of suffering but also as a model of the acknowledgment and articulation of grief. The fact that apparently no one before Bernard had gone that far in the re-evaluation of the concept of the lament for a deceased person,[74] seems to support my view.

The immediate continuation of the text further confirms to me that Bernard uses the concept of penance as a validation of his affective experience: From now on, in the second part, Bernard focuses on the justification of his mourning. Why would that be necessary if there was only a spiritual connotation to the concept of penance? This suggests to me instead that Bernard had a sense of exposing himself by using the concept in a new way.[75]

The notion of having to appease God in order to be consoled, reveals the inherent conflict, namely that Bernard can only value his affect states if they are in harmony with his understanding of God's requirements. This makes a continuous examination and justification of his feelings necessary. At this point, Bernard can avoid the conflict between his feelings and what he perceives to be God's demand by the compromise he presents. Yet, in my view, as I will demonstrate below, the outcome of this text is determined by this conflict.

In the second part Bernard attempts to reconcile and to consolidate his main themes: the validity of his mourning, and the need to be united with God.

Bernard's defense of his mourning has a dynamic quality: It is not aimed at maintaining a *status quo* but provides a springboard for bolder testimonies about his affective experience, and these in turn make further defensive strategies necessary to corroborate his stance. This interplay structures and intensifies the second part of the sermon.

Bernard first distinguishes between his own and worldly mourning:

> And I implore you, let not mere conventional respect, but your human affection,[76] draw you to me in my sorrow. Day after day we see the dead bewailing the dead (see Mt 8:22): floods of tears, but all to no purpose [*fletum multum, et fructum nullum*[77]]. Not that I condemn the affection they show, unless it be out of all proportion,[78] but the reason that inspires it. The former springs from nature, the disturbance it causes is but a consequence of sin; the latter however is sinful vanity. Their weeping, if I mistake not, is solely for the loss of earthly glory, because of the misfortunes of the present life. Those who so weep should themselves be wept for.

Obviously, Bernard's purpose is to refute his own doubts about his mourning. The distinction he makes sounds rather rational, and the question that follows reveals that he is not fully convinced by it: 'Can it be possible that I am one of them?'. His answer brings him back to his lament: 'My emotional outburst is certainly like theirs, but the cause, the intention, differs. I make no complaint at all about the ways of this world (1 Co 7:33). But I do lament the loss of a loyal helper, one whose advice on the things of God was always reliable. It is Gerard for whom I weep . . .'.[79] That Bernard here, as above, does not go beyond the notion of the spiritual purpose to Gerard's services is in line with his evaluation of his needs for Gerard (mentioned above) and most likely an honest statement on his part.

In the next section, Bernard justifies his pain by defending himself against the accusations of a fictitious opponent: 'I am that unhappy portion prostrate in the mud, mutilated by the loss of its nobler part, and shall it be said to me: "Do not weep"? My very heart is torn from me and shall it be said to me: "Try not to feel it"? But I do feel it intensely in spite of myself . . . I feel it and go on grieving. . . .' Bernard turns the meaning of his feelings around by once more using the idea of penance to vindicate the impact the pain has on him: 'He who chastises me will never be able to accuse me of hardness and insensibility. . . .'[80] Insensitivity is now perceived as arrogance. This justification facilitates a bold declaration of the significance of his affectivity:

> I have made public the depth of my affliction [*affectum*]; I make no attempt to deny it.[81] Will you say then that this is carnal? That it is human, yes, since I am a man. If that does not satisfy you, yes, I am carnal. Yes, I am carnal, sold under sin (Rom 7:14), destined to die, subject to penalties and sufferings. I am certainly not insensible to pain; to think that I shall die, that those who are mine will die, fills me with dread. And Gerard was mine, so utterly mine. . . .

A poignant statement about his self-experience containing an allusion to Job, concludes this section: 'And it is he who has gone from me (Jb 6:10). I feel it, the wound is deep'.[82]

Bernard makes it clear that his sensitivity to pain belongs to his human condition which is inevitably marked by sin and thereby subject to death, penalties, and suffering. He disarms the imagined accusation—reflecting his own doubts?—that his affective experience should be called carnal by affirming the carnal as part of the human condition with its frailty and shortcomings. What matters for our purpose is that Bernard uses here his compassion with the deficient human condition, even his insistence on it, to attest again to the legitimacy and significance of his mourning. In other words, subject to suffering, he wants to have the right to feel and to articulate it and to have it responded to. As in the beginning, Bernard is seeking his monks' compassion: 'My sons, . . . grieve for your father's misfortune . . . for you can see how heavy [is] the penalty I have received from God's hand for my sins'.[83] Again he responds to an anticipated criticism of his pain:

> Can any man lightly say that I can get along without Gerard, unless he be ignorant of all that Gerard meant to me? I have no wish to repudiate the decrees of God (Jb 6:10), nor do I question that judgment by which each of us has received his due: he the crown he had earned, I the punishment I deserved.

Only twice in the whole text does Bernard turn to his monks for understanding. There is a specific meaning to this. In both places, Bernard has taken a risk and become especially vulnerable, earlier by allowing himself to show his pain, here by claiming his human nature in order to affirm his pain. This suggests to me that he cannot rely on God's acceptance of his reaction to the loss which he views as God's punishment.

Furthermore, concerned that his lament could be perceived as complaint, Bernard introduces a new element by carefully distinguishing between his lament and a reproach of God's judgment, between being human and being impious: 'Shall I find fault with his judgment because I wince at the pain? This latter is but human, the former is impious. It is but human and necessary that we respond to our friends with feeling. . . .[84] By this he creates a space in the hope of reconciling his need for the articulation of his painful affect with his need for a close relationship with God. Ultimately, I think, the fictitious opponents refer to God, for it is God he has to console.

The ensuing reflections on friendship bring Bernard back to Gerard and to his experience of being alone in his grief. This serves as a transition to the next section where Bernard returns to death personified to contrast it with the scene in the first part. The transition concludes with the following sentence: *Solus ego patior quod solent pariter pati qui se diligunt, cum se amittunt.*[85] This is a variation of an idea in the first death scene. There he played with the opposition *amare* - *amittere* (SC 26.4).[86] Here, Bernard continues by connecting *amittere* with *praemittere* in the hope of following Gerard rather than losing him: *Utinam non te amiserim, sed praemiserim! Utinam vel tarde aliquando 'sequar te quocumque ieris'* (Lc 9:57; Rv 14:4).[87] This marks a decisive difference between the two passages addressing the personified death. In the first instance Bernard emphasised his loss and the fundamental difference between his own and his brother's fate, here Bernard attempts to establish a connection by merging his own with Gerard's experience of a victory over death which re-enacts Christ's redemption. Bernard describes the miracle of Gerard's death:

> . . . *videre hominem in morte exsultantem et insultantem morti. Ubi est, mors, victoria tua? Ubi est, mors, stimulus tuus?* (1 Co 1:55). *Iam non stimulus, sed iubilus. Iam cantando moritur homo, et moriendo cantat.*[88]

Bernard's paradoxical language reflects Gerard's triumph over death: *stimulus* is changed to *iubilus*, and *mori* is absorbed and enclosed by *cantare*. The implication is: 'You are dead, O death. . . .' Here, this does not mean only that death is defeated and ridiculed but also that the evil nature of death is transformed through irony and becomes part of the process of salvation: 'Begetter of sorrow, you have been made a source of gladness; an enemy to glory, you have been made to contribute to glory; the gate of hell, you have been made the threshold of heaven; the very pit of perdition, you have been made a way of salvation, and that by a man who was a sinner'.[89] While the ridicule of death is quite common, the renaming is unusual.[90] I think that this shows that Bernard liked to go to the extreme: his adaptation of traditional themes to his distinct context renders his language original and poignant, and often gives his style a heightened affective quality. Yet more specifically, the paradoxical speech can be seen as Bernard's attempt to express the transformations, the fluidity of the process of his affective experience: life turns into death, a cruel death into a force in the service of salvation.

Bernard concludes his description of Gerard's death: *Sic cantabat quem nos lugemus: in quo et meum, fateor, luctum paene in cantum convertit, dum intentus gloriae eius, propriae fere miseriae obliviscor.*[91] Twice Bernard adds the word 'almost' (*paene, fere*): His mourning was *almost* changed into song, and he *almost* forgot his own misery. This is an indication of Bernard's precision and honesty about his experience.

This scene with death reverses and surpasses the first (SC 26.4). The transformation of death goes beyond Gerard's individual death and has implications as well for Bernard. First of all, it means that Gerard, following the example of Christ, becomes a spiritual guide. This is quite different from Bernard's attempt (in SC 26.5) to achieve a connection with Gerard by means of an abstract and at that point experience-distant syllogism.[92] Beyond that, this second scene confirms that death, personified as devil, is now abolished and therefore concedes its former place to God.[93] Bernard carefully and slowly prepared both these shifts in the foregoing sections: he approached God's anger directly; he introduced the idea of mourning as penance; and he declared his acceptance of God's judgment.

Bernard's indication of the change in his state of mind leads back to his lament and also forms a transition to the next passage:

> *Sed revocat me ad me pungens dolor, facileque a sereno illo intuitu, tamquam a levi excitat somno perstringens anxietas. Plangam igitur, sed super me, qui super illum vetat ratio. Puto enim, si opportunitas daretur, modo diceret nobis: 'Nolite flere super me, sed super vosmetipsos flete'* (Lc 23:28).[94]

The distinction between mourning for himself and mourning for Gerard, between his own experience and that of Gerard, allows him to stay with his feelings. As above in SC 26.6, Bernard substantiates his reasoning with Gerard's anticipated response. The biblical passage (Lk 23:28) most often cited in prohibiting lamentation for the dead and suggesting tears of penance instead,[95] is used by Bernard to support the concept of penance to justify his mourning.[96]

Yet, just because Bernard assigns a new meaning to the concept of penance in this context, the idea of mourning not for his brother but for himself seems to require further clarification and justification. To make his point Bernard uses biblical examples that do not simply match his own case. He starts with the example of David who mourns *for* Absalom, Saul, and Jonathan to establish two objectives. First, he differentiates from this his own mourning that is not for Gerard, and lists three reasons for it. This leads to the conclusion that he does not mourn for but because of Gerard: *plango postremo, etsi non super te, propter te tamen.*[97] This distinction in turn allows him to go even further: *Hinc prorsus, hinc afficior graviter, quia vehementer amo.*[98] The notion of mourning for himself that could be understood in the context of spiritual penance has now been clearly identified as a concept of mourning that is caused by his strong love for Gerard. This motivation for mourning can no longer be mistaken for penance. The fact that at this point he refutes an anticipated objection appears to confirm that he has ventured into unknown territory: *Et 'nemo mihi molestus sit'* (Gal 6:17), *dicens non debere sic affici. . . .*[99] The second reason behind his use of the example of David is that he has a right to be deeply affected by his brother's death, for David yielded to his love for his parricidal son Absalom without injury to faith and without offending the judgment of God. Bernard rounds off his argument emphatically: 'And see, a greater than Absalom is here'.[100]

Transcending the authority of David, Bernard moves on to the example of Christ as a climax. The statement that Christ wept when he looked at Jerusalem and foresaw its destruction serves as further justification for the validity of his grief: *Et ego propriam, et quae in praesenti est, desolationem non sentiam? Plagam meam recentem et gravem non doleam? Ille compatiendo flevit, et ego patiendo non audeo?*[101] The juxtaposition of *pati* and *compati* is used to distinguish between Christ's and Bernard's experience in order to substantiate his mourning.[102] Further to affirm that his mourning is legitimate and no contradiction of his faith, Bernard emphasizes that 'at the tomb of Lazarus Christ neither rebuked those who wept nor forbade them to weep, rather he wept with those who wept (Rm 12:5) . . . These tears were witnesses to his human nature, not signs that he lacked trust'.[103] The resurrection of Lazarus provides the ultimate proof that Christ's mourning did not interfere with his faith.

Bernard then applies the same interpretation to himself: 'In the same way, our weeping is not a sign of lack of faith; it indicates the human condition. Nor do I rebuke the striker if I weep on receiving the blow, rather do I invite his mercy, I try to mitigate his severity. You hear the heavy note of sorrow in my words (Jb 6:3), but I am far from murmuring'.[104] As above in SC 26.9, sensitivity to pain and tears are associated with the human condition and here, in addition, with the human nature of Christ. Why does Bernard have to defend again his experience of pain after all his foregoing efforts culminated in an identification with Christ? He faces here the smiting, not the compassionate, God, and the example of Lazarus does not help him to come to terms with that.[105] Christ's mourning was validated and ended in the resurrection of Lazarus. Yet Gerard does not rise from his grave, and thus for Bernard the conflict remains.

Returning to the idea of not questioning God's judgment (SC 26.10) Bernard now goes a step further by distinguishing between God's mercy and his judgment, between his goodness and his justice. At this point, he perceives God's severity as justice rather than as anger, and for the first time he praises God and speaks to God directly. Bernard wants to show that his grief does not interfere with his acceptance of God's justice. To him this means that God's justice as well as God's goodness deserves praise. What are the implications of this shift? First of all, his feelings are centered around God: there is the requirement of having to appease God in order to sustain the bond. Above, in SC 26.8, where his mourning was embedded in the concept of penance, it was seen as the means of consoling God.[106]. At that point, there was no conflict between his affect and the need to comply with God's requirements. Here, as we saw, he attempts to evoke God's mercy and to mitigate his severity, yet here this undertaking turns out to preclude his mourning:

In a first step Bernard points out his own fairness by referring back to a statement in SC 26.10 that he deserved the punishment of his misery.[107] By deferring to the concepts of fairness and justice, Bernard indicates that he dismisses and bypasses the experience of his pain. He then introduces a new thought by reminding himself that God had also given Gerard to him: *Tu dedisti Girardum, tu abstulisti* (Jb 1:21) *et si dolemus ablatum, non tamen obliviscimur quod datus fuit, et gratias agimus quod habere illum meruimus, quo carere in tantum non volumus, in quantum non expedit.*[108] He expresses his gratitude to God and gives a somewhat defensive explanation to missing Gerard. Yet in his effort to demonstrate God's justice Bernard refers to an agreement he had made with God. When Gerard had been very ill on their trip to Italy the previous year, Bernard had prayed that God would let Gerard return home before his death,[109] and had said that he would not argue if God took Gerard away afterwards. 'Since then I lost sight of my agreement with you, but you did not forget. I am ashamed of these sobs of grief that go to prove I broke the agreement'.[110] To summarize his legalistic defense of God's right—and perhaps to some extent the whole sermon—Bernard in a typical manner reduces his statement to a poignant phrase: *Quid plura?*

Repetisti commendatum, recepisti tuum.[111] God took only what was his, and therefore, because of the legitimacy of God's action, the articulation of his pain becomes unwarranted.

The result of his reasoning is not only that God is just but also that God is right and that he is wrong in stating his pain over Gerard's death. Bernard lost the sense of the validity of his feelings. He began this passage by asserting that his mourning would not repudiate God's judgment in order to substantiate the expression of his pain. To prove this, he demonstrates that God's judgment is just; this in turn invalidates his hurt, and thus he ends up feeling ashamed of articulating his grief. Now he perceives the expression of his pain as arguing with God, as a challenge to God's justice. The earlier distinction between the reproach of God's judgment and the manifestation of his pain is lost. This could mean that the distinction was a rationalization on his part to begin with. Yet the essence of it is that Bernard has to surrender his own feelings if he cannot harmonize them with God's requirement of him. And in this instance, his attempt to achieve a reconciliation is undermined, for the argument he uses to justify his mourning turns out to invalidate it.

The phrase quoted above introduces the concluding sentence: *Finem verborum indicunt lacrimae; tu illis, Domine, finem modumque indixeris.*[112] The first part represents a cliché,[113] but as usual, Bernard makes it meaningful by integrating it into his specific context, and therefore, it can and must be taken seriously. First, it provides a frame: Bernard had opened his lament by saying that his grief forced him to interrupt his discourse. The ending surpasses the beginning: the tears now force him to end his lament. On the surface, this appears as an effective rhetorical climax, indicating the intensity of Bernard's grief. In this case, the ending would feel like an artificial maneuver. Yet, if we take the context into account, this ending seems to summarize Bernard's state of mind accurately: although he still acknowledges his strong feelings, he does not support them because they are in conflict with God. Ashamed of his mourning, he is therefore left with nothing more to say. Yet by his wish that God may end his tears, Bernard seems to look for a resolution to his struggle: If he puts God in charge of his tears, he can hope for comfort and an end to his grief on the one hand, and on the other, he does not have to suppress them by forcing moderation and a limit on them. I see this ending as a compromise: Bernard attempts to achieve a reconciliation between his experience of mourning and his faith in God.

Before resuming his explanation of the Song of Songs in the next sermon, Bernard gives closure to his grief for Gerard. The fact that he can now refer to his foregoing lament as a tribute of human affection paid to Gerard shows that he has detached himself from his experience of grief.[114] In the same vein, he gives reasons for the need to stop mourning; they consist of traditional arguments against bereavement. The tone is rational and calm: 1. 'As he [Gerard] is in the state of happiness it is improper to prolong our mourning for him. . . .' 2. 'Even though we do shed tears in our troubles, our grief should not be excessive.' 3. 'or it will seem to express our regret for the service we have lost rather than our love for him'.[115] Bernard is now concerned that his mourning has become excessive,[116] that his mourning means that he is selfish because his experience is not congruent with that of Gerard, and because grieving the loss focuses on his need for Gerard.[117] The concluding sentence on his mourning expresses his wish that the knowledge that Gerard is with God may ease the pain of the bereavement and may make his loss more bearable. Bernard's use of the form of a wish seems to reflect his genuine experience and describe exactly his affect states. In this passage, Bernard yields to the traditional view of mourning, but we can still catch a glimpse of the complexity of his experience.

This ending shows that Bernard could not reconcile this tension. All his attempts to affirm his experience of grief ultimately failed because he associated with grief the defectiveness of human nature. When he uses the argument of man's deficiency to assert and validate his experience of pain, it is undermined by the same token, as there is ultimately still a negative value attached to the human condition. By associating his mourning with the human nature of Christ, Bernard found a space for assigning a positive meaning to painful affect. I think that it is rather significant that this is different from Bernard's concept of merging with Christ's passion, where man's experience is left out.[118] Here, Bernard's own personal pain is in the center, and he uses the human nature of Christ to affirm his mourning. While suffering with Christ leads to God's divine nature, here there is no direct identification possible. Bernard's solution to the problem of making the transition to God, who does not suffer but who caused his grief by taking Gerard away, is to disavow his grieving. The ending appears to be successful from the vantage point of Bernard's journey to God, as he achieves the needed tie with God which takes priority over his grief. Yet this is not a mystical journey resulting in a sense of a union with God based on love. Bernard's love, longing, loneliness—all these feelings are centered on his brother. He merely praises God for being good and just: God constitutes the center of Bernard's existence, but in this text, he is not the object of Bernard's love. Being in harmony with God's judgment seems not to relieve his grief but to require him to repress his affect.

The ending re-establishes a reliable order based on God's justice.[119] This movement back could be understood as an almost inevitable counteraction to Bernard's articulation of his grief experience and thereby to his dread about leaving solid ground. The order provides the necessary containment for his venture into the realm of human affects.[120] Bernard's thinking and language are saturated by tradition, but the vehicle of tradition also aids the exploration of a new dimension of human experience.

NOTES

1. SC 26.9; SBOp 1:177,16. 'I have made public the depth of my affliction, I make no attempt to deny it' (CF 7:69). See below n.81. *Affectus* is here translated with the specific content of the affect. *Affectus* can be translated with 'affect', as long as we take Bernard's understanding into account. Affects are determined by a dynamic concept: they are a striving force, they impact man and move him either towards God or away from God. On *affectus* see Ulrich Köpf, *Religiöse Erfahrung in der Theologie Bernhards von Clairvaux*, Beiträge zur historischen Theologie 61 (Tübingen, 1980) 136-143. Köpf (143) makes the connection between Bernard's concept of affect and that of experience. See also Wilhelm Hiss, *Die Anthropologie Bernhards von Clairvaux*, Quellen und Studien zur Geschichte der Philosophie 7 (Berlin, 1964) 97ff, and Peter von Moos, *Consolatio. Studien zur mittellateinischen Trostliteratur über den Tod und zum Problem der christlichen Trauer*, Münstersche Mittelalter Schriften 3 (Munich, 1971), C 783.

2. Christine Mohrmann's studies on Bernard's style and on the Latin of the Fathers of the Church need to be mentioned as well in this respect: 'Observations sur la langue et le style de S. Bernard', SBOp 2 (1958) IX-XXXIII, and *Études sur le latin des chrétiens*, [2]1 and 2 (Rome: Edizioni di storia e letteratura, 1961).

3. Jean Leclercq, *Nouveau visage de Bernard de Clairvaux. Approches psycho-historiques* (Paris: Cerf, 1976); *A Second Look at Saint Bernard* (Kalamazoo: Cistercian Publications, 1990)

4. Leclercq (*Nouveau visage*, 60) states the necessity of examining how Bernard's language reflects his psychology. Leclercq focuses his psychological exploration primarily on the mechanisms of aggression and repression. See also his 'Aggressivité et répression chez Bernard de Clairvaux' *Revue d'histoire de la spiritualité* 52 (1976) 155-172.

My interpretation is guided primarily by the intersubjective perspective elaborated by Robert Stolorow, George Atwood, and Bernard Brandchaft, eds. *The Intersubjective Perspective* (Northvale, NJ: Aronson, 1994), George Atwood and Robert Stolorow, *Faces in a Cloud: Intersubjectivity in Personality Theory* (Aronson, 1993), Robert Stolorow and George Atwood, *Contexts of Being: The Intersubjective Foundations of Psychological Life* (Hillsdale, NJ: The Analytic Press, 1992), and Robert Stolorow, Bernard Brandchaft and George Atwood, *Psychoanalytic Treatment: An Intersubjective Approach* (The Analytic Press, 1987).

5. See e.g. Jean Leclercq, *L'amour des lettres et le désir de Dieu. Initiation aux auteurs monastiques du moyen âge* (Paris: Cerf, 1957) 202f. [*The Love of Learning and The Desire for God* (New York: Fordham, 1961, 1977)].

6. *liber experientiae* SC 3.1; SBOp 1:14,7. See Friedrich Ohly, *Hohelied-Studien. Grundzüge einer Geschichte der Hoheliedauslegung des Abendlandes bis um 1200* (Wiesbaden, 1958) 143, 136.

7. '. . . it is the *affectus*, not the intellect, which has spoken, and it is not for the intellect to grasp' (SC 67.3; CF 40:6).

8. The most extensive study on Bernard's concept of 'experience' has been done by Köpf (*Religiöse Erfahrung*). Jean Mouroux examines the concept of Bernard's 'experience' in the framework of a theology of the christian experience ('Sur les critères de l'expérience spirituelle d'après les sermons sur le cantique des cantiques', *ASOC* 9 [1953] 3/4: 253-267). Brian Stock ('Experience, Praxis, Work, and Planning in Bernard of Clairvaux: Observations of the *Sermones in Cantica*', in *The Cultural Context of Medieval Learning*, Boston Studies in the Philosophy of Science 26 [Dordrecht/Boston, 1975] 223ff and 265ff) on the other hand, focuses on the pragmatic aspect of Bernard's 'experience'. Bernard himself mixes the different aspects of the affective experience when he uses the phenomenology of affects as a metaphor for the love of God: 'The *affectus* have their own language, in which they disclose themselves even against their own will. Fear has its trembling, grief its anguished groans, love its cries of delight. Are the lamentations of the mourner, the sobs of those who grieve, the sighs of those in pain, the sudden frenzied screams of those in fear, the yawns of the replete—are these the result of habit? Do they constitute a reasoned discourse, a deliberate utterance, a premeditated speech? Most certainly such expressions of feeling are not producd by the processes of the mind, but by spontanenous impulses. So a strong and burning love, particularly the love of God does not stop to consider the order, the grammar, the flow, or the number of words it employs, when it cannot contain itself...' (SC 67.3; CF 40:6f).

9. On Bernard's affective style, see my '*Nam iteratio affectionis expressio est.* Zum Stil Bernhards von Clairvaux', *Cîteaux* 36 (1985) 5–20, and *Studien zur Paronomasie bei Bernhard von Clairvaux,* Dokimion 5 (Fribourg, Switzerland: University Press, 1979).

10. Leclercq poses the question whether Bernard's art of writing disguises or allows us to track the spontaneous play of psychological mechanisms (*Nouveau visage*, 36). For Leclercq there is a potential dichotomy between Bernard's stylistic devices and his sincerity, see e.g. *Nouveau visage,* 48 and 58, and *L'amour des lettres*, 248f. Elsewhere, Leclercq has made a more general statement: 'Between

the produced work and the sincerity of the author, there is nearly always in the middle ages a screen of rhetoric; literary techniques tend to become defence mechanisms' ('Modern Psychology and the Interpretation of Medieval Texts', *Speculum* 48 [1973] 476). In my view, stylistic devices such as exaggerations reflect more Bernard's affectivity than his subservience to the laws of rhetoric. Bernard's style is interesting because he has the freedom and the ability to use literary techniques in the service of articulating affect, and this is not necessarily a conscious process on his part.

A comparison with Nicholas of Clairaux, Bernard's secretary who imitated Bernard's language, highlights the contrast: Nicholas' style is formalized, stereotyped, lacking Bernard's mastery and creative spontaneity. He depicts idealistic positions that reflect his notion of how he thinks it ought to be rather than his affective experiences. It is the effort itself he makes to present a certain image which reveals his psychology. See my 'The Style of Nicholas of Clairvaux's Letters', CS 98 (Kalamazoo: Cistercian Publications, 1987) 195-210.

11. The term *experientia* is not present in this text, but *affectus* appears twelve times, the verb *affici* three times; and the affect determines the experience. In addition, Bernard is making use of an extensive vocabulary for the articulation of affects around grief—affects such as love, the bitter and sharp pain of separation, loss, abandonment, misery, sadness, loneliness, suffering, feeling wounded.

12. See above, n.1.

13. Only after I had completed this article, was I informed of M.B. Pranger's recent study which includes a chapter on SC 26 (*Bernard of Clairvaux and the Shape of Monastic Thought: Broken Dreams* [Leiden: Brill, 1994].

14. See von Moos, *Consolatio*, C 828ff.

15. Although von Moos points out Bernard's sense of alienation, distance from God ('Gottferne': *Consolatio*, C 743, 763, 765, 828), he uses a structural model based on the rhetorical tradition that does not take this aspect into consideration.

16. For an example of Bernard's use of the model of the gradual ascent, see my 'The Compositional Structure of Bernard's Eighty-Fifth Sermon on the Song of Songs', CS 84 (Kalamazoo: Cistercian Publications, 1985) 86-108, and 86, n.4, for references on the literary tradition of the theme of the gradual ascent.

17. Leclercq has shown that Bernard's texts are composed with art, see *Recueil d'études sur saint Bernard et ses écrits, 3* (Rome: Edizioni di storia e letteratura, 1969) 56-67, 105-135, 137-162, 180-188. Von Moos (*Consolatio*, C 799) uses the image of a spiral as well.

18. The variances between the two existing divisions of the text—the older one deriving from later manuscripts and the one in use today that was introduced much later by Mabillon (see Leclercq, SBOp 1: lxiii)—reflect this difficulty.

19. The division in two parts in combination with the distinction of a gradual ascent is also present in SC 85, see my 'Compositional Structure', 91f and 285. The difference in structure between the two texts regarding the structure is that in SC 26 all the divisions are blurred and do not follow an explicit plan.

20. There is a connection between the two parts concerning the content, and Bernard prepares for the transition, see von Moos, *Consolatio*, C 734ff.

21. SC 26.2; SBOp 1:171,3f. 'Besides all that, the sorrow that oppresses me since my bereavement compels me to come to an end' (*On the Song of Songs* 2, transl. by Kilian Walsh, CF 7 [Kalamazoo: Cistercian Publications, 1976] 60). The latin text is quoted in the main text where the english translation cannot render the stylistic aspects that are involved.

22. I agree with Brian McGuire ('Monks and Tears', in *The Difficult Saint: Bernard of Clairvaux and his Tradition*, CS 126 [Kalamazoo: Cistercian Publications, 1991], 141) that Bernard's description of the sudden outburst of his grief is to be understood not in a literal sense, but rather as an expression of his self-state. The text reflects an affective not an historic truth. There is also an example of this affective meaning in Bernard's Ep 144.4, written to his monks in Clairvaux in 1137 on a trip to Italy: Bernard declares that the letter had been written with tears and sobs: *certe cum lacrimis et singultibus ista dictavi* (SBOp 7:346,8). There his statement indicates the intensity of missing his monks.

23. He hereby follows Gregory the Great; see von Moos, *Consolatio*, C 777. A sentence that follows shortly reflects these two aspects: 'I, whose life is bitterness (Jb 3:20), what do I have to do with this canticle?' (CF 7:60).

24. SC 26.3; CF 7:60. *Sed feci vim animo meo ac dissimulavi usque huc, ne affectus fidem vincere videretur* (SBOp 1:171,10f).

25. 'How long shall I keep my pretence while a hidden fire burns my sad heart, consumes me from within?' (CF 7:60).

26. SC 26.3; SBOp 1:171,6. 'A concelaed fire creeps forward with full play, it rages more fiercely.' (CF 7:60).

27. On these style figures see the references in n.9.

28. SC 26.3; SBOp 1:171,7f. 'Overpowering sorrow distracts my mind, the displeasure of the Lord drains my spirit dry' (CF 7:60). 'Displeasure' in the english translation reduces the intensity of the perceived affect on God's part.

29. SC 26.3; CF 7:60f.

30. SC 26.3; CF 7:61.

31. SC 26.3; CF 7:61.

32. On the concept of compassion, see von Moos, *Consolatio*, C 149.

33. On the concept of bereavement in the medieval christian tradition, see von Moos, *Consolatio*, C 131-150. McGuire (*Tears*, 140-148) does not take into account the complexity of the issue of the tears of human loss. He does not clearly distinguish between brotherly compassion and Bernard's self-experience, hereby following Bernard's own shifts in his thinking.

34. Augustine, *Confessiones*, 9:12,29ff. See von Moos, *Consolatio*, C 742.

35. Augustine, *Confessiones*, 9:12,33.

36. SC 26.4; CF 7:61.

37. It is an indication of the quality of Bernard's style that the rhetorical rules serve a distinct purpose, i.e. that the formal elements acquire meaning.

38. SC 26.4; SBOp 1: 172,6-8. 'I was frail in body and he sustained me, faint of heart and he gave me courage, slothful and negligent and he spurred me on, forgetful and improvident and he gave me timely warning.' (CF 7:61).

39. Mt 25:35f, quoted by von Moos, *Consolatio*, C 749. Bernard makes the parallel structure of the sentence more rigorous. The idea behind the biblical passage is: ' . . . as you did it to one of the least of these my brethren, you did it to me' (Mt 25:40).

40. SC 26.4; SBOp 1:172,9f. 'We loved each other in life: how can it be that death separates us?' (CF 7:61).

41. Most likely this is an association to 1 S 15:32: *Siccine separat amara mors?*.

42. SC 26.4; SBOp 1:172,22f. 'Why, I ask, have we loved, why have we lost each other?' (CF 7:62).

43. SC 26.4; CF 7:61f.

44. See von Moos, *Consolatio,* C 757. On the tradition of the paradox of life and death, see von Moos, *Consolatio,* C 754, A 754.

45. The idea of the spiritual fruit is connected with the allusion to the biblical image of the tree that will be cut down if it fails to produce any good fruit (Mt. 3:10); see von Moos, *Consolatio,* C 750.

46. In the previous section the two words are already connected with each other: *qui illum amisissem, omnes miserarentur* (SC 26.3; SBOp 1:171,15). '. . . all took pity, not so much on him who had gone as on me who had lost him' (CF 7:60f.).

47. SC 26.4; SBOp 1:172,23. 'O cruel circumstance! But pity pertains only to my lot, not to his' (CF 7:61).

48. CF 7:62.

49. SC 26.5; SBOp 1:173,12.

50. SC 26.5; SBOp 1:173,13f. '. . . he who is united to the Lord becomes one spirit with him, his whole being somehow changed into a movement of divine love' (CF 7:63).

51. SC 26.5; SBOp 1:173,15-17. 'But God is love, and the deeper one's union with God, the more full one is of love. And though God cannot endure pain, he is not without compassion for those who do'(CF 7:63).

52. SC 26.5; SBOp 1:173,17–20. 'Therefore you too must of necessity be merciful, clasped as you are to him who is Mercy, though you no longer are miserable; and though you no longer suffer, you can still be compassionate. Your love has not been diminished but only changed' (CF 7:63. The translation has been changed). In Hum 12 Bernard differentiates the two natures of Christ in terms of the relation of *misericordia* and *miseria*: while the mercy of the divine nature is free from misery, the mercy of the human nature is attached to misery (SBOp 3:25). Gerard is thereby associated with Christ; see below, p.202.

53. CF 7:63.

54. SC 26.6; CF 7:64.

55. The english translation of Bernard's text is unclear: 'This is how it must be.' (CF 7:64).

56. This might also be an indication that Bernard is here not operating within the theology of his experience but is referring to his psychology that cannot necessarily be easily accommodated to his spirituality.

57. CF 7:64.

58. CF 7:65.

59. SC 26.7; CF 7:66.

60. 2 S 19:1.

61. SC 26.8; SBOp 1:176,8. In Ep 159:2, a letter written in 1133 to Pope Innocent in the name of the Bishop of Paris on the subject of the murder of Prior Thomas of Saint Victor, Bernard refers also to 2 S 18:33: 'It would be much better for me to die instead of you [*pro te*] than to survive you [*post te*]' (SBOp 7:368,9f). In the context of this letter, the wish of dying instead of Thomas is an expression of compassion. In SC 26.8 the antithesis of *mori pro te - vivere post te* is condensed to *mori post te*. There might also be an allusion to Jb 6:8. In a letter to Suger, the abbot of Saint Denis, written in 1150 regarding Suger's imminent death, Bernard uses the phrase 'to come after you', playing with the verb *venire*: '. . . *cum perveneris quo nos praevenis, ut et nobis cito detur venire post te et ad to pervenire*' (Ep 266.2; SBOp 8:176,12f).

62. See above, p.191.

63. Von Moos, *Consolatio*, C 777. Gregory's passage referring to Jb 6:10 (Moralia sive Expositio in Iob, 7:2,11) is quoted by von Moos, *Consolatio*, A 777.

64. Bernard had expressed above the wish to die at once. Von Moos (*Consolatio, C* 777) comes to a different understanding of the meaning of this passage. In the lament for Humbert, another fellow monk who died 10 years later, in 1148, Bernard in reference to Jb 6:9–10, expressed the wish to be killed all at once by God's blows (*Utinam quem flagellas, occidas semel*), connected with the hope that God would transform the blows into favors. (Humb 6; SBOp 5:445,24–446,4). Bernard closes a letter, written in 1151, stating that his slowly declining health might mean that he does not deserve to be killed all at once (*occidatur semel*) and to enter quickly into life (Ep 270.3; SBOp 8:180,14f).

65. This sentence also indicates the presence of anger that is directed towards himself as he identifies with God's perspective.

66. . . . *me occidit, cum succidit illum* (SC 26.8; SBOp 1:176,13). In Jb 6:9 *succidat* corresponds to Bernard's *occidit.*

67. Bernard resumes here the image of the tree, see above n.45.

68. SC 26.8; CF 7:67.

69. In SC 55.3, Bernard uses the metaphor of the tears of penance in the traditional sense: 'I shall strive to correct the evils by better conduct, to wash them away with tears, to chastise them with fastings and other exercises of the holy discipline' (CF 31:85).

70. The english translation is unclear: 'but without ceasing to mourn' (CF 7:67).

71. SC 26.8; CF 7:67. The connection of a lament with Mt 5:5 is unusual, see von Moos, *Consolatio*, C 777.

72. See von Moos, *Consolatio*, C 777.

73. See below, SC 26.9, p.200.

74. See von Moos, *Consolatio*, C 777.

75. Reinhard Schwarz who examines Bernard's concept of penance ('Bernhard von Clairvaux' in *Vorgeschichte der reformatorischen Busstheologie*, Arbeiten zur Kirchengeschichte 41 [Berlin 1968] 83-104), does not mention this text.

76. The antithesis *affectus - usus* replaces the common antithesis *ratio - usus.* See von Moos, *Consolatio*, A 781. This is again an indication of Bernard's emphasis on affect as opposed to reason in coping with his grief. In the *Vita Sancti Malachiae* where Bernard presents the rational aspect, he opposes *usus* to *ratio*: *Luctus iste usu se, non ratione tuetur* (V Mal 75; SBOp 3:378,7). Bernard depicts here his notion of the ideal harmony including faith and affect, governed by the order of reason: *Vicit fides, triumphat affectus, res in suum devenit statum; cuncta geruntur ex ordine, cuncta ex ratione procdunt* (V Mal 74; SBOp 3:378,1-3).

77. SC 26.8; SBOp 1:176,25.

78. *Non culpamus affectum, nisi cum excedit modum* (SC 26.8; SBOp 1:176,25f). The appeal for moderation is part of the christian and ancient tradition of the literature of bereavement. See Hiss, *Anthropologie*, 103f, n.94. In Ep 374 written in 1148 on the death of Malachy, Bernard cautions that there should be measure in our grief: *modum tamen adhibere necesse est* (Ep 374.1; SBOp 8:335,13). See also V Mal 75; SBOp 3:378,4. For sources on the idea of moderation see von Moos, *Consolatio* T 379ff.

79. SC 26.8; CF 7:68.

80. Following Augustine, Bernard protests against the stoic doctrine of apathy. See Hiss, *Anthropologie*, 103, n.94. Von Moos (*Consolatio*, C 788) suggests that Bernard follows here the interpretation of Job by Gregory the Great.

81. See the title of this article. The reference to Jn 1:20 where John reveals himself. 'He declared, he did not deny, but declared', gives even more weight to his pronouncement [*confessio*]: The declaration of the impact of his affects on him is indeed seen as a self-declaration.

82. SC 26.9; CF 7:69.

83. In the lament for Humbert (see above, n.64), this causal connection is made explicit: The death of Humbert is seen as having been caused by the sins of Bernard and his monks (Humb 7; SBOp 5:447,2).

84. SC 26.10; CF 7:69.

85. SC 26.10; SBOp 1:178,9f. 'All by myself I experience the sufferings that are shared equally by lovers when compelled to remain apart.' (CF 7:70).

86. See above, p.192. Von Moos (*Consolatio,* C 798) expresses his surprise about Bernard's freedom to use this image that is determined entirely by human affect and refers to the sphere of carnal love. This shows again that Bernard goes beyond the traditional boundaries of spiritual love in order to express his feelings.

87. SC 26.11; SBOp 1:178,11f. 'Would that I have not lost you, but have sent you on before me! Would that one day, however far off, I may follow you wherever you go!' (CF 7:70). In the letter to Suger, (see above, n.61) Bernard expresses the same idea by juxtaposing *perire* (to go away by perishing) with *praeire* (to go before): *non possum perdere sic dilectum usque in finem. Non mihi perit, sed praeit . . .* (Ep 266.2; SBOp 8:176,9f). In this case the emphasis on the ongoing connection is meant to reassure primarily the dying Suger rather than Bernard.

88. SC 26.11; SBOp 1:178,17-20. ' . . . to see a man exulting in the hour of death, and mocking its onset. "O death, where is your victory?" A sting no longer but a shout of joy. A man dies while he sings, he sings by dying' (CF 7:70).

89. SC 26.11; CF 7:70. *Usurparis ad laetitiam, mater maeroris; usurparis ad gloriam, gloriae inimica; usurparis ad introitum regni, porta inferi, et fovea perditionis ad inventionem salutis, idque ab homine peccatore . . . Mortua es, o mors, . . .* (SBOp 1:178,20-24).

90. I am following here von Moos, *Consolatio*, C 804f.

91. SC 26.11; SBOp 1:179,7-9. 'This is how he sang, the man we mourn for; and he could well have changed my mourning into song, for with my mind fixed on his glory, the sense of my own misery had begun to fade' (CF 7:71).

92. See above, pp.193f.

93. On the concept of death as devil see von Moos, *Consolatio*, C 805f., A 806.

94. SC 26.12; SBOp 1:179,10-13. 'But the pang of sorrow quickly recalls me to myself from that serene vision; I am roused, as from a light sleep, by a gnawing anxiety. I continue to lament, but over my own plight, because reason forbids me to mourn for him. I feel that given the occasion, he would now say to us: "Do not weep for me, but weep for yourselves" (Lk 23:28)' (CF 7:71).

95. See von Moos, *Consolatio*, C 811, T 309ff.

96. Von Moos (*Consolatio*, C 811) thinks that Bernard no longer makes the distinction between lament and penance, that it becomes the same. This view does not take into account the complexity and problematic nature of Bernard's attempt to validate his affective experience.

97. SC 26.12; SBOp 1:179,23f. 'In the first place I bewail my own wounds and the loss this house has suffered; I bewail the needs of the poor, to whom Gerard was a father; I bewail above all the state of our whole Order, of our religious life, that derived no small support from your zeal, your wisdom and your example, O Gerard; and finally, though my mourning is not for you, it is because of you' (CF 7:71f).

98. SC 26.12; SBOp 1:179,24f. 'My deepest wound is in the ardor of my love for you' (CF 7:72).

99. SC 26.12; SBOp 1: 179,25f. 'And let no one embarrass me by telling me I am wrong in yielding to this feeling . . .' (CF 7:72).

100. SC 26.12; CF 7:72. This is an allusion to Mt 12:42 (*ecce plus quam Salomon hic*) referring to Christ. On this passage, see von Moos, *Consolatio*, C 813. This sentence associates Gerard with Christ as above in SC 26.11, but it might also serve as a prelude to the example of Christ that follows.

101. SC 26.12; SBOp 1:180,1-3. 'And shall I not feel my own desolation that even now presses upon me? Shall I not grieve for the heavy blow so recently received? Christ's tears were tears of compassion, and shall I be afraid to weep in my suffering?' (CF 7:72. The translation mistakenly reads: 'David's tears . . .').

102. See above, p.194, where Bernard uses this pair to make a different point.

103. CF 7:72 (I corrected 'human kindness' to 'human nature'). Von Moos (*Consolatio*, A 814) indicates Ambrose (*De excessu fratris* [*Satyri*] 1:10f) as the most likely source.

104. SC 26.13; CF 7:72. *Sic nec fletus utique noster infidelitatis est signum, sed conditionis indicium; nec, quia percussus ploro, arguo ferientem, sed provoco pietatem, severitatem flectere satago. Unde et verba dolore sunt plena* (Jb 6:3), *non tamen murmure* (SBOp 1:180,8-11).

105. Von Moos (*Consolatio*, C 830) distinguishes two aspects of the argumentation of consolation: one representing the theology of suffering justifies and transforms the mourning, the other one eschatological, opposes the mourning.

106. See above, p.198.

107. See above, p.201.

108. SC 26.13; SBOp 1:180,17-20. 'You gave me Gerard, you took him away: and if his removal makes me sad, I do not forget that he was given to me, and offer thanks for my good fortune in having had him. I regret his departure only to the extent that it is of no avail' (CF 7:73. The last sentence of the translation has been modified).

109. Bernard points out his responsibility as abbot to give Gerard back to his monks who had entrusted Gerard to him, which matches his legal reasoning. Interesting is also that on the same trip Bernard himself had been ill and expressed in two letters (written in the fall of 1137) his strong wish to return to his monks and to die among them (Epp 144,145).

110. SC 26.14; CF 7:73 (For the translation of *praevaricatio* the word 'unfaithfulness' in the english translation has been replaced by the more legal term 'breaking of the agreement').

111. SC 26.14; SBOp 1:181,5f. 'What more shall I say? You entrusted Gerard to us, you have claimed him back; you have but taken what was yours' (CF 7:73).

112. SC 26.14; SBOp 1:181,6f. 'These tears impose an ending on my words; may you, O Lord, impose an ending and moderation on them' (This is my own translation).

113. For examples, see von Moos, *Consolatio*, T 46ff, T 1703ff.

114. Von Moos (*Consolatio*, C 830, 849) holds the view that Bernard in this conclusion overcomes the stance of self-centered bereavement by the idea of sharing Gerard's joy, and by finding meaning in the work of God.

115. SC 27.1; CF 7:74.

116. On the requirement for moderation, see above n.78.

117. See above, p.196.

118. Man is encouraged to examine not what he suffers but what Christ has suffered: *Non interroges, o homo, ea quae pateris, sed quae passus est ille* (Epi 1.2; SBOp 4:293,13f).

119. This distinguishes God not only from the realm of human feelings but from death that was characterized as erratic and envious.

120. Hiss (*Anthroplogie*, 39) points out that for Bernard God remains always the essential point of reference, that his stance is truly theocentric; but that his stance can also rightfully be called anthropocentric, since for Bernard nothing is of meaning that does not refer to man and to his existence.

Jean Leclercq's Attitude Toward War

Eoin de Bhaldraithe

When Jean Leclercq wrote on 'Saint Bernard's Attitude toward War',[1] he warned us that our present-day views on armed conflict should not prejudice our study of Bernard. Yet Leclercq's own attitude seems to have affected his study considerably. We would like to offer a summary of his views, quoting directly some of his more surprising statements. Then we will try to assess his approach especially by contrasting it with that of Thomas Merton. Next we will look at the ideals of the military orders and see what they owe to Bernard. Some examples of his subsequent influence will bring us down to our own day and how we now look on Bernard's 'pagans'.

We begin with a story which shows that an exact replica of Bernard's attitude to war survives today. His nonacentenary in 1990 was the occasion for a study of the history of catholic teaching on peace.[2] I received a letter asking what were my sources for Bernard's claim that he worked miracles while preaching the crusade. I went first to his encyclical on the crusade and read the several versions that exist but to no avail. Eventually in *De consideratione*, where Bernard ponders on the failure of the crusade, I found the reference in the footnotes of the Migne edition.[3]

After a few hours of this research, I heard on a news bulletin a summary of Saddam Hussein's message to his soldiers on the first day of the Gulf War. They were fighting the forces of infidelity. They knew that God was on their side. Even if they were not to win they would still fight bravely for 'our people love martyrdom'.

It was exactly Bernard's message. For Bernard the Muslims were infidels and were to be killed; God, speaking through the pope, had ordered the crusade. Those who died fighting for Christ would undergo a joyful martyrdom. The similarity would hardly have been noticeable if one had not been reading Bernard. Of course, Sadam Hussein was using an extreme islamic approach to stir his people to war. Yet it is a remarkable feature of the conflict that the presidents of Iraq and the United States both asked their people to pray for victory.

The christian preaching of the crusade had furnished the soldiers with strong motives, so eventually muslim theology found it necessary to provide counter motivation. The west may have abandoned strict crusade thinking but its counterpart survives among the Muslims.[4]

ASSESSING BERNARD

Leclercq's Attitude to Bernard

In his contribution to a history of spirituality, Leclercq dealt with the military orders.[5] We will summarize here Leclercq's views on Bernard at that time: In the treatise for the Templars, Bernard had shown that they were truly religious as there was nothing lacking to their evangelical perfection. Yet the historian must ask how the mildness of the gospel could be reconciled with the laws of war. Those military monks were founded for a defensive war but some were later 'ordered to drive back the pagan Slavs'.[6] Bernard forbade killing in lawful defence. The death of a military monk 'was not generally considered to be a martyrdom'.[7]

Thirteen years later Leclercq published his main study on war.[8] He begins by telling us that while many have seen Bernard 'as merely the representative of a long christian tradition of violence', he believes that his hero was really an evangelical 'peacemaker' (1).[9] It is hard for us to realize how much violence there was in the twelfth century, indeed 'violence and religion tended to be at each other's service' (2). Clerics were exempt from armed combat, yet it was a holy or sacred duty.

Leclercq went on to outline church teaching on violence at the time. Augustine had already said it was proper for the secular power to coerce heretics. In doing so 'he managed to rise above his own strong personal aversion' (6). Anselm of Lucca, asked by Gregory VII to write on the subject (8), was the first to claim that the church itself and not just the secular power, could use force. War could be waged to correct heretics, defend widows and orphans and cure malefactors. Basically violence must be accompanied by love.

For Bernard the monks formed a 'peace corps'. By recruiting so many monks 'Bernard appeared as the greatest non-violent leader of his time' (13). There were two ways to the heavenly Jerusalem; one was holy war, the other was monastic life in which Sunday was usually a day of devotion to the new Jerusalem.

Leclercq now comes to the actual wars. 'Bernard tried to have as few wars as possible' and 'he advocated the least possible violence' (14). He told King Louis VII that war involves murder. The widows and orphans produced by war suffer most. Religious war, however, was different. Urging Henry I of England to take up the sword in favour of Innocent II Bernard said that 'by the justice of our cause we appease God' (17). The spiritual and temporal powers must defend one another. If one must fight, let it be against the enemies of the church and then the war will be just. In this Bernard faithfully followed Anselm.

Bernard opposed attacks on Jews during the Crusade. Yet it was often necessary to defend the church against heretics. While faith should not be imposed, princes could use coercion and persecution when it seemed necessary. The concept of 'persecution' comes from Anselm and stands for 'the prevention of wrong-doing and a subsequent coercion in favour of good conduct'(19). Bernard recommended it to the inhabitants of Toulouse. Yet they were to practise 'hospitality' to the poor. Jesus remains the 'perfect model of non-violence' (20).

The pagan Wends interfered with the Crusade so Bernard urged a crusade against them 'to destroy them entirely or preferably to convert them' (21). Leclercq prefers a missionary interpretation of this famous phrase but 'the alternatives are not that clear-cut' (21).

The Muslims in the Holy Land were, of course, Bernard's main opponents. His famous crusade was 'oriented towards the reestablishment of peace' (22). His attitude was only a continuation of his approach to the Templars.

In the treatise written for them, Bernard said that the Templars could not 'kill pagans unless it was impossible to do otherwise'. Killing is allowed for self-defense. The Templar *securus interimit, interit securior.* 'It is better to be the victim of violence than the instigator' (24) is Leclercq's interpretation of the phrase.[10] Their death in war is glory, joy, exultation and beatitude. But in the end their life of war was subordinated to prayer.

Next Leclercq introduces us to some contemporary critics of the military orders' ideal (25–29). Isaac of Stella he quotes as saying that the new militia was really a new monstrosity. Its members thought that it was lawful to despoil and kill pagans; if they themselves died in the process they were martyrs. Leclercq insists that Bernard avoids mention of spoliation; 'on the contrary, he had preached voluntary poverty' (28). What Isaac meant was that lawful violence must be accompanied by a right intention.

Edessa fell to the Muslims in 1145, so on 31 March 1146 Bernard preached the crusade at Vézelay. While the Pope asked him to preach in France Bernard, 'contrary to the intentions of the Pope' (30–31), tried to involve all the other christian nations. The fact that he thus involved a number of princes and was not able to unite them as he thought he could, 'led to their defeat' (31). In his encyclical to them he simply uses the ideas of Anselm of Lucca as Urban II had done before him.

For Bernard the expedition was to be ascetic and expiatory. His crusader mystique was simply an application of the Templar ideal. The intention had to be right. But he also flattered young noblemen by appealing to their bravery.

Leclercq was not quite so sure that Bernard's missionary intention towards the Muslims was as clear as it was towards the Wends. The Jews are subject to the christian princes, so we should patiently await their conversion. Not so with the Muslims. Palestine was Christ's land. Those who had taken it over should be driven back.

Bernard had agreed with those who thought that the Orthodox in Constantinople should be attacked. Their separation by schism constituted a violent situation, according to Leclercq. They were to be conquered 'not as schismatics, but as the political adversaries of the crusaders' (35).

Leclercq wondered if the facts he had uncovered justified Bernard's attitude towards the crusade. His true weakness was not his religious motivation but his lack of political realism. An historian, P. Lorson, is quoted as saying that Bernard's encyclical on the crusade was written at 'a moment of collective, and perhaps individual, psychosis', but it is not quite clear whether Leclercq agrees (38).

Finally he declares that Bernard was 'fundamentally' a man of peace, thus recalling his initial statement as in a biblical *inclusio*.[11]

Assessment of Leclercq's Attitude

Leclercq mentions 'the moral programme proposed in the new testament' (6) but we are at a loss to see what he thought it was.[12] 'Pacifists and war-mongers', normally, 'accuse each other of being unfaithful to some text of the gospel' (8). Those are presented as two extremes and it is implied that while a Christian would not be eager for war, he should hardly be a pacifist either.

On the other hand we were told that Bernard would be seen as a 'peacemaker' (1). He was pulled in two ways by the gospel and society, by non-violence and violence, which seems to equate the gospel with non-violence. Indeed his statement that by recruiting so many Cistercians, Bernard was a great 'non-violent leader' (13) is an obvious allusion to Gandhi, but it is unworthy of the great Hindu as he did not call some to non-violence and others to violence.

Bernard claims that widows and orphans suffer most in war (16), but Leclercq placed this alongside the view of Anselm that one could go to war for the sake of widows and orphans (9) and offers no explanation of the contradiction.

To prove that Isaac of Stella was concerned with right intention, he quoted him as saying, 'When something may be lawfully done, will one not be tempted to do it for mere pleasure?' (29) Yet the true meaning is that an enemy will freely kill christians when he finds that they believe killing is lawful.[13] Bernard does avoid mentioning spoliation, but the fact that he preaches voluntary poverty does not offset this, as that refers to individuals and it is the community that would acquire the spoil.

Leclercq's conclusion, that there was nothing wrong with Bernard's religious motivation, only with his political realism (35), seems to say that if the crusade succeeded, all would have been well as it was really from God.

Leclercq claimed that it was the division among the leaders that caused the crusade to fail. In fact, two tactical decisions led to the debacle. King Louis VII decided to go to Jerusalem to pray at the holy sepulchre before attacking Nur ad-Din in Aleppo claiming that his crusader vow obliged him to do so. On his return to Acre the decision was taken to attack instead Unur of Damascus simply because he was a Muslim even though he was an ally of the Palestinian Franks.[14]

'It was a decision of utter folly', says Steven Runciman, taken mainly because Damascus is mentioned in scripture.[15] 'It was here that the holy blindness of this religious crusade of Saint Bernard's revealed itself with an astonishing clarity', says Karen Armstrong.[16] Leclercq's view cannot be taken as serious historical interpretation.

He quotes Bernard as saying that the Templars could not kill pagans unless it was impossible to do otherwise as killing was allowed only for self-defence (23–24). Yet what Bernard actually says is that they are not to be killed if there is some other way of preventing them from oppressing the faithful, but now 'it is better that they be killed'.[17] In our own day 'self-defence' is the most usual justification for war and so does Leclercq allow present day attitudes to influence him. It is all the more surprising as he had admitted in his earlier work that Bernard, in this Templar treatise, taught that killing for self-defence was forbidden.[18]

He probably goes furthest when he tries to defend Bernard's attitude to the Orthodox. To describe the schism as 'a violent situation' is to give a new meaning to the word 'violent' (35) as well as ignoring the fact that it takes two to make a schism. When Leclercq wrote this, the Second Vatican Council had described those schismatics as 'still joined to us in closest intimacy'.[19] Even at the time of Bernard it is doubtful if there actually was a schism as the crusaders received communion while in Byzantium.[20]

In sum, Leclercq says that the Orthodox were not to be attacked as schismatics, but their schism was violent anyhow. Possibly he had borrowed unconsciously from the catholic paramilitaries in Ireland who were claiming at the time that they were not killing protestants as protestants but as something else.

When Leclercq speaks of as few wars as possible and as little violence as possible, he does not seem to have thought of the possibility of not fighting for the Holy Land at all. We conclude that in seeking to defend his hero, Leclercq has involved himself in a number of serious contradictions.

In the Middle Ages, if someone was to be canonized, it was necessary to write a biography enumerating the miracles the holy person had performed. Today miracles are less important to us, but after all we have learnt from Gandhi, we would wish our heroes to be people of peace. This is what Leclercq seeks to prove about Bernard, so his essay is in honourable continuity with medieval hagiography.

Thomas Merton's Attitude to Bernard

The best way to show the limitations of Leclercq's scholarly approach is to present the different attitude of Thomas Merton. Already in 1954 he was saying that the crusading Bernard was 'a temptation, perhaps even a scandal'.[21] Some say that 'the Bernard of the Crusade was not the true Bernard', but Merton thought that he may in fact have been more himself at Vézelay than at Clairvaux.[22]

At this time Merton held that it was Catholic doctrine that the pope could ask christian armies to defend the divine order.[23] Yet this view did not lead him to defend Bernard. We have described elsewhere how Merton later became a virtual pacifist by reading Roland Bainton's history of attitudes to war and peace.[24] Origen had been fully pacifist but Augustine changed the tradition. This realization gave Merton the strong basis for his convictions on peace. If he had not come to see that Augustine had departed from the tradition and that the Church was basically following his position, Merton could never have proclaimed his own doctrine with such assurance.

His role in opposing the Vietnam War is now a matter of history. His teaching has been enshrined in the pastoral letter on peace issued by the bishops of the United States. This document has won the freedom of the Church for the pacifist position which had been regarded as heresy since the Middle Ages.[25]

Since Merton was not defending Bernard, he could let reality speak for itself and does not hesitate to use the word 'scandal'. Yet this honesty did not impede Merton from admiring Bernard's mystical writings. As he says, people tend to create two Bernards since those who read his spiritual treatises would not usually be interested in his teaching on war.[26] Leclercq had not studied early christian doctrine on peace and was still trying to defend the old catholic position.[27]

Old Testament Authority

Leclercq insisted that Bernard did not innovate but followed Anselm of Lucca, whom he quotes as saying that 'Vengeance should be exercised not through hatred but through love' (8). This is clearly the doctrine of Augustine.[28] Bernard, however, says that the Templar hates those who hate God.[29] This is a quotation from Psalm 138. He then cites the books of Judges and Maccabees. Those were favourite reading in the refectories of The Templars, whose rule may have come from Bernard himself.[30] The book of Judges had been transformed into 'a kind of chivalry novel'.[31] Certainly Bernard would later use this book to apologise for the defeat of the crusade and, as we shall claim, to write the programme for the next two crusades.[32] So it seems that Bernard is really departing from Anselm and Augustine and taking the Old Testament as his authority. The christian warrior need not fight with reluctant love but should do so with enthusiastic hatred. Perhaps it was not a great transition as Augustine's argument involved some sophistry. Bernard was saying that if Christians are going to fight they should do it wholeheartedly.

THE IDEALS OF THE KNIGHTS

We now look at some sources which throw further light on the ideals of the military orders.

The Letter of Hugh of Saint Victor

A manuscript in Nîmes preserves the only copy of a letter to the Templars attributed to Hugh of Saint Victor.[33] It comes between the latin Rule and Bernard's *De laude*. Leclercq surmised that it was really written by Hugh de Payns, first Master of the Knights.[34] Later he accepted the arguments of Clement Schlafert and agreed that the attribution in the manuscript was more likely to be genuine.[35]

We can deduce that there was a crisis of confidence among the Templars. Some of them doubted whether they were full religious while others had qualms about their military activities. Most seriously, it would seem, the brother servants, divided between equerries and *conversi*, were 'murmuring' against the knights who were all from the nobility.

Schlafert claims that Hugh spoke with an authority second only to that of Bernard himself, affirming them in their vocation and justifying their warfare. Isaac of Stella attacked *De laude* and this letter on similar terms—which confirms its high authority.[36] The Master himself, as a member of the Order, would not have carried much weight in the crisis. Indeed it is implausible that he would have left for the West and sought to solve the problem by writing home.

Bernard's work is of a higher literary quality and gives a stronger answer to the same doubts. Hugh's letter would have been superfluous if Bernard's masterpiece had already existed. The earliest date for both is 1129 when Hugh de Payns came to the Council of Troyes seeking affirmation for his Order.[37] It would seem that the Victorine letter was written soon afterwards. The Templar Master had to ask Bernard three times for a reply, so *De laude* must have come a year or so later and certainly before Hugh's death in 1136.

We quote a few lines from the letter attributed to Hugh of Saint Victor:

> [The devil] suggests hatred and anger when you kill and suggests greed when you despoil. You repel his attacks because when you kill you do not hate unjustly and when you despoil you do not desire unjustly. . . . you do not hate the man but the iniquity . . . you take from them what is justly forfeited for their sins and what is justly due to you for your labour.[38]

Hugh here is very close to Augustine; one kills the enemy with love. Hatred is to be avoided but, as we saw, Bernard would encourage it. Gaetano Raciti has pointed out that when Isaac of Stella says that the new militia 'lawfully despoils and religiously kills', he is making a sarcastic reference to those words of Hugh, just as he ironically echoes the words of *De laude*.[39]

All indications then urge us to accept the letter as having come from Hugh of Saint Victor. The contrast between the two lets us see how Bernard's ideas went beyond those commonly accepted in the Church of his day.

Knighting and Profession

Their dedication to battle prevented the knights from being ordained as priests. A few brothers were ordained to serve as chaplains, so they, like Bernard, could not wield the sword. They could only exhort their brethren to fight as Gratian would say in his Decree.[40]

The profession ceremony was preceded by the conferring of the order of knighthood. The ceremony as used by the Knights Hospitallers is given by Jacques Paul Migne in his work on the religious orders.[41] A liturgical ceremony like this would have been standard for all military orders. Further we can deduce that it was very ancient. The theology of violence it contains is similar to that of Bernard, so we can presume that its inspiration goes back to his time.

First a priest blessed the sword, saying, 'Use this sword to defend yourself and the holy Church of God and to rout the enemies of the cross of Christ and of the christian faith. . . .'

Then a knight, usually the superior, questioned the novice, 'What do you ask?'. He replied, 'The Order of Chivalry'. The knight then said, 'It is a noble and salutary thing to serve the poor of Jesus Christ and to accomplish the works of mercy, and to make yourself available for the defence of the faith. This Order is given only to those who deserve it by the ancient nobility of their lineage.'

The knight next gave the sword to the novice, saying, 'Take this sword. Its brightness means that it is inflamed with faith; its point means hope; its hand-piece signifies charity. Use it virtuously for your own defence and that of the catholic faith. Do not be afraid to enter into dangers for the name of God.'

The knight then wiped the sword on the novice's arm and put it into the scabbard saying, 'As you put this sword into its scabbard clean and polished, so may you never draw it to strike a person unjustly or stain it in any way.'

The novice then stood up and brandished his sword three times. The knight stated that this signifies challenging the enemies of the catholic faith with hope of success. The knight then took the sword again and hit the novice on the shoulder three times in a gesture we are familiar with from the conferring of knighthood by british monarchs.

The rest of the ceremony is like most other professions. As well as keeping the Rule he is asked to have a burning heart for the defence of the faith of Jesus Christ against its enemies 'so that he will the more easily call you to his kingdom'. Then he took an oath on the missal to keep all the rules, including chastity. The habit of the Knights Hospitaller had an eight pointed star and each point was held to represent one of the beatitudes. While this helped to offset the strong military language, it was a very real consecration of violence.

The Master's Oath

In his account of the Templars, Migne gives the text of an oath taken by a newly elected Master, equivalent to a provincial in later times. It is found in a manuscript of the abbey of Alcobaza in Portugal and is reported by several historians of the Cistercian Order. Those indicate clearly that it applied to the whole Order and not just to the portuguese houses.[42]

> I swear that I will defend not only by words but also by the force of arms and by all my power the mysteries of the faith . . . I promise also to be obedient to the Master general of the order according to the statutes prescribed for us by our Father Saint Bernard.

So Bernard, regarded as their founder and legislator, was much more an authority figure for them than for the Cistercians.

The superior continued by promising, 'that I will give aid against the infidel kings and princes; that in the presence of three enemies I will not flee, but will decapitate them if they are infidels.' This shows how seriously the word 'infidel' was taken. Apparently it would be acceptable to flee in the presence of four enemies, but with two or three the knight had to stand his ground. There is very little sign here of any missionary intention or of Augustine's idea of accompanying violence with love. Its spirit is authentically bernardine.

The very close links of the Templars with the Cistercians are exhibited as he continued, 'I will not refuse help to religious persons especially to the religious of Citeaux and their abbots, since they are our brothers and companions; I will help them in word, in works and even by arms.' We see then that the Templars regarded themselves as the armed wing of the Cistercians, who were hardly a medieval 'peace corps'.

The contrast between *De laude* and the letter of Hugh shows that Bernard innovated by advocating hatred. The ceremony of knighthood consecrated violence while the Master's oath illustrated the bernardine approach to infidels.

SUBSEQUENT INFLUENCE OF BERNARD

We would now like to outline briefly some of the later influence of the military orders, and more important perhaps, Bernard's bearing on the rise of the mendicant orders. Finally we shall see how his influence can also be felt in some contemporary war situations.

The Military Orders

We have seen how Leclercq stated that the military orders were founded to fight defensive wars, but the german knights were an exception as they were 'ordered to drive back the pagan Slavs'.[43] No reason is given as to why such an exception was made. Desmond Seward and Manfred Hellmann[44] also simply indicate which areas they were given to conquer but make no effort to say why. Those Slavs were basically the same people as Bernard's 'Wends', certainly when viewed from Clairvaux. So it is most likely that the german knights were carrying out his policy of converting or exterminating them.

Seward devotes part of his book on *The Monks of War* to the german and iberian military orders. He tells us how surprised he was to find so many similarities between the Nazis and the prussian knights. The activities of the iberian orders reminded him of how the Spanish and Portuguese treated the native Americans. Thus two very sad chapters in modern history have their roots in the military orders and in the theological foundation Bernard laid for them.

The Poverty Movement

I once asked Jean Leclercq about Bernard's attitude to heretics, especially as it can be seen in sermons 64 to 66 on the Canticle. He was unaware of how this was related to the origin of the friars and expressed surprise when I showed him an article of Sophronius Clasen on the poverty movement.[45] The Waldenses, for example, held that all Christians were bound to poverty and forbidden to kill anyone. This was also taught by Saint Basil the Great to those preparing for baptism and represents the common position of the early Church.[46]

Bernard insisted that the celibate men and women of the poverty movement were to be placed in separate monasteries. If they refused they were to be considered guilty of heresy, that is 'eliminated from the church'.[47] Bernard's views soon became official policy. Some thirty years after his death the members of the movement were forbidden to preach.[48] After another thirty years, however, Innocent III allowed many poverty groups back into the church. They could retain their ideals provided they recognized the hierarchy. The Franciscans, consisting of friars, nuns and persons living in the world, are the best known group, orally approved in 1209 or 1210.[49] Church law had hitherto allowed ordination only for a particular church. That was now changed and absolute ordination was permitted so that friars could be ordained and preach.[50] For the women, however, Bernard's policy prevailed and they were subjected to enclosure.

The membership of persons living in the world was finally approved in 1221, despite the Fourth Lateran Council decrees of six years earlier, which had followed Bernard.[51] Known as the third order, these 'tertiaries' had the ideal of non-violence extended even to them. They were not to take up lethal weapons against anyone or bear them about, a fact proudly quoted by the bishops of the United States in their pastoral letter on peace.[52] But there were inevitable compromises.

In the cathedral of Toledo, there is an altar painting of Saint Francis with the Master of the Knights of Santiago.[53] The latter wears the habit of his order over the gilded armour of a Master. Seeing the two of them together, one realizes that the franciscan habit is not only one of poverty but also of non-violence. The Francis of this picture follows the Sermon on the Mount but only as a counsel. He agrees that the Master is not bound by it.

The Francis of this picture would not criticize the crusades. He would be more faithful than most to Bernard's stipulation that one must seek to convert Muslims before killing them—whence his preaching to the Sultan. The Waldenses opposed crusading, but Francis could not do so if he were to have a place inside the 'official church.'

Poverty and non-violence were accepted as long as they were regarded as optional for individuals and not required of the whole

Church. For eight centuries after Bernard his policy of enclosure was applied to all women religious; today it still applies to some.

The War In Lebanon

Seward describes how the battle of Acre began in 1290. The Christians in the city were generally at peace with the surrounding Muslims, who crowded into the market place to sell their produce. As virtual rulers, the knights were satisfied with the co-existence. A small band of crusaders arriving from Italy, however, went straight to the market place and, despite the pleas of the knights, began cutting the throats of Muslims. This led to the battle and downfall of Acre.

The action of the italian crusaders reminds us of a contemporary tragedy. The Maronites are Christians and Catholics. France created Lebanon for them by cutting it off from Syria and including just enough Muslims to ensure a Catholic majority. They were soon outnumbered, however, but the Lebanese government never allowed a census as it would have revealed that the Christians had become a minority.[54]

In December 1975, four Christians were killed in east Beruit. The maronite political leader told his men to set up checkpoints on the ring road and kill forty Muslims. When the latter heard what was going on they set up their own blockade at the other end of the road and started killing Christians. On that Black Saturday three hundred Muslims and three hundred Christians had their throats cut.[55] We can easily see the parallel with the throat cutting which precipitated the fall of Acre.

Later, at the invitation of the Maronites, Israel invaded Lebanon and this further revived the longstanding christian-muslim rivalry.[56] In the following statement made in 1985 by the Hizb Allah, usually regarded as an extremist group, we will recognize many of the crusading sentiments, coming now from muslim lips.

> In the name of God, the merciful and the compassionate. To him who scattered America's dreams in Lebanon and who resisted the Israeli occupation . . . to paramount martyr, Raghib Harb, may God be pleased with him . . . We beseech God . . . to give us victory over the tyrants.
>
> We consider ourself a part of the islamic nation in the world which is facing the most tyrannical arrogant assault

> from both the East and the West. God is behind us, supporting us with his care . . . and giving us his dear and resounding victory against them.
>
> Nearly 100,000 is the number of the victims of the crimes perpetrated against us by America, Israel and the Phalange (the Maronite party). Our objective is submission by the Phalange to just rule.
>
> God, may he be praised, says, 'Let there be no compulsion in religion'. . . . Therefore, we do not want Islam to rule in Lebanon by force, as the political Maronism is ruling at present.
>
> We wish to address a few words to the Christians in Lebanon, especially to the Maronites. The policy followed by the leaders of political Maronism is incapable of achieving peace. . . . The time has come for the fanatical Christians to come out of the tunnel of sectarian loyalty. We are confident that Christ, God's prophet, peace be upon him, is innocent of the massacres perpetrated by the Phalange in his name and in yours.[57]

This will give some flavour of the thought of an extreme islamic group. If the language were changed about, with Christians speaking to Muslims, it would be very close to that of Bernard. God's cause and martyrdom are identical. 'The islamic nation' corresponds to medieval Christendom. It is more moderate, however, in asking simply for just rule and in revering Christ.

Ethnic Cleansing

Writing twenty years ago, Leclercq described the conflict of Bernard's time as belonging to 'remote historical periods' (1). Yet in our own day the current war in former Yugoslavia looks remarkably similar with the same catholic, orthodox and muslim contendants. It has brought the term 'ethnic cleansing' into everyday use. This procedure too was prescribed by Bernard. After his visit to Toulouse in 1145, he wrote to thank the people who welcomed him.

> We rejoiced at your devotion to us and at your zeal and hatred of the heretics so that each of you could say, 'Did I not hate those who hate you, Lord? With a perfect hate

> have I hated them and they became my enemies.' . . . The truth was manifested through us, not only in word but in power. So were caught the wolves who came to you in sheep's clothing. . . . So dearly beloved, persecute and apprehend them and do not desist until they perish (*depereant*) completely and flee from all your territory for it is not safe to sleep near to serpents.[58]

Incomprehensibly, Leclercq describes this as 'encouraging the people of Toulouse to defend themselves' (20). Bernard is now recommending perfect hatred of heretics. Ten or fifteen years earlier, when writing *De laude*, Bernard had reserved hatred only for pagans and did not use the word 'perfect'. He said, not that heretics should be killed, but that the territory should certainly be 'religiously' cleansed. Yet the word 'perish' is ambiguous, apparently allowing for some deaths in the purifying process.

We can say that Bernard here established the programme for the crusade of Innocent III against the Cathars of some sixty years later; it was also the programme for the better known persecution of the Huguenots.

This is a side of the story we cannot follow here. A short passage from Armstrong, however, captures the reality succinctly. Innocent III in 1207 wrote to King Philip

> urging him to take an army to fight the heretics in the region of Languedoc, offering him indulgences that were similar to those given to people who went on a crusade to the holy Land to fight the Muslims. For the first time in Europe, a Pope was calling upon Christians to kill other Christians: Innocent was setting a precedent for a new kind of holy war that would become an incurable disease in Europe. It looked forward to the wars and persecutions waged by catholics and protestants against one another, to the wars of religion in the seventeenth century and to the bitter, endless struggle in Northern Ireland today.[59]

Without Bernard there would have been wars but he supplied a religious motive for some of the worst of them. In this section we have seen his greater or lesser influence on such varied topics as nazi ideals, new world colonialism, franciscan poverty, women's enclosure, the war in Lebanon, ethnic cleansing in former Yugoslavia, and the troubles in Ireland.

ARE MUSLIMS CHRISTIAN?

For Bernard it was axiomatic that Muslims were pagans and infidels. The attitude is very well explained by R.W. Southern. The early success of the crusades brought only reactions of 'triumph and contempt' towards the conquered.[60] Fairy tale lives of Mohammed circulated during Bernard's life time. The author of the *Gesta Dei per Francos* could not say whether his picture of the Prophet was true or false, but this he could say: 'it is safe to speak evil of one whose malignity exceeds whatever ill can be spoken'.[61] According to Southern this frankish picture had little contact with reality but 'a profound influence on future thought'.[62] It is from the same milieu that Bernard's theological view of Islam arose.

Some centuries earlier, Islam had simply been regarded as one more christian heresy. Saint John Damascene includes Mohammed in his book on heresies.[63] Many of the statements in the Koran should be laughed at, he says, yet Mohammed held that there is one God, and that Christ is the Word and Spirit of God. He was the prophet and servant of God but not his son. It was not Christ himself but only his shadow that was crucified. Muslims accuse Christians of adoring the cross, he wrote. Mohammed allowed four wives and divorce. He insisted on circumcision. This summary of Damascene's treatise on Islam shows that he regarded Muslims clearly as Christians but seriously in error.[64]

Southern outlines the growth in understanding of Islam during the Middle Ages. In the fifteenth century, Nicholas of Cusa was one of the earliest textual critics and has to his credit the demonstration that the *Donation of Constantine* was a forgery.[65] When he turned his attention to the Koran he claimed that it consisted of a basic layer of nestorian christianity with many jewish corrections superimposed.[66] But even as he was engaged in this conciliatory research, others were advocating 'a return to more warlike and spirited virtutes, as depicted in the epics of the early crusades'.[67]

As we come to understand better the primitive christianity which has survived in the East, and which we unfairly label 'nestorian', our understanding of Islam can only be improved. Today our church claims to have 'a high regard for Muslims'.[68]

CONCLUSION

The various points we have studied allow us to give a clearer picture of the development of church teaching on peace and war than has been possible hitherto.

The Apostolic Tradition of the early third century witnesses to the original approach that a soldier who killed somebody was to be excluded from the Church.[69] This continued as the normal canon law in the eastern church with Saint Basil insisting on a three year exclusion from Holy Communion for soldiers who killed in war.

In the West, Augustine said that it was lawful for the state to go to war for a religious purpose but even then the soldier had to exclude hatred from his heart and kill with love. Yet it is not clear that such a one would be allowed to Holy Communion. It seems that it was some centuries later before the penitentials acknowledged an exception for religious war.

Anselm of Lucca took a new approach when he said that not only the state but the church itself, in practice the pope, could initiate war. Bernard decided that Augustine's love was not necessary and justified hatred on Old Testament terms. The fact that 'pagans' held the Holy Land was sufficient reason to kill them. At home he prescribed religious cleansing of heretics.

Bernard still held to the traditional view that forbade killing in self-defence. The scholastics of the following century would come to allow this and war would be permitted for any just reason.

With all respect to the great Jean Leclercq, Bernard does indeed take his place as one of the most extreme in a long line of christian advocates of violence. Bernard's attitude was certainly not 'in keeping with the spirit of the gospel and was even opposed to it'.[70] Accordingly, 'we beg pardon of God and of our separated brothers and sisters, just as we forgive them that offend us'.[71]

NOTES

1. J. Leclercq, 'L'attitude spirituelle de S. Bernard devant la guerre', *Collectanea Cisterciensia* 36 (1974) 195–225; in English, 'Saint Bernard's Attitude toward War',

J. R. Sommerfeldt, ed., *Studies in Medieval Cistercian History* 2 CS 24 (Kalamazoo: Cistercian 1976) 1–39. This is 'the fundamental study' according to I. Biffi, 'La Cristologia di San Bernardo "pellegrino" in Terra Santa', *La Scuola Cattolica* 120 (1992) 15–47.

2. E. de Bhaldraithe, 'St Bernard, Thomas Merton, and Catholic teaching on peace', *Word and Spirit: A Monastic Review* 12 (1990) 54–79.

3. PL 182:745; the editor, J. Mabillon, refers us to the similar claim of miracles wrought during Bernard's visit to Toulouse.

4. K. Armstrong, *Holy War: The Crusades and their Impact on Today's World* (London: Macmillan, 1988). At the end of her research, she says that she is 'now convinced that the crusades were one of the direct causes of the conflict in the Middle East today' (xiii).

5. 'The Military Orders', J. Leclercq, F. Vandenbroucke, L. Bouyer, *The Spirituality of the Middle Ages*, A History of Christian Spirituality 2 (London: Burns & Oates, 1968) 133–136 (original French 1961).

6. *Ibid.* 136.

7. *Ibid.* Leclercq means 'lawful *self*-defence'.

8. Leclercq, 'L'attitude'; henceforth, numbers in the text will refer to the english translation, 'Bernard's Attitude'.

9. In a note, Leclercq refers to the Beatitudes in Matthew 5.

10. But surely the proper paraphrase would be, it is safe (in the eyes of God) to kill but it is better to be killed.

11. In *A Second Look at Bernard of Clairvaux*, CS 105 (Kalamazoo: Cistercian, 1990; originally published as *Nouveau Visage de Saint Bernard* Paris, 1976) Leclercq discusses Bernard's conflicts over Morimund, Robert, Anacletus, and Abelard (87–102) but does not mention the Templars or the crusades.

12. He cites a study by R.A. McCormick, 'The Morality of War' *New Catholic Encyclopedia* 14:802 which deals with the just war, beginning with Augustine, but has no discussion of the New Testament.

13. The original Leclercq refers to seems to be, *Quare non faciet libenter quod factum reperiet licenter* even though this is from 48.8 and the previous sentence quoted is from 48.10. The translation of A. Hoste, G. Raciti, *Isaac de l'Etoile: Sermons* III, SCh 339 (Paris: Cerf, 1987) is 'Pourquoi ne fera-t-il pas à plaisir ce qu'il constatera fait à loisir?' (160).

14. See, for example, S. Runciman, *A History of the Crusades* 2 (Cambridge: 1952) Chapter 3: 'Fiasco', 278–88.

15. *Ibid.* 281.

16. Armstrong, *Holy War*, 152.

17. Tpl 4; SBOp 3: 217: *Nunc autem melius est ut occidantur.* ET *Bernard of Clairvaux, Treatises* 3, CF 19 (Kalamazoo: Cistercian, 1977) 135.

18. Leclercq-Vandenbroucke-Bouyer, *Spirituality*, 136.

19. 'Decree on Ecumenism', from A. Flannery, *Vatican Council II* (Dublin: Dominican, 1980) 465.

20. F. Dvornik, 'Eastern Schism', *New Catholic Encyclopedia* 5:24–25.

21. Thomas Merton, *The Last of the Fathers* (London: Hollis, 1954) 40.

22. *Ibid.*

23. *Ibid.* 41.

24. R. Bainton, *Christian Attitudes Toward War and Peace. A Historical Survey and Critical Re-evaluation* (London: Hodder and Stoughton, 1961); Bhaldraithe, 'Bernard, Merton' 70.

25. U.S. Bishops, *The Challenge of Peace: God's Promise and Our Response* (Washington: NCCB–London: CTS, 1983).

26. *The Last of Fathers*, 40.

27. As well as the article by McCormick, he cites two standard Catholic studies from the 1930s ('Attitude', 6); cf. 'Catholic Position' in Bhaldraithe, 'Bernard, Merton' 58–59. Runciman's chapter on 'Holy Peace and Holy War' is particularly good on how the western church, following Augustine, was 'less enlightened' than the East. The virtual pacifism of the Byzantine Empire caused most of the misunderstandings with the crusaders. *Crusades* 1 (1951) 83–92, especially 83–84.

28. E.g. Letter 173 on compelling heretics by charity (PL 33: 755–56); *De civitate Dei* 19:7 on the wise man reluctantly waging just war (PL 41:634). Bhaldraithe, 'Bernard, Merton' 57–58.

29. Tpl 8; SBOp 3: 221; CF 19: 140.

30. D. Seward, *The Monks of War: The Military Religious Orders* (London: Methuen, 1972) 22–23, who relies on M. Melville, *La Vie des Templiers* (Paris, 1951). Leclercq commends this chapter in which Seward shows the cistercian and bernardine dimensions of the templar vocation ('Attitude' 24). M. Barber, *The New Knighthood: A History of the Order of the Temple* (Cambridge: University, 1994) does not mention Seward.

31. Melville, *Vie des Templiers*, 81–83.

32. Bhaldraithe, 'Bernard, Merton', 60, 65.

33. C. Schlafert, 'Lettre inédite de Hugues de Saint-Victor aux chevaliers du Temple', *Revue d'ascétique de mystique* 34 (1958) 275–99.

34. J. Leclercq, 'Un document sur les débuts des Templiers', *Revue d'histoire ecclésiastique* 52 (1957) 81–91.

35. When 'Un document' was reprinted in *Recueil d'études sur saint Bernard et ses écrits* 2 (Rome: Edizioni di Storia e Letteratura, 1966) 87–99, Leclercq added a note acknowledging that the attribution to Hugh de Payns was only a conjecture (98–99). Yet in 'L'attitude spirituelle' (1974) he refers to this reprinting but still says it is probably by the Temple Master ('Attitude' 25). Barber argues in favour of Hugh of Saint Victor but seems unaware of Leclercq's added note; *New Knighthood* 343, note 10.

36. Hoste-Raciti, *Isaac*, SCh 339: 310–311, note complémentaire 28: *novae militiae monstrum*.

37. Barber, *New Knighthood*, accepts 1129 rather than 1128 as the date of Troyes (9).

38. Original in Schlafert, 'Lettre inédite', 292–93.

39. Hoste-Raciti, *Isaac*, note complémentaire, SCh 339: 310.

40. F. H. Russell, *The Just War in the Middle Ages* (Cambridge: University, 1975) 76.

41. J. P. Migne, *Dictionnaire des ordres réligieux* II (Paris, 1848) 849–53.

42. Migne, *Dictionnaire* III (Paris, 1850) 613–14. Quoted more fully in Bhaldraithe, 'Bernard, Merton', 62.

43. Leclercq-Vandenbroucke-Bouyer, *Spirituality*, 136.

44. M. Hellmann, 'Teutonic Knights', *New Catholic Encyclopedia* 13:1025–28.

45. S. Clasen, 'Poverty Movement', *New Catholic Encyclopedia* 11:682–83, a summary of his monograph on the subject.

46. See our assessment of Basil, reported in A, Kavanagh, *On Liturgical Theology* (New York: Peublo, 1984) 155–58.

47. *Sermones in Cantica* 66.14; SBOp 2: 187; CF 31: 206.

48. Clasen, 'Poverty Movement', 652.

49. *Ibid.* 652–53. The Humiliati were the first group to have the ban of the church lifted. They formed a model for the Dominicans, Franciscans, and others. M. Lambert, *Medieval Heresy: Popular Movements from the Gregorian Reform to the Reformation* (Oxford: Blackwell[2], 1992) 91–98.

50. C. Vogel, 'Titre d'ordination et lien du presbytre à la communauté locale dans l'église ancienne', *La Maison Dieu* 115 (1973) 70–85; E. de Bhaldraithe, 'Private Mass, Parish Mass' *Religious Life Review* 33 (1994) 233–38.

51. Clasen, 'Poverty Movement', 653.

52. U.S. Bishops, *Challenge of Peace*, 33.

53. Plate 12 in Seward, *Monks of War.*

54. K. Salibi, *A House of Many Mansions: The History of Lebanon Reconsidered* (London: Tauris, 1988).

55. R. Fisk, *Pity the Nation: Lebanon at War* (Oxford: University Press, 1991).

56. Z. Schiff, E. Ya'ari, *Israel's Lebanon War* (New York: Simon & Schuster, 1984). The authors are particularly clear on how Israel was invited in.

57. 'Text of Open Letter Addressed by Hizb Allah to the Downtrodden in Lebanon and in the World', A.R. Norton, *Amal and the Shi'a: Struggle for the Soul of Lebanon* (Austin: University of Texas, 1987) Appendix B, 167–187. The martyr mentioned was a suicide bomber.

58. *Letter* 242; SBOp 8: 128; English in B.S. James, *The Letters of St Bernard of Clairvaux* (London: Burns & Oates, 1953) 389–390, where *odium* is translated as 'eager dislike'. P. Riché, 'Saint Bernard et l'hérésie', *Bulletin de Littérature Ecclésiastique* 93 (1992) 17–26, includes a good description of heresy at the time of Bernard. He plays down the significance of the letter to Toulouse, saying that Bernard gave them prudent advice (*des conseils de prudence*, 24).

59. Armstrong, *Holy War* 296.

60. R. W. Southern, *Western Views of Islam in the Middle Ages* (Cambridge, Mass: Harvard, 1962) 28.

61. *Ibid.* 31.

62. *Ibid.* 33.

63. *De haeresibus liber*; PG 94:763–74.

64. On the intriguing question of 'Muslim Christology', see K.W. Tröger, 'Jesus, the Koran, and Nag Hammadi', *Theology Digest* 38 (1991) 213–18.

65. Southern, *Western Views*, 92.

66. *Ibid.* 93–94.

67. Notably Jean Germain, Chancellor of the Order of the Golden Fleece; *ibid.* 94–98.

68. 'Declaration on Non-Christian Religions', Flannery, *Vatican II*, 739. For an ironic commentary see T. Michel, 'Christian-Muslim dialogue in a changing world', *Theology Digest* 39 (1992) 303–20.

69. Bhaldraithe, 'Merton, Bernard', 76 note 8.

70. 'Decree on Religious Liberty', Flannery, *Vatican II*, 809.

71. 'Decree on Ecumenism', *ibid.* 460.

Bernard of Clairvaux On the Truth Accessible Through Faith

John R. Sommerfeldt

BERNARD'S EPISTEMOLOGY is a subject both fascinating and crucially important for the study of twelfth-century thought. It is a subject with which I have been engaged for some forty years. In my efforts I have, of course, benefitted enormously from Jean Leclercq's critical edition of Bernard's works and from the vast array of his books and articles on Bernard. But I have also—as have many others, both beginning students and more advanced scholars—rejoiced in his humble and generous personal response to my endeavors.

The very first paper I wrote on Bernard, back in the mid–1950s, was entitled 'The Attitude of Bernard of Clairvaux Toward Reason: The Conflict with Abelard'. The paper eventually saw the light of day in 1961, published in an abbreviated form in the *Papers of the Michigan Academy*, with the likewise abbreviated title 'Abelard and Bernard of Clairvaux'.[1] Because that journal did not have a wide circulation, I sent offprints to the giants of medieval scholarship—among them, of course, Jean Leclercq—boldly and brashly offering a correction to their opinions on the question. The response I received from Father Jean was amazingly generous and encouraging. It included this sentence: 'I hope you will be able to go on in your studies on Bernard and Abelard.' Little did he—or I—know that forty years later I would still be exploring Bernard's epistemology and benefitting from his counsel almost to the day of his death.

As an example of his encouragement, I give this passage from a paper he delivered before the Stubbs Society at Oxford in 1973:

> There is still a great deal to be said on all these points, for Bernard's genius defies categorization. The most original contribution to work in this field has been made by John Sommerfeldt, director of the Institute of Cistercian Studies at West[ern] Michigan University. He is concentrating his research on Bernard's epistemology, for he thinks that Bernard's concept of knowledge should give us the key to his apparent inconsistencies. According to this theory Bernard has a specific and unique logic arising from his personal spiritual inspiration, difficult to define and impossible to classify in the categories with which we are familiar.[2]

'The most original contribution in this field has been made by' should have read 'the only one foolish enough to work in this field is', but one can imagine how such a passage encouraged me to continue my virtually solitary task. I have done much less well at it than Jean Leclercq's description would indicate, but the praise mistakenly given has inspired me to offer my thoughts on one aspect of Bernard's epistemology in this volume commemorating a scholar-monk who was a patient mentor and who continues to be a source of inspiration.

The epistemological method, the means to truth, which Bernard saw as fundamental to his culture, society, and the individual persons who live within them, is faith. This is not because Bernard denies that non-Christians can achieve knowledge[3] or even the happiness of salvation without the christian faith,[4] but because faith is a means to truth which he assumes and assigns to all classes and all callings in his christian society.

What did Bernard mean by 'faith'? Bernard relies on the apostle Paul for one definition: 'The apostle quite rightly defines faith as the substance of things hoped for [Heb 11:1], for clearly no one can hope without confidence, anymore than one can paint on a void'.[5] More helpful is Bernard's definition in *On Consideration*: ' . . . Faith is a sort of voluntary and certain foretaste of truth not yet apparent. . . .'[6] This phrase is indeed pregnant with meaning:

faith is the result of choice; the knowledge which results is both certain and not clearly comprehended.

The certainty of the knowledge received in faith Bernard repeatedly asserts. In the *Fifty-ninth Sermon on the Song of Songs*, for example:

> What is heard [in faith] confirms what is seen, so that the witness of the two [Mt 18:16]—I speak of the ear and the eye—is validated. That is why the Lord said: 'Go and tell John'—for he was speaking to John's disciples—'what you have heard and seen' [Lk 7:22]. He could not have expressed to them more briefly or more clearly the certainty of faith.[7]

One ' . . . sees through faith . . .'[8] as well as hears, and what one sees and hears is the truth: 'What wonder is there if the ears catch the truth, since faith comes from hearing and hearing by the word of God [Rm 10:17], and the Word of God is Truth [Jn 17:17]?'[9] The source of the knowledge conveyed in faith is God, Truth himself. Bernard defends his teaching on baptism, for example, by an appeal to John the Baptist: ' . . . But if we deny to the herald of Truth what we give to another, contrary to the proclamation of Truth, this is not only an injury, it is blasphemy. Clearly it contradicts not only John, but the Truth.'[10] One should believe the testimony of the Truth, as David did: ' "I have believed" [Ps 115:10], he says, the words of the Truth: "Whoever follows me does not walk in darkness" [Jn 8:12]. What is he confessing? That in believing I have known the Truth.'[11]

If the Truth is the source of the knowledge given in faith, one can, through faith, gain ' . . . knowledge of God [2 Co 10:5], which is the christian faith. . . .'[12] This knowledge fills Bernard with confidence in the accessibility of Truth:

> Pursue him; follow him; seek him. Do not let that inaccessible brightness [1 Tm 6:16] or loftiness deter you from seeking him or despair of finding him. 'If you can believe, all things are possible to the believer' [Mk 9:22]. 'The Word is near you', Paul says, 'in your mouth and in your heart' [Rm 10:8]. Believe, and you have found him. For to believe is to have found. The faithful know that Christ lives in their hearts through faith [Eph 3:17]. What is nearer? So, seek

> him fearlessly; seek him faithfully. 'The Lord is good to the soul seeking him' [Lm 3:25]. Seek in longing; follow in action; find in faith. What does faith not find? It attains the inaccessible; it discerns the unknown; it comprehends the boundless; it apprehends that least experienced; it somehow encompasses even eternity itself in its vast embrace. I speak in faith: I believe in—though I do not understand—the eternal and blessed Trinity. I hold fast by faith what I cannot grasp with my mind.[13]

Although faith based on God's authority, and reason leading to understanding, are parallel means to the truth,[14] faith is, in some cases, a surer guide to reality than either reason or the senses. In Bernard's *Twenty-eighth Sermon on the Song of Songs*, he expands the words of Christ to Mary after the resurrection, 'Do not touch me' to:

> Faith is ignorant of ignorance; faith, in comprehending the invisible, does not feel the poverty of the senses. It even crosses the limits of human reason, the capacity of nature, the bounds of experience. Why do you ask the eye that for which it does not suffice? Why does the hand endeavor to explore that which is beyond its reach? What information the eye or the hand will bring back is little. Well will faith tell of me, not diminishing my majesty. Learn to possess certainly, to follow completely that which faith commends. 'Do not touch me, for I have not yet ascended to my Father' [Jn 20:17].
>
> As if he wished to be or could be touched by her after he would be ascended. Yet he could be touched, but by affection not the hand, by desire not the eye, by faith not the senses. 'Why do you seek to so touch me', he says, 'would you weigh the glory of the resurrection with a physical sense? Do you not know that, when I was still mortal, the eyes of the disciples could not even briefly bear the glory of my transfigured body that was still destined to die [Mt 17:6]? Indeed, I continue to accommodate your senses by bearing the form of the servant whom you are accustomed to seeing. But my glory has been made too wonderful for

> you, fashioned so that you cannot fathom it [Ps 138:6]. So, defer your decision; suspend your judgement; in such matters do not believe the determination of your senses for what is reserved for faith. Faith will determine more worthily and more surely what it comprehends more fully. In faith's mystical and profound embrace, it grasps what is the length, width, height, and depth [Eph 3:18]. What eye does not see, what ear does not hear, what surpasses the human heart [1 Co 2:9], faith carries within herself as if wrapped in a covering, as if kept under a seal.'[15]

Faith, then, leads one surely to truths not ascertainable by other means.

But the truths ascertained by faith are, as yet, cloudy and unclear. Bernard acknowledges this in his *On Consideration*:

> These two [faith and understanding] possess certain truth. But faith possesses truth hidden and obscure. . . . Faith possesses no uncertainty, or, if it does, it is not faith but opinion. How, then does it differ from understanding? Even though faith is no more uncertain than understanding, still it is obscure, as understanding is not.[16]

Farther on in the same book, Bernard gives the example of the Christian's knowledge of the existence of the Trinity:

> Does anyone ask how this [unity in Trinity] can be? Let it suffice for such a one to hold that it is indeed so, and this not as evident from reason or as an uncertain opinion, but as convinced by faith. This is a great mystery, worthy of veneration not of investigation. How can plurality exist in unity—and such a unity—and unity in plurality? To scrutinize this is temerity; to believe it is piety; to know it is life—and life eternal [Jn 17:3].[17]

Faith, then, allows one to know with certainty the otherwise unknowable, with a knowledge which transcends the penetration and clarity of understanding.

The knowledge gained from faith is not only certain and cloudy, it is also the result of choice. Faith is a gift from God, but that gift can be rejected. Bernard's model of acceptance is Mary's response to the annunciation; he counsels her rhetorically:

> Blessed Virgin, open your heart to faith, your lips to consent, your womb to the Creator. Behold, the one desired by all the nations [Hg 2:8] stands at the gate and knocks [Rv 3:20]. Oh if, at your delay, he should pass by, and you should have to seek in sorrow him whom your soul loves [Sg 3:1–4]! Rise up! Run! Open! Rise up by faith; run by devotion; open by consent![18]

Freedom of choice, without which it is impossible to be truly human,[19] necessitates a voluntary response to the gift of faith.

Bernard believes faith is also necessary to the human being—at least to live human life fully as a Christian—because much of the knowledge imparted in faith is otherwise inaccessible. Bernard writes in his *First Sermon for the Feast of Pentecost*:

> Today the Holy Spirit reveals to us something about himself, just as before we came to know something about the Father and the Son. For a complete knowledge of the Trinity is life eternal [Jn 17:3]. Now, however, we know in part [1 Co 13:9]; we believe the rest which we are not at all capable of understanding. About the Father, I know his creation, since his creatures cry out: 'He made us, and not we ourselves' [Ps 99:3]. 'For, from the creation of the world, the invisible things of God are clearly seen, understood by the things that are made' [Rm 1:20]. But to comprehend his eternity and immutability is too much for me: 'He lives in light inaccessible' [1 Tm 6:16]. About the Son too, I know by his grace something great: his incarnation. For 'who will explain his generation?' [Is 53:8]. Who can comprehend the equality of the begotten with the begetter? About the Holy Spirit, I likewise know something—obviously by inspiration—if only his procession, that he proceeds from the Father and the Son. This 'knowledge is made wonderful to me; it is powerful, and I cannot master it' [Ps 138:6]. For there are two questions here: from where and to where does he proceed. His procession from the Father and the Son covered his hiding place with darkness [Ps 17:12]. But today his procession begins to become known to humans, and it is now manifest to the faithful.[20]

If God's eternity and immutability, the incarnation of the Son, and the procession of the Holy Spirit are beyond what the human mind can discover for itself, that information—some of it, Bernard thinks, necessary to human fulfillment[21]—must be revealed by God's inspiration and known through faith.

Baptism is a case in point for Bernard; he writes to Hugh of Saint Victor:

> This is not something which, even without any promulgation, the natural law would not allow to remain unknown—for example, the precept 'What you do not wish done to you, do not do to another' [Tb 4:16, cited RB 61.14]. This is rather a positive prescription, not a natural precept. For what is there in nature or reason that teaches that no mortals can receive internal and eternal salvation if their bodies are not moistened outwardly with a visible element? The sacrament of God, the Most High, is to be received not discussed, venerated not judged. It arises from faith; it is not innate. It is sanctioned by tradition not discovered by reason.[22]

Information of this kind must be revealed: 'One person does not understand the thought of another, unless that person makes it known. How much less can anyone investigate the divine counsel, except him to whom God wishes to reveal it?' [Mt 11:27].[23]

Although Bernard thinks one need know only that necessary to one's fulfillment,[24] knowledge about God is indeed necessary. He writes the cardinal deacon, Peter:

> If knowledge of God is the cause of a person's being something at all, ignorance makes that person nothing. But he, who 'calls those who are not, as well as those who are' [Rm 4:17], has mercy on those brought down to nothingness [Ps 72:22]. He feeds us with hidden manna [Rv 2:17], of which the apostle says: 'Your life is hidden with Christ in God' [Col 3:3]. Because we cannot yet contemplate by sight or, surely, embrace through love, he gives us that manna, in the meantime, both to taste through faith and to seek through desire. By these two we are brought into being a second time, and we take hold of 'some beginning at

> being his creatures' [Jm 1:18], to be transformed at some time 'into the perfect Man, fully mature with the fullness of Christ' [Eph 4:13]. And this will no doubt be when justice will be transformed into judgement [Ps 93:15], that is, when faith will be transformed into understanding, when the justice which is clearly from faith [Rm 9:30] will be transformed into the judgement of full knowledge, and when the desire of the pilgrim will be exchanged for the fullness of delights. If faith and desire start the absent [on their way], understanding and love will truly consummate [the journey for] those present.[25]

Faith is necessary to the pilgrim setting out on the path to truth and happiness; faith's limitations will be resolved in the blessed state at the end of that path.

God's revelation of himself as Truth, and the truths which flow from that, are expressions of his mercy:

> . . . Faith comes by hearing [Rm 10:17]; as long as the soul walks by faith and not by sight [2 Co 5:7], she must put more reliance on the instruction she hears than on that revealed by sight. It is pointless for her to strain eyes unpurified by faith, when only those who are clean of heart [Mt 5:8] are promised the riches of this vision. It is truly written: 'By faith he cleanses their hearts' [Ac 15:9].[26]

Mercy leads to the gift of faith; by the same token, the faith of the believer leads to God's mercy. Bernard gives a concrete example in his *Steps of Humility and Pride*:

> We read in the gospel [Mk 10:46–52; Lk 18:35–43; Jn 9] of two blind men. The one received his sight, the other recovered it; one lost his sight and the other never had it, since one had been blinded and the other had been born blind. The one who had lost his sight merited marvelous mercy by his miserable and manifold moanings. The case of the one born blind shows still greater mercy and marvel, for no sight had preceded his prayers; he had never sensed the blessing of his illuminator. Of him, not the other, it was said: 'Your faith has made you whole' [Lk 18:42; Mk 10:52].[27]

The mercy of God is also made manifest through faith. Bernard writes of faith's testimony to those mercies in his *On the Need for Loving God*:

> If we wish to have Christ as our frequent guest, it is necessary for us to keep our hearts always fortified with the testimonies of our faith [see Eph 3:17], our faith in the mercy of him who died and in the power of him who rose. As David said: 'These two things I have heard, that power belongs to God and mercy to you, O Lord' [Ps 61:12–13]. About both these 'the testimonies are ever so believable' [Ps 92:5]. Christ died for our sins and rose again for our justification [Rm 4:25]. He ascended [Mk 16:19] for our protection, sent the Spirit [Jn 16:7] for our consolation [Ac 9:31], and one day will return [Ac 1:11] for our fulfillment. He surely showed his mercy by his death, his power in the resurrection, and both of these in each of the rest.[28]

God's merciful and loving purpose, then, in giving faith to humans, is to promote their spiritual welfare by making known to them that which will promote their well-being, both immediate and ultimate. Bernard affirms this in his *Twenty-eighth Sermon on the Song of Songs*:

> So that you may know that in promoting the soul's spiritual welfare, the Holy Spirit follows this order—first preparing the hearing, then gladdening the sight—he says: 'Hear, O daughter, and see' [Ps 44:11]. Why strain your eye? Prepare your ear. Do you wish to see Christ? First prepare yourself to hear him, then to hear about him, so that, when you do see, you may say: 'As we have heard, so we have seen' [Ps 47:9]. The brightness is boundless; the sight is so scanty it cannot see it. You can by hearing but not by looking. When God cried out: 'Adam, "where are you"' [Gn 3:9], the sinner that I am did not any longer see him—but I heard him. But the hearing—if it be grateful, watchful, and faithful—will restore the sight. Faith will purge the eye confused by ungodliness. Obedience will open the eye closed by disobedience; thus the psalmist says: 'From your commands, I have gained understanding' [Ps 118:104]. The observance of the commands restores to the intellect that which transgression has carried off.[29]

Faith so restores the human being that it is efficacious for salvation even without baptism;[30] even martyrdom draws its efficacy from the faith that informs it.[31]

Thus, faith not only involves a certain, though unclear, comprehension of truth, it involves a voluntary response.[32] And so faith is a matter of both intellect and will.[33] The soul's volitional response to the gift of faith should be love: 'Faith surely enjoins on me the need for loving him all the more whom I perceive as so much greater than I, for I receive from him not only the gift of myself, but of himself.'[34] Bernard's models in this loving response to faith are Martha and Mary, the sisters of Lazarus:

> When Jesus asked where they had laid him, Martha answered: 'Come and see' [Jn 11:34]. Why did she stop at that? Martha, you have given us a wonderful example of faith. Surely you do not begin to doubt now? When you said 'Come and see', was your hope not strong enough to add: 'and raise him up'? If you had no hope, you would not have troubled the Master with a useless visit. It is rather that faith will sometimes gain what prayer hardly dares ask. . . . O you two holy sisters, friends of Christ, if you really love your brother, why do you not ask for him the mercy of one whose power you cannot doubt, about whose love you can have no hesitation [Jn 11:3]? But their answer comes: 'We are praying, praying all the better when we voice no prayer. We trust all the more strongly when we seem to doubt. We show our faith; we show our love. . . .'[35]

Faith requires not merely the intellect's assent in belief, it also requires loving action: 'While in the flesh the soul walks by faith [2 Co 5:7], which clearly is necessary to acting in love [Ga 5:6]. If it does not act, it is dead' [Jm 2:20].[36]

To be sure, faith must precede the loving response which is necessary to good works; Bernard is no pelagian or semi-pelagian.[37] He tells his brothers in his *Fifth-first Sermon on the Song of Songs*:

> . . . Faith must come before good works. Without faith, moreover, it is impossible to please God, as Paul attests [in Heb 11:6]. Still more, he teaches: 'All that does not proceed from faith is sin' [Rm 14:23]. Hence, there is no

> fruit without flower or good work without faith. But it is also true that faith without works is dead [Jm 2:20], just as a flower appears useless when no fruit follows. 'Prop me up with flowers, encompass me with apples, for I languish with love' [Sg 2:5]. Therefore, the mind accustomed to quiet receives consolation from good works rooted in unfeigned faith [1 Tm 1:5]. . . .[38]

But faith must be lived to be genuine: 'Clearly not everyone who has faith lives by faith. For "faith without works is dead" [Jm 2:20] and cannot give the life which it lacks.'[39]

By his gift of faith, God also provides a guide to good works: 'True and full faith complies with all [God's] precepts. . . .'[40] To those who do have faith and comply with the precepts of faith Bernard promises an appealing reward. He has the Father tell them: 'Be beautiful and touch me; be faithful, and you are beautiful.'[41] To the faithful are promised the beauty of complete fulfillment: 'Possess faith, possess dutiful love, possess wisdom—but the wisdom of the saints, which is fear of the Lord [Ps 110:10; Si 1:16]—and you have what is yours.'[42]

Faith, then has both profound soteriological as well as epistemological consequences. The very lack of clarity of the knowledge conferred in faith is a blessing to pilgrims on their path to truth and happiness:

> It is good that faith is shadowy. It tempers the light to the dim-sighted eye and prepares the eye for the light. It is written: 'By faith he cleanses their hearts' [Ac 15:19]. Faith, therefore, does not extinguish the light but protects it. All that which an angel sees clearly, the shadow of faith delivers to me, stored up now in the embrace of the faithful, to be revealed in due time. Is it not expedient to hold that which is obscure when you cannot comprehend it in its nakedness? The Lord's mother so lived in the shadow of faith that it is said of her: 'Blessed are you who have believed' [Lk 1:45]. Even the body of Christ was a shadow for her, as we hear: 'The power of the Most High will cover you with its shadow' [Lk 1:35]. This is no mean shadow which is formed by the power of the Most High. Truly there was power in Christ's flesh which overshadowed the Virgin, since, by the

> enveloping shield of his quickening body, she could bear the presence of his majesty and sustain the inaccessible light [1 Tm 6:16]—something impossible to mortal woman. That was power indeed, by which all opposing power was defeated. Both the power and the shadow [Lm 4:20] put demons to flight and shield humans—surely a quickening power, surely a refreshing shadow. We who walk by faith [2 Co 5:7] live in the shadow of Christ. . . .[43]

But the shadow of faith brings no uncertainty and will lead, in due time, to the understanding of the blessed:

> Just as faith leads to full knowledge, so desire leads to perfect delight. Just as it is said: 'Unless you believe, you will not understand' [Is 7:9, LXX], so it can be equally, though not absurdly said: 'If you do not desire, you will not perfectly love.' Understanding, therefore, is the fruit of faith, perfect love the fruit of desire. For now, 'the just live by faith' [Rm 1:17]; then the blessed by understanding.[44]

NOTES

1. *Papers of the Michigan Academy of Science, Arts, and Letters* 46 (1961) 493–501.

2. Jean Leclercq, 'Saint Bernard in Our Times', trans. Garth L. Fowden. Published as a pamphlet (by the Stubbs Society) (Oxford: Impensis Roberti Lyle & prostant venales apud G.L.J.S; Printed for the Society at Holywell Press in Alfred Street, [1973] p. 9). Also in M. Basil Pennington (ed.), *Saint Bernard of Clairvaux: Studies Commemorating the Eighth Centenary of His Canonization*, CS 28 (Kalamazoo, Michigan: Cistercian Publications, 1977) pp. 13–14.

3. See Dil 2.6; SBOp 3:123; CF 13:98.

4. For examples, see SC 14.1–2 (SBOp 1:75–77; CF 4:97–99) and Ep 363.6–7 (SBOp 8:316).

5. QH 10.1; SBOp 4:442–43; CF 25:192. Here, as elsewhere, the translation is mine; I have, however, included a citation to the most readily available, good translation.

6. Csi 5.3.6; SBOp 3:471; CF 37:145.

7. SC 59.9; SBOp 2:140; CF 31:128.

8. SC 70.2; SBOp 2:209; CF 40:38.

9. SC 28.7; SBOp 1:197; CF 7:94.

10. Bapt 3.13; SBOp 7:194. In translating selections from Bernard's *On Baptism* I have here, as elsewhere, followed the translation of this treatise by High Feiss in '*Bernardus Scholasticus*: The Correspondence of Bernard of Clairvaux and Hugh of Saint Victor on Baptism', in John R. Sommerfeldt (ed.), *Bernardus Magister: Papers Presented at the Nonacentenary Celebration of the Birth of Saint Bernard of Clairvaux,*

Kalamazoo, Michigan, Sponsored by the Institute of Cistercian Studies, Western Michigan University, 10–13 May 1990, CS 135 ([Kalamazoo]: Cistercian Publications; [Saint-Nicholas-lès-Cîteaux]: Cîteaux: Commentarii Cistercienses, 1992) pp. 349–78.

11. Hum 4.15; SBOp 3:28; CF 13:43.

12. Tpl 3.5; SBOp 3:218; CF 19:135.

13. SC 76.6; SBOp 2:257–58; CF 40:114–15.

14. Bapt 2.6 (SBOp 7:189), and 5.18 (SBOp 7:198).

15. SC 28.9; SBOp 1:198; CF 7:95–96.

16. Csi 5.3.5–6; SBOp 3:470–71; CF 37:144–45.

17. Csi 5.8.18; SBOp 3:482; CF 37:163.

18. Miss 4.8; SBOp 4:54; CF 18:54.

19. See my *The Spiritual Teachings of Bernard of Clairvaux*, An Intellectual History of the Early Cistercian Order, [1]; CS 125 (Kalamazoo, Michigan: Cistercian Publications, 1991) pp. 9–11.

20. Pent 1.1; SBOp 5:160–61; CF 53:69–70.

21. See V Nat 3.3; SBOp 4:213.

22. Bapt 1.2; SBOp 7:186. Bernard does not mean that all must undergo a baptism with water to be saved, as the rest of the letter-treatise makes clear.

23. Bapt 1.3; SBOp 7:186.

24. See SC 37.1; SBOp 2:4; CF 7:181.

25. Ep 18.2; SBOp 7:67.

26. SC 41.2; SBOp 2:29; CF 7:205.

27. Hum 22.54; SBOp 3:57; CF 13:80.

28. Dil 3.9; SBOp 3:126; CF 13:101.

29. SC 28.7; SBOp 1:196–97; CF 7:93–94.

30. Bapt 2.6 and 8; SBOp 7:189 and 191. Faith, Bernard believes, surely sufficed for salvation before the institution of baptism. See Bapt 2.8; SBOp 7:190.

31. Bapt 2.8; SBOp 7:191.

32. See above, pp. 240–241.

33. For a discussion of the intellect and will, see *Spiritual Teachings*, pp. 7–11.

34. Dil 5.15; SBOp 3:131; CF 13:108.

35. Hum 22.52; SBOp 3:55–56; CF 13:78–79. Mary—this time the mother of Jesus—is also a model of this sort of response to faith; see Hum 22.53; SBOp 3:56; CF 13:79.

36. Dil 11.32; SBOp 3:146; CF 13:123. The necessity of living out one's faith in loving service is discussed in *Spiritual Teachings*, pp. 173–81.

37. The primacy of grace in Bernard's soteriology is discussed in *Spiritual Teachings*, pp. 27–30 and 145–50.

38. SC 51.2; SBOp 2:84–85; CF 31:41.

39. SC 48.7; SBOp 2.71; CF 31:18.

40. Bapt 2.8; SBOp 7:191.

41. SC 28.10; SBOp 1:198–99; CF 7:96.

42. Csi 2.6.13; SBOp 3:421; CF 37:63.

43. SC 31.9–10; SBOp 1:225; CF 7:132.

44. Ep 18.2; SBOp 7:67.

Aelred of Rievaulx and Isaiah

Thomas Renna

It is I Yahweh Sabaoth who speaks. I will rise against them and wipe out the name and remnant from Babylon.

THE BOOK OF ISAIAH has received a lot of attention. Modern scholars continue to debate the question of authorship and historical context. Current scholarship focuses on the unity of themes, the result of post-exilic redactions.[1] Some think that the oracles against the foreign nations (chapters 13–24) of First Isaiah were a form of salvation prophecy.[2] Others believe they were intended to accuse Israel, as well as the foreign nations, of sin, especially pride,[3] and to assert that the God of Israel controlled the destiny of *all* nations. Scripture scholars have been sensitive to the oracles' connections with other parts of the Bible, but the fate of the oracles—and indeed the Book of Isaiah itself—has rarely been taken beyond the New Testament. The reason for this neglect, it would seem, is that the historical development of Isaiah interpretations seems self-evident and unchanging. Isaiah foretold the coming of the Messiah. The Gentiles accepted Jesus as the Messiah, while the Jews did not. What more can be said? This messianic theme, in fact, pervades virtually all patristic and medieval commentaries and homilies on Isaiah.

Unfortunately there is no survey of medieval commentaries on Isaiah. A recent critique of Isaiah hermeneutical development makes only a passing allusion to the medieval tradition.[4] The first post-biblical commentary was apparently written by Origen, whose lost work probably emphasized the salvific work of Christ and his Church.[5] While Eusebius of Caesarea's commentary[6] seems to have had little influence on later greek writers, the major commentaries of Cyril of Alexandria (*c*.370–444)[7] and Theodoret of Cyrrhus (393–458) certainly did.[8] Other greek commentators, such as John Chrysostom,[9] have little to say about the so-called burdens of Isaiah.

Jerome was probably the first latin author to envision Isaiah's denunciation of foreign nations as a kind of self-contained section of Isaiah. It is entirely possible that Jerome, who translated ten of Origen's sermons on Isaiah, relied heavily on Origen for this part of his monumental commentary on Isaiah, now available in a modern edition and the subject of a major study.[10] While much of Jerome's commentary consists in a close textual analysis, several recurring themes are relevant here: God permitted the Babylonians to destroy the earthly Jerusalem as a punishment of the Jews.[11] So too, Jerome frequently adds, the Romans leveled the Holy City as divine punishment for the Jews' rejection of the Messiah.[12] The Word was sent to the Gentiles after the Jews lost their inheritance because of their blasphemies and idolatries. Zion and Jerusalem together express the same idea: the Christian Church.[13] For Jerome, Isaiah is above all the prophet of the Church,[14] the mystical body of all believers, both jewish Christian and gentile Christian. The oracles against the nations, according to the allegorical sense, were directed primarily against jewish arrogance and unbelief.[15] Carnal Israel is a type of the future time.[16] Zion is *speculatio*, which represents the Church.[17] Carnal Israel foretold the coming of the spiritual Israel, the Church, with its ecclesiastics and evangelical doctrine.[18] When the Jews rejected Jesus as the Messiah, the Word of God was taken to the Gentiles.[19] Finally, the nations represent virtues[20] and vices, especially pride.[21] Thus Jerome connects certain vices to the individual soul (in addition to the Church), which must overcome them. Many of these motifs are expanded in Jerome's sermons on the psalms.[22]

Jerome treated the Burdens of Isaiah as a distinct subdivision of his commentary.[23] While his main interest is the Church, there are suggestions of specific virtues suitable for the new Israelites, although not specifically ascetics and monks. Echoes of Jerome can be found in Augustine[24] and Ambrose.[25] While the Carolingians generally showed little interest in Isaiah, a notable exception is Haymo of Auxerre (d.*c.* 866), a monk at Saint Germain of Auxerre who also wrote long commentaries on the Letters of Paul, the Apocalypse, the Song of Songs, and the minor prophets.[26]

While Haymo of Auxerre clearly used Jerome's commentary on Isaiah, there are substantial theological differences between the two. Haymo's interpretation reflects the troubles of the mid-ninth century: Isaiah is above all the prophet of the *Church.* Not only the Church as the body of Christ,[27] but also the Church as an institution, organized around the hierarchical *sacerdotium* and the sacraments.[28] As with Jerome, Haymo sees the Jerusalem of Deutero-Isaiah as a foreshadow of the visible Church.[29] Whereas Jerome usually equates Zion with Jerusalem,[30] Haymo often distinguishes between Zion, the earthly City of the ancient Hebrews, and the 'new' Jerusalem, the present Church,[31] which will ultimately be perfected and completed as the celestial Jerusalem.[32] Haymo's entire commentary is based on this distinction between the jewish city and the 'gentile' city.

Again and again Haymo returns to this theme, no matter the text he is supposedly explaining. Jews and Gentiles together make up the Church universal.[33] Haymo's argument, however, is not always easy to follow, since his commentary is also a *catana* of undigested quotes and paraphrases. Yet despite the myriad of meanings assigned to Zion and Jerusalem, the principal motif is constant: the Church began as a union of Jew and Gentile, and developed as a union of the two, soon to be continued in eternity.[34] Jerome, no friend of Jews, had had a penchant for designating the Church as the true Zion, the true Jerusalem, the true Israel; Haymo preferred to emphasize the providential merging of the two chosen peoples, Jews and Gentiles. The primitive Church was not some idealized archetype of the Church—as it would become for many twelfth-century reformers—; rather, the *ecclesia primitiva* consisted of newly converted Jews who began to add pious Gentiles to their ranks.[35] Together the circumcised and the uncircumcised built the one *ecclesia.*[36] Again taking his cue from Jerome, Haymo accuses the unbelieving Gentiles of idolatry and the unbelieving Jews of infidelity.[37] The apostles converted both groups by their word and example.[38] The Gentiles came to the faith without the benefit of prophets, patriarchs, and the Law.

While Jerome was content to allude briefly to the various 'orders' in the Church, Haymo gets very specific, with emphasis on the preaching prelates.[39] (Haymo does not dwell on the ecclesiastical function of monks, who are designated as the virgins, continent, or eunuchs,[40] and generally defined as those who abandon the world.) Finally, for Haymo, Isaiah was the prophet of christian virtues, particularly humility, chastity, and charity.[41] In typically carolingian fashion Haymo repeatedly alludes to the virtues expected of *all* Christians. Monks or ascetics are not assigned any special virtues. His catalogue of right behavior includes perseverance, simplicity of heart, right belief (presumably aimed against Adoptionism, celtic practices, and residual paganism), faith, and good works.[42] Somewhat more than Jerome Haymo sets Christ against Antichrist, the offspring of the Jews.[43]

Did Haymo intend to exhort his contemporaries in the carolingian empire? It is difficult to be sure, since he avoids explicit references to events or persons. The peace and unity theme[44] is reminiscent of Alcuin and many ninth-century commentators. Possibly the Antichrist refers, at least in part, to the Spanish Moors and the Vikings from the north, or perhaps to any evil force disrupting the carolingian *pax*. The constant references to preaching prelates[45] and just princes[46] were probably aimed at curbing inter-christian conflicts. The allusions—both positive and negative—to the Jews may be simply a rhetorical plea to christian leaders to work harder for a united and peaceful Christendom. A *leitmotif* in Haymo's commentary on Isaiah is *conversion*,[47] the need to transform one's life of vice to the life in Christ. Basically Haymo's vision of the Church rests on individual moral behavior. Institutional reform will presumably follow.

Aelred of Rievaulx, the only early Cistercian to write on Isaiah, did not merely repeat a venerable tradition. Aelred's set of sermons on the so-called Burdens of Isaiah represents a major shift in interpretation. The abbot of Rievaulx, indeed, changed the direction of Isaiah hermeneutics to one more suited to monastic ideals. How does Aelred fit into these patristic and carolingian isaiaic traditions? While Aelred's debt to Jerome is obvious, the influence of Haymo is less clear. The latter's emphasis on Jewish-Gentile unity and on the present Church is perhaps the greatest point of similarity. But no matter the number of passages which echo Jerome or Haymo, the cistercian abbot made the Burdens of Isaiah into a different kind of work. Aelred's sermons differ in structure, content, and purpose.

Aelred isolates the Burdens of Isaiah from the totality of the Book of Isaiah. His sermon cycle on Isaiah 13–24 revolves around specific themes, with relatively few digressions. The sermons deal largely with only three of the Burdens: Babylon, Philistia, and Moab. For the most part, the sermons are set around groups of three ideas. Most prominent is that of the three foreign nations as representative of three vices. Babylon represents the love of the world;[48] Moab the world's wisdom, chararcterized by idle curiosity and vanity;[49] Philistia pride and vain glory.[50] Babylon itself contains three kinds of reprobates, who are themselves mirror-images of the three types of the elect.[51] The first *ordo* of the elect are those who are not yet of the elect, namely the Jews and pagans. The second are sinful Christians who are not as yet justified. The third are justified but not yet glorified (entered into heaven).[52] Aelred's use of the three evil foreign nations to illustrate some corresponding virtue or state of life is the basic methodology followed throughout the entire set of sermons on the Burdens of Isaiah.

Just as the three nations represent humankind's failings, they also suggest, by contrast, three states of perfection: conversion, purgation, and contemplation.[53] The evils of Moab prefigured the three grades of humility.[54] From this humility comes perfection, chastity, and tranquillity.[55] Good conversation, good works, and good intention can effectively overcome the luxury, cupidity, and vanity of Moab.[56] Just as the exterior is related to the interior, so every vice is related to its opposite, corresponding virtue.[57]

Aelred's allusions to the various types of virtues are, to be sure, patristic and carolingian. But Aelred relates these groups of virtues—usually in threes—to the monastic life. His point is not simply that Moab prefigured some particular monastic practice or behavior, but that the particular vice in question continues to trouble the contemporary monk, who can combat the temptation by practicing the appropriate virtue. Aelred's sermons on the Burdens of Isaiah were not classroom exercises on technical points of exegesis. He intended his listeners to apply his exhortations to everyday concerns.

His extended assault on the philosophers,[58] for example, is not a plea to keep liberal studies out the cloister; it is a call for *conversio*. Philosophers engage in useless dialectics, but monks should begin their spiritual progress by turning away from worldly wisdom. (This process was not of course considered a one-time event, but rather an ongoing struggle throughout the monk's earthly pilgrimage.) If this were not enough, Aelred concludes by incorporating the philosophers within the elect.[59] It is useful for monks to meditate on the plight of the philosophers, since their attachment to secular wisdom can indirectly teach them to rise to the *sapientia* of Christ. Even now, the philosophers are coming to Christ and his sacraments.

Aelred frequently juxtaposes the vices of the foreign nations to specific vitures. Moab, which is the discord of vices, also intimates frugality as opposed to luxury, patience to anger, chastity to lust, and charity opposed to cupidity.[60] This is not simply the conventional typology of the Old Testament prefigurations. Aelred's intent is that the recognition of a specific vice is the initial step in the practice of its opposite, corresponding virtue. In the Church all orders, gifts, and virtues are united in one charity, just as a cithera has many chords.[61] Aelred never lets his listeners forget that he is talking about virtues applicable to the cloister. The monk must be particularly attuned to the importance of vigils, fasts, and contrition of heart.[62] Moab's vanity can be conquered by regular monastic discipline and by contemplation.[63] One must flee the world and climb to the mountain of contemplation, itself joined to charity.[64] The monk is in a constant state of conversion as he moves away from vice and secular wisdom towards charity and union with God.

Throughout the sermons on Isaiah peace and concord are contrasted with the confusion of Babylon. Yet for Aelred peace is not simply a social ideal or even an interior state; it is a virtue desirable for monks. We must strive for interior peace, even though true peace is impossible here below.[65] The tabernacle of David is the Church, wherein are mercy and truth, peace and justice.[66] Unlike Babylon, in the Church holy souls are united as a single heart and voice.[67] Even the peace of Jerusalem—conventionally applied in twelfth-century exegesis and homelitics to the blessed in heaven—is associated with the practice of the monastic life. 'Our peace' (of monks) is simultaneouly Christ and the monastic community united in charity and hope (in heaven).[68] The peace of Jerusalem (that is, the life of heaven insofar as it is experienced here below) is found by living in and like Christ in unity and charity.[69] In Babylon there is only confusion and work. In the peace of Jerusalem monks 'rest' in the practice of virtues.[70] Zion at once suggests the Church and the poor in spirit who are included in it.[71] In the patristic tradition of Zion as *speculatio* Aelred has Christ founding Zion as the contemplative soul.[72] For the abbot of Rievaulx the peace of Christ and the peace of Jerusalem both apply to the monk's interior progress. His use of models taken from jewish prefigurations of christian states of perfection are meant to have a practical effect: to exhort monks to improve their behavior, individually and communally.

But there are three subjects which seem at first sight less 'monastic'. First, the three ages of the Church: apostolic community, persecution, and the conversion of the secular princes, with the added comment that the evils of persecution have returned in our day.[73] This historical scheme, appearing as it does as the conclusion in the final sermon (as if this were a major theme in the entire set of sermons), comes as something of a jolt. Did Aelred want it to be taken literally? What are these 'persecutions' of modern times? It has been suggested on the basis of these and other passages that Aelred, as a witness to the turmoil of the reign of King Stephen, took a pessimistic view of contemporary England.[74] This theory would seem to be correct—although the evidence is admittedly slight—but in the context of the Burdens of Isaiah the *principal* function of the three ages of the Church is as a metaphor of the three progressions of the monk's life: conversion, penance, contemplation.[75] Indeed Aelred establishes a typology of the three evil nations as counterpoints to the three eras of the Church; allegorically this tripartite division applies to the holy soul's advancement towards perfection.[76] This is not to say that Aelred lacked a sense of the historical evolution of the Church. But in the context of the Burdens of Isaiah the historical stages are mainly intended to illustrate the nature of interior progression towards the divine.

Second, why the constant referral to the conversion of the Jews, a hope that appears in other of Aelred's writings?[77] Aelred Squire suggests that he had direct or indirect contact with the Jews in nearby York.[78] Then again, the necessity of the Jews' conversion before Christ's second coming was a staple in patristic exegesis. However this may be, this theme in the Burdens of Isaiah acts as a pointer to the conversion of the monastic audience; more precisely, the imminent conversion of the Jews, as foretold by Isaiah, serves as a guide for the ongoing conversion of those in the cloister.[79] The Jews will return to the fold in the same way the soul will 'return' to God, an action anticipated in this life. The 'reunion' of Jews and Gentiles was for Aelred a metaphor for the harmony which should prevail in the monastery.

Third, the Antichrist motif appears more often in the De La Bigne 1677 text of Aelred's sermons than in the deficient Migne copy.[80] Since Antichrist is not related to the contemporary Church, it is uncertain why Aelred used the idea so extensively. The key may be in his reference to Antichrist in the world.[81] The monk is engaged in the never-ending struggle against worldly temptation. The Antichrist is Babylon or the *saeculum*. The City of Man is opposed to the City of God. Antichrist is Satan who tempts the monk with memories of the world outside.

Did Aelred know the *Burdens of Isaiah* of Gottfried of Admont (benedictine abbot, d.1165)?[82] Probably not, since there is no evidence that this work was known in England.[83] Gottfried based his tract on man's ten senses, five of the soul and five of the body. He makes the 'vocation' of the Jews and Gentiles equivalent to conversion and confession.[84] The Jews represent the perfection of faith; the Gentiles, unity. The true penance and true humility of the interior man is superior to the penance and humility of the exterior man.[85] There are three kinds of penance as there are three kinds of compunction. But the differences between Aelred and Gottfried are more apparent than the similarities. When Gottfried makes Moab represent prelates who live carnally,[86] he does not explain how the proper behavior of prelates relates to monks, as does Aelred. Gottfried's school-like design of the ten visions with their corresponding human senses left little room for development. Aelred's more flexible plan of only three oracles allowed for a progression of the interior life, much in the manner of his *Jesus at Twelve*.

Aelred has little in common with the long commentary on Isaiah by Hervé of Burgidol (*c.*1075–*c.*1150). Although generally not as attuned to the interior dimension of the prophets' visions (which are of three basic types: corporeal, spiritual, and intellectual[87]) as Aelred, Hervé did not neglect the holy soul. He often refers to Jerusalem to mean heaven.[88] *Ecclesia* is frequently contrasted with *Synagoga* and the Jews.[89] Hervé refers to the Church more often than does Aelred. The Church requires its good pastors who preach the Word.[90] The *onus Tyri* is juxtaposed with monks and monasteries.[91]

CONCLUSION

1) Aelred utilized a minor literary genre—an exposition of the *Burdens of Isaiah*—to explain the spiritual development of the monk. This set of sermons is not a treatise on the soul's ascent to God, but an exhortation to holiness.

2) In the wider context of Isaiah exegesis Aelred's *Burdens of Isaiah* represents a shift away from the conventional emphasis on ecclesiology and jewish/gentile dichotomy. Aelred diminishes the prophetic thrust of Isaiah hermeneutics in favor of a description of *how* the ascetic attains the contemplative ideal. Isaiah foretold not so much the coming of Christ and his Church as the process by which one achieves union with Christ in this life.

3) Aelred gave his monks a lesson in how to read the scriptures. While Aelred's allegorical methods may have been somewhat old-fashioned, even in his own day, his interpretations were not. He tried to get away from the rigid classification of virtues so common in carolingian exegesis. Commonplace allegories, often far-fetched and detached from social reality, were often repeated without purpose. Aelred wanted to make the Old Testament prophets—always a difficult subject for young monks—a living voice which was immediately relevant. The Holy Spirit was using Isaiah, Aelred assured his charges, to reveal the meaning of the *vita monastica*. What appears at first sight a tale of horrors—the foreign nations condemned by Yahweh—is actually a concealed lecture in the school of the cloister.

Aelred's *Burdens of Isaiah* does not easily fit into the 'monastic' category as opposed to the 'scholastic'. The literary structure of the work could be either. While some scholastic influence is evident—such as discussions of the functions of the soul—the schoolmen are severely criticized. The relatively tight organization has more in common with twelfth-century moral treatises than with carolingian scriptural exegesis. Certainly Aelred intended his sermons to be eminently practical.

4) In the history of homiletics, the *Burdens of Isaiah* is typical of a genre becoming popular in the twelfth century: the cycle of

sermons on a small number of themes. The Burdens should be compared to Aelred's three sermons on Saint Benedict.

5) The Burdens typify the twelfth-century tendency among monastic writers to stress the interior dimension of standard biblical and exegetical images. Even the common virtues, such as penance, are viewed from the contemplative perspective.

6) There is something very *English* about Aelred's sermons on Isaiah. The author's recoil from schism and conflict may reflect the times of King Stephen. Aelred's faith in prelates and princes is reminiscent of the Venerable Bede, who based his *History of the English People* on the twin contributions of bishops and kings. Like Bede Aelred urged secular and ecclesiastical leaders to adopt something of the spirituality of the cloister. For Bede the latter was ideally represented by the celtic tradition in England. For Aelred it was the Cistercian Order. 'I Yahweh will turn Babylon into a marshland and sweep it with the broom of destruction.' Was this a warning to England?

But have no fear, ye monks of Rievaulx, for 'Yahweh has laid the foundations of Zion, and there the poor of his people shall find refuge.'

NOTES

* The author wishes to thank Saginaw Valley State University for providing a generous research grant which made this study possible. An earlier version of this article was read at the 29th International Congress on Medieval Studies, Western Michigan University, 6 May 1994.

1. See, e.g., C. R. Seitz, *Zion's Final Destiny: The Development of the Book of Isaiah* (Minneapolis: Augsburg Fortress Press, 1991); 'Isaiah, Book of (First Isaiah),' *Anchor Bible Dictionary* (New York: Doubleday, 1992) 3: 472–88; *Isaiah 1–39. Interpretation* (Louisville: John Knox Press, 1993). Also: R. Clements, 'Beyond Tradition-History: Deutero-Isaianic Development of First Isaiah's Themes,' *Journal for the Study of the Old Testament* 31 (1985) 95–113; *Isaiah 1–39. New Century Bible Commentaries* (Grand Rapids: Wm. B. Eerdmans, 1980).

2. See C. Westermann, *Grundformen prophetischen Rede* (2nd ed., Munich, 1964); trans. as *Basic Forms of Prophetic Speech*, London, 1967).

3. See G. R. Hamborg, 'Reasons for Judgement in the Oracles against the Nations in the Prophet Isaiah,' *Vetus Testamentum* 31.2 (1981) 145–59. For other studies of Isaiah's oracles against the nations (chapters 13–24) in the context of the Book of Isaiah as well as of other biblical books, see R. Clements, *Prophecy and Tradition* (Oxford: Basil Blackwell 1975), Chap. 5; J. N. Hayes, 'The Usage of Oracles against Foreign Nations in Ancient Israel,' *Journal of Biblical Literature* 87

(1968) 81–92; S. Erlandsson, *The Burden of Isaiah. A Study of Isaiah 13.2–14.23* (Lund: CWK Gleerup, 1970); D. Christensen, *Transformations of the War Oracle in Old Testament Prophecy* (Ann Arbor, 1975); F. Huber, *Jahwe, Juda und die anderen Völker beim Propheten Jesaja* (Berlin-New York, 1976); D. Jones, 'The *Traditio* of the Oracles of Isaiah of Jerusalem,' *Zeitschrift für die Alttestmentliche Wissenschaft* 67 (1955) 226–46; M. Cahill, 'The Oracles against the Nations: Synthesis and Analysis for Today,' *Louvain Studies* 16/2 (1991) 121–36; G. I. Davies, 'The Destiny of the Nations in the Book of Isaiah,' *The Book of Isaiah*, ed. J. Vermeylen, *Bibliotheca Ephemeridum Theologicarum Lovaniensium* 81 (Leuven: University Press, 1989) 93–120, and A. K. Jenkins, 'The Development of the Isaiah Tradition in Isaiah 13–23,' *Ibid.*, pp. 237–51; this entire collection (over 450 pp.) is excellent.

4. J. J. Schmitt, *Isaiah and His Interpreters* (New York-Mahwah: Paulist, 1986) 22.

5. Only some of Origen's homilies on Isaiah have survived. See *Homiliae in Visiones Isaiae*, PG 13:219–54. The Burdens of Isaiah are not included in these nine homilies. Jerome's translation in PL 24:801–936.

6. J. Ziegler, ed., *Der Jesajakommentar. Die Griechischen Christlichen Schriftsteller* (Berlin: Academie, 1975); Eusebius on the Burdens of Isaiah is in PG 24:183–254.

7. Burdens of Isaiah in PG 70:345–556. Cyril alludes to the mysteries of Christ (360D), Christ's Church (380C, 548A, 570AB), holy city Jerusalem as the Church (368B, 388C, 502B), peace of Christ (384B, 562B), Zion is *speculatio* and Jerusalem is *visio pacis* (562AB). Cf. 1144–48 (Zion and Jerusalem). See A. Kerrigan, *St. Cyril of Alexandria: Interpreter of the Old Testament*. Analecta Biblica (Rome: Biblical Institute 1952).

8. J.-N. Guinot, ed., *Commentaire sur Isaïe*, Sources Chrétiennes 295 (Paris: Cerf, 1982); 64–169. A fairly literal commentary, with little interpretation. Later, Theodore refers to Jerusalem as a type of the Church and the heavenly City; SCh 315:252–67.

9. J. Dumortier, ed., *Commentaire sur Isaïe*, SCh 304 (Paris: Cerf, 1983) does not treat the Burdens of Isaiah. See also Potamius, PL 8:1415–16; Zeno, PL 11:462–73; Paterius, PL 79:947–50.

10. Pierre Jay, *L'Exégèse de Saint Jérôme d'après son 'Commentaire sur Isaïe'* (Paris: Études Augustiniennes, 1985); brief allusions to the *iuxta historiam* and the Burdens or Visions of Isaiah on pp. 64–65, 344–48. Jay's work focuses on Jerome's exegetical methods, particularly on the differences between the literal and spiritual interpretations.

11. M. Adriaen, ed., *S. Hieronymi Presbyteri Opera, Commentariorum in Esaiam* in Corpus Christianorum Series Latina, vol. 73A (Turnhout, 1963), p. 503.

12. CCSL 73A:575–76, 672–74.

13. CCSL 73A:521, 542–43, 565, 567, 574, 579–81, 606, 610.

14. CCSL 73A:521, 546, 559, 567, 575.

15. CCSL 73 (1963) 166–69, 187, 190, 266, 267.

16. CCSL 73:266, lines 24–27.

17. CCSL 73:276–77. See also CCSL 73:211, 223, 232, 252, 254, 259, 260; CCSL 73A:521.

18. CCSL 73:267–68.

19. CCSL 73:166–67, 267–74; CCSL 73A:489.

20. CCSL 73:179; CCSL 73A:565.

21. CCSL 73:169, 191, 240.

22. G. Morin, ed., CCSL 78 (1958) pp. 117, 291; CSEL 54 (1910) ed. I. Hilberg, *Ep.* 46.3, p. 332.

23. See Jerome's reference to Bishop Amabilus in the beginning of the Burdens of Isaiah, Bk. 5, line 1; CCSL 73:158; P. Jay, *L'exégèse de saint Jérôme*, pp. 64–65 (references to the visions of Isaiah in Jerome's letters 71 and 72), 282–87 (typology in commentary on Isaiah).

24. Especially in his sermons on the Psalms. For Zion/Jerusalem and the Church see E. Dekkers, J. Fraipont, edd., *Enarrationes in Psalmos*; CCSL 38 (1956), pp. 64, 615; CCSL 39:824–25. In a forthcoming study in *Collectanea Augustiniana* I discuss the role of Zion in Augustine's sermons on the Psalms.

25. Although Ambrose did not write a commentary on Isaiah he often refers to Jerusalem as the Church; *De Abraham* 64; CSEL 32/1:618, 698; CSEL 62:290f.; CSEL 73:331; Jerusalem as the soul: *Obitu. Val.* 78, CSEL 73:365; PL 16:1060, 1113, 1142, 1191, *et passim*. Some patristic and medieval commentaries on Isaiah listed in L. Alonso-Schökel, 'Isiae,' *Dictionnaire de spiritualité* 7/2 (1971) 2077–78.

26. H. Barré, 'Haymon d'Auxerre,' *Dictionnaire de spiritualité* 7/1: pp. 91–97.

27. *Expositio in Isaiam*, PL 116:715–1086 at 995.

28. The Church consists of three orders: preachers, virgins, and the continent, expressed as Noah, Daniel, and Job (PL 116:998). Other treatments of the various *ordines* in the Church, with emphasis on the place of bishops: PL 116:968C, 1031, 1035, 1037 (ministers and doctors), 1040 (the 'walls' of the Church, the preachers and doctors, protect the Church against heresy).

29. PL 116:978A,982B. Also 984, 995, 1031, 1047.

30. CCSL 73A:277, 574.

31. PL 116:967, 975, 982, 1008, 1031, 1047, 1067, 1075, 1079 (*Hierusalem, id est praesens Ecclesia, vel coelestis*), 1085 (*Erit Ecclesia futura ex praesenti Ecclesia, quia ex praesenti Ecclesia construentur . . .*).

32. PL 116:978, 982, 1008, 1009, 1031, 1048 (*visio pacis*), 1049, 1072 (celestial Jerusalem contains angels and saints), 1075 (present Church and heavenly Jerusalem); *patria* (1005 and 1011).

33. PL 116:985, 993. Also PL 116:996, 998, 999, 1000, 1004, 1005, *passim*.

34. Jews and Gentiles constitute the one, universal Church; PL 116:985, 1009. Believing Jews and the newly converted Gentiles began the expansion which will eventually include the whole world.

35. PL 116:986, 1033. Also: PL 116:968, 970, 976, 979 (Zion as the Church), 985, 1023, 1034–35, 1037, 1047, 1050 (Zion as the primitive Church), 1079.

36. PL 116:998, 999.

37. PL 116:1005C, 1017C. Also PL 116:1044–45, 1048.

38. PL 116:969, 998, 1008, 1038.

39. PL 116:998, 1022, 1031, 1035, 1037, 1049.

40. PL 116:998, 1007.

41. PL 116:982, 1005, 1023, 1035, 1046, 1083.

42. PL 116:982A. Also 995A, 999, 1006A, 1009, 1031–32, 1046C, 1072, 1083D, 1003.

43. PL 116:1025–26. '*debemus intelligere Antichristum, qui ex populo Judaeorum nascetur*' (1026A).

44. E.g., PL 116:996, 1021.

45. PL 116:969, 948, 998, 1001, 1002, 1023.

46. PL 116:983, 1032–33, 1036, 1039.

47. E.g., PL 116:1005–06.

48. *Sermones de oneribus*, PL 195:374. The following discussion is based on the 'long text' (printed in Cologne 1618 and Lyon 1677), as opposed to the 'short text' printed in Migne from the Tissier edition. The long text is closer to the manuscripts. See note 62 below. For a discussion of the long and short texts and the manuscript tradition, see Charles Dumont, 'Autour des sermons *De oneribus* d'Aelred de Rievaulx,' *Collectanea O. C. R.* 19 (1957)–114–21. The manuscripts and editions are listed in A. Hoste, *Bibliotheca Aelrediana. Instrumenta Patristica* 2 (The Hague: Martinus Nijhoff, 1962) 54–61. While a consideration of the MSS is beyond the scope of this study, a modern critical edition would be most welcome. Comparisons of the Lyon 1677 ed. and the Ordinary Gloss start from note 63 below.

49. PL 195:455–57.

50. PL 195:449.

51. PL 195:366–367A.

52. PL 195:367.

53. PL 195:499.

54. PL 195:473CD.

55. PL 195:473D–474A.

56. PL 195:474D–475A.

57. PL 195:486, 476B, 497AB.

58. PL 195:456, 498. Cf. Thomas Merton, 'St Aelred of Rievaulx and the Cistercians,' *Cistercian Studies Quarterly* 22 (1987) 55–75 at 68–71.

59. PL 195:458A.

60. PL 195:497C.

61. PL 195:496BC.

62. PL 195:486C. The sins of Moab are often related to the holy soul which strives to practice the opposite virtues. E.g., Sermon 24: *Domum animae intellige conscientiam, in qua omnes mentis Thesauros reponit, ubi locum quietis invenit, quam a tumultu saeculi, mundique pertubationibus fugientem, laeto sinu suscipit, et omnes qui exterius sentiuntur, lenit sua tranquillitate dolores. Quid horum non agit sana ac secura conscientia, in qua vastate est civitas vitiorum, et murus currit passionum? Dibon quae interpretatur fluxus eorum, teneritudinem exprimit affectionis, quae per illicita quaeque defluens devaricabat pedes suos omni transeunti. Haec a collionie Moabiticae corruptionis purgate in ipsa conscientia, de imis ad alta conscedit, de vitiis ad virtutes, de initiis bonae vuluntatis ad effectum boni operis*, in Marguerin De La Bigne, *Maxima Bibliotheca veterum patrum* (Lyon 1677) vol. 23: p. 59FG. This passage is not in PL 195, but would be inserted in PL 463D after *esse facillima.* I have used the De La Bigne edition in the Rare Book Room of the library of the University of Chicago. (There is also a copy of De La Bigne in Special Collections, library of Xavier University, Cincinnati.) Aelred's Burdens of Isaiah are in De La Bigne, pp. 3–76. The PL sermon numbering is one ahead of the De La Bigne text. Thus sermon 6 in De La Bigne is sermon 7 in PL. After a careful comparison of the De La Bigne and the PL texts, I estimate that 10–15% of the De La Bigne ed. is omitted from PL. (Another edition of the long text is found in the *Magna bibliotheca Patrum*, vol. 13 [Cologne, 1618]). Interestingly many passages concerning the Church, Antichrist, the soul and virtues, and virtues/vices are missing in the shorter text. There is no modern study of Aelred's sermons on Isaiah, although historians often cite passages from them. See Aelred Squire, 'The Literary Evidence for the Preaching of Aelred of Rievaulx,' *Cîteaux* 11 (1960) 165–79, and *Aelred of Rievaulx A Study*, CS 50 (Kalamazoo, 1981) pp. 133–46; A. Hoste, *Bibliotheca Aelrediana* (The Hague,

1962) pp. 55–61; A. Le Bail, 'Aelred,' *Dictionnaire de spiritualité* (Paris, 1938) 1:225–34 at 229; A. Hallier, *The Monastic Theology of Aelred of Rievaulx* CS 2 (Kalamazoo, 1969) p. 44, *et passim*.

63. PL 195:484A & D. Cf. 433D, followed (not in PL) by *Quis eius recolens exteriora, et nunc videns interiora, non miretur lupum in ove, in agno leonem, in monacho furem tanto tempore lativisse? Felix qui haec videns inclinatur timens sibi, compatiens illi, sicque manus suas lavat in sanguine peccatoris*; De La Bigne, 43H. Also PL 195:409–410. For his sermons on the Burdens of Isaiah Aelred probably used some version of the Ordinary Gloss. The Strassburg edition of 1481 juxtaposes Moab's pride and vanity with true penance, although the latter is not explicitly related to monastic discipline; Karlfried Froehlich and M. T. Gibson, *Biblia Latina cum Glossa Ordinaria: Facsimale Reprint of the Editio Princeps Adolph Rusch of Strassburg 1480/81*, 4 vols. (Brepols: Turnhout, 1992), vol. 3: p. 29vr. Isaiah is vol. 3, pp. 653r–701v; Chaps. 13–24 of Isaiah is 24v–42v. For this edition and the problems of the Ordinary Gloss see the Introduction in vol. 1, and M. T. Gibson, 'The Twelfth Century Glossed Bible,' *Studia Patristica* 23 (Louvain, 1990) 232–44, and 'The Place of the Glossa Ordinaria in Medieval Exegesis,' *Ad Litteram: authoritative texts and their medieval readers*, eds. Kent Emery, M. Jordan (Notre Dame: University Press, 1992) pp. 5–27; R. Wielockz, 'Autour de la Glossa Ordinaria,' *Recherches de théologie ancienne et médiévale* 49 (1992) 222–28; B. Smalley, 'Glossa Ordinaria,' *Theologische Realenzyklopädie* 13 (1984) 452–57; J. de Blic, 'L'oeuvre exégetique de Walafrid Strabon et la Glossa Ordinaria,' RTAM 16 (1949) 5–28; *Dictionnaire de théologie catholique* 15:2 (1950), cols. 3499–3503; E. Bertola, 'La "Glossa Ordinaria" biblica ed i suoi problemi,' RTAM 41 (1978) 34–78. Cf. PL 195:484A (*contemplatio*) and *Glossa Ordinaria*, 1480 ed. [henceforth *GO* 1480] 29r.

64. PL 195:484D–485A.

65. PL 195:426. Cf. the commonplace contrast between carnal and spiritual circumcision; PL 195:489D–490A (carnal, sensual (philosophers and heretics, and spiritual) and *GO* 1480, 28vr, 30r.

66. PL 195:486C: *Tabernaculo David, id est, in Ecclesia, quae adhuc peregrinatur in terra, in qua misericordia et veritas obviaverunt sibi, justitia et pax osculatae sunt* [cf. Ps 85:10]. PL 486C. Cf. De La Bigne, 33DH, inserted in PL 416A after *dilexit talia*: *Nec instante tunc extremo indicio, a bonis ulterius habitabitur, nec a sanctis praedicatoribus in ea fundamentum illud, quod Christius est, ulterious collocabitur, nec ponet ibi tentoria Arabs, Christus scilicet tabernacule sua, id est, perfectos saeculo abrenuntiantes, nec invenient ibi requiem sancti angeli, vel viri perfecti animarum nostrarum pastores, quorum requies est optima bonorum, pax et concordia subditorum.* This is part of a long passage on peace which is omitted in PL. Also PL 195:417CD, 396D. For tabernacle and Moab in *GO* 1480, see 29r.

67. PL 195:381–82.

68. PL 195:422. The peace of Jerusalem and Christ is something which applies to the brethren collectively and individually. This *pax* is at work here and now—to be completed in heaven. See also PL 195:426, 440.

69. The following passages are in De La Bigne but not in PL: *eius itaque utentes exemplo, quoniam post dulce convivium iam a mensa surreximus, post modicum disessari praecipimus, obsecramus, monemus, ne discedatis ab Ierosolymis*—De La Bigne, 37BC, inserted in PL 422A after *discederent*. De La Bigne, 37C inserted in PL 195:422B after *restituat*: *Accedite nunc filii mei dulcissimi, et in signum pacis, et charitatis, quam commendavi vobis, date osculum patri, simulque omnes oremus, ut Dominus prosperum iter nobis faciat, et redeuntes vos in hac ipsa pace invenire concedat.* De La Bigne 37G in

PL 422C after *Haec in pas: quam ut meministis commendavi nobis. Cum me lex ordinis cogeret ad tempus separari a vobis, quam nunc rediens ad vos Deo gratias, inveni in vobis, pax utique Christi.*

70. PL 195:422D–423AB. Cf. GO 1480, 28v, 29v, 30v, 32v, 37v. The GO 1480 does not relate Jerusalem to the monastic life, although it does set virtues off against vices, e.g., 34v. The *GO* 1480 echoes the patristic/medieval commonplace that Egypt represents the *mundum* (33v–34v). Although Aelred does not deal with Egypt as one of the Burdens, he alludes to Moab as the *mundum*; PL 455–56, *passim*.

71. PL 195:429A. Not in PL: *Ipsa est ecclesia de gentibus Sion, scilicet quam fundavit Dominus . . . ipsa soli illi sperabant, qui fuerint pauperes populi eius, id est Sion*—De La Bigne, 54 GH inserted in PL 453C: *Eia fratres charissimi, si praeoccupatus fuerit quis in aliquo delicto, vel praeter solitum tentatione pulsatus, videat ne forte ante ruinam exaltatum sit cor, quoniam si ipsius peccati causam defleverit, facilius pro comisso veniam impetrabit. Efficietur enim pauper spiritu, humilis mente, quia non hi, qui confident in divitiis suis, sed qui in christiana paupertate gloriantue, sperabunt in Domino. Verumtamen potest per speculum, quod interpretatur Sion, spiritus scientia exprimi, in qua anima constans, virtutum fructus a furibus bestiisve conseruat. Sed in hac scientia, quam in anima sancta fundat Dominus, non superbi confidant, non sperent elati, sed pauperes populi eius.*'; De La Bigne, 55F inserted in PL 455A after '*pauperes ejus.*'

72. PL 195:454D–455A. Sion is the Church; De La Bigne, 54H. On *clama civitas*: Bigne, 55ABC has inserted in PL 195:453C: *civitas animam appelat, quae pro diverso statu diverse fortitur nomina, nunc Jericho, nunc Jerusalem, nunc Babylonis digna vocabulo. Huius muri, sunt virtutes vel vitia; domus, dona naturae; populus, affectiones et cogitationes. . . . Tunc autem civitas clamare dicitur, quando anima totam se in se, et ad se colligit, et ita in vocem vel laudis, vel confessiones, vel doloris vel orationis erumpit.* The holy city of God is the Church; De La Bigne, 54EF. See also PL 478D–479AB, 480B. Cf. GO 1480: *Ad monte Hierusalem: vel potius ad`ecclesiam quae est in contemplatione tamquam speculationis filia*, 29r; cf. PL 195:484A.

73. PL 195:498A–499AB. Same text in De La Bigne, 75G. Persecution in GO 1480 is incidental, e.g., 32v, 34r.

74. Squire, *Aelred of Rievaulx*, pp. 134–46. In *Jesus at the Age of Twelve*, Pt 2, chap. 16, Aelred bewails the imminent third age of the Church, when charity grows cold; ed. A. Hoste, SCh 60 (Paris, 1958) pp. 82–84; CF 2 (Kalamazoo, 1971) pp. 20–21. See A. Squire, 'Historical Factors in the Formation of Aelred of Rievaulx,' COCR 19 (1960) 262–82; M. Dutton, "The Conversion and Vocation of Aelred of Rievaulx: A Historical Hypothesis," ed. D. Williams, *England in the Twelfth Century* (Woodbridge 1990) 31–49.

75. Cf. the states of the Church as election, persecution, and peace; PL 195:385D. See also PL 401–402: the three states of the Church are preaching, persecution, and peace.

76. PL 195:499CD–500A. Same text in De La Bigne. *GO* 1480 occasionally refers to *anima* (28v; cf. PL 455A, De La Bigne 55) but not in the sense of Aelred's spiritual progressions.

77. E.G., *Jesus at the Age of Twelve*, Chaps. 17–18; SCh 60: 84–90; CF 2: 21–24. The Jews appear only in passing in *GO* 1480, 29r.

78. Squire, *Aelred of Rievaulx*, pp. 141–42.

79. PL 195:416, 419, 420, 445–48.

80. PL 195:401D, 404D, 420, 421, 427, 428, 429, *et passim*. Bigne (not in PL), 26CD, 27C, 28G, 29BCE, 33DHG, 34C, 36D.

81. E.g., PL 195:427–28.

82. PL 174:1157–1210. Geoffrey is not listed in David N. Bell, *An Index of Cistercian Authors and Works in Medieval Library Catalogues in Great Britain*, CS 132 (Kalamazoo, 1994).

83. PL 174:1157–59.

84. PL 174:1161.

85. PL 195:1166–67.

86. PL 195:1164.

87. *Commentariorum in Isaiam, Libri Octo*; PL 181:17–204 at 19–20. Cistercians seem to have been familiar with this important commentary.

88. PL 181:151, 154 (Jerusalem as Church), 155, *et passim*. Sion is the Church (264). Sion is *speculatio* and Jerusalem is *visio pacis* (238, 244, 302). The Burdens of Isaiah are in cols. 151–239.

89. PL 174:264, 266, 268, 279–80, *passim*.

90. PL 174:208, 219, 221, 266.

91. PL 174:222, 224, 225–28. Rupert of Deutz' commentary on Isaiah omits the Burdens; CCCM 23 (1972). Thomas Aquinas shows little interest in the interior aspects of Isaiah's visions, although he often alludes to the virtues. His exegesis of the Burdens is in *Opera Omnia* vol. 18 (Paris, 1876), pp. 747–779.

Aimery of Limoges, Patriarch of Antioch: Ecumenist, Scholar and Patron of Hermits

Bernard Hamilton

I FIRST MET Father Jean at the Spoleto Conference on the *alto medioevo* in 1956. I was a student at the British School at Rome and had just begun work on my Ph. D. thesis. Jean immediately took a friendly interest in my research, which involved the impact of Cluny and Camaldoli on tenth-century Rome, introduced me to some of the eminent scholars who were present, and helped me to gain access to the archive of Saint John Lateran. We remained firm friends ever afterwards and over the years I have received a stream of learned and supportive postcards from him from all over the world, as well as the gift of a huge number of offprints. Since I came to live in Nottingham I have seen Jean regularly when he visited the nearby Mount Saint Bernard Cistercian Abbey, and it has been a pleasure over the years to have him stay with me and meet the rest of my family.

Father Jean has been an important influence on my work: partly through his advice; partly through the opportunities which he has given me of meeting with other scholars sharing similar concerns (for example, by inviting me to speak at the Congress on Saint Peter Damian at Ravenna in 1972); but chiefly because his scholarship and his monastic profession were so firmly integrated that his life gave me an insight into the learned monastic tradition of the Middle Ages which I could not have obtained from research alone. One of the greatest satisfactions of my academic career was to know that he approved of my book on *Religion in the Medieval West.*

I have chosen this subject as my way of saying thanks, because Aimery of Limoges combined many of the characteristics of Father Jean in his life: he was a distinguished scholar, he was untiring in his zeal for the unity of Christendom, and he combined a very active life with a high regard for the eremitical ideal.

Aimery of Limoges, third Latin Patriarch of Antioch, has undoubtedly been the victim of character assassination. William of Tyre, writing about the deposition of Ralph of Domfront, the second Latin Patriarch, in 1140, says of the choice of his successor:

> the clergy of Antioch and specially those who had plotted to depose the Lord Ralph, at the bidding and suggestion of the prince and chiefly, it is said, through bribery, elected a certain subdeacon of the church called Aimery. He came from Limoges, and was an uneducated man and not at all honourable in his conduct. The aforesaid Lord Ralph had appointed him dean . . . intending thereby to place him under an obligation and to ensure his loyalty to himself, but this was a vain hope for from that time forward he is said to have joined with Ralph's enemies, and unmindful of the good faith he owed to his benefactor he had plotted his downfall.[1]

The reason for William's antipathy is not known: he was only a child at the time of Aimery's succession, and the two men seldom met in adult life. Most probably it reflected the dispute over ecclesiastical jurisdiction in the County of Tripoli. In Orthodox times the sees of Tripoli, Tortosa, and Jubail, together with those of Beirut, Sidon, and Acre, had formed part of the ecclesiastical province of Tyre. When Tyre was captured by the Franks in 1124 and a latin archbishop enthroned there, his claim to jurisdiction over the three northern dioceses was contested by the patriarch of Antioch. This led to prolonged litigation in the papal courts. This revolved round the question whether the Orthodox provincial boundaries should continue to be observed, or whether, as Paschal II had ruled in 1111, ecclesiastical boundaries should follow newly established political boundaries in the Latin East. In 1139 Pope Innocent II upheld the claim of the archbishop of Tyre to jurisdiction over the three northern seas, but interestingly this ruling was never enforced, not even by Alberic of Ostia, the cardinal who presided at the legatine synod of 1140 convoked specifically to regulate the affairs of the Church of Antioch, and at which Aimery's predecessor, Ralph of Domfront, was deposed. The tripolitan sees therefore remained under the jurisdiction of Antioch, and this was a major source of grievance to William of Tyre, who as archbishop was deprived of half of his province.[2] His antipathy to Aimery may well have arisen because of this dispute.

William's unflattering portrait has undoubtedly influenced modern scholars who have written about Aimery, but attention has recently been drawn to a range of evidence which makes it possible to achieve a more balanced view of his personality and achievements. Rudolph Hiestand has drawn attention to *La Fazienda de ultra mare*, a pilgrim's guide to the Holy Land, written for Archbishop Raymond of Toledo (1124/5–1152) by Aimery, archdeacon of Antioch.[3] Hiestand argues convincingly that his author must be Aimery of Limoges, and from the correspondence which is annexed to the work it is clear that he knew Raymond of Toledo well. Given their respective life spans, Aimery was clearly much younger than Raymond and it is therefore reasonable to infer that he had been Raymond's pupil before he went to live in the Latin East. This would give an approximate date of birth of 1110 for Aimery. Raymond of Toledo was one of the leaders of the intellectual revival in Western Europe in the early twelfth century, and was the patron of a school of translators of classical and arabic works into Latin. *La Fazienda* makes it plain that Aimery had studied in Toledo and had received an excellent academic training, for it is written in Castilian, and is based in part on a study of the hebrew text of the Old Testament as well as on the Vulgate text. On internal evidence the treatise was written before 1144, and almost certainly dates from before Aimery's appointment as dean of Antioch in 1140.[4]

Aimery was probably attracted to the latin East because of his intellectual interests, and he also had connections there. His uncle, Peter Armoin, was part of the entourage of Prince Raymond of Poitiers, who had appointed him castellan of Antioch.[5] Raymond was concerned to give office to men from his native Aquitaine in order to counter the power of the Normans who had ruled in Antioch since the First Crusade, and Peter Armoin's well qualified nephew, who was destined for a career in the church, soon attained preferment. Aimery cannot have come to the Levant until after 1136, when Raymond came to power, and his rise was meteoric. Raymond was involved in a bitter power struggle with the Patriarch Ralph of Domfront, a very ambitious man who attempted to make the prince a vassal of the church.[6] When Aimery arrived in Antioch the office of archdeacon was vacant, because the previous holder, Lambert, had been deposed by Ralph at the beginning of his reign.[7] The patriarch must have been responsible for Aimery's appointment: his abilities were undoubted and Ralph may well have thought that Prince Raymond would see this appointment as a conciliatory gesture. But in 1139 Ralph decided for tactical reasons to reinstate archdeacon Lambert, and that was the occasion, I infer, for Aimery's promotion to dean.[8]

Late in 1140 Ralph of Domfront was deposed by a legatine synod and was imprisoned in a monastery on the Black Mountain.[9] Aimery of Limoges was elected as new patriarch: he was an obvious choice, since he was a man of mature life, who already held senior office in the church, who was well educated and had been respected and promoted by the previous patriarch, but who also enjoyed the full confidence of Prince Raymond. William of Tyre implies that Aimery was not elected until after the legate had left for Rome in 1141 and the first secure reference to him as patriarch is found in a document of 1143.[10] Although this implies that the pope had confirmed Aimery's appointment by that date, his position was again put in doubt when Ralph of Domfront escaped from prison and fled to Rome where he appealed in person against his deposition. William of Tyre relates that the pope reinstated Ralph and that he was preparing to return to Antioch, when he was poisoned.[11] He does not date these events, but in 1145 the bishop of Jabala was sent by Prince Raymond to lodge a complaint about the patriarch to the new pope, Eugenius III, and Cahen rightly interprets this as a request to reverse his predecessor's decision to reinstate Ralph.[12] So far as is known that judgment was not revised, but with Ralph's death Aimery's position became secure. It is generally assumed that Ralph died before 1149, though there is one piece of evidence which might suggest a later date. When in 1149 Cardinal Guido of Florence, Eugenius III's legate, convoked a synod in Jerusalem, Aimery forbade any of his suffragans to attend, because of the political crisis in North Syria following the battle of Inab. The bishop-elect of Tripoli, who obeyed this injunction, had his appointment quashed by the legate and had later to go to Rome to be reinstated by the pope. It is possible, as Cahen suggests, that Aimery feared that if his patriarchate was represented at the synod his own position would be called in question because Ralph of Domfront was still alive, but it is more likely that Aimery was unable to be present himself because of the situation in north Syria and did not want the question of the province of Tyre reopened in his absence.[13] After this time Aimery's patriarchal status was never called in question. Eugenius III recognised it: when he wanted a copy of the homilies of Saint John Chrysostom on Saint Matthew's Gospel, he asked Aimery to procure a latin translation for him. Aimery sent him a copy of the greek text instead, which was then translated by Burgundio of Pisa, who presented it to the pope in 1151.[14]

As well as being a gifted scholar Aimery had considerable gifts of leadership which were frequently called upon during his long reign. This first happened when, on 29 June 1149, Prince Raymond was killed, together with many of his knights, at the battle of Inab by the army of Nur ad-Din of Aleppo. Raymond's heir, Bohemond III, was a minor and government devolved on Raymond's widow, the twenty-one year old Constance, hereditary princess of Antioch. In that emergency she received the full support of the Patriarch Aimery: even William of Tyre relates that he 'proved himself to be a true guardian of the stricken province', raising an army of mercenaries at his own expense.[15] Inevitably this led Aimery's enemies to accuse him of wishing to rule Antioch himself. Baldwin III of Jerusalem was anxious that his cousin Constance should remarry, and in 1152 convoked a *curia generalis* at Tripoli which she attended with the barons of Antioch, and at which Aimery of Limoges and his suffragans were also present, together with several members of the royal family. Not even the admonitions of her aunts, Queen Melisende of Jerusalem and Hodierna, Countess of Tripoli, could persuade Constance to take a husband, and William of Tyre reports that the patriarch was thought to be responsible for her intransigence:

> because he was a clever and subtle man he was said to have encouraged her in this mistaken course of action, so that he might in the meantime more freely rule the whole land, which he was very desirous of doing.[16]

William was not writing from personal knowledge; he was a student in Western Europe at this time,[17] and he may simply have been repeating a malicious rumour because he disliked Aimery. Nevertheless, his observation gains a certain force from what happened next. In 1153 Constance of Antioch did remarry: her husband was Reynald of Chatillon and Aimery is said to have been critical of the new prince. Moreover, the Church of Antioch was rich whereas recent territorial losses had impoverished the prince whose defence expenditure nevertheless remained extremely high. The reason for this disparity in income is not known, because the archive of Antioch has never been found and there is very little evidence about the property of the patriarch or of the rest of the church in the twelfth century. Nevertheless, all contemporary writers are unanimous in asserting that Aimery of Limoges was rich. It would appear from William of Tyre's account that Reynald sequestered some church property and when Aimery protested, imprisoned him in the citadel of Antioch. He humiliated the patriarch by causing him to sit bareheaded on the roof of the keep throughout a summer's day, for good measure pouring honey over his head, which made him a prey to mosquitoes and midges. William of Tyre gives his only sympathetic account of Aimery on this occasion—perhaps because he disliked Reynald of Chatillon even more—describing the patriarch as 'a very old priest, the successor of Peter, prince of the Apostles, a sick man, almost continually ailing'.[18] This seems for the most part to be invention. Aimery at this time was probably aged about forty-four, and appears to have had robust health: he was certainly to live an active life for another forty years.

Nevertheless, the news of this very public quarrel disturbed the court of Jerusalem and Baldwin III sent the bishop of Acre and Ralph the Chancellor of the Kingdom to restore peace. Reynald agreed to release Aimery and to return all church property. The patriarch nevertheless refused to go on living in Antioch and went into exile in Jerusalem in 1153.[19] He was still there in 1158 when Theodora Comnena, niece of the Emperor Manual and bride of

King Baldwin III, reached the Holy Land. At that time the pope had not ratified the appointment of Amalric of Nesle, the new patriarch-elect of Jerusalem; and because this marriage was of the greatest diplomatic importance and the rites needed to be performed with the fullest solemnity, Aimery of Limoges was commissioned to anoint Theodora as queen and to solemnize her marriage to the king.[20] This was the only occasion on which a Latin Patriarch of Antioch exercised full liturgical functions in the Catholic cathedral of Jerusalem.

The Emperor Manuel campaigned in Cilicia and Syria in the winter of 1158–9, and Aimery accompanied Baldwin III who went to meet him when the emperor visited Antioch at Easter 1159.[21] Prince Reynald did not seek to reopen his quarrel with the patriarch, who was therefore able to stay on in the city after Baldwin left. He and Reynald were not required to work together for long. In November 1161 Reynald was captured by the governor of Aleppo and spent the next fifteen years in prison.[22] This led to a contest between Princess Constance who wished to act as regent, and the barons who wished to make Bohemond III prince, although he was still underage, which was only resolved in *c.* 1163, when Aimery and the High Court invoked the military aid of prince Thoros of Cilicia and placed Bohemond III in power.[23] About a year later, on 10 August 1164, the confederate christian armies of north Syria were defeated at the battle of Artah by Nur ad-Din and Bohemond was taken prisoner. As in 1149 Aimery of Limoges took charge of the government during this emergency and sent an appeal for help to Louis VII of France.[24] But Nur ad-Din made no attempt to attack Antioch, fearing Byzantine reprisals if he did so, for not only had Manuel established his protectorate there in 1159, he had also, in 1161, married Bohemond's sister, Mary. Nur ad-Din therefore released Bohemond on bail and he went to Constantinople to ask his imperial brother-in-law to pay his ransom and Manuel agreed to this on condition that a greek patriarch was restored to Antioch.[25]

Aimery of Limoges, like his latin predecessors, claimed to be the lawful successor of Saint Peter in the see of Antioch and to have canonical jurisdiction over all the Orthodox as well as the Latins in his patriarchate. The Byzantine rulers contested this claim; when Manuel's father, John II, had restored byzantine rule in Cilicia in 1138, he had expelled the latin bishops and replaced them by

Greeks,[26] and all the Comnenian Emperors had appointed titular Orthodox patriarchs of Antioch who lived in Constantinople.[27] In 1165 Bohemond III returned to Antioch with the current titular patriarch, Athanasius III, and Aimery was required to cede his cathedral to his greek rival. He did so with an ill grace, anathematizing all the Latins in Antioch who accepted Athanasius as their canonical superior, and went to live in his castle of al-Qusair.[28] Athanasius' installation provoked no reaction either from the court of Jerusalem or from the pope. The Franks in the East realised the importance of the byzantine protectorate and did not wish to offend the emperor: William of Tyre does not even mention the restoration of Anastasius III in his official history of the crusader kingdom. Pope Alexander III was likewise unwilling to antagonize Manuel, who was an important ally in his struggle against the western emperor, Frederick Barbarossa.[29]

Aimery was restored to power by what he certainly regarded as an act of God. In 1170 there was a severe earthquake in north Syria and Athanasius was mortally wounded when the sanctuary of Antioch cathedral collapsed during the liturgy. Aimery was therefore left in undisputed possession of his see,[30] for although Manuel appointed a new titular Orthodox patriarch, Cyril II, he did not attempt to instal him in power at Antioch. But as overlord of the principality, he did in *c.* 1177 arrange a marriage between Bohemond III, who had recently become a widower, and his own great-niece Theodora.[31] Alexander III seems to have feared that this might lead to the restoration of a greek Patriarch, and in 1178 wrote urging the clergy and people of Antioch to resist any attempt to make their church subject to that of Constantinople.[32] This is an indication of how much the political situation had changed since 1165. Having in 1177 brought his long war against the Emperor Frederick to an end at the Peace of Venice, Alexander was in a position to take a firm stand about the rights of the latin patriarch of Antioch, while Manuel did not wish to antagonize the pope, since he was seeking western allies.[33] This was the context of William of Tyre's embassy to Constantinople in the winter of 1178–9, on behalf of Baldwin IV of Jerusalem. Since he went by way of the Third Lateran Council he would also have had the opportunity to speak to the pope about the needs of the latin East. On his way back to Jerusalem in the spring of 1180, William reports that his mission called at Antioch, where 'we carried out with the prince and the lord patriarch the business enjoined upon us by his imperial highness'. This business was, of course, confidential, and the only indication which William gives of its nature is when he speaks of the time spent at Manuel's court as 'very useful to us and to our church'. This may indicate that Manuel had been persuaded by William—who had been advised by the pope and the court of Jerusalem—not to seek to restore an Orthodox patriarch in Antioch. Certainly William's guarded account seems to indicate that Manuel treated Aimery as legitimate incumbent in 1180.[34]

When Manuel died in the autumn of that year, Bohemond promptly repudiated his byzantine wife Theodora, and married Sibyl, a frankish noblewoman who was said to be of doubtful moral character. Aimery of Limoges refused to recognise the legitimacy of this marriage and excommunicated the prince. The quarrel between them then escalated, for Bohemond began seizing church property, while the patriarch withdrew with his supporters to al-Qusair, placing Antioch under an interdict. Civil war broke out: the Patriarch's supporters were led by Reynald Masoier, lord of al-Marqab, and Bohemond laid siege to the patriarch's castle. Baldwin IV of Jerusalem was rightly disturbed by news of this, since it jeopardized the security of north Syria, and he sent an impressive delegation to Antioch to mediate peace, led by the new Patriarch of Jerusalem, Heraclius, the Masters of the Temple and the Hospital, Count Raymond of Tripoli and Bohemond's stepfather, Reynald of Chatillon. After lengthy negotiations the envoys succeeded in producing a compromise solution: Bohemond would restore confiscated church property, but would remain excommunicated until he regularized his marriage (though as Cahen pointed out, the church soon came to accept Sibyl as lawful princess of Antioch).[35]

This quarrel bears a striking similarity to that between Aimery and Reynald of Chatillon thirty years earlier. No marriage irregularities had been at issue then, and it seems probable that the chief problem in 1180–81, as in 1153, was that of church property, and that Bohemond's divorce was simply a catalyst in this dispute. Whereas prince Reynald had won his struggle with Aimery and had been able to exclude him from Antioch for several years, Bohemond III was forced to make peace with him. By 1180 Aimery had become an elder statesman in the Latin East: he had held office for forty years and had an international reputation, and his exclusion would have caused protests throughout the Catholic world. Indeed, it was Bohemond, not the patriarch, who was weakened by this quarrel, since a substantial group of noblemen left his service and entered that of Thoros the Roupenid, Lord of Cilicia.[36]

Throughout Aimery's long term of office the lands of the church of Antioch had been contracting. At its greatest extent the latin patriarchate was made up of six archbishoprics and ten bishoprics in addition to the patriarchal see. Rafaniyah had been lost to the Muslims in 1137, and the archbishops of Mamistra and Tarsus had been driven from their sees by John Comnenus in *c.* 1138, before Aimery came to power. In the first eleven years of his reign the county of Edessa with its three archbishoprics of Edessa, Hierapolis, and Quris were lost to the Muslims, as were the sees of Artah, Marash, and Kesoun and the archdiocese of Apemea in the principality of Antioch. These events effectively reduced the suffragan sees of Antioch to six: Latakia, Jabala, Valania, in the principality; and Tortosa, Tripoli, and Jubail in the County of Tripoli; and this explains why Aimery was determined to retain control over those three northern sees of the province of Tyre.[37] Even there his authority was not unchallenged, for in 1152 the Knights Templar acquired the fief of Tortosa, where their powers of exemption greatly reduced the authority of the latin bishop.[38] Because of the steady decline of his ecclesiastical jurisdiction, Aimery might have been notable chiefly for his strenuous intervention in the secular affairs of the principality. But in fact he was an important religious leader because of his dealings with the oriental Christians in his patriarchate.

Although Aimery's friendly relations with the separated Eastern Churches was rooted in part in a common antipathy to the byzantine Church, it was no doubt also stimulated by the efforts which the Emperor Manuel made to restore unity between the Church of Constantinople and the non-Chalcedonian Christians of the East. From 1170–2 Theorianus, the Emperor's envoy, presided at a series of negotiations with representatives of the Jacobite and Armenian Churches, trying to unite them with the Orthodox Church, but the discussions proved inconclusive.[39]

Aimery began to develop close relations with the Jacobites when their new patriarch, Michael the Syrian, was elected in 1166. He fixed his see at Mardin in northern Iraq[40] but soon established friendly relations with his frankish neighbours. In 1168 he went on pilgrimage to Jerusalem and returned home by way of Antioch. At that time the Orthodox Patriarch Athanasius III was in power, but Michael ignored him and paid his respects to Aimery at his castle of al-Qusair.[41] Michael claimed to be lawful patriarch of Antioch, and his preference for meeting his latin rather than his greek rival is explained by a comment in his history:

> The Franks never made any difficulty about matters of doctrine, or tried to formulate it in one way only for Christians of differing race and language, but they accepted as a Christian anybody who venerated the cross without further examination.[42]

No doubt this had been true of all the frankish prelates who had ruled in north Syria since the First Crusade, but Michael was writing out of his own experience of Aimery of Limoges. The Greeks were much more concerned with theological exactitude—which the Jacobites resented.

In personal terms Michael had much in common with his fellow patriarch, for he too was a scholar and the author of a very important history. He stayed in Antioch until Easter 1169, and according to the anonymous syriac *Chronicle of 1234* was allowed by the frankish authorities to be solemnly enthroned in the cathedral and presumably to preside at the Jacobite liturgy there.[43] This may indeed have happened, even though Michael himself says nothing about it, because the greek patriarch was not popular with the frankish rulers who may have felt no scruples about offending him. Certainly Michael's long stay at Antioch led him to form an enduring friendship with Aimery and the Franks.

Michael the Syrian came to Antioch again in 1178 and Aimery of Limoges invited him to attend the Third Lateran Council which was going to meet at Easter 1179. Michael declined, but when he learned that the Cathar heresy was on the council's agenda he wrote a treatise against it for the consideration of the pope.[44] Aimery's invitation was revolutionary: Michael had not made any profession of Catholic faith or even expressed a wish to be in communion with the Roman See. Moreover he claimed to be the lawful incumbent of the see of Antioch. But Aimery seems to have supposed that Michael's presence at the Council might be the first step in restoring unity between the Catholic and Jacobite churches. Michael remained a loyal friend to the Franks until his death in 1199, appointing as his vicar in Antioch his own brother Athanasius who had fled there from Jerusalem in 1187 after its capture by Saladin.[45] The Jacobite Church in Michael's reign never entered into communion with the Latins, and political circumstances would certainly have made that very difficult because most Jacobites lived under Muslim rule, but nevertheless the warmth of the relations between the two communities was appreciable, and that was a consequence of Aimery's efforts.

When Aimery became patriarch, the Armenians of Cilicia were under byzantine rule and had little direct contact with the church of Antioch because the Emperor John had driven the latin hierarchy from the province and replaced them with Greeks.[46] The Catholicus of Armenia, Gregory III (1113–66), while maintaining friendly contacts with the papacy, lived in muslim territory and had no close dealings with the Franks of Antioch.[47] Relations between the two churches improved after Cilicia regained her independence in *c.* 1172, and Rupen III (1175–87) who wanted a frankish alliance, allowed latin archbishops to be restored at Tarsus in 1178 and at Mamistra by 1186.[48] The chief link between the Armenians and Aimery would seem to have been Saint Nerses of Lampron, armenian archbishop of Tarsus, a churchman of truly ecumenical spirit, who made no difficulty about admitting a rival latin archbishop in his own see. As he later explained to Leo the first-crowned, when he had visited the Crusader States he had observed the Latin Church in action and had found many things about it which were admirable. He had received a particularly warm welcome at Antioch:

> The latin churches of the East as well as those of the West showed their approval of my sound views before the arrival of the Roman Emperor [Frederick I in 1190]. At a synod of bishops, finding that I was well instructed in their disciplines and that I was extending the benefits of this to my own country through the practice of good works, they glorified the heavenly Father. I also recall how the churches of the Latins and the Greeks at Antioch, solemnly greeted me as Paul, unworthy though I am, and said that I was the

> worthy successor in that Apostle's see [of Tarsus]. Those churches opened their doors to me and their clergy listened attentively to my preaching.[49]

These discussions culminated in 1184 in the dispatch of an embassy to Pope Lucius III by the Catholicus Gregory IV with a profession of faith. Lucius obviously regarded this as an act of submission to the Holy See and sent a *pallium* to the Catholicus, together with a text of the *Rituale Romanum*. The Armenians may not have understood this exchange in the same way as the Catholic authorities, but there seems no doubt that they wished to establish full communion with the Roman Church. Aimery's name is not directly mentioned in the negotiations, but he must have been involved in them, since by recognising the Armenians the pope was licensing an alternative Catholic hierarchy within the jurisdiction of the latin patriarch of Antioch. Saint Nerses translated the Roman Ritual into Armenian, because it would form the basis for bringing the practices of his church into conformity with those of the Roman see.[50] Lucius III obviously thought that full religious unity had been restored with the Armenian Church, and in 1184 he ordered armenian clergy in the diocese of Valania, who had no bishop of their own, to obey the latin bishop.[51] Pope Clement III likewise assumed that the union was in force and wrote about this to the Catholicus Gregory IV in 1189.[52] Relations between the Armenian Church and the Latins remained cordial in the years immediately following the Third Crusade, and this culminated in the formal act of union in 1198.[53] Aimery of Limoges did not live to see this, but there is no doubt that by his tactful handling of the situation he had contributed in a very central way towards it.

His greatest success in promoting unity with the oriental churches was with the Maronites. William of Tyre relates how in *c.* 1181 they renounced their error, by which he presumably means Monotheletism, and

> returned to the unity of the Catholic Church, receiving the orthodox faith and being willing to embrace and devoutly observe all the traditions of the Roman Church.[54]

The Maronites lived in the County of Tripoli, and therefore within the latin patriarchate of Antioch. William of Tyre gives a more triumphalist account of the union than the facts warrant, for in 1181 only some of the maronite hierarchy came into communion with Rome, while there was strong opposition to this on the part of many others. Nevertheless, the union was slowly implemented: in 1215 the maronite patriarch attended the Fourth Lateran Council, and the union, although it has had a chequered history, has survived until the present day.[55] The settlement which Aimery of Limoges devised for the Maronites was to become the blueprint for uniate churches of the eastern rite. The Maronites preserved their own liturgy, canon law and forms of religious observance insofar as these were compatible with Catholic norms. They retained their own hierarchy, which was subject to the maronite patriarch who was answerable to the pope alone, and the local Catholic hierarchy had no jurisdiction over the Maronite Church.[56]

Thus by the time of his death Aimery had succeeded in taking the first steps towards union with all three of the main groups of non-byzantine Christians living in his patriarchate, although full union had not yet been achieved with any of them. It was a remarkable achievement, because it involved the recognition of independent ecclesiastical jurisdictions within his own patriarchate, and, as future events were to show, this was the way forward in ecumenical relations between Rome and the eastern Churches.

Aimery believed that the orthodox Christians, both Syrians and Greeks, were in full communion with the Western Church already. There were a substantial number of them in the city of Antioch and among the monasteries on the Black Mountain and he had no doubt that they owned him canonical obedience.[57] So far as I am aware he did not recognise the existence of the titular Orthodox patriarchs who succeeded Athanasius III, Cyril II (*c.* 1173–9) and Theodore IV Balsamon (pre 1189 – post 1195), a learned canonist who had a profound contempt for the Latin Church which he regarded as schismatic.[58] But Aimery's attitude to the greek members of his flock was in no way negative. He corresponded with Hugo Eteriano, the pisan scholar who was one of the Emperor Manuel's principal advisers on western affairs.[59] In 1176 he wrote to thank Hugo for sending him a copy of his treatise on the procession of the Holy Spirit, a matter about which he wished to be fully informed because it was the chief point of theological contention between the Orthodox and Latin churches. Aimery's letter implies that he had by this time learned Greek, for he speaks of 'reading with admiration the books written both in Latin and Greek which you have sent'.[60] He also asks Hugo to procure more books for him: a copy of Saint John Chrysostom's commentary on the pauline Epistles; a history of the Byzantine Empire 'from the time at which their emperors split away from the Roman Empire until the present day'; and finally a copy of the acts of the Council of Nicaea 'which we have heard is held by the Lord Emperor'.[61] Aimery was obviously wishing to be better informed about the history of the byzantine church and people and about the way in which they understood the faith. His purpose may have been polemical, but it may equally well have been eirenical: a desire to understand the Orthodox and to promote true unity among the Greeks and Latins in his obedience whom he believed were members of the one Church. This would certainly have been in keeping with the rest of his dealings with eastern Christians.

Aimery was also concerned with the spiritual needs of Latin Christians under his care. One such group were the hermits who lived on the Black Mountain of Antioch. This is known from the writings of Gerard of Nazareth who had himself been a hermit there and who later during Aimery's reign became Bishop of Latakia (1139–61). He relates how Aimery enacted that every solitary who lived on the Black Mountain must have a spiritual director. This was no doubt a necessary reform, for, as Gerard's writings make plain, large numbers of Latins, as well as of oriental Christians, lived as hermits on the Black Mountain in the twelfth century, and although some of them lived in community, like those of Jubin, others had no training at all in the religious life.[62] Aimery's legislation was evidently found beneficial and was continued after his death: in 1235 Pope Gregory IX sent an instruction to the Minister of the hermits of the Black Mountain.[63]

According to a treatise by the Dominican Stephen of Salagnac (†1291), Aimery of Limoges was also responsible for drawing up the first rule for the hermits of Carmel.[64] It is known that both greek and latin hermits were living on Carmel in the twelfth century and it is therefore possible that Aimery was asked to advise them, or that they adopted the same kind of rule which he had drawn up for the hermits of the Black Mountain.[65] Nevertheless, there is no contemporary evidence for this, and it is *prima facie* unlikely that a patriarch of Antioch would have been able to exercise that degree of religious influence in the patriarchate of Jerusalem, even though he did live there for some years in Baldwin III's reign.[66]

Saint Nerses of Lampron was favourably impressed by the charity of the latin clergy of Antioch towards the poor during Aimery's reign, and the patriarch clearly set his fellow priests a good example, for Michael the Syrian records with admiration his generosity to the poor during the drought which afflicted Syria in 1178.[67] He was also concerned with maintaining the defences of his patriarchate. Not only did he improve the fortifications of his own castle of al-Qusair—which might be regarded as simple self-interest[68]—he also seems to have used his early links with Castile to persuade the Master of the Order of Santiago to undertake the defence of the antiochene frontier in 1180.[69] It is also very much to Aimery's credit that in 1186 he encouraged his friend, Reynald Mazoier, to sell his great lordship of al-Marqab to the Knights of St. John because he could no longer satisfactorily undertake its defence. The lordship encompassed most of the bishopric of Valania, which consequently came under the influence of the Order and was lost to the secular church,[70] and Aimery must have been aware that the sale would be potentially damaging to his own ecclesiastical interests.

When the news of the disastrous frankish defeat at Hattin reached Antioch, Aimery sent a mission to England, led by the bishop of Jabala, to invoke the assistance of Henry II, perhaps building on earlier links between the principality and the angevin crown.[71] When Saladin campaigned in north Syria in 1188, he failed to capture Antioch city and certain other fortresses, including the patriarch's castle of al-Qusair.[72] Although a late source, the *Anonymi Rhenani Historia*, relates that Aimery of Limoges bought off an attack, this does not find support in contemporary sources.[73] al-Qusair was a well fortified castle: Bohemond III had not been able to capture it, and it was later to resist the Mamluks for some years after they captured Antioch in 1268.[74] Saladin did not return to the north, and the lands of Antioch remaining in frankish hands were confirmed to them by him in the Treaty of Jaffa in 1192, a pact subsequently ratified by Prince Bohemond who visited the sultan at Beirut in October 1192.[75]

Saladin's conquests had diminished the ecclesiastical powers of the patriarchate and these were not restored in Aimery's lifetime. The dioceses of Latakia, Jabala, and Jubail all passed into muslim hands.[76] Thus by the time Aimery died he had only five suffragans: the archbishops of Tarsus and Mamistra, whose powers were nominal; the bishop of Tortosa, who was overshadowed by the Knights Templar; the bishop of Valania who was virtually a chaplain of the Knights of Saint John; and the bishop of Tripoli, who alone had any real power.

According to the contemporary chronicle of Michael the Syrian, Aimery died in 1193 in his castle of al-Qusair and was buried in Antioch cathedral. Michael adds 'they appointed in his place an aged priest called Ranulf'.[77] Cahen, who points out that the death of an unnamed patriarch of Antioch is also recorded in the *Bustan* for 1193, accepts this dating, but this is not without problems:[78] no other source mentions Ranulph, and the Old French Continuation of William of Tyre ascribes to Aimery a leading role in the events of 1193–4. In October 1193, Bohemond III and some of his chief supporters were seized and imprisoned by Leo II of Cilicia who then attempted to gain control of Antioch with the help of frankish dissident noblemen who had been in his service since 1181. This led to a riot in the city, and the Patriarch Aimery presided over an assembly in the cathedral at which a commune was set up and Bohemond's eldest son Raymond recognised as regent. Aimery, Raymond, and his brother Bohemond [IV] then appealed to Henry of Troyes, ruler of Jerusalem, to mediate with Leo. He did so in 1194 and Bohemond III was released, but the commune of Antioch remained in existence and was the earliest such body to be formed in the Frankish East.[79] This kind of initiative is so much in keeping with the rest of Aimery of Limoges' career that I am reluctant to attribute it to an otherwise unknown Patriarch Ranulph on the sole evidence of a passage in Michael the Syrian. Since Cahen wrote, Ruth Morgan has edited the earliest redaction of the Old French continuation of William of Tyre, and this names Aimery as the patriarch in 1194.[80] *The Chronicle of the Holy Land* which forms part of the *Gestes des Chiprois* contains this entry:

> In the year 1196 died Saladin . . . And in this same year died Aimery, Patriarch of Antioch, and Peter of Angouleme, who was bishop of Tripoli, succeeded him.[81]

Saladin, of course, died in 1193, as Michael the Syrian says Aimery did: and Peter of Angouleme did become patriarch of Antioch, although there is no evidence apart from this entry of his holding office until 1197.[82] No final resolution of this problem is possible unless fresh evidence comes to light; but one suggestion would be that Michael the Syrian gives correct information under the wrong date: that Aimery died in 1196, and that Ranulph did briefly succeed him as patriarch-elect but that his appointment never received papal confirmation.

Aimery of Limoges may justly be counted one of the greatest churchmen to hold office in the Crusader States. He ruled the Church of Antioch for almost sixty years and was distinguished by his learning, his desire to promote unity between Catholics and oriental Christians, and his concern for the spiritual wellbeing of solitaries. But he coupled those qualities with considerable force of character and political, diplomatic and even military skills, which earned him a place among the great secular leaders of the Latin East.

Notes

1. *Willelmi Tyrensis Archiepiscopi Chronicon*, XV.18; ed. R. B. C. Huygens (identification des sources historiques et détermination des dates par H-E. Mayer, G. Rösch), *Corpus Christianorum Continuatio Medievalis*, 63, 63A (Turnhout, 1986) [henceforth WT], pp. 699–700.

2. *Ibid.*, XVI.14; pp. 650–1; J. G. Rowe, 'The Papacy and the Ecclesiastical Province of Tyre', *Bulletin of the John Rylands Library*, 43 (1960–1) 160–89.

3. M. Lazar, ed., *La fazienda de ultra mar*, Acta Salamanticensia. Filosofia y Letras, 18 (2) (Salamanca, 1965).

4. R. Hiestand, 'Un centre intellectuel en Syrie du Nord? Notes sur la personnalité d'Aimery d'Antioche, Albert de Tarse et *Rorgo Fretellus', Le Moyen Age*, 100 (1994) 8–16. Hiestand points out that *La Fazienda* must have been written before 1145 because the author does not know about the finding of the head of Saint John the Baptist at Sebastea in that year. For Raymond of Toledo, see J. Kritzeck, *Peter the Venerable and Islam* (Princeton, 1964) 53–55.

5. WT XV.16; p. 697.

6. B. Hamilton, 'Ralph of Domfront, Patriarch of Antioch (1135–40), *Nottingham Medieval Studies*, 28 (1984) pp. 1–21.

7. WT XIV.10; p. 642.

8. *Ibid.*, XV.15; p. 695. Aimery had become dean by April 1140; G. Bresc-Bautier, ed., *Le cartulaire du chapitre du Saint-Sépulcre de Jérusalem, Documents relatifs à l'histoire des croisades publiés par l'Académie des Inscriptions et Belles-Lettres*, 15 (Paris, 1984), nos. 76, 77, pp. 178, 182.

9. R. Hiestand, 'Ein neuer Bericht über das Konzil von Antiochia 1140', *Annuarium Historiae Conciliorum*, 20 (1988) 314–50.

10. WT XV.18; pp. 699–700. P. Pelliot, 'Mélanges sur l'époque des croisades', *Mémoires de l'Institut national de France, Académie des Inscriptions et Belles-Lettres*,

44/1 (1960) 9–10, argued that Aimery was not confirmed in office until 1142. He cites William of Tyre's assertion that Amalric of Jerusalem was crowned 'on 18 February 1163 in the twentieth year of the Lord Aimery, third Latin patriarch of the holy church of Antioch' (WT, XIX.1; p. 864). This is congruent with a privilege for Venice issued by Prince Roger of Antioch: *factum anno principatus VII, Aimerico patriarcha.* The seventh year of Raymond's reign began in 1143, although the editors wrongly date this charter to 1140 (G. L. F. Tafel and G. M. Thomas, eds., *Urkunden zur älteren Handels- und Staatsgeschichte der Republik Venedig mit besonderer Beziehung auf Byzanz und die Levante, Fontes rerum austriacarum*, section III, 12–14, 3 vols [Vienna, 1856–7], I, no. xlvi, pp. 102–3).

11. WT XV.17; p. 699.

12. Otto of Freising, *Chronica, sive historia de duabus civitatibus*, VII. xxxiii; ed. A. Hofmeister, *Monumenta Germaniae Historica Scriptores* [henceforth *MGH SS*] *rerum Germanicarum in usum scholarum separatim editae* (Hanover, Leipzig, 1912) pp. 363–4; cf. C. Cahen, *La Syrie du nord à l'époque des croisades et la principauté franque d'Antioche* (Paris, 1940) p. 504.

13. Continuator of Sigebert of Gembloux, *Historia Pontificalis*, xxxvi; *MGH SS*, 20: pp. 540–1; Cahen, *Syrie*, p. 505; B. Hamilton, *The Latin Church in the Crusader States. The Secular Church* (London, 1980) 41–2.

14. E. Martène & U. Durand, eds., *Veterum Scriptorum et Monumentorum amplissima collectio*, 9 Vols (Paris, 1724–33) 1: 817–18.

15. WT XVII.10; pp. 772–4.

16. *Ibid.*, XVII.18; p. 786.

17. *Ibid.*, XIX.12; 879–82; R. B. C. Huygens, 'Guillaume de Tyr étudiant. Un chapitre (XIX, 12) de son "Histoire" retrouvé', *Latomus* 21 (1962) 811–29; P. W. Edbury & J. G. Rowe, *William of Tyre. Historian of the Latin East* (Cambridge, 1988) p. 15.

18. WT XVIII.1; p. 809: . . . *sacerdotem longevum, Petri apostolorum principis successorem, virum egrotativum, pene perpetuo infirmantem.* The account is substantially confirmed by Michael the Syrian, *Chronicle*, ed. with French trans. by J. B. Chabot, 4 vols (Paris, 1899–1924) [henceforth MS], XXI.viii; III, pp. 411–412.

19. WT XVIII.1; p. 809. His presence in Jerusalem is attested in a document of 1155, ed. Bresc-Bautier (n. 8 above), no 37, p. 106.

20. WT XVIII.xxii; p. 843; B. Hamilton, 'Women in the Crusader States: the Queens of Jerusalem 1100–90', in D. Baker, ed., *Medieval Women* (Oxford, 1978) 157–8.

21. WT XVIII.25; p. 847; John Cinnamus, *Epitome rerum ab Ioanne et Alexio Comnenis gestarum*, ed. A. Meineke, *Corpus Scriptorum Historiae Byzantinae* (Bonn, 1836) p. 187; P. Magdalino, *The Empire of Manuel Komnenos 1143–1180* (Cambridge, 1993) pp. 66–72.

22. The date is sometimes given as 1160, but see B. Hamilton, 'The Elephant of Christ: Reynald of Châtillon', *Studies in Church History* [henceforth *SCH*] 15 (1978) p. 98, n. 13.

23. MS XVIII.x; vol. 3: p. 324.

24. Cahen, *La Syrie*, pp. 408–9; R. Röhricht, *Regesta Regni Hierosolymitani* (*MXCVII–MCCXCI*), 2 vols (Oeniponti, 1893–1904) I, no. 405.

25. R-J. Lilie, *Byzantium and the Crusader States, 1096–1204*, revised edn. 1988, English trans. J. C. Morris & J. E. Ridings (Oxford, 1993) pp. 184–93; MS XVIII.xi; vol. 3: 326.

26. Odo of Deuil, *De Profectione Ludovici VII in Orientem*, ed. & trans. V. G. Berry (New York, 1948) p. 68.

27. Hamilton, *Latin Church*, pp. 173–5.

28. MS XVIII.xi; vol. 3: 326; King Fulk had captured al-Qusair with the help of the Patriarch Bernard of Valence in 1134, *ibid.*, XVI, v. vol. III, p. 234, and it may have been granted to the patriarchs from that time. P. Deschamps, *Les chateaux des croisés en Terre Sainte.* III. *La défense du comté de Tripoli et de la principauté d'Antioche* (Paris, 1973) pp. 351–7.

29. Lilie, *Byzantium and the Crusader States*, pp. 189–93; P. Lamma, *Comneni e Staufer. Ricerche sui rapporti fra Bisanzio e l'Occidente nel secolo XII*, 2 vols (Rome, 1955–7).

30. MS XIX.vi; vol. 3: 339.

31. Cahen, *La Syrie*, pp. 419–20; C. M. Brand, *Byzantium Confronts the West, 1180–1204* (Cambridge, Mass., 1968) p. 22.

32. S. Löwenfeld, *Epistolae Pontificum Romanorum ineditae* (Leipzig, 1885) p. 164.

33. Magdalino, *Manuel*, pp. 98–104.

34. WT XXII.4; pp. 1009–1011.

35. *Ibid.*, XXII.6–7; pp. 1013–1017; Cahen, *La Syrie*, p. 423, n. 6.

36. Listed in WT XXII.7; p. 1016.

37. Hamilton, *Latin Church*, pp. 38–41.

38. J. Riley-Smith, 'The Templars and the castle of Tortosa in Syria: an unknown document concerning the acquisition of the fortress', *English Historical Review*, 84 (1969) pp. 278–88.

39. P. Tekeyan, *Controverses christologiques en Arméno-Cilicie dans la seconde moitié du xiie siècle (1165–98), Orientalia Christiana Analecta* 124 (Rome, 1939) 14–42.

40. MS XIX.ii; vol. 3: 329–331.

41. *Ibid.*, XIX.iii; 3: 332.

42. *Ibid.*, VI.i; 3: 222.

43. *Anonymi Chronicon ad annum Christi 1234 pertinens*, trans. A. Abouna, introduction etc., J. M. Fiey, *Corpus Scriptorum Christianorum Orientalium*, Scriptores Syri, 154 (Louvain, 1974), *Historia Ecclesiastica*, p. 230.

44. MS XX.vii; vol. 3: 377–8.

45. *Ibid.*, XXI.vii; viii; vol. 3: 409, 411–412.

46. See n. 26 above.

47. B. Hamilton, 'The Armenian Church and the Papacy at the time of the Crusades', *Eastern Churches Review* X (1978) pp. 65–8.

48. MS XX.vii; vol. 3: 377 (Tarsus); J. Delaville Le Roulx, *Cartulaire général de l'Ordre des Hospitaliers de St Jean de Jérusalem (1100–1310)*, 4 vols (Paris 1894–1906) [henceforth *CGOH*], no. 783 (Mamistra).

49. Saint Nerses of Lampron, 'Lettre adressée au roi Léon II', *Recueil des Historiens des Croisades* [henceforth *RHC*], *Documents Arméniens*, ed. E. Dulaurier (Paris, 1869), i: pp. 592–3.

50. *Pontificia Commissio ad redigendum codicem iuris canonici orientalis, Fontes*, series III, [henceforth *CICO*] vol. I, *Acta Romanorum pontificum a s. Clemente I . . . ad Coelestinum III . . .* (Vatican City, 1943), no. 395, pp. 811–13.

51. *CICO*, vol. III, *Acta Honorii III et Gregorii IX (1216–41)*, ed A. L. Tautu (Vatican City, 1950), no. 132, pp. 178–80.

52. This is a reissue of Lucius III's bull, P. Jaffé, W. Wattenbach, S. Löwenfeld, *Regesta Pontificum Romanorum ab condita ecclesia ad annum post Christi natum 1198*, 2 vols (Leipzig, 1885–8), no. 16463.

53. Hamilton, 'Armenian Church', *Eastern Churches Review* 10 (1978) pp. 70–1.

54. WT XXII.9; p. 1018.

55. K. S. Salibi, 'The Maronite Church in the Middle Ages and its Union with Rome', *Oriens Christianus*, 42 (1958) 92–104.

56. For the later history of the Union, see P. Dib, 'Maronites', *Dictionnaire de Théologie Catholique*, ed. A. Vacant and others, 30 vols (Paris, 1903–50) 10/1: cols, 1–142.

57. S. Runciman, 'The Greeks in Antioch at the time of the Crusades', *Proceedings of the International Congress of Byzantine Studies, Thessalonica, 1953*, vol II (Athens, 1956) pp. 583–91.

58. Hamilton, *Latin Church*, p. 178

59. A. Dondaine, 'Hugues Éthérien et Léon Toscan', *Archives d'histoire doctrinale et littéraire du moyen age* 19 (1952) 67–134; 'Hugues Éthérien et le concile de Constantinople de 1166', *Historisches Jahrbuch* 77 (1958) pp. 473–83.

60. *Propterea libros de processione Spiritus Sancti, quos tam Graece quam Latine scriptos misistis, cum magna suscipimus cordis alacritate, et mox ut in perlegendis illis studii nostri curam potuimus adhibere, vestrum ingenium et facundiam et modum loquendi, plurimum sumus admirati.* ed. E. Martène & U. Durand, *Thesaurus Novus Anecdotorum*, 5 vols (Paris, 1717) 1: 480.

61. This correspondence can be precisely dated to 1176 because Hugo says that he is sending the books by the hand of Prince Reynald. Martène-Durand, 1: 479–81. Reynald's only visit to Constantinople occurred in that year; B. Hamilton, 'Manuel I Comnenus and Baldwin IV of Jerusalem', in J. Chrysostomides, ed., *Kathegetria. Essays presented to Joan Hussey for her 80th birthday* (Camberley, 1988) 360–1.

62. B. Z. Kedar, 'Gerard of Nazareth, a neglected twelfth-century writer in the Latin East', *Dumbarton Oaks Papers*, 37 (1983) pp. 55–77. The passage about Aimery (p. 74) reads: *sedulus vitae monasticae promotor fuit . . . Legem tulit, ne quis in Monte Nigro sine maiore inspectore viveret solitarius.*

63. L. Auvray, ed., *Les Registres de Grégoire IX*, 3 vols (Paris, 1896–1955), no. 2660.

64. *De quattuor in quibus Deus ordinem Praedicatorum insignivit*, a work completed after Stephen's death by Bernard Gui in 1304. Melchior de Ste Marie, 'Carmel. Origine', *Dictionnaire d'histoire et de géographie écclesiastiques*, vol. 11: col 1073.

65. John Phocas, 'A general description . . . of the Holy Places of Palestine', in J. Wilkinson, *Jerusalem Pilgrimage 1099–1185*, Hakluyt Society, ser. II, no. 167 (London, 1988) pp. 335–6.

66. A. Jotischky, *The Perfection of Solitude: Hermits and Monks in the Crusader States* (Pennsylvania State University Press, 1995) pp.100-138.

67. MS XX, vi; vol. 3: 374.

68. See n. 28 above.

69. *Bullarium Equestris Ordinis S. Iacobi de Spatha*, eds., A. F. Aguado de Cordova, A. A. Aleman et Rosales, I. L. Agurleta (Madrid, 1719) pp. 22–3.

70. *CGOH*, no. 783; cf. *CGOH*, no. 799 about the ecclesiastical consequences of this sale.

71. *The Chronicle of the Regions of Henry II and Richard I* [published as *The Chronicle of Benedict of Peterborough*], ed. W. Stubbs, Rolls Series, 49 (I, II) (London, 1867), 2: p. 38; the Pipe Roll for 1178–9, for example, records the presence in England of Robert, an envoy from Manuel Comnenus, and Prince Bohemond of Antioch;

A. A. Vasiliev, 'Manuel Comnenus and Henry Plantagenet', *Byzantinische Zeitschrift* 29 (1929–30) 233–44.

72. M. C. Lyons & D. E. P. Jackson, *Saladin. The Politics of the Holy War* (Cambridge, 1982) 286–91.

73. *Anonymi Rhenani Historia*, c. xlv, *RHC, Historiens Occidentaux*, 5 vols (Paris, 1844–95), 5: p. 521.

74. Deschamps, *Les chateaux des croisés*, 3: pp. 351–7.

75. Cahen, *La Syrie*, pp. 432–3; Lyons & Jackson, *Saladin*, pp. 360, 362.

76. Hamilton, *Latin Church*, p. 48.

77. MS XXI.viii; vol. 3: 412.

78. Cahen, *La Syrie*, pp. 507–9.

79. M. R. Morgan, ed. *La continuation de Guillaume de Tyr (1184–1197), Documents relatifs à l'histoire des croisades publiés par l'Académie des Inscriptions et Belles-Lettres*, 14 (Paris, 1982) pp. 168–70, 177; J. Prawer, 'The "community of Antioch"', *Crusader Institutions* (Oxford, 1980) pp. 68–76, has no doubt that the patriarch involved in this was Aimery of Limoges.

80. Ruth Morgan argued that the compiler of manuscript d, which she edited, had access to the lost chronicle of Ernoul, or to a manuscript closely related to it, which gives this continuation a special value for the period to 1197; *La continuation*, p. 8. See also M. R. Morgan, *The Chronicle of Ernoul and the Continuations of William of Tyre* (Oxford, 1973).

81. 'Chronique de Terre Sainte', in G. Raynaud, ed., *Les Gestes des Chiprois, Société de l'Orient latin, sér. historique*, vol. 5 (Geneva, 1887) p. 15.

82. Hamilton, *Latin Church*, p. 214–15.

'In Their Mother Tongue': A Brief History of the English Translation of Works by and Attributed to Saint Bernard of Clairvaux: 1496–1970

David N. Bell

ALL CISTERCIAN scholars are indebted to Dom Jean Leclercq and his colleagues for the splendid edition of the *Sancti Bernardi Opera* published in eight volumes between 1957 and 1977.[1] This is, and will remain, the standard edition of the latin text of Bernard's works, but since latin literacy is a declining commodity, and since the number of those who can read the language with ease and enjoyment is ever decreasing, what is a pleasure for some may be a problem for many.[2] It follows, therefore, that the need for vernacular translations of medieval texts becomes more and more pressing as the years go by, and Cistercian Publications deserves all credit for its attempts at satisfying this need and for providing an interested public with up-to-date versions of a large number of treatises which, otherwise, would repose unread and unappreciated in the pages of the Migne Patrology or the *Corpus Christianorum*.

The first volume of the complete bernardine canon to be published by Cistercian Publications appeared in 1971,[3] but the history of the english translation of works attributed to the abbot of Clairvaux began almost six centuries earlier. We must note, however, that at that date it was not Bernard but *pseudo*-Bernard who was being put into English, and, as we shall see, that tradition was hardly to change for more than three hundred years. There are manuscript versions of English translations of the *ps.*-bernardine *Meditationes piisimae de cognitione humanae conditionis*, the *Epistola de perfectione vitae* (commonly known as the *Golden Letter*, and to be distinguished from the *Epistola ad fratres de Monte Dei* of William of Saint-Thierry which also appears under this title), the *Liber de modo bene vivendi*, a work usually attributed to Bernard but possibly by Thomas of Froidmont, the *Speculum peccatoris*, the *Epistola de cura et modo rei familiaris utilius gubernandae*, commonly ascribed to Bernard Silvestris, and various pseudonymous poems, prayers and sentences.[4]

Even in Latin the *Meditationes piisimae* had always been extremely popular,[5] and this popularity is reflected in the fact that it was the first work of which an english translation was to appear in print. The *Medytacōns of saynt Bernarde . . . translated fro laten in to englissh by a deuoute Student of the vnyuersytee of Cambrydge* was published at Westminster by Wynkyn de Worde in 1496 and again in 1499,[6] and these editions represent the only works attributed to Bernard to appear among the *incunabula*. In the years following their publication, however, a considerable number of treatises—almost all of them pseudonymous—appeared in print, and this flurry of activity, which lasted until about 1640, represents the first of three main periods in the history of the translation of the bernardine and *ps.*-bernardine *corpus*. It was to be followed by two dismal centuries, from about 1640 to 1840, when little of any consequence was produced; and it was not until about 1843 that we see a resurgence of interest in translating Bernard. But, as we shall see, the translations which were produced then were different both in character and in intent from those of the earlier centuries.

Between 1496 and 1950 at least 141 editions of translations of bernardine and *ps.*-bernardine works appeared in print,[7] and if we divide up these four and a half centuries into fifty year periods and note the number of editions published in each period, we arrive at the following table:

Period	*Number of Editions*
1496–1550	21
1551–1600	15
1601–1650	18
1651–1700	4
1701–1750	9

1751–1800	4
1801–1850	12
1851–1900	27
1901–1950	31

These figures demand explanation. Why is it that in the second half of the seventeenth century we see such a decline in the numbers of editions published, and why do the numbers increase so noticeably in the first half of the nineteenth century?

The period from 1496 to 1650 covers the reigns of the Tudors and the Stuarts and it was a period in which english religious literature (for which there was always an immense demand[8]) still owed a great deal to its medieval latin heritage. It was also a period of great religious controversy[9] in which Roman Catholicism underwent considerable vicissitudes, sometimes being proscribed and sometimes encouraged, and the bernardine translations reflect the unsettled times. In 1545, for example, Thomas Paynell dedicated his translation of the *Liber de modo bene vivendi*[10] to a twenty-nine year old woman who would later become Mary I, but Paynell (anticipating the vicar of Bray) also dedicated other works to Elizabeth I and skilfully contrived to stay out of trouble.[11] The recusant Antony Batt, on the other hand, had no time for such equivocation and in 1631, in the comparative safety of the English College at Douai, published his *Hive of Sacred Honie-Combes*, a large compilation of mainly *ps.*-bernardine texts, very well translated, for the 'poore afflicted . . . Catholiques of England'[12] and dedicated it to Henrietta Maria, the pro-Catholic queen of Charles I. But the 'true Catholicks' for whom William Crashaw published his *Manuall* in 1613 and for whom he translated the *ps.*-bernardine *Visio Philiberti* or *Dialogus animae et corporis damnati* into English verse,[13] were not Roman Catholics at all. Crashaw was a strong and fervent Protestant and, for him, 'true' Catholicism was the pure tradition of the early Church which Roman Catholicism had obscured, defaced, and suppressed.[14] He was well aware that the *Visio* 'was made in the Mist of Popery, euen not long after the Diuell was let loose; yet it is not tainted with Popish corruption, nor scarce smels of any superstition, whereas it is stuft with godly truthes and wholsome intructions'.[15]

We must also note that the works which were produced during this period continued to reflect the medieval popularity of texts attributed to Bernard rather than texts actually written by him, and of the nearly sixty editions published between 1496 and 1650, all but three are of pseudonymous works. There were, for example, nineteen editions of the *Golden Letter*,[16] ten of 'blessed Saint Barnards verses conteynyng the vnstable felicitie of this wayfaring worlde',[17] nine of the *Meditations*,[18] five of the *Visio Philiberti*,[19] and two different translations of the *Liber de modo bene vivendi*.[20] Of genuine works we have only Richard Whytford's version of the *De praecepto et dispensatione*, translated in 1532 for the Bridgettine sisters of Syon,[21] Antony Batt's translation of the *De diligendo Deo* included in his *Hive of Sacred Honie-Combes* published in 1631,[22] and Henry Hawkins' English version of Giovanni Pietro Maffei's Italian paraphrase of the Life of Saint Malachy of Armagh published in 1632.[23]

This pseudonymous tradition, in fact, was to continue until the early nineteenth century, for if we examine the eighty editions published between 1496 and 1842, we find that the *Meditations, Golden Letter*, *Visio Philiberti*, and 'blessed Saint Barnards verses' account for about 80% of them, and that the only genuine works of the saint to be available in English in their entirety were the three mentioned above—*De praecepto et dispensatione, De diligendo Deo*, and the *Vita S. Malachiae*—and the sermon *ad clericos de conversione* first translated in 1677.[24]

The dramatic decline in the number of translations which began in the middle of the seventeenth century coincided with the Civil War, the execution of Charles I, the establishment of the Commonwealth, and the triumph of Puritanism. Religious life in England at this time was in a state of great confusion and, as John Moorman says, 'the dark shadow of Calvin lay over the land'.[25] 'Popish' books were proscribed and religious works had to conform to 'the ancient doctrine of the primitive Church, both in faith and good manners, and to the doctrine established in the Church of England'.[26] Such times were not conducive to the translation and publication of works by manifestly Catholic writers, and when Bernard was translated at all, he was generally translated with polemical or apologetic intent. Such was John Panke's *Collectanea. Ovt Of St Gregory the Great, and St Bernard the Deuout, against the Papists who adhere to the doctrine of the present Church of Rome, in the most fundamentall points betweene them and us* published at Oxford in 1618;[27] and although *A Mirror That flatters not: Or, A Looking-glass For All New-Converts To whatsoever Perswasion, Roman-Catholicks, Conformists, or Non-Conformists*, which contains translations of the sermon *ad clericos de conversione* and three of the *Parabolae*, was published in London in 1677 (two editions) and 1685 as the author's appeal to end sectarian animosity,[28] it cannot be said to have had much—or indeed any—success. It was not that the Puritans were averse to bernardine exegesis, especially the exegesis of the Song of Songs,[29] but the Bernard they read was Bernard in Latin (for they were learned men), and the Bernard who appears in their works is a Bernard transformed and transmuted in the furnaces of Puritanism.[30]

A far greater enemy than Protestantism, in fact, was the rise of Reason after the Restoration in 1660 and the growing aversion to any form of what became known, and disparaged, as 'enthusiasm'. 'Science, philosophy, theology—all were to be judged at the bar of Reason; and knowledge or opinions which were not founded upon a sound rational basis had little chance of being accepted'.[31] Bernard's passionate outpourings were alien to the sober piety of the times, and when, in the second half of the eighteenth century, the preaching of John Wesley and his followers brought new life to this moribund spirituality, it did not bring back Bernard. Wesley, it is true, loved and esteemed certain writers of the Catholic spiritual tradition (one of his favourite works was Thomas à Kempis's *Imitation of Christ*), but Bernard was not among them;[32] and although early Methodism was nothing if not emotional, the age of Wesley was also the age of 'No popery!' The Catholic Relief Act of 1778 had led to such serious rioting—the Gordon Riots[33]—that it had to be withdrawn, and the last years of the eighteenth century were marked by intense and violent anti-Catholic sentiment. It is hardly surprising, therefore, that bernardine translation reached its nadir in the second half of the eighteenth century when only two pseudonymous works appeared in print: an edition of a version of the *Visio Philiberti* which had first appeared in 1640,[34] and three editions of George Stanhope's popular *Pious Breathings*, first published in 1701, which contained his translation of the *Meditationes piisimae*.[35]

In the first decades of the nineteenth century, the tide began to turn. The idea of reform was in the air and, as John Moorman has it, 'there were few institutions so much in need of reform as the Church'.[36] Moreover, the number of Roman Catholics in England was rapidly increasing as a result of immigration from Ireland, and although most men and women of the time still distrusted the pope and his church, the victorian spirit of toleration saw the Roman Catholic Relief Act, 'the most decisive of the Emancipation measures',[37] passed in 1829. Three years later this reforming spirit was manifested in the revolutionary Reform Act of 1832; the Reform Act led, if indirectly, to the Irish Church Act of 1833; and it was the Irish Church Act which provoked John Keble, on 14 July 1833, to preach the Assize Sermon at Oxford on 'National Apostasy' in which he accused Parliament of a 'direct disavowal of the sovereignty of God'.[38] The Oxford Movement had begun.

The Oxford Movement ushered in a period of intense activity and equally intense controversy in the English church, and its theology, administration, worship, ritual—its whole life, in fact—was irreversibly transformed. There was a renewal of theological scholarship, a renaissance of interest in the church's patristic and medieval foundations (witness the excellent translations in the *Library of the Fathers*), a reintroduction of the romanticism and enthusiasm which had been so disparaged by Caroline piety (the figure of Frederick Faber springs immediately to mind), the formation and reformation of a multitude of religious orders, most of them Anglican,[39] and, among many, a great revival of interest in the teachings of the Roman Catholic church. For Newman, indeed, 'it was not the Primitive Church that should be taken as the model, but that church which showed most signs of holiness, of being the true body of Christ',[40] and for Newman and many others, that church was the Church of Rome.

It cannot come as a surprise, therefore, to find that from such fertile soil there should sprout new translations of Bernard of Clairvaux. Sometimes, it is true, the translators sought to portray the saint as a proto-Protestant[41]; but for the most part the new translations were translations of a romantic, passionate, Catholic, Marian Bernard, whose writings were more suited to the times than they had been for more than two centuries.[42]

Thus, in 1843, there appeared the first English translation of the four homilies *super 'Missus est'*, the object of the anonymous translator being firstly, to supply 'some appropriate matter for contemplation at a time apt, above all others in the Sacred Year, to open the heart of Christians, and suggest the desire of peaceful devotion as a refuge from distracting controversy'; and secondly, to encourage 'more reverent and loving thoughts than all of us have been accustomed to entertain towards her, whose august privilege is indissolubly blended in the memory of the Church with the sweetly solemn Mystery of Advent and Christmas'.[43] Another version of the homilies, likewise anonymous, was published with other marian material in 1867;[44] a third version, with even more material in praise of Mary, in 1886;[45] and yet another version, 'chiefly for convents', in 1909.[46]

Meanwhile, in 1861, the Rev'd William B. Flower, 'late Scholar of S. Mary Magdalene College, Cambridge, and British Chaplain, Baden Baden', had published his translation of forty-six selected *Sermons for the Seasons of the Church*;[47] 1881 saw the first new translation for two hundred fifty years of Bernard's *De diligendo Deo*;[48] and in 1889 there was published the first volume of Samuel J. Eales' projected translation of the *opera omnia* of Saint Bernard—a sound, if fairly literal translation based on Mabillon's edition—which was to remain the only available translation of many important bernardine works, including the letters and the sermons *in Cantica*, for more than half a century.[49]

Eales was not, in fact, the first to envisage such a complete translation. A similar project had already been proposed more than forty years earlier by the tractarian cleric Frederick Oakeley and Professor John Sherren Brewer of King's College, London, who, like Oakeley, had also been deeply influenced by the Oxford Movement. Oakeley and Brewer had progressed to the stage of assigning the various works of Bernard to a team of translators, both clerical and lay, when the conflicts and controversies aroused by the Oxford Movement forced the project to be abandoned. Of the intended translation only a tiny fraction ever appeared in print: a selection of twenty-four letters, translated by 'One of the Lay Contributors to the Intended Translation of St. Bernard's Works', which were published in the pages of *The British Magazine* in 1847.[50]

The publication of Eales' *magnum opus* between 1889 and 1896, even though it was incomplete, effectively ended the dominance of *ps.*-Bernard, and although interest in the pseudonymous works did not entirely disappear, it was certainly very much diminished. The Middle English translation of the *Psalterium S. Bernardi* or *Eight Verses of St Bernard* which appeared in 1842 was published for its language, not its content;[51] the 1867 and 1927 editions of *The Paradyse of Daynty Deuises* reflected an interest in Richard Edwards, not Bernard of Clairvaux;[52] the numerous English versions of the *ps.*-bernardine hymn *Jesu dulcis memoria* published between 1845 and 1931 were intended primarily for devotional or liturgical use, not as contributions to bernardine scholarship;[53] and the version of the *Epistola de cura et modo rei familiaris utilius gubernandae* which appeared in 1904 was produced in a very limited edition as a monument to fine printing and binding.[54] The only important *ps.*-bernardine works to be translated during the entire period from the late nineteenth century to 1970 were the *Vitis mystica*, translated by W. R. Bernard Brownlow in 1873[55] and again by Samuel Eales in 1889;[56] the *Liber de modo bene vivendi* translated by C. B. Tyrwhitt in 1886 for the Anglican sisters of the Community of the Holy and Undivided Trinity in Oxford;[57] the *Instructio sacerdotis de praecipuis mysteriis nostrae religionis* published in 1954 by Sister R. Penelope Lawson of the Anglican Community of Saint Mary the Virgin;[58] and, in 1956, Geoffrey Webb and Adrian Walker's *The School of Self-Knowledge*, 'A Symposium from Mediaeval Sources', which contained paraphrased selections from the *Meditationes piisimae* and *De conscientia aedificanda*.[59]

In fact, of the fifty or so bernardine translations which appeared between the publication of Eales' volumes and 1970, all but the few mentioned above were of the genuine *corpus*; and by 1970 most, though not all, of the genuine works of Bernard were available in English translation.

Of the sermons, those on the Song of Songs were retranslated by Ailbe J. Luddy of Mount Melleray, who also translated the entire series of sermons *de tempore* and *de sanctis*, the four homilies *super 'Missus est'*, the sermon *ad clericos de conversione*, and a selection of the sermons *de diversis*.[60] The seventeen sermons on Psalm 90 [91] *'Qui habitat'* were translated (with some omissions) in 1953 by Sister Penelope Lawson under the title *Lent with Saint Bernard*;[61] and seven years later Leo Hickey produced another version of the sermons on the nativity.[62]

Of the treatises, we find three different translations of the *De gradibus humilitatis et superbiae*,[63] four more versions of the *De diligendo Deo* (and surely enough is enough);[64] an excellent translation by Watkin W. Williams of the *De gratia et libero arbitrio*;[65] an equally sound translation by Hugh J. Lawlor of the *Vita S. Malachiae*;[66] and two different translations of the *De consideratione*, one by George Lewis in 1908 and the other by Ailbe Luddy in 1921.[67] But the interested reader who wished to consult an English version of the *De praecepto et dispensatione* was still dependent on Richard Whytfield's version published in 1532,[68] and *ep.* 42 to Henry of Sens *de moribus et officio episcoporum*, *ep.* 77 to Hugh of Saint-Victor *de baptismo*, the *Apologia*, *In laude novae militiae*, *Officium de Sancto Victore*, most of the sermons *de diversis*, and one or two minor pieces still awaited English translation.

As for the letters, they were translated (with some omissions) in 1953, at the request of the abbot of Caldey, by Father Bruno Scott James,[69] and it is difficult to see how his translation can be improved.

Many of these translations appear in series, and the series in which they appear differ in their intentions. Some are scholarly rather than devotional; other are devotional rather than scholarly. An example of the former is the *Translations of Christian Literature* series published in the 1920s by the S.P.C.K., the educational arm of the Church of England, a series which reflects not only the purposes of the Society but the spirit of ecumenism which was much in the air at the time. The series included Mills' translation of the *De gradibus humilitatis et superbiae*, Williams' translation of the *De gratia et libero arbitrio*, and Lawlor's translation of the *Vita S. Malachiae.*[70] These volumes—and most others in this series—are first-class translations, with excellent introductions and copious annotations, and they remain of great benefit to all students of medieval monastic literature.[71] The same cannot always be said of the versions which have appeared in those series which emphasize devotion rather than scholarship and which reflect the reawakening of interest in spirituality and mysticism which began in 1911 with the publication of Evelyn Underhill's extraordinarily popular *Mysticism*.[72]

In the *Fleur de Lys Series*, for example, published by Mowbray's in the 1950s and '60s we find a version of the *De gradibus humilitatis et superbiae*, together with the sermons on Psalm 90 [91], a translation of the *ps.*-bernardine *Instructio sacerdotis de praecipuis mysteriis nostrae religionis*, an abridgement of the *Meditationes piisimae*, and a paraphrase—it can hardly be termed a translation—of the first part of the *Vita prima S. Bernardi* by William of Saint-Thierry.[73] The quality of these translations varies considerably. Those by Sister

Penelope Lawson, though too often edited and abbreviated, are generally sound; those by Geoffrey Webb and Adrian Walker are generally poor. We also find that introductions are brief and annotations minimal, and one is led to conclude that devotional people are not intelligent, and that intelligent people cannot be devout.[74]

The volumes published by Cistercian Publications have done much to demonstrate the absurdity of this conclusion. The first volume of the Cistercian Fathers Series was published in 1971 'primarily to provide cistercian monks and nuns with good English translations of the Fathers of the Order,'[75] but it was also hoped that the volumes would reach a wider audience and would also be of use to 'religious, scholars and the concerned laity'.[76] The astonishing increase of interest in cistercian studies which has occurred during the last twenty years is, to a great extent, due to the efforts of Cistercian Publications and bears eloquent testimony to the fact that the love of learning and the desire for God are not mutually incompatible.

So where do we go from here? There is really no point in retranslating works which have already been well translated, and there is no need whatever for yet another version of the *De diligendo Deo*. What we might do, perhaps, is to glance again at the contents of medieval monastic libraries—not just cistercian libraries—and determine what the monks and nuns actually read, heard read, used, or studied. All of us, from personal experience, are aware of the disparity between the number of the books we own and those we have actually read; and it is, I think, somewhat anomalous that John of Forde's commentary on the Song of Songs—a rare work which enjoyed only the most limited circulation—is easily available in English translation whereas the *ps.*-bernardine *Meditationes piisimae*, which were to be found in every monastic library, often in multiple copies,[77] are not available in a critical edition and have not been translated into English in their entirety since 1701.

Thanks to the work of Cistercian Publications, the entire *corpus* of the genuine works of Bernard will soon be available in English, and future translators might find it rewarding to turn their attention away from these *opera vera* to those delightful, insightful, pseudonymous, popular, and important *dubia* and *spuria* which were so widely read and so remarkably influential in the monastic and literary culture of the High Middle Ages.

Abbreviations

B J. de la Croix Bouton, *Bibliographie Bernardine, 1891–1957*, Commission d'histoire de l'ordre de Cîteaux, v (Paris, 1958).

'Bibliography' D. N. Bell, 'A Bibliography of English Translations of Works By and Attributed to St Bernard of Clairvaux: 1496–1970', forthcoming in *Cîteaux*.

EBR 1–3 H. S. Bennett, *English Books and Readers* (1) 1475 to 1557(Cambridge, 1970[2]); (2) 1558 to 1603 (Cambridge, 1965); (3) 1603 to 1640 (Cambridge, 1970).

J L. Janauschek, *Bibliographia Bernardina* (Vienna, 1891; repr. Hildesheim, 1959).

M E. Manning, *Bibliographie Bernardine (1957–1970)*, Documentation cistercienne, 6 (Rochefort, 1972).

PL *Patrologia Latina*, ed. J.-P. Migne.

STC A. W. Pollard & G. R. Redgrave, revd. by W. A. Jackson *et al.*, *A Short-Title Catalogue of Books Printed in England, Scotland, and Ireland 1475–1640* (London, 1986[2]).

Walther H. Walther, *Initia carminum ac versuum medii aevi posterioris Latinorum* (Göttingen, 1969[2]).

Wing *Short-Title Catalogue of Books Printed in England, Scotland . . . 1641–1700*, compiled by Donald Wing (New York, 1972).

Although this present article cites most important english translations of bernardine and *ps.*-bernardine works, it is intended to be a history, not a comprehensive bibliography. Selections from Bernard, for example, are for the most part excluded, and details of reprints and later editions are provided only when necessary. For a comprehensive annotated bibliography, see my 'Bibliography'.

Notes

1. *Sancti Bernardi Opera*, ed. J. Leclercq, C. H. Talbot, & H. Rochais (Rome: Editiones Cistercienses, 1957–77).
2. The problem is far from new: see *EBR* 1:152–77.
3. See nn. 75–76 below.
4. See, for example, R. E. Lewis, N. F. Blake, & A. S. G. Edwards, *Index of Printed Middle English Prose* (New York/London, 1985) nos. 213, 245, 461, 575, 787; P. S. Jolliffe, *A Check-List of Middle English Prose Writings of Spiritual Guidance* (Toronto, 1974) 75 (D.12), 76 (E.1) = 133–4 (O.1), 96–7 (H.14) = 141 (O.24), 100 (H.19) = 143 (O.33), 101 (H.23) = 143 (O.36); and P. Revell, *Fifteenth Century English Prayers and Meditations: A Descriptive List of Manuscripts in the British Library* (New York/London, 1975) 32 (#111), 69 (#206), 98 (#284). For further discussion, see Part I of my 'Bibliography'. Latin texts of the *Meditationes*, *Epistola de perfectione vitae*, and *Liber de modo bene vivendi* may be found in *PL* 184: 485–508, 1173–4 (under the title *Varia et brevia documenta pie seu religiose vivendi*), and 1199–1306; of the *Speculum peccatorum* in *PL* 40: 983–92; and of the *Epistola de cura et modo rei familiaris utilius gubernandae* in *PL* 182: 647–51 (*Ep.* 456 *ad Raymundum*).

5. See D. N. Bell, *An Index of Authors and Works in Cistercian Libraries in Great Britain*, CS 130 (Kalamazoo, 1992) 48, and *idem*, *An Index of Cistercian Authors and Works in Medieval Library Catalogues in Great Britain*, CS 132 (Kalamazoo, 1994) 172–3.

6. The 1496 edition is *STC* 1916 (J 191); the 1499(?) edition is *STC* 1917. The date of this second printing is not quite certain since both editions have the same colophon. Another edition appeared in 1525 (*STC* 1918; J 448). Janauschek (J 494) also reports a 1545 edition, but this appears to be an error: I can find no trace of it and it is not recorded in *STC*. I suspect that 1545 is simply an error for 1525. In the preface to his translation, the 'deuoute Student' makes it quite clear that demand for an English version of the work was very great (see *EBR* 1: 67).

7. I say 'at least' because I may well have missed some later reprintings of earlier editions. My main sources have been the catalogues of the British Library, Bodleian Library, Cambridge University Library, and Library of Congress, together with the bibliographies by Janauschek (J), Bouton (B), and Manning (M). Between 1950 and 1970 another fourteen translations appeared.

8. See *EBR* 1: 57–8, 65–76; *EBR* 2: 112–56; and *EBR* 3: 87–117. 'From the time of the beginning of printing in England religious works had provided the greater part of many printers' output and although by the seventeenth century other kinds of literature took a more prominent place, it still remained true that religious works of many kinds made a brave show on the booksellers' stalls' (*EBR* 3: 87).

9. For a brief account of the mass of controversial literature being produced in the first half of the seventeenth century, see *EBR* 3: 88–91. 'Controversy was in the air', says the author, 'and the breath of their nostrils to some' (p. 88).

10. *A compēdius & a moche fruytefull treatyse of well liuynge, cōtaynyng the hole sūme and effect of al vertue. Wrytten by S. Bernard & translated by Thomas Paynell* (London: Thomas Petyt, c. 1545 [the date in the colophon—1541—is faked]) (*STC* 1908; J 499).

11. On Paynell (fl. 1528–67), see *DNB* 15: 572–7.

12. *A Hive of Sacred Honie-Combes Containing Most Sweet and Heavenly Covnsel: Taken Ovt of the Workes of the Mellifluovs Doctor S. Bernard, . . . Faithfully translated into English by the R. Fa. Antonie Batt* (Doway [Douai]: Peter Avroy for John Heigham, 1631) (*STC* 1922), sig. *3v. The work is now available in facsimile reproduction as vol. 194 in the series English Recusant Literature 1558–1640, Menston: The Scolar Press, 1974. For a detailed list of contents, the reader is referred to my 'Bibliography'.

13. *Querela sive Dialogus Animae & Corporis Damnati . . . The Complaint or Dialogve, Betwixt the Soule and the Bodie of a damned man . . . Supposed to be written by S. Bernard . . . and now published out of an ancient Manuscript Coppy by William Crashaw*, published together with Crashaw's *Manuale Catholicorum . . . A Manuall for true Catholicks . . .* (London: N. O[kes] for L[eonard Becket], 1613) (*STC* 1908.5). Later editions: 1616, 1622, and 1632. The *Visio Philiberti*, beginning 'Noctis sub silentio' (Walther 11894) or 'Vir quidam extiterat' (Walther 20421), is the well-known poem often attributed to Hildebert of Le Mans or Walter Mapes and edited by Thomas Wright in his *Latin Poems Commonly Atributed to Walter Mapes*, Camden Society, 16 (London, 1841) 95–106.

14. See *Querela sive Dialogus*, 114.

15. *Ibid.*, sig. A3v. On Crashaw (1572–1626), see *DNB* 5: 36–8.

16. The history of the translation of the *Golden Letter* is somewhat complicated

and is examined in detail in the Appendix to my 'Bibliography'. There were, in fact, two different contemporary translations, one by Richard Whytford and the other anonymous. The Whytford translation appears in *STC* 1912, 1913, 1914, 23966, 23967, 23967.5, 23968, 23988, 25413, and 25413.5; the anonymous translation in *STC* 1915, 1915.5 (formerly *STC* 1911), 23963, 23964, 23964.3, 23964.7, and 23965; and both translations appear (unintentionally) in *STC* 25412. Antony Batt also included a translation in his *Hive of Sacred Honie-Combes*, 421–26.

17. 'The Translation of the blessed Saint Barnards verses, conteynyng the vnstable felicitie of this wayfaring worlde' refers to the well-known *ps.*-bernardine poem *De contemptu mundi, inc.* 'Cur mundus militat' (Walther 3934). It forms the preface to Richard Edwards, *The Paradyse of Daynty Deuises* first published in 1576 (*STC* 7516; J 626) and reprinted numerous times thereafter. Later editions: 1577(?), 1578, 1580, 1585, 1590(?), 1596, 1598(?), 1600, 1606, 1810, 1812, 1867 and 1927. It must be noted, however, that this large number of editions is not a testimony to the popularity of *ps.*-Bernard, but to the popularity of Edwards' collection.

18. For the 1496, 1499 and 1525 editions of the translation by the 'deuoute Student of the vnyuersytee of Cambrydge', see n. 6 above. A second translation appeared in 1611 in *Saint Bernard, His Meditations: or, Sighes, Sobbes, and Teares, vpon our Sauiours passion. Also his Motives to Mortification, with other Meditations. All done . . . by W.P. Maister of Artes, in Cambridge. The second edition much amended* (London, [T. Creede] for A. Johnson, 1611 [1610]) (*STC* 1919). The *Most Devovt and Diuine Meditations of Saint Bernard Concerning the knowledge of humane Condition* has a separate title-page and numeration. The first edition may have been published in 1608, but no example of it has been found. Later editions: 1614 and two editions in 1631. Another translation is included in Antony Batt's *Hive of Sacred Honie-Combes* (see n. 12) 1–56 and a translation of selected excerpts in *The yong mans gleanings. Gathered ovt of Diuers Most Zealous and Deuout Fathers, and now published for the benefit of euerie Christian Man, which wisheth good successe to his soule at the later day. By R. B. Gent* (London: John Beale for Benjamin Lightfoote, 1614) (*STC* 1064.5) 90–102.

19. See n. 13 for four editions of Crashaw's translation. A new translation was published as a broad-sheet ballad c.1640: *Saint Bernards Vision. Or, a briefe Discourse . . . betweene the Soule and the Body of a damned man newly deceased . . .* (London: for J. Wright, 1640[?]) (*STC* 1910; J 1001). Later editions: 1683(?), 1730(?) and 1776.

20. For Paynell's translation (c. 1545), see n. 10. Antony Batt's translation, *A Rule of Good Life: Written by the mellifluous Doctor S. Bernard*, was printed at Douai by Laurence Kellam in 1633 (*STC* 1923; J 963) and has been reprinted as vol. 79 in the series English Recusant Literature 1558–1640, Menston: The Scolar Press, 1971. The other pseudonymous texts translated during this period will be found listed in the index to my 'Bibliography'.

21. See J. Hogg, *Richard Whytford's The Pype or Tonne of the Lyfe of Perfection with an Introductory Study of Whytford's Works*, Vol. 1, Part 2 (Salzburg, 1989) 57–9, 100–39 (*STC* 25421). We should note, however, that Whytford did not intend to produce a literal translation and did not hesitate to make his own additions when he thought it necessary (see *ibid.*, 55, n. 6). Cf. n. 23 below.

22. Batt, *Hive of Sacred Honie-Combes*, 457–514.

23. G. P. Maffei, *Fuga Saeculi. Or the Holy Hatred of the World. Conteyning the Liues of 17. Holy Confessours of Christ, Selected out of Sundry Authors. Written in*

Italian by the R. Fa. Iohn-Peter Maffaeus of the Society of Iesus. And translated into English by H[enry] H[awkins] (Paris [*sic*, but actually St Omer: English College Press], 1632) (*STC* 17181; J 961) 1–63. Maffei, like Whytford, was quite prepared 'to cut of al superfluityes, to reduce scattered Narrations to the order of Tymes, or Kinds; and finally to modify those passages, which transferring the thoughts to things dishonest or hurtfull (as somtymes it happens) the chaster Eares, or more delicate Consciences, in some manner, come to be offended'. In the sixteenth and seventeenth centuries, it mattered little to the reader that a translation might be two steps removed from the original (see *EBR* 2: 103).

24. The translation appears in *A Mirror That flatters not* (see n. 28 below) 1–42. For those readers who would include the *Parabolae* among the genuine works of Bernard (I prefer to class them as *dubia*), English translations of *Parabolae* I-V appeared in Batt's *Hive of Sacred Honie-Combes*, 546–74 and 583–97; of *Parabolae* I-III in *A Mirror That flatters not*, 43–57 (but the last pages of Wing 1982 are misnumbered); and of *Parabola II* in *The Holy War. By Saint Bernard*. [Translated by Samuel R. Maitland] (Gloucester: Hough & Jew, 1827) (J 1927).

25. J. R. H. Moorman, *A History of the Church in England* (London, 1953) 247.

26. See *EBR* 3: 43, 49–51 and Chapter III *passim*.

27. *STC* 19169; J 891. The work was reprinted, with modernized orthography, in 1835 as *Romanism Condemned by the Church of Rome; or, Popery Convicted of Idolatry, Apostacy & anti-Christianity, from its own Highest Authorities* (Salisbury: J. Hearn, Jun., 1835).

28. Wing 1981, 1982, and 1980A. 'The Conversion which will make us happy in the other World', says the translator on his title-page, 'is the Conversion describ'd by St. Bernard; not the simple Change to such a Church, Perswasion or Communion'. The Latin text of the sermon *de conversione* is to be found in *SBOp* 4: 69–116 and of the three *Parabolae* in *SBOp* 6/2: 261–7 (I), 267–73 (II), and 274–6 (III).

29. See G. S. Wakefield, 'The Puritans', in *The Study of Spirituality*, ed. Cheslyn Jones *et al.* (Oxford, 1986) 444.

30. See *ibid.* In the second half of the seventeenth century the only bernardine translations to appear were the three editions of the *Mirror That flatters not* (n. 28) and the 1683(?) edition of the *Visio Philiberti* (n. 19).

31. Moorman, 254.

32. 'Anxious to provide his disciples with solid spiritual reading, [Wesley] became, within Protestantism, one of the great popularizers of his beloved *Imitation* as well as of Teresa of Avila, Ignatius of Loyola, Francis de Sales and Fénelon. Apart from the Quakers . . . no one did so much to rebuild the bridges on the spiritual plane between Catholicism (old and new) and a renewed Protestantism' (L. Bouyer, *A History of Christian Spirituality, III: Orthodox Spirituality and Protestant and Anglican Spirituality* [New York, 1969] 193).

33. See Moorman, 312, and J. Paul de Castro, *The Gordon Riots* (London, 1926).

34. For the 1776 edition of the *Visio Philiberti*, see n. 19.

35. *Pious Breathings. Being the Meditations of St Augustine, His Treatise of the Love of God, Soliloquies, and Manual. To which are added Select Contemplations from St Anselm, & St Bernard. Made English by George Stanhope, D.D., Chaplain in Ordinary to His Majesty* (London: Printed for S. Sprint, T. Bennet, R. Parker, J. Bullord, and M. Gilliflower, 1701) (J 1378) 355–414. There were a number of later editions of this work, all of which are listed in my 'Bibliography'.

36. Moorman, 329.

37. *The Oxford Dictionary of the Christian Church*, ed. F. L. Cross (Oxford, 1958) 252.

38. See S. Neill, *Anglicanism* (Penguin Books, 1960) 255.

39. The whole story may be read in P. F. Anson, *The Call of the Cloister: Religious Communities and Kindred Bodies in the Anglican Communion* (London, 1964[4]).

40. Moorman, 344.

41. A good example is the Rev'd Richard Collins' *On the Necessity of Conversion. A Letter to the Clergy of the Deanery of Boroughbridge. A New Edition, to which is now subjoined a Translation of the Letter of S. Bernard to Thomas of Beverley on the Same Subject* (Leeds: T. Harrison, 1856) (J 2256), in which the author attempts to show that for Bernard, 'conversion' means 'the act of justification by God's Holy Spirit' (p. 7) or, in other words, justification by faith. John Panke had done much the same thing two and a half centuries earlier: in his *Collectanea* (n. 27) he concluded that both Gregory the Great and Saint Bernard 'taught the same doctrine to their churches & hearers, which the church of England teacheth to hers' (sig. A6[r]).

42. Cf. G. S. Wakefield, 'Anglican Spirituality', in *Christian Spirituality, III: Post-Reformation and Modern*, ed. L. Dupré & D. E. Saliers (New York, 1989) 279.

43. *Four Homilies of S. Bernard, Abbot, upon the Incarnation of Our Lord Jesus Christ, commonly called 'Super Missus est'* (Edinburgh: R. Grant & Son; Aberdeen: A. Brown & Co.; London: J. Leslie, 1843) (J 2077) vii.

44. *The Glories of the Virgin Mother, and Channel of Divine Grace. From the Latin of St. Bernard. By a Catholic Priest* (Boston: Patrick Donahoe, 1867) (J 2426). For a detailed account of the contents of this collection, see my 'Bibliography'.

45. *Behold your Mother! The Virgin Mother of God, by S. Bernard, Father and Doctor of the Church, First Abbot of Clairvaux, Containing all that he has expressly written in praise of our Blessed Lady. Arranged and Translated by a Secular Priest [A. P. J. Cruikshank]. With Introduction on the Doctrine of S. Bernard with regard to the Immaculate Conception* (London: Thomas Richardson & Son, 1886) (J 2680). For a detailed account of the contents of this collection, see my 'Bibliography'.

46. *Sermons of St. Bernard on Advent and Christmas, including the Famous Treatise on the Incarnation called 'Missus est.' Compiled and translated at St. Mary's Convent, York, from the Edition (1508), in black-letter, of St. Bernard's Sermons and Letters. [Chiefly for convents]. With Introduction by the Right Rev. J. C. Hedley, O.S.B.* London: R. & T. Washbourne; New York: Benziger Bros., 1909 (B 183).

47. Published in London by Joseph Masters and at Baden Baden by D. R. Marx (J 2334).

48. *Saint Bernard on the Love of God*, tr. Marianne Caroline & Coventry Patmore (London: Kegan Paul & Co., 1881) (J 2612). A second edition was published in 1884 (J 2661).

49. *Life and Works of Saint Bernard, Abbot of Clairvaux, edited by Dom John Mabillon . . . , translated and edited with additional notes by Samuel J. Eales* (London: John Hodges, 1889–96) (J 2722). Four volumes were published: the first two contain most of the Letters (*Epp.* 1–145 [excluding the two letter-treatises, *ep.* 42 *de moribus et officio episcoporum* and *ep.* 77 *de baptismo*, which still await translation]; and 146–380); the third completes the Letters (*Epp.* 381–490) and also contains nineteen sermons *de tempore* (including those *super Missus est*); the fourth contains the 86 sermons *in Cantica*. A second edition was published in 1912. The selection of 31 sermons published in 1901 by Bruce Blaxland, *The Song of Songs. Selections from the Sermons of S. Bernard. With notes and introduction by Bruce Blaxland*, Library of Devotion (London: Methuen & Co.; New York: E. S. Gorham, 1901), is not a

new translation but a reprint of that of Eales. For a note on the *Library of Devotion*, see n. 71 below.

50. See *The British Magazine and Monthly Register of Religious and Ecclesiastical Information* . . . 31 (1847) 49–61, 190–198, 321–327, 428–443, containing an anonymous translation of *Epp.* 76 and 78–100. *Ep.* 77 to Hugh of Saint-Victor *de baptismo* was not included on the grounds that it was a treatise rather than a letter.

51. *A Paraphrase on the Seven Penitential Psalms, in English Verse, supposed to have been written by Thomas Brampton S.T.P. in the year 1414; together with a legendary Psalter of Saint Bernard, in Latin and in English verse. With notes by William Henry Black*, Percy Society, Early English Poetry, vol. 7 (London: T. Richards, 1842; repr. New York/London: Johnson Reprint Co., 1965) (J 2064) 51–4.

52. See n. 17.

53. See J. Julian, *A Dictionary of Hymnology* (London, 1907 [revd. ed.]; repr. New York, 1957) 1: 585–9. The versions by Caswall, Horst, Edersheim and Crippen are complete; those by Copeland and Charles are reduced and I have not included them. Neither have I included the many hymns based on selected stanzas of the poem (see *ibid.*, 587–9) nor such oddities as David Stanley Smith's *Ave Maria: A rhapsody for chorus, semi-chorus, soli, and orchestra* (London, 1917) or John Bacchus Dykes's *Jesus, the Very Thought of Thee . . . hymn-anthem for choir and congregation with soprano and alto solos* (Chicago: Hall & McCreary Co., 1947). Translations of the poem produced after 1909 are listed in my 'Bibliography'. A similar devotional/liturgical translation was Emily Mary Shapcote's verse rendering of the *Oratio ad membra Jesu Christi patientis*: *Rhythmical Prayer to the Sacred Members of Jesus Hanging on the Cross. Ascribed to St. Bernard. Rendered into English Rhythm by E. M. Shapcote, Tertiary of St. Dominic* (London: Burns & Oates, 1879) (J 2590). The *oratio*, printed in *PL* 184: 1319–24, may have been the work of Arnulf of Bohéries, and a new verse-translation was published by Sr Sheryl Chen in *Cistercian Studies Quarterly* 29 (1994) 25–40.

54. *The Proverbys of Saynt Bernarde. The Doctrynall Principlis and Proverbys Iconomie or Howsolde Keeping, sent from Saynte Bernard unto Raymonde, Lord of Ambrose Castelle. Le Regisme de mesnaige selon saint Bernard* (London: Caradoc Press, 1904).

55. *'Vitis Mystica,' or, The True Vine: a Treatise on the Passion of Our Lord: (Ascribed to S. Bernard)*, tr. W. R. B. Brownlow (London: R. Washbourne, 1873) (J 2498). For the Latin text, see *PL* 184: 635–740.

56. *The Mystic Vine; Vitis Mystica. A Meditation on the Passion of Our Lord and Saviour Jesus Christ, treated mystically and devotionally*, tr. Samuel J. Eales (London: Swan Sonnenschein & Co., 1889). A second edition was published in 1892. The *Vitis mystica* may possibly be a work of Bonaventure, and an edited translation of the shorter recension was published under his name in 1955: *The Mystical Vine: A Treatise on the Passion of Our Lord by Saint Bonaventure*, tr. 'A Friar of S.S.F.', Fleur de Lys Series, 5 (London: A. R. Mowbray & Co., 1955). On the Society of Saint Francis, see Anson (n. 39), 200–08.

57. *'How to Live Well' . . . (Attributed to S. Bernard)*, tr. C. B. Tyrwhitt (Oxford: Printed at the Convent, [S. Giles' Road West,] 1886). On the Community of the Holy and Undivided Trinity, see Anson, 288–97.

58. *The Threefold Gift of Christ. By Brother Bernard*, tr. 'A Religious of C.S.M.V.' [Sr R. Penelope Lawson], Fleur de Lys Series, 4 (London: A. R. Mowbray & Co., 1954). On the Community of St Mary the Virgin at Wantage, see Anson, 242–59.

59. Published as no. 8 in the Fleur de Lys Series by A. R. Mowbray & Co. Ltd., London, 1956.

60. *Saint Bernard's Sermons on the Canticle of Canticles*, tr. 'A Priest of Mount Melleray' [Ailbe J. Luddy] (Dublin: Browne & Nolan, 1920) (two volumes) (B 228); and *St Bernard's Sermons for the Seasons & Principal Festivals of the Year*, tr. 'A Priest of Mount Melleray' [Ailbe J. Luddy] (Dublin: Browne & Nolan, 1921–23) (three volumes) (B 276; repr. Westminster, Md: The Carroll Press, 1950). The sermon *ad clericos de conversione* was also translated by Watkin W. Williams: *Of Conversion. A Sermon to the Clergy by Saint Bernard of Clairvaux. The Text of the Anchin Manuscript with a Translation and Notes* (London: Burns, Oates and Washbourne, 1938) (B 505). In the same year the same publisher also printed an edition of Williams' translation without the latin text. The earliest translation of the sermon had appeared in 1677 (n. 28).

61. *Lent with St Bernard. A Devotional Commentary on Psalm Ninety-One*, tr. 'A Religious of C.S.M.V.' [Sister R. Penelope Lawson], Fleur de Lys Series, 1 (London: A. R. Mowbray & Co.; New York: Morehouse-Gorham Co., 1953) (B 933). Sister Penelope also published edited and abridged selections from the sermons *in Cantica* and the sermons *de tempore* and *de sanctis*: *Saint Bernard on the Song of Songs. Sermones in Cantica Canticorum*, tr./ed. 'A Religious of C.S.M.V.' (London: A. R. Mowbray & Co., 1952) (B 706), and *St. Bernard on the Christian Year. Selections from his Sermons*, tr. 'A Religious of C.S.M.V.' (London: A. R. Mowbray & Co., 1954) (B1007).

62. *Saint Bernard. The Nativity*, tr. Leo Hickey, Spiritual Classics, 1 (Chicago/Dublin/London: Scepter, 1959) (M 28).

63. *Saint Bernard: The Twelve Degrees of Humility and Pride*, tr. Barton R. V. Mills, Translations of Christian Literature, II Latin Texts (London: S.P.C.K.; New York/Toronto: The Macmillan Co., 1929); *The Steps of Humility, by Bernard, abbot of Clairvaux*, tr. George B. Burch (Cambridge, Mass.: Harvard University Press, 1940) (B 513) (later editions: 1942, 1950, 1963); *The Steps of Humility*, tr. Geoffrey Webb & Adrian Walker, Fleur de Lys Series, 13 (London: A. R. Mowbray & Co.; New York: Morehouse-Gorham Co., 1957). The translations by Mills and Burch are excellent; the version by Webb & Walker may be ignored.

64. For Batt's translation, see n. 22; for the Patmores' translation, see n. 48; *Saint Bernard on Loving God*, tr. William Harman van Allen, Caldey Books, 1 (Tenby: Caldey Abbey, 1909) (van Allen's translation is reproduced in *On Loving God and Selections from Sermons by St Bernard of Clairvaux*, ed. Hugh Martin, Treasury of Christian Books [London: SCM Press, 1959]. The selections from the sermons *in Cantica* are taken from Eales' translation [n. 48]); *The Book of Saint Bernard on the Love of God*, ed./tr. Edmund G. Gardner (London/Paris/Toronto: J. M. Dent & Sons; New York: E. P. Dutton & Co., 1916) (B 215); *Saint Bernard on the Love of God*, tr. Terence L. Connolly, first printed for private circulation in 1935 and then commercially in London (by Burns, Oates & Co.) and New York (by Spiritual Book Associates) in 1937 (B 464), with later editions in 1943 and 1951; *Saint Bernard: On the Love of God; De Diligendo Deo*, tr. by 'A Religious of C.S.M.V.' [Sr R. Penelope Lawson] (London: A. R. Mowbray & Co.; New York: Morehouse-Gorham, 1950) (B 658), reprinted in the Fleur de Lys series, 17 (1961) (M 30) and reissued in a new format in 1982.

65. *The Treatise of St. Bernard, abbat of Clairvaux, concerning Grace and Free Will, addressed to William, abbat of St. Thierry*, tr. Watkin W. Williams, Translations of Christian Literature, II Latin Texts (London: S.P.C.K.; New York: The Macmillan Co., 1920) (B 237).

66. *S[t] Bernard of Clairvaux's Life of S[t] Malachy of Armagh*, tr. H. J. Lawlor,

Translations of Christian Literature, V: Lives of the Celtic Saints (London: S.P.C.K.; New York: The Macmillan Co., 1920) (B 227).

67. *Saint Bernard, On Consideration*, tr. George Lewis, Oxford Library of Translations (Oxford: Clarendon Press, 1908); *St. Bernard's Treatise on Consideration*, tr. 'A Priest of Mount Melleray' [Ailbe J. Luddy] (Dublin: Browne & Nolan, 1921) (B 232).

68. See n. 21.

69. *The Letters of St. Bernard of Clairvaux*, tr. Bruno S. James (Chicago: H. Regnery, 1953; repr. New York, n.d.) (B 850); *St. Bernard of Clairvaux Seen through his Selected Letters*, tr. Bruno S. James, foreword by Thomas Merton (Chicago: H. Regnery, 1953). James's translation does not include the three long letter-treatises *ep.* 42 *de moribus et officio episcoporum*, *ep.* 77 *de baptismo*, and *ep.* 190 *de erroribus Petri Abaelardi*. The first two still await English translation.

70. See nn. 63, 65, and 66.

71. The same may be said of the volumes in the *Oxford Library of Translations* (n. 67 [Lewis's translation of the *De consideratione*] and the *Library of Devotion* (n. 49 [Blaxland's selection of the sermons *in Cantica*]). The latter, according to the blurb, was 'a series of the masterpieces of devotional literature. The books are edited with sympathetic and scholarly care, and are furnished with such Introductions and Notes as may be necessary to explain the standpoint of the author and the obvious difficulties of the text, without unnecessary intrusion between the author and the devout mind'.

72. See C. J. R. Armstrong, *Evelyn Underhill (1875–1941)* (London/Oxford, 1975) 95–157; Wakefield, 'Anglican Spirituality' (n. 42) 282.

73. See nn. 63, 61, 58, and 59. The *Vita prima* is paraphrased in *St. Bernard of Clairvaux: The Story of his Life as recorded in the Vita Prima Bernardi . . .* , tr. Geoffrey Webb & Adrian Walker (London: A. R. Mowbray & Co., 1960).

74. Much the same impression is given by such other devotional series as the *Treasury of Christian Books* (n. 64 [Martin's *On Loving God*]; *Caldey Books* (n. 64 [Van Allen's translation of the *De diligendo Deo*]), a series of books deemed likely 'to be of service, not only to the friends of Caldey but to Catholics generally, in helping them in their lives and habits of devotion'; and the *Spiritual Classics* (n. 62 [Hickey's translation of the sermons for the Nativity]), which has a useless introduction, no notes, and no biblical references.

75. *The Works of Bernard of Clairvaux, Volume One: Treatises I*, CF 1 (Spencer, Mass.: Cistercian Publications, 1970) ix.

76. *Ibid.* The texts included in this first volume—the *Apologia, De praecepto et dispensatione, Prologus in Antiphonarium*, and *Officium de Sancto Victore*—were chosen, said Father Basil Pennington, 'because, unlike most of the other works of St Bernard, they have never before to our knowledge been published in English' (ix). Father Pennington overlooked Whytford's version of the *De praecepto et dispensatione.*

77. See n. 5. There were, for example, at least seventeen copies at Syon and twenty-one at Peterborough (Bell, *Index of Cistercian Authors and Works in Medieval Library Catalogues* 121–2, 138).

What We Are Not Supposed To Know

G. R. Evans

ANCIENT PHILOSOPHY and early christian thought both have a good deal to say on the subjects of forbidden knowledge and forbidden knowing. The problem of the debt of the Christian to the secular tradition is, of course, a running question for historians of the early christian period. It can illuminate the earlier scene to take a look at it from the vantage-point of the Middle Ages, a period when scholars secure in a comparatively developed christian tradition addressed the philosophical questions raised in secular authors, both before (when it took one kind of ingenuity) and after they got possession of the bulk of Aristotle again in the twelfth and thirteenth century (when it took another).

I want to take advantage of the insights that angle of view affords us, and explore the continuing western latin tradition on what seem to be five distinguishable themes in this debate.

1. It is argued sometimes that the actual process of enquiry is bad for human beings
2. and sometimes that it offends God or the gods. It is variously argued
3. that the object or content of forbidden knowledge is bad for human beings and
4. that it is inappropriate for human beings (because it is proper only for God or the gods).

5. Fifthly, there is a body of discussion which suggests that there is a time for everything and the time for the revelation of the forbidden knowledge is not yet, or not everyone is yet ready for it.

1. Sometimes the actual process of enquiry is bad for human beings

The first question is why it should be bad for human beings to want to find things out, and why God or the gods should object to their trying to do so. We had better get 'invention' out of the way before we begin. Mediaeval scholars, reared on Cicero's *De inventione*,[1] thought of 'invention' as lying in the province of rhetoric. There it meant the cataloguing of standard arguments for rapid retrieval when needed by the orator. So 'invention' was not primarily a process of exploration and enquiry.[2] It was not really an exercise in seeking out new knowledge.

The machinery

The literature relevant to our present inquiry points us in another direction, towards discussion of a structure of powers or faculties, more or less hierarchically arranged. Sense, imagination, reason and understanding, *sensus* (or *sensualitas*), *imaginatio*, *ratio* and *intelligentia* form a double ladder for taking in and organising ideas. The senses make their observations. *Imaginatio* is the bridge. It exercises itself upon things not present to sense but of a character the senses could perceive if they were. Reason puts in order what the senses tell it about the things they observe. Understanding brings order to the otherwise confused representations of absent things which the imagination makes. It is the *imaginatio* above all which is the faculty given to abuse of the process of enquiry, because it operates at the dangerous point of junction of sense and the higher intellectal and rational powers.

This mechanism, it is argued, sometimes goes wrong, especially at the point where there is a disruption of the working of the machinery proper to human intellectual nature, and there lies the harm. 'Action which flows from nature is smooth, pleasant: that which is done against nature does violence to the agent, in some degree—that is to say, is painful,' as Aristotle would argue.[3] From the mediaeval Christian vantage-point, especially under the influence of Augustine, the disruption involved results from sin and it damages the individual in whom it occurs because it diverts the process of discovery from its proper object, which is God.

Augustine explored some of the implications in the part of his *Confessions* which follows the autobiographical account of how he became a Christian. This is a foundation-text for the mediaeval discussion. In Book X (29–43) he looks at the ways in which the soul can be tempted in directions away from the divine intention for human nature. One of these is the temptation of the pleasures of the senses (*concupiscentia carnis*); another the temptation to misuse reason; the third is the temptation to reach too high for human nature, which includes in its crudest form worldly ambition *(ambitio saeculi)*.[4] This last includes the greater and satanic danger of falling into spiritual pride. When the powers or faculties of the soul fall into a wrong relationship with one another, the results, says Augustine, are disorderly and painful. The person who succumbs to these temptations disintegrates. Sensation ought to be subordinate to reason, but it can get out of hand and overrule the judgement. Will ought also to be subordinate to reason, but if will becomes dominant, uncontrollable *curiositas* results (X.35). At the final stage, when sound judgement vanishes altogether in a state of pride the individual has no defence against Satan, for whom also the sin of pride was the end of the story.

There is, of course, a great deal more to be said about this crucial point of juncture between sense and the higher intellectual and rational powers. One of the newly-discovered sermons of Augustine points out that the senses need external aids (the eye cannot see without light). They also need internal assistance. No sense can perceive what is proper to the others because each reports for itself to a central point, a *sensus interior*, to which the separate senses are subject, and whose instruments they are. This is (loosely) identified in Augustine with the mind (*mens*), though it would be unwise to place too much reliance on the choice of term. Augustine's vocabulary is to some degree exploratory.

The relationship of this *interior sensus* to the God in whose divine image it was made is not explored in this sermon, but the notion of the inner judge is comprehensively developed by many mediaeval authors.[5] Anselm of Canterbury, for example, speaks of a *sensus interior.* This seems to him, as the Augustine, to lie beyond the senses themselves. He calls it *opinio,* thus seeing it as a judge which can be mistaken. The senses report accurately enough, but the *sensus interior* sometimes reads what they say wrongly. For example, a stick standing upright in water looks as though it is broken at the point where it meets the surface, but this is what we would now call an optical illusion.[6]

This account of a structure which is hierarchical, in which the senses feed what they take in 'upwards', across a point of juncture with a faculty or faculties which process it imaginatively and intellectually. This is taken more or less for granted in many of the authors I shall be citing and seems to derive in mediaeval usage largely from this material in Augustine, and from Boethius' account in his commentary on Porphyry.[7] There is a useful contrast here between a christian and a secular emphasis. Augustine, takes imagination to be a *genus visionis,* a mode of seeing *secundum spiritum,* by which we image or 'imagine' spiritually those things which we experience through the bodily senses.[8] It is a *visio spiritualis,* by which 'we think in imagination of absent bodily things or recollect in memory those we have known'.[9] Human sinfulness may confuse the process. In Boethius *imaginationes* are characterised as intrinsically *confusas atque inevidentes,* and as needing ordering simply because they are raw until understood, just as sensations are raw until reasoned with. Thus the christian assumptions may be overlaid on the secular without undue difficulty, and without disturbing the underlying pattern of the explanation of the process.

This dual line of thinking is developed in the Middle Ages in various ways. One way is much concerned with the machinery, and we might call it, in a modern sense, almost a 'scientific' approach. Godfrey of Saint Victor, for example, explains in his *Microcosmus* that *sensualitas* is like earth, *obtusa* and *immobilis*. Imagination is like water, *obtusa sed mobilis.* It lifts itself as if from the earth up to images of absent bodily things, but like water it does not form peaks above the level of those bodily things.[10] *Ratio* is like air, *subtilis, obtusa et mobilis. Intelligentia* is like fire, *subtilis, acuta et mobilis.*[11] In a similarly 'scientific' vein, medical studies of the twelfth-century attempted to put imagination especially firmly on a scientific footing as a mechanism. A pregnant woman who has some immoderate longing puts her hand on her face or some other part of her body. The infant, when it is born, will have a birthmark in that same place on its own body, in the shape of the thing she desired. Why is this? When the mother desires something, the spirit 'is moved'. By imagination it makes a form resembling the thing desired, which the spirit adopts, so that when the mother presses part of the body with her hand the spirit retains the impression.[12]

The same group of sources, concerned with mechanism and not metaphysics, suggests that imagination is stronger in wakefulness than in sleep.[13] But in sleep the spirit can reach down to levels where it can stir life forces which ultimately reach the brain.[14] And post-coitally, when the animal spirit has been stirred in the brain, it represents different images to the soul, which prompts particular thoughts.[15]

The Boethian explanation (which we find in the *De Trinitate*) of the principle that mathematics forms a bridge between physics and theology proved relevant here. But it made it necessary to impute to *imaginatio* the very power of organisation which Boethius denies in the *Commentary* on Porphyry. Physics deals with the concrete things of nature, theology with the purely speculative. Mathematics treats the concrete as though it were abstract. In much the same way, explains the twelfth-century Hugh of Saint Victor in his *Didascalicon*, the imagination works to bring pattern and order to the muddle of sense-impressions.[16] Such untidinesses of borrowing are a not uncommon mediaeval phenomenon, of course, and again they do not make unworkable the superimposition of christian preoccupations upon the ancient secular philosophical account.

This tension between *imaginatio,* seen as a faculty of abstraction and ordering, and *imaginatio,* seen as a faculty which reaches for things unseen and gets itself into confusion, generated a good deal of the mediaeval uncertainty as to whether imagination was to be regarded with respect or suspicion—which was our starting question. This is where we come up hard against the question why seeking to discover should be bad for human beings. This can be expected to be especially noticeable when the Augustinian line, which takes in sin, is in play rather than the more strictly mechanistic 'Boethian' one. In the thirteenth century Gilbert of Tournai outlines in his *De modo addiscendi* procedures for inculcating good habits of learning into children. These include the right use of the faculties. For example, reason works as it should when it seeks to lift itself up to the contemplation of the Creator humbly; then it experiences the delight of wisdom.[17] But if reason is infected by an abuse of *imaginatio*, it develops *vitia*. A fourfold sickness results: imaginativeness, idleness of thought; false discretion of judgement; wrongheaded deliberateness of counsel. *Imaginatio* represents to reason the appearance of things seen.[18] It runs backwards and forwards between mistress and slave (that is between reason and the senses), like a handmaid; and whatever it seizes upon outwardly through the bodily sense it represents inwardly to the reason. For reason cannot itself go outside and the bodily sense cannot enter in; and so imagination assists the reason where sense fails it. It does so ceaselessly.[19] But imagination is frequently *bestialis* and only sometimes *rationalis*. It is bestial when through it we run about the things we see or feel with a wandering mind without steadiness or profit, as the beasts do.[20] We begin to see that wanting to find things out is bad for us when it diminishes us in our natures to a level lower than that at which they were created to operate, so that we are attracted to objects worthy only for lower beings.

Godfrey of Saint Victor is another author to explore the modes of right and wrong relationship between the senses and imagination. Giving spiritual assent is a matter of focussing that which is otherwise dispersed and scattered in one's being. Some of this fragmentation is external and some internal. That which is outside is *per sensus*; that which is *intra me* is *per ymaginationes*.[21] But when the imagination allows the health-giving thoughts and meditations and pleasures and wishes to stray in a fleshly direction in the wrong manner it becomes bound to the *consensus carnis*.[22] The theme is the same. It goes to a bodily level; it becomes worthy of a beast.

Classical and late antique greek thought was sensitive to the powerful attractiveness of the senses in the perpetual war of flesh with spirit. Christianity took the notion over, with modifications to accommodate the idea of sin, but still with the same strong sense that the flesh was dangerously seductive, that attractiveness of the senses could be purified away. Albertus Magnus in the thirteenth century mentions the argument that prophecy has this effect. 'Nothing is imagined which is not received by the senses; but in the imaginative prophetic vision that is not always the case, as is clear from Ezekiel's vision of the four animals.' There was no sense-impression to prompt that.[23] Under the inspiration of the Spirit the senses need not be a source of problems. Nevertheless, in general they could be expected to be so.

Christian theology involves faith and looks to salvation. It has many extra dimensions over and above, or different in emphasis from, those of the secular classical tradition in its attitude to the pathways of enquiry which this machinery makes it possible to explore. The idea of theological study as a 'way' or path ,not only of enquiry and discovery, but of approaching God himself, is not peculiarly christian, but its approach is to a quite distinctively christian God, and it definitively involves an entering into relationship with him.[24] 'The greater discovery, we say, is to find God,[25] says Ramon Lull (c. 1235–1315). There are three ways of enquiring about God (*deum investigare*), says Faber Stapulensis at the end of the Middle Ages: by imagination, reason, understanding (*imaginatione, ratione, intellectu*). The first is *infra nos*, the second *secundum nos*, the third *supra nos*.[26] This is again a motif which derives from the hermetic tradition, and which is commonplace in the earlier Middle Ages.[27]

2. The process of enquiry can offend God or the gods

Why should the imperfect operation of this machinery be offensive to God or the gods? There are perhaps two main points to be made here. To christian scholars a serious danger of the misuse of the image-forming faculty of imagination must be idolatry. Abelard—in a familiar enough tradition—argues in the *Sic et Non* that God cannot be known by means of corporeal images. 'If I imagine any 'form' or thing 'formed' to myself in place of you, God, I commit idolatry, says William of Saint Thierry, also in the twelfth century.[28] The faculty should be used as an instrument or vehicle through which God can make himself known to the soul; but he not humankind, is the image-maker here, and if humankind tries to make the images itself, it will get them wrong and, by implication, offend the real image-maker.[29]

This is part of the long patristic and mediaeval debate about the Genesis text on *imago et similitudo*, which seems to many mediaeval scholars to imply a distinction between the two in its assertion that human beings are made in the 'image' and 'likeness' of God (Genesis 1:26). Hugh of Saint Victor suggests that while image has to do with *figura*, similitude belongs to *natura*. Bodily nature cannot approach the likeness of the divine nature, because it is so far removed from it in its own nature.[30] Peter Abelard stresses the limitations and incompleteness of the 'similitude' of humanity to God. Whereas an image is a 'close likeness', one may speak of 'a likeness' of some sort, even if there are not many points of resemblance.[31] So the essence of the matter seems to be that presumptuous image-making or the claiming of image and likeness beyond what is proper to the creature are alike an offence to the Creator, conceived of as he must be by christian scholars. Both can be thought of as idolatry. The force of this is felt in the christian tradition in ways which do not apply in secular classical thought. (The gods there are offended by rather different human presumptions.) Nevertheless, the beast-like tendencies of inappropriate image-making are bad consequences of misplaced enquiry there, too, and that can be read as an offence to the gods because it takes human beings in the reverse direction from the *deificatio* for which they should, especially in the hermetic tradition, be striving.

Limitation is not the same thing as misrepresentation. It is the way things are for creatures to have the capacities proper to their natures, as Aristotle might put it. Creaturely limitation is in accordance with God's intention, says the Christian tradition. We are, in our capacities, ultimately what he has made us. It is, however, also possible for the divine image in humanity to be 'deformed' (*imago deformata).* The natural *imago Dei* in human beings consists in the power and possibility of knowing God, loving him and enjoying him, says the twelfth century Achard of Saint Victor.[32] The good image thus formed in the course of the right sort of enquiry is in accordance with the right use of imagination, reason and memory; as the soul images, reasons upon and commits to memory the words of divine Wisdom which are heard in the Scriptures.[33] A wrong image offends God because it is a distortion of the true worship due to him, and also because it taints the soul in which it lodges and makes it what it ought not to be. It is a disruption of right order.

This has a bearing on the reasons why God should be offended by inappropriate inquiries. The notion of right order (*rectus ordo*) is strong in Gregory the Great and especially in Anselm, where it is developed in terms of an obligation to do what is appropriate to one's nature. To go beyond that, as the angels who fell are described as doing in the *De casu diaboli*, is to seek to disrupt God's intention. That can reasonably be seen as offending him.

3. The object or content of forbidden knowledge is bad for human beings

Curiositas is a classical neologism, seemingly tossed off by Cicero in a letter to Atticus.[34] It remains a rare word before Apuleius, who has Lucius punished for his curiosity in *The Golden Ass.*[35] But already in Cicero's own philosophical writings it was beginning to diversify.[36] He regards it as a natural quality of human wit.[37] But he sometimes colours it with a sense of *cupiditas* for learning, knowing, investigation *(discendi, noscendi, investigandi).*[38] *Curiositas* is also capable of vanity in *The Republic.*[39] These two broad shadings reflect a preexisting distinction. Behind the Latin stand at least two ideas in greek minds: the creditable desire for knowledge and something more unworthy, even culpable, in which the desire for knowledge is distorted, even defeated, by the very qualities of curiosity itself.[40] Curiosity looks for knowledge.[41] But it may paradoxically itself block the way to knowledge. (Zeno of Verona explains that curiosity makes a person guilty *rather than* giving him the knowledge he seeks.[42] Cassiodorus suggests that it is only when grace helps us that we can be worthy to find anything out through curiosity, and this implies that without the aid of grace curiosity is a pretty weak instrument.)[43]

This double recognition that curiosity is merely human and in fact even a good and necessary characteristic of the human mind which would advance in knowledge; and that it is at times a vice, continues in early christian authors. Apponius, expounding the Song of Songs, finds the *curiositas humana* intrinsically limited.[44] Tertullian speaks of the *curiositas humana*;[45] as something superstitious.[46] Augustine of the *vitium curiositatis humanae.*[47] For Augustine, too, curiosity easily becomes vanity when it is applied to certain studies.[48] Petrus Chrysologus describes *curiositas humana* in terms of the pursuit of 'worldly wisdom'.[49]

So in these foundational texts for the christian tradition we begin to perceive again the parallel ciceronian tracks for the meaning of *curiositas*: a sense in which it is a desirable trait, a prompter to sound learning, to the desire to understand what was not understood before; and a sense in which it is a disorderly (and therefore powerful) appetite for unsuitable or inappropriate[50] or simply surplus[51] knowledge, or a desire for what is outward rather than inward, and therefore unworthy of a creature with the *interior homo* of the soul.[52]

The first meaning, in which curiosity is a *good* appetite for knowledge, appears actually to be contrasted with *curiositas* in a text of Augustine. He describes how different is the progress towards laying hold on the eternal, from 'vain and evanescent curiosity'.[53] Curiosity will pass away with the transient things it delights in.[54] Elsewhere he exhorts his listener to rein in his curiosity so that it may lead him in good not bad ways.[55] He certainly recognises that 'good' curiosity exists. 'Let curiosity lead you to know what he means when he says, "He who eats my flesh and drinks my blood remains in me, and I in him."[56]

Curiosity desires cognition, then, but *cognitio* cannot be certain except insofar as it is knowledge of the eternal and unchanging.[57] It may appear misleadingly in the first sense, as Augustine perceives in the *Confessions*, where *curiositas affectare videtur studium scientiae*.[58] In the second sense, Augustine speaks of its unworthy objects.[59] In that second sense, as Eve and Pandora found to everyone's cost, it can be sharpened to irresistibility by being knowledge forbidden. Augustine notes the way it is emboldened to break the commandments so as to experience everything.[60]

The undesirable element of *curiositas* in stoic thought too was its tendency to lack of moderation. Varro provides an etymology in his *De lingua latina*, deriving it from *cura*. He says that that is formed from 'heart' and 'burn', so that it indicates an essentially immoderate desire.[61] Cicero has a similar notion.[62] *Curiositas* in the Vulgate (Numbers 4,20) refers to an inordinate tendency. It makes demands.[63] Curiosity is a dangerous presumption' (*periculosa praesumptio*).[64]

Curiosity has certain companion-faults. *Curiositas* is linked in a trio with fleshly lust and pride by Augustine.[65] Aelred of Rievaulx has it in another trio, with the desire for wrong, *appetitus noxiae*, which he defines as empty knowledge (*inanis scientiae*), with the wish to know a great deal about other people's lives, not so as to imitate but so as to envy them, if something good emerges, or to insult them if something bad is revealed; and lastly with the immoderate interest in worldly affairs.[66] Aelred has a further trio, of wandering thoughts, the kindling of unworthy interest, curiosity (*vagatio, suspicio, curiositas*).[67]

A crucial aspect of *curiositas* for mediaeval authors is its relation to *veritas*. For Tertullian, *curiositas* is opposed to the *simplicitas veritatis*.[68] Augustine points out that illicit curiosity lacks truth.[69] Here Augustine's discussion (*Confessiones* X.35) is central.[70] He stresses that curiosity pretends to be serious study in search of science and learning. But it can be distinguished from legitimate seeking for pleasure by its objects, and it is the unworthiness of those objects with which we are concerned here. Curiosity is trivial in its tastes; the least little thing excites it.

The search for pleasure is marked by aesthetics. *Curiositas* is more often defined as *desiderium oculorum*, 'desire of the eyes',[71] than in any other way. That is a natural association when epistemology is heavily dependent on a doctrine of illumination. Thus it is to be contrasted with faith, for one may be led by what one sees and not by the unseen things of faith.[72] But other senses are involved too. The senses look for visual beauty, harmonious sounds, lovely scent, fine flavours and pleasurable tactile sensations. Curiosity rushes to see a mangled corpse, and things similarly shocking and dangerously exciting to the other senses attract it too. Similarly, curiosity is drawn to astrology or necromancy.[73] It trusts oracles.[74] It is inseparable from the world and life of pagan religions in general.[75]

To the learned mediaeval mind, curiosity has a series of related faults which arise from the principles Augustine outlines. It is liable to be idle, that is, thoughtlessly or without proper direction drifting towards its unworthy or even harmful objects. When Jesus said that he did not know the time of the Last Judgement (Mk 13:32), Bernard of Clairvaux suggests, he simply wanted to stop the idle curiosity of his disciples.[76] In the view of Bernard of Clairvaux, *curiositas* is first step of Satan's sin of pride.[77] Indeed Satan fell through curiosity.[78] This is what is happening when a hitherto good monk starts glancing about him and taking a constant interest in what others are doing, being a busybody, and thus 'wandering away from himself.[79] Geoffrey of Auxerre, in his *Colloquy of Simon and Jesus*,[80] points to the abuse which occurs when clerics give up their duty to be content with no more than they need and look for wealth to squander in pleasure, vanity and 'curiosity'.[81] 'Although I ought to be discharging the task of a wise man, it behoves me to become a fool; I should have prepared a fitting sermon,' confesses Achard of Saint Victor to his audience. The reason for his improvidence has been the curiosity and restlessness of his spirit, which, when it should have stayed at home and thought of God, has been wandering about outside.[82] Much later in the Middle Ages, among the Lollard dissenters, we find reference to idle curiosity in the study of the arts.[83] Geoffrey of Auxerre describes how ambition, curiosity and pleasure-seeking go together, and they are not of God but of the world.'[84]

4. Some knowledge is inappropriate for human beings because it is proper only for God or the gods

The problem we must touch on in this penultimate section has partly to do with novelty. A sense that something uncomfortably new is being said is expressed by Nicholas of Dresden: *haec, inquam, sunt inconsueta et appellacio inaudita*.[85] One difficulty lay with the continuing suspicion that the Devil is behind novelty.[86] The Church has always said there is a sacrifice in the Mass, so those who deny it hold a *nova fides*, and that means they are not of the Church,[87] says Johannes Eck in 1526. We say that new dogmas, at war with the faith or the Church are all lying innovations of devils, and are at war with the unity of the Church and with truth and *sinceritas*, says Johannes Dietenberger in 1532.[88] The point here is that God is the creator, and if human beings try to 'innovate' they go beyond their creaturely limitations and insult the source of all that is good.

There is also felt to be presumption in trying to be novel, a setting of oneself up above one's neighbour and the opinions of the Fathers and the whole Church, as Eck puts it. The presumptions are so swollen up that they not only think they know better than their brothers and neighbours, but they also, in their inflated and swelling rashness, prefer their own views to those of the holy Fathers of the Church.[89] Here there is again an echo of the debate about *rectus ordo*.

5. There is a time for everything and the time for the revelation of the forbidden knowledge is not yet, or not everyone is yet ready for it

But it is not always the case that learning something new is not what God wants. Mystery religions keep their secrets from all but the initiated. The *disciplina arcani* in early Christianity followed the same principle. This sort of thinking could be supported from tradition on the basis that it is God's intention that later generations should learn what earlier ones did not yet see. Learning has to go on. This is the other implication of the principle that everything was not taught to the apostles at once. 'The Holy Spirit does not teach the apostles all truth,' points out Wyclif, 'because there were many things they did not know after his coming, as is clear from the election of Matthias, and many similar things.'[90] The Holy Spirit taught the apostles truths, but only those which it was right for them to know, comments Wyclif.[91] Augustine wrote the *De consensu evangelistarum*. But something still remains to be done, says Jean Gerson. He did not solve all the problems. 'I have tried to continue what he began.'[92] So the living should teach the living.[93] Thus there is a promise of unfolding, an expectation that further truths new to the learner will be revealed. It is not necessarily always newness in itself which is wrong, but seeking something new at the wrong time, or in the wrong circumstances or when not qualified to know it.

Most challenging of all perhaps in this context is Nicholas of Cusa's concept of 'learned ignorance', which makes the principle of 'folly for God' philosophically newly profound. 'A man—even one very well versed in learning—will attain unto nothing more perfect than to be found to be most learned in ignorance which is distinctively his. The more he knows that he is unknowing, the more learned he will be.'[94]

Conclusion

Mediaeval Christianity had, then, a heightened consciousness of paradoxes which the classical tradition had begun to perceive and which had been sharpened and multiplied in early christian struggles with them. At the heart of the problem is the difficulty which the christian latin tradition in the West had, especially from Augustine's time, about the aspiration of mind and spirit towards things unseen and as yet unknown. That was, on the one hand, its proper direction, for in that inaccessible light (*lux inaccessibilis*) lay God himself.[95] It was also, as Hugh of Saint Victor recognised, sometimes an intrinsically noble vocation, leading men so to despise wealth and honours, so to bear injuries with gladness, as to dedicate themselves the more freely to the contemplation of higher things unimpeded by unworthy desires.[96] Hugh saw too that wonder at creation was edifying, and led to questioning, questioning to investigation, and investigation to a rational grasp.[97] But it was also dangerous, because it could lead into realms where lay various profound dangers to the soul. Some mediaeval scholars tried to tame those dangers by being scientific. Others tried to find safe paths by way of a developing tradition of spirituality in which love and divine guidance were protective. But both routes depended substantially upon the assumptions of the earlier work, and from these we do not find our mediaeval authors breaking away altogether.

Notes

1. Insofar as they were taught rhetoric from classical sources.

2. For most of the Middle Ages this was understood to be the case largely on the basis of Cicero's description in the *De inventione*, of the way to find arguments for a specific purpose.

3. There is a convenient short summary of Aristotle in this area in A. H. Armstrong and R. A. Markus, *Christian Faith and Greek Philosophy* (London, 1960) 113.

4. See on all this Robert Crouse, 'In multa defluximus: *Confessions* X.29–43 and St. Augustine's theory of personality', *Neoplatonism and Early Christian Thought*, ed. H. J. Blumenthal and R. A. Markus (London, 1981) 181–185.

5. F. Dolbeau, 'Nouveaux sermons de saint Augustin pour la conversion des pa•ens et des donatistes (II),' *Revue des Études Augustiniennes* 37 (1991) 261–306, para. 6, 276–7.

6. *De veritate*, VI; *Anselmi Opera Omnia*, 6 vols., ed. F. S. Schmitt (Rome–Edinburgh, 1938–68), 1:183,23–184,2.

7. Boethius, *In Porphyrii Isagoyen Commentarium*; CSEL 48: 135–136.

8. Augustine, *Contra Adimantum* XXVII.2; CSEL 25: 186–187.

9. *De Musica* VI.xi.32: *Corpora absentia imaginaliter cogitamus sive memoriter recordantes quae novimus*. R. Schneider, *Seele und Sein* (Stuttgart, 1957) p. 206ff. assembles a useful list of references in connection with *phantasia*.

10. Godfrey of Saint Victor, *Microcosmus*, 19; ed. P. Delhaye (Lille–Gembloux, 1951) p. 46: A *sensualitate quidem velud a terra usque ad ymagines absentium corporum se elevat, sed ultra nichil prevalens more aqua circa corpora fluctuat.*

11. *Ibid.*

12. *The Prose Salernitan Questions*, B 35; ed. B. Lawn, (London, 1979), p. 19: *In fantastica cellula multum commovetur et per imaginationem similis forma representatur, unde spiritus in se formam suscipit. So ergo mater manu comprimit aliquam partem, spiritus sibi retentus immutate humorem secundum se.*

13. *The Prose Salernitan Questions*, 245; p. 121.

14. *The Prose Salernitan Questions*, B 37; p. 20. *Si ergo contingat nervos non ex toto opilari, spiritus transcurrit ad inferiora unde movet spiritum vitalem, quo moto movetur et cor et pulmo, et dum imaginatio inducitur in fantastica cellula, movet cerebrum.*

15. *The Prose Salernitan Questions*, 42; p. 21: *Dum enim spiritus animalis in cerebro commovetur diversas anime representat imaginationes, unde sequitur diversitas rationum.*

16. Hugh of Saint Victor, *Didascalicon*, II.iii; ed. H. Buttimer (Washington, 1939) p. 26: *Quia per instrumenta sensuum non uniformiter ad sensibilia comprehendenda descendit, eorumque similitudinem per imaginationem ad se trahit.*

17. Gilbert of Tournai, *De modo addiscendi*, IV.xx; ed. E. Bonifacio (Turin, 1953) p. 227.

18. *Ibid.: Cum eidem rerum visibilium repraesentat speciem.*

19. *Ibid.: Eidem ministrare non desinit.*

20. Gilbert of Tournai, *De modo addiscendi*, IV.xxii; ed. E. Bonifacio (Turin, 1953) p. 233: *Bestialis quando per ea quae vidimus aut sentimus vagando mente discurrimus sine gravitate sine utilitate, sicut et bestiae.*

21. Godfrey of Saint Victor, *Microcosmus*, 19, Chapter 204; ed. P. Delhaye (Lille–Gembloux, 1951) p. 224.

22. *Microcosmus*, 19, Chapter 156; p. 173.

23. Albertus Magnus, *Quaestiones, De prophetia* I,a.2, iv.i.2; ed. A. Fries, W. Kübel, H. Anzulewicz (Aschendorff, 1993) p. 67.

24. Jacobus Faber Stapulensis, *The Prefatory Epistles*; ed. F. Rice (New York–London: Columbia University Press, 1972) p. 5. *Eo ordine eaque facilitate nobis scientiarum et virtutum viam patefecit, ut plane videatur ab illo divino munere nullum excludi voluisse, cui quantulumque mentis adesset, divinius id bonum putans quod pluribus cognoscere profuturum.*

25. Raymond Lull, *Liber de inventione maiore*; ed. J. Stöhr, *Opera Latina*, (Palma, 1960) Vol. 2:300. *Inventio maior, dicimus, quod est invenire Deum.*

26. Stapulensis, *The Prefatory Epistles*; Rice, p. 224.

27. For example, in Alan of Lille at the end of the twelfth century. The theme of 'ways' also appears in other methodological contexts. Juan de Torquemada (388–1468), writing in defence of converted Jews, speaks of ways of 'proving' which are useful in this particular case. The first two ways are by the Scriptures and by reason. The third way depends on the promises made by God to the Israelites: *tertia via . . . ex promissionibus divinis factis populo israëitico.* There remains a fourth way, which is by the actions or deeds which Christ did among the Jews for the salvation of the human race:

Juan de Torquemada, OP *Tractatus contra Madianitas et Ismaelitas*; ed. N. I. Martinez et V. P. Gil (Burgos, 1957), Chapter 5, p. 71, Chapter 6, p. 75. *Superest iam quarta via, videlicet ex gestis specialiter per Christum apud genus iudeorum in executione divine providentie circa salutem humani generis, ostendere quod genus iudeorum non fuerit a Deo per totum reprobatum et dampnatum.* Jean Gerson (1363–1429) uses a different 'quadrivial' approach in the *De consolatione theologiae*. The consolation of theology lies first in hope through the contemplation of divine justice; second in Scripture through its revelation of the *regiminis mundi*; thirdly, in patience in the zeal for moderation; and fourthy in learning, through a quiet conscience. Jean Gerson, *De consolatione theologiae; Oeuvres complètes*, ed. P. Glorieux (Paris, 1973) IX:185.

28. *Oratio Domni Willelmi*, 35; Guillaume de Saint-Thierry, *La contemplation de dieu*, ed. J. Houlier (Paris, 1968): *Si formam aliquam vel formatum aliquid imaginer michi pro te deo meo: idolatra fio. Oratio Domni Willelmi*, 48; Guillaume de Saint-Thierry, *La contemplation de dieu*; ed. J. Hourlier (Paris, 1968): *Remotis omnibus usitatis locorum veo localium imaginationibus intellige te deum in se ipso invenisse, ipso ostendente qui tanto verius et certius est, quanto ex seipso, in se ipso, per se ipsum est quod est.*

29. Richard of Saint Victor, *De Trinitate* 6.XXI; ed. J. Ribaillier (Paris, 1958) p. 258: *Ex his licet perpendere quae sit figura spiritualis substantiae. Procul dubio, dante Domino, eadem perfectionis forma potest informare animam tuam et animam meam. Si itaque juxta voluntatis similitudinem Patris ac Filii conformitatem vel configuratione, quaerimus. . . . .*

30. Hugh of Saint Victor, *De sacramentis christianae fidei*; PL 176:264D: *Imago pertinet ad figuram, similitudo ad naturam. Haec autem in anima sola facta sunt, quia corporea natura similitudinem capere non potuit Divinitatis, quae ab eius excellentia et similitudine in hoc ipso longe fuit quod corporea fuit.*

31. Peter Abelard, *Theologia scholarium*, 45–6; CCCM XII: 418: *Imago quippe expressa alicuius similitudo vocatur; similitudo autem dici potest, etsi non multum id cuius similitudo est exprimat.*

32. Achard of Saint Victor, *Sermons inédits*; ed. J. Châtillon (Paris, 1970) pp. 29–30: *Consistit in potentia vel possibilitate cognoscendi Deum, et diligendi , et perfruendi. Que imago post peccatum et per peccatum corrupta et deformata, sed non penitus deleta est.*

33. *The Prose Salernitan Questions*, 169; p. 88: *Tamen quia anima, spiritibus mediantibus, suas replet operationes scilicet imaginationem, rationem, et memoriam, auditis verbis sapientis anima intenta imaginatur, ratiocinatur, et audita memorie commendat.*

34. 2.12.2, 19th April, 59, and see on this A. Labhardt, '*Curiositas*, Notes sur l'histoire d'un mot et d'une notion', *Museum Helveticum* 17 (1960) 206–224.

35. See J. Mette on *curiositas* in Apuleius' *Golden Ass*, in *Festschrift Bruno Snell* (Munich, 1956) 227–235.

36. Labhardt, '*Curiositas*', 206–7.

37. Cicero, *De otio*, 5.3: *Curiosum nobis natura dedit ingenium.*

38. In the *De divinatione*, for example, we find: *illum autem id diutius facere non potuisse elatumque cupiditate respexisse.* Cicero, *De divinatione* 1.49.

39. Laelius, *Republic*, I.xix. See, too, Robért Joly, '*Curiositas*', L'Antiquité classique, 30 (1961) 33–44.

40. The Latin renders at least two Greek terms: *philomatheia* (love of learning) and *polypragmosyne* (being busy about a great many things).

41. Johannes de Forda, *Super extremam partem Cantici canticorum Sermones cxx*, Sermo 101, CCCM, 18: 686; CF 47:7.

42. Zeno of Verona, *Tractatus*, Book i, 50; CCSL 22:124.

43. Cassiodorus, *Expositio psalmorum*; Psalm xc; CCSL 98: 831.

44. Apponius, *In Canticum canticorum expositio*, ed. H. Bottino and J. Martini, PL *Supplementum* (Paris 1958) p. 167. (See also the edition of B. de Vregille and L. Neyrand, CCSL 19)

45. *Ad nationes* 1.1.3; CCSL 1: 11; *Apologeticum* i; CCSL 1: 25–26.

46. *Apologeticum*, 25; CCSL 1: 135–137.

47. Augustine, *Sermo* 277.13.13; PL 38:1264. *Contra Julianum* 6.7.17; PL 44:832.

48. This issue is discussed at length, especially in connection with the liberal arts, in H. Marrou, *Saint Augustin et la fin de la culture antique* (Paris, 1959).

49. Petrus Chrysologus, *Sermo* 11, line 5; *Collectio Sermonum*; CCSL 24:174.

50. Augustine, *De diversis quaestionibus octoginta tribus, Questio 68;* CCSL 44A:174.

51. Fulgentius of Ruspe; CCSL 91:477.

52. Gregory the Great, *XL Homiliarum in Evangelia libri duo*, Book II, Homily 36. iv. l; PL 76:1263, quoted by Bede, *In Lucae Evangelium expositio*, IV.xiv, l; CCSL 120:279.

53. Augustine, *De vera religione*, xxix.l; CCSL 32:221.

54. Augustine, *De catechizandis rudibus*, xxvi.l; CCSL 46:174.

55. *Enarrationes in Psalmos*, Psalm 103, *Sermo*, iii, para. 10, CCSL 40:1509: *Esto curiosus, providus*, so that no one may misapprehend your *curiositas*.

56. Augustine, *Sermones*, 132; PL 38:735.

57. Augustine, *De vera religione*, lii; CCSL 32:252.

58. *Confessiones* ii.6; CCSL 27:24.

59. Augustine, *De vera religione*, xlix; CCSL 32:248; *De Genesi contra Manichaeos*, ii; PL 34:210.

60. Augustine, *De genesi ad litteram libri duodecim*, xi; CSEL 28/1:365,10.

61. *De lingua latina*, ed. P. Flobert (Paris, 1985) 6:46: *Quod cor urat; curiosus, quod hac praeter modum utitur.*

62. Cicero, *De finibus.*, 4.12: *insatiabilis quaedam e cognoscendi rebus [natura] voluptas.* Idem. 1.44: *Natura inest in mentibus nostris insatiabilis quaedam cupiditas veri videndi.*

63. Quodvultdeus, *Sermo 2, De symbolo* II, xi; CCSL 60:347: *Curiositas exigat.*

64. Defensor Locogianensis, *Liber scintillarum*, lxx, *Sententia* 19; CCSL 117: 211.

65. Augustine, *Enarrationes in Psalmos*, Psalm 8, para.xiii; CCSL 38:56; *Sermones*, 284; PL 38:1291: *Voluptas carnis, superbia et curiositas.*

66. Aelred of Rievaulx, *Compendium speculi caritatis*, Chapter 53; CCCM 1:34.

67. Aelred of Rievaulx, *Sermones, Sermo* xliii; CCCM 2:338.

68. *Adversus Marcionem* 2.21.2; CCSL 1:499.

69. Augustine, *Sermones, Sermo* 122A, p. 256, line 23.

70. H. Blumenberg, '"Curiositas" und "veritas" zur Ideengeschchte von Augustine, *Confessiones* X.35', *Studia Patristica*, 6 (Berlin, 1962) 294–302.

71. Augustine, *In Johannis epistulam ad Parthos tractatus*, ii; PL 35:1996. Cf. Agobard of Lyons, *De spe et timore*; CCCM 52:146.

72. Quodvultdeus, *Sermo I, De Symbolo*, vii; CCSL 60:323–325.

73. Augustine, *In Johannis epistulam ad Parthos tractatus*, ii, PL 35:1996.

74. Augustine, *De civitate Dei*, V.xxi; CCSL 48:157.

75. See Augustine's discussion, *De civitate Dei* vii. 34–5; CCSL 48:214–215.

76. Bernard of Clairvaux, *De gradibus humilitatis* III.10; *Sancti Bernardi Opera* 3, ed. J. Leclercq and H. M. Rochais (Rome, 1963) 23–24.

77. *Ibid.*, X.28; SBOp 3:38.

78. *Ibid.*, X.38; SBOp 3:45.

79. *Ibid.*, X.28–38; SBOp 3:38–45.

80. Geoffrey of Auxerre, *De colloquio Symonis et Iesu* 17.33; PL 184:449.

81. *Ibid.*

82. Achard of Saint Victor, *Sermons inédits*; ed J. Châtillon (Paris, 1970) 101, Sermon for the Feast of Saint Augustine: *Cuius improvidentie causa est precipua curiositas et inquietudo spiritus mei qui, cum deberet intus quiescere domique residere et his que Dei sint vacare, foris vagatur, mobilis et instabilis, huc ac illuc discurrens.*

83. Thomas Netter, *Fasciculi Zizaniorum* XII; ed. W. Waddington Shirley (London, 1858) 368, the 'Lollard Conclusions' brought before Parliament in the last decade of the fourteenth century: *Quod multitudo artium non necessariarum usitarum in nostro regno nutrit multum peccatum in wast [= waste, i.e. English], curiositate, et inter dysgysing. Istud ostendit ex parte experientia et ratio, quia natura cum paucis artibus sufficit ad necessitatem hominis.*

84. Geoffrey of Auxerre, *De colloquio Symonis et Iesu* 19.16–21; PL 184:450: *Ambitio, curiositas et voluptas non ex patre sunt, sed ex mundo. . . . in 'concupiscientia carnis' universa, accipie corporalium sensuum delectationem, qua quidem ne ipsa curiositas caret; ac deinceps 'concupiscentiam oculorum', quaecumque ad humanum diem, quenmpropheta minime concupivit, et saecularem gloriam et extrinsecam pertinent vanitatem.*

85. P. de Vooght, 'Le dialogue "De purgatorio" (1415) de Nicolas de Dresde', *Recherches de Théologie ancienne et médiévale* 42 (1975) 132–223, p. 164.

86. Beryl Smalley, 'Ecclesiastical attitudes to novelty, c. 1100–1250, *Studies in Church History* 12 (1975) 113–133.

87. Johannes Eck, *De sacrificio missae* I.1 (1526); ed. E. Iserloh, V. Pfnür, P. Fabisch, Corpus Catholicorum 36 (1982) p. 14: *Hoc novum est monstrum a Luthero invectum, a veteribus et priscis hereticis ignoratum, ab omnibus Christi fidelibus absconditum, . . . Necesse est spurium esse et adulterum, qui novam fidem, contempta ecclesia, inducat.*

88. Johannes Dietenberger OP, *Phimostomus scripturariorum: Köln 1532*; Chapter I.i; ed. E. Iserloh, Corpus Catholicorum 38 (1985) p. 6: *Nova dogmata, fidei vel ecclesae pugnantia . . . dicimus omnes adventitias mendacesque daemoniorum eorundemque satellitum doctrinas.*

89. Johannes Eck, *De Sacrificio Missae*, I.i; 13: *Adeo enim* intumuerunt, *ut non solum altius saperent, quam eorum confratres et proximi, set et iudicia eorum, sententiare sanctorum patrum ecclesiasticorum, sanctorum patrum ac totius ecclesiae, inflata praesumptione ac turgida temeritate, praeferrent.*

90. John Wyclif, *Sermones*, Sermon 28; ed. J. Loserth (London, 1887ff.) 3 vols., 1:190: *Spiritus Sanctus non docebit apostolos omnem veritatem, cum multa post adventum Spiritus Sancti ignorarunt; ut patet de eleccione Matthie et multis similibus.*

91. Wyclif, Sermon 28; p. 191: *Veritates non omnes sed pertinentes distincte doceb it apostolos, cum eis congruerit ipsas noscere.*

92. Jean Gerson, *Monotessaron*, ed. P. Glorieux, *Oeuvres complètes* (Paris, 1973), IX:248: *Tentavimus . . . continuare prout inchoaverat. Visus est protinus labor vix explebilis, maxime propter ordinis rerum gestarum incertitudinem.*

93. Wyclif, Sermon 33; p. 225: *Deus enim qui posuit omnia in mensura ordinavit viventes eiusdem generis consulentes viventibus.*

94. Nicholas of Cusa, *De docta ignorantia*, I.i.4; ed. P. Wilpert, revised H. G. Senger (Hamburg, 1970) p. 6.

95. I Timothy 6:16. Cf. Anselm, *Prosologion*, I; ed. F. S. Schmitt *Opera Omnia*, (Rome–Edinburgh, 1938) p. 98.

96. Hugh of Saint Victor, *Didascalicon*, III.xiv; ed. C. H. Buttimer (Washington, 1939) p. 64.

97. Hugh of Saint Victor, *De Meditatione;* ed. R. Baron, *Six opuscules spirituels*, Sources chrétiennes 155 (Paris, 1969).

The Light Imagery of Saint Bernard's Spirituality and Its Evidence in Cistercian Architecture

Emero Stiegman

BERNARD OF CLAIRVAUX saw the world, not 'as a harmony of many colors,' but 'as a monochrome in black and white'. When Erwin Panofsky makes this comment, he seems to speak for many students of spirituality as well as of the arts—those who wonder why the abbot could not be more inclusive in his appreciation of human experience, why he subjected himself to an asceticism so comprehensive as to subsume the arts.[1] Reflecting upon the assessment of this renowned art historian, we may well conclude that, although it is in a misapprehension of the saint's spiritual vision that this judgment speaks for many, Bernard did indeed see the world in black and white.

It is not unusual for misconceptions of monastic asceticism to be expressed with a kind of sympathy and in a language constituting an elliptical theological argument.[2] According to the view I have cited, Bernard, a man of superior sensibility and saintly honesty, simply lacked a christian philosophy which might have enabled him, as it enabled others, to embrace the beauty of creation. However wrong this may be, it has the merit—beyond formalism, beyond the observation of institutional continuities—of working from the premise that the abbot's art, even as his spirituality, is to be accounted for in the way he saw the world. Regardless of the theoretical explanation we may settle for, we sometimes become aware of an identity between the quest for God, with the 'asceticism' accompanying it, and the desire to respond more fully to the beautiful, with the discipline enjoined by the desire itself. Questions regarding the perception of reality in a notable figure, saint or artist, can initiate a study in either spirituality or art history.[3] When we have satisifed ourselves with the more proximate historical reasons for Saint Bernard's artistic legislation, there remains room for speculation about a possible reason within the declared ascetical reasons—i.e., a reason both deeper and more heuristic than those generally ascribed to asceticism.[4] We may ask how he saw the world. Attempting an explanation that would move beyond institutional history and an aligning of practices with one or another of the monastic virtues, I would like to study Bernard's artistic renunciation of color, and the biblical roots of this—including concommitantly his 'imageless' contemplation—as the manifestation of a spirituality whole and entire.

The appropriateness of my concluding a study of spirituality with some remarks on cistercian architecture is grounded in the fact that, time and again, what has sent me back for second thought into Saint Bernard's writings has been the witness of the buildings as phenomena, resistant at times to the 'interpretations' of the literary and theological guilds. The suggestions I offer regarding architecture will be those of an amateur who feels that—despite the difficulty of locating a starting point in the hermeneutical circle revolving between works and words—sometimes the more usable beginning is the building; sometimes Bernard's architecture appears to warrant more than a specialized interest in the student of spirituality. The suggestions, nevertheless, will be appended as a codicil to this study in bernardine spirituality.

I propose to move toward the following conclusions: (1) For Saint Bernard the language of color is unsuited to represent the monastic quest, where the experience of God can be spoken of only in terms of light and darkness. (2) In the light-darkness antinomy of the johannine New Testament, Bernard finds a primal generative image of the human spiritual struggle, an image stressing directness, urgency, totality. His employment of it is not to be explained wholly as a principle of the faith, in the narrow sense of 'belief', but must be accounted for as a perception of the world, what might be called an experiential *sense* of the real (grounded in faith), with inevitable effects in the arts. (3) Approaching the cistercian monastery church as the site for Bernard's type of contemplative prayer leads to a positive evaluation of architectural features which gothic art strove to eliminate.

No attempt to situate Bernard in his era, to understand him through comparisons and contrasts, is possible without the assistance of Jean Leclercq's lifelong work. The great and beloved Benedictine seems to have recognized in Bernard's case a special necessity for resisting the favorite labor-saving device of scholar's, the absorption of the subject into an accomodating *Zeitgeist.* With a broad awareness of the twelfth century and an incomparable knowledge of the monastic tradition—its history, customs, spirituality, prophets, literature and art, imagery and vocabulary—Dom Jean was able to comment upon his special saint with an authority that has been hardly resisted. Yet he warned frequently that Bernard was a difficult writer.[5] Perhaps none knew more intimately than he that, because of Bernard's grounding in an era that leapt mightily beyond its recent past, and because of a solidarity with the great patristic writers which seemed in some respects to make him impervious to major currents of his day, the saint's thought could not be safely categorized. And yet, to Leclercq, there was no more reliable teacher of basic christian spirituality than this archetypal monk addressing his community: Bernard was the tradition. We have come to see so much of this as true that we see also our debt to Leclercq as beyond the recognition of superior scholarship.

Light Imagery in the Twelfth Century

The sources of our knowledge regarding aesthetic theories in the twelfth century are comprised in largest part of the first medieval attempts to formulate a theology of art. Without surprise, the works of Gilbert Crespin, Rupert of Deutz, Theophilus, Heraclius, Hugh of Saint Victor, together with all the hexameral literature of the school of Chartres, give evidence of the strong sway of Augustine. At Chartres the rediscovered *Timaeus* of Plato is clearly in evidence. In many places, when not altogether obvious, the influence of Dionysius the pseudo-Areopagite, through the translation and commentary of John Scotus (Eriugena), may be suspected.[6] It is not always possible to distinguish these three intellectual vectors, and for our purposes it is not necessary. What concerns us is a trait these sources have in common: their account of the beautiful, couched largely in terms of light, is linked to a cosmological mysticism.[7]

Consider, first, the perennial presence of Augustine. Mystical prayer in this tradition begins its ascent to God, frequently, in the perception of the Creator immanent in the world.[8] Secondly, the *Timaeus*, rediscovered at Chartres, is a late and quite this-worldly Plato, one of the principal stimuli of the new interest in nature. Here *the many* are points of departure for the quest for *the One* from which they emanate (a light image). Finally, third, in the mystical theology of Dionysius light so constitutes the essence of everything it illuminates that the world itself is a theophany.

A useful way to relate cistercian sensibilities to this background is to compare the light imagery of Saint Bernard to that of abbot Suger of Saint Denis (d. 1151). Historians interested in 'the vision in which the [gothic] cathedral originated' have tended to ask of Suger's meagre and mediocre writings more than these can yield.[9] What would seem evident is that the man who claims responsibility for the artistic program of the first gothic church was not only fascinated by color but argued, in the dionysian language of Eriugena, that color is of special value to the monk's contemplation. By viewing many-colored gems, he is 'transported from this inferior to that higher world in an anagogical manner'.[10] The variety of colors apprises him of 'the diversity of the sacred virtues'—i.e., of God's multiform power in creation.[11]

Tracing the true inspiration of Suger's art, however, is not that simple. He may be engaged merely in a diplomatic exercise, as Conrad Rudolph contends, appealing to the vision of the monastery of Saint Denis' pseudo-patron saint and, with pretentions to monastic contemplation, placating leaders of the reform movement, prominent among whom would be Bernard of Clairvaux.[12] Dionysius was a very philosophical mystic, one for whom the biblical story is hardly ever the starting point of his ascent to God. Finding in Suger's text on stained glass windows nothing but explanations of their iconography—no mention made either of their revolutionary architectural character or of the overwhelming psychological effect of great expanses of stained glass as such—one is therefore led to suspect that even what may be dionysian in the program at

Saint Denis was the work of a scholarly intermediary. Grover Zinn, granting that role, very plausibly, to Hugh of Saint Victor, calls attention to strong augustinian elements in this 'dionysian' source.[13]

And yet, if we are to discover how Suger envisioned the gothic, a style essentially linked to effects from which Saint Bernard turned away, we may have to be reconciled to dealing with his text in a way that is more hypothetical and inferential than directly probative. Panofsky is right in believing that what Suger needed from the dionysian system was a view of the world in which there was 'no insurmountable chasm' and 'no dichotomy' between things, 'from the highest, purely intelligible sphere of existence to the lowest'.[14] One can infer that, whether he learned this from Dionysius or not, this is the way Suger desired to view reality and this is what the gothic program meant to him.

Again, for our purposes, it does not greatly matter whether the builder of Saint Denis, in his presentation to the public, was more a clever apologist than a forthright devotee; he was certainly a spokesman for the light mystique of his times. He was listened to. His building style overwhelmed the western tradition for centuries. Let us look briefly at this light mystique, searching out clues to Suger's experience of it.

Consider, first, his near-obsessive repetition of gem catalogues. The golden altar frontal of Saint Denis' upper choir was ornamented with 'a multifarious wealth of precious gems, hyacinths, rubies, sapphires, emeralds and topazes, and also an array of different large pearls'.[15] What immense satisfaction the author takes in these colorful gems: new liturgical furnishings are described, not by the features of their design, but according to the variety of gems that ornament them. So it is for the cross of Saint Eloy 'and that incomparable ornament commonly called "the Crest"',[16] for the candlesticks at the side of the altar,[17] the golden crucifix,[18] the chalice,[19] two vases,[20] and a special porphyry vase.[21] He reports that the hunt for precious gems pushes on relentlessly.[22]

We move from gems to stained glass. Suger has been credited with leading the building campaign by which stained glass windows were to become so nearly contiguous and so enormous as to create the feeling of an uninclosed building, a place of prayer with glass walls. What students first read about gothic regards the maximization of space for stained glass, 'the principle of Gothic style', its 'leading idea'.[23] For all Suger's lines explaining biblical narrative and the allegories configured on glass, we can hardly doubt that the basic effect of the windows he speaks of had to do much less with iconography than with an ineffable quality of light.

How are we to explain the powerful pre-critical impact of gothic stained glass? Sunlight streams through this poured rock which we call glass, opening the inner constitution of it as a special color, different from what is disclosed in the adjacent piece of glass, creating the mystery of translucence. With instant insight, we recognize light passing through an object and declaring a quality of color otherwise invisible to be of a special revelatory character: only by a force beyond itself is the object attractive, and only through the medium of the object does this force reach us. In its vibrant radiance of color, this earth-stuff becomes one with the light.[24] From deep within the ruby or emerald bursts a fire, from within the pearl (though not truly translucent), a soft iridescent glow. Every variation on a color reveals a qualitatively different object, because the difference among colors is qualitative. (The human response tends this way, even for those acquainted with the theory of wavelength and of spectral analysis.) There are meanings which are 'felt or intuited aesthetically'.[25]

Writing about the great windows of Saint Denis, Suger, strangely, had nothing to say that might point to a spiritual meaning he saw in them or even to the architectural innovation they constituted.[26] As we know, what his efforts brought him to, with the assistance of theologians and one or more unknown master builders, was the conception of a church that stood as the symbol of a translucent cosmos.[27] In the heaven of the cathedral, one gazed upon a kind of mandala of dazzling complexity, where colors in scattered patches and areas of interfusion shone through a wondrously complex and ordered geometry of stone tracery.[28] Here one realized that the divine Light radiated in presence and power through all the multiplicity of creation, binding all to Itself.

Suger spoke of a mystical meaning found in assembled gems and did not predicate these ideas of his windows.[29] I believe that, in so far as the gems and the windows share in the metaphors of translucence and variety of color, we may cautiously infer that the experience he describes as his response to gems represents as well his experience of the stained glass window, though (not to his honor as builder) in his prose he seems to place more mystical effectiveness on the gems. The hypothesis fairs well when set against testimonies in the era. What Hugh of Saint Victor, for example, writes in commenting upon the mystical theology of Dionysius can be read as an altogether convincing analysis, in theological terms, of the stained glass window's effect, and the same metaphorical dynamic emerges in Suger's description of the contemplative prayer induced by precious gems in his church.[30]

We are now in a different spiritual country from that of Saint Bernard.

We have spoken of the metaphor of translucence as a 'mystery'. Unlike our era, the twelfth century reveled in what M.-D. Chenu calls 'an authentic feeling for mystery', 'a taste for the marvelous'.[31] An openness to accepting wondrous objects and startling occurrences as *praeter naturam* prevailed; and only slowly did theologians define the distinguishing marks between these and what christian faith knew to be the mystery of grace, *super naturam*. Again, the experience of mystery was not always objectified. 'Often', writes Chenu, 'their spontaneous practice of symbolism was not suficiently self-conscious to lead to explicit analysis of the laws underlying their work'.[32]

This mystery of translucence is cognitively pre-christian; it is experienced before associations of faith modify it. With christian iconography, the artist baptizes a natural form. What shines through creation and is revealed of God now becomes the Christ-event, in promise and fulfillment. Upon the philosophical mysticism that discerns a Great Power in the world is now imposed an invitation to christian contemplation. And yet, this doctrine accepted in faith remains the theoretical ground upon which we base our interpretation of a natural marvel, one of the outstanding displays of twelfth-century mystagogy. Not, of course, that the sacred story cannot completely inform our reception of the window's light; only that the fracturing and ordering of the light retains so glorious an effect in its own right that the faith perspective converting it will have continually to be re-imposed. Underlying the christian artifact is an awesome earth mystique, a signifying which occurs within devout viewers whether they choose to recognize it or not.

With this in mind, one speaks of the prayerful frame of mind induced by awesome spectacles, like a great gothic rose window, as pertaining to philosophical or cosmological mysticism. God's becoming present to us through our experience of creation is a phenomenon explained in the doctrine of Dionysius. But is it not explained in the teachings of William of Conches and Bernardus Silvestris and their colleagues in the school of Chartres, and in the universally disseminated writings of Augustine as well? If one tends to suspect, *a priori*, the presence of Dionysius more than that of others, it is because of this thinker's drive to state his entire system in terms of light—e.g., that light was the very being of what became visible by it.[33] In its relevance to Saint Bernard, the critical category to which we are brought in our search for 'the vision in which the cathedral originated' is, not *dionysian* or *augustinian*, but *philosophical*. In this philosophical mysticism, two ideas predominate: first, that all creation is a theophany; and, second, that all things form a continuum of being and beauty, so that nothing need be rejected.[34]

In our study of the spirituality of Saint Bernard, we have remained a while with his monastic counterpart, Suger, in the hope of learning how this epoch-making builder's art, illuminated as far as possible by his undistinguished writing, might reveal his spirituality. Let us turn now to a great spiritual writer, whose architecture can contribute to our grasp of his text more than has been asked of it thus far. The simple black and white art of Bernard was to the sumptuously chromatic art of Suger what the either-or spirituality of Clairvaux was to the all-enfolding view of human existence ambitioned by those who conceived Saint Denis. The vision of these latter, with Suger at their head, produced in the cathedrals that followed their lead what were 'arguably the finest achievements in the history of western architecture'.[35] To Suger, all the world shone with the muted glory of God; the house of God, then, should radiate the divine presence. What did the abbot of Clairvaux find problematic about that?

Bernard and the Cistercians

As the Cistercians exult in the imagery of light, the dionysian mind is not much in evidence. In the hymns of their liturgy, we observe a grateful acceptance of the way the Divine Office sacralizes time: each of the canonical hours contains a hymn alluding to the cycle of changes in the light of day. Some typical remarks can be cited, largely from two collections by M.-M. Davy.

William of Saint Thierry was fond of the metaphor of noonday: 'The noon of the Bridegroom', 'The repose of high noon', 'the knowledge of the noon-day light'.[36] He compared different states of fervor to the bright light of morning and the fading light of evening.[37] In the *Vita prima*, he describes the joy of Bernard as a constant radiance.[38] Aelred of Rievaulx, who refers to large effects in ecclesiastical art as 'those tiny external glories', advises us, born though we be with the color of the earth, to attire ourselves in the colors of virtue.[39] (Even so slight and unusual a nod to color by Aelred breaks ranks with Bernard.) Guerric of Igny speaks frequently of our humanity as that darkness from which we emerge into light in the resurrection of Christ.[40] Gilbert of Hoyland remarks that the contemplative's *otium spiritus* is brought about not by liquor but by light. The Word, he says, in hiding himself within a shadow, *is* shadow—i.e., Christ.[41]

All these Cistercian Fathers treat the theme of light in a manner similar to Saint Bernard, though occasionally some sign does emerge of Stephen Harding's generation with its more lenient attitude toward color—especially with Aelred: when counseling the recluse to attend to the inner person rather than to take pleasure in ornamenting the monastic environment, he described the virtues of the bride as beautiful colors on her many-colored robe.[42] (Elaborating the same theme, Bernard in SC 27. 3–4 had spoken of the virtues on the bride's robe simply in terms of degrees of brightness.) In the end, at least because of what we know of Bernard's powerful influence over the architecture of the Order and the legislation regarding the arts, it is he who is of central importance in the question of cistercian aesthetics.

The first thing to observe in Saint Bernard's handling of light imagery is his resolute turning away from the entire phenomenon of color. This may not place us at the heart of the matter, but it points the way. Some samples: he gently mocks the monk who believes a sacred image is holy in proportion to the degree of its coloration (*eo creditur sanctior quo coloratior*).[43] He tells the well dressed prelate in the *De moribus* that what is seen in a person's interior (*in abscondito*) does not come in colors.[44] In the Second Sermon in Lent, we read that from perseverance in the virtues comes the uncolored unity of good conversation.[45] In the *Super cantica* [SC], Christ takes pleasure in the gift of love, not in the color of the lover.[46] Again, the divine Word does not enter through the eyes because he has no color.[47] Then, no beauty can be compared to the soul, certainly not the colored cheek for which corruption waits.[48] In another place: do not let carnal imagination envisage the colored corruption of the flesh . . . for the soul is not painted in visible colors.[49] Bernard invites us to reflect upon what the color of sadness and jealousy must be like that God turns away from them.[50] Color seems to represent false value: the Word gladdens the heart, 'not with the charm of color, but with the love it bestows'.[51]

There are very many other such remarks, all pressing us to take notice of how regularly the author uses color as a metaphor for impurity, superficiality, or vain pretention. I can find no countervailing figurative use of color in Saint Bernard. Among the spiritual senses, he seems to say, true sight does not dwell on surfaces and is, in effect, color-blind.

This list of references could suggest a certain habit of mind in the author, particularly as the list might be vastly extended. From a catalogue of random quotations, however, no matter how abundant, we can come to no conclusion. We might strengthen our case by indicating where major pericopes on the subject of light occur. For instance, an extended passage in SC 15 extolling the name of Jesus is virtually an ode to the divine light. In SC 82.2–4 there are several pages dedicated to discussing the fall of Adam and Eve in terms of light and darkness with many references, all derogatory, to color. It interests the artist in every reader to see Eve's temptation conceived entirely as the problem of a kind of absolute aesthetic sensibility: as Eve contemplates the fruit of desire, she is asked:

> Why do you imprint upon your soul a different form, or rather, deformity? For what it delights to possess it fears to lose. Now fear is a color: while it pigments your freedom it covers it and renders it untrue to itself (*sibimet dissimilem*).[52]

The fifth book of *De consideratione* explains that the monk does not need sensory aids to contemplation; the argument is made largely (in the johannine manner) with reference to the eternal Word as light, the world as darkness, and human sight as unable to discern the light. Some of the marian texts, especially the sermon for the

Sunday within the octave of the Assumption, speak of the woman clothed with the sun: Mary is the model disciple, illustrating the transformation that the light of the Word must accomplish in the darkness of the soul: *mulier amicta sole* (Apoc 12:1) is paralleled to *induimini Dominum Jesum Christum* (Rom 13:14).

But, the finest opportunity for observing the treatment which characterizes our author will present itself if we follow him as he reflects upon the many appeals to the language of light and darkness in his favorite biblical book, the Song of Songs. The *Super Cantica* holds the central position in the bernardine canon. It occupied the last eighteen years of the saint's life, and as the word shared most intimately with his monks it documents his innermost spirit. The commentary arrives as far as chapter 3, verse 1, of the Song of Songs. There are nine verses referring to light in this stretch of the biblical text; and much of Bernard's spiritual doctrine is drawn together around these images of light. Let us survey them, at least in concentrated summary.

(1) 'I am very dark but comely [*nigra sum sed formosa*] . . . like the tents of Kedar, like the curtains of Solomon' (Song 1:5). Bernard's discussion of this darkness of the bride is book-length; it covers SC 25, 26, 27, and 28. One who knows that only God is light, knows that all creation is darkness. The holy soul, made in God's image, but having lost much of the divine likeness, glories even in her weakness; she humbly proclaims both the fact of her darkness and her hope in God's love.

Bernard makes capital of the tidy *nigra-sed-formosa* contrast to ground the concept of *compunctio*—that fusion of humility and hope, or detachment and desire, which marks the start of the spiritual journey. One finds this traditionally monastic view of the inner struggle, in Leclercq's account, as 'the point of departure for all Bernard's doctrine'.[53] In the darkness of the bride, we find the theme the abbot developed in the first of his publications, *The Steps of Humility and Pride*. The text of the Song provides, above all, a uniquely appropriate figure for what is the axis of his anthropology, the doctrine that, though our likeness to God has been darkened in sin, we retain the divine image: we are dark in our loss of likeness to God, but bright in our retention of God's image. The unit SC 25–28 is an extended development of a beauty preserved even in our blackened souls.[54]

Within this context, sermon 27 explains why the soul is God's best dwelling place, and in the process provides us with the bernardine text that, more than any other, can be suggestively associated with architecture. The light imagery slides into spacial imagery.[55] God's earthly house is to be marked by those traits that reflect the soul's reality, a lowly but expectant emptiness and the expansive grandeur befitting God's image: 'She is black like the tents of Kedar. . . . beautiful like the curtains of Solomon'.[56] This 'temple bright with light'[57] has a black-and-white beauty: 'Any distinctions that exist there [in the soul's true home, heaven] do not consist of colors but of degrees of bliss'.[58] Bernardine spirituality becomes aesthetics, then, at its very foundation.

A lesser reflection on our blackness is that, as color, it is superficial: one may be 'black without . . . beautiful within'.[59] Darkness represents our earthly condition, not always the effect of a sinfulness in which God's likeness is lost, but the limitations of creaturehood and of our bodiliness. The saints (e.g., Paul) can be abject in appearance. Yet Bernard will more often link darkness to the sinfulness that characterizes all humanity, emphasizing the inclusion of the humanity of Christ, in whom he says, 'I recognize the form of our darkened nature . . . the garment of the first sinful humans'.[60]

(2) 'Do not gaze at me because I am swarthy, because the sun has scorched me [*decoloravit me*]' (Song 1:6). This verse, ancillary to the preceding one, is treated by the abbot in SC 28, the concluding sermon of the group noted above. Bernard explores the senses in which the swarthiness of the bride can be commended. He takes full advantage of the image of a divine sun that removes earthly glitter from the beloved, uncoloring her and leaving her, in her own eyes, in the truth of her darkness. Those who gaze at her, failing to recognize their own blackness, have not yet begun the process of their purification.

The darkness of the human Christ, referred to in item (1) above, offers Bernard a lead into the theme that underlies much of his light imagery—i.e., the superiority, during this interim before the beatific vision, of that hearing which is faith over the seeing which is sensory experience and unaided reason. The centurion on Calvary recognized Christ 'by the voice . . . not by the face'.[61] Bernard enjoys playing on the idea in epigrammatic fashion. The eyes, he concedes, are a nobler power, but vision is reserved for heaven.[62] The theme is resumed at SC 41.2.

Since the light reaching our corporeal eyes may leave us deceived, we must attend to the way God chooses to reach us. The contrast between *revealing* and *concealing* is a theme deriving from Bernard's light imagery. Do not look for wisdom with your eyes, 'because flesh and blood will not reveal it to you, but the Spirit [cf. Mt 16:17]'.[63] Mary in the garden at Easter was not allowed to touch the risen Saviour 'because she depended more on what she saw than on what she heard'.[64] What she saw concealed the reality of Christ's risen state.[65] Late in the *Super Cantica*, Bernard reflects that the Scriptures themselves, in as much as they are human words, not only reveal but also conceal the mind of God; for, they 'speak wisdom concealed in a mystery'.[66] Their light is not accessible to merely human effort.

The light of the world does not reveal what the soul thirsts for. In the imperfection of the Creator's mediated presence within a world that is, in this, unlike God, God is absent. (We would not call this attitude apophatic, because Bernard does not invite attention to *objects* which mediate God's presence only as inadequate.[67]) It is a matter, not of theological aesthetics, but of judgment regarding what is appropriate and effective for certain persons in certain conditions: 'All things are lawful', the abbot reminds us, 'but not everything is to be recommended'.[68] Bernard the reformer sees the monk as someone who seeks God by 'rushing' in the 'most direct' way, walking a 'straight path', according to the *rectissima norma* of the Rule.[69] To such a person, an art that draws the viewer toward the world, where *something* of God may be discovered, can seem ill advised.

Earthly light conceals; earthly beauty distracts. One may say that the exclamation in the *Confessions* (11.4), 'You who made these things are beautiful, for they are beautiful' truly represents Augustine's contemplation. (In fact, in Book Ten the bishop attempts an expository retracing of his ascent from earthly beauty to that beauty which is God.) Comparable reflections in Bernard lack this character.[70] In the mystical encounter, Bernard hears the Word encourage the soul to seek the beauty of God in the sufferings of Christ, in 'the little bundle of myrrh' kept by the bride between her breasts (Song 1:12; SC 45.4). 'Contemplate me in the spirit', says the Bridegroom (SC 45.5).

(3) 'Tell me where you pasture your flock, where you make it lie down at noon' (Song 1:7). Here again, there is a great expanse of development. Sermons 31, 32, and 33 are dedicated to the mystical noontide [*meridies*]. The theme is taken up again at length in SC 48.6–8. Already we have noticed in Bernard (SC 28, above) certain images of light which are derogatory: e.g., 'the brightness of eternal light . . . *dimmed* in the flesh';[71] or, 'Why wish to touch what is *ugly* [*deformis*, referring to the body of Christ] . . . ?'[72] 'Under these forms he possessed neither beauty nor majestly'.[73] Particularly striking is his use of Ps 18:6, 'He pitched his tent in the sun' (*In sole posuit tabernaculum suum*), where the sun stands for Christ's body: our author marvels that 'he who dwells in unapproachable light should deign to reveal his presence openly and in the light . . . namely in the body'.[74] That sun which is Christ, then, is not overwhelmingly bright. We are dealing with an element in Saint Bernard's theology which caused Déchanet in 1953 to observe that anthologies never reproduced quotations which would illustrate it.[75] This element, which figures largely in determining the specific difference between the abbot's light imagery and the work of others, and which manifests a telling trait of his spirituality, is the *umbra Christi*, Christ as shadow.

Bernard insisted there were two ways of knowing Christ: according to the flesh and according to the spirit. In his human form, Christ is the sacrament of God, guiding us and making the divine lovableness visible. But carnal love for the human Christ, a stage of development, must be transcended: we must love him who is Spirit according to the Spirit.[76] He read in Saint Paul that, in his resurrected condition, Christ is no longer accessible to us in the images of his humanity (2 Cor 5:16). The abbot was one of the first to cultivate a vividly pictorial devotion to the humanity of Christ, but then 'Saint Bernard reverted to the early tradition of the Church'.[77] He writes, 'Christ the Lord is a Spirit before our face; under his shadow we shall live among the nations [Lam 4:20]'.[78] Bernard longs to see him 'in the form of God, no longer in shadow [*non in umbra*]'.[79] Since the Christ of images is not the eternal light but a shadow, the author counsels his monks that, in contemplation, there is no need for 'representations which belong to the weakness of his humanity'.[80]

Here we can see how cistercian artistic legislation forbidding narrative imagery in the oratory—to the great extent that it represented Bernard—was grounded in a Christology, and only consequently in asceticism.

Carnal love for the human Christ, that shadow of the Godhead, extends to the *memoria Christi* found in the New Testament. But, the esteem Bernard exhibits for the mediatory function of Christ's humanity is not extended to the literal text. The question of inspiration, then, is considered generally from the point of view of spiritual exegesis.[81] We saw something of this, above, speaking of language as a concealment of the divine light.[82]

Bernard does not always speak of Christ as shadow; he is not averse to citing from the fourth Gospel, 'I am the light of the world' (Jn 8:12).[83] Nevertheless, one looks for reasons to explain why a text like Jn 1:4, 'In him was life, and the life was the light of all people' (*In ipso vita erat, et vita erat lux hominum*) occurs never once in the entire bernardine corpus.[84] My own suspicion is that a rhetorical identification of the divine life, coming to us through Christ, with the eternal light of God in Christ, would set up an awkward inconsistency of imagery in a text which frequently figured the human Christ as a shadow. Christ as exemplar can be the light of the world while remaining, in Bernard's imagery, a shadow with respect to that light which is to be equated with the divine life.

Grateful as he is for the sacramental value of Christ's humanity, Bernard longs to move beyond the shadow, to 'lie down at noon' (Song 1:7) in contemplation of the eternal Word. In sermon thirty-three, which completes this unit, he writes:

> I too have the Word, but the Word made flesh; and the Truth is set before me, but in the sacrament. . . . in this life I have to be content with the husk, as it were, of the sacrament, with the bran of the flesh, with the chaff of the letter, with the veil of the faith. And these are the kind of things whose taste brings death, unless they are seasoned in some way with the first fruits of the Spirit.[85]

The light image 'veil of the faith' receives its content from the accompanying complex of appositive images, all of which form a lament for the darkness of the human condition.

It will be readily seen what a difference there is between Bernard's attitude towards the restricted light of earthly existence as expressed in the image of shadow (*umbra*) and that of Hugh of Saint Victor, commenting upon Dionysius. Where Bernard stresses the absence of that eternal light which is the soul's true Bridegroom, Hugh pauses to take pleasure in the revelation made possible by the divine light filtering through created things. He writes:

> [The divine light] is veiled only that it may be more revealing. . . . Its shading is our illumination. . . . Somehow, our weak eyes see the sun comfortably when it is covered by a cloud.[86]

Two viewers see the same reality, but from different perspectives.

(4) 'Your cheeks are comely as the turtledove's, (5) your neck as jewels. We will make you ornaments of gold, studded with silver' (Song 1:10–11). These images describing the physical charm of the bride are explained in SC 40 and 41 respectively. The author acknowledges that the imagination is stirred by color here, and he immediately warns, 'You must not give an earthbound meaning to this coloring of the corruptible flesh'. The incorporeal soul, he says, has no color. He reads the face of the bride as 'the mind's intention' (SC 40:1) and the neck as 'the soul's intellect' (SC 41:1).[87] After this quick transposition, the objects of color are dropped from consideration. Gold and silver are perceived, in the hebrew manner, more as degrees of brightness than as colors; e.g., even as pure white light: 'Gold signifies the splendor of the divine nature'.[88]

It must not be supposed, of course, that in working such transpositions to the spiritual, the abbot failed to understand that the things of the world mediated the divine prerogatives.[89] In a Christmas sermon—to choose one example—he waxed eloquent over the way the power, wisdom, and goodness of the Creator might be seen in creation itself.[90]

He makes brief mention of the splendid appearance of the bride (SC 41:1) and then, by slight of hand, maneuvers our attention to a part of her image not spoken of in the text of the Song—her ears. The jewel-like quality of her neck, he writes, refers to ornaments given her and hanging from her ears, the organ of faith.[91] Faith comes by hearing (Rom 10:17), he says, as he renews a favorite theme. It is worth sharpening our focus on this *tour de force* of imagination for the way it uncovers Bernard's determination to turn the light imagery of the Song into a message of faith rather than of vision and to shift emphasis from the mind's seeing to the heart's listening.

That the bride is beautiful in the eyes of her divine lover and that she is ravished by the beauty of her spouse remain dominant motifs, in the *Super Cantica* just as in the Canticle, even while Bernard struggles to monitor carefully the human allure of vision, recognized both in a self-gratifying contemplation and in the drive of the curious intellect. He is never ingenuous regarding images of light. Though the soul longs for contemplation (SC 40), she may be called to care for the needs of others, mothering the Bridegroom's children (SC 41). The language of love and of marriage abounds here.

While trying to learn the function of light imagery in Bernard's work, particularly here in his masterpiece, we need to remember that the kiss of lovers (SC 2–8)—and not an image of light—is clearly the figure the author finds most functional. The kiss is that contact of the Holy Spirit which gives love as well as knowledge (SC 8.6). In a special way we observe what Bernard considers the alternative to his affective mysticism—to notice, for example, that he finds danger in approaching God *per ea quae facta sunt* (Rom 1:20; SC 8.5), through the sensible world.[92] The context is that of the Cistercians among enthusiasts for cosmological mysticism rather than that of Paul among the Romans. 'This revelation [the kiss] which is made through the Holy Spirit', Bernard writes, 'not only conveys the light of knowledge but also lights the fire of love'.[93] Again: 'The favor of the kiss bears with it a twofold gift, the light of knowledge and the fervor of devotion'.[94] The abbot does not condemn as unloving all whose mystical approach has a philosophical dimension, but in these sermons he is not overly cautious in setting up a simple alternative to his concept of 'the kiss', nor in associating it with light images proper to cosmological reflection, nor in betraying his ambivalence regarding these images.

Saint Bernard's insistence upon a starting point in the frequently dim and ungratifying light of faith must be recognized as characterizing his contemplation. Even when forming, in one short paragraph (SC 15.6), a collage of thirteen scriptural light images as applied to Christ, he contrives to turn them all into metaphors of faith.[95] Denis Farkasfalvy remarks that, unlike the dionysian manner of John Scottus Eriugena, engaging in a philosophical approach to mysticism, Bernard moves immediately from the eternal Word (Jn 1:1) to the Word made flesh (Jn 1:14): we know God in the humanity of Jesus. This elimination of philosophical avenues to contemplation convinces Farkasfalvy of the correctness of earlier studies which concluded to no discernible influence of the pseudo-Areopagite upon Bernard.[96] The abbot of Clairvaux determined not to tarry in the shadow of Christ *inter gentes*, but he would always begin there.

To recognize precisely where we discern a distinction, it must not be supposed that by 'philosophical' approaches to contemplation we mean those that fail to transcend reason. The reference is, instead, to authentically christian prayer which rises from sublime suggestions in nature, where metaphysical intuitions incite the mind to seek the Creator.[97] Dionysian mysticism was of this type. But, with differences of its own, so was the mysticism of Saint Augustine.[98] Bernard's strong personal preference for a different approach is stated clearly and in extended form in his exposition on the Bridegroom's intimate rooms (SC 23.11–17).[99] Elsewhere, he coins the untranslatable epigram, *Contemptus omnium otium dederit* (Detachment from all things makes possible a resting in God), where among the implications of Saint Bernard's *contemptus* I would read an exclusion of cosmological curiosity.[100]

(6) 'Behold, you are beautiful . . . your eyes are doves' (Song 1:15). In SC 45, 'Your eyes are doves' returns to the theme of *seeing* noted in item (2) above: how one sees God, and what our human eyes do not see. This is developed through an unusually sustained use of the language of light and darkness; the progress of the bride, for example, is 'from brightness to brightness' (SC 45.5).[101]

In the dove, Bernard reads humility. The eyes of the humble are 'spiritually enlightened' and prepared to accept the Word's invitation: 'From now on, . . . contemplate me in the spirit, because Christ the Lord is a spirit before your face'.[102] But, in preparation, we must look upon the light of him who has abandoned his divine light, the human Christ. The abbot extols two kinds of light, that of the eternal Word and that of Christ in his human nature:

> How beautiful you appear to the angels, Lord Jesus, in the form of God, eternal, begotten before the daystar . . . the

> radiant light of God's glory . . . untarnished brightness of eternal light!. . . . How beautiful you are to me, Lord,. . . . When you divested yourself of the native radiance of the unfailing light . . . your love shone out more brightly. . . . Star out of Jacob, how brilliant your rising above me! How pleasant your light as you come to me in darkness, rising from on high!. . . . And how you rose from the heart of the earth, gleaming after your setting, Sun of Righteousness![103]

This exultation in the humanity of Christ, in the language of light—Jesus is the divine light that comes to us in darkness—can restore balance to what we have had to emphasize in Bernard's light imagery—i.e., the christological implications in the *umbra Christi* figure. Contemplating the light of Christ in his human nature marks a stage in the development of the soul, a dwelling in the 'shadow' of Christ, as we have said. But, it is in this privation of light that his love 'shone out more brightly'. Bernard knew that sensible images are necessary in forming the soul. 'It is not the spiritual which is first but the physical [*animale*]', he repeats.[104] He is not disregarding the creation.

But monks, he believes, hear the call of the Bridegroom, 'From now on . . . contemplate me in the Spirit'. In SC 62, Bernard discusses the preparation of 'the inner eye', 'the eye that is pure and simple', as the necessary condition for seeing in the Spirit.[105] The principle is that one knows by assimilation: like knows like. Our vision is spiritualized as we are 'transformed into his likeness from one degree of glory to another'.[106] But, it must be recognized that 'We are transformed [only] when we are conformed'.[107] The true mystic, then, explores first, not the mystery and majesty of God, but God's will. The call to contemplation can indeed be answered, for 'Truth does not withold its vision from the pure of heart'.[108]

With these qualifications, the author narrows the scope of light imagery in its more conventional religious usage, even as he commits occasional passages to luxuriating in it. His more ordinary manner can be observed in SC 74, on the visit of the Bridegroom: the mystical encounter is a dialogue, more a voice than a vision.

(7) 'In his shadow I sat' (Song 2:3) is reflected upon in SC 48:5–8. The rich theme of Christ's humanity, our comfortable shade, is taken up anew, with emphasis upon the exclusiveness of Christ as

our way to God. In images of light and of the tree, sermon 48 offers a clear and relatively comprehensive exposition of that bernardine Christology the trademark of which is the *umbra Christi.*

First, we encounter Bernard's ambivalence. The reference to Lam 4:20,—'Christ the Lord is a spirit before our face; in his shadow we shall live among the nations'—looks in two directions; but it would be wrong to take the second clause for mere resignation. The author explains that 'his shadow is his flesh; his shadow is faith'.[109] Or, 'through his flesh he is the shadow of faith, through his spirit he is the light of the mind'.[110] Bernard speaks of that 'shadow for which I longed' and warmly encourages us, while still in the flesh, to 'live in his shadow . . . so that one day you may reign in his light'.[111] To understand the meanings behind Bernard's shadow image—behind what I have referred to as a seemingly derogatory slant—we must be responsive to both sides of his ambivalence. He leaves the shadow of the Word's humanity in quest of the eternal light. Nevertheless, the human Christ is to be sought, first as the object of faith, without which we can never come to the light of the Spirit; and second, as that shadow within which we can truly rest. The connotations in this latter dimension of the image regard both what the generation as a whole saw—that, in the human Christ, God had tempered the divine light to human eyes—and that, in the contemplation of Christ, one beheld specifically the love and the lovableness of God.

Bernard does not miss the opportunity of appealing to the *umbra* figure to argue for *rest* as his contemplative ideal.[112] Christ's shadow is 'where the bride rests'.[113] The prophet of Lam 4:20 said that in his shadow we live; 'the bride, however, enjoying a privilege, boasts that she alone is seated beneat it [the tree which is Christ]'.[114] 'To be seated is to be at ease', and this is a greater thing than simply to live there.[115] The bride, therefore, 'in loving commitment, is sweetly at rest'.[116]

Yet, although the *memoria Christi* is necessary, consoling, and challenging, Bernard looks to the time when this *umbra* of faith will yield to the light of vision. We see something of his nostalgia for heaven in the adverbs *nondum* and *interim* (*not yet* and *meanwhile*): 'We, however, who have not yet deserved to be rapt into paradise, . . . let us meanwhile be fed with the flesh of Christ, . . . [and] preserve the faith . . .'.[117]

It is more than nostalgia; it is a desire for God that will push Bernard to anticipate the divine presence in prayer, to live even here 'by his understanding . . . no longer in the shadow but in the light'.[118] He believes in order to understand.[119] First, then, he wishes to come to the shadow, 'and then to pass on to that of which it is the shadow'.[120] This drive to *pass on* and to move ahead comes from deep within the abbot's spirituality. He refuses to dally even for a moment. He feels called to the highest possibilities. His is the monastic simplicity of the most direct way. An expression of this is his frequent appeal to the *se extendere* of Phil 3:13—as, for example, 'He is . . . "a spirit before our face," that is, in the future, provided we forget what lies behind and strain forward (*nosmetipsos extendimus*) to what lies ahead'.[121] From the comfortable shadow of Christ in the flesh, Bernard must move ahead to the light of the eternal Word, beyond images and beyond color. His life is a preparation for 'the advance of the dawn', the coming of the Bridegroom.[122]

Therefore, in practice, what is meant, above all, by the contrast between Christ as *Spiritus* and Christ as *umbra* is that monks at prayer cannot forever content themselves with the iconography of the New Testament story but must move beyond images toward a contemplation of the eternal Word. Not every physical environment, of course, will be equally supportive of this silence of the mind.

Another aspect of this Christology can be seen in those images of sermon 48 leading up to the reflection upon *umbra*. The text of the Song (2:3) reads, 'As an apple tree among the trees of the wood, so is my beloved among the sons'. Bernard wonders whether this is not small praise to bestow upon the Bridegroom. He explains by comparing the apple tree to other trees.

Can we conclude to anything truly determinative in Bernard's spirituality through an exercise in decoding such imagery? Let us stop here and acknowledge that we are apt to discover within ourselves a certain resistance to this way of addressing the most serious concerns of the spirit. We are inclined to read with a concealed condescension this quest for spiritual meanings in Scripture by way of lengthy obervations on apple trees—as if the hidden things of God were to be found under the rhetorical ornaments of a hebrew poem.

Yet, a little time with the text makes altogether plain that answers to some important questions we would pose to Saint Bernard will be found—remarkably free of ambiguity—not in an analytic tract, but here, among the trees. The abbot fully intended his figures to communicate a clear doctrine.

We retrace Bernard's steps, then, from our light image, (Christ the shadow) to another one, (Christ the shading apple tree), and from there to his imagistic starting point, the earth. This text on the *umbra Christi* (SC 48), the most explicit and clarifying in Bernard's works, opened with the verse, 'As a lily among thorns, so is my love among maidens' (Song 2:2), and explained that the place of thorns was the world—'this curse-laden earth of ours', where we dwell 'while the soul is in the flesh'.[123] But the soul exposed to tribulations and 'the disquietude of temptations' while in the world must take courage, for Jesus said, 'I have overcome the world' (Jn 16:38).[124] The suggestions of John's gospel go beyond the short quotation; they issue from Bernard's bundling of everything in the human condition into a category called 'the world' standing against the Word. We must come back to this.

In the continuing dialogue of the Song, the beloved addresses the Bridegroom, as we have seen, as an apple tree among the trees of the wood. Christ is different from 'the other trees'.[125] They give shade but are 'sterile trees that bear no fruit suitable for human food'.[126] (Though many trees bear fruit, only one yields 'human' food.) He alone 'gives life to the world' (Jn 6:51).[127] The other trees are 'the world':

> For the other trees of the wood may indeed provide a comforting shadow, but not a life-giving food, not enduring fruits of salvation. There is only one 'author of life' [Acts 3:5], 'one mediator between God and man, the man Jesus Christ' [1 Tim 2:5].[128]

Let us here make an incidental observation linking the preceding thoughts to cistercian art. The manner in which Bernard speaks of Christ as the only way to God—not a communal christian doctrine to this effect—rules out the possibility that he shared in his era's openness to cosmological mysticism, and therefore to the color mystique of the gothic. The only element of the creation which makes God present to us is the human Christ; 'the other trees' may seem to provide shade, tempering the divine light, but their food is not for humans; their shade is not salutary. 'Unless you believe [unless you seek God in Christ] you will not understand'.[129] Beyond this, Bernard's determination to build on faith and to move past it into imageless contemplation of Christ as Spirit rules out any role for specific symbols, either sensible or intellectual, in the environment of prayer.

The burden of proof for these conclusions is not placed entirely upon one text, even though the text provides an ample and leisurely discussion; the same ideas issue from the other sermons to which our inquiry into light imagery has sent us—and with unrivalled clarity in SC 23 on the chambers of the Bridegroom.

It may be objected we have insufficient evidence that Bernard was addressing questions of contemplative methods as related to sacred art in this sermon (SC 48). On the other hand, one may not succeed in discovering other possible points of reference for the exclusionary comparison the abbot makes between Christ as mediator of the divine presence and those elements of the creation in which that function might be sought. Bernard did not have a separate spirituality held in reserve for sacred art.

(8) 'Until the day breathes forth life and the shadows lie prostrate' (Song 2:17). In sermon 72 Bernard explains that the Word, which is our daylight, is the life that breathes within us; the day of the Saviour will dispel the night of this world.[130] But, he writes, 'There is also a day with an evil significance [Job 3:3; Jer 20:14] which is cursed by the Prophets'.[131] The remark prefaces a lengthy consideration of instances in which the pattern of light imagery dissipates. For example, 'Shadows' refer to those hostile powers which the Apostle Paul called . . . the princes of darkness [Eph 67:12], . . . children of night [1 Th 5:5]'.[132] Again, 'The hour of darkness . . . shall pass [Lk 22:53]';[133] or, 'The night is the devil [2 Cor 12:7]'.[134] 'Night is the Antichrist [2 Th 2:8]'.[135] 'Is not the Lord the day?. . . . He puts the shadows to flight with the breath of his mouth [Job 15:30]'.[136] Our first parents were plunged into terrible darkness, 'counting the darkness as light and light as darkness [Is 5:20]'.[137] There are many other such items in the collection.

Reflecting upon original sin, upon the fact that 'in this day [when our first parents sinned] we are all born',[138] the author turns the physical light of day into an image of our ongoing struggle with hostile powers and of our moral fragility: this day is one 'in which the flesh does not cease to struggle against the spirit'.[139] At this point, we find a proliferation of the pauline language of *flesh* and *spirit* (with reminiscences of Gal 5:17 and Rom 7:23), introduced to regulate the highly varied light imagery and offer theological clarification of it. In SC 72:8–11 this terminology becomes dominant. It is as if, with this great rush of light images threatening to complicate the rather simple schema from which he derives special meaning, a schema that brackets all extended meanings, the author calls upon an organizing principle underlying his thought. Paul's spirit and flesh are matched to the light and darkness of John's gospel [Jn 1:5, 8:12]. Light can be distinguished now as 'according to the flesh' or 'according to the spirit', as can also darkness. In fact, it may be helpful at this point to tabulate, even if in a somewhat *a priori* way and without references, how this distinction is played out in Saint Bernard's writings, acknowledging meanwhile (as the author does here in SC 72) occasional usages outside the pattern. Helpful, because *caro* and *spiritus* are key concepts issuing from the abbot's Christology: what functions in us *according to the spirit* is the operation of the risen Lord in his community; what moves within us *according to the flesh* either repudiates our divine destiny restored in Christ or is ignorant of it.[140] Bernard's duplication of Paul's *caro-spiritus* is faithful to the Apostle—e.g., it is not an equivalent of body-soul—but no more simple than in the New Testament. The expression '*in* the flesh' (*in carne*)—e.g., 'the aspiring soul who is still in the flesh'[141]—may imply no antagonism to 'in the Spirit' (*in Spiritus*), but may refer merely to the *interim* of our earthly sojourn. The sense of the light image is greatly changed by the implication of *in carne* instead of *secumdum Carnem*. Here, then, are light (white), darkness (black), and color as metaphors in Bernard's usage:

LIGHT

(A) *according to the flesh* or *in the flesh*
- God of the philosopher
- Human knowing, wisdom

(B) *according to the spirit:*
- God of revelation, Creator, Redeemer
- The Word in the Trinity (Jn 1)

— Revelation brought by Christ
— The revealing Spirit working in humans
— Vision (in relation to faith's dark glass)

DARKNESS

(A) *according to the flesh* (held as darkness by the world), *in the flesh*
— Human ignorance
— Pain and loss

(B) *according to the spirit* (a darkness contrary to the world's darkness)
— The nothingness from which creation is made
— All creatures (Gen 3:19; Ps 103:15)
— The humanity of Christ (umbra)
— Faith (in relation to vision)
— Light according to the flesh
— Sorrow for sin, penance

COLOR

(A) *according to the flesh* or *in the flesh*
— Qualitative differences in things
— An indefinite variety emanating from the One

(B) *according to the spirit*
— Inexhaustible potentialities of the Creator revealed in creation (Bernard neither denies this nor makes habitual appeal to it.)
— The potential allure of created things, the confusion introduced into the choice between God vs not-God

(9) Finally, 'In my bed night after night [*per noctes*] I sought him whom my soul loves' (Song 3:1). Sermon 75, while expounding the necessity of seeking the Lord when he is not perceived as present (a theme continued in SC 84, 85, and 86), is a study of various meanings for darkness (night). The reason the Bridegroom conceals himself as in darkness is that the desire, affection, and love of the soul (*desiderium . . . affectus . . . negotium amoris*) may increase.

We meet again a substantial development of the theme of Christ the shadow: 'If we think of Christ in a wordly way, we do not know him' (Cf. 2 Cor 5:16).[142] He is a Spirit (Lam 4:20): 'He is not here, he is risen' (Mk 16:6).[143] Bernard dwells insistently upon the fact that the error of monks who seek Christ now in his human nature lies in their belief that the risen Lord would be *on earth*. He writes, 'I say the world . . . is almost all night, and always plunged in complete darkness. . . . light has nothing to do with darkness'.[144] And later: 'He has arisen from the heart of the earth, but did not remain on earth'.[145]

To seek the Bridegroom at night, then, means to pursue him in his humanity. The bride acted this way only when she was spiritually young, when she lay in a little bed (*in lectulo meo*). Now the meaning of night expands:

> Those who are ignorant are ignorant at night, and likewise those who seek seek at night. . . . Now the day shows openly what the night concealed. . . . It is night, then, when the Bridegroom is being sought, for if it were day, he would be seen among us [2 Thess 2:7].[146]

Different moral meanings are grouped into the commonality of *night*:

> The faithlessness of the Jews, the ignorance of pagans, the perversity of heretics, even the shameless and degraded behavior of Catholics—these are all nights. For surely it is night when the things which belong to the Spirit of God are not perceived?[147]

Another meaning, the opposite of 'the day of salvation' (2 Cor 6:12), had been given earlier: 'The night is coming when no-one can work' (Jn 9:4).[148]

Johannine Dualism

As we see, then, Bernard's reflections on light and darkness are occasioned by the content of the biblical text he means to elucidate. This, I believe, is because his spirituality is, to some extent and in a way not yet remarked upon, formed at this sapiential source.[149]

The Song of Songs is grouped with the wisdom writings of the Old Testament, where the broad picture is of a dual reality: the eternal Wisdom which is light; and the world which, lacking Wisdom, is darkness. The Song of Songs, in that extended meaning cherished in both jewish and christian tradition, transposes Wisdom to Beauty. The ethical duality now regards divine love. This radical delineation of all reality into two contraries is continued and seen from the perspective of the end-time in the apocalyptic tradition.

With this I am not trying to suggest that the johannine corpus is enfolded within a world of exclusively biblical thought, proof against any larger intellectual environment. Exegetes have generally acknowledged that John is the most greek of the gospels; and their awareness of this greek character has been at the root of some nervous questions regarding the gospel's authorship and setting. What is of interest to my project is that hint of the wisdom quest in John, the element which points simultaneously to both the wisdom tradition of the Old Testament and the Greeks' love of wisdom, their *philosophia*. The useful reflection is that the Bible's wisdom literature, including the Song of Songs, and greek philosophy, which deals heavily in the light imagery so irresistible to the twelfth century, represent—side by side—the closest possible juncture of these two traditions.[150] We recall that, for this reason among others, some books of Israel's wisdom caused grave worry to both Jews and Christians who set out to fix the canon.

We have not generally thought of Saint Bernard's spirituality as growing out of the biblical traditions of wisdom and apocalyptic; or, to claim less, we have not been called to reflect upon how these sources colored his thought; but perhaps, when we observed something of its johannine character, we should have. Gilson contended that chapter four of Saint John's first epistle, on love, formed a center for the most important 'doctrinal bloc' of the abbot's spirituality, orienting even the contents of the fourth gospel.[151] Although the point has never been in dispute, one should notice that, in summarizing what Bernard drew from this center, Gilson took no account of what biblical scholars refer to as a 'johannine dualism' encapsulated in the antinomy of light and darkness. The exhortation to love in 1 Jn 4, for example, is framed within that chapter's general caution to 'test the spirits', to distinguish those of the world from those who confess that Jesus is from God, to separate truth from falsity, to espouse love and not fear. This antithetical manner of thinking, characteristic of the fourth gospel, corresponds to what has been frequently noted in Saint Bernard's writing, that sharp divide and great chasm between a total commitment to the divine Lover and everything perceived as threatening compromise—the either-or.[152] To downplay this cast of the abbot's mind is to misrepresent it, whatever one's interest in spirituality. If we are to discover a dimension of bernardine spirituality which manifests itself in visual art, we must pay careful attention to precisely this. Let us attempt, then, to clarify the meaning of 'johannine dualism'.

Bultmann speaks of it as a dualism of decision, ethical rather than cosmological.[153] The distinction would not be encouraging to anyone who sought to enfold Bernard into the light mystique of his era. (Schillebeeckx further justifies the terminology, speaking of 'an existential dualism, really a form of the monism of grace'.[154]) The progressive discovery after 1947 of the Dead Sea Scrolls (one of whose manuscripts is entitled 'The War of the Sons of Light against the Sons of Darkness') has revealed an apocalyptic language so similar to the johannine writings that scholars who had long pondered over the authorship of the fourth gospel began to speculate upon links to the community of the scrolls, the Essenes, centering on Qumran. Early diffident suggestions of indirect influence have been rapidly yielding to the conclusion that 'the johannine prophet', the principal authority behind the writings ascribed to John the Evangelist, was a Christian who may well have passed his early years among the Essenes, for 'the Evangelist had dualism in his bones'.[155] When a theologian like Schillebeeckx, surveying and summarizing the views of exegetes (1977), speaks of johannine origins as in the tradition of wisdom literature, he is virtually reassuring believers that such dualism characterizes much of the Old Testament and, although mediated by sectarian Jews at Qumran, it was not a heterodox mindset.[156]

Nevertheless, Qumran connections are meaningful. Some groups of former jewish sectaries, it seems, heirs to the essene tradition, belonged to the johannine congregation. It would have been necessary that in their quest for the light they receive a proclamation emphasizing the uniqueness (or exclusiveness) of Christ as the revelation of God. The congregation would account to some extent for the peculiar style we are speaking of.[157]

Consider the opening of John's gospel, 'In the beginning was the Word . . .':

> In the word was life, and the life was the light of human beings, and the light shines in the darkness, and the darkness has never mastered it. . . . He was in the world, and the

> world came about through him, and the world did not know him. (Jn 1:3–10)[158]

Students of the text have, as we have seen, noticed that this *logos* hymn has deep roots in wisdom literature, where the world is *skotia*, darkness. It is not in essence evil; it is simply not-God, not-light. (One is reminded that for Bernard, unlike for most of the tradition, the *regio dissimilitudinis*, region of unlikeness, where one dwells after having lost the divine likeness in sin, is not sin, but simply the earth.) The light of Wisdom divides humankind; it brings on a crisis, forces a decision. In the fourth gospel, to one side and to the other, are the Word and the world, truth and falseness, life and death (or judgment, implying condemnation). Contrast and antagonism are present, however, not merely in occasional verbal pairings; conflict is the very form of this gospel, presented as an extended trial, as the struggle of two parties in dispute.[159] But, the model received, ultimately from the wisdom books, is worked out in John on a grid of very few metaphors, most of them interchangeable, constantly repeated. The words *light*, *life*, and *world* are used many times more often in John than in the three Synoptics combined.[160] We are in a realm of simple antitheses, of crisis, of radical discontinuity. The inevitability of either accepting or rejecting the light which is Christ dominates the whole fourth gospel.

When it is suggested, then, that Saint Bernard is johannine, we must not think only of a gentle insistence upon love; we must see the relentless pattern of having to decide—clearly, definitively, urgently—in favor of God or of the not-God, of light or of darkness. In the fourth gospel this is not a doctrine different from primordial Christianity; it is a style, the reflection of a certain community's experience. In Saint Bernard, it is that rude spirituality of the *either–or*: rarely missed is the opportunity of increasing the tension and broadening the gap between moral alternatives, or strenuously urging a choice of the most direct way as against every other way. It is the voice of monastic reform, of the desert fathers. Its pedigree is irreproachable.

The abbot's frequent use of the fourth gospel has not gone unnoticed. Among his several fine studies on Bernard and the Bible, Denis Farkasfalvy has done a comprehensive survey of the saint's one hundred forty-five quotations and reminiscences of John's prologue.[161] He demonstrates that, even when Bernard amasses clusters of references to John, the theological meaning is usually (with some notable exceptions) pauline.[162] As to the johannine language, 'These texts hardly ever play a decisive role in determining Bernard's theological teaching'.[163] Of special significance to our inquiry is the instance of *caro* in Jn 1:14, *et verbum caro factum est*: while Bernard's epistemology relies heavily upon this statement—we know the eternal Word only in the humanity of Christ—the meaning assigned to *caro* is taken from Paul's antinomy of *caro* and *spiritus* (e.g., Rom 1:3–4; 8:4; 1 Cor 1:26), where *caro* means not body but humanity, always with implications of human misery.[164] Bernard does not apply the term to the humanity of the risen Christ, who according to the duality established is entirely *spiritus*.[165]

A question, then, is forced upon us: if Bernard's frequent use of those antitheses which characterize the fourth gospel (especially of light and darkness) is merely a stylistic matter, as distinguished from substantive theological thought, is it possible to claim that his spirituality is significantly colored by johannine dualism? 'Theological doctrine' is a narrower concept than spirituality. There is no tension between the statements that Bernard's theology is dominantly pauline and that his spirituality has a strong johannine slant. Nothing in a good writer is merely a stylistic matter. If one assigns to the province of rhetoric Bernard's penchant for formulating the largest issues in sharp and simple johannine antitheses, can one then claim that this rhetoric plays no major role in bernardine spirituality?

Pauline theology is very accomodating to the spirituality we have been describing. The example of pauline thought we have seen above, the duality of spirit and flesh, is a powerful antithesis. Scholars have pointed to a kind of 'radicalizing' of soteriological doctrine in Paul and have found this drive toward mutually exclusive dualities second only to that of John.[166] It was easy, then, for Bernard to formulate his pauline Christology in the johannine form of light against darkness, the Word against the world, truth against falseness, life against judgment. It is enough to claim that this rhetoric or style establishes for Bernard's thought a major element in its expressiveness and tone. Johannine dualism is not a distinct doctrine in the New Testament; it is a perspective, a viewing of human existence from the point of a particular experience. It is an attitude.

Our question cannot be dismissed as merely technical—a matter of choosing the correct academic drawer for filing bernardine spirituality away. To say that Bernard's doctrine is pauline is to say, among other things, that it conceives the relation of Creator and creation, Redeemer and redeemed, in the radically distinct way of *Spirit* and *flesh*. To say it is johannine is to point, beyond the centrality of love, to the necessity of a simple vital decision for *light* against *darkness*, excluding all ambiguities and delays. In each case, what is sought is the clearest tracing of scriptural roots. In each case too, what is discovered is an insistence upon seeing the human situation in terms of mutually exclusive images. What John adds to Paul is an urgency, a deepening and generalizing of the dualistic exclusivity which is already there.

Bernard does indeed, most frequently, conceptualize the christian kerygma in the special manner of Paul; but, beyond this, I would argue, something in his intimate response to Christ—that pressing sense of a call in all areas of life to a decision of utter clarity and of a growing 'from brightness to brightness' (SC 45.5)—is characteristic of the johannine writings, where the master metaphors coalesce around the starkly differentiated images of light and darkness. Then, whether the dualism observed be thought of as stylistic or formal in some other sense, there can be no doubt that, in its ubiquity, it discloses Bernard's own perceptions and is not simply an extrinsic homiletic ornamentation.

While contending that Bernard's frequent references to John do not determine his 'theological teachings', Farkasfalvy would seem to leave ample room for the effect we are here pointing to when he notes that the 'atmosphere' created by these allusions is 'rich in implications of both a theological and emotional nature'.[167] What Bernard implies through this style, specifically and habitually, should be sought through an awareness of the function it exercises in its source, the fourth gospel. This, I hope, makes clear the necessity of our brief exposition of johannine dualism. Even the pericope on love in 1 Jn 4 is developed, as I have shown, within the context of this dualism—a fact which adds an undercurrent of meaning to Gilson's claim that Bernard's most fundamental 'doctrinal bloc' is johannine.

The severe insistence we have been noticing regarding the discontinuity between alternatives has always been the religious foundation of that approach to the arts which declines to accept aesthetic stimulation, intellectual as well as sensory, as a starting point for the ascent to God. The discontinuity may be associated simply with the gap between good and bad will—i.e., it may be prudential. This insistence underlay the tradition of reform monasticism, of some major reformers of the sixteenth century, of the Puritans, of twentieth-century crisis theology. Something of its truth has been respected even by those whose aesthetics rest upon different principles. Augustine, we have seen, invoked the divine immanence in the world and moved prayerfully to the Creator through the beauty of creation. He saw God's goodness 'participated' to the things of earth and to the creative mind of human beings, and in this he is the traditional apologist of all religious art. Saint Bernard did not propose to his monks this manner of contemplation, though he was augustinian in his understanding of God's presence in the world. The dualism of decision which we have been studying in the fourth gospel—not unknown to Augustine, whose thought included the irreducible duality of the city of God and the city of man—conditioned Bernard's spirituality generally and his aesthetics particularly. Together with all those similarly affected by johannine dualism, or more generally by the dichotomous view of wisdom literature, he belongs to what might be called the 'other' tradition of art—the one that Suger, even as he pretended to adhere to it, recognized as different. Certain attempts to rehabilitate Bernard must be judged as condescending.

Reform monasticism, we remember, conceived itself as within the family of the Fathers of the Desert, those who looked for an alternative to the lost opportunity of physical martyrdom. Try for a moment to imagine these johannine figures speaking the lines of Abbot Suger, who sought in architecture that 'superior, well-tempered harmony' which 'equalizes by proper composition the disparity between things human and divine'.[168] Not likely. And no more likely is it that Bernard and the Cistercians shared a common spirituality and a common aesthetics with the great builders of high romanesque or with Suger and the early gothic.[169] What we find in bernardine literature creates significant tensions within the larger tradition.

Although the expression I take from Scripture scholars, 'johannine dualism', has no vogue in cistercian studies, something of what it intends to label has always been noted. We have pointed out above that Bernard's distinctiveness in the broad tradition of augustinian spirituality—his difference—was a matter not of doctrine but of prudential judgment; that for the abbot the *quaerere Deum* of monasticism was to be interpreted through the Rule's insistence upon a radical simplicity—i.e., upon *haste* along the most *direct* path to God. In our effort to verify that the pattern of Bernard's foundational decisions was johannine, and to clarify what that means, we should not fail to observe that another way of speaking of this radical simplicity is to refer to it as *eschatological.* What can this clarify? How is the johannine eschatological?

Choosing to see the world in black and white, as we learn from his light imagery, was the saint's way of hastening, of not being deterred, as he moved to the great encounter with God. When he reflected upon biblical texts, the level of meaning in which he took greatest delight was the one which regards our final destiny (*quo tendimus*). This anagogical perspective can be made to encompass the whole of human life, and in Saint Bernard the comtemplative it did. Here the end-time (*eschaton*) of eschatology is, not merely a time after death, but a time in which our lives are lived in the risen Christ. Heaven is not only hereafter but now—most especially in the longing expectation of the Bridegroom's visit. Choosing to attend only to the white light of the Word and to see all else as darkness is to cultivate an eschatological consciousness. If we do not relate those decisions of Bernard which become attitudes—e.g., decisions regarding the arts—to this perspective, we misconceive his either-or spirituality, and we fail to appreciate what is going on psychologically in his art.

In a discussion regarding the perils of confusion in the concept *eschatology*, G. B. Caird cites a text which was, incidentally, a favorite of Bernard, found thirty-three times in his works, Rom 13:11–14, where God and this world are characterized as light and darkness. It is Caird's example of an eminently correct view of christian eschatology, having nothing to do (he contends) with an imminent end of the world:

> You know what time it is. . . . the night is far gone, the day is near. Let us then lay aside the works of darkness and put on the armor of light; let us live honorably as in the day . . .

> Put on the Lord Jesus Christ, and make no provision for the flesh, to gratify its desires. (Rom 13:11–14)[170]

The author concludes his study: 'Wherever in the course of time men and women come face to face, whether for judgment or for salvation, with him who is the beginning and the end, that event can be adequately viewed only through the lenses of myth and eschatology'.[170A] On Bernard's contemplative path, coming face to face with the eternal Word occupies all the longing of monks, because he is light, while their involvements in other things concern 'the works of darkness'. In his exposition of the text of Rom 13:11–14, the abbot unfailingly focuses upon its light imagery to communicate the eschatological dimension of his doctrine. It would be helpful to glance at least at the instances which occur in the *Super Cantica*, following the sequence of the sermons.

(1) In sermon fifteen, without quoting the fourth gospel, Bernard develops the statements of Rom 13:12–13 as an example of Jesus' character as light of the world, a lamp to every eye. He assembles around the text several New Testament metaphors of light.[171]

(2) Sermon thirty-three dwells upon the brightness of the Word Incarnate. The sun—the creation and the created condition of Christ—only concealed his rays. The author interprets Rom 13:12, 'The day is near', as meaning that the Word is coming. The sense is clearly a contemplative one, regarding intimate moments of prayer rather than the day of final judgment.[172] (When we put aside the apocalyptic last-day connotation in 'the day is near' and allow present-day relevance to take the foreground, the expression becomes a model statement of traditional monastic understanding of anagogy as found in Bernard.)

(3) A second pericope in sermon thirty-three takes up the theme 'works of darkness' (Rom 13:12–13). These are the bogus splendor put on by many who pursue office in the Church, their ornaments, their painted *objects d'art*, their music, and their drinking.[173]

(4) The 'sleep' from which we must be roused (Rom 13:11) is spoken of in sermon fifty-two not as the physical death from which all will one day rise, but as a state of spirit lacking inner illumination.[174]

(5) We find 'the works of darkness' (Rom 13:12) again in sermon sixty-one. The abbot warns lest this be misunderstood as referring

to the protective shadows found in the Song—'the clefts of the rock' or 'the crannies of the wall'. These works are, instead, our preoccupations with earthly matters.[175]

(6) Sermon seventy-two (which we have looked at already) dwells on the contrast between night and day in Rom 13:11–14. 'The night', says Bernard, 'is the devil. . . . night is the Antichrist. . . . Is not the Lord the day?. . . . He puts the shadows to flight with the brightness of his coming. . . . Finally, when what is perfect comes, what is partial will disappear'.[176] In the author's elaboration, there is a fine fusion of the pauline text with the light imagery and the eschatological urgency of John. Rev 1:1 is cited on 'what must *soon* take place', *quae oportet fieri cito*; and also 1 Jn 2:18: 'Children, it is the last hour! . . . . now Antichrists multiply' (*Filioli, novissima hora est:. . . . et nunc Antichristi multi facti sunt*). This is not a reference to a future age.

This eschatological perspective of Saint Bernard, made evident regularly in the pleasure he takes in the anagogical sense of Scripture and illustrated here in his comments on a pauline text, finds its most frequent and most suitable expression in his manner of manipulating the light imagery of the fourth gospel—in the johannine dualism of light and darkness. At the same time, no reading of the johannine corpus could justify narrowing our interest in it to dualism as a formal feature of the Gospel. Bernard's manner of fusing John and Paul—of linking them by a stylistic element they share—urges the question whether he is johannine in form and pauline in content. Does he find in John the substance of choice, or merely the urgency of choosing? For the past five centuries the christian tradition of the West has been divided in its reflection upon humanity's bonding with the divine: the old Church speaks of a growth in *love*, while the heirs of the great Reformers—forever cautious about tendencies to obscure the extent to which all that is salvific is received—have spoken about accepting the gift of *faith*. In this, the chosen prophet of the Reformation has been Paul; the favorite source of those who speak of the supremacy of love (1 Cor 13 notwithstanding) has been John. It would be perhaps disingenuous to paper over the difference by arguing either that, theologically, faith and love are identical, or that the different languages contain no variance in perception.

The question regarding pauline rather than johannine content—Bernard's manner of conceiving the place of faith and of love—

forces upon us the recognition that the dichotomy of light and darkness refers to two values, polarity (or qualitative discontinuity) and directionality (or quantitative continuity). The first has to do with the decision of faith and is best configured in the image of conversion. In accepting Christ we 'turn around', we move one way rather than the other, its polar opposite. The image permits of no gradations. One could not properly attribute the necessity for faith and decision to one book of the New Tewstament rather than another. Yet, Bernard (with all christian tradition) finds greatest clarity on the role of faith in Paul, even when his chosen language is that of John's antinomy of light and darkness. Directionality, on the other hand, while deriving from polarity, regards the movement that is to follow upon decision. Here darkness is not merely the contrary of light; it is considered as on a quantitative continuum with light: the soul is to move on to ever greater light. In this, *conversion* is a less appropriate model than *growth*. One grows in love; and, after Gilson's exposition of the *schola caritatis*, commentators have generally observed that johannine texts on love hold the center in Bernard's work. The great decision is to be continually reaffirmed, for 'on the road of life not to progress is to regress'.[177] (This is a dominant message in such early works as *The Steps of Humility and Pride* and *On Loving God*.) Directionality here is the coordinate part of polarity in Johannine light imagery.

We must let this large question lie, making only two comments. First, returning full-circle to Gilson's most important 'doctrinal bloc', it seems evident that 1 Jn 4, on love, is the perspective in which Bernard saw the gospel. *What* one is to choose is returning Christ's love progressively or remaining indifferent to it. Second, all the bernardine texts we have seen which reflect upon how monks approach God in prayer narrow the parametars to Christ as sole mediator, to an ascent beginning in the Word made flesh—i.e., to faith. While Bernard's mysticism moves ahead in love from this point, it turns away from every other starting point, such as awe before the things of nature. Our brief account of the johannine character of Bernard's spirituality, of the deep significance of its vocabulary of light, can lead those with a specialized interest in cistercian art to recognize the fact that this imagery, probably more than any other stylistic constituent, will satisfyingly bridge the divide between two cistercian media, literature and architecture.

Cistercian Art, an Expression of Bernard's Johannine Dualism

Without pretending to the kind of analysis that a firm grip on architectural history could make possible—the history of a specific building in an historical setting—let me suggest, with very few and briefly considered examples, the kind of clarification that Bernard's literary manner with light imagery can bring to cistercian architecture. The fact that not everything we observe pertained to the Cistercians alone should lead us to further inquiries into the history of that reformed monasticism of which the Cistercians were the maturation; it does not invalidate our obervations. The johannine dichotomous point of view offers us a series of dualities in accord with which we may attempt a reading of Saint Bernard's abbey church.

It is not necessary to assume that the man we think of as responsible for 'Cistercian architecture' personally engineered its defining solutions. For our purposes, it is enough to claim that he oversaw and approved what those who had absorbed his spirit must have proposed and built.

Like *light-darkness*, *inside-outside* is a dichotomous construct usable for setting up a perspective, applicable especially well, for example, to the walls of the oratory. Light, obviously, enters the building from *outside*. Other elements of the program declare themselves when viewed in the perspective of *upper-lower*, *heaven-earth*, *now-then* (with Bernard's special *interim*), *Spirit-flesh*, *image-likeness*. Always, what is of aesthetic interest is the mutually exclusive nature of the two terms of the duality, the refusal to reconcile opposites, to make accomodations in the name of continuity. Bernard's light imagery leads us to posit that, in architecture, a cistercian solution is one which contrives to manipulate visual elements in such a way as to create an environment suggestive of these dualities.

Perhaps color is the most arresting example: between light and darkness there is no dionysian hierarchy of being, no intermediate realities qualitatively different; there are only degrees of brightness. The spectrum of color, in so far as it graduates light into a continuum of kinds, is the metaphor for a contrary view of the world. We can link this perception to cistercian illuminated manuscripts after about 1150: General Chapter had decided they should be 'of one color'.[177A] This is usually applied to the rejection of colored glass.

In that dimension of Bernard's spirituality which his light imagery opens to us, we see 'spiritual' reasons that cannot be separated from the specifically aesthetic reasons why Bernard stood apart from Suger's mystique of color; and, emphatically to our point, we are led into discovering the aesthetic strength he saw in his own architectural program, in his world of black and white.

It must be said in passing that if we speak of Bernard's decisions in this matter as 'asceticism', we must expand that concept beyond the stereotype of exercises in penance or self-improvement, because in the abbot there is no divide between asceticism and contemplation.[178] This builder, as known through his writings, is not interested in 'giving up' beauty but in turning toward that quiet inner emptiness where the white light of divine beauty can be more easily received. The literary evidence that he thought of the oratory as an image of the monk's soul—the more interiorizing and intimate element of the Heavenly Jerusalem typology—is abundant.[179] The soul is made in the image of God and, even after losing the divine likeness through sin retains its essential beauty. Corresponding to it, a material house of God would have to be beautiful, even while accepting that discipline which the lost likeness makes appropriate to the soul—the emptying out, the silencing, the enlarging.

What we see of asceticism in the oratory, its poverty, reflects a condition believed appropriate to the soul. While it is true that this concerns the avoidance of all pampering of the flesh (e.g., sensory displays) and a sharing of this world's good with the needy, the deeper truth is that these objectives are conditions for rendering the soul free for prayer. Only awareness of this last real purpose offers clues to something aesthetically positive about the building. Now we become sensitive to that darkness which is the human Christ, the darkness of faith, which alone opens us to the divine light of the Word. The dramatic shaft of white light bursting through a high window is only an environmental suggestion of the divine Spouse's desire to visit, when he chooses, to enter the soul empty of material and spiritual pretentions. The emptiness of the building fosters consciousness of another world, creates an air of expectancy. Only knowledge of the meaning asceticism has for Bernard can suggest *what* is here to be expected.

Like poverty, the cistercian norm of practicality must not be abandoned to those who would see it as the denial of aesthetic meaning. Planning the oratory had to be practical, functional; but one can appreciate the extent to which this end was achieved only through an understanding of the function which the building was to house. Our exploration of the place of prayer in Bernard's life and of the character of his prayer—his kind of contemplation—pertains to the question of practicality. Of central concern is the over-all effect of the building, the experience it fosters as an ensemble. Leclercq concludes that in Bernard's aesthetics only this mattered. The chant, for example, was good, not when it satisfied certain ideological norms, but when it made the singer prayerful; and writing was well done, not when the rules were meticulously followed, but when, in sum, it was pleasing.[180] The monastery church, then, would be practical when it was an authentic *oratorium*, fostering the *praxis* for which it had been envisioned.

We cannot leave the topic of artistic asceticism without asking why Bernard does not strip down language the way he does the other arts. Bernard is biblical in a sense that, perhaps, has not been sufficiently clarified. Not only does he move *toward* the Scriptures—seeking, for example, the contemplative starting point we have spoken of; he *moves from* the Scriptures, with a mind-set originating within the culture of the sacred writers. He represents an impetus originating in the Scriptures. Gerhard von Rad, after surveying the Chosen People's achievements in art, concludes that 'Israel's artistic charisma' is the *word*, that they 'lacked all critical reflection on the phenomenon of beauty and on artistic reproduction as such'.[181] Bernard is as striking an example as can be found of a biblical bias in the arts.[182] When the augustinian tradition moves away from this—in metaphysics or in cosmological mysticism—Bernard resists it.

But, let us return to fenestration. First, the absence of clerestory windows in a Cistercian oratory lends emphasis to the East-West directionality of the lighting, the orienting of the church. This, together with the low placement of smaller windows in the transverse bays of the aisles (as at Fontenay)—they are beneath the level of all the west-end windows—causes all the interior contours to be edged in white light. Each dark volume is made discreet by the etching of its borders. The deep-shadow areas of the oratory had their meaning, the meaning of shadows in Bernard's spirituality, and were not merely tolerated as something which available technology could not overcome.

Looking for facile lexical equivalents of such shadows in Bernard's text, however, is the wrong method. The interpretation of any image in isolation is hazardous. In our efforts to be put in touch with our response to the oratory building we must not be deterred by Bernard's capacity to make a figure in the Scriptures 'mean' anything he happens to need in fleshing out his argument. There are incidental meanings (as in SC 62.1, where the wall, made up of many stones, means the communion of saints), and there are systematic meanings—those that are repeated and become part of a consistent image complex. What matters is the vision that emerges from the larger context of the saint's work.

Consider the framing of the window openings: in some churches, like Le Thoronet and Bonmont, there is none at all; the stone perimeters of a small rose window (the *oculus*) are completely unsculpted, creating the sence of a violent entry of light—white light, rushing through a hole in the thick wall rather than through a window calculated to receive it, penetrating the darkness of the interior—not dissipated, modulated, or controled—an image of two graphically distinguished worlds, inside and outside.

Or, consider the treatment that a large church, like Pontigny, gives the uncolored roses of the transepts: a set of slender engaged columns stands at either side of the opening. While one cannot say with confidence what such a detail 'means', it can rouse us to remembering something of the light imagery of Bernard's spirituality, and at that point the simple columns take on the formal function of expectant sentinals, or of candlesticks, flanking the highest solemn entranceway of white light. Such arrangements seem to lay stress on an inside-outside feeling, rather than to blur it, as the gothic window sets out to do. This determination to separate darkness from light, inside from outside, is, I think, the expression of a spirituality based on johannine antinomies.

If light is God and darkness is humanity, then windows are the portals of the divine and walls are the confinement of the human. In a building where color is banned as a mere surface phenomenon, the walls are not ornamented with tapestries or paintings; the surface spaces are not articulated through systems of responds and recessed geometrical areas. If the ambition of the gothic builder was to thin the wall, lighten it, and have it recede indefinitely, the cistercian builder of the golden age was content to accept the wall, almost to call attention to its mass (as becomes evident in some cloister arcades), and to emphasize its character as enfolding and containing. One may suspect that the heaviness of cistercian walls signifies our humanity, particularly the body. It would be an insightful suspicion, for the author of the *Super Cantica* spoke that way: he envisioned the Bridegroom as beyond the wall of our flesh but coming towards it for a visit. 'Our flesh is the wall', he wrote, speaking of our creatureliness.[183] In another place we read, 'As long as this mere crumbling wall of the body stands, this ray of intense brightness will pour itself in, not through open doors, but through chinks and crevices'.[184] (The *oculus* of Le Thoronet is a 'chink' in the armor of its darkness.) Nevertheless, the cistercian wall is of noble substance and carefully crafted, even as the human being, despite the darkness of its dissimilitude, is made in the image of the Light, and therefore capable of welcoming the light.

Bernard writes, in metaphors of light and darkness, about the spiritual duality of the soul's imperishable image and its lost likeness, and, in a building of physical light and darkness, he gives this duality plastic form. Is not the oratory, like the soul, 'dark but beautiful' (*nigra . . . sed formosa*)? The experience of the building, as the abbot wished it to be, can be put in his own words: 'How lowly! Yet, how sublime! . . . an earthly tent and a heavenly palace . . . a body doomed to death and a temple bright with light . . . She is black but beautiful' (Song 1:4).[185]

No sooner have we said that something in the oratory 'signifies' something else than we must retract the statement. To claim symbolic meaning for anything here is to struggle against what seems rather obvious in the intentions behind cistercian building legislation: no part of the building is to call attention to itself. Let us say, then, with respect to any element of the oratory, that the builder hoped to draw foreseeable affective responses to his work along the lines of the spirituality expressed in the work. If we say the building tended to tranquilize the praying monk and to turn him in on himself, we mean it did this through the creation of an atmosphere rather than through any object or part.[186] One can well ask how a particular element contributed to such an atmosphere. Certainly, sentinels or candlesticks flanking transept rose windows, the wall of the flesh, and the darkness of our humanity are all overly specific metaphors and have a ring of arbitrariness. But they are simply efforts to form a literary transposition of a building which can correctly be assumed to match *in some way* a literarily recorded spirituality. Although that way will not amount to the translation of one medium into another—the comparisons affirmed must be immediately denied—it can assist in giving content in a specific instance to what has been called the symbolic power of forms.[187]

As an expression of bernadine spirituality, the romanesque thickness, heaviness, and plainness of the cistercian oratory walls communicate their shadows and enclosure to us easily. Bernard's builders vested these plain surfaces and the volumes they defined with a feeling that imposes itself on those who respond to them for what they concretely are, rather than as to a preliminary stage in the technological march toward the gothic. An evolutionistic formalism blunts our capacity to respond just as surely as the unmonitored reaching for literary equivalents.

The discontinuity of black and white provides the key to a feature of cistercian architecture which of itself is not an image of light.[188] Characteristic of the oratory is the way engaged columns leading downward from the vaults end abruptly on the wall and are 'supported' by a wall brace called a corbel. At Fontenay a different solution creates the same effect: the columns above the nave arcade end on a massive and ostentatiously terminal base, that member which 'grounds' a column. Here, instead, this bottom or ending of the engaged column supporting the vault remains high above the floor. Why forego the effect, both charming and monumental, of the gothic nave, where the responds seem to grow out of the earth and spread like branches from the springing of the vault? Because something of this dwelling place of the Word is from *above* and is not to be perceived as from the earth *below*. One might attempt being more specific, speaking of the divine image as distinguished from the lost likeness, of the soul as distinguished from the body, but that would be to go beyond (and therefore outside of) the effect envisioned. In this temple, 'both lowly and sublime' (SC 27.11), the *below* is discontinuous with the *above*, even as black is with white.

Several things, then, have come to our attention which can be enlisted as evidence in support of the argument that the oratory embodies meanings literarily expressed in johannine dichotomous light imagery. We have observed the borders of deep-shadow volumes defined in light, the mural values which so bluntly lock the outside away from the inside, the window treatment which emphasizes privation of the light, and the configuration of responds which keep apart rather than join the vault and the floor. We may well feel inclined to entertain the hypothesis that, what is being suggested by such things taken together (again, environmentally) is the unbridgeable separateness of opposites, both ontological and moral. The cistercian oratory, in this view, embodies what we may call the johannine principle of discontinuity.

We have seen, however, that a static polarity does not exhaust the content of Bernard's johannine vision. How does cistercian architecture represent the dynamic directionality consequent upon this—i.e., how does the building speak for the possibility of spiritual growth? A necessary preface to any attempt at an answer must be that in Bernard, as in the Bible generally, uses of *darkness* referring to anything other than the absence of light are merely instances of extended meanings (see the discussion of Song 2:17, from SC 72, above). Otherwise, Bernard could not read black shadows and white light on a quantitative continuum, as he does. As it is, however, the temple receiving the Word is not only beautiful but black (Song 1:5), a self-contradictory condition in any world of meaning other than one in which darkness is itself but a relatively low degree of light.

In the world of the oratory, Christ himself is a darkness (*umbra*) as is also the holy soul (*nigra sed formosa*) still struggling *in carne*; and the white light entering the building is the promise of a vision that pertains to the blessed, anticipated in the contemplative monk's desire. The decision at Fontenay to open as much window space in the east-end as the structure would allow and to place windows in the west-end only in the upper half of the wall results in a concentration of light upon the front area of the nave (on the stalls of the choir monks) and in an illumination of the vault. Should one insist upon a reductionist explanation here, refusing any openness to spiritual meanings because 'functional' reasons are available? We would do well to say no, acknowledging the suggestiveness of a lighting arrangement in which the light of the divine Spouse was situated at the site of prayer, where the soul could, in intention, move from the shadow of Christ's humanity to the light which he inhabited as risen Lord.

Perhaps also the glazing of the oratory windows, in the monochrome gray of the grisailles studied by Helen Zakin, spoke of degrees of light and darkness—not in isolation, but as a midpoint in the range of brightness.[189]

Without this dynamic dimension in the johannine duality, as Bernard reads it, not only would cistercian spirituality be falsified in the dichotomy of black and white—deprived of an image of growth—but the oratory could not come to the mature architectural integration one discovers in it.

Finding the meaning of light in cistercian architecture cannot be an attempt to restate a building in literary terms. We will not arrive at meaning by identifying the tenor of what is judged, all too questionably, to be a symbol.[190] Always, in the arts, the *what* is known only through the *how*; content, we are forever reminded, cannot be isolated from style. Our aesthetic perceptions will not be greatly aided by the information that light stands for God, for his presence, for grace, or for Truth. We need, beyond this, to observe *how* what stands for God is made to relate to what stands for the not-God. We must notice the arrangements determining a characteristic relationship between light and darkness. Just as in the abbot's writings this stylistic analysis is undertaken with the aid of literary discipline—theological curiosity is not enough—so in the architecture which he oversaw the study of style requires (I am not slow to concede) disciplined art criticism. And yet, knowing how he expressed himself in one art—knowing what we might call his literary spirituality—will be of great assistance in discerning his architectural spirituality—e.g., in corroborating a reading of his buildings, or (more dangerously) in supplying artistic hypotheses for approaching them. Saint Bernard possessed but one imagination.

Nothing in a cistercian oratory means anything, I suspect, except as a contribution to the building's effect. When we describe this effect (or, better, undergo it) with historical correctness—the experience of now which reproduces the experience of then—we shall speak, coincidentally (as it were), out of the text of Bernard's johannine spirituality. Having responded sensitively to the oratory's style of illumination, we knew already the mind of the builder, which is also recorded in his spiritual writings.

CONCLUSION

The effectiveness with which cistercian architecture induces a consciousness of something awesomely simple at the core of human life can lead one to a surer reading of Bernard's text.

The imagery of black and white safeguarded a disposition at the heart of this saint's spirituality. The profound significance given by others to graduated color expressed a contrary ideal and experience. One side spoke for the exclusiveness of decision, the denials inherent in every affirmation. The other clung to the inclusiveness of vision, the grateful awareness of all God's gifts. (The saint's black and white was itself visionary, but in a manner that bound it to the decision of love.) While it is true that Bernard made his case in the name of monasticism, it would be a dangerous evasion to decline further evaluation. Leclercq defined monastic life as 'une forme de vie religieuse qui n'a pas de fin sécondaire'.[191] There can be, however, no multiplicity of *primary* ends in any form of religious life. The will to eliminate painful choices through cultivated thinking must be reliquished. The monastic vision will always be a point of recall, a witness to the necessity of certain exclusions. Leclercq continues: 'C'est cet exclusivisme . . . qui détermine les éléments distinctifs de la spiritualité monastique'.[192] The spiritualities of black and white and of color are coordinates, separated only by a line of necessity known in experience. Here one accepts the truth, not choosing but being chosen.

Much of the meaning of Bernard's imagery of black and white, of light and darkness, centered upon his style of prayer. He believed monks should advance to a mystical encounter with God free of all earthly images. Again, Leclercq defines the situation: 'À deux milieux de vie ont répondu deux modes differents de réflexion religieuse'.[193] The *theologia* of monks (from the origins of their tradition) was a style of prayer that moved to contemplation.[194] But, since this is the path of the advanced, we are left with the necessity of beginnings that are closer to the earth.[195] The contrast in the two systems of light imagery regards an abstract directionality. In concrete experience, all good souls will find themselves from time to time in Bernard's world of black and white.

The fact that prayer conditioned Bernard's elimination of color makes clear that his policies were oriented to vision as well as to decision. Suger's reflection on variety in color was that this spoke for the multiplicity of God's powers in creation. Bernard would have thought of this as theoretically correct but, for himself personally, practically unmanageable. The reasons in aesthetics why one might at times prefer a scheme of black and white may not be different from the reasons in spirituality why the Cistercians banned color in the oratory. Since visual reality is more multiform than is dreamed of in your philosophy, to 'see' anything appreciatively one must limit what is to be looked at. One pleased in the vision of black and white has chosen terminals within which variety can be measured and the measure enjoyed. The Dionysian intuition is correct: different colors show many things, black and white show the range of one thing. The range regards light in itself, in the wholeness of white, or in brightness as such. The ascetical choice—an exercise in the economy of means—is accounted for, ultimately as ambition rather than renunciation.

As to the inclusiveness of Bernard's appreciation of human experience, we must rest content in the awareness that he does not condemn what he turns away from. Nothing is so significant and seminal in his spirituality as his respect for experience:[196] we are to respond to God, not as declaring principles and formulating commandments, but as speaking intimately to us in the reality of our lives. On the one hand, there is the full array of human possibilities, the chromatic splendor of creation; on the other, there is the concrete truth of the limited and wounded individual soul. We choose in the end, not according to norms, but according to our vision of the right fit: 'All things are lawful', Bernard explains, 'but not everything is to be recommended'.[197] His spirituality defines a direction for the monk, but describes as well something of the truth of the human condition as such. In the crisis of decision, Saint Bernard believes, the splendid variety of cosmic color fades away revealing a clean demarcation between darkness and light; under pressure of the desire for ultimate beauty, the color of the surface world may yield to the truth of black and white.

NOTES

1. Erwin Panofsky, *Abbot Suger and the Abbey Church of Saint-Denis and Its Art Treasures*, 2nd ed. Gerda Panofsky-Soergel (Princeton: Princeton University Press,

1979) 26: 'Suger had the good fortune to discover, in the very words of the thrice-blessed Saint Denis, a Christian philosophy that permitted him to greet material beauty as a vehicle of spiritual beatitude instead of forcing him to flee from it as though from a temptation; and to conceive of the moral as well as the physical universe, not as a monochrome in black and white but as a harmony of many colors.' In this volume, Panofsky translates and comments on *Sugerii abbatis Sancti Dionysii liber de rebus in administratione sua gestis* [hereafter *Adm.*], which he dates 1144–1149, and *Libellus alter de consecratione ecclesiae sancti Dionysii* [hereafter *Cons.*] which is dated to 1144–1147. References hereafter will cite chapter and page number.

2. It is not helpful to pretend that asceticism is an unproblematic concept. In 'Ascèse, ascétisme,' *Dictionnaire de Spiritualité* [DSp], J. De Guibert laments a poverty in Catholic theology on the general theory of asceticism (col. 1001). In 'Asceticism', in Karl Rahner, et al., *Sacramentum Mundi: An Encyclopedia of Theology*, 6 vols. (New York: Herder and Herder, 1968–70) 1:110–116, Friedrich Wulf distinguishes between moral and mystical asceticism, showing how they cannot be separated, but concedes that 'The traditional [in a quantitative sense] Catholic view places the main emphasis on moral asceticism' (p. 111). The ascetical element in cistercian spirituality and art, however, is (as we shall see) dominantly mystical.

3. For example, Otto von Simson, *The Gothic Cathedral: Origins of Gothic Architecture and the Medieval Concept of Order* (New York: Pantheon Books, 1962), studies Suger, seeking 'the vision in which the cathedral originated' (p. xix).

4. Conrad Rudolph, 'The "Principal Founders" and the Early Artistic Legislation of Cîteaux,' in Meredith Parsons Lillich, ed. *Studies in Cistercian Art and Architecture*, Vol. 3, CS 89 (Kalamazoo, Mich.: Cistercian Publications, 1987) 1–45, esp. pp. 12–21. The author describes the situation in which Bernard was 'in legislative control' (p. 13) and was therefore 'the moral author' of the artistic legislation of the Order. Also, Conrad Rudolph, *The 'Things of Greater Importance': Bernard of Clairvaux's Apologia and the Medieval Attitude Toward Art* (Philadelphia: University of Pennsylvania Press, 1990) 193–201. Rudolph inquires into Bernard's motives for 'artistic asceticism' and demonstrates that what the saint saw as threatened in the 'luxurious art' (p. 7) of the era were the very foundations of monasticism. The author's understanding of Bernard's asceticism goes well beyond that conventional acceptance here referred to. I would like, nevertheless, to explore further what would perhaps fall under Bernard's 'internal spiritual objections' (p. 200) to some common monastic building practices, specifically those involving the use of color.

5. Jean Leclercq, 'Un guide de la lecture pour St. Bernard,' *La Vie Spirituelle* 102 (1960) 440–47, at p. 440. Other works of Leclercq referred to in this study, besides the critical edition of Saint Bernard (cited below), are the following: *The Love of Learning and the Desire for God: A Study of Monastic Culture* (New York: Fordham University Press, 1961); *Études sur le vocabulaire monastique du moyen âge* (Rome, 1961); 'Théologie traditionelle et théologie monastique,' *Irénikon*, 37/1 (1964) 50–74; 'La crise du monachisme aux XIe et XIIe siècles,' *Aux sources de la spiritualité occidentale: étapes et constantes* (Paris, 1964) 175–99; 'Les caractéristiques de la spiritualité monastique,' *Aux sources*, 306–312; *Témoins de la spiritualité occidentale* (Paris: Cerf, 1965); 'Essais sur l'esthétique de S. Bernard,' *Studi medievali* 9 (1968) 688–728; 'S. Bernard, théologien de la vie Cistercienne,' *Collectanea Cisterciensia* 30 (1968) 245–271; 'Saint Bernard et l'Écriture Sainte' in *Saint Bernard mystique* (Paris, 1948) 483–489; *Saint Bernard et le 12e siècle monastique: Écriture Sainte et*

vie spirituelle, DSp 4 (1958) col. 187–194; 'Saint Bernard et la tradition biblique d'après les Sermons sur le Cantique,' *Sacris Erudiri* 9 (1960) 225–248.

6. We will speak of pseudo-Dionysius simply as Dionysius. For the larger context of dionysian thought, see Frederick Copleston, SJ, *A History of Philosphy, Vol. 2: Medieval Philosophy, Part 1: Augustine to Bonaventure* (1950; Garden City, NY: Doubleday, Image Books, 1962) 106–115. The philosopher-theologian embodies many ideas of the fifth-century Neoplatonist Proclus; that he was probably a syrian ecclesiastic is 'reasonable' (p. 108). For an analysis of dionysian mysticism (and for a current bibliography), see Bernard McGinn, *The Foundations of Mysticism*, Vol. 1 of *The Presence of God: A History of Western Christian Mysticism*, 4 vols. (New York: Crossroad, 1991) pp. 157–182, 388–395; for differences between Augustine and Dionysius, pp. 158, 161, 169, 171; also Paul Rorem, 'The Uplifting Spirituality of Pseudo-Dionysius,' in Bernard McGinn and John Meyendorff, eds. *Christian Spirituality: Origins to the Twelfth Century*, Vol. 16 of World Spirituality (New York: Crossroad, 1986) 132–151.

7. On the growing fascination with light as symbol in the era, see Edgar DeBruyne, *Études d'esthétique médiévale*, 3 vols. (Bruges: De Tempel, 1946) 3:37.

8. I have studied this in 'Metaphysics in the Prayer of St. Augustine,' *Congresso Internazionale su S. Agostino nel XVI Centenario della Conversione, Rome, 15–20 settembre 1986, Atti II; Studia Ephemeridis 'Augustianum'* (Rome, 1987) 59–77.

9. For 'the vision . . .' see Von Simson in n. 3, above. This author's case for a dionysian inspiration in the gothic is wholly circumstantial and, I believe, largely creditable. In developing his proposition (pp. 102–111) that the works of Suger betray 'a definite metaphysical system' (p. 102), the author surveys the situation of the times, turning up truly suggestive elements. The effort is so valuable that one wants to close an eye to the excessive degree to which Von Simson reads the dionysian system in Suger's very text and concludes accordingly that it was the principal influence upon the Gothic. When the same method is used to bring Saint Bernard into the gothic synthesis, however, it collapses. The author, strangely reversing his field, forces himself into the untenable position (p. 43) of having to discourage those who would understand the spirituality of Bernard in relation to his art from giving great weight to the saint's writings, especially the *Apologia*. On the other hand, Conrad Rudolph, *Artistic Change at St.-Denis: Abbot Suger's Program and the Early Twelfth-Century Controversy over Art* (Princeton, NJ: Princeton University Press, 1990) pp. 51, 70, rejects Von Simson's claim that Suger's writings betray the influence of Dionysius and concludes rhetorically: 'What is Pseudo-Dionysian about Suger's art program?' (p. 50) Perhaps there is a commonality between moving, on the one hand, from the hypothesis that Suger's gothic manifests the influence of Dionysius to the conclusion that his *text* can demonstrate this and, on the other hand, moving from the demonstration that Suger's *text* does not reveal a significant knowledge of the dionysian system to the conclusion that his art program is not dionysian. A writer like Suger, whose philosophical exposition is tainted, as Rudolph shows, by political objectives and whose analytic talent is obviously slight cannot be counted on to lead us to the wellsprings of his creation. Artists can be inarticulate. After careful exploration, one must conclude that Suger's text offers very limited access to his art.

10. *Unde, cum ex dilectione decoris domus Dei aliquando multicolor, gemmarum speciositas ab exintrinsecis me curis devocaret, . . . videor videre me quasi sub aliqua extranea orbis terrarum plaga, . . . demorari, ab hac etiam inferiori ad illam superiorem anagogico more Deo donante posse transferri.* (*Adm.* 33, pp. 62–64) Panofsky (p. 21) explains that the

notion of anagogy here, taken from the phrase of Eriugena, refers to a movement from the material to the immaterial world. The traditional *anagogia*, instead, had to do with the eternal destiny of humans, *quo tendimus*—as, for example, in the works of Saint Bernard. On the dionysian language of Eriugena, see Panofsky, p. 21.

11. Adm 33, p. 62: *sanctarum etiam diversitatem virtutum.*

12. Conrad Rudolph, *Artistic Change at St-Denis*, p. 75. The author sees 'the pressure of the opposition Suger faced' as accounting for much in the literary presentation of Saint Denis to the public.

13. Grover A. Zinn, Jr., 'Suger, Theology, and the Pseudo-Dionysian Tradition,' in Paula L. Gerson, ed., *Abbot Suger and Saint-Denis, A Symposium* (New York: Metropolitan Museum of Art, 1986; Abrams, 1988), 33–40, finds close correspondence between the language of Suger's poem for the gilt-bronze doors of the west façade's central portal and the thought of Hugh of Saint Victor (p. 36). Hugh at times represents Pseudo-Dionysius as the source of his thought though it is Hugh's own (p. 35, nn. 24, 25). Rudolph, *Artistic Change at St-Denis*, argues for a participation by Hugh in Suger's art program 'far more direct . . . and far more fundamental than just the area of Pseudo-Dionysian light mysticism alone' (p. 33).

14. Panofsky 19. A good example of the hypothetical approach is M. F. Hearn, *Romanesque Sculpture: The Revival of Monumental Stone Sculpture in the Eleventh and Twelfth Centuries* (Cornell University Press, 1980) 169–175, and esp. 187–189, where the author builds a plausible argument for dionysian influence upon romanesque sculpture by demonstrating the interpretive power of dionysian doctrines (his hypothesis) when applied to specific works.

15. *Adm.* 31, p. 54: . . . *gemmarum preciosarum multiplicem copiam, jacinctorum, rubetorum, saphirorum, smaragdinum, topaziorum necnon et opus discriminantium unionum.*

16. The sight of these reminds Suger of Ezechiel 28:13: *Omnis*, inquam, *lapis preciosus operimentum tuum, sardius, topazius, jaspis, crisolitus, onix et berillus, saphirus, carbunculus et smaragdus.* He is pleased to find all of these there, except the carbuncle. (*Adm.* 33, p. 62).

17. *Adm.* 33, p. 60: *Collateralibus quidem candelabra viginti marcarum auri . . . ibidem deponentes, jacintos, smaragdines, quascumque gemmas preciosas apposuimus, et apponendas diligenter quaeritare decrevimus.*

18. *Adm.* 32, p. 56: *Hinc est quod preciosarum margaritarum gemmarumque copiam circumquaque per nos et per nuncios nostros quaeritantes, quam preciosiorem in auro et gemmis tanto ornatui materiam invenire potuimus.*

19. *Adm.* 34A, p. 78: *Comparavimus etiam praefati altaris officiis calicem preciosum, de uno et continuo sardonice. . . .*

20. *Adm.* 34A, p. 78: . . . *in eodem vase, gemmis auroque ornato. Adm.* 34 A, p. 78: *Vas quoque aliud, huic ipsi materia . . . cujus versiculi sunt isti: Dum libare Deo gemmis debemus et auro, Hoc ego Suggerius offero vas Domino.*

21. *Adm.* 34A, p. 78: *Et versus hujusmodi eidem vasi inscribi fecimus: Includi gemmis lapis iste meretur et auro. . . .*

22. 'And we gave orders carefully to look out for others to be added further': *Et apponendas diligenter quaeritare decrevimus.* (*Adm.* 33, pp. 60–61)

23. E. H. Gombrich, *The Story of Art*, 15th ed. (Englewood Cliffs, N.J.: Prentice Hall, 1989) 138.

24. Lynn Thorndike, 'Some Medieval Texts on Colours,' *Ambix: The Journal of the Society for the Study of Alchemy and Early Chemistry* (Cambridge) 7 (February

1959) 1–24: In western alchemic tradition, the change of materials rises through four stages, each manifested in a different color.

25. Frank Burch Brown, *Religious Aesthetics: A Theological Study of Making and Meaning* (Princeton: Princeton Univeristy Press, 1989) 118. The author speaks here of Dionysius' language on the luminous 'super-essential darkness' that is God.

26. In a statement like the following, for example, one notices (precisely in a passage given to engineering details) the absence of any reference to that complex of solutions which makes the large windows possible: ' . . . that elegant and praiseworthy extension, in [the form of] a circular string of chapels, by virtue of which the whole [church] would shine with the wonderful and uninterrupted light of most luminous windows, pervading the interior beauty' (. . . *illo urbano et approbato in circuitu oratoriorum incremento, quo tota clarissimarum vitrearum luce mirabili et continua interiorem perlustrante pulchritudienem eniteret*): *Cons.* 4, pp. 100–101. We would be gratified to read how it became possible to make the light of the windows *continua*, because that is a critical merit in the builder.

27. Von Simson, pp. 96–102, discusses the question, 'To what extent was Suger himself responsible for Saint-Denis?' After reviewing relationships among patrons, technicians, and artisans in the twelfth century, and pointing to Suger's uncommon knowledge of architectural engineering, the author accepts the view that the abbot himself was 'the "leader" of the great enterprise.' He concretizes this: those who assisted Suger bore the relationship of contractors to 'the modern architect' (p. 98). This seems, however, an extremely generous and somewhat gratuitous specification of the abbot's 'leadership.' Cf. Bill Risebero, *The Story of Western Architecture* (Cambridge, Mass.: MIT Press, 1979) 61–62. From awareness of what was achieved at Saint Denis, in point of both technique and novelty of design, and of the larger currents of the age, Risebero would deny Suger the role of architect.

28. Hugh of Saint Victor, commenting upon his dionysian text, refers to the way a complex of many different things may suddenly coalesce into a unity suggestive of the divine: 'There is a kind of similitude . . . in which certain glances, as it were, at different likenesses produce a single image' (*Est tamen aliqua similitudo . . . in qua quasi speculamina quaedam diversorum proportionum unam imaginem effingunt*). *Expositio in hierarchiam caelestem* 2; PL 175:948. Cited (at greater length) in Von Simson, p. 121, n. 87.

29. See n. 10, above.

30. Von Simson, pp. 120–121, and n. 87. Although the author's case is more inferential than he acknowledges, his extended quotations from Hugh of Saint Victor suggest powerfully that Hugh indeed envisioned the stained glass window as a demonstration of dionysian theory.

31. M.-D. Chenu, OP, *Nature, Man, and Society in the Twelfth Century: Essays on New Theological Perspectives in the Latin West*, trans. Jerome Taylor (Chicago: University of Chicago Press, 1968). See 'The Symbolist Mentality,' pp. 99–145, at pp. 129 and 130.

32. Chenu, *Nature, Man, and Society*, p. 130.

33. The thesis is traced through the works of Dionysius in Étienne Gilson, *History of Christian Philosophy in the Middle Ages* (New York: Random House, 1955) p. 83, documented on pp. 597–598—e.g., *De coelesti hierchia* 3.1; 3.2 (PG 3:164–165).

34. The theme is developed in the opening long paragraph of *De consecratione* (*Cons.* 1, pp. 82–85).

35. Risebero, *The Story of Western Architecture*, p. 62.

36. M.-M. Davy, *Initiation à la symbolique romane (XIIe Siècle)*, Nouvelle Edition (Paris: Flammarion, 1977) p. 52, quotes from M.-M. Davy ed., *Guillaume de St Thierry, Commentaire sur le Cantique des Cantiques* 142 (Paris: 1958) 176–177.

37. *Commentaire sur le Cantique*, 83, No. 54, quoted in Davy, *Initiation*, p. 52.

38. Quoted in M.-M. Davy and I. P. Renneteau, 'La lumière dans le Christianisme,' Book 2 of M.-M. Davy et al., *Le thème de la lumière dans le Judaïsme, le Christianisme, et l'Islam* (Paris: Berg, 1976) p. 237.

39. Aelred of Rievaulx, *A Rule of Life for a Recluse*, trans. Mary Paul Macpherson OCSO, in *Aelred of Rievaulx: Treatises & The Pastoral Prayer*, CF 2 (Kalamazoo: Cistercian Publications, 1971) p. 71.

40. Davy and Renneteau 237, quoting *Guerric d'Igny, III[e] sermon pour l'Epiphanie*, trans. John Morson and Hilary Costello (Paris: 1970) p. 275.

41. *Tractatus ascetici*, I, 7; PL 184:256B; quoted in Davy, *Initiation*, 53.

42. *A Rule of Life for a Recluse*, 72.

43. Apo 12, in Jean Leclercq and H. M. Rochais, edd. *S. Bernardi Opera*, [SBOp], 8 Vols. (Rome: Editiones Cistercienses, 1957–1977) Vol 3:105, 17–18.

44. Mor 42.8: SBOp 7:107,5: *Nam quae videntur in abscondito nullis apparent fucata coloribus.*

45. Quad 2.6; SBOp 4:363,23–24: *Hinc nempe virtutum perseverantia, hinc conversationis pulchrae discolor unitas.*

46. SC 31.6; SBOp 1:223,17–18: *grata quippe amoris munere, non colore.*

47. SC 74.5; SBOp 2:242,24: *sane per oculos non intravit, quia non est coloratum.*

48. SC 25.6; SBOp 1:167,3: *non facies colorata vicina putredini.*

49. SC 40.1; SBOp 2:24,15: *vide autem ne carnaliter cogites colorata carnis putrdinem.*

50. SC 71.3; SBOp 2:216: *adverte qualis color tristitiae seu invidiae sit, qui Dei a se avertit aspectus.*

51. SC 31.6; SBOp 1:223,17–18: *grata quippe amoris munere, non colore.*

52. SC 82.4; SBOp 2:294–295: *Quid tu animae tuae alteram formam, immo deformitatem, imprimis alienam? Enim vero quod delectat habere, id etiam perdere timet; et timor color est. Is libertatem, dum tingit, tegit, et eam nihilominus sibimet reddit dissimilem.*

53. Jean Leclercq, 'Essais sur l'esthétique de S. Bernard', p. 696. Regarding this experience of inner struggle, the author remarks: 'All his theology is but a reflection . . . on this primary datum' (p. 696). In *The Love of Learning* (pp. 37–41), Leclercq explains *compunctio*, and traces it to Gregory the Great. He advances the discussion in 'S. Bernard et l'expérience chrétienne' (pp. 261–275): in Bernard, one follows the soul's passage from the consciousness of sin to the embrace of hope.

54. This unit continues the anthropological reflections begun in SC 24. Some of the principal appeals to image and likeness are found in the following places: SC 24.5–7 (SBOp 1:156–159); SC 25.7 (1:167,6–10); SC 27.3 (1:183, 11–18); SC 27.6 (1:185,22–26); SC 27.9 (1:188,8–10). A good discussion of Bernard's treatment is Michael Casey, *Athirst for God: Spiritual Desire in Bernard of Clairvaux's Sermons on the Song of Songs*, CS 77 (Kalamazoo: Cistercian Publications, 1988) 133–170.

55. Bernard exhorts the soul to enlarge itself: 'Then the width, height and beauty of your soul will be the width, height and beauty of heaven itself' (. . . *tunc prorsus latitudo caeli, latitudo tuae animae, et altitudo non dispar, sed nec dissimilis pulchritudo*). SC 27.11; SBOp 1:190,13–14.

56. SC 27.1; SBOp 1:182,2–3: . . . *porro discussum et declaratum, quomodo nigra sicut tabernacula Cedar. . . . sicut pelles Salomonis formosa.*

57. SC 27.14; SBOp 1:191,18: *templum lucis.*

58. SC 27.5; SBOp 1:184,24–25: *Divisiones autem sunt, non colorum, sed beatitudinum.*

59. SC 25.3; SBOp 1:164,14: *cum . . . nigredo color sit.* SC 25.5; SBOp 1:166,9: *Propterea etsi nigra foris, sed intus formosa. . . .*

60. SC 28.2; SBOp 1:193,21–23: *Agnosco denigratae formam naturae; . . . protoplastorum peccantium habitum.*

61. SC 28.4; SBOp 1:195,6–7: *Ex voce agnovit Filium Dei et non ex facie.*

62. SC 28.5; SBOp 1:195,18–19: *Dignum quidem fuerat per superiorum oculorum fenestras veritatem intrare ad animam; sed hoc hobis, o anima, servatur in posterum cum videbimus facie ad faciem.*

63. SC 28.8; SBOp 1:197,15–16: *Ne quaeras sapientiam in oculo carnis, quia caro et sanguis non revelat eam, sed spiritus.*

64. SC 28.8; SBOp 1:197,21–23: *Merito carnem redivivam Verbi tangere prohibetur mulier carnaliter sapiens, plus quippe tribuens oculo quam oraculo, id est carnis sensui quam verbo Dei.*

65. 'Why wish to touch what is ugly? Have patience that you may touch the beautiful.' (*Quid deformem vis tangere? Expecta ut formosum tangas.*) SC 28.10; SBOp 1:198,27–28.

66. SC 74.2; SBOp 2:240,17–19: *Nos quidem in expositione sacri mysticique eloquii caute et simpliciter ambulantes, geramus morem Scripturae, quae nostris verbis sapientiam in mysterio absconditam loquitur.* For this reading of the text, see Thomas Merton, 'The Cistercian Fathers and Their Monastic Theology. Part One, Saint Berrnard: V, The Mystical Doctrine of Saint Bernard's Sermons on the Canticle of Canticles,' ed. Chrysogonus Waddell, OCSO in *Liturgy O.C.S.O.*, 28/3 (1994) 29–74, at pp. 40–41.

67. See Thomas Merton, 'The Cistercian Fathers and Their Monastic Theology.' After surveying the doctrine of the *Super Cantica* in terms of images other than light, Merton remarks that Bernard's doctrine is 'eminently a mysticism of light' (p. 51)—i.e., the stress is on the cataphatic, on gratitude and joy.

68. Apo 4.7; SBOp 3:87,24 (cf 1 Cor 10:22): *Omnia licent, sed non omnia expediunt.*

69. RB73: *Caeterum ad perfectionem conuersationis qui festinat . . . ad celsitudinem perfectionis. Quae enim pagina aut qui sermo diuinae auctoritatis Ueteris ac Noui Testamenti non est rectissima norma uitae humanae? Aut quis liber sanctorum catholicorum patrum hoc non resonat ut recto cursu perueniamus ad creatorem?* John Chamberlin ed., *The Rule of St. Benedict: The Abindgdon Copy, edited from Cambridge, Corpus Christi College MS. 57* (Toronto: Pontifical Institute of Mediaeval Studies, 1982) 72,24–32. This is the concept appealed to as an explanation of cistercian 'simplicity', in the Foreword to *The Spirit of Simplicity Characteristic of the Cistercian Order: An Official Report demanded and approved by the General Chapter* [authored by J.-B. Chautard OCSO], *Together with Texts from St. Bernard of Clairvaux on Interior Simplicity*, Translation and Commentary by A Cistercian Monk of Our Lady of Gethsemani [Thomas Merton], Cistercian Library 3, (Trappist, Kentucky: Abbey of Our Lady of Gethsemani, 1948) i-vi. The writer of the Foreword states, 'We may sum up the teaching of Saint Bernard and of the *Little Exordium* in a few brief words by saying that, for them, simplicity consisted in *getting rid of everything that did not help the monk to arrive at union with God by the shortest possible way*' (p. iii).

70. On Bernard in relation to Augustine, see my 'Metaphysics in the Prayer of St. Augustine.' p. 71 (above, note 8).

71. SC 28.2; SBOp 1:193,9–12: *Splendor et figura substantiae Dei obnubiletur in forma servi, candor vitae aeternae nigrescat in carne.*

72. SC 28.10; SBOp 1:198,27–28: *Quid deformem vis tangere? Expecta ut formosum tangas.*

73. SC 45.6; SBOp 2:53,13–14: *In his namque, iuxta Prophetam, non erat ei species neque decor* [Is 53:2].

74. SC 53.7; SBOp 2:100,6–11: *Sane enim non invenio alibi, ubi in sole posuerit tabernaculum suum, id est in luce et in manifesto suam ubi in sole posuerit tabernaculum suum, id est in luce et in manifesto suam sit dignatus exhibere praesentiam ipse lucis inaccessibilis habitator, nisi utique in terris. . . . in sole posuit tabernaculum suum, corpus videlicet. . . .* Other instances are these: SC 6.3 (SBOp 1:27,13); SC 22.3 (1:31,9); 1 Epi A. 1 (4:292,20); and SC 29.8 (1:208,19), where *in sole ponens* is glossed as *Dedi te in lucem gentium.*

75. Dom Jean-Marie Déchanet, OSB, 'The Christology of St. Bernard,' *Cistercian Studies*, Vol. 2 of *St. Bernard Theologian* (Berryville, Va., 1962) 37–51, at p. 43. The author speculates that this may be 'because of their distinctly Eastern and somewhat Originist flavor' (p. 43). He dismisses any possibility that Bernard's approach would worry a theologian.

76. In SC 20.6–8 (SBOp 1:118–120), Bernard explains that images of the human Christ which stir the heart are a gift of the Holy Spirit. Here, as in many places where the commonplace metaphor would refer to light, he seems to avoid images of light: Spirits have *tongues* of their own; the presence of the Word does not touch *the eye* but makes glad *the heart.*

77. Déchanet, 'The Christology of St. Bernard', p. 43.

78. SC 31.8; SBOp 1:224,26–27: *Spiritus ante faciem nostram Christus Dominus; in umbra eius vivemus inter gentes* (Lam 4:20). Déchanet (p. 44) alludes to a parallel usage in William of Saint Thierry, *Epistola ad Fratres de Monte Dei*, 1. 14. 43 (PL 184:336 AB)

79. SC 31.8; SBOp 1:224,2: *Videbimus eum et nos sicuti est, hoc est in forma Dei, et non in umbra.*

80. SC 45.6; SBOp 2:53,11–13: *Existimo enim nequaquam hac vice eius sensibus importatas imagines carnis, aut crucis, aut alias quascumque corporearum similitudines infirmitatum.*

81. Denis Farkasfalvy, O.Cist, *L'inspiration de l'écriture sainte dan la théologie de saint Bernard.* Studia Anselmiana 53 (Rome: Herder, 1964) p. 127.

82. See nn. 66 and 67.

83. Of the seven reminiscences of this text in Bernard's works, three are in the *Super Cantica*: SC 21.2 (SBOp 1:123,27); SC 48.6 (2:71,8); and SC 72.9 (2:231,17).

84. Denis Farkasfalvy, O.Cist., 'Use and Interpretation of Saint John's Prologue in the Writings of Saint Bernard,' *Analecta Cisterciensia* 35 (1979) 205–226. The author finds the omission surprising, given Bernard's very frequent use of John's prologue. He suspects the reason may be that the sentence is too abstract for Bernard's concrete imagery (p. 206).

85. *Habeo et ego Verbum, sed in carne; et mihi apponitur veritas, sed in sacramento. . . . me oportet interim quodam sacramenti cortice esse contentum, carnis furfure, litterae palea, velamine fide. Et haec talia sunt quae gustata afferunt mortem, si non de primitiis Spiritus quantulumcumque accipiant condimentum.* SC 33.3; (SBOp 1:235,10–15)

86. Ejus igitur obumbratio nostri est illuminatio. . . . Quemadmodum infirmi oculi solem nube tectum libere conspiciunt. (*Expositio in hierarchiam caelestem* 2; PL 175:946) Cited in Von Simson, p. 121 n. 87. This reflection is not altogether absent

from Bernard's text. See, e.g., SC 41.3; (SBOp 2:30,25–26) on images of earthly things which 'temper the intensity of divine light' (quodam modo adumbratus purissimus ille ac splendidissimus veritatis radius).

87. SC 40.1; SBOp 2:24,21–22: Cogita animae faciem, mentis intentionem. SC 41.1; SBOp 2:28,23–24: Nihil . . . elucet quam ipsum animae intellectum colli nomine designari.

88. SC 41.3; SBOp 2:30,8: Aurum divinitatis est fulgor.

89. Panofsky (p. 26), for example, as we have noted at the start, contrasted Bernard, who 'disapproved of art', to Suger, who 'had the good fortune to discover' that the beauty of God shone through the world and might then be seen in art.

90. Nat V, 3.8 (SBOp 4:217,5): Quanta videlicet sit in creatione potentia, quanta in positione sapientia, in compositione quanta benignitas. See also SC 23.11 (SBOp 1:145,24–146,15) on the contemplative room from which one beholds the Bridegroom as he 'formulates plans as guidelines in weight, measure and number for all things created'. Not Bernard's favorite room, this is still what he recognizes as a place of contemplation.

91. '[The companions of the Bridegroom] try to console the bride with the promise that until she can see in the beatific vision him for whom she longs so ardently, they will make her beautiful and costly pendants for her ears. The reason for this I think is that faith comes by hearing [Rom 10:17].' Nunc autem vide ne forte magis sodalibus eius congruentiusque assignemus, sponsam quasi consolantibus tali promissione, quod donec perveniat ad visionem eius, cuius desiderio sic flagrat, facturi sint illi muraenulas pulchras et pretiosas, quae sunt aurium ornamenta. Atque hoc propterea, ut opinior, quia fides ex auditu . . . . SC 41.2 (SBOp 2:29,14–18)

92. Saint Paul's remark (Rom 1:19), writes Bernard, that God was revealed to the Romans, does not mean that they received the divine kiss. 'The Apostle actually tells us the means by which they knew; they perceived him in the things that he had made. From all this it is clear that even their knowledge was not perfect, because they did not love.' Denique ipse Apostolus dicat per quid cognoverint; Per ea, inquit, quae facta sunt, intellecta conspexerunt. Unde et constat quia nec perfecte cognoverunt, quem minime dilexerunt. SC 8.5 (SBOp 1:39,1–3)

93. SC 8.5; SBOp 1:38,21–23: Porro revelatio quae per Spiritum Sanctum fit, non solum illustrat ad adnitionem, sed etiam accendit ad amorem.

94. SC 8.6; SBOp 1:39,22–24: Utrumque enim munus simul fert osculi gratia, et agnitionis lucem, et devotionis pinguedinem.

95. See SC 15.6 (SBOp 1:85,28–86, 8) on the name of Jesus.

96. Denis Farkasfalvy, O.Cist., 'Use and Interpretation' (note 84) p. 212, n. 23 for bibliography. Leclercq, 'Essais sur l'ésthetique de saint Bernard,' p. 691, writes that Bernard mistrusted any philosophical role in contemplation, because it threatened the primacy of Scripture.

97. Bernard McGinn, *The Foundations of Mysticism*, p. 161, speaks here of the 'cosmological': 'His [Dionysius's] presentation is far more cosmological and "objective" than what we have seen in Origen and especially Evagrius.' Bernard's monastic tradition stems from Origen and Evagrius.

98. See my 'Metaphysics in the Prayer of Saint Augustine', pp. 76–77. Augustine, in the metaphysical language of his prayer, engages in a form of play rather than in an intellectual quest requiring metaphysics. Yet, reflection upon the nature of things (*natura rerum*) is ordinarily his beginning for an ascent to God.

99. Bernard acknowledges that moving to God through the wonders of creation is profoundly christian. Yet, he prefers—'I do not speak for others,' he says—a more restful engagement with the Bridegroom. He leaves what in his esteem is the room of *studium* in favor of the room of *otium*. SC 23.15 (SBOp 1:148,18–19)

100. SC 74.3 (SBOp 2:241,8–90) See Jean Leclercq, *Études sur le vocabulaire monastique du moyen âge* (Rome, 1961), s.v. *otium*. The word is contrasted to *cura, negotium, studium*—involvement with changing things.

101. SC 45.5; SBOp 2:53,1–2: Sane ducenda es de claritate in claritatem. For more on seeing and hearing, see SC 53.

102. SC 45.5; SBOp 2:52,25: Nunc copiam habeto videndi. SC 45.5; SBOp 2:52,23–24: 'Iam me,' inquit, 'intuere in spiritu, quia spiritus ante faciem tuam Christus Dominus.'

103. SC 45.9; SBOp 2:55,8–20: Quam pulcher es angelis tuis, Domine Iesu, in forma Dei, . . . in splendoribus sanctorum ante luciferum genitus, splendor et figura substantiae Patris, et quidam perpetuus minimeque fucatus candor vitae aeternae? Quam mihi decorus es, Domine me, in ipsa tui huius positione decoris! . . . ibi pietas magis emicuit, ibi caritas plus effulsit, ibi amplius gratia radiavit. Quam clara mihi oriris stella ex Iacob, quam lucidus flos de radice Iesse egrederis, quam iucundum lumen in tenebris visitasti me, oriens ex alto! . . . . Quam denique rutilans post occasum, Sol iustitiae, de corde terrae resurgis!

104. SC 60.2; SBOp 2:143,2–3: Non enim prius quod spirtuale est, sed quod animale [cf. 1 Cor 15:46].

105. SC 62.7; SBOp 2:160,2: . . . *in sanando oculo interiori*. SC 62.4; SBOp 2:157,18–190: Tantum affer purum et simplicem oculum.

106. SC 62.5; SBOp 2:158,19: In eamdem imaginem transformamur de claritate in claritatem [2 Cor 3:18].

107. SC 62.5; SBOp 2:158,20: Transformamur cum conformamur.

108. SC 62.8; SBOp 2:160,26: Non est quod se veritas deneget intuendam puro cordi.

109. SC 48.6; SBOp 2:70,25–26: Umbra eius, caro eius; umbra eius, fides.

110. SC 48.7; SBOp 2:72,4: Ipse per carnem umbra est fidei, ipse intelligentiae lumen per spiritum.

111. SC 48.6; SBOp 2:70,16: Sub umbra eius quem desideraveram sedi. SC 48.7; SBOp 2:72,2–3: Et tu ergo vide ut vivas exemplo Prophetae in umbra eius, ut quandoque et regnes in lumine eius.

112. In SC 23, as we have seen, Bernard uses *rest* as a criterion among three types of contemplation. See SC 23.15 (SBOp 1:148,17–19).

113. SC 48.8; SBOp 2:73,2: ubi sponsa pausat.

114. SC 48.8; SBOp 2:72,20–21: 'Sedimus' dixit, sed singulariter: 'sedi,' ut agnoscas praerogativam.

115. SC 48.8; SBOp 2:72,16–17: Sedere enim quiescere est. Plus est autem quiescere in umbra quam vivere. . . .

116. SC 48.8; SBOp 2:72,23: devota et amans, suaviter requiescit.

117. SC 48.8; SBOp 2:72,10–13: Nos vero, qui nondum in paradisum, . . . rapi meruimus, Christi interim carne pascamur, . . . fidem servemus.

118. SC 48.6; SBOp 2:71,6: At qui vivit ex intellectu, beatus est, quia vivit non in umbra iam sed in lumine.

119. SC 48.6; SBOp 2:71,10: Nisi credideritis, ait, non intelligetis [cf. Is 7:9]

120. SC 48.6; SBOp 2:71,9–10: Prius est venire ad umbram, et ita ad id, cuius umbra est pertransire.

121. SC 48.7; SBOp 2:72,5–8: Spiritus ante faciem nostram, id est in futuro se tamen quae retro sunt obliviscentis, ad ea quae ante sunt nosmetipsos extendimus [cf. Phil 3:13]. Denis Farkasfalvy, O.Cist., 'The Use of Paul by Saint Bernard As Illustrated by Saint Bernard's Interpretation of Philippians 3:13,' in John R. Sommerfeldt, ed., *Bernardus Magister*, CS 135 (Kalamazoo: Cistercian Publications, 1992) 161–168, speaks of Bernard's never resting content with ordinary things, at pp. 162–163, and of his very frequent reference to the *se extendere* of Phil. 3:13 as an encouragement to self-transcendence.

122. SC 48.8; SBOp 2:72,26–27: Eritque, cum declinaverint umbrae, crescente lumine. . . .

123. SC 48.1; SBOp 2:67,6–8: Attende pessimum germen eius, cui maledictum est, terrae nostrae. . . . . Donec ergo in carne est anima, inter spinas profecto versatur.

124. SC 48.2; SBOp 2:68,3: Sed confidite, inquit, quia ego vici mundum.

125. SC 48.6; SBOp 2:70,18: Nam cetera quidem silvarum ligna . . . .

126. SC 48.3; SBOp 2:68,29–69,2: Denique nec sponsa magni aestimasse videtur, quae hoc in lignis silvarum tantum efferre curavit, nimirum sterilibus nec fructus humano victui aptos ferentibus.

127. SC 48.5; SBOp 2:70,14–5: Solus panis vivus qui descendit de caelo, et dat vitam mundo.

128. SC 48.6; SBOp 2:70,18–21: Nam cetera quidem silvarum ligna, etsi solatii umbram habent, sed non vitae refectionem, non fructus perpetuos salutis. Unus est enim vitae auctor, unus mediator Dei et hominuum homo Christus Iesus.

129. In *De diligendo Deo*, Bernard sees faith from a different perspective. To show that God should be loved by all human beings, the author must begin in a faith more broadly conceived, one that can be demanded even of those who have not heard of Christ. (Contrast, e.g., Dil 6 and 7.) The *Super Cantica*, his most intimate communication with his monks, had no need to take up this apologetic position.

130. The Vulgate *donec adspiret dies* is rendered 'until the day breathes forth *life*' in the Cistercian Fathers series (trans. Irene Edmonds). This is indeed the sense of *adspiret*, as Bernard's context makes clear. Were Bernard ever to have referred to Jn 1:4, 'The life was the light of all people', this would have been the inevitable place of reminiscence; but, he never cited this verse.

131. SC 72.4; SBOp 2:228,10–11: Est et in mala significatione dies, cui maledixere Prophetae.

132. SC 72.5; SBOp 2:228,15–17: Ego tamen umbrarum nomine hoc loco magis arbitror disignatas contrarias potestates . . . principes tenegrarum ab Apostolo perhibentur.

133. SC 72.5; SBOp 2:228,25: transibit hora et potestas tenebrarum.

134. SC 72.5; SBOp 2:228,29: Nox diabolus est.

135. SC 72.5; SBOp 2:229,1–2: Nox etiam Antichristus, quem Dominus interficiet spiritu oris sui.

136. SC 72.5; SBOp 2:229,3–4: Numquid non Dominus dies est? . . . spiritu oris sui fugat umbras.

137. SC 72.7; SBOp 2:230,10–11: In tenebris ambulant nescientes, ponentes tenebras lucem et lucem tenebras.

138. SC 72.8; SBOp 2:230,19: In hac die nascimur universi.

139. SC 72.8; SBOp 2:230,24–25: dum non cesset in ea caro concupiscere adversus spiritum.

140. Though the duality flesh-spirit is not restricted to Paul in the New Testament, it is truly 'pauline,' at least in the sense that Paul was the first to relate the doctrine of the Spirit to Christology. On this, see Ernst Käsemann, *Commentary on Romans*, trans. Geoffrey Bromiley (Grand Rapids, Mich.: Eerdmans, 1980) 198–252, esp. p. 213. For Paul's characteristic use of the duality, see Charles H. Giblin, SJ, *In Hope of God's Glory: Pauline Theological Perspectives* (New York: Herder and Herder, 1970) pp. 86–88 on Gal 16–26, and pp. 391–392 on Rom 8:1–13. The author explains that the terms of the duality must be understood 'in a dialectical context, that is, in relation to that with which it [either word] is contrasted in a specific context' (p. 87).

141. SC 7.8; SBOp 1:35,21–22: Et vide familiare amicumque colloquium animae in carne suspirantis cum caelestibus potestatibus. In the sermon we are considering, we read, 'Eve living within our flesh' (Eva utique vivente in carne nostra). SC 72.8 (SBOp 2:230,20)

142. SC 75.2; SBOp 2:248,18–19: Et si cognovimus Christum secundum carnem, sed nunc iam non novimus (cf. 2 Cor 5:16).

143. SC 75.7; SBOp 2:251,14: Surrexit, non est hic (Mk 16:6).

144. SC 75.10; SBOp 2:253,2–9: Quid dico, quia noctes habet mundus, cum pene ipse totus sit nox, et totus semper versetur in tenebris? . . . . nulla societas luci ad tenebras.

145. SC 75.12; SBOp 2:254,6–7: Surrexit de corde terrae, sed super terram non remansit.

146. SC 75.9; SBOp 2:252,22–26: . . . dici potest quod qui ignorant, nocte ignorent, ac per hoc qui quaerunt, nocte quaerant. . . . Porro dies palam facit quod nox abscondit. . . . Nox est itaque donec quaeritur sponsus, quoniam si dies esset, de medio fieret, et minime quaereretur.

147. SC 75.10; SBOp 2:253,4–6: Nox est iudaica perfidia, nox ignorantia paganorum, nox haeretica pravitas, nox etiam catholicorum carnalis animalisve conversatio. Annon nox, ubi non percipiuntur ea quae sunt Spiritus Dei?

148. SC 75.4; SBOp 2:249,19–22: Dominus aperte praenuntiat venire noctem, quando nemo potest operari. . . . Et ideo dies salutis. . . .

149. The pioneer in efforts to trace the biblical roots of Bernard's spirituality was Jean Leclercq. See, for example, the following studies: J. Leclercq, 'Saint Bernard et l'Écriture Sainte' in *Saint Bernard mystique* (Paris, 1948) 483–489; 'Saint Bernard et le 12e siècle monastique: Écriture Sainte et vie spirituelle', DSp 4/25 (1958) col. 187–194; 'Saint Bernard et la tradition biblique d'après les Sermons sur le Cantique,' *Sacris Erudiri* 9 (1960) 225–248.

150. John L. McKenzie, SJ, *Dictionary of the Bible* (New York: Macmillan, 1965) 929–933, s.v. 'Wisdom, Wisdom Literature,' remarks with respect to wisdom writings other than the hebrew scriptures: 'The conception of wisdom was substantially the same everywhere, with important modifications introduced in the OT' (p. 929).

151. Étienne Gilson, *The Mystical Theology of Saint Bernard*, trans. A.H.C. Downes (London, 1940; Kalamazoo: Cistercian Publications, 1990) 20–25.

152. Yves Congar, OP, 'The Ecclesiology of Saint Bernard,' in *Saint Bernard Theologian*, Part 1: *Cistercian Studies*, 1 May 1961 (Berryville, Virginia) [trans. from *Saint Bernard théologien*, Actes du congrès de Dijon 115–119 septembre, *Analecta sacri ordinis Cisterciensis* 9 (Rome: Curia generalis S.O.C., 1953)] pp. 81–141. The author contrasts Bernard's 'either/or' to spiritualities that seek 'a synthesis between the spiritual and temporal, between culture and faith' (p. 99).

153. Rudolph Bultmann, *Theology of the New Testament* 2 (London, 1952) 21.

154. Edward Schillebeeckx, *Christ: The Experience of Jesus as Lord*, trans. John Bowden (New York; The Seabury Press, Crossroads Book, 1980) p. 340.

155. John Ashton, *Understanding the Fourth Gospel* (Oxford: Clarendon Press, 1991) 237. Ashton reviews the scholarship on johannine dualism, pp. 205–237. What he contends regarding 'the profoundly dualistic nature of the evangelist's thinking—in terms not of his receptiveness to new ideas but of his own gut reactions' (p. 237) is what earlier advocates (e.g., Brown, Charlesworth, Schnackenburg) put forward more timidly. A similar case is made by John Painter, *The Quest for the Messiah: The History, Literature, and Theology of the Johannine Community*, 2nd Revised Ed. (Nashville: Abbingdon Press, 1993) discussing dualism in pp. 36–47 of his treatment of Qumran.

156. Schillebeeckx, *Christ: The Experience of Jesus as Lord*, p. 340. The author cites (p. 341) as examples of darkness in the Wisdom books Prov 30:1–14; Job 28; Ecclesiastes; Wisdom 7 and 9. We may remark, beyond this, that the light imagery of the wisdom books fits the larger context of the hebrew Scriptures. Note, for example, how the theme of Incarnate Light coming into a world of darkness (Jn 1:5) is traceable, not only to wisdom imagery, but to Is 9:2: 'The people that walk in darkness have seen a great light'.

157. Ashton, *Understanding the Fourth Gospel*, p. 168, rejects the notion of jewish sectarianism, preferring to speak of Judaism as at a stage in which much dissent was countenanced.

158. Jn 1:3–10: In principio erat Verbum. . . . In ipso vita erat, et vita erat lux hominum: Et lux in tenebris lucet, et tenebrae eam non comprehenderunt. . . . In mundo erat et mundus per ipsum factus est et mundus eum non cognovit.

159. Ashton, *Understanding the Fourth Gospel*, p. 228.

160. C. K. Barrett, 'John and the Synoptic Gospels,' *Expository Times* 85 (1974) 228–231.

161. Farkasfalvy, 'Use and Interpretation of Saint John's Prologue in the Writings of Saint Bernard,' pp. 205–226.

162. Farkasfalvy, 'Use and Interpretation,' 224, 226. For Bernard's pauline orientation generally, see Farkasfalvy, 'L'inspiration de l'écriture sainte,' 133.

163. Farkasfalvy, 'Use and Interpretation,' 224.

164. Regarding the importance in Bernard's epistemology of the fact that the eternal light of the *Verbum* has become flesh, see Denis Farkasfalvy, O.Cist., 'La Conoscenza di Dio secondo San Bernardo,' in *Studi su S. Bernardo di Chiaravalle, nell'ottavo centenario della Canonizzazione* (Rome, 1975) 201–214.

165. Farkasfalvy, 'Use and Interpretation,' 225.

166. Brevard S. Childs, *Biblical Theology of the Old and New Testaments: Theological Reflections on the Christian Bible* (Minneapolis: Fortress Press, 1992) p. 246, speaking of divine righteousness in relation to God's people, says, 'Paul radicalized the doctrine. . . . The Apostle argued for the sharpest possible polarity . . . .' The duality is also expressed in terms of Spirit and flesh. Ernst Käsemann, *Commentary on Romans*, p. 212, speaking of Paul's doctrine of the Spirit, remarks, 'Apart from the johannine view, it is the most sharply delineated in the NT.'

167. 'Use and Interpretation,' 209.

168. *Cons.* 1, p. 83.

169. In 'A Tradition of Aesthetics in Saint Bernard,' *Bernardus Magister*, ed. John R. Sommerfeldt, CS 135 (Kalamazoo: Cistercian Publication and *Cîteaux, Commentarii Cistercienses*, 1992) 129–147, I strove to identify a broad aesthetical

tradition to which Bernard belonged. Here, instead, I specify ways in which he is distinct within that tradition.

170. G. B. Caird, *The Language and Imagery of the Bible* (Philadelphia: Westminster Press, 1980) citation at p. 269.

170A. Caird, p. 271.

171. SC 15.6; SBOp 1:86,5–11.

172. SC 33.5; SBOp 1:236,25–237,5.

173. SC 33.15; SBOp 1:244,13–18.

174. SC 52.3; SBOp 2:91,21–92,8.

175. SC 61.2; SBOp 2:149,19.

176. SC 72.5; SBOp 2:228,29–229,13. Nox diabolus est, nox angelus Satanae. . . . Nox etiam Antichristus . . . . Numquid non Dominus dies est? Dies plane illustrans et spirans: spiritu oris sui fugat umbras. . . . Denique cum venerit quod perfectum est, tunc evacuabitur quod ex parte est [cf 1 Cor 13:10].

177. 3 Pur 2; SBOp 4:340,11: In via vitae non progredi regredi est.

177A. Rudolph, 'The "Principal Founders"' (note 4), pages 21–22, argues for 1149–50 as the date of statute 80 in cistercian art legislation.

178. I have attempted to explain and illustrate this in 'Action and Contemplation in Saint Bernard's Sermons on the Song of Songs,' Introduction to *Bernard of Clairvaux on the Song of Songs III*, trans. Kilian Walsh OCSO and Irene M. Edmonds, CF 31 (Kalamazoo: Cistercian Publications, 1979) vii–xxv, at pp. xiii–xviii.

179. For example, Bernard dedicates SC 27 to a systematic reflection upon the text, 'I am beautiful like the curtains of Solomon,' where the soul of the bride is shown to be the chosen dwelling of the Word. The virtuous person is a heaven, he says (SC 27.8), and speaks of spatial dimensions of the soul; and after having specified a meaning or function for each dimension, he recapitulates, 'the width, height, and beauty of your soul will be the width, height, and beauty of heaven itself'—latitudo caeli, latitudo tuae animae, et altitudo non dispar, sed nec dissimilis pulchritudo (SC 27.ll; SBOp 1:190,11–12). Most suggestive of all is the author's account of the psychological atmosphere that the dwelling-place of God must create: 'If she is to become heaven, the dwelling-place of God, it is first of all essential that she be empty of all these defects. Otherwise how could she be still enough to know that he is God?' The latin text makes available something of the architectural sensitivity of the builders of the oratory in their insistence upon the elimination of colorful artistic devices: the author plays upon the word *vacare* (to empty out), giving it, within the brevity of two short sentences, a triple sense—to empty the mind of distractions; to remain still, as enjoined by Ps 85:11 (Be still—*vacare*—and know that the Lord is God); and to pray, in the manner of the contemplative's complete withdrawal from the images of workaday life—the lexical sense of *vacare* in the monastic tradition is *to pray, to contemplate*. The text reads: Oportet namque primo quidem his omnibus vacuam esse animam, ut caelum fiat atque habitatio Dei. Alioquin quomodo poterit vacare et videre, quoniam ipse est Deus? (SC 27.10; SBOp 1:189,4–6) Perhaps a good beginning for the accumulation of the 'evidence' that I insist is there is in the sign found in many cistercian monasteries today above the entrance to the oratory: *Domus Dei*, the house of God. A rapid glance at *domus* and its variants in the *Thesaurus Sancti Bernardi Claravallensis*: *Concordantiae* (Corpus Christianorum) will turn up the following instances in which Bernard associates the material building with the soul (the apparatus: Volume: page, line, paragraph, item number): 6B. 87. 25. 36 Sent 3; 5. 375. 16. 1 Ded 2; 4. 215. 16. 5 NatV. 3; 5. 239. 11. 1 Assp

3; 2. 154. 15. 1 SC 62; 5. 388. 20. 1 Ded 5; 6B. 96. 2. 5 Sent 3; 5. 403. 4. 5 Mart; 4. 177. 23. 4 AdvA 3; 5. 235. 23. 6 Assp 2; 5. 237. 3. 8 Assp 2; 3. 222. 8. 9 Tpl; 2. 276. 2. 6 SC 79; 5. 376. 4. 1 Ded 2; 6B. 94. 22. 53 Sent 3; 6A. 258. 25. 4 Div 42; 6B. 94. 25. 53 Sent 3+; 5. 376. 19. 2 Ded 2; 5. 395. 1. 8 Ded 5; 5. 372. 15. 3 Ded 1. Among the above, we find the author's reflection that God said, 'We will make our dwelling place with him. Therefore, I already know where a house is to be prepared for him, for nothing other than his own image can hold him'—Mansionem apud eum faciemus. Itaque iam scio, ubi paranda sit domus ei, quoniam non capit eum nisi imago sua. The thought continues with the explanation that it is the soul which is *capax Dei*. He cites Acts 17:24: 'He who is Lord of heaven and earth does not live in shrines made by human hands ' (2 Ded 2; SBOp 5:376,19). Special significance springs from the setting—the dedication of a church building. On another such occasion, Bernard reminded his monks that the house dedicated by the hand of a bishop was really for us rather than for God; God's dwelling is in the soul (3 Ded 1; SBOp 5:372,15).

180. Leclercq, 'Essais sur l'esthétique de S. Bernard,' p. 693.

181. Gerhard von Rad, *Old Testament Theology* (New York: Harper and Row, 1962) 364–365. James Alfred Martin, Jr., *Beauty and Holiness: The Dialogue between Aesthetics and Religion* (Princeton, N.J.: Princeton University Press, 1990), cites von Rad and adds that 'the suspicion of beauty' is 'part of the legacy of Biblical religion' (p. 11).

182. For an unconscious defense of this bias, see Bernard J. F. Lonergan, SJ, *Method in Theology* (New York: Herder and Herder, 1972) pp. 70–73, on 'linguistic meaning': 'By its embodiment in language, . . . meaning finds it greatest liberation' (p. 70).

183. SC 56.1; SBOp 2:114,20: Caro paries est.

184. SC 57.8; SBOp 2:124,13–16: Sed sane non per ostia aperta, sed per angusta foramina is tantae claritatis radius se infundet, stant adhuc dumtaxat hoc ruinoso pariete corporis.

185. SC 27.14; SBOp 1:191,16–19: O humilitas! o sublimitas! . . . et terrenum habitaculum, et caeleste palatium . . . et corpus mortis, templum lucis. . . . Nigra est sed formosa.

186. A problematic item in this regard is the floral theme of some grisaille glass. Bernard speaks of the lily in Song 2:1 as 'the most shining white flower, beautifully and appropriately disposed in the form of a crown,' *candissimo flore, pulchre ac decenter disposito in coronam* (SC 70.5; SBOp 2:210,27–28), and explains this as a figure of Christ's humanity and of his resurrection. (This image may, incidentally, contribute towards explaining why, in a building type so spare in ornament, variations on the lily-or-crown-like figure are played out on the capitals of many engaged columns at Fontenay and Pontigny, where there were also lily patterns in some of the grisailles.) Helen Zakin, *French Cistercian Grisaille Glass* (New York: Garland, 1979), gives illustrations of lily patterns in the Pontigny windows (pp. 239–247; plates 29–37), cites Bernard generously, and concludes that the lily motif of the windows has 'the significance attributed to that flower by Saint Bernard' (p. 161). This is plausible; and, in the architecture of the oratory, it is the only instance (to my knowledge) of an image in which claims for a discrete symbolic meaning cannot be made to yield easily to environmental meanings. For this reason, I believe that also this floral motif was meant to be excluded from consideration as an object of contemplation. Its symbolic function is radically muted.

187. François Bucher, 'Cistercian Architectural Purism,' *Comparative Studies in Society and History*, Vol 3 (1960–1961) 89–106, at p. 103, speaks of the oratory as having 'a passive interior which would in effect be neutral,' one in which 'all the elements . . . throw us back upon ourselves'.

188. Bucher, 'Cistercian Architectural Purism,' 89. In C. Hugh Holman and William Harmon, eds., *A Handbook to Literature*, 6th edit. (New York: Macmillan, 1992) p. 288, we read that some literary scholars (e.g., Cleanth Brooks) speak of a 'functional metaphor', describing the way a certain figure may be 'able to have "referential" and "emotive" characteristics and to go beyond them and become a direct means in itself of representing a truth incommunicable by any other means.' Similarly, I would say, an architectural form may 'function' as a symbol without standing apart from the ensemble to which it contributes, and in this should be distinguished from symbols in general.

189. Helen Jackson Zakin, *French Cistercian Grisalle Glass*, pp. 141–170, studies iconographic problems in cistercian art. Her observations on vegetal imagery (pp. 154 ff.) and geometric imagery (pp. 161 ff.) are proof that it is possible to push the thesis of the unornamented cistercian oratory too far. At the same time, Zakin's search for *symbolism* in the cistercian use of light (e.g., pp. 144–154) puts some stress on what seems to be a cardinal principle of this architecture—that no part or detail is to call attention to itself. The author safeguards the principle in her interpretation of patterns which occur in several media—they work towards a 'unified visual effect, a total visual environment which may have been unique to the Cistercians' (p. 166)—but runs contrary to it in seeking a highly specific tenor (see following note) of all light images. Our contention is that, although Bernard offers such a tenor in his prose, he does not intend it to come to explicit notice in the oratory, where imagery is wholly environmental. Geometric imagery, for example, speaks archtypically of order, even without recourse to 'Saint Augustine's numerical concepts' (p. 164).

190. Holman and Harmon, eds., *A Handbook to Literature*, p. 288, explain the analysis of metaphor, from I. A. Richards, in terms of *vehicle* (carrier of a concept, the referring image) and *tenor* (the concept, the subject of the comparison, that which is referred to).

191. Leclercq, 'Les caractéristiques de la spiritualité monastique,' p. 306.

192. 'Les caractéristiques' 307.

193. Leclercq, 'Théologie traditionelle et théologie monastique,' p. 55.

194. Leclercq, Études sur le vocabulaire monastique du moyen âge, pp. 70–80 for 'monachisme et théologie'.

195. McGinn, *The Foundations of Mysticism*, p. 174, writes: 'It is only in and through the full appropriation of the cataphatic moment, however—that is, by immersion in the beauty of the universe—that we can dialectically attain the negation of representations necessary for discovering that God is always more than we can conceive.'

196. It is easy for those familiar with the monastic tradition to overlook this and to fail to see what Bernard's principal contribution to western thought has been—i.e., the making possible of a reappropriation of this fundamental element of the tradition. Despite numerous inaccuracies in reading Bernard, Norman F. Cantor, *The Civilization of the Middle Ages*, revised ed. (New York: Harper Collins, 1993) pp. 339–343, does not fail here, where many a true expert is myopic: he pronounces Bernard's evaluation of individual experience 'the most potentially revolutionary doctrine of the twelfth century' (p. 338). Although monastic apologists will insist

that what is 'revolutionary' here is not new, Cantor is, in substance, right: for posterity, Bernard illuminates from within what, in institutional history, forever tends to become opaque.

197. Apo 4.7; SBOp 3:87,24–25; cf. 1 Cor 10:22: *Omnia licent, sed non omnia expediunt.*

Who Founded the Order of Citeaux?[1]

Brian Patrick McGuire

Prologue: Remembering Jean Leclercq

ONE OF MY STUDENTS has described his experience of researchers in terms of two personality types.[2] The first goes about work with a sense of trying to dominate a given area. Once the project is complete and the results clear, this type of researcher defends the conclusions fiercely and is not interested in discussing them with anyone. The second type of researcher is dedicated not so much to conclusions as to discussions of methods, data, and results. This researcher does not feel obliged to mark out territory and to keep off intruders. On the contrary, he or she welcomes dialogue.

If I can take this distinction into the territory of feudal imagery, one researcher resembles the feudal lord who builds a castle and surrounds it with a moat. The second simply puts up a little house and invites friends and colleagues to enter as guests. This researcher has no illusion of reaching timeless results, knowing that each generation of historians creates its own interpretations. In the pursuit of objective truths, this researcher admits and even welcomes many different approaches to understanding.

Such a researcher was Jean Leclercq. When I first met him at Kalamazoo in 1978 and when he lectured in Copenhagen in 1983, he was not concerned with building research moats and castles. I remember strolling with him up our main pedestrian mall in Copenhagen, with his hand locked into my arm. It was a delight to be with this inimitable monk, writer, and researcher. Here was a person who loved the life of the monk and dedicated himself to the study of monasticism in its historical development. Leclercq invited me to come to visit him in his little house, his monastery. I never made it to Clervaux, but he shared his research home with me many times in the coming years through his unforgettable (and almost illegible) notes and postcards, scribbled with references and suggestions. With me as with so many others, Jean Leclercq was always willing to share with others the contents of his intellectual and spiritual home.

Now that Jean Leclercq has got his wish of conversations with Saint Bernard, we who are left behind can best honor Dom Jean not by considering his work sacred but by following his example and maintaining a dialogue with each other. This attitude seems all the more important as we approach 1998 and the nine hundredth anniversary of the foundation of the monastery of Cîteaux. In what follows I will not always be in agreement with Jean Leclercq's own evaluation of Cîteaux's early years and with his emphasis on Saint Bernard's role in creating the Order of Cîteaux. In disagreeing with a father about the cistercian fathers, I ask the reader to look upon my role not as that of *enfant terrible* but as that of a dedicated, questioning visitor to the cistercian foundation, past and present.

Scholarly Disarray on the Eve of 1998

Almost forty years ago, the scholar who did the most to upset the once comfortable story of the foundation of Cîteaux, Jean Lefèvre, admitted that a lifetime's work left only doubt about how the Order had begun:

> To whom attribute the fatherhood of the practical points of the reform? To Robert of Molesme alone? To Alberic, his successor? To the two first abbots conjointly, since the second continued what the first started? These passion-stirring

> questions are without an answer, and the cistercian origins remain surrounded by numerous obscurities. . . . the first and most important <stage>, that of 1098–1100, escapes us almost completely. One must simply admit: a thousand interpretations, no matter how ingeniously conceived, will never replace the documents we do not have.[3]

Our predicament today is that there is no post-Lefèvre consensus on the early years of Cîteaux. We are in the painful situation of realizing that as we approach 1998 we know less about the foundation of Cîteaux than our scholarly predecessors thought they knew in 1898. My contention is that the documents we need are available, but that we have not considered them properly, to a large extent because Lefèvre and others have left us in total confusion concerning the dates for these sources.

There is hope for a re-orientation of our knowledge. In what follows I will try to avoid questions of dating and to leave to the scholarship of Chrysogonus Waddell of Gethsemani Abbey the task of providing a new critical edition of the documents for 1998. Instead, I will ask a much simpler question: what did the early Cistercians want to tell their readers through their documents about who they were? By this, I hope to shed light on the meaning of the cistercian establishment and to find the person responsible for the conversion of a single monastic house into an order with regularized bonds among the houses.

In 1986 Jean-Baptiste Auberger contributed to the discussion about the origins of Cîteaux with his *L'unanimité cistercienne primitive: mythe ou realité?*[4] Auberger's conclusions have been clarified in a recent article by H. E. J. Cowdrey of Oxford, and they have been challenged in a paper given at Kalamazoo in 1994 by Christopher Holdsworth of Exeter.[5] As Holdsworth pointed out, Auberger's book for several years received little attention, and we are now indebted to Cowdrey for getting to the essence of a work whose lavish format and many illustrations make it appear more formidable than its thesis perhaps is.

Cowdrey summarizes the 'Auberger thesis' as follows: there are two traditions for early Cîteaux, one that derives from Cîteaux itself, and one that comes from Clairvaux. The first tradition, found in the *Exordium Parvum*, emphasizes the desire of the early monks at Cîteaux to live according to the Rule of Saint Benedict with greater strictness. Here the key word is *artius*, underlining a concern for a more ascetic orientation and openly criticizing the way of life which the brothers had left at Molesme. The second tradition, that of Clairvaux, is reflected in the *Exordium Cistercii*, which has much more positive things to say about Molesme and which points out that the first Cistercians desired to follow the Rule in a more spiritual manner. The key word is *altius*. As Cowdrey concludes, 'For the one tradition, the change was from bad to good, but for the other, from good to better.'

The Clairvaux-Citeaux Opposition as a Misconception

Christopher Holdsworth's careful analysis of the Auberger thesis has convinced me that there are substantial problems with Auberger's attempt to distinguish between the desires and goals of a Stephen Harding at Cîteaux and a Bernard at Clairvaux. Instead of trying to summarize Holdsworth's arguments before he himself has published his paper, however, I would like to add my own comment to Auberger's distinction between two early traditions.

The Cistercians in the twelfth and early thirteenth centuries speak with two voices: one polemical and one loving. In the early sources we hear a mixture of these two voices. The *Exordium Parvum* brings together documents and narrative in the hope of convincing anyone who questions the legitimacy of the cistercian foundation that everything was done as it should have been done. The collection was meant to show potential enemies of the Order that there was nothing questionable about its origins.

> We Cistercians, the original founders of this monastery, make known to our successors through this present writing how canonically, by what authority, and by which persons, as well as what period of time, their monastery and manner of living had its beginning.[6]

These words were probably not written down before the middle of the twelfth century, as a preamble to a text whose origins are obscure but probably much earlier. What matters is not so much its date as its purpose: to respond to all who might challenge the monks by claiming that Cîteaux was founded in an uncanonical manner and without the authorization of the proper church authorities.

The importance of this *legitimist* approach was widely recognized in the accounts later drawn up for other cistercian houses, as in the chronicle for Fountains Abbey in Yorkshire and the *Exordium Carae Insulae*, the Øm Abbey Chronicle in Denmark.[7] As the Danish monks wrote in about 1200, imitating the tone and posture of the *Exordium Parvum*:

> Desiring to hand over to the knowledge of those who come after us, how this house, which is called Øm, began, we wish at the same time to make known at what time and by what persons it was built, and with what privileges it was confirmed. . . . so that if by chance at any time some lay or clerical person should be tempted to disturb or take away its possessions, once he has known the truth of its foundation and the respect imposed by its founders, he will cease from the work of evil he has begun.[8]

The phrase *cognita veritate fundationis et reverentia fundatorum* is the give-away expression. The Øm monks, like their predecessors at Cîteaux, wanted to make known to all potential challengers that their birthright was unassailable. The seeming lack of chronology both in the *Exordium Parvum* and in its imitator accounts from Øm, Fountains, and elsewhere is the result of the fact that the monks start with the most dramatic and important event the foundation of the house, and then afterwards provide information about the circumstances behind it. The greater strictness of the new monastery is of importance here as a signal to potential enemies of Cîteaux that their move from Molesme cannot be condemned as a lack of stability. The monks' change of place has to be commended as a desire for a more ascetic observance of the Rule of Saint Benedict.

This documentary form contrasts markedly with the *Exordium Cistercii*, which speaks a language of love and community and does not include evidence from charters to strengthen its narrative. This *Exordium* evinces self-confidence in the cistercian vocation and uses the foundation story as a kind of *exemplum* in order to encourage future monks to follow the original pattern.[9] What Auberger thinks of as a reflection of a Clairvaux mentality is rather an indication of a cistercian posture intended for preaching to the converted and reminding them of the meaning of their conversion. Here what matters is a more spiritual life (*altius*) and not the need to defend the legitimacy of the original foundation.

I do not want to exclude the possibility that Bernard may have contributed to the formulation of the *Exordium Cistercii*, but I think it is misleading to limit the origins of this account to Clairvaux. Auberger's attempt to distinguish between a Cîteaux and a Clairvaux tradition founders on the twelfth-century cistercian sense of audience. When they spoke to those who loved them, monastic writers expressed themselves quite differently than they did when they felt obliged to justify their break with the past. What we meet in the early documents is not two different traditions but two different approaches to expressing the same identity.[10]

THE EVIDENCE OF THE *CARTA CARITATIS PRIOR*

However many difficulties we may have in dating the *Exordium Parvum* and the *Exordium Cistercii*, there is one document from the early Cîteaux tradition whose *terminus ante quem* provides no problems. The so-called *Carta Caritatis Prior* had to have been drawn up by 1119, when Pope Calixtus II, the former archbishop Guy of Vienne, confirmed the document.[11] The papal bull is addressed to 'the venerable Stephen abbot of the monastery of Cîteaux and his brothers' but mentions 'the consent and common deliberation of the abbots and brothers of your monasteries'. The bull takes for granted that Cîteaux had already placed itself at the head of a group of monasteries.[12] We thus have a document which indicates that within twenty years of the foundation of Cîteaux, a structure of organization existed in order to ensure mutual cooperation. The *caritas* here points to a sense of harmony and respect that were to be obtained by living up to the contents of the pact.

The fourth provision of the *Carta Caritatis* gives us a good idea of how this harmony was to be achieved. It describes a procedure for visitation by the abbot of Cîteaux (here still called the New Monastery) to houses that had submitted themselves to his authority:

> When, however, the abbot of the New Monastery comes to any of these monasteries for the sake of a visit, the local abbot should yield his place to him everywhere in the monastery, in recognition of the fact that the church of the New Monastery is mother of his church. . . .
>
> . . . Also the abbot of the New Monastery should be careful not to presume to deal with anything or to give orders about or handle anything concerning the material goods of the place to which he has come, against the will of the brethren. But if he understands that the precepts of the rule or of our order are being violated in that place, with the advice of the abbot, and with him present, he should charitably apply himself to make the correction. But if the local abbot is not there, he should nonetheless correct what he finds amiss.[13]

Such a provision could be seen merely as a safeguard of the authority of the abbot of Cîteaux. But if we look at the language in terms of the references and tradition on which it surely drew, the passage comes across as an assertion of a desire to follow the Rule of Saint Benedict. In his seventy-first chapter Benedict asked the brothers to obey each other and to respect hierarchy in the internal life of the individual monastery:

> Obedience is a blessing to be shown by all, not only to the abbot but also to one another as brothers, since we know that it is by this way of obedience that we go to God. Therefore, although orders of the abbot or of the priors appointed by him take precedence, and no unofficial order may supersede them, in every other instance younger monks should obey their seniors with all love and concern. Anyone found objecting to this should be reproved.[14]

Similarly, the *Carta Caritatis* here was asking abbots to obey each other and to respect hierarchy in the relationships among their monasteries. The internal mechanisms of the Rule for the single house were applied to the external workings or interrelationships among monastic houses. Respect, hierarchical order, obedience were still required, but now they were to extend beyond the monastery and to regulate relationships among monasteries.

It has become fashionable to point out how the founders of Cîteaux, in claiming to return to the letter of the Rule of Saint Benedict, actually created structures, such as visitations and the General Chapter, which were never anticipated in the Rule.[15] But if we remember that the Rule emphasizes the importance of the abbot, then the *Carta Caritatis* can be read as underlining the Rule in making sure that the abbot will be able to rule his house well. In the cistercian foundation, the abbot was given a support system: a father abbot, the abbot of his founding house, who would respect his prerogatives but be able to intervene if necessary. Cooperation and interdependency existed in a clear hierarchy among abbots, just as Benedict required hierarchy among the monks within the monastery. An internal ordering of duties and obligations now became externalized, but with continuing emphasis on the primacy of the abbot.

This mode of organization was a far cry from that which Cluny represented. There there was only one abbot, that of Cluny, and the subservience of houses in the congregation was underlined by the fact that their leaders had only the status of priors.[16] Cluny sought to preserve Benedict's Rule by allowing one single abbot for all its houses, while Cîteaux interpreted the Rule as an invitation to maintain the integrity of each abbot over his monastic house, while at the same time acknowledging his dependence upon a father abbot and ultimately upon the abbot of Cîteaux. The genius of Cîteaux rests in a conviction that the abbot's authority and the mutual love of the brethren are strengthened by a back-up or support system of other abbots and other monasteries.

The early Cistercians were convinced that their new degree of organization and interdependency made it possible for them to live in greater conformity with the Rule of Saint Benedict. Outside intervention was allowed, but it had to be moderated according to the wishes of the local abbot and his brethren. The abbot of Cîteaux could visit and regulate affairs at a monastery only because its abbot and monks wanted him to be there. Like the abbot described in the Rule (ch. 3), Cîteaux's abbot could act only with the consent of those dependent on him. What appears to us as *innovatio* must have been for the early Cistercians much more a *renovatio* to the spirit of the Rule of Saint Benedict.

Amid the scholarly debates of the last decades, there seems so far to have been no one who has tried to deny that behind the

Carta Caritatis Prior stood Stephen Harding, the abbot of the New Monastery. He made Cîteaux the unchallenged mother house of the new Order, as we can hear in the second provision, asking members of other houses 'that they observe the Rule of the blessed Benedict in everything, just as it is observed in the New Monastery'.[17] In making this request, he had already assured daughter houses that no 'material advantage' (*nullius commodi corporalis exactionem*) would be taken from them (*Carta Caritatis Prior*, ch. 1, the chapter heading). Their membership in this new mode of monastic cooperation would be based on consensual mutuality and not on economic subservience. All houses were to have the same liturgical books and customs, so that all the monks could live together without *discordia* and 'in one form of charity and one rule and similar usages'.[18]

Stephen Harding as Decision-Maker

Stephen Harding has been called a monarchical abbot, as if he went about directing early Cîteaux with little concern for the views of the brethren.[19] I think this term is unfortunate, unless it is meant merely as a reflection of the kind of abbot Benedict recommends in his Rule. Certainly Benedict's abbot has great discretionary powers over his monks, but at the same time he is required to take into account their desires and advice. Stephen seems to me to have followed the Rule in asserting the abbot's authority. As Cîteaux acquired daughter houses, he devised legal mechanisms for maintaining that abbatial authority in a wider context. What mattered always was respect for the local abbot and a link between him and other abbots, all bound together in a consultative network with the abbot of Cîteaux.

A good example of how Stephen combined advice-taking with decision-making can be found in a matter that takes us outside Cîteaux and perhaps to the town of Troyes. Stephen himself described how he had been disconcerted by various conflicting biblical texts, especially in books of the Old Testament. To resolve some of the questions, he had gone to Jews and discussed with them in French (*lingua romana*) what they had in their own writings. Some of the scriptures which had raised problems for Stephen were not at all to be found in the Jewish texts.[20]

Stephen's willingness to confer with jewish scriptural scholars reveals a man of imagination and flexibility. At a time when a fanaticism generated by the First Crusade was bringing about Western Europe's first pogroms against Jews,[21] Stephen turned to jewish scholars for solid advice. In doing so, he was not alone, for the jewish point of view was very evident in theological debates in the twelfth century, as we can see from Abelard's writings.[22] But Stephen was especially bold because he himself went to the Jews and because he was willing to submit to them the question of the reliability of biblical texts. Here, as in the formulae of the *Carta Caritatis*, Stephen Harding expresses himself as a person willing to experiment and improvise in order to find new solutions to old problems of authority.

The same willingness to experiment by looking at other traditions is seen in Stephen Harding's letter on the chant. Here, in accord with the Rule of Saint Benedict, he appealed to the 'common consent' of the brethren in making an important decision: limiting hymns to those which Saint Ambrose was thought to have composed.[23] As in trying to determine the rightful contents of the Bible, Stephen went back to the sources and did his best to be faithful to them. While he was looking for something that no longer could be found, his passion for origins was in both cases combined with an attention to authorities.

Consultation, whether with the brethren or of recognized authorities, characterizes Stephen Harding's dealings. As abbot of a monastery that from 1113 was sending out daughter houses, Stephen wanted very much to live according to the Rule. His sense of allegiance to its letter and spirit had taken him from Molesme to the New Monastery. In his zeal for conserving the Rule, he questioned everything, from biblical and liturgical texts to the contents of monastic life. He was determined to get right Benedict's formulae for regulating human and institutional relationships.

Stephen Harding's Personality

Who was Stephen Harding? As we have seen him so far, he combined personal authority with an ability to focus contact and cooperation among monks and monasteries. If we can believe the much later hagiographical source composed for Stephen's friend of youth, Peter of Jully, Stephen took a long time to find his way.[24] Around the time of the Norman Conquest, a young Stephen had left a traditional monastic house at Sherborne in the West Country and in Burgundy later joined forces with another Englishman, Peter, who is called *clericus*. They visited cathedral schools, went to Rome, sought a kind of regularized daily life, and ended up at Molesme in order to live a life that in terms of the Rule of Saint Benedict continued what Stephen had begun at Sherborne and yet was quite different.

There is a tradition that Stephen at some point temporarily left Molesme with others in order to found a hermitage.[25] Whatever the truth of the story, it represents the spirit of restlessness and experimentation that characterizes the founders of Cîteaux. They were men who had done the rounds of the intellectual and spiritual possibilities available at the end of the eleventh century. They were dissatisfied with established ways and wanted to make a physical and spiritual space and to distance themselves from traditional modes of monastic life.

Many decades later, Stephen as abbot of Cîteaux wrote to the monastery at Sherborne where he had lived as a boy and told its monks in the most diplomatic of manners that he still valued them and their vocation. Chrysogonus Waddell has deftly interpreted this seemingly vague letter of goodwill as a tactful assurance to a traditional monastery that it had nothing to fear from the 'invasion of the whites' in England.[26] According to Waddell, Stephen may have been aware of fear in the old monasteries that the cistercian expansion would challenge their standing. Stephen explained in language that would have warmed any monk's heart that he still shared a bond with Sherborne and had great respect for everything it represented:

> . . . I was a monk of yours, and with my staff I passed over and beyond the sea so that in me, the very least of all of you and of no importance whatever when I was with you, the Lord might show forth the riches of his mercy and provoke you to emulation of me. For living fountain that he is, he filled the empty vessel: for so he willed; that you, who were so much better for the holiness of your family-line,

> would have the courage to hold fast and strong to monastic observance, would dare to presume on the Lord.[27]

We do not know how the monks at Sherborne reacted to such encouragement, but the letter conveys loyalty and devotion to the world from which Stephen had emerged.

Stephen's thoughtfulness and concern about the spread of his Order are also reflected in the stories told about him in the *Exordium Magnum Cisterciense.*[28] I am aware that these tales were written down six decades after his death and so give us no more than a pale reflection of the oral traditions that must have circulated about him earlier in the twelfth century. Yet such stories combine traditional materials with flashes of insight into the mind and heart of a man whom the author of the *Exordium Magnum* experienced as being fondly remembered by those who had known him.

Conrad of Eberbach, the compiler of the *Exordium Magnum*, lived in the 1180s and early 1190s at Clairvaux, where he may have begun his work.[29] He hints at no difference between a Cîteaux and a Clairvaux tradition concerning the early decades of the Order. Just as he celebrated Bernard in twenty chapters of the second distinction of his work, so he dedicated nine chapters of the first distinction to Stephen. He first tells how Stephen was in doubt over the success of his foundation and was given reassurance by a dead monk who appeared to him.[30] Secondly Conrad tells an amazing story, in view of hagiographical conventions and Bernard's canonization two decades earlier, about how Bernard as a novice at Cîteaux had once skipped some penitential psalms he had promised himself to say in silence after Compline. Abbot Stephen Harding accused Bernard for his oversight, and Conrad uses the word *negligentia,* one of the key words in the *Exordium Magnum* in its repeated warnings against a decline in monastic asceticism: 'Understanding that he had been caught by the spiritual man, <Bernard> fell at his feet, confessed his neglect and asked for his indulgence.'[31] Bernard was quickly and easily forgiven, of course, but this incident served as a lesson to him: 'He was found to be more solicitous in both private and public observances' (*tam privatis quam publicis observationibus sollicitior inveniri*).

We may exaggerate in using this story as a key to the relationship between Stephen Harding and Bernard, but Conrad clearly intended to show that Stephen as abbot knew better than Bernard as novice. Bernard did not come to the monastic life fully formed. He had to learn how to become a good monk according to the Rule, and to do so he was in need of a teacher who was more aware of him than Bernard was of himself.

A third story in its homeliness recalls similar tales about desert fathers and the means by which the Lord took care of them.[32] Stephen had been bled, as was the monastic custom, but the monastery was so poor that the cellarer had no food he could give him to make up for the loss of strength and supply consolation. But suddenly he saw a great bird that dropped a fish from its claws before the brothers, providing Stephen's extra meal.[33] This story, unlike the one about Bernard, is not taken from Conrad of Eberbach's usual source, the *Liber Miraculorum* compiled in the late 1170s by Herbert of Clairvaux. Here Conrad seems to have been drawing on an oral tradition at Cîteaux.

A fourth tale reminds the reader (perhaps deliberately) of a similar theme in the *Vita Prima* of Saint Bernard: how the monks' lack of food was taken care of.[34] But my favorite story concerns how Stephen was seen going into church in the evening after making a sign. When a monk who was sufficiently close to him to be able to question him about such a personal matter asked Stephen what the meaning was, Stephen told him:

> To all the thoughts which because of the office entrusted to me I am forced to admit during the day for the disposition of the house, I say that they are to remain outside and are by no means to dare to come in with me. They are to wait for me until I find them here tomorrow after prime has been said.[35]

Once again there is a homely, familiar quality to the anecdote, a surprising evocation of a man who is remembered not so much as a miraclemaker but as someone for whom the Lord cared and who took care of his monks.

A final description of Stephen is provided by a reference to his abbatial staff, kept at Cîteaux in the time of Conrad, as a reminder of his humility. This staff is said to resemble the walking sticks commonly used to support the old and handicapped and shows how Stephen hated every indication of pride in office.[36] In Conrad's day

Stephen had become an historical memory: the staff was locked away in the sacristy at Cîteaux and seems to have been looked upon both as relic and a museum piece.

Such stories are more than attractive bits of hagiography. They witness to a living tradition at Cîteaux-Clairvaux kept alive by a desire to remain close to the ideals and attitudes of the early years. For Conrad at Clairvaux and at Eberbach, Stephen Harding of Cîteaux was at the very centre and point of departure for the earliest tradition of the Order in all its purity.

My attention to what is nothing more than an *exemplum* tradition may surprise a reader who may be expecting chronological proximity to the first years at Cîteaux to determine the meaning of the monastic constitution as interpreted by Stephen Harding. But I find in the stories so lovingly told in the *Exordium Magnum* an indication of a living twelfth-century tradition about the importance of Stephen in the formulation of cistercian life. In such stories I see a striking tribute to the centrality of Stephen Harding not only for Cîteaux but also for the Order of Cîteaux.

Stephen as Founder of the Order of Citeaux

Robert of Molesme founded a monastery at Cîteaux, while Stephen Harding founded the Order of Cîteaux.[37] Here the *Carta Caritatis Prior* is the central document. By 1119 Stephen had worked out for the monasteries attached to Cîteaux a way by which their abbots and monks were to be bound with Cîteaux in love and loyalty. He had formulated a set of practices that would ensure regular contacts between Cîteaux and its daughters and would guarantee the integrity of the abbatial office in each monastery. Benedict's emphasis on the authority of the abbot would be respected and secured by giving the abbot of each house a support system through visitations by the father abbot. The latter, however, was not looked upon as a monarch who could interfere at will. As in the Rule, consultation and dialogue were integral parts of the workings of authority.

The General Chapter, as described in the seventh chapter of the *Carta Caritatis Prior*, also emphasized dialogue. This assembly has usually been seen in the light of the decisions recorded in Jean-Marie

Canivez's collection of its statutes.[38] Recent work, however, has questioned Canivez's criteria for selection, and monastic historians such as Chrysogonus Waddell and Constance Berman are looking at the decisions of the General Chapter with fresh eyes.[39] I want to contribute to this debate by pointing out that, just as with the device of visitations, so too with the General Chapter, we need to look at them as provisions intended basically to extend the Rule of Saint Benedict from the individual monastery to a group of monasteries. A consultative process which had previously been a means for regulating behavior in one house was now to be used for all the houses in the new order.

Benedict did not speak of a daily chapter but made it clear, as we already have seen, that all things should be done on the advice of the community, at least of its senior members (ch 3). In his famous chapter 71 on mutual obedience, Benedict had insisted that a monk who was criticized by the abbot or by one of the seniors had to ask for forgiveness and make satisfaction. By the eleventh century, the chapter meeting of the individual house was organized as a means both for discussing necessary business and for regulating the monks' behavior. Here one monk could proclaim another for not living up to the Rule.[40]

Stephen Harding, with his genius for innovation through renovation, simply moved this structure of discussion and discipline from the chapter of the individual monastery to a chapter for the Order as a whole. The General Chapter should be seen as nothing more than the implementation of debate and observance for all the houses:

> . . . there let them treat of the welfare of their own souls; if something is to be emended or added to in the observance of the Holy rule or of the order, let them so ordain, and let them re-establish among themselves the good of peace and charity. But if any abbot proves to have been less zealous for the Rule or too intent on things secular, or habitually prone to any vice, let him there be charitably proclaimed. Let the one proclaimed ask the pardon and fulfill the penance assigned him for the fault.[41]

When we read such passages, we see clearly our mistake in looking at the General Chapter in its original form as a legislative body handing down rules for all the houses. In the first decades, and in the design of Stephen Harding, the General Chapter was meant simply to enforce the Rule as it already existed. The Chapter would maintain harmony and discipline among the monastic houses belonging to the Order, just as the local chapter was intended to keep harmony and discipline among the members of the monastery. In the same way as a monk could be proclaimed at chapter and admonished to change his habits, so too an abbot could be proclaimed at General Chapter. As with the practice of visitation, Stephen Harding transferred an attitude and mode of behavior from a single monastery to the order of monasteries grouped together under the monastery of Cîteaux.

Cîteaux's first daughter house, La Ferté, was founded in 1113, and only after this point must it have become necessary to consider such a transference of individual monastery practices into a larger context. I would think that 1115–19 would have been the crucial years for Stephen's extension of the Rule of Saint Benedict from the single house to a religious order. The formulation, acceptance, and observance of these provisions are to my mind what made Cîteaux into an order. They are not a collection of legal statutes so much as a rethinking and extrapolation of the Rule of Saint Benedict from the traditional single monastery model to a group model.

In retrospect such a structure might seem quite obvious, but in the context of what was then available for imitation, the cluniac monarchical model, Stephen was a pioneer. He respected the integrity of the abbot and yet linked him with other abbots in mutual concern for the bonds of christian charity and monastic discipline.

What about Alberic, the prior at Cîteaux who became abbot on Robert's return to Molesme, probably already in 1098 or soon after, and who lived until 1108? We know of him in the *Exordium Parvum*'s statement, however late it may be, that his desire for a more perfect way of life had caused much resentment among the brothers at Molesme and had even led to his being physically abused.[42] Alberic deserves to be remembered for his courage and determination to continue the experiment after the central figure had disappeared. He had to pick up the pieces and bear the humiliation of Robert's departure. It was Alberic who made sure that the proper contacts were made with Rome in order to get the papal privilege that guaranteed the new foundation from outside interference.[43] But Alberic does not speak to us through any document in the way Stephen Harding communicates his personality in the *Carta Caritatis Prior.* If we can allow ourselves to accept the slender evidence about the early years of Cîteaux, it seems possible to divide the years between 1098, the original foundation, and 1133, the resignation of Stephen Harding from the abbacy, into three separate periods. The first period, 1099–1108, under Alberic, may be called *the survival years.* Those remaining from Robert's foundation stuck it out, in spite of shame and contempt, and did their best to continue the experiment. From 1108, when Stephen took over as abbot, until 1119, when the *Carta Caritatis Prior* was approved by Calixtus II, we witness *the formative years,* when Stephen came to formulate the structures of cooperation and discipline which he took from the Rule of Saint Benedict and molded into a new regularized form of contact among monasteries. Finally, from 1119 until 1133, when Stephen resigned at the General Chapter, we have *the fruitful years.* During this period Stephen's structural bonds began to operate among the monasteries, not in the sense of a fully regulated and automatically functioning legal body, but in terms of regular contacts and consultation.

I hope this understanding of Stephen's contribution has deepened the appreciation of him already present in J.B. Dalgairns' now classic *Life of St. Stephen Harding*, first published in 1844 and edited in 1898 by John Henry Newman. As Dalgairns wrote of Stephen: 'He was the spiritual father of St. Bernard, and was, it may be said, the principal founder of the *Order* of Cistercians.'[44]

Responding to Jean Leclercq

In following Dalgairns and placing Stephen at the center of the birth of the Order of Citeaux, I realize that I am opposing some of the last articles Jean Leclercq published, especially a long piece on Saint Bernard and the paternity of Cîteaux.[45] Here Leclercq pointed out that Bernard spent a few months with his friends and companions in a kind of experimental monastic life before entering Cîteaux with them.[46] Leclercq considers the Bernard who entered Cîteaux in 1112 to have already been formed in his monastic vocation and practically to have refounded Cîteaux by his entrance.[47]

Dom Jean reviews almost all the sources we have concerning the activities of Stephen Harding and reduces them to indications that Stephen was doing what many other monastic or church reformers were doing at the time in correcting biblical texts or reviewing the liturgy.[48] The originality of Stephen's insights or methods is thus questioned and even denigrated. Stephen's delight in lavish illustrations is for Leclercq an indication that the abbot of Cîteaux had no sense of the ascetic reforms that a Bernard brought to the art and architecture of the Order. Here, as in practically everything else, Leclercq makes Bernard into the real founder of the special cistercian asceticism which attracted so much attention and had great success in the twelfth century.

In this area I think the compiler of the *Exordium Magnum* had a sense of proportion that Jean Leclercq, in his long attachment to Saint Bernard, here lacked. As we have already seen, Conrad of Clairvaux and Eberbach found it important to include a story about how Bernard did not enter Cîteaux fully-formed and complete in the monastic life. He had to learn from his abbot, Stephen, that a promise was a promise. Bernard's youthful forgetfulness about his vow concerning the penitential psalms required a word of correction from Stephen. Conrad ignored what we think of as the usual hagiographical tendency to makes saints perfect from childhood and allowed for development in Bernard's monastic vocation.

I would contend that Jean Leclercq failed to consider this evolutionary side of Bernard and succumbed to a traditional hagiographical tendency to have the saint emerge fully formed from childhood and youth. At the same time, I think our modern master exaggerated Bernard's involvements. What I find in Bernard's writings, especially in his letters concerned with the monastic life, is not an attention to detail and everyday practice in the monastery, but a concern with human personalities, intentions, attitudes and ideals. Bernard looks for the 'big picture', and did not 'waste time' with organizational machinery. I cannot imagine the abbot of Clairvaux sitting patiently through a General Chapter at Cîteaux while administrative minutiae were being discussed. Perhaps he did so out of obedience, but his thoughts would have been elsewhere!

The tendency to make Bernard into the dynamo behind the establishment and success of the Cistercian Order distorts Bernard's genius for grasping a problem not in terms of its details but in the light of its significance for the monastic life as a whole. Just as Stephen Harding became an innovator in his conscientious imitation of Benedict's attention to the content of everyday life in a monastery, so too Bernard of Clairvaux brought innovation by imitating Benedict's attention to asceticism and mutual concern in the monastic community. Both sides of Benedict, legislation and love, are present in twelfth-century monasticism, and both were necessary to make the Cîteaux experiment into a success. With an abbot like Bernard, Stephen Harding had a publicist for his cause who could not be stopped. And with an abbot such as Stephen, Bernard had a father and authority figure who was down-to-earth and concerned about how legal structures could function in a just and caritative manner.

It does Bernard no credit to make him into the be-all and end-all of cistercian life in the twelfth century. Recent research has come more and more to emphasize the varieties of the cistercian experiment in various parts of Europe.[49] However much the personality and writings of Bernard overshadow all our other sources from the twelfth century, it is the organizational genius of Stephen Harding in the *Carta Caritatis* that provided the foundation for the structure from which Bernard could benefit.

In a manuscript from the Clairvaux daughter of Beaupré, which I elsewhere have dated to about 1200, Stephen Harding is called the 'main initiator of this order' (*ipsius ordinis precipuus iniciator*).[50] I think this formula comes as close as any to capturing the reality of Stephen Harding's contribution to the foundation of the Order of Cîteaux. He is not the single founder, but he is the central person behind the establishment of the Order.

Cistercian monks today choose to join Stephen with Alberic and Robert and to celebrate the feast of the founders of Cîteaux, without distinguishing among the individual contributions. This liturgical solution is indicative of an Order which for all its quarrels and splits through the centuries has time and again gone back to its origins in order to find new life and sustenance.

As an historian, however, I have felt obliged to distinguish among the contributions of the founders. I look upon Robert as a restless man who was after something better. Alberic I consider to have been Robert's close friend, who had the courage to continue the new foundation without Robert. In Stephen I see an administrative and organizational genius who built on familiar language and experience in the monastic inheritance and made a new structure. Without such a foundation, Bernard would have been unable to make his own unique contribution.

It is fashionable nowadays to 'deconstruct' the Order of Cîteaux and to point out that the sources even for the twelfth century do not point to the unity and unanimity that used to be considered the Order's trademark.[51] I am fascinated by much of the new work emerging from this decentralist viewpoint. It corresponds to what I found years ago in working on the Cistercians in Denmark. More importantly, this approach can contribute not only to our understanding of Cîteaux but also to a larger appreciation of the development of monastic and christian life in the Middle Ages and in our own time.

A few central texts, however, have an importance which cannot be ignored. Among them, the *Carta Caritatis* has grown in my appreciation during the last decade. When I looked at it in the 1980s for evidence of monastic friendship, I was disappointed by what seemed a sterile list of administrative regulations. Today I see in this source a fresh and inspired understanding of the Rule of Saint Benedict that could underpin new and lasting bonds among monastic houses. Behind the *Carta Caritatis Prior* I detect the mind and work of Stephen Harding. He thus becomes the rightful founder of the Order of Cîteaux.

Yet I still wonder. Jean Leclercq once challenged me by claiming that only monks can study monks. He may have been right, even though the very concept of the cistercian scholar nowadays welcomes us confused seculars into a world once mainly reserved for those who had taken vows. In the *translatio studii* that has taken place in the last decades between Europe and North America and between monks, nuns and seculars, Jean Leclercq remains the giant to whom we all refer. But in remembering Jean Leclercq, I prefer to think of him as the attentive and even somewhat mischievous figure who kidnapped and delighted my then two-year old son with Kalamazoo's famed ice cream. For years thereafter, Dom Jean sent us postcards of clowns. In some sense Jean Leclercq thought of himself as God's clown, performing for the Lord and not taking too seriously his role as world authority on monastic culture. With Jean Leclercq we are all clowns acting in God's great and painful circus.

Notes

1. This is a revised and expanded version of a paper presented at the 1995 Cistercian Studies Conference at Kalamazoo. I am grateful to Dr E. Rozanne Elder of the Institute of Cistercian Studies of Western Michigan University for making it possible for me to include this paper in the present collection. Also I am in debt to Chrysogonus Waddell of Gethsemani Abbey for invaluable advice and guidance. Finally I want to thank James France of Oxfordshire for kindly sending me photocopies of articles not easily available to me in Denmark.

2. This student is Oluf Schönbeck from the Department of Religious History, Copenhagen University. His observations are contained in a paper he wrote for me in 1990 entitled 'Cîteaux 1098–1119' and which revived my interest in a subject which I had long since dismissed as too difficult and controversial.

3. Jean Lefèvre, 'Que savons-nous du Cîteaux primitif?', *Revue d'histoire ecclésiastique* 51 (1956) 5–41, p 41. Translated by Bede Lackner, *The eleventh-century Background of Cîteaux* (CS 8, 1972) p. 261, n. 114. For a response, see J. Winandy, 'Les origines de Cîteaux et les travaux de M. Lefèvre', *Revue Bénédictine* 67 (1957) 49–76. Also helpful are: Chrysogonus Waddell, 'The *Exordium Cistercii* and the Summa Cartae Caritatis: A Discussion Continued', *Cistercian Ideals and Reality*, ed. John R. Sommerfeldt (CS 60, 1978) 30–49, and Christopher Holdsworth, 'The Chronology and Character of Early Cistercian Legislation on Art and Architecture', *Cistercian Art and Architecture in the British Isles*, ed. Christopher Norton (Cambridge, 1986) 40–55.

4. Published in the series Cîteaux: Studia et Documenta 3 (Achel, Belgium).

5. H. E. J. Cowdrey, "'Quidam Frater Stephanus Nomine, Anglicus Natione": The English Background of Stephen Harding', *Revue Bénédictine* 101 (1991) 322–40, esp. 323–5. Christopher Holdsworth has been kind enough to entrust me with a copy of his paper from the Cistercian Conference in 1994, and I look forward to its publication.

6. Trans. Bede Lackner in appendix to Louis Lekai, *The Cistercians: Ideals and Reality* (Kent State University Press: Ohio, 1977) p. 451. Latin text in Jean de la Croix Bouton and Jean Baptiste Van Damme, *Les plus anciens textes de Cîteaux*, Citeaux. Commentarii Cistercienses. Studia et Documenta 2 (Achel, 1974) p. 54. The edition will, we hope, be replaced in 1998 by the fruits of Chrysogonus Waddell's textual labors.

7. L.G.D. Baker, 'The Genesis of English Cistercian Chronicles', *Analecta Cisterciensia* 25 (1969) 14–41.

8. *Scriptores Historiae Danicae Minores* 2, ed. M.Cl. Gertz (Copenhagen, 1922; reprinted 1970) p. 158. My translation. See my *Conflict and Continuity at Øm Abbey* (Museum Tusculanum: Copenhagen, 1976), especially chapter 3, 'The Opening of the Exordium 1: Cistercian Polish vs. real Problems'.

9. Contained in Bouton and Van Damme (note 6 above) pp. 110–14 and translated by Lackner, pp. 443–45

10. After completing this section, I checked R.W. Southern's now classic description of the Cistercians in *Western Society and the Church in the Middle Ages*, The Pelican History of the Church 2 (Harmondsworth, 1970). Southern says about the two cistercian voices: 'The first Cistercians spoke equally confidently with two voices. The first was the voice of the military aristocracy from which they sprang, and this voice is most clearly heard in their legislation. The second voice was the

one which they used in the cloister—it was the voice of mutual friendship, of introspection and spiritual sweetness.' (p. 257)

11. Text in Bouton and Van Damme (note 6 above), p. 104.

12. Here and in what follows I use the Latin text of Bouton and Van Damme (note 6 above) and the English translation made in 1983 for private distribution by Martinus Cawley and John Baptist Hasbrouck of Guadalupe Abbey, Oregon, and by Chrysogonus Waddell. I hope this excellent translation is reprinted for wider distribution in 1998.

13. Trans. Cawley, Hasbrouck and Waddell (note 12 above), p. 13.

14. Trans. in *RB 1980: The Rule of St. Benedict*, ed. Timothy Fry (Liturgical Press: Collegeville, Minnesota) p. 293.

15. As in Lekai (note 6 above), pp. 31–2.

16. There were, of course, variations on this pattern, situations in which other houses with abbots maintained some type of bond with Cluny but did not give up their independence. The result was not the well-consolidated structure of an *ordo religiosus* which Cîteaux came to head. See C.H. Lawrence, *Medieval Monasticism* (Longman: London and New York, 1984 and later) esp. pp. 84–5.

17. Translation as in note 12 above, p. 4.

18. Chapter 3 in the *Carta Caritatis Prior*, text in Bouton and Van Damme (note 6 above), p. 92.

19. See Lawrence (note 16 above), p. 156: 'At the beginning the organisation was monarchic: the abbot of Cîteaux had absolute and undivided powers over his daughter-houses.' H.E.J. Cowdrey, *Revue Bénédictine* 101 (1991), p. 324: ' . . . the earliest documents of Stephen's abbacy indicate that he at first exercised strong personal, even monarchical authority—a veritable *paternalisme abbatial*.'

20. 'Unde nos multum de discordia nostrorum librorum quos ab uno interprete suscepimus ammirantes, Iudeos quosdam in sua scriptura peritos adiuimus, ac diligentissime lingua romana ab eis inquisiuimus de omnibus illis scripturarum locis. . . . Qui suos libros plures coram nobis reuoluentes, et in locis illis ubi eos rogabamus, hebraicam siue chaldaicam scripturam romanis uerbis nobis exponentes, partes vel uersus pro quibus turbabamur minime reppererunt.' The so-called Encyclical of Stephen Harding; text in Yolanta Załuska, *L'enluminure et le scriptorium de Cîteaux au xiie siècle*, Cîteaux Commentarii Cistercienses. Studia et Documenta 4 (Cîteaux, 1989) p. 274.

21. See Norman Cohn's now classic *The Pursuit of the Millennium* (Oxford University Press: New York, 1970), esp. 'The poor in the first crusades', pp. 61–70.

22. See *A Dialogue of a Philosopher with a Jew, and a Christian*, trans. Pierre J. Payer (Pontificate Institute of Mediaeval Studies: Toronto, 1979).

23. 'Mandamus filiis sancte ecclesie: nos hos hymnos quos beatum ambrosium archiepiscopum constat composuisse . . . cummunique fratrum nostrorum consilio ac decreto statuisse, ut amodo a nobis omnibus posteris nostris, hii tantum nullique alii canantur.' Printed in Chrysogonus Waddell, 'The Origin and Early Evolution of the Cistercian Antiphonary', *The Cistercian Spirit: A Symposium In Memory of Thomas Merton*, ed. M. Basil Pennington, CS 3 (1973) p. 206.

24. See the life of Peter of Jully found in PL 185:1255–70. Peter died in 1136 but this source was not composed before 1160, so it is late. See G. Maton, 'Pietro di Jully, beato', *Bibliotheca Sanctorum* 10 (1968), p. 704.

25. See Bede Lackner, *The Eleventh-Century Background* (note 3 above), pp. 235–6.

26. 'Notes towards the Exegesis of a Letter by Saint Stephen Harding', *Noble*

Piety and Reformed Monasticism, ed. E. Rozanne Elder, CS 65 (Kalamazoo, 1981) 10–39, esp. p. 33.

27. *Ibid.*, p. 35.

28. I use the critical edition, *Exordium Magnum Cisterciense sive Narratio de Initio Cisterciensis Ordinis*, ed. Bruno Griesser, Series Scriptorum S. Ordinis Cisterciensis (Editiones Cistercienses: Rome, 1961), abbreviated as EM, with the number of the book or *distinctio* in roman numerals, and the chapter in arabic.

29. See my 'Structure and Consciousness in the *Exordium Magnum Cisterciense*: The Clairvaux Cistercians after Bernard', *Cahiers de l'Institut du Moyen Age grec et latin* 30 (Copenhagen, 1979) 33–90, esp. pp. 37–40.

30. EM I.22, pp. 80–82. Part of this story (p. 82) is taken, as Bruno Griesser points out in the notes, from the *Vita Prima* of Saint Bernard (I.3.18, PL 185:237). The story of a dead monk returning in order to inform a doubting brother about some important event is, of course, very common in monastic literature.

31. EM I.23, p. 82: 'Et intelligens a viro spiritali se esse deprehensum procidit ad pedes eius negligentiam confitens atque indulgentiam petens.'

32. One thinks, for example, of Anthony and Paul at their meeting in the desert, as described by Jerome, when a raven dropped to them a loaf of bread. Contained in PL 23:17–28. See Helen Waddell's translation, *The Desert Fathers* (University of Michigan Press: Ann Arbor, 1966) p. 35.

33. EM I.24, p. 83, told as a story of love for Stephen by the cellarer, and so in the same tradition of ascetic friendship and devotion blessed by the gift of food as Jerome celebrated in his story of Paul the Hermit and Anthony: 'Et sincera caritate abbatem suum diligens discurrebat, si forte alicuibi aliquid inveniret, unde caritatem, quae intus ardebat, etiam foris ostenderet, cum ecce grandis quaedam avis advolat non mediocris quantitatis piscem unguibus ferens. . . .'

34. EM I.25, p. 83. See the much more concrete story in *Vita Prima* 1.6.27; PL 185:242.

35. EM I.26, p. 84: 'Omnibus, inquit, cogitationibus, quas ex iniuncto officio pro dispositione domus per diem admittere cogor, dico, ut foris remaneant nec prorsus ingredi mecum praesumant, sed exspectent, quousque cras dicta prima hic eas inveniam.'

36. EM I.27, p. 84, entitled 'De sincera humilitate ipsius': ' . . . ferula pastoralis eius, cum qua in festivis processionibus incedere solebat . . . quae usque hodie in Cisterciensi secretario ob reverentiam tanti patris conservata et in magna veneratione habita, non multum a communibus sustentatoriis, quibus senes et debiles inniti solent, distare videtur.' See the illustrations of the abbatial staffs attributed to Robert of Molesme and Bernard: *Saint Bernard et le monde cistercien*, Léon Pressouyre and Terryl N. Kinder (Paris, 1990) pp. 56–7.

37. I am grateful to James France of Oxfordshire for this formulation. Mr France is completing for 1998 an important survey on how cistercian monks and nuns have been portrayed in art, and so he has also been attentive to the ways Stephen Harding is illustrated.

38. *Statuta Capitulorum Generalium Ordinis Cisterciensis* 1, Bibliothèque de la Revue d'Histoire ecclésiastique 9 (Louvain, 1933).

39. Father Chrysogonus promises us a much-needed new edition of the statutes. In April 1995 Constance Berman gave at the Medieval Centre in Copenhagen a talk entitled, 'Was there an Order of Cîteaux in the twelfth century?'. Her point is that it is not until late in the century that we find regular yearly decisions at the Chapter which deal with individual houses, instead of reassertions for the

whole Order of practices already outlined in the early literature. Professor Berman's conclusion is that the General Chapter only slowly evolved into the legislative body it has been traditionally seen as having been almost from the beginning.

40. As seen in the rulebook written by Ulrich of Hirsau and reflecting practices at Cluny. See Lawrence, *Medieval Monasticism* (note 16 above), p. 100.

41. *Carta Caritatis Prior*, ch. 7, trans. by Waddell *et al.* (note 12 above), p. 19.

42. Bouton and Van Damme (note 6 above), ch. 9, p. 69: '. . . multumque diu nitendo laboraverat, ut ad illum de Molismo transmigrarent fratres locum, et pro hoc negotio multa obprobria, carcerem et verbera perpessus fuerat.'

43. *Exordium Parvum*, ch. 10, as in Bouton and Van Damme (note 6 above).

44. I have used the edition of Dalgairns edited by Herbert Thurston and published in 1898 by The Newman Bookshop, Westminster, Maryland. Note that Jean-Baptiste Van Damme in his popular *Les trois fondateurs de Cîteaux*, Pain de Cîteaux 29 (1966), emphasizes that Robert of Molesme, Alberic and Stephen all are to be considered as founders of Citeaux.

Basil Pennington was even more democratic when he asserted that 'the actual founders of the Order of Cîteaux were the abbots gathered in the General Chapter of 1123'. See his 'Discerning the Spirits and Aims of the Founders', *The Cistercian Spirit. A Symposium In Memory of Thomas Merton*, ed., M. Basil Pennington, CS 3 (1973) p. 16. Pennington prefaced this conclusion, however, with the remark (pp. 15–16): 'If the title of founder of the Order of Cîteaux can be claimed for any single man, Stephen Harding would be that man.'

45. 'La "paternité" de S. Bernard et les débuts de l'ordre cistercien', *Revue bénédictine* 103 (1993) 445–81. This article is summarized in 'Saint Bernard and the Beginnings of the Cistercian Order', *Cistercian Studies Quarterly* 29 (1994) 379–93. I will not deal here with Leclercq's 'Le témoignage de Guillaume de Malmesbury sur S. Etienne Harding', *Studia Monastica* 36 (1994) 13–19, where Dom Jean tries to demolish the witness of William of Malmesbury to Stephen Harding's importance at Cîteaux as a result of excessive patriotism. Although I agree that William's description needs to be looked at critically, I find Leclercq's conclusions too radical.

46. 'La paternité', p. 458: 'A Châtillon, Bernard crée, si l'on peut ainsi parler, un "pré-Clairvaux" dont il est le père, qui passera par Cîteaux, où Bernard gardera ce rôle.' Cf. *Vita Prima* 1.3.15; PL 185:235–36.

47. As 1La paternité', p. 471: 'Si l'Ordre de Cîteaux existe, c'est à cause de S. Bernard. Sans lui l'abbaye de Cîteaux aurait continué à décliner lentement, s'acheminant vers sa fin.' In view of the work done by historians such as Louis Lekai to point out how the Cistercian texts posterior to about 1120 exaggerate the idea of decline at Cîteaux prior to Bernard's entrance, it is surprising to see how Leclercq accepts this out-of-date interpretation of Cîteaux's situation in 1112–13. One aspect of Leclercq's presentation which does offer a helpful new perspective, however, is his contention that monastic life at Jully resembled that of Cîteaux but was established at the time Bernard joined Cîteaux, and with Bernard's involvement ('La paternité', pp. 459–61).

48. See 'La paternité', pp. 472–74.

49. See the overview provided by Kaspar Elm, 'Questioni e risultati della recente ricerca sui cistercensi', *I cistercensi nel mezzogiorno medioevale*, ed. Hubert Houben and Benedetto Vetere (Congedo Editore, 1994) 7–31.

50. Paris Bibliothèque nationale MS latin 15912, f. 147va: 'Sancte recordationis Stephanus quondam cistercii abbas et ipsius ordinis precipuus iniciator, vir

conspicue sanctitatis omniumque virtutum gratia decoratus apparuit.' This remark is contained in a version of Herbert of Clairvaux's *Liber miraculorum* not found in the published version in PL 185. See my 'The Cistercians and the Rise of the Exemplum', *Classica et Mediævalia* 34 (1983) 211–67.

51. As in the survey of Kaspar Elm, note 49 above.

A Bibliography of the Works of Jean Leclercq

Compiled by Michael Martin

The bibliography below is based in part on five previous bibliographies:

Louis Leloir, OSB, in *Bernard of Clairvaux: Studies presented to Dom Jean Leclercq* Cistercian Studies Series 23 (Cistercian Publications, 1972) 215–264 [through 1972].

Réginald Grégoire, OSB, in *Studia Monastica* 10 (1968) 331–359 [through 1968]; *Studia Monastica* 20 (1978) 409–423 [1968–1977]; *Studia Monastica* 30 (1988) 417–440 [1978–1988].

Jean-Marie Christiaens, OSB, in *Monastic Studies* 16 (1985) 253–260 [addenda to the 1968–1977 bibliography of Grégoire].

I. Books

1. Translation and Introduction, Smaragdus of Saint-Mihiel [Smaragde] (†825) *La voie royale; Le diademe des moines* (La Pierre-qui-Vire, 1940/1949) pp. 259.

2. *Jean de Paris et l'ecclésiologie du XIIIe siècle* (Paris: Vrin, 1942) pp. 268.

3. *La spiritualité de Pierre de Celle (1115–1183)* Études de théologie et d'histoire de la spiritualité, 7 (Paris: Vrin, 1946) pp. 246.

4. *Pierre le Vénérable* (Saint-Wandrille: Éd. de Fontenelle, 1946) pp. 407.

5. In collaboration with J. P. Bonnes *Un maître de la vie spirituelle au XIe siècle: Jean de Fécamp* (Paris: Vrin, 1946; 1986) pp. 236.

6. *Analecta Monastica.* Première série, Studia Anselmiana, 20 (Rome: Pont. Institutum S. Anselmi, 1948) pp. 240.

7. *Saint Bernard mystique* (Bruges et Paris: Desclée de Brouwer, 1948) pp. 494.

8. *La vie parfaite. Points de vue sur l'essence de l'état religieux* (Turnhout et Paris: Brepols, 1948) pp. 170; *The Life of Perfection* (Collegeville, MN, 1961) pp. 125; *La vita perfetta* (Milan: Ancora, 1961); *La vida perfecta* (Barcelona: Herder, 1965).

9. *Lettres d'Yves de Chartres.* Édition critique et traduction précédées d'une introduction (Paris: Les Belles-Lettres, 1949) pp. 313.

10. *Un humaniste ermite. Le B^x Paul Giustiniani (1476–1528)* (Rome: Ed. Camaldoli, 1951) pp. 182; Italian edition (S. Eremo Tuscolano: Frascati, 1975).

11. *Analecta Monastica.* Deuxième série, Studia Anselmiana, 31 (Rome: Pont. Institutum S. Anselmi, 1953) pp. 206.

12. *Études sur S. Bernard et le texte de ses écrits.* Analecta S. Ordinis Cisterciensis, 9 (Rome: Apud Curiam Generalem Sacri Ordinis Cisterciensis, 1953; 1955) pp. 247.

13. *La dottrina del beato Paolo Giustiniani* (Frascati, 1953); *Seul avec Dieu. La vie érémitique d'après la doctrine du B^x Paul Giustiniani* Preface by Thomas Merton (Paris: Plon, 1955) pp. 175; *Alone with God* (New York: Farrar, Strauss and Cudahy, 1961; London, The Catholic Book Church, 1961; 1962; and London: Hodder and Stoughton, 1962) pp. 192; Spanish edition (Medellín, 1976); *Il richiamo del deserto. La doctrina del Beato Paolo Giustiniani* Spiritualità/Maestri, 8 (Rome: Ed. Paoline, 1977) pp. 174.

14. *L'amour des lettres et le désir de Dieu. Initiation aux auteurs monastiques du moyen âge* (Paris: Cerf, 1957; 1963) pp. 269; *The Love of Learning and the Desire for God* (New York: Fordham Univ. Press, 1961, 1974, 1977, 1982 and New York: Mentor Omega Book, 1962); *Wissenschaft und Gottverlangen* (Düsseldorf: Patmos-Verlag, 1963); *Cultura umanistica e desiderio di Dio* (Florence: Ed. Sansoni, 1965); *Cultura y vida cristiana* (Salamanca: Ed. Sigueme, 1965); English edition (London: S.P.C.K., 1977); *Cultura y vida cristiana* 2nd Italian edition (Firenze: Sansoni Editore Nuova, 1983);

Cultura umanistica e desiderio di Dio: studio sulla letteratura monastica del medio evo (Firenze: Sansoni, 1988) pp. 382; *L'amour des lettres et le désir de Dieu. Initiation aux auteurs monastiques du moyen âge* 3e éd. corr. (Paris, 1990).

15. In collaboration with C. H. Talbot and H. Rochais. *S. Bernardi Opera* Vol. I (Rome: Éditiones Cistercienses, 1957) pp. 264; Vol. II (1958) pp. 328; In collaboration with H. Rochais, Vol. III (1963) pp. 532; Vol. IV (1966) pp. 496; Vol. V (1968) pp. 452; Vol. VI/1 (1970) pp. 416; Vol. VI/2 (1972) pp. 305; Vol. VII (1974) pp. 408; Vol. VIII (1977); Also available on CD-Rom: *CETEDOC: Library of Christian Latin Texts* CLCLT 1 (Turnhout: Brepols, 1991; CLCLT 2, 1994) 1 disc + 1 manual.

16. *L'idée de la royauté de Christ au moyen âge.* Coll. Unam Sanctam (Paris: Cerf, 1959) pp. 235.

17. *S. Pierre Damien ermite et homme d'Église* (Rome: Ed. Storia e Letteratura, 1960) pp. 284; *S. Pietro Damiano eremita e uomo di Chiesa* (Brescia: Morcélliana, 1972) pp. 294.

18. *The History of Medieval Spirituality* (Typescript, privately reproduced and distributed by the Benedictine Institute of Sacred Theology, June, 1960, St. John's University, Collegeville, MN.) pp. 139.

19. F. Vandenbroucke and L. Bouyer, eds., in collaboration with Jean Leclercq. *La spiritualité du moyen âge* (Paris: Aubier, 1961), Leclercq wrote Part I of Vol. 2, 'De saint Grégoire le Grand à saint Bernard, du VIe au XIIe siècle,' pp. 9–272; Revised and augmented edition (Paris: Aubier, 1966); *The Spirituality of the Middle Ages* (New York: Desclée, 1968) and London: Burns & Oates, 1968) pp. 602; *La Spiritualità del medioevo de san Gregoria a san Bernardo (sec. VI-XII).* Storia della spiritualita cristiana, 3/1 (Bologna: Dehoniane, 1969; 1986) pp. 383; American editions (New York: Seabury Press, 1968; 1977; 1981; 1982).

20. *Études sur le vocabulaire monastique du moyen âge.* Studia Anselmiana, 48 (Rome, 1961) pp. 186.

21. *Recueil d'études sur S. Bernard et ses écrits* I (Rome: Edizioni Storia e Letteratura, 1962) pp. 370; II (1966) pp. 405; III (1969) pp. 436; IV, Storia e Letteratura, 167 (1987) pp. 435; V (1992) pp. 510.

22. *La liturgie et les paradoxes chrétiens* (Paris: Cerf, 1963) pp. 306;

La liturgia y las paradojas cristianas (Bilbao: Ed. Mensajéro, 1967); *La liturgia e i paradossi cristiani* (Rome: Ed. Paoline, 1967).

23. *Otia monastica. Études sur le vocabulaire de la contemplation au moyen âge.* Studia Anselmiana, 51 (Rome, 1963) pp. 186.

24. *Aux sources de la spiritualité occidentale: étapes et constantes.* Tradition et spiritualité, 4 (Paris: Cerf, 1964) pp. 318; *Espiritualidad occidental. Fuentes* (Salamanca: Ed. Sigueme, 1967).

25. *Témoins de la spiritualité occidentale* (Paris: Cerf, 1965) pp. 410; *Espiritualidad occidental. Testigos* (Salamanca: Sigueme, 1967).

26. *Chances de la spiritualité occidentale* (Paris: Cerf, 1966) pp. 382.

27. *S. Bernard et l'esprit cistercien* (Paris: du Seuil, 1966) pp. 190; French edition reprints (Paris: Éditions du Seuil, 1975; 1978); *Bernard of Clairvaux and the Cistercian Spirit.* Cistercian Studies Series 16 (Kalamazoo, MI: Cistercian Publications, 1976) pp. 175; *S. Bernard e lo spirito cisterciense* (Torino, 1976) pp. 130; *San Bernardo: monje y profeta (1090–1153)* (Madrid: Bibliotheca de Autores Cristianos, 1990) pp. 165; *Bernhard von Clairvaux. Entschiedenheit in Demut,* Aus dem Französischen von Willy J. Helg, P. Alberich Martin Altermatt, O.Cist, Meister des Glaubens, 3 (Würzburg: Echter Verlag/Freiburg (Schweiz): Paulusverlag, 1991).

28. *Aspects du monachisme hier et aujourd'hui* (Paris: Éd. de la Source, 1968) pp. 368; *Aspects of Monasticism.* Cistercian Studies Series 7 (Kalamazoo, MI: Cistercian Publications, 1978) pp. 343.

29. *Vie religieuse et vie contemplative.* Coll. Renouveau (Gembloux-Paris: Éd. Duculot, 1969) pp. 274; *Vida religiosa y vida contemplativa* (Bilbao: Mensajero, 1970) pp. 252; *Vita religiosa e vita contemplativa* (Assisi: Cittadella editrice, 1972) pp. 211; *Contemplative Life.* Cistercian Studies Series 19 (Kalamazoo, MI: Cistercian Publications, 1978) pp. 193.

30. *Le défi de la vie contemplative.* Coll. Renouveau (Gembloux-Paris: Éd. Duculot, 1970) pp. 374; *El desafío de la vida contemplativa* (Bilbao: Mensajero, 1971) pp. 300.

31. *Moines et moniales ont-ils un avenir?* (Bruxelles-Paris: Lumen vitae, 1971) pp. 264.

32. *Nouveau visage de Bernard de Clairvaux. Approches psycho-historiques* (Paris: Cerf, 1976) pp. 180; *A Second Look at Bernard of Clairvaux* Cistercian Studies Series 105 (Kalamazoo, MI: Cistercian Publications, 1990) pp. 150.

33. *Libérez les prisonniers. Du bon larron à Jean XXIII* (Paris: Cerf, 1976) pp. 166.

34. *Monks and Love in Twelfth Century France. Psycho-historical Essays* (Oxford: Clarendon Press, 1979) pp. 146; *L'amour vu par les moines du XII*[e] *siècle* (Paris: Cerf, 1983) pp. 160; *I monaci e l'amore nella Francia del XII secolo* (Rome: Jouvence, 1984) pp. 184.

35. *Monks on Marriage. A Twelfth-Century View* (New York: Seabury Press, 1982) pp. 136; *Le mariage vu par les moines au XII*[e] *siècle* (Paris: Cerf, 1983) pp. 162; *I monaci e il matrimonio. Un'indagine sul XII secolo* (Torino: Società Editrice Internazionale, 1984) pp. 230.

36. *La femme et les femmes dans l'œuvre de saint Bernard* (Paris: Téqui, 1983) pp. 144; *La donna e le donne in San Bernardo.* Biblioteca di Cultura Medievale. Di fronte e attraverso, 149 (Milan: Jaca Book, 1985) pp. 144; *Women and Saint Bernard of Clairvaux.* Cistercian Studies Series 104 (Kalamazoo, MI: Cistercian Publications, 1989) pp. 175.

37. Bernard McGinn and John Meyendorff, eds., in collaboration with Jean Leclercq *Christian Spirituality: Origins to the Twelfth Century.* World Spirituality, 16 (New York: Crossroad, 1985; 1992); Leclercq wrote 'Monasticism and Asceticism- Part II: Western Christianity,' pp. 113–131; and, 'Prayer and Contemplation- Part II: Western,' pp. 415–426.

38. *Nouvelle page d'histoire monastique. Histoire de l'A.I.M. 1960–1985.* Secretariat de l'Aide Inter-Monasteres, 7, rue d'Issy, F–92170 Vanves (Vanves, 1986) pp. 222; *Venticinque anni di storia monastica. A.I.M. 1960–1985* (Parma: Tipolitografia Benedettina Editrice, 1988) pp. 246.

39. *Bernard de Clairvaux.* Bibliothèque d'histoire du christianisme, 19 (Paris: Desclée, 1989) pp. 166; *Bernhard von Clairvaux. Ein Mann prägt seine Zeit* (München: Verlag Neue Stadt, 1990); *Bernardo de Claraval* (Valencia: Edicep, 1991) pp. 237; *Bernardo di Chiaravalle* (Milan: Vita e pensiero, 1992) pp. 174.

40. *Umanesimo e cultura monastica* (Milan: Jaca Book, 1989) pp. 168.

41. *Esperienza spirituale e teologia: alla scuola dei monaci medievali.* Biblioteca di Cultura Medievale. Di fronte e attraverso, 262 (Milan: Jaca Book, 1990) pp. 195.

42. *Il monachesimo occidentale oggi.* Orizzonti monastici, 4 (Seregno: Abbazia San Benedetto, 1992) pp. 96.

43. *Regards monastiques sur le Christ au Moyen Âge.* Jésus et Jésus-Christ, 56 (Paris: Desclée/Groupe Mame, 1993) pp. 251.

44. *Momenti e figure di storia monastica italiana* a cura di Valerio Cattana OSB. Italia benedettina 14 (Cesena, Badia di Santa Maria del Monte: Centro storico benedettino italiano, 1993) pp. 679.

45. *Di grazia in grazia. Memorie. Presentazione* di Inos Biffi, Biblioteca di cultura medievale 330 (Milan: Jaca Book, 1993). [Leclercq's autobiography. The French text remains unpublished.]

46. *'Ossa humiliate' I: Frammenti di spiritualità monastica* (Seregno: Abbazia San Benedetto, 1993) pp. 100.

47. *La figura della donna nel medioevo* (Milan: Jaca Book, 1994) pp. 213. [Selection of articles.]

1939

48. 'Jean de Paris. Le Christ médicin,' *La vie spirituelle* 59 (1938–1939) 293–300.

49. 'La théologie comme science d'après la littérature quodlibétique,' *Recherches de théologie ancienne et médiévale* 11 (1939) 351–374.

50. 'La renonciation de Célestin V et l'opinion théologique en France du vivant de Boniface VIII,' *Revue d'histoire de l'Église de France* 25 (1939) 1–12; Charles T. Wood, ed. *Philip the Fair and Boniface VIII* (New York, 1967) 42–46; *Felipe el Hermoso y Bonifacio VIII* (Uteha, Mexico, 1967).

51. 'Des stations romaines au missel jociste,' *La vie sprituelle* 59 (1939) 307–309.

1940

52. 'La realeza de Jesucristo en las obras de Santo Tomás,' *Ciencìa Tomista* 59 (1940) 144–156; Reprinted in Jean Leclercq, *L'idée de la royauté de Christ au moyen âge* Coll. Unam Sanctam (Paris: Cerf, 1959).

1941

53. 'Les bénédictins en France au temps de Philippe le Bel et de Boniface VIII,' *Revue Mabillon* 31 (1941) 85–100; 32 (1942) 1–14.

1942

54. 'Un témoignage du XIIIe siècle sur la nature de la théologie,'

Archives d'histoire doctrinale et littéraire du moyen âge 13 (1940–1942) 301–321.

55. 'La royauté du Christ dans les lettres des papes du XIIIe siècle,' *Revue historique du droit français et étranger* (1942) 112–120; Reprinted in Jean Leclercq, *L'idée de la royauté de Christ au moyen âge* Coll. Unam Sanctam (Paris: Cerf, 1959).

56. 'Une Lamentation inédite de Jean de Fécamp,' *Revue bénédictine* 54 (1942) 41–60.

57. 'Un ancien recueil de leçons pour les vigiles des défunts,' *Revue bénédictine* 54 (1942) 16–40.

58. 'Cluny et le Concile de Bâle,' *Revue d'histoire de l'Église de France* 28 (1942) 1–15.

59. 'Cluny pendant le Grand Schisme d'Occident,' *Revue Mabillon* 32 (1942) 1–14.

1943

60. 'Prédicateurs bénédictins aux XIe et XIIe siècles,' *Revue Mabillon* 33 (1943) 48–73.

61. 'La consécration légendaire de la basilique de Saint-Denis et la question des indulgences,' *Revue Mabillon* 33 (1943) 74–84.

1944

62. 'L'idée de la royauté du Christ au XIIIe siècle,' *L'année théologique* 5 (1944) 217–242; Reprinted in Jean Leclercq, *L'idée de la royauté du Christ au moyen âge.* Coll. Unam Sanctam (Paris: Cerf, 1959).

63. 'Les méditations d'un moine du XIIe siècle,' *Revue Mabillon* 34 (1944) 1–19.

64. 'L'interdit et l'excommunication d'après les lettres de Fulbert de Chartres,' *Revue historique de droit français et etranger* (1944) 67–77.

65. 'Dévotion privée, piété populaire et liturgie au moyen âge,' *Études de pastorale liturgique* (Rome, 1944) 149–183.

66. 'Lecture et oraison,' *La vie spirituelle* 70 (1944) 392–402.

1945

67. 'L'exégèse médiévale,' *Bulletin Thomiste* 7 (1942–1945) 59–67.

68. 'Le sermon sur la royauté du Christ au moyen âge,' *Archives d'histoire doctrinale et littéraire du moyen âge* 14 (1943–1945) 143–180;

Reprinted in Jean Leclercq, *L'idée de la royauté de Christ au moyen âge*. Coll. Unam Sanctam (Paris: Cerf, 1959).

69. 'Fleury au moyen âge,' Introduction to *Saint-Benoît-sur-Loire* Coll. 'Églises et monastères de France' (Paris: Cerf, 1945) 10–12.

70. 'Le *De grammatica* de Hugues de Saint-Victor,' *Archives d'histoire doctrinale et littéraire du moyen âge* 14 (1943–1945) 263–322.

71. 'L'Ascension, triomphe du Christ,' *La vie spirituelle* 72 (1945) 289–300; Reprinted in Jean Leclercq, *La liturgie et les paradoxes chrétiens* (Paris: Cerf, 1963).

72. 'L'amitié dans les lettres au moyen âge,' *Revue du moyen âge latin* 1 (1945) 391–410.

73. 'Un nouveau fragment du Traité, De unitate divinae essentiae et pluralitate creaturarum?' *Revue du moyen âge latin* 1 (1945) 173–177.

74. 'Un sermon prononcé pendant la guerre de Flandre sous Philippe le Bel,' *Revue du moyen âge latin* 1 (1945) 165–172.

75. 'Un traité De fallaciis in theologia,' *Revue du moyen âge latin* 1 (1945) 43–46.

76. 'Un art liturgique populaire,' *Cahiers de l'art sacré* 2 (1945) 17–23.

77. 'Les paradoxes de l'économie monastique,' *Economie et humanisme* 4 (1945) 15–35.

78. 'Une série de bénédictions pour les lectures de l'Office,' *Ephemerides liturgicae* 59 (1945) 318–321.

79. 'Comment fut construit Saint-Denis,' Coll. 'La Clarté-Dieu' (Paris, Cerf, 1945) 1–56.

80. 'Les anges au Baptême,' collection *Bible et Missel* (Paris: Cerf, 1945) 1–16; *Les anges au Baptême* (Paris: Cerf, 1946) pp. 16; Reprinted in Jean Leclercq, *La liturgie et les paradoxes chrétiens* (Paris: Cerf, 1963).

81. Review of P. Salmon *Le lectionnaire de Luxeuil*. In *La Maison-Dieu* 3 (1945) 119–124.

1946

82. 'La Collection des Lettres d'Yves de Chartres,' *Revue bénédictine* 56 (1945–1946) 108–125.

83. 'Deux sermons inédits de S. Fulgence,' *Revue bénédictine* 56 (1945–1946) 93–107.

84. 'Les décrets de Bernard de Saintes,' *Revue du moyen âge latin* 2 (1946) 167–170.

85. 'Technique et rédemption. La mystique du vol,' *Revue nouvelle* 3 (1946) 161–170.

86. 'Victor Leroquais,' *Revue du moyen âge latin* 2 (1946) 126–128.

87. 'La Chaise-Dieu au moyen âge,' Introduction to Paul Deschamps *La Chaise-Dieu* Les monastères de France, 3 (Paris: Cerf, 1946) 9–11.

88. 'Plaidoyer pour le temps présent,' *Revue nouvelle* 4 (1946) 3–7.

89. 'Pour l'iconographie des Apôtres,' *Revue bénédictine* 56 (1945–1946) 216–217.

90. 'Les méditations eucharistiques d'Arnauld de Bonneval,' *Recherches de théologie ancienne et médiévale* 13 (1946) 40–56.

91. 'Médiévisme et unionisme,' *Irénikon* 19 (1946) 6–23.

92. 'L'idée de la royauté du Christ dans l'œuvre de Saint Justin,' *L'Année théologique* 7 (1946) 83–95; Reprinted in Jean Leclercq, *L'idée de la royauté de Christ au moyen âge* Coll. Unam Sanctam (Paris: Cerf, 1959).

93. 'Katolsk Blomstring i Frankrig,' *Catholica* 3 (1946) 121–130.

94. 'Le genre épistolaire au moyen âge,' *Revue du moyen âge latin* 2 (1946) 63–70.

95. 'Recherches sur d'anciens sermons monastiques,' *Revue Mabillon* 36 (1946) 1–14.

96. 'Aux origines du cycle de Noël,' *Ephemerides liturgicae* 60 (1946) 7–26.

97. 'Le sermon, acte liturgique,' *La Maison-Dieu* 8 (1946) 27–46; Reprinted in Jean Leclercq, *La liturgie et les paradoxes chrétiens* (Paris: Cerf, 1963).

98. 'Deux anciennes versions de la Légende de l'Abbé Macaire,' *Revue Mabillon* 36 (1946) 65–79.

99. 'Le magistère du prédicateur au XIIIe siècle,' *Archives d'histoire doctrinale et littéraire du moyen âge* 15 (1946) 105–147.

100. 'Bénédictions pour les lectures de l'Office de Noël,' *Miscellanea Giovanni Mercati* II (Rome, 1946) 1–7.

101. 'Pierre le Vénérable et l'invitation au salut,' *Bulletin des missions* 20 (1946) 145–156; Reprinted in Jean Leclercq, *Témoins de la spiritualité occidentale* (Paris: Cerf, 1965).

102. 'L'epiphanie, fête du sacre,' *La vie spirituelle* 75 (1946) 6–17;

Reprinted in Jean Leclercq, *La liturgie et les paradoxes chrétiens* (Paris: Cerf, 1963).

103. 'Aspects de la dévotion mariale au moyen âge,' *Cahiers de la vie spirituelle 'La Sainte Vierge, Figure de l'Église'* (Paris, 1946) 241–261; Reprinted in Jean Leclercq, *La liturgie et les paradoxes chrétiens* (Paris: Cerf, 1963).

104. 'Catholica Unitas,' *Cahiers de la vie spirituelle* 'La Communion des Saints' (Paris, 1946) 37–53; English in *Worship* 8 (1961) 470–485.

105. 'La lecture divine,' *La Maison-Dieu* 5 (1946) 21–33; Reprinted in Jean Leclercq, *La liturgie et les paradoxes chrétiens* (Paris: Cerf, 1963).

106. 'Points de vue sur l'histoire de l'état religieux,' *La vie spirituelle* 74 (1946) 816–833; 75 (1946) 127–137.

107. 'Un sermon inédit de S. Thomas sur la royauté du Christ,' *Revue thomiste* 46 (1946) 152–166; Reprinted in Jean Leclercq, *L'idée de la royauté de Christ* (Paris: Cerf, 1959) 79–107.

108. 'Dom Germain Morin,' *La Maison-Dieu* 6 (1946) 160–162.

109. Review of I. Herwegen, *Sinn und Geist der Benediktinerregel.* In *La Maison-Dieu* 6 (1946) 135–139.

1947

110. 'Le latin chrétien, langue d'Église,' *La Maison-Dieu* 11 (1947) 55–75.

111. 'Le florilège d'Abbon de Saint-Germain,' *Revue du moyen âge latin* 3 (1947) 113–140.

112. 'Inédits bernardins dans un manuscrit d'Engelberg,' *Revue Mabillon* 37 (1947) 1–16; Reprinted in Jean Leclercq, *Recueil d'études sur S. Bernard et ses écrits* II (Rome: Ed. Storia e Letteratura, 1966).

113. 'Les études universitaires dans l'Ordre de Cluny,' *Mélanges bénédictins* (1947) 351–371.

114. 'Une prière des moines de Saint-Airy,' *Revue bénédictine* 57 (1947) 224–226.

115. 'Passage authentique inédit de Guitmond d'Aversa,' *Revue bénédictine* 57 (1947) 213–214.

116. 'Autour d'un manuscrit de la Règle du Maître,' *Revue bénédictine* 57 (1947) 210–212.

117. 'Prédication et rhétorique au temps de Saint Augustin,' *Revue bénédictine* 57 (1947) 117–131.

118. 'Simoniaca heresis,' *Studi Gregoriani* I (Rome, 1947) 523–530.

119. 'Symbolique chrétienne de la lune,' *Lunaires, Cahiers de Puésie* 4 (1947) 133–148.

120. 'Fragmenta Reginensia,' *Ephemerides liturgicae* 61 (1947) 289–296.

121. 'Une lettre inédite de Saint Pierre Damien sur la vie érémitique,' *Studia Anselmiana*, 18–19 (Rome, 1947) 283–293.

122. 'Le IIIe livre des homélies de Bède le Vénérable,' *Recherches de théologie ancienne et médiévale* 14 (1947) 211–218; Corpus Christianorum Series latina, 122 (1955) 381–384.

123. 'Un miracle de Notre-Dame à Avesnes au XIe siècle,' *Société archéologique et historique d'Avesnes 'Mémoires'* 18 (1947) 79–85.

124. 'L'idéal du théologien au moyen âge. Textes inédits,' *Revue des sciences religieuses* 21 (1947) 121–148.

125. 'Les prières inédites de Nicolas de Clamanges,' *Revue d'ascétique et de mystique* 23 (1947) 170–183.

126. 'La vie évangélique selon la Règle de saint Benoît,' *La vie spirituelle* 76 (1947) 848–855.

127. 'La royauté du Christ dans la spiritualité française du XVIIe siècle,' *La vie spirituelle, Supplément* 1 (1947) 216–229, 291–307.

128. 'Un opuscule inédit de Jean de Limoges sur l'exemption,' *Analecta Sacri Ordinis Cisterciensis* 3 (1947) 147–154.

129. 'Un recueil espagnol d'opuscules ecclésiologiques au XIVe siècle,' *Analecta Sacra Tarraconensia* 20 (1947) 2–6.

130. 'Introduction,' *Sermons [de] Leon le Grand* Sources chrétiennes 22, Dom René Dolle, translator and notes (Paris: Éditions du Cerf, 1947) 7–62; 2nd edition (1965) 7–55.

131. 'Jours d'ivresse (Sobria ebrietas),' *La vie spirituelle 'Le huitième jour'* 76 (1947) 574–691; Reprinted in Jean Leclercq, *La liturgie et les paradoxes chrétiens* (Paris: Cerf, 1963).

132. Review of J. Travers, OP *Valeur sociale de la liturgie d'après S. Thomas d'Aquin* (Paris, 1946). In *La Maison-Dieu* 12 (1947) 145–152.

1948

133. 'La Sainte Église et la rémission des péchés,' *Cahiers de la vie spirituelle 'L'Église et le pécheur'* (Paris, 1948) 12–28; Reprinted in Jean Leclercq, *La liturgie et les paradoxes chrétiens* (Paris: Cerf, 1963).

134. 'L'Église pénitente,' *Cahiers de la vie spirituelle 'L'Église et le pécheur'* (Paris, 1948) 226–235.

135. 'La voie royale,' *La vie spirituelle, Supplément* 2 (1948) 338–352.

136. 'Le doigt de Dieu,' *La vie spirituelle* 78 (1948) 492–507; *Worship* 7 (1962) 426–437; Reprinted in Jean Leclercq, *La liturgie et les paradoxes chrétiens* (Paris: Cerf, 1963).

137. 'Une homélie-prière sur le Saint-Esprit,' *Revue d'ascétique et de mystique* 24 (1948) 80–86.

138. 'Smaragde et la grammaire chrétienne,' *Revue du moyen âge latin* 4 (1948) 15–22.

139. 'Pour l'histoire de deux processions,' *Ephemerides liturgicae* 62 (1948) 83–88.

140. 'Les inédits africains de l'homéliaire de Fleury,' *Revue bénédictine* 58 (1948) 53–72; Partially reprinted in *Patrologiae latinae, Supplementum* 3: 1412–1424.

141. 'Nouveau témoin du Conflit des Filles de Dieu,' *Revue bénédictine* 58 (1948) 110–124.

142. 'La vie économique des monastères au moyen âge,' *Inspiration religieuse et structures temporelles* (Paris, 1948) 211–259.

143. 'L'idée de la royauté du Christ au XIVe siècle,' *Miscellanea Pio Paschini*, Lateranum 14 (Rome, 1948) 405–425; *Revista española de teologia* IV (1950) 249–265; Reprinted in Jean Leclercq, *L'idée de la royauté de Christ au moyen âge* (Paris: Cerf, 1959).

144. 'Les deux compilations de Thomas de Perseigne,' *Mediaeval Studies* 10 (1948) 204–209.

145. 'Tables pour l'inventaire des homéliaires manuscrits,' *Scriptorium* 2 (1948) 195–214; Partially reprinted by C.L. Smetana, *Traditio* 15 (1959) 165–180.

146. 'La discrétion bénédictine,' *Prudence chrétienne* (Paris, 1948) 100–107.

147. 'Les manuscrits des bibliothéques d'Espagne,' *Scriptorium* 3 (1948) 140–144.

148. 'Les études médiolatines en Espagne,' *Revue du moyen âge latin* 4 (1948) 440–447.

149. 'Un florilège attribué à un moine de Poblet,' *Analecta Sacra Tarraconensia* 21 (1948) 153–156.

1949

150. 'Le centenaire de la liberté religieuse au Danemark,' *La vie*

intellectuelle (1949) 112–125.

151. 'Documents pour l'histoire des chanoines réguliers,' *Revue d'histoire ecclésiastique* 44 (1949) 556–569.

152. 'Une nouvelle édition des œuvres de S. Bernard,' *Revue d'histoire ecclésiastique* 44 (1949) 194–197.

153. 'Le commentaire du Cantique des cantiques attribué à Anselme de Laon,' *Recherches de théologie ancienne et médiévale* 16 (1949) 29–39.

154. 'Textes et manuscrits de quelques bibliothéques d'Espagne,' *Hispania sacra* 2 (1949) 91–118.

155. 'Smaragde et son œuvre. Introduction à la traduction de La Voie Royale,' *La Pierre-qui-vire* (1949) 3–23; Reprinted in Jean Leclercq, *Témoins de la spiritualité occidentale* (Paris: Cerf, 1965).

156. 'L'idée de la royauté du Christ pendant le grand Schisme et la crise conciliaire,' *Archives d'histoire doctrinale et littéraire du moyen âge* 24 (1949) 249–265; Reprinted in Jean Leclercq, *L'idée de la royauté du Christ au moyen âge* (Paris: Cerf, 1959).

157. 'Un tratado sobre los nombres divinos en un manuscrito de Cordoba,' *Hispania Sacra* 2 (1949) 327–338.

158. 'Sermons de l'école de S. Augustin,' *Revue bénédictine* (1949) 100–113.

159. 'Bref discours pastoral attribuable à Paulin d'Aquilée,' *Revue bénédictine* 59 (1949) 157–160.

160. 'Saint Bernard et Origène d'après un manuscrit de Madrid,' *Revue bénédictine* 59 (1949) 183–195; Reprinted in Jean Leclercq, *Recueil d'études sur S. Bernard et ses écrits* I (Rome: Storia e Letteratura, 1962).

161. 'Sermon ancien sur les danses déshonnêtes,' *Revue bénédictine* 59 (1949) 196–201.

162. 'Saint Jerôme docteur de l'ascèse d'après un centon monastique,' *Revue d'ascétique et de mystique: 'Mélanges Marcel Viller'* 25 (1949) 140–145.

163. 'Recherches dans les manuscrits cisterciens d'Espagne, I. Textes relatifs aux institutions et à la liturgie,' *Analecta Sacri Ordinis Cisterciensis* 5 (1949) 109–112.

164. 'Recherches dans les manuscrits cisterciens d'Espagne, II. Textes hagiographiques; III. Textes doctrinaux,' *Analecta Sacri Ordinis Cisterciensis* 5 (1949) 114–119.

165. 'Manuscrits cisterciens dans des bibliothéques d'Italie,' *Analecta Sacri Ordinis Cisterciensis* 5 (1949) 94–108.

166. 'Les manuscrits des bibliothéques d'Espagne. Notes de voyage,' *Scriptorium* 3 (1949) 140–144.

1950

167. 'L'idéal monastique de Saint Odon d'après ses œuvres,' *À Cluny. Congrès scientifique, 9–11 juillet 1949* (Dijon, 1950) 227–232; Reprinted in Jean Leclercq, *Témoins de la spiritualité occidentale* (Paris: Cerf, 1965).

168. 'Vienne (Concile de), XVe concile œcuménique (1311–1312),' *Dictionnaire de Théologie Catholique* XV/2 (Paris, 1950) 2973–2979.

169. 'L'édition de Saint Bernard,' *Revue d'histoire ecclésiastique* 45 (1950) 715–727.

170. 'Vivre à Dieu seul,' *Rythmes du monde* 2 (1950) 28–31.

171. 'Les manuscrits cisterciens du Portugal,' *Analecta Sacri Ordinis Cisterciensis* 5 (1950) 131–139.

172. 'Textes et manuscrits cisterciens en Suède,' *Analecta Sacri Ordinis Cisterciensis* 6 (1950) 125–130.

173. 'L'office divin et la lecture divine,' *La Maison-Dieu* 21 (1950) 60–70; Reprinted in Jean Leclercq, *La liturgie et les paradoxes chrétiens* (Paris: Cerf, 1963).

1951

174. 'Origène au XIIe siècle,' *Irénikon* 24 (1951) 425–439.

175. 'L'exégèse médiévale de l'Ancien Testament,' *L'Ancien Testament et les chrétiens* (Paris, 1951) 168–182.

176. 'Le traité de Guillaume de Saint-Jacques sur la Trinité,' *Archives d'histoire doctrinale et littéraire du moyen âge* 25–26 (1951) 89–102.

177. 'Lettres du temps de Saint Bernard,' *Studien und Mitteilungen zur Geschichte des Benediktiner-Ordens* 63 (1951) 1–7; Reprinted in Jean Leclercq, *Recueil d'études sur S. Bernard et ses écrits* II (Rome: Ed. Storia e Letteratura, 1966).

178. 'Une épître d'Innocent II à l'évêque Henri de Bologne,' *Rivista di storia della Chiesa in Italia* 5 (1951) 263–265.

179. 'Saint Bernard et ses secrétaires,' *Revue bénédictine* 61 (1951) 208–229; Reprinted in Jean Leclercq, *Recueil d'études sur S. Bernard et ses écrits* I (Rome: Ed. Storia e Letteratura, 1962).

180. 'Manuscrits cisterciens dans les bibliothèques d'Italie,' *Analecta Sacri Ordinis Cisterciensis* 7 (1951) 71–77.

181. 'L'ancienne version latine des sentences d'Evagre pour les moines,' *Scriptorium* 5 (1951) 195–213.

182. 'Textes cisterciens dans des bibliothèques d'Allemagne,' *Analecta Sacri Ordinis Cisterciensis* 7 (1951) 46–70.

1952

183. 'Une élévation sur les Gloires de Jérusalem,' *Mélanges Lebreton* (Paris, 1951–1952) 326–334.

184. 'Le mystère de l'autel,' *La Maison-Dieu* 29 (1952) 60–70; Reprinted in Jean Leclercq, *La liturgie et les paradoxes chrétiens* (Paris: Cerf, 1963).

185. 'Anciennes sentences monastiques,' *Collectanea Ordinis Cisterciensium Reformatorum* 14 (1952) 117–124.

186. 'Passage supprimé dans une épître d'Alexandre III,' *Revue bénédictine* 62 (1952) 149–151.

187. 'Contemplation et vie contemplative du VIe au XIIe siècle,' *Dictionnaire de spiritualité* 2 (Paris, 1952) 1929–1948.

188. 'Une ancienne rédaction des coutumes cisterciennes,' *Revue d'histoire ecclésiastique* 47 (1952) 172–176.

189. 'Les manuscrits de l'abbaye de Liessies,' *Scriptorium* 6 (1952) 51–62; Reprinted in *Mémoires de la Société historique et archéologique de l'arrondissement d'Avesnes* 19 (1948–1953).

190. 'Les écrits de Geoffroy d'Auxerre,' *Revue bénédictine* 62 (1952) 274–291; Reprinted in Jean Leclercq, *Recueil d'études sur S. Bernard et ses écrits* I (Rome: Ed. Storia e Letteratura, 1962).

191. 'Textes sur S. Bernard et Gilbert de la Porrée,' *Mediaeval Studies* 14 (1952) 107–128; Reprinted in Jean Leclercq, *Recueil d'études sur S. Bernard et ses écrits* II (Rome: Storia e Letteratura, 1966).

192. In collaboration with J. Laporte, 'Bénédictions épiscopales dans un manuscrit de Huesca,' *Hispania Sacra* 5 (1952) 79–101.

193. 'L'éloge funèbre de Gilbert de la Porrée,' *Archives d'histoire doctrinale et littéraire du moyen âge* 19 (1952) 183–185.

194. 'Le commentaire de Teuzon sur la Règle bénédictine,' *Studien und Mitteilungen zur Geschichte des Benediktiner-Ordens* 64 (1952) 5–12.

195. 'Pour l'histoire de l'expression philosophie chrétienne,' *Mélanges de science religieuse* 9 (1952) 221–226.

196. 'Dévotion et théologie mariales dans le monachisme bénédictin,' H. du Manoir, *Études sur la Sainte Vierge* II (Paris, 1952) 547–578.

197. 'Carême et pénitence,' *La Maison-Dieu* 31 (1952) 44–59; Reprinted in Jean Leclercq, *La liturgie et les paradoxes chrétiens* (Paris: Cerf, 1963) 114–132.

1953

198. 'Le texte complet de la vie de Christian de l'Aumône,' *Analecta Bollandiana* 71 (1953) 21–52.

199. 'Le premier traité authentique de Saint Bernard,' *Revue d'histoire ecclésiastique* 48 (1953) 196–210; Reprinted in Jean Leclercq, *Recueil d'études sur S. Bernard et ses écrits* II (Rome: Ed. Storia e Letteratura, 1966).

200. 'Le mystère de l'Ascension dans les sermons de Saint Bernard,' *Collectanea Ordinis Cisterciensium Reformatorum* 15 (1953) 81–88; 'The Mystery of the Ascension in the Sermons of Saint Bernard,' *Cistercian Studies* 25 (1990) 9–16.

201. 'Drogon et Saint Bernard,' *Revue bénédictine* 63 (1953) 116–131; Reprinted in Jean Leclercq, *Recueil d'études sur S. Bernard et ses écrits* I (Rome: Ed. Storia e Letteratura, 1962).

202. 'Sermon pour l'Assomption restitué à Saint Bernard,' *Recherches de théologie ancienne et médiévale* 20 (1953) 5–12; Reprinted in Jean Leclercq, *Recueil d'études sur S. Bernard et ses écrits* II (Rome: Ed. Storia e Letteratura, 1966).

203. 'Un document sur Saint Bernard et la seconde croisade,' *Revue Mabillon* 43 (1953) 1–4; Reprinted in Jean Leclercq, *Recueil d'études sur S. Bernard et ses écrits* II (Rome: Ed. Storia e Letteratura, 1966).

204. 'Les sermons de Bernard sur le psaume *Qui habitat*,' *Bernard de Clairvaux* (Paris, 1953) 435–446; Reprinted in Jean Leclercq, *Recueil d'études sur S. Bernard et ses écrits* II (Rome: Ed. Storia e Letteratura, 1966); 'Die Ansprache des hl. Bernhard zum Psalm *Qui habitat*,' *Cistercienser Chronik* 99 (1992) 27–38.

205. 'Der Heiliger Bernhard und wir,' *Einführung zu Bernhard von Clairvaux. Die Botschaft der Freude* (Einsiedeln, 1953; 1954; 1977) 9–37; *Ora et labora* 14 (Milan, 1959) 1–12.

206. 'S. Bernardo maestro di carità,' *Camaldoli* (1953) 151–155.

207. 'S. Bernard et la dévotion joyeuse,' *S. Bernard homme d'Église* (Desclée de Brouwer, 1953) 237–247.

208. 'Une vie qui donne le change,' *S. Bernard homme d'Église* (Desclée de Brouwer, 1953) 195–201.

209. 'L'image de Saint Bernard dans les manuscrits,' *Saint Bernard et l'art des Cisterciens* (Dijon, 1953) 22–24.

210. 'Les sermons synodaux attribués à Saint Bernard,' *Revue bénédictine* 63 (1953) 292–309; Reprinted in Jean Leclercq, *Recueil d'études sur S. Bernard et ses écrits* I (Rome: Ed. Storia e Letteratura, 1962).

211. 'Saint Bernard et la théologie monastique du XIIe siècle,' *Analecta Sacris Ordinis Cisterciensis* 9 (1953) 7–23.

212. 'Écrits monastiques sur la Bible aux XIe–XIIIe siècles,' *Mediaeval Studies* 15 (1953) 95–106.

213. 'Die Verbreitung der bernhardinischen Schriften im deutschen Sprachraum,' *Bernhard von Clairvaux Mönch und Mystiker* (Mainz, 1953) 176–191; French in Jean Leclercq, *Recueil d'études sur S. Bernard et ses écrits* II (Rome: Ed. Storia e Letteratura, 1966).

214. 'Les manuscrits de l'abbaye d'Hautmont,' *Scriptorium* 7 (1953) 59–67.

215. 'Vivre à Dieu seul,' *Moines. Témoignages. Cahiers de la Pierre-qui-vire* (Bruges-Paris, 1953) 189–194.

216. 'Nouveaux témoins sur Origène au XIIe siècle,' *Mediaeval Studies* 15 (1953) 104–106.

217. 'Notre Dame abbesse,' *'Priez sans cesse.' Trois cents ans de prière* (Paris, 1953) 175–177.

218. 'Un nouveau manuscrit d'Echternach à Luxembourg,' *Scriptorium* 7 (1953) 219–225.

219. 'Un témoignage sur l'entretien des manuscrits,' *Scriptorium* 7 (1953) 260.

1954

220. 'Grandeur et misère de la dévotion mariale au moyen âge,' *La Maison-Dieu* 38 (1954) 122–135; Reprinted in Jean Leclercq, *La liturgie et les paradoxes chrétiens* (Paris: Cerf, 1963).

221. 'Poèmes sur la bataille de Courtrai conservés à Tolède,' *Handelingen van het Genootschap 'Société d'Emulation' te Brugge* 91 (1954) 155–160.

222. 'Saint Bernard docteur,' *Collectanea Ordinis Cisterciensium Reformatorum* 16 (1954) 284–286; Reprinted in Jean Leclercq, *Recueil d'études sur S. Bernard et ses écrits* II (Rome: Ed. Storia e Letteratura, 1966).

223. 'Saint Bernard et la dévotion médiévale envers Marie,' *Revue d'ascetique et de mystique* 30 (1954) 361–375; Partially reprinted in Jean Leclercq, *Témoins de la spiritualité occidentale* (Paris: Cerf, 1965).

224. 'Epîtres d'Alexandre III sur les Cisterciens,' *Revue bénédictine* 64 (1954) 68–42.

225. 'Saint Bernard théologien,' *San Bernardo* (Milan, 1954) 30–41; Reprinted in Jean Leclercq, *Témoins de la spiritualité occidentale* (Paris: Cerf, 1965).

226. 'Un coutumier de Saint-Martial,' *Revue Mabillon* 44 (1954) 37–42.

227. 'Pour l'histoire de l'enluminure cistercienne,' *Scriptorium* 8 (1954) 142–143.

228. 'Gratien, Pierre de Troyes et la seconde croisade,' *Studia Gratiana* II (Bologna, 1954) 585–593.

229. 'Recherches sur les sermons sur les Cantiques de Saint Bernard,' *Revue bénédictine* 64 (1954) 208–223; 65 (1955) 71–89, 228–258; 66 (1956) 63–91; 69 (1959) 237–257; 70 (1960) 562–590; Reprinted in Jean Leclercq, *Recueil d'études sur S. Bernard et ses écrits* I (Rome: Ed. Storia e Letteratura, 1962).

230. 'S. Bernard et la tradition mariale de l'Église,' *Marie* (Nicolet, Québec, 1954) 33–36.

1955

231. 'Points de vue sur le grand schisme d'Occident,' *1054–1954. L'Église et les Églises* (Chevetogne, 1955) 223–240.

232. 'Manuscrits cisterciens dans diverses bibliothèques,' *Analecta Sacri Ordinis Cisterciensis* 11 (1955) 139–148.

233. 'La poste des moines,' *Cahiers de Saint-André* 12 (1955) 74–77.

234. 'Lettres de Mabillon et de Rancé sur Saint Bernard,' *Revue Mabillon* 45 (1955) 29–35; Reprinted in Jean Leclercq, *Recueil d'études sur S. Bernard et ses écrits* II (Rome: Ed. Storia e Letteratura, 1966).

235. 'Un recueil d'hagiographie colombanienne,' *Analecta Bollandiana* 73 (1955) 193–196.

236. 'Messes pour la profession et l'oblation monastiques,' *Archiv für Liturgiewissenschaft* 4/1 (1955) 93–96.

237. 'Sermon sur la Divisio Apostolorum attribuable à Gottschalk de Limbourg,' *Sacris erudiri* 7 (1955) 219–228.

238. 'Lettres de vocation à la vie monastique,' *Analecta Monastica* III, Studia Anselmiana, 37 (Rome, 1955) 169–197.

239. 'La vêture ad succurrendum d'après le moine Raoul,' *Analecta Monastica* III, Studia Anselmiana, 37 (Rome, 1955) 158–168.

240. 'Lettres d'Odon d'Ourscamp, cardinal cistercien,' *Analecta Monastica* III, Studia Anselmiana, 37 (Rome, 1955) 145–157.

241. 'Le sermon de Grossolano sur le chapître monastique,' *Analecta Monastica* III, Studia Anselmiana, 37 (Rome, 1955) 138–144.

242. 'Saint Bernard à Jumièges,' *Jumièges. Congrès scientifique du XIIIe centenaire* (Rouen, 1955) 791–796; Reprinted in Jean Leclercq, *Recueil d'études sur S. Bernard et ses écrits* II (Rome: Ed. Storia e Letteratura, 1966).

243. 'Un nouveau manuscrit d'Hautmont,' *Scriptorium* 9 (1955) 107–109.

1956

244. 'Sermons de l'école de S. Bernard dans un manuscrit d'Hauterive,' *Analecta Sacri Ordinis Cisterciensis* 12 (1956) 3–26; Reprinted in Jean Leclercq, *Recueil d'études sur S. Bernard et ses écrits* I (Rome: Ed. Storia e Letteratura, 1962).

245. 'Pierre le Vénérable et les limites du programme clunisien,' *Collectanea Ordinis Cisterciensium Reformatorum* 18 (1956) 84–87; Reprinted in Jean Leclercq, *Témoins de la spiritualité occidentale* (Paris: Cerf, 1965).

246. 'Documents sur la mort des moines,' *Revue Mabillon* 45 (1955) 165–180; 46 (1956) 65–81.

247. 'Bénédictions pour les leçons de l'office dans un manuscrit de Pistoie,' *Sacris erudiri* 8 (1956) 143–146.

248. 'Littérature et vie mystique,' *Collectana Ordinis Cisterciensium Reformatorum* 18 (1956) 269–302; Reprinted in Jean Leclercq, *L'amour des lettres et le désir de Dieu. Initiation aux auteurs monastiques du moyen âge* (Paris: Cerf, 1957).

249. 'Les collections de sermons de Nicolas de Clairvaux,' *Revue bénédictine* 66 (1956) 269–302; Reprinted in Jean Leclercq, *Recueil*

d'études sur S. Bernard et ses écrits I (Rome: Ed. Storia e Letteratura, 1962).

250. 'Aspects historiques du mystère monastique,' *Convivium* 24 (1956) 641–649; 'Epilogo,' *Il monachesimo nell'alto medioevo e la formazione della civiltà occidentale* (Spoleto, 1957) 609–622; Partially reprinted in Jean Leclercq, *Témoins de la spiritualité occidentale* (Paris: Cerf, 1965).

251. 'Saint Antoine dans la tradition monastique médiévale,' *Antonius Magnus Eremita , 356–1956* Studia Anselmiana, 38 (Rome, 1956) 229–247.

252. 'L'archétype clarévallien des traités de Saint Bernard,' *Scriptorium* 10 (1956) 229–232; Reprinted in Jean Leclercq, *Recueil d'études sur S. Bernard et ses écrits* II (Rome: Ed. Storia e Letteratura, 1966).

253. 'Pierre le Vénérable et l'érémitisme clunisien,' *Petrus Venerabilis, 1156–1956,* Studia Anselmiana, 40 (Rome, 1956) 99–120.

254. 'Voyage rétrospectif aux eaux de Vichy et autres lieux,' *Bulletin de la Société d'histoire et d'archéologie de Vichy et des environs* 56 (1956) 171–190.

255. 'Maria christianorum philosophia,' *Mélanges de science religieuse* 13 (1956) 103–106.

256. 'Les peintures de la Bible de Morimondo,' *Scriptorium* 10 (1956) 23–26.

257. 'Un homme agréable,' *Cahiers de Saint-André* 13 (1956) 115–118; Italian in *Vita monastica* 15 (1961) 71–74; Reprinted in Jean Leclercq, *Témoins de la spiritualité occidentale* (Paris: Cerf, 1965).

258. 'Textes et manuscrits cisterciens dans diverses bibliothèques,' *Analecta Sacri Ordinis Cisterciensis* 12 (1956) 289–310.

1957

259. 'Un document sur les débuts des Templiers,' *Revue d'histoire ecclésiastique* 52 (1957) 81–91; Reprinted in Jean Leclercq, *Recueil d'études sur S. Bernard et ses écrits* II (Rome: Ed. Storia e Letteratura, 1966).

260. 'Comment aborder Saint Bernard,' *Collectanea Ordinis Cisterciensum Reformatorum* 19 (1957) 18–21.

261. 'Regula magistri et Règle de Saint Benoît,' *Revue d'ascétique et de mystique* 40 (1957) 101–105.

262. 'Les deux rédactions du Prologue de Pierre Lombard sur les Épîtres de S. Paul,' *Miscellanea Lombardiana* (Novara, 1957) 109–112.

263. 'Disciplina,' *Dictionnaire de spiritualité* III (Paris, 1957) 1291–1302.

264. 'Guerric et l'école monastique,' *Collectanea Ordinis Cisterciensium Reformatorum* 19 (1957) 238–248; Partially reprinted in Jean Leclercq, *Témoins de la spiritualité occidentale* (Paris: Cerf, 1965).

265. 'Nouvelle réponse de l'ancien monachisme aux critiques des cisterciens,' *Revue bénédictine* 67 (1957) 77–94; Reprinted in Jean Leclercq, *Recueil d'études sur S. Bernard et ses écrits* II (Rome: Ed. Storia e Letteratura, 1966).

266. 'Inédits de S. Pierre Damien. Un ancien catalogue des Manuscrits de Font Avellane. Sur l'authenticité des poèmes de S. Pierre Damien,' *Revue bénédictine* 67 (1957) 151–174.

267. 'Deux opuscules sur la formation des jeunes moines,' *Revue d'ascétique et de mystique* 33 (1957) 387–399.

268. 'Y a-t-il une culture monastique?' *Il monachesimo nell'alto medioevo e la formazione della civiltà occidentale* (Spoleto, 1957) 339–356; Reprinted in Jean Leclercq, *Témoins de la spiritualité occidentale* (Paris: Cerf, 1965).

269. 'Saint Pierre Damien poéte,' *La vie spirituelle, Supplément* 43 (1957) 423–440.

270. In collaboration with R. Floreville, 'Un débat sur le sacerdoce des moines au XIIe siècle,' *Analecta Monastica* 4, Studia Anselmiana, 41 (Rome, 1957) 8–118.

271. 'Pour une histoire humaine du monachisme au moyen âge,' *Analecta Monastica* 4, Studia Anselmiana, 41 (Rome, 1957) 1–7.

272. 'Saint Pierre Damien écrivain,' *Convivium* 25 (1957) 385–399; Reprinted in Jean Leclercq, *S. Pierre Damien ermite et homme d'Église* (Rome: Ed. Storia e Letteratura, 1960).

273. 'Documents sur S. Pierre Damien,' *Rivista di storia della Chiesa in Italia* 11 (1957) 106–113.

274. 'Le jugement du B^x Paul Giustiniani sur S. Pierre Damien,' *Rivista di storia della Chiesa in Italia* 11 (1957) 423–426.

275. 'Gébouin de Troyes et S. Bernard,' *Revue des sciences philosophiques et théologiques* 41 (1957) 632–640; Reprinted in Jean Leclercq, *Recueil d'études sur S. Bernard et ses écrits* I (Rome: Ed. Storia e Letteratura, 1962).

276. 'Cluny fut-il ennemi de la culture?' *Revue Mabillon* 47 (1957) 172–182.

277. 'La collection des sermons de Guerric d'Igny,' *Recherches de*

théologie ancienne et médiévale 24 (1957) 15–26; Reprinted in Jean Leclercq, *Recueil d'études sur S. Bernard et ses écrits* I (Rome: Ed. Storia e Letteratura, 1962).

278. 'Deux épîtres de S. Bernard et de son secrétaire,' *Studien und Mitteilungen zur Geschichte des Benediktiner-Ordens* 69 (1957) 227–231; Reprinted in Jean Leclercq, *Recueil d'études sur S. Bernard et ses écrits* 2 (Rome: Ed. Storia e Letteratura, 1966).

279. 'S. Bernard en microssillons,' *Collectanea Ordinis Cisterciensium Reformatorum* (1957) 398–402.

280. 'Saint-Germain-des-Prés au moyen âge,' *Revue d'histoire de l'Église de France* 43 (1957) 3–12; *La vie spirituelle* 99 (1958) 504–514; *Mémorial du XIV*e *centenaire de l'Abbaye de Saint-Germain-des-Prés* (Paris, 1959) 3–12; Reprinted in Jean Leclercq, *Aux sources de la spiritualité occidentale* (Paris: Cerf, 1964).

281. 'Saint-Germain et les bénédictins de Paris,' *Revue d'histoire de l'Église de France* 43 (1957) 223–230; *Mémorial du XIV*e *centenaire de l'Abbaye de Saint-Germain-des-Prés* (Paris, 1959) 223–230.

282. Review of J. Huijben and P. Debongnie, *L'auteur ou les auteurs de 'l'Imitation de Jésus-Christ'* (Louvain, 1957). In *Convivium* 4 (1957) 757–759.

1958

283. 'Saint Bernard et le XIIe siècle monastique,' *Dictionnaire de spiritualité* 4 (Paris, 1958) 187–194.

284. 'Introduction,' *S. Bernard. Textes choisis, 'Les écrits des saints'* (Namur, 1958) 1–15.

285. 'Le cloître est-il un paradis?' *Le message des moines à notre temps* (Paris, 1958) 141–159.

286. 'L'idée de la seigneurie du Christ au moyen âge,' *Revue d'histoire ecclésiastique* 53 (1958) 57–68; Reprinted in Jean Leclercq, *L'idée de la royauté du Christ au moyen âge* (Paris: Cerf, 1959).

287. 'La vie et la prière des chevaliers de Santiago d'après leur règle primitive,' *Liturgica* 2, Scripta et Documenta, 10 (Montserrat, 1958) 347–357.

288. 'Fragmenta mariana,' *Ephemerides liturgicae* 72 (1958) 292–305.

289. 'La crise du monachisme aux XIe et XIIe siècles,' *Bullettino dell'Istituto Storico Italiano per il Medio Evo e Archivio Muratoriano*

70 (1958) 19–41; Reprinted in Jean Leclercq, *Aux sources de la spiritualité occidentale* (Paris: Cerf, 1964); English in Noreen Hunt, ed. *Cluniac Monasticism in the Central Middle Ages* (London, 1971) 217–242.

290. 'Nouvelles lettres de Pierre de Celle,' *Analecta Monastica* 5, Studia Anselmiana, 43 (Rome, 1958) 160–179.

291. 'Aspects littéraires de l'œuvre de S. Bernard,' *Cahiers de civilisation médiévale* 1 (1958) 425–450; Reprinted in Jean Leclercq, *Recueil d'études sur S. Bernard et ses écrits* III (Rome: Ed. Storia e Letteratura, 1969) 13–36.

292. 'Virgile en enfer d'après un manuscrit d'Aulne,' *Latomus* 17 (1958) 731–736.

293. 'Les sources chrétiennes,' *La vie spirituelle* 98 (1958) 654–661.

294. 'Les Distinctiones super Cantica de Guillaume de Ramsey,' *Sacris erudiri* 10 (1958) 329–352.

295. 'Le poème de Payen Bolotin contre les faux ermites,' *Revue bénédictine* 68 (1958) 52–86.

1959

296. 'Documents on the Cult of St. Malachy,' *Seanchas Ardmhacha,* Journal of the Armagh Diocesan Historical Society 3 (1959) 318–322; Reprinted in Jean Leclercq, *Recueil d'études sur S. Bernard et ses écrits* II (Rome: Ed. Storia e Letteratura, 1966).

297. 'Richesses spirituelles du XIIe siècle,' *La vie spirituelle* 100 (1959) 298–306.

298. 'De l'humour à l'amour à l'école de S. Bernard,' *La vie spirituelle* 101 (1959) 182–203; Italian in *Ecclesia* 18 (1959) 377–383; Reprinted in Jean Leclercq, *Témoins de la spiritualité occidentale* (Paris: Cerf, 1965).

299. 'Visages de S. Bernard, notes pour un commentaire du disque S. Bernard,' *Encyclopédie sonore* (Paris: Hachette, 1959) pp. 16.

300. 'Le Sacré-Coeur dans la tradition bénédictine au moyen âge,' *Cor Jesu* 11 (1959) 3–28.

301. 'The Unity of Prayer,' *Worship* 33 (1959) 408–417; *Paroisse et liturgie* 42 (1960) 277–284; *Erbe und Auftrag* 37 (1961) 458–470; *Rivista di ascetica e mistica* 6 (1961) 9–24; *Seminarios* 24 (1964) 401–415; Reprinted in Jean Leclercq, *La liturgie et les paradoxes chrétiens* (Paris: Cerf, 1963); *Cuadernos monásticos* 7 (1972) 79–110; *Monastic Studies* 10 (1974) 71–86.

302. 'Meditation as a biblical reading,' *Worship* 33 (1959) 562–568; *Paroisse et liturgie* 42 (1960) 357–362; Reprinted in Jean Leclercq, *La liturgie et les paradoxes chrétiens* (Paris: Cerf, 1963).

303. 'Une doctrine de la vie monastique dans l'École du Bec,' *Spicilegium Beccense I. Congrès international du IX*[e] *centenaire de l'arrivée d'Anselme au Bec* (1959) 477–488; Reprinted in Jean Leclercq, *Témoins de la spiritualité occidentale* (Paris: Cerf, 1965).

304. 'Grammaire et humour dans les textes du moyen âge,' *Convivium* 3 (1959) 270–276; *Annales de la Société royale d'archéologie de Bruxelles* 50 (1961) 150–156.

305. 'Les Psaumes 20–25 chez les commentateurs du haut moyen âge,' *Richesses et déficiences des anciens psautiers latins* (Rome, 1959) 213–229.

306. 'Pour l'histoire des traités de S. Bernard,' *Analecta Sacri Ordinis Cisterciensis* 15 (1959) 56–78; Reprinted in Jean Leclercq, *Recueil d'études sur S. Bernard et ses écrits* II (Rome: Ed. Storia e Letteratura, 1966).

307. 'Textes et manuscrits cisterciens à la Bibliothèque Vaticane,' *Analecta Sacri Ordinis Cisterciensis* 15 (1959) 79–103.

308. 'Un missel de Montiéramey,' *Scriptorium* 13 (1959) 247–249.

309. 'Les premières journées vannistes,' *Studia monastica* 1 (1959) 453–454.

310. 'Anciennes prières monastiques,' *Studia monastica* 1 (1959) 379–392.

311. 'Un témoignage sur l'influence de Grégoire VII dans le réforme canoniale,' *Studi Gregoriani* 6 (1959) 173–227.

312. 'Vie divine et vie humaine,' *Étudiants catholiques de Nancy* 37 (1959) 28–30.

313. Review of M. Pacaut *La théocratie*. In *Revue belge de philologie et d'histoire* 37 (1959) 474–476.

1960

314. 'Mérites d'un réformateur et limites d'une réforme,' *Revue bénédictine* 70 (1960) 232–240; Reprinted in Jean Leclercq, *Témoins de la spiritualité occidentale* (Paris: Cerf, 1965).

315. 'Formes anciennes de l'office marial,' *Ephemerides liturgicae* 74 (1960) 89–102.

316. 'Une thèse de thèologie sur Aelred de Rievaulx,' *Collectanea Ordinis Cisterciensium Reformatorum* 12 (1960) 49–50.

317. 'The Meaning of Life,' *Worship* 34 (1960) 178–184.

318. 'Un guide de lecture pour S. Bernard,' *La vie spirituelle* 102 (1960) 440–447.

319. 'La spiritualité du VIe au XIIe siècle, de S. Benoît à S. Bernard, Bibliographie organisée,' *La vie spirituelle* 102 (1960) 563–566.

320. 'Lettre d'un moine à son abbé,' *Studi médievali* 1 (1960) 687–700.

321. 'S. Bernard éditeur d'après les Sermons sur l'Avent,' *Mélanges d'archéologie et d'histoire publiés par l'École française de Rome* 72 (1960) 373–396; Reprinted in Jean Leclercq, *Recueil d'études sur S. Bernard et ses écrits* 2 (Rome: Ed. Storia e Letteratura, 1966).

322. 'Spiritualité vanniste et tradition monastique,' *Revue d'ascétique et de mystique* 36 (1960) 323–335; Reprinted in Jean Leclercq, *Témoins de la spiritualité occidentale* (Paris: Cerf, 1965).

323. 'L'authenticité bernardine du sermon in celebratione adventus,' *Mediaeval Studies* 22 (1960) 214–231; Reprinted in Jean Leclercq, *Recueil d'études sur S. Bernard et ses écrits* II (Rome: Ed. Storia e Letteratura, 1966).

324. 'Sermon sur l'unité dans un manuscrit des Dunes,' *Cîteaux* 11 (1960) 212–213.

325. 'S. Liudger, un témoin de l'évangélisme au VIIIe siècle,' *La vie spirituelle* 102 (1960) 144–160; *Erbe und Auftrag* 37 (1961) 292–305; Reprinted in Jean Leclercq, *Témoins de la spiritualité occidentale* (Rome: Ed. Storia e Letteratura, 1965).

326. 'S. Anschaire, apôtre des scandinaves,' *La vie spirituelle* 103 (1960) 415–431; *Saint Anschaire: Moine de Corbie, Missionnaire en Scandinavie* (Saint-Riquier, 1960) pp. 21; Reprinted in Jean Leclercq, *Témoins de la spiritualité occidentale* (Rome: Ed. Storia e Letteratura, 1965).

327. 'L'obbedienza religiosa secondo la regola di S. Benedetto,' *Vita monastica* 61 (1960) 51–63; *American Benedictine Review* 16 (1965) 183–193.

328. 'Une parenthèse dans l'histoire de la prière continuelle: la *Laus Perennis* du haut moyen âge,' *La Maison-Dieu* 64 (1960) 90–101; Reprinted in Jean Leclercq, *La liturgie et les paradoxes chrétiens* (Paris: Cerf, 1963).

329. 'L'abbé Lebeuf, liturgiste,' *Nouvelle Clio* 3 (1960) 157–162.

330. 'Mönchtum und Peregrinatio im Frühmittelalter,' *Römische*

Quartalschrift 55 (1960) 212–225; Enlarged redaction in *Aux sources de la spiritualité occidentale* (Paris: Cerf, 1964).

331. 'The Monastic Tradition of Culture and Studies,' *American Benedictine Review* 11 (1960) 99–131.

332. 'Sancta simplicitas,' *Collectanea Ordinis Cisterciensium Reformatorum* 22 (1960) 138–148; Reprinted in Jean Leclercq, *Chances de la spiritualité occidentale* (Paris: Cerf, 1966).

333. 'The Sacraments of the Easter Season,' *Worship* 34 (1960) 296–306.

334. 'S. Bruno et le rayonnement de l'idéal cartusien,' *La vie spirituelle* 102 (1960) 652–664; Reprinted in Jean Leclercq, *La spiritualité du moyen âge* (Paris: Aubier, 1961).

335. 'Le B[x] Paul Giustiniani et les ermites de son temps,' *Problemi di vita religiosa in Italia nel Cinquencento* (Padoue, 1960) 225–240; Reprinted in Jean Leclercq, *Témoins de la spiritualité occidentale* (Paris: Cerf, 1965).

336. 'Spiritualité et culture à Cluny,' *Spiritualità Cluniacense* (Todi, 1960) 103–151; Partially reprinted in Jean Leclercq, *Aux sources de la spiritualité occidentale* (Paris: Cerf, 1964).

337. 'S. Bernard et la tradition biblique d'après les Sermons sur les Cantiques,' *Sacris erudiri* 11 (1960) 225–248; Reprinted in Jean Leclercq, *Recueil d'études sur S. Bernard et ses écrits* I (Rome: Ed. Storia e Letteratura, 1962).

338. 'The liturgical roots of the Devotion to the Sacred Heart,' *Worship* 34 (1960) 551–566; *La vie spirituelle* 104 (1961) 377–393; *Primer Congreso internacional sobre el culto al Sagrado Corazón de Jesús* (Barcelona, 1961) 351–359; *Beilage zum Kirchlichem Anzeigen* 17 (Luxembourg, 1962) 1–7, 28–29; Reprinted in Jean Leclercq, *La liturgie et les paradoxes chrétiens* (Paris: Cerf, 1963).

339. 'Liturgy and mental prayer in the life of St Gertrude,' *Sponsa Regis* 31 (1960) 1–5; Reprinted in Jean Leclercq, *La liturgie et les paradoxes chrétiens* (Paris: Cerf, 1963).

340. 'Une nouvelle thèse de théologie monastique,' *Collectanea Cisterciensia* 22 (1960) 49–50.

341. Review of W. Hafner *Der Basiliuskommentar zur Regula S. Benedict*. In *Bibliothèque de l'École des Chartes* 118 (1960) 209–211.

1961

342. 'Textes et manuscrits cisterciens dans des bibliothèques des

États-Unis,' *Traditio* 17 (1961) 163–183.

343. 'Introduction,' *Lettres choisies de Saint Bernard* Coll. Les écrits des Saints (Namur: Éd. du Soleil Levant, 1961) 9–16.

344. 'Monachesimo ed esilio,' *Vita monastica* 15 (1961) 99–106; Reprinted in Jean Leclercq, *Aux sources de la spiritualité occidentale* (Paris: Cerf, 1964).

345. 'Le monachisme clunisien,' *Théologie de la vie monastique* (Paris, 1961) 447–457.

346. 'Le monachisme du haut moyen âge (VIIIe–Xe siècles),' *Théologie de la vie monastique* (Paris, 1961) 437–445; English in *Sponsa Regis* 23 (1961) 165–172.

347. 'Sur le statut des ermites monastiques,' *La vie spirituelle, Supplement* 58 (1961) 384–394; Reprinted in Jean Leclercq, *Aux sources de la spiritualité occidentale* (Paris: Cerf, 1964).

348. 'À la découverte d'Odon de Morimond,' *Collectanea Ordinis Cisterciensium Reformatorum* 23 (1961) 307–313; Reprinted in Jean Leclercq, *Témoins de la spiritualité occidentale* (Paris: Cerf, 1965).

349. 'La séparation du monde dans le monachisme au moyen âge,' *Problèmes de la religieuse d'aujourd'hui: La séparation du monde* (Paris, 1961) 75–94; *La separación del mundo* (Madrid, 1963) 77–97; *La separazione del mondo* (Alba, 1963) 82–104; Reprinted in Jean Leclercq, *Aux sources de la spiritualité occidentale* (Paris: Cerf, 1964).

350. 'Monachisme et pérégrination du IXe au XIIe siècles,' *Studia monastica* 3 (1961) 33–52; Reprinted in Jean Leclercq, *Aux sources de la spiritualité occidentale* (Paris: Cerf, 1964).

351. 'On monastic priesthood according to the ancient medieval tradition,' *Studia monastica* 3 (1961) 137–155.

352. 'La theographia de Longuel de Clairvaux,' *Cîteaux* 3 (1961) 212–225.

353. 'Opuscules tirés de manuscrits monastiques,' *Archivum Latinitatis Medii Aevi* 2–3 (1961) 141–143.

354. 'An Itinerary,' *Worship* 8 (1961) 521–527.

355. 'S. Martin dans l'hagiographie monastique du moyen âge,' *S. Martin et son temps. Mémorial du XVIe centenaire des débuts du monachisme en Gaule 361–1961* Studia Anselmiana, 46 (Rome, 1961) 175–188.

356. 'Note sur le devoir d'état dans la spiritualité ancienne,' *Christus* 29 (1961) 71–74; *The Benedictine Review* 17 (1962) 12–14.

357. 'Caratteristiche della spiritualità monastica,' *Problemi e orientamenti di spiritualità monastica, biblica e liturgica* (Rome, 1961) 327–

336; Spanish in *Cistercium* 87 (1963) 153–156; Reprinted in Jean Leclercq, *Aux sources de la spiritualité occidentale* (Paris: Cerf, 1964).

358. 'Nieuwe stromingen in het oude monachisme,' *Abdijleven* 3 (Achel, 1961) 53–58.

359. In collaboration with H. Rochais, 'La tradition des sermons liturgiques de S. Bernard,' *Scriptorium* 15 (1961) 240–284; Reprinted in Jean Leclercq, *Recueil d'études sur S. Bernard et ses écrits* II (Paris: Cerf, 1966).

360. 'La vie contemplative dans S. Thomas et dans la tradition,' *Recherches de théologie ancienne et médiévale* 28 (1961) 251–268.

361. 'Exercices spirituels,' *Dictionnaire de spiritualité* IV (1961) 1900–1907.

1962

362. 'Culte liturgique et prière intime dans le monachisme du moyen âge,' *La Maison-Dieu* 69 (1962) 39–55; Reprinted in Jean Leclercq, *Aux sources de la spiritualité occidentale* (Paris: Cerf, 1964).

363. 'S. Romuald et le monachisme missionnaire,' *Revue bénédictine* 72 (1962) 307–323; Partially reprinted in Jean Leclercq, *Témoins de la spiritualité occidentale* (Paris: Cerf, 1965).

364. 'Pour une histoire de la vie à Cluny,' *Revue d'histoire ecclésiastique* 57 (1962) 386–408, 783–812; Partially reprinted in Jean Leclercq, *Aux sources de la spiritualité occidentale* (Paris: Cerf, 1965); German in *Cluny* Wege der Forschung, 241 (Darmstadt: Wissenschaftliche Buchgesellschaft, 1975) 254–318.

365. 'Une thèse sur Cîteaux dans la tradition monastique,' *Collectanea Ordinis Cisterciensium Reformatorum* 24 (1962) 358–362.

366. 'Deux opuscules médiévaux sur la vie solitaire,' *Studia monastica* 4 (1962) 93–109.

367. 'Un congrès sur l'érémitisme,' *Studia monastica* 4 (1962) 404–407.

368. 'La flagellazione volontaria nella tradizione spirituale dell' occidente,' *Il movimento dei Disciplinati nel Settimo centenario del suo inizio* (Pérouse, 1962) 73–83; French in Jean Leclercq, *Témoins de la spiritualité occidentale* (Paris: Cerf, 1965).

369. 'Spiritualitas,' *Studi medievali* 3 (1962) 279–296.

370. 'Une homélie de Volcuin de Sittichenbach,' *Studi medievali* 3 (1962) 315–339.

371. 'Textes et manuscrits cisterciens dans diverses bibliothèques,' *Analecta Sacri Ordinis Cisterciensis* 18 (1962) 121–134.

372. 'Theology and Prayer,' *Father Cyril Gaul Memorial Lectures* 2 (St. Meinrad, IN, 1962) 1–23; *Encounter* 24 (1963) 349–364; *Seminarios* 9 (1963) 466–484; *La preghiera nella Bibbia e nella tradizione patristica e monastica* (Rome, 1964) 951–971; Reprinted in Jean Leclercq, *Chances de la spiritualité occidentale* (Paris: Cerf, 1966); 'Teología y oración,' *Revista San Anselmo* 4/15 (1985) 71–80.

373. 'Le sacerdoce des moines,' *Bulletin du Comité des études. Compagnie St-Sulpice* 38–39 (1962) 394–422; *Irénikon* 36 (1963) 5–40; *Selecciónes de teologia* 3 (1964) 267–272; *Monastic Studies* 3 (1965) 53–86; Reprinted in Jean Leclercq, *Chances de la spiritualité occidentale* (Paris: Cerf, 1966).

374. 'Le nouveau catalogue des manuscrits théologiques de la bibliothèque universitaire de Bâle,' *Scriptorium* 16 (1962) 76–78.

375. 'Pour une histoire intégrale du monachisme,' *Analecta Monastica* VI, Studia Anselmiana, 50 (1962) 1–3.

376. 'Un traité sur la profession des abbés au XIIe siècle,' *Analecta Monastica* 6, Studia Anselmiana, 50 (1962) 177–191.

377. 'Über das Einsiedlerleben im Mittelalter,' *Geist und Leben* 35 (1962) 378–382.

378. 'La spiritualité des chanoines réguliers,' *La vita comune del clero nei secoli XI et XII* (Milan, 1962) 117–135; Reprinted in Jean Leclercq, *Témoins de la spiritualité occidentale* (Paris: Cerf, 1965).

379. Review of E.S. Creenhill, *Die geistigen Vorausetzungen der Bilderreihe des 'Speculum virginum'*. In *Cahiers de civilisation médiévale* 5 (1962) 477–479.

380. Review of Maurice Bevenot, *The Tradition of Manuscripts*. In *The Heythrop Journal* 3 (1962) 187–189.

1963

381. 'Les études bernardines en 1963,' *Bulletin de la Société internationale pour l'étude de la philosophie médiévale* 5 (1963) 121–138.

382. 'L'*Exordium cistercii* et la *Summa cartae caritatis* sont-ils de Saint Bernard?' *Revue bénédictine* 73 (1963) 88–89; Reprinted in Jean Leclercq, *Recueil d'études sur S. Bernard et ses écrits* 2 (Rome: Ed. Storia e Letteratura, 1966).

383. 'Eremus et Eremita,' *Collectanea Ordinis Cisterciensium Refor-*

matorum 25 (1963) 8–30; Reprinted in Jean Leclercq, *Chances de la spiritualité occidentale* (Paris: Cerf, 1966).

384. 'Monasticism and St. Benedict,' *Monastic Studies* 1 (1963) 9–23; Reprinted in Jean Leclercq, *Aux sources de la spiritualité occidentale* (Paris: Cerf, 1964).

385. 'Regola benedettina e prezenza nel mondo,' *La bonifica benedettina* (Rome, 1963) 17–25; *Monastic Studies* 2 (1964) 51–63; *Erbe und Auftrag* 40 (1964) 224–233; Reprinted in Jean Leclercq, *Aux sources de la spiritualité occidentale* (Paris: Cerf, 1964).

386. 'Christusnachfolge und Sakrament in der Theologie des Heiligen Bernhard,' *Archiv für Liturgiewissenschaft* 8 (1963) 58–72; English in *Cistercian Studies* 9 (1974) 36–54; French in *Collectanea Cisterciensia* 38 (1976) 263–282; Italian in *Ora et Labora* 41 (1986) 26–36, 71–78.

387. '*Umbratilis.* Pour l'histoire du thème de la vie cachée,' *Revue d'ascétique et de mystique* 156 (1963) 491–504; Reprinted in Jean Leclercq, *Chances de la spiritualité occidentale* (Paris: Cerf, 1966).

388. 'Introduction,' Baudouin de Ford, *Le sacrement de l'autel.* John Morson and Elisabeth de Solms, eds., Sources chrétiennes, 93–94 (Paris: Cerf, 1963) 7–51.

389. 'Le monachisme en Islam et en chrétienté,' *Images de Toumiline* (March, 1963) 1–5.

390. 'La rencontre des moines de Moissac avec Dieu,' *Annales du Midi* 75 (1963) 405–417; *Moissac et l'Occident au XIe siècle. Actes du Colloque international de Moissac 1963* (Toulouse, 1964) 81–93; Reprinted in Jean Leclercq, *Témoins de la spiritualité occidentale* (Paris: Cerf, 1965).

391. 'Caelestinus de caritate,' *Cîteaux* 3 (1963) 202–217.

392. 'Une paraphrase en vers de proverbes bibliques attribuable à Jean de Lodi,' *Studi medievali* 4 (1963) 325–349.

393. 'La joie dans Rancé,' *Collectanea Ordinis Cisterciensium Reformatorum* 25 (1963) 206–215; Reprinted in Jean Leclercq, *Témoins de la spiritualité occidentale* (Paris: Cerf, 1965).

394. 'L'érémitisme en Occident jusqu'à l'an mil,' *Le millénaire du Mont-Athos* 1 (Chevetogne, 1963) 161–180; *L'eremitismo in Occidente nei secoli XI e XII* (Milan, 1965) 27–44.

395. '*Sedere.* À propos de l'hésychasme en Occident,' *Le millénaire du Mont-Athos* 1 (1963) 253–264; Reprinted in Jean Leclercq, *Chances de la spiritualité occidentale* (Paris: Cerf, 1966).

396. 'L'Écriture Sainte dans l'hagiographie monastique du haut moyen âge,' *La Biblia nell'alto medioevo* (Spoleto, 1963) 103–128.

397. 'Problèmes de l'érémitisme,' *Studia monastica* 5 (1963) 197–212.

398. 'Une vie de Jérôme d'Ancône par Ludovico Brunori,' *Traditio* 19 (1963) 371–409.

399. 'Les études dans les monastères du Xe au XIIe siècle,' *Los monjes y los estudios* (Poblet, 1963) 106–117.

400. 'Culture monastique et retour à l'unité,' *Irénikon* 3 (1963) 406–408.

401. 'La dévotion médiévale envers le Crucifié,' *La Maison-Dieu* 75 (1963) 119–132.

402. 'Note sur la manière de citer Mabillon,' *Studia monastica* 5 (1963) 423–424.

403. Review of Demosthenes Savramis, *Zur Siziologie des byzantinischen Mönchtums*. In *The Catholic Historical Review* (1963) 509–510.

1964

404. 'Il ritiro come esercizio di vita solitaria,' *Vita monastica* 77 (1964) 55–62; Reprinted in Jean Leclercq, *Chances de la spiritualité occidentale* (Paris: Cerf, 1966).

405. 'Le Haut Moyen Âge. Introduction,' and 'Spiritualité monastique du VIe au XIIe siècle,' *Dictionnaire de spiritualité* [s.v. 'France,'] V (1964) 805–806, 818–847; *Histoire spirituelle de la France* (Paris, 1964) 64–110.

406. 'Théologie traditionnelle et théologie monastique,' *Irénikon* 37 (1964) 50–74; *Seminarios* 25 (1965) 203–223; Spanish in *Cistercium* 24 (1972) 23–46; Reprinted in Jean Leclercq, *Chances de la spiritualité occidentale* (Paris: Cerf, 1966).

407. 'Un traité de Jérôme de Matelica sur la vie solitaire,' *Rivista di storia della Chiesa in Italia* 18 (1964) 13–22.

408. 'Preface,' J. Hourlier *S. Odilon, abbé de Cluny* (Louvain, 1964) 5–7.

409. 'Méditations d'un moine de Moissac au XIe siècle. Présentation,' *Revue d'ascétique et de mystique* 40 (1964) 197–200.

410. 'Méditations d'un moine de Moissac au XIe siècle. Textes,' *Revue d'ascétique et de mystique* 40 (1964) 201–210.

411. 'Ancien sermon monastique dans le manuscrit Palat. Lat. 295,' *Mélanges Eugène Tisserant* 6 (1964) 577–582.

412. 'Aspects spirituels de la symbolique du livre au XIIe siécle,' *L'homme devant Dieu. Mélanges H. de Lubac* (Paris, 1964) 63–72.

413. 'De quelques procédés du style biblique de S. Bernard,' *Cîteaux* 5 (1964) 330–346; Reprinted in Jean Leclercq, *Recueil d'études sur S. Bernard et ses écrits* 3 (Rome: Ed. Storia e Letteratura, 1969).

414. 'Marie reine dans les sermons de S. Bernard,' *Collectanea Cisterciensia* 26 (1964) 265–276; *Ora et labora* 21 (1966) 70–79.

415. 'Problèmes et orientations du monachisme,' *Études* (May, 1964) 667–684; Spanish in *Cistercium* 16 (1964) 163–177; Italian in *Ora et labora* 19 (1964) 162–177; *Tijdschrift voor geestelijk leven* 10 (1964) 730–754; Reprinted in Jean Leclercq, *Chances de la spiritualité occidentale* (Paris: Cerf, 1966).

416. 'Un réformateur, S. Bernard,' *Lettre de Ligugé* 104 (1964) 7–9.

417. 'Petulance et spiritualité dans le commentaire d'Helinand sur le Cantique des cantiques,' *Archives d'Histoire Doctrinale et Litteraire du Moyen Âge* 31 (1964) 37–59.

418. 'S. Bernard écrivain d'après d'Office de S. Victor,' *Revue bénédictine* 74 (1964) 155–169; Reprinted in Jean Leclercq, *Recueil d'études sur S. Bernard et ses écrits* II (Rome: Ed. Storia e Letteratura, 1966).

419. 'Überlegung und Neubesinnung im heutigen Mönchtum,' *Das Wagnis der Nachfolge* (Paderborn, 1964) 59–94; Reprinted in Jean Leclercq, *Chances de la spiritualité occidentale* (Paris: Cerf, 1966).

420. 'Nouveau sermon d'Isaac de l'Étoile,' *Revue d'ascétique et de mystique* 40 (1964) 277–288.

421. In collaboration with J. Figuet, 'La Bible dans les homélies de S. Bernard sur *Missus est*,' *Studi medievali* 5 (1964) 3–38; Reprinted in Jean Leclercq, *Recueil d'études sur S. Bernard et ses écrits* 3 (Rome: Ed. Storia e Letteratura, 1969) 213–248.

422. 'Notes sur la tradition des épîtres de S. Bernard,' *Scriptorium* 18 (1964) 198–209; Reprinted in Jean Leclercq, *Recueil d'études sur S. Bernard et ses écrits* 3 (Rome: Ed. Storia e Letteratura, 1969) 307–322.

423. 'Un dialogo riuscito,' *Studi cattolici* 45 (1964) 102–105.

424. 'Textes et manuscrits cisterciens dans diverses bibliothèques,' *Analecta Sacri Ordinis Cisterciensis* 20 (1964) 218–231; Partially reprinted in Jean Leclercq, *Recueil d'études sur S. Bernard et ses écrits* III (Rome: Ed. Storia e Letteratura, 1969) 336–342.

425. 'L'assemblée locale dans la communion de l'Église universelle,' *La Maison-Dieu* 79 (1964) 81–105.

426. 'Présent et avenir du monachisme africain,' *Christus* 44 (1964) 567–574; Italian in *Ora et labora* 20 (1965) 97–103; Reprinted in Jean Leclercq, *Chances de la spiritualité occidentale* (Paris: Cerf, 1966).

427. 'Une lettre de l'abbé de Pontigny à un bourgeois de Provins au XIIIe siècle,' *Bulletin de la Société d'histoire et d'archéologie de l'Arrondissement de Provins (Seine-et-Marne)* (1964) 67–68.

428. 'Preface,' D. Farkasfalvy *L'Inspiration de l'Écriture Sainte dans la théologie de Saint Bernard*. Studia Anselmiana, 53 (Rome, 1964) 7–9.

429. Review of R.W. Southern, *St. Anselm and his Biographer*. In *Medium Aevum* 33 (1964) 222–227.

430. In collaboration with R. Grégoire, Review of *Corpus consuetudinum monasticarum* I et II, *Studi medievali* 5 (1964) 658–668.

1965

431. 'Deux questions de Berthaud de Saint-Denys sur l'exemption fiscale du clergé,' *Études d'histoire du droit canonique dédiées à G. Le Bras* (Paris, 1965) 607–617.

432. 'Culte et pauvreté à Cluny,' *La Maison-Dieu* 81 (1965) 33–50; Reprinted in Jean Leclercq, *Témoins de la spiritualité occidentale* (Paris: Cerf, 1965).

433. 'Le monachisme africain d'aujourd'hui et le monachisme antique,' *Irénikon* 28 (1965) 33–56; *Monastic Studies* 4 (1966) 137–160; Italian in *Ora et labora* 20 (1955) 97–103, 172–177; 21 (1966) 11–22; Reprinted in Jean Leclercq, *Chances de la spiritualité occidentale* (Paris: Cerf, 1966).

434. 'Les relations entre le monachisme oriental et le monachisme occidental dans le haut moyen âge,' *Le millénaire du Mont-Athos* II (Chevetogne, 1965) 49–80.

435. 'Problems Facing Monachism Today,' *American Benedictine Review* 16 (1965) 47–60; *Geist und Leben* 38 (1965) 214–223;

Reprinted in Jean Leclercq, *Chances de la spiritualité occidentale* (Paris: Cerf, 1966); Reprinted in Jean Leclercq, *Recueil d'études sur S. Bernard et ses écrits* 3 (Rome: Ed. Storia e Letteratura, 1969) 249–266.

436. 'Pour l'histoire de l'obéissance au moyen âge,' *Revue d'ascétique et de mystique* 41 (1965) 125–143.

437. 'L'érémitisme et les Cisterciens,' *L'Eremitismo in Occidente nei secoli XI e XII* (Milan, 1965) 573–576; Reprinted in Jean Leclercq, *Témoins de la spiritualité occidentale* (Paris: Cerf, 1965).

438. 'Epilogue,' *L'Eremitismo in Occidente nei secoli XI et XII* (Milan, 1965) 593–595.

439. 'Compte-rendu de voyage en Afrique 1965,' *Bulletin de liaison des monastères d'Afrique* 2 (1965) 23–29.

440. 'L'obéissance, éducatrice de la liberté, dans la tradition monastique,' *La liberté évangélique, principes et pratique* (Paris, 1965) 55–85; Spanish in *Cuadernos monásticos* 8 (1973) 227–248.

441. 'The Role of Monastic Spirituality Critically Discussed,' *Worship* 39 (1965) 583–596; *Protestants and Catholics on the Spiritual Life* (Collegeville, MN, 1966) 20–33; *La vie spirituelle* 114 (1966) 623–644; *Cuadernos monásticos* 2 (1966) 1–31; Reprinted in Jean Leclercq, *Aspects du monachisme hier et aujourd'hui* (Paris: Éd. de la Source, 1968); Reprinted in Jean Leclercq, *Recueil d'études sur S. Bernard et ses écrits* 3 (Rome: Ed. Storia e Letteratura, 1969) 213–248.

442. 'Prières médiévales pour recevoir l'Eucharistie, pour saluer et pour bénir la croix,' *Ephemerides liturgicae* 79 (1965) 327–340; Reprinted in Jean Leclercq, *Recueil d'études sur S. Bernard et ses écrits* III (Rome: Ed. Storia e Letteratura, 1969) 213–248..

443. 'Charlemagne et les moines,' *Collectanea Cisterciensia* 27 (1965) 242–245; *Vita monastica* 20 (1966) 43–48; Reprinted in Jean Leclercq, *Chances de la spiritualité occidentale* (Paris: Cerf, 1966).

444. 'Postface,' *La notion de mépris du monde dans la tradition spirituelle occidentale. Revue d'ascétique et de mystique* 41 (1965) 287–290; *Le mépris du monde* Problèmes de vie religieuse (Paris, 1965) 55–58.

445. 'La vie monastique est-elle une vie contemplative?' *Collectanea Cisterciensia* 27 (1965) 108–120; Spanish in *Schola caritatis* 42 (1967) 141–145; Reprinted in Jean Leclercq, *Chances de la spiritualité occidentale* (Paris: Cerf, 1966).

446. 'Deux nouvelles revues monastiques,' *Studia monastica* 7 (1965) 201–206.

447. 'Sermon de Philippe le Chancelier sur S. Bernard,' *Cîteaux* 16 (1965) 205–213; Reprinted in Jean Leclercq, *Recueil d'études sur S. Bernard et ses écrits* III (Rome: Ed. Storia e Letteratura, 1969) 325–336.

448. 'Documents sur les fugitifs,' *Analecta monastica* VII, Studia Anselmiana, 54 (Rome, 1965) 87–145.

449. 'De la tradition comme ouverture au présent,' *Rythmes du monde* 39 (1965) 5–15; *Monastic Studies* 4 (1966) 1–15; Reprinted in Jean Leclercq, *Chances de la spiritualité occidentale* (Paris: Cerf, 1966).

450. With E. Francechini, 'Presentation' of Jonas. M. Tosi, E. Cremona and M. Paramidani, eds. *Vita Columbani et discipulorum eius* (Piacenza, 1965) xiv-xv.

451. 'Orientations du monachisme en Afrique,' *Rythmes du monde* 39 (1965) 19–20.

452. 'Problèmes et perspectives du monachisme africain,' *Christus* 49 (1965) 120–135; Italian in *Ora et labora* 21 (1966) 101–113.

453. 'Hélinand de Froidmont ou Odon de Cheriton?' *Archives d'histoire doctrinale et littéraire du moyen âge* 32 (1965) 61–69.

454. 'Textes contemporains de Dante sur des sujets qu'il à traités,' *Studi medievali* 6 (1965) 491–535.

455. In collaboration with G. Gartner, 'S. Bernard dans l'histoire de l'obéissance monastique,' *Anuario de estudios medievales* 2 (1965) 31–62; *Cistercian Studies* 3 (1968) 207–234; Reprinted in Jean Leclercq, *Recueil d'études sur S. Bernard et ses écrits* 3 (Rome: Ed. Storia e Letteratura, 1969) 267–303.

456. 'Cultura spirituale e ideale riformatore dell'abbazia di Pomposa nel sec. XI,' *Analecta Pomposiana* 1 (1965) 73–88; Reprinted in Jean Leclercq, *Témoins de la spiritualité occidentale* (Paris: Cerf, 1965).

457. 'Nouveaux aspects littéraires de l'œuvre de S. Bernard,' *Cahiers de civilisation médiévale* 8 (1965) 299–326; Reprinted in Jean Leclercq, *Recueil d'études sur S. Bernard et ses écrits* 3 (Rome: Ed. Storia e Letteratura, 1969) 57–104.

458. 'Comment vivaient les frères convers,' *Analecta Cisterciensia* 21 (1965) 239–258; *I laici nella società religiosa del secoli XI e XII* (Milan, 1967) 152–182.

459. 'Gilbert Crispin,' *Dictionnaire de spiritualité* 6 (1965) 369–370.

460. 'Giustiniani Paul,' *Dictionnaire de spiritualité* 6 (1965) 414–417.

461. 'Prières attribuées à Guillaume et à Jean de Fruttuaria,' *Monasteri in Alta Italia* (Turin, 1966) 157–166.

462. 'Clôture et ouverture,' *'In Unitate'* 7 (1965) 1–2.

1966

463. 'L'univers religieux de S. Colomban et de Jonas de Bobbio,' *Revue d'ascétique et de mystique* 42 (1966) 15–30; Reprinted in Jean Leclercq, *Aspects du monachisme hier et aujourd'hui* (Paris: Éd. de la Source, 1968) 193–212; Italian in *Atti del Convegno internaz. di studi colombiani. Bobbio 28–30 agosto 1965. Colombano pioniere di civilizzazione cristiana europea* (Bobbio, 1974) 95–100; English in *Aspects of Monasticism* (Kalamazoo, 1978) 187–206.

464. 'À propos d'un séjour de S. Ignace à Montserrat,' *Christus* 50 (1966) 161–172; Italian in *Ora et labora* 26 (1971) 129–137; Reprinted in Jean Leclercq, *Aspects du monachisme hier et aujourd'hui* (Paris: Éd. de la Source, 1968); Reprinted in Jean Leclercq, *Recueil d'études sur S. Bernard et ses écrits* 3 (Rome: Ed. Storia e Letteratura, 1969) 267–303.

465. 'La vie contemplative et le monachisme d'après Vatican II,' *Gregorianum* 47 (1966) 495–516; *Écoute* no. 151 (1966) 1–27; Italian in *Ora et labora* 22 (1967) 18–35; English in *Cistercian Studies* 2 (1967) 53–75; Reprinted by *Asirvanam Monastery, Kengeri* (Bangalore, 1967) pp. 16; *Cuadernos monásticos* 3 (1967) 51–91; Partially translated in 'Vita contemplativa e monachesimo secondo il Concilio Vaticano II,' (Sorrento: Monastero San Paolo, 1967) pp. 32; Reprinted in Jean Leclercq, *Aspects du monachisme hier et aujourd'hui* (Paris: Éd. de la Source, 1968) 11–37; 'Monastic Life after the Second Vatican Council,' *The Downside Review* 86 (1968) 13–30.

466. 'Jérôme de Matelica et Aegidius Ghiselini,' *Rivista di storia della Chiesa in Italia* 20 (1966) 9–17.

467. 'Le formulaire de Pontigny,' *Miscellanea Populetana* (Poblet, 1966) 229–265.

468. 'L'art de la composition dans les sermons de S. Bernard,' *Studi medievali* 7 (1966) 128–153; Reprinted in Jean Leclercq, *Recueil d'études sur S. Bernard et ses écrits* 3 (Rome: Ed. Storia e Letteratura, 1969).

469. 'Petrus Damiani,' *Die Heiligen in ihrer Zeit* (Main, 1966) 540–541.

470. 'Petrus Venerabilis,' *Die Heiligen in ihrer Zeit* (Main, 1966) 1–4.

471. 'Sur le caractère littéraire des sermons de S. Bernard,' *Studi medievali* 7 (1966) 701–744; Reprinted in Jean Leclercq, *Recueil d'études sur S. Bernard et ses écrits* 3 (Rome: Ed. Storia e Letteratura, 1969) 163–210.

472. 'Un formulaire écrit dans l'Ouest de la France au XIIe siècle,' *Mélanges offerts à René Grozet* (Poitiers, 1966) 765–775.

473. 'Livres et lectures dans les cloîtres du moyen âge,' *Nouvelle revue luxembourgeoise* 3 (1966) 243–252; Italian in *Vita monastica* 19 (1965) 122–134; Reprinted in Jean Leclercq, *Aspects du monachisme hier et aujourd'hui* (Paris: Éd. de la Source, 1968) 295–307.

474. 'Nouvel itinéraire en Afrique,' *Bulletin de liaison des monastères d'Afrique* 5 (1966) 66–72.

475. 'La royauté du Christ. Les Pères,' *Assemblées du Seigneur* 88 (Saint-André, 1966) 64–79.

476. 'Bible et réforme grégorienne,' *Concilium* 17 (1966) 57–68; Spanish edition, 404–420; Dutch edition, 61–76; Portugese edition, 56–68; American edition, 63–77; English edition, 34–41; German edition, 507–514.

477. 'Liturgie monastique ou liturgie des monastères?' *Liturgie et monastères. Études* 1 (Saint-André, 1966) 11–18.

478. 'Galvano di Levanto e l'Oriente,' *Venezia e l'Oriente fra Medioevo e Rinascimento* (Florence, 1966) 403–416.

479. 'Sur le rôle des contemplatifs dans la société de demain,' *Collectanea Cisterciensia* 28 (1966) 125–137; *Cistercian Studies* 1 (1966) 117–129; Reprinted in Jean Leclercq, *Chances de la spiritualité occidentale* (Paris: Cerf, 1966).

480. 'L'art de la composition dans les traités de S. Bernard,' *Revue bénédictine* 76 (1966) 87–115; Reprinted in Jean Leclercq, *Recueil d'études sur S. Bernard et ses écrits* 3 (Rome: Ed. Storia e Letteratura, 1969); Reprinted in Jean Leclercq, *Aspects du monachisme hier et aujourd'hui* (Paris: La Source, 1968) 279–294.

481. 'Cluniazensische Reforms,' *Sacramentum Mundi Theologisches Lexikon für die Praxis* 1 (1966) 795–799.

482. 'Un trappiste malgache au XVIIe siècle?' *Collectanea Cisterciensia* 28 (1966) 68–70.

483. 'Preface,' R. Grégoire *Les homéliaires du moyen âge. Inventaire et analyse des manuscrits* (Rome, 1966) v-vii.

484. 'Notes Abélardiennes,' *Bulletin de philosophie médiévale* 8–9 (1966–1967) 59–62.

1967

485. 'Contemplant sur la montagne,' *La vie spirituelle* 116 (1967) 377–387; Reprinted in Jean Leclercq, *Aspects du monachisme hier et aujourd'hui* (Paris: Éd. de la Source, 1968) 39–49.

486. 'Les leçons d'un millénaire monastique,' *La vie spirituelle* 116 (1967) 91–107; Reprinted in Jean Leclercq, *Aspects du monachisme hier et aujourd'hui* (Paris: Éd. de la Source, 1968).

487. 'L'érémitisme en Occident,' *Lettre de Ligugé* 121 (1967) 10–19.

488. 'La professione secondo battesimo,' *Vita religiosa* 3 (1967) 3–8.

489. 'Témoignages contemporains sur la théologie du monachisme,' *Gregorianum* 48 (1967) 49–76; Italian in *Ora et labora* 22 (1967) 78–87; English in *Cistercian Studies* 2 (1967) 189–220; Reprinted in Jean Leclercq, *Aspects du monachisme hier et aujourd'hui* (Paris: Éd. de la Source, 1968) 99–133.

490. 'La récréation et le colloque dans la tradition monastique,' *Revue d'ascétique et de mystique* 43 (1967) 3–20; Spanish in *Cuadernos monásticos* 12 (1977) 195–202.

491. '*Lectulus*. Variazioni su un tema biblico nella tradizione monastica,' *Biblia e Spiritualità* (Rome, 1967) 417–436; Reprinted in Jean Leclercq, *Chances de la spiritualité occidentale* (Paris: Cerf, 1966).

492. 'Une bibliothèque vivante,' *Millénaire monastique du Mont Saint-Michel* II (Paris, 1967) 247–255; *Vita monastica* 20 (1966) 217–230.

493. 'Prières d'apologie dans un sacramentaire du Mont-Saint-Michel. Jean de Fécamp au Mont Saint-Michel,' *Millénaire monastique du Mont Saint-Michel* II (Paris, 1967) 357–361.

494. 'S. Bernard prêcheur d'après un exemple inédit,' *Mélanges offerts à M.D. Chenu* (Paris, 1967) 345–362; Reprinted in Jean Leclercq, *Recueil d'études sur saint Bernard et ses écrits* IV, Storia e Letteratura, 167 (Rome: Edizioni di Storia e Letteratura, 1987) 81–93.

495. 'Genèse et évolution de la vie consacrée,' *Cahiers de la Revue diocésaine de Tournai* 7 (Tournai, 1967) 2–27; *Monastic Studies* 5 (1968) 59–85; *Theology Digest* 28 (1968) 212–228; Reprinted in Jean Leclercq, *Aspects du monachisme hier et aujourd'hui* (Paris: Éd. de la Source, 1968).

496. 'Le monachisme contesté,' *Nouvelle revue théologique* 99 (1967) 607–618; Italian in *Ora et Labora* 22 (1967) 164–173; Reprinted in Jean Leclercq, *Aspects du monachisme hier et aujourd'hui* (Paris: Éd. de la Source, 1968) 135–151.

497. 'Eucharistie et monachisme d'après un ouvrage récent,' *Collectanea Cisterciensia* 29 (1967) 116–118.

498. 'Impressions sur le monachisme africain et malgache,' *Parole et mission* 10 (1967) 480–499; *Rythmes du monde* 14 (1966) 165–176; Italian in *Vita monastica* 21 (1967) 38–47, 97–106; Reprinted in Jean Leclercq, *Aspects du monachisme hier et aujourd'hui* (Paris: Éd. de la Source, 1968) 323–342.

499. 'St Bernard on the Church,' *The Downside Review* 85 (1967) 274–294.

500. 'Monasticism and angelism,' *The Downside Review* 85 (1967) 127–137; Reprinted in Jean Leclercq, *Aspects du monachisme hier et aujourd'hui* (Paris: Éd. de la Source, 1968) 153–166.

501. 'Dévoloppement de la liturgie du Sacré-Coeur,' *Assemblées du Seigneur* 56 (Paris, 1967) 7–12.

502. 'Saint Bernard et l'expérience chrétienne,' *La vie spirituelle* 117 (1967) 182–198; *Worship* 41 (1967) 222–233; J. Sudbrack and J. Walsh, eds. *Grosse Gestalten christlicher Spiritualität* (Wurzburg, 1969) 122–136; Reprinted in Jean Leclercq, *Aspects du monachisme hier et aujourd'hui* (Paris: Éd. de la Source, 1968) 261–277.

503. 'L'avenir des moines,' *Irénikon* 40 (1967) 189–220; *Cistercian Studies* (1967); Italian in *Ora et Labora* 23 (1968) 49–58, 324–328; Reprinted in Jean Leclercq, *Aspects du monachisme hier et aujourd'hui* (Paris: Éd. de la Source, 1968) 167–189.

504. 'Fragmenta monastica, (Sermon dans un manuscrit de Venise: sermo [Sancti Bede] Ad Monachos,' *Benedictina* 14 (1967) 23–26.

505. 'Pour l'histoire du vocabulaire latin de la pauvreté,' *Melto* 3, Mélanges Mgr Pierre Dib (Beyrut, 1967) 293–308.

506. 'Observations sur les sermons de S. Bernard pour le Carême,' *Cîteaux* 18 (1967) 119–129; *Collectanea Cisterciensia* 35 (1973) 173–

185; Reprinted in Jean Leclercq, *Recueil d'études sur saint Bernard et ses écrits* IV, Storia e Letteratura, 167 (Rome: Edizioni di Storia e Letteratura, 1987) 95–106; 'Bemerkungen zu den Predigten des hl. Bernhard für die Fastenzeit,' *Cistercienser Chronik* 97 (1990) 1–9.

507. 'Itinéraire monastique à Madagascar,' *Bulletin de liaison des monastères d'Afrique* 6 (1967) 30–33.

508. 'Questions des XIIIe et XIVe siècles sur la juridiction de l'Église et le pouvoir séculier,' *Studia Gratiana* 12, Collectanea Stephan Kuttner, 2 (1967) 309–324.

509. 'Il s'est fait pauvre,' *La vie spirituelle* 117 (1967) 501–518; Reprinted in Jean Leclercq, *Aspects du monachisme hier et aujourd'hui* (Paris: Éd. de la Source, 1968) 51–67.

510. 'S. Bernard écrivain d'après les Sermons sur le Psaume *Qui habitat*,' *Revue bénédictine* 77 (1967) 364–374; Reprinted in Jean Leclercq, *Recueil d'études sur saint Bernard et ses écrits* IV, Storia e Letteratura, 167 (Rome: Edizioni di Storia e Letteratura, 1987) 107–122.

511. 'Le cheminement biblique de la pensée de S. Bernard,' *Studi medievali* 8 (1967) 835–856; Reprinted in Jean Leclercq, *Recueil d'études sur saint Bernard et ses écrits* IV, Storia e Letteratura, 167 (Rome: Edizioni di Storia e Letteratura, 1987) 11–34.

512. 'Maria contemplativa ed attiva,' *Miles Immaculatae* 3 (1967) 425–429; *Mount Carmel* 16 (1968) 87–91; Reprinted in Jean Leclercq, *Vie religieuse et vie contemplative* (Gembloux-Paris: Éd. Duculot, 1969) 265–270.

513. 'Tradition et évolution dans le passé et le présent de la vie religieuse,' *Revue diocésaine de Tournai* 22 (1967) 398–420; *Vivre ensemble l'aujourd'hui de Dieu. La vie religieuse, signe du royaume pour tous les hommes, 3–8 avril 1967* (Ramegnies-Chin-lez-Tournai, 1968) 79–98; Reprinted in Jean Leclercq, *Aspects du monachisme hier et aujourd'hui* (Paris: La Source, 1968) 69–97; *Strukturen christlicher Existenz. Beiträge zur Erneuerung des christlichen Lebens Pater Friedrich Wulf zum sechzigsten Geburtstag* (Würzburg, 1968) 263–281; Reprinted in Jean Leclercq, *Vie religieuse et vie contemplative* (Gembloux-Paris: Éd. Duculot, 1969) 11–39; *Rinnovamento della vita religiosa* (Rome, 1970) 27–58.

514. 'Jean de Gorze et la vie religieuse au Xe siècle,' *Saint Chrodegang* (Metz, 1967) 133–151; Reprinted in Jean Leclercq, *Aspects du*

monachisme hier et aujourd'hui (Paris: Éd. de la Source, 1968) 235–259.

515. 'L'eremitisio ieri e oggi,' *Vita religiosa* 3 (1967) 243.

516. 'Un fondateur monastique au XIIIe siècle. Pour un portrait spirituel de S. Silvestre Guzzolini,' *Inter fratres* 27 (1967) 10–24; Italian in *Ora et Labora* 24 (1969) 68–79; *The Downside Review* 87 (1969) 1–10.

517. [Correspondence between Jean Leclercq and John Moffit] John Moffit, *Papers: of John Moffit* (Archive/manuscript control at University of Virginia, 1967; 1982).

518. 'Benedictine spirituality,' *New Catholic Encyclopedia* 2 (1967) 285–288, 491.

519. 'Gilbert Crispin,' *New Catholic Encyclopedia* 6 (1967) 477.

520. 'Ivo of Chartres,' *New Catholic Encyclopedia* 7 (1967) 777–778.

521. 'Monastic Schools,' *New Catholic Encyclopedia* 9 (1967) 1031–1032.

522. 'Theology and Prayer,' *New Catholic Encyclopedia* 14 (1967) 64–65.

1968

523. 'Chronique de l'actualité contemplative,' *Nouvelle revue théologique* 90 (1968) 66–78; Reprinted in Jean Leclercq, *Vie religieuse et vie contemplative* (Gembloux-Paris: Éd. Duculot, 1969).

524. 'Un témoin de la dévotion médiévale envers S. Pierre et les Apôtres,' *Gregorianum* 49 (1968) 134–154.

525. 'Alle origini della vita religiosa e dei voti,' *Vita religiosa* 4 (1968) 3–10.

526. 'Variazioni sui millenari monastici,' *Bollettino della Deputazione di Storia patria per l'Umbria* (Perugia, 1968) 186–191.

527. 'Les formes successives de la lettre-traité de S. Bernard contre Abélard,' *Revue bénédictine* 78 (1968) 87–105; Reprinted in Jean Leclercq, *Recueil d'études sur saint Bernard et ses écrits* IV, Storia e Letteratura, 167 (Rome: Edizioni di Storia e Letteratura, 1987) 265–283.

528. 'Preface,' W. Tunynk *Vision de paix* (Paris, 1968) 5–15.

529. 'Le rôle des moines dans le mouvement liturgique,' *Paroisse et liturgie* 3 (1968) 248–255.

530. 'S. Bernard et les jeunes,' *Collectanea Cisterciensia* 30 (1968) 147–154; Reprinted in Jean Leclercq, *Vie religieuse et vie contemplative* (Gembloux-Paris: Éd. Duculot, 1969); Italian in *Ora et Labora* 37 (1982) 173–180.

531. 'Les intentions des fondateurs de l'Ordre cistercien,' *Collectanea Cisterciensia* 30 (1968) 233–271; *Cistercian Studies* 4 (1969) 21–61; English in *The Cistercian Spirit. A Symposium* Cistercian Studies Series, 3 (Spencer, MA: Cistercian Publications, 1970) 88–133; Spanish in *Cistercium* 22 (1970) 285–299.

532. 'Le monachisme en marche,' *Vivante Afrique* 256 (May-June, 1968) 1–4.

533. 'Contemplation et vie contemplative hier et aujourd'hui,' *Vie consacrée* 40 (1968) 193–226; *Écoute* 170 (1969) 1–19; Reprinted in Jean Leclercq, *Vie religieuse et vie contemplative* (Gembloux-Paris: Éd. Duculot, 1969).

534. 'Fragmenta monastica, II. Oraisons á S. Pierre et aux Apôtres,' *Benedictina* 15 (1968) 14–18.

535. 'Relation de voyage dans les monastères d'Asie,' *Bulletin de liaison des monastères d'Afrique* 7 (1968) 7–21; *The Examiner* (6 April 1968) 5–9.

536. 'Un renouveau après bien d'autres,' *Informations catholiques internationales* (15 December 1968) 38–40; Dutch edition, ibid.; Spanish edition, ibid.

537. 'An experiment in Indianizing the Church,' *The Examiner* (6 April 1968); *Cistercian Studies* 3 (1968) 183–186.

538. 'Essais sur l'esthétique de S. Bernard,' *Studi medievali* 9 (1968) 688–728; Reprinted in Jean Leclercq, *Recueil d'études sur S. Bernard et ses écrits* 4, Storia e Letteratura, 167 (Rome: Edizioni di Storia e Letteratura, 1987) 35–77.

539. 'Problèmes monastiques d'Extrême-Orient,' *Rythmes du monde* 42 (1968) 214–232; *A New Charter for Monasticism* (Notre Dame-London, 1970) 280–300.

540. 'Die Mönche,' *Der grosse Entschluss* 24 (1968–1969) 28–31, 119–121, 224–226, 372–374, 532–535; *Der grosse Entschluss* 25 (1970) 177–180, 416–418.

541. 'La confession louange de Dieu,' *La vie spirituelle* 118 (1968) 253–265; *Worship* 42 (1968) 159–176; *Cistercian Studies* 4 (1969) 192–212; Reprinted in Jean Leclercq, *Vie religieuse et vie contemplative* (Gembloux-Paris: Éd. Duculot, 1969).

542. 'Continuité et vérité,' *La Maison-Dieu* 80 (1968) 131–141; *El oficio divino hoy* (Barcelona, 1969) 191–205; *Erbe und Auftrag* 45 (1969) 280–288; Reprinted in Jean Leclercq, *Le défi de la vie contemplative* (Gembloux-Paris: Éd. Duculot, 1970).

543. 'Le chapitre des coulpes,' *La vie des communautés religieuses* 26 (1968) 108–117; Italian in *Vita religiosa* 4 (1968) 439–447; Reprinted in Jean Leclercq, *Le défi de la vie contemplative* (Gembloux-Paris: Éd. Duculot, 1970).

544. 'Mönchtum in den jungen Kirchen,' *Liturgie und Mönchtum* 43 (1968) 69–76.

545. 'Problèmes du monachisme chrétien en Asie,' *Collectanea Cisterciensia* 30 (1968) 15–52; *Parole et mission* 11 (1968) 437–465; Italian in *Ora et Labora* 24 (1969) 2–32; Italian in *Vita monastica* 22 (1968) 147–159; Reprinted in Jean Leclercq, *Vie religieuse et vie contemplative* (Gembloux-Paris: Éd. Duculot, 1969).

546. 'L'humanisme littéraire de S. Bernard,' M. de Gandillac and E. Jeauneau, eds. *Entretiens sur la renaissance du XII*[e] *siècle* (Paris-La-Haye, 1968) 295–308.

547. Review of B. de Gaiffier, *Études critiques d'hagiographie et d'iconologie*. In *Studi medievali* 9 (1968) 235–240.

1969

548. 'Vie monastique,' *Orval. Neuf siècles d'histoire 1069–1969* (Orval, 1969) 217–222.

549. 'Une rédaction en prose de la *Visio Anselli* dans un manuscrit de Subiaco,' *Benedictina* 16 (1969) 188–195.

550. 'Humanisme des moines au moyen âge,' *Dictionnaire de spiritualité* VII (1969) 960–970.

551. '*Ad ipsam sophiam Christus.* Le témoignage monastique d'Abélard,' *Sapienter ordinare. Festgabe für Erich Kleineidam* (Leipzig, 1969) 179–198; *Revue d'ascétique et de mystique* 46 (1970) 161–182.

552. 'Lettres d'Amérique latine,' *Bulletin de l'A.I.M.* 10 (1969) 21–34; Italian in *San Benedetto* 14 (1970) 72–78.

553. 'Foreword,' A. Hallier OCSO, *The Monastic Theology of Aelred of Rievaulx* Cistercian Studies Series, 2 (Spencer, MA: Cistercian Publications, 1969) xv–xvii.

554. 'Les lettres de Guillaume de Saint-Thierry à S. Bernard,' *Revue bénédictine* 79 (1969) 375–391; Reprinted in Jean Leclercq,

Recueil d'études sur saint Bernard et ses écrits 4, Storia e Letteratura, 167 (Rome: Edizioni di Storia e Letteratura, 1987) 349–370.

555. 'The Exposition and Exegesis of Scripture from Gregory the Great to Saint Bernard,' *Cambridge History of the Bible. The West from the Fathers to the Reformation* (Cambridge, 1969) 183–197.

556. 'San Maiolo fundatore e riformatore di monasteri a Pavia,' *Atti nel 4° convegno internazionale di studi sull'alto mediaevo* (Spoleto, 1969) 155–173; Partially reprinted in Jean Leclercq, *Aspects du monachisme hier et aujourd'hui* (Paris: Éd. de la Source, 1968).

557. 'Producción y consumo según Isaac de Stella,' *Cistercium* 20 (1969) 211–220; French in *Collectanea Cisterciensia* 31 (1971) 159–166; English in *Cistercian Studies* 4 (1969) 267–274.

558. 'Tâtonnements du monachisme dans le tiers-monde,' *Parole et mission* 12 (1969) 587–591.

559. 'Humanisme et foi chrétienne,' *Parole et mission* 12 (1969) 623–627.

560. 'A monastic pioneer of the thirteenth century: A spiritual portrait of St Sylvester Guzzolini,' *The Downside Review* 87 (1969) 1–16.

561. 'Actualité de l'humour,' *La vie spirituelle* 121 (1969) 263–271; Italian in *Monastica* 12 (1971) 42–47; Reprinted in Jean Leclercq, *Le défi de la vie contemplative* (Gembloux-Paris: Éd. Duculot, 1970).

562. 'Derniers souvenirs de Thomas Merton,' *Bulletin de l'A.I.M.* 9 (1969) 17–21; *Collectanea Cisterciensia* 39 (1969) 9–14; Italian in *Ora et Labora* 24 (1969) 121–125; Reprinted in Jean Leclercq, *Le défi de la vie contemplative* (Gembloux-Paris: Éd. Duculot, 1970).

563. 'Le monachisme dans un monde en transformation,' *La vie spirituelle* 121 (1969) 5–31; *Geist und Leben* 42 (1969) 118–137; *American Benedictine Review* 22 (1971) 187–207; Reprinted in Jean Leclercq, *Le défi de la vie contemplative* (Gembloux-Paris: Éd. Duculot, 1970).

564. 'Confession et louange de Dieu chez S. Bernard,' *La vie spirituelle* 120 (1969) 588–605; English in *Cistercian Studies* 4 (1969) 199–212; Spanish in *Cistercium* 21 (1969) 211–220.

565. 'Prière et vitesse,' *La vie spirituelle* 120 (1969) 191–224; C. Mooney, ed. *Prayer. The Problem of Dialogue with God* (Paramus-London, 1969) 23–46; Italian in *Monastica* 12 (1971) 54–78; Reprinted in Jean Leclercq, *Le défi de la vie contemplative* (Gembloux-Paris: Éd. Duculot, 1970).

566. 'Espérance et esthétique,' *Lettre de Ligugé* no. 138 (1969) 5–7; Italian in *Monastica* 11 (1970) 30–33.

567. 'Ugo di Cluny,' *Bibliotheca sanctorum* 12 (1969) 752–755.

568. 'Impressions sur le monachisme en Inde,' *Parole et mission* 12 (1969) 405–424; Reprinted in Jean Leclercq, *Le défi de la vie contemplative* (Gembloux-Paris: Éd. Duculot, 1970).

569. 'La rencontre des moines d'Asie à Bangkok,' *Parole et mission* 12 (1969) 390–404; *Collectanea Cisterciensia* 31 (1969) 91–96; Italian in *Ora et Labora* 24 (1969) 163–170; *Il tetto* 7 (1970) 78–88; *Erbe und Auftrag* 47 (1971) 68–74; Reprinted in Jean Leclercq, *Le défi de la vie contemplative* (Gembloux-Paris: Éd. Duculot, 1970).

570. 'Present day problems in monasticism,' *The Downside Review* 87 (1969) 135–156; *Rythmes du monde* 45 (1969) 7–23; *A New Charter for Monasticism* (Notre Dame-London, 1970) 23–44; Reprinted in Jean Leclercq, *Le défi de la vie contemplative* (Gembloux-Paris: Éd. Duculot, 1970).

571. 'Pour une spiritualité de la cellule,' *Collectanea Cisterciensia* 3 (1969) 74–82; Italian in *Ora et Labora* 25 (1970) 103–110; Reprinted in Jean Leclercq, *Le défi de la vie contemplative* (Gembloux-Paris: Éd. Duculot, 1970).

572. 'Problèmes de la prière dans les communautés religieuses,' *La vie des communautes religieuses* 27 (1969) 2–13; Reprinted in Jean Leclercq, *Le défi de la vie contemplative* (Gembloux-Paris: Éd. Duculot, 1970); English in *Tjurunga* 9 (1972) 68–82.

573. 'Monastic Culture as a Link with Antiquity,' Charles R. Young, ed., *The Twelfth-Century Renaissance* (Holt, Rinehart and Winston, 1969) 41–50.

574. Review of M.D. Knowles and D. Obolensky, *Nouvelle histoire de l'Église, 2: Le moyen âge*. In *Cahiers de civilisation médiévale* 12 (1969) 84–86.

575. Review of D.E. Luscombe, *The School of Peter Abelard*. In *The Ampleforth Journal* 74 (1969) 411–412.

1970

576. 'Introduction,' to 'Apologia to Abbot William,' *Bernard of Clairvaux, I. Treatises, 1* Cistercian Fathers Series, 1 (Spencer, MA: Cistercian Publications, 1970) 3–30; *Cistercians and Cluniacs: St. Bernard's 'Apologia' to Abbot William* Cistercian Fathers Series, 1A (Spencer, MA: Cistercian Publications, 1970) 3–30.

577. 'Introduction' to 'St Bernard's Book on Precept and Dispensation,' *Bernard of Clairvaux, I. Treatises. 1* Cistercian Fathers Series, 1 (Spencer, MA: Cistercian Publications, 1970) 73–102.

578. 'Qu'est-ce que vivre selon une règle?' *Collectanea Cisterciensia* 32 (1970) 155–163; Italian in *Ora et Labora* 25 (1970) 145–151; Reprinted in Jean Leclercq, *Moines et moniales ont-ils un avenir?* (Bruxelles-Paris: Éd. Lumen vitae, 1971).

579. 'Deux nouveaux Docteurs de l'Église,' *La vie spirituelle* 123 (1970) 135–146; Italian in *Monastica* 12 (1971) 49–57.

580. 'Le diverse forme divita religiosa,' *Studi Francescani* 67 (1970) 105–115; Reprinted in Jean Leclercq, *Moines et moniales ont-ils un avenir?* (Bruxelles-Paris: Éd. Lumen vitae, 1971).

581. 'Les contemplatives peuvent-elles se gouverner elles-mêmes?' *Vie consacrée* 42 (1970) 3–28; English in *Cistercian Studies* 5 (1970) 111–130; Italian in *Vita monastica* 24 (1970) 78–103; Reprinted in Jean Leclercq, *Moines et moniales ont-ils un avenir?* (Bruxelles-Paris: Éd. Lumen vitae, 1971).

582. 'Attualità della communità apostolica,' *Servizio della parola* no. 21 (1970) 10–14; Reprinted in Jean Leclercq, *Moines et moniales ont-ils un avenir?* (Bruxelles-Paris: Éd. Duculot, 1971).

583. 'A Sociological Approach to the History of a Religious Order,' *The Cistercian Spirit. A Symposium* Cistercian Studies Series, 3 (Spencer, MA: Cistercian Publications, 1970) 134–143.

584. 'Bref traité sur la confession dans un manuscrit d'Orval,' *Recherches de théologie ancienne et médiévale* 27 (1970) 142–147.

585. 'Profession according to the Rule of St Benedict,' *Cistercian Studies* 5 (1970) 252–277; M. Basil Pennington, ed. *Rule and Life. An Interdisciplinary Symposium* Cistercian Studies Series 12 (Spencer, MA: Cistercian Publications, 1971) 117–150.

586. 'The Priesthood in the Patristic and Medieval Church,' *The Christian Priesthood* (London-Denville, NJ, 1970) 53–75.

587. 'La rencontre des moines d'Extrême-Orient,' *Bulletin de l'A.I.M.* 11 (1970) 29–35; English edition, ibid.

588. 'Un témoin de l'antiféminisme au moyen âge,' *Revue bénédictine* 80 (1970) 304–309.

589. 'Monastic historiography from Leo IX to Callistus II,' *Studia monastica* 12 (1970) 57–86; French in *Il monachesimo e la riforma ecclesiastica (1049–1122)* (Milan, 1971) 271–301.

590. 'Violence and the devotion to St Benedict in the Middle

Ages,' *The Downside Review* 88 (1970) 344–360; *Mélanges de science religieuse* 28 (1971) 3–15.

591. 'Attualità di una crisi mediaevale,' Preface to G. Lunardi *L'ideale monastico nelle polemiche del Seculo XII sulla vita religiosa* (Noci, 1970) 5–8.

592. 'Vieni e Seguimi,' *Monastica* 11 (1970) 3–10.

593. 'L'humanisme des moines au moyen âge,' *A Giuseppe Ermini, I, Studi mediaevali* (1970) 69–113.

594. 'Thèmes pour une réflexion chrétienne sur l'Expo 70,' *Nouvelle revue théologique* 102 (1970) 634–648; *The Japan Missionary Bulletin* 24 (1970) 347–353, 413–418; Italian in *Monastica* 11 (1970) 31–46.

595. 'Il monachesimo cristiano e gli altri,' *Vita religiosa* 6 (1970) 180–184; Reprinted in Jean Leclercq, *Moines et moniales ont-ils un avenir?* (Bruxelles-Paris: Éd. Duculot, 1971).

596. 'Existe-t-il une prière contemplative?' *La vie des communautés religieuses* 28 (1970) 194–199; Italian in *Ora et Labora* 28 (1970) 1–5; *Spiritual Life* 17 (1971) 34–39.

597. 'Presentazione,' Ferruccio Gastaldelli, ed. *Goffredo di Auxerre 'Super Apocalypsim'* (Rome, 1970) 7–8.

598. 'Teologia de la vida monastica, estratto e Conferencia de D. Jean Leclercq à Montreal,' *La Saulsaie* 4 (1970) 19–60.

599. Review of S. Giuliani, *Profilo di un santo. S. Silvestro abate.* In *Rivista di storia della Chiesa in Italia* 24 (1970) 244.

600. Review of G. Sprunk, *Kunst und Glaube in der lateinischen Heiligenlegende* (München, 1970). In *Rivista di storia della Chiesa in Italia* 25 (1970) 240–242.

1971

601. 'La rencontre des monachismes,' *Parole et mission* 14 (1971) 340–348.

602. 'St Bernard and the Rule of St Benedict,' M. Basil Pennington, ed., *Rule and Life. An Interdisciplinary Symposium* Cistercian Studies Series, 12 (Spencer, MA: Cistercian Publications, 1971) 151–168; 'San Bernardo y la Regla de San Benito,' *Cuadernos monásticos* 28 (1990) 307–321.

603. 'Teologia de la vida monastica,' *Cuadernos monásticos* 6 (1971) 9–60.

604. 'Monachesimo femminile,' *Dizionario degli instituti di perfezione* (Rome, 1971) 31–36.

605. 'Recherches sur la collection des épîtres de S. Bernard,' *Cahiers de civilisation médiévale* 14 (1971) 205–219; Also see [606].

606. 'Lettres de S. Bernard: histoire ou littérature?' *Studi medievali* 12/1 (1971) 1–74; Reprinted along with [620] in Jean Leclercq, *Recueil d'études sur S. Bernard et ses écrits* 4, Storia e Letteratura, 167 (Rome: Edizioni di Storia e Letteratura, 1987) 125–225.

607. 'Le cloître est-il une prison?' *Revue d'ascétique et de mystique* 47 (1971) 407–420.

608. 'Prière monastique et accueil,' *Collectanea Cisterciensia* 33 (1971) 379–400; *Vita Monastica* 26 (1972) 96–125.

609. 'Marginalité et accueil,' *Collectanea Cisterciensia* 33 (1971) 401–405.

610. 'L'encyclique de S. Bernard en faveur de la croisade,' *Revue bénédictine* 81 (1971) 282–308; Reprinted in Jean Leclercq, *Recueil d'études sur S. Bernard et ses écrits* IV, Storia e Letteratura, 167 (Rome: Edizioni di Storia e Letteratura, 1987) 227–246.

611. 'À propos de l'encyclique de S. Bernard sur la croisade,' *Revue bénédictine* 82 (1972) 312.

612. 'Multipluralism. Benedictine life in the Church today,' *The Ampleforth Journal* 76 (1971) 75–83; Italian in *Ora et Labora* 26 (1971) 158–166; *Cistercian Studies* 7 (1972) 77–84.

613. 'Une réunion de contemplatives à Obout,' *Bulletin de l'A.I.M.* 12 (1971) 26–31; English edition, ibid.

614. 'Une expérience pascale,' *Collectanea Cisterciensia* 33 (1971) 120–123.

615. 'Note sur la tradition monastique d'Occident,' *Collectanea Cisterciensia* 33 (1971) 102–104.

616. 'Consécration religieuse et vie contemplative,' *La vie des communautés religieuses* 29 (1971) 2–19.

617. 'Vie monastique masculine et vie monastique féminine,' *Supplément à la Lettre de Ligugé* 149 (1971) 3–9; *Cistercian Studies* 6 (1971) 327–333; Italian in *Ora et Labora* 27 (1972) 3–8.

618. 'Le Commentaire d'Étienne de Paris sur la Règle de S. Benoît,' *Revue d'ascétique et de mystique* 47 (1971) 129–144.

619. 'Introduction,' Thomas Merton *Contemplation in a World of Action* (New York, 1971) ix-xx.

620. 'Culture and the Spiritual Life,' *Review for Religious* 30 (1971) 167–178.

621. 'Un formulaire de chancellerie de l'abbaye d'Orval,' *Cîteaux* 21 (1970) 300–301.

622. 'S. Gérard de Csanád et le monachisme,' *Studia monastica* 13 (1971) 13–30.

623. 'La figura di Pier Damiano. Ermite et homme d'Eglise,' *Testi e documenti di vita sacerdotale e di arte pastorale XVII* (Rome, 1971) 105–113.

624. 'Deux témoins de la vie des cloîtres au moyen âge,' *Studi medievali* 12/2 (1971) 987–995.

625. 'Prière des heures et civilisation contemporaine,' *La Maison-Dieu* 83 (1971) 34–45; Italian in *Monastica* 13 (1972) 21–30.

1972

626. 'Notes abelardiennes,' *Bulletin de Philosophie médiévale* 13 (1972) 71–74.

627. 'Évangile et culture dans la tradition bénédictine,' *Nouvelle revue théologique* 104 (1972) 171–182; *Revue historique ardennaise* 7 (1972) 143–149.

628. 'S. Bernard de Clairvaux et la communauté contemplative,' *Collectanea Cisterciensia* 34 (1972) 36–84; English in *Cistercian Studies* 7 (1972) 97–142; M. Basil Pennington, ed. *Contemplative Community. An Interdisciplinary Symposium* Cistercian Studies Series 21 (Washington D.C.: Cistercian Publications, 1972) 61–113.

629. 'Pour un portrait spirituel du B[x] Bernardo Tolomei,' *Saggi e ricerche nel VII Centenano della nascita del b. Bernardo Tolomei (1272–1972)* Studia Olivetana, 1 (Monte Oliveto Maggiore, 1972) 11–21; Italian in *L'Ulivo* 2 (1972) 24–31; German in *Der Grüss* 68 (1973) 59–65.

630. 'Pédagogie et formation spirituelle du VIe au XIIe siècle,' *La scula dell'Occidente latino nell'alto medio evo* (Spoleto, 1972) 42–72.

631. 'Un tour du monde monastique par les Mers du Sud,' *Bulletin de l'A.I.M.* 13 (1972) 7–17; English edition, ibid.

632. 'Scopis mundatum (Matth. 12, 44, Mc 11, 25). Le balai dans la Bible et dans la liturgie d'après la tradition latine,' *Epektasis. Mélanges offerts au Cardinal Jean Daniélou* (Paris, 1972) 129–137; Italian in *Monastica* 14 (1973) 5–13; 'La escoba en la Biblia y en

la liturgia segun la tradición latina,' *Cuadernos monásticos* 12 (1977) 459–466.

633. 'L'ascèse de la prière,' *Seminarium* 12 (1972) 12–25; *Monastic Studies* 8 (1972) 89–102; Italian in *Monastica* 13 (1972) 38–48; Spanish in *Cuadernos monásticos* 9 (1974) 75–84; English in *Word and Spirit* 4 (1983) 117–131.

634. 'New Forms of Contemplation and of the Contemplative Life,' *Theological Studies* 33 (1972) 307–319.

635. 'Les chapitres généraux de Cîteaux, de Cluny et des Dominicains,' *Concilium* 7 (1972) 91–97.

636. 'The Definitive Character of Religious Commitment,' *American Benedictine Review* 23 (1972) 181–205; Spanish in *Vida religiosa* 34 (1973) 375–388.

637. 'Jean de Fécamp,' *Dictionnaire de spiritualité* 8 (1972) 445–448.

638. 'The relevance of prayer today,' *Encounter* 17 (1972) 3–13.

639. 'Pour l'histoire du canif et de la lime,' *Scriptorium* 26 (1972) 46–52.

640. 'Preface,' Francis Acharya, *Kurisumala Ashram. Chronique de Douze Années* (Vanves, 1972) 1–6.

641. 'The experience of God and prayer for Christians of our time,' *Spiritual Life* 18 (1972) 246–255.

642. 'La experiencia de Dios en grupos,' *Cuadernos monásticos* 7 (1972) 137–152; French in *L'expérience de Dieu dans la vie monastique* (La Pierre-Qui-Vire, 1973) 160–176; Italian in *Dio vivo o morto?* (Subiaco, 1973) 139–152.

643. 'Lecture, culture et vie spirituelle,' *La vie des communautés religeuses* 30 (1972) 205–218.

644. 'Le thème de la jonglerie chez S. Bernard et ses contemporains,' *Revue d'histoire de la spiritualité* 48 (1972) 386–399; Reprinted in René Louis and Jean Jolivet, eds., *Pierre Abélard. Pierre le Vénérable* Colloques Internationaux du Centre National de la Recherche Scientifique, 546 (Paris: CNRS, 1975) 671–687.

645. 'Un livre intitulé Jesus,' *Nous, gens de la Bible* (Paris, 1972) 24–28; Italian in *Monastica* 14 (1973) 26–30; 'Un libro titulado Jesus,' *Revista San Anselmo* 1 (1982) [numéro spécial] 5–11.

646. 'Prologue,' A. Magarinos *Sacerdotes de ayer* (Madrid, 1972) 9–19.

647. Review of Richard E. Weingart, *The Logic of Divine Love* (Oxford 1970). In *Medium Aevum* 41 (1972) 59–61.

648. Review of H. Steger, *Philologia Musica.* In *Rivista di storia della Chiesa in Italia* 26 (1972) 176–177.

649. Review of F. C. Gardiner, *The Pilgrimage of Desire.* In *Cahiers de civilisation médiévale* 15 (1972) 82–83.

650. Review of M. Aubran, *La vie de S. Étienne d'Obazine.* In *Medium Aevum* 41 (1972) 143–144.

651. Review of R. Hostie, *Vie et mort des Ordres religieux.* In *Bulletin de l' A.I.M.* 14 (1972) 88–89.

1973

652. 'Evangelio y cultura en la historia de la autoridad monástica,' *Vida religiosa* 34 (1973) 31–46; French in *La vie des communautés religieuses* 32 (1974) 79–93; Italian in *Ora et Labora* 30 (1975) 116–128; Spanish in *Studia Silensia* 1 (1975) 327–342.

653. 'La influencia de los religiosos en la animación espiritual de nuestro tiempo,' *Presencia de los religiosos en la nueva sociedad* Instituto de vida religiosa (Madrid: Publicaciónes Claretianas, 1973) 111–135; French in *La vie des communautés religieuses* 32 (1974) 47–64.

654. 'Las consecuencias de la evolución litúrgica para la oración de las comunidades religiosas,' *Vida religiosa* 34 (1973) 245–259; French in *La vie des communautés religieuses* 35 (1977) 66–83; Italian in *Ora et Labora* 34 (1979) 5–21.

655. 'Vie sacramentelle et vie monastique,' *La vie des communautés religieuses* 31 (1973) 177–192.

656. '*Ioculator et saltator*: S. Bernard et l'image du jongleur dans les manuscrits,' *Translatio studii. Manuscript and Library Studies honoring Oliver L. Kapsner* OSB (Collegeville, MN, 1973) 124–148.

657. 'L'idiot à la lumière de la tradition chrétienne,' *Revue d'histoire de la spiritualité* 49 (1973) 289–304; 'L'idiota e la tradizione cristiana,' *Dostoevskij nella coscienza d'oggi* Quaderni S. Giorgio (Firenze: a cura di Sante Graciotti, 1981) 93–106.

658. 'Modern Psychology and the interpretation of mediaeval texts,' *Speculum* 48 (1973) 476–490; German in *Erbe und Auftrag* 51 (1975) 409–426; Italian in *Nuova Rivista Storica* 60 (1976) 150–168.

659. 'S. Pierre Damien et les femmes,' *Studia Monastica* 15 (1973) 43–56; German in *Erbe und Aufrag* 51 (1975) 270–281; English in *Cistercian Studies* 9 (1974) 354–355; *Tjurunga* 7 (1974) 33–46.

660. 'Nos communautés sont-elles une transparence de l'Évangile?' *La vie des communautés religieuses* 31 (1973) 226–235; Spanish

in *Cuadernos monásticos* 8 (1973) 603–611; Italian in *Ora et Labora* 30 (1975) 51–59.

661. 'Le monachisme comme phénomène mondial,' *Le Supplément* 26 (1973) 461–478; 27 (1974) 93–119; Italian in *Ora et Labora* 31 (1976) 20–34, 73–82; English in *Cistercian Studies* 21 (1986) 277–310.

662. *Saint Bernard in Our Times. A lecture delivered before an open meeting of the Stubbs Society* Printed for the Society (Oxford, 1973) pp. 20; French in *Collectanea Cisterciensia* 36 (1974) 3–23; Reprinted in M. Basil Pennington, ed., *St. Bernard of Clairvaux: Studies Commemorating the Eighth Centenary of his Canonization* Cistercian Studies Series, 28 (Kalamazoo, MI: Cistercian Publications, 1977) 1–26.

663. 'Thomas Merton: Voortduren de Vernieuwing,' *De Nieuwe Boodschap* 100 (1973) 190–192; English in Patrick Hart, ed. *Thomas Merton Monk. A Monastic Tribute* (New York, 1974) 93–104; Revised edition, Patrick Hart, ed., *Thomas Merton Monk,* Cistercian Studies Series 52 (Kalamazoo, MI: Cistercian Publications, 1983) 93–104.

664. 'Para descolonizar o monaquismo,' Interview by R. Laurentin *Igreja e Missão* 25 (1973) 439–448.

665. 'Bangalore: Une centaine de participants la deuxième *Rencontre des moines d'Asie,*' *Informations Catholiques internationales* (1 décembre 1973) 30.

666. 'Faut-il partout des maisons de prière?' *Église et mission* (1973) 2–10; Italian in *Monastica* 14 (1973) 32–40.

667. *Départ et envoi dans le monachisme du haut moyen âge* (Paris: Centre de recherches de théologie missionnaire, 1973) pp. 9.

668. Review of A.E. Angenendt, *Monachi Peregrini: Studien zu Pirmin und den monastischen Vorstellungen des frühen Mittelalters* (München, 1973). In *Rivista di storia della Chiesa in Italia* 27 (1973) 581–582.

1974

669. 'Jalons dans une histoire de la théologie spirituelle,' *Seminarium* 14 (1974) 113–122; Italian in *Ora et Labora* 30 (1975) 15–24.

670. 'Aux origines bibliques du vocabulaire de la pauvreté,' *Études sur l'histoire de la pauvreté (Moyen âge XVIe siècle)* Publications de la Sorbonne, Études, 8 (Paris, 1974) 35–43.

671. 'Les controverses sur la pauvreté du Christ,' *Études sur*

l'histoire de la pauvreté (Moyen âge XVIe siècle) Publications de la Sorbonne, Études, 8 (Paris, 1974) 45–56.

672. 'Pour l'histoire de l'encyclique de S. Bernard sur la croisade,' *Études de civilisation médiévale. IXe-XIIe siècle. Mélanges E.-R. Labande* (Poitiers: C.E.S.C.M., 1974) 479–494; Reprinted in Jean Leclercq, *Recueil d'études sur S. Bernard et ses écrits* 4, Storia e Letteratura, 167 (Rome: Edizioni di Storia e Letteratura, 1987) 247–263.

673. 'Problèmes des *Indices* de S. Bernard,' *Cîteaux* 25 (1974) 257–270; Reprinted in Jean Leclercq, *Recueil d'études sur S. Bernard et ses écrits* IV, Storia e Letteratura, 167 (Rome: Edizioni di Storia e Letteratura, 1987) 385–400.

674. *S. Giovanni Gualberto e il Concilio Vaticano II* (Vallombrosa, 1974) pp. 20; Reprinted in G. Zambernardini, *Trilogia del nono centenario S. Giovanni Gualberto, II. Cammina colla Chiesa* (Vallombrosa, 1977) 55–76.

675. 'Attitude spirituelle de S. Bernard devant la guerre,' *Collectanea Cisterciensia* 36 (1974) 195–225; English in John R. Sommerfeldt, ed., *Studies in Medieval Cistercian History* II, Cistercian Studies Series, 24 (Kalamazoo, MI: Cistercian Publications, 1976) 1–39.

676. 'New journey round the world via the Philippines,' *Bulletin de l'A.I.M.* 17 (1974) 49–56; French edition, ibid.

677. 'Liturgy and Contemplation,' *Monastic Studies* 10 (1974) 71–86; Italian in *Monastica* 23 (1983) 12–16.

678. 'The Imitation of Christ and the Sacraments in the teaching of St Bernard,' *Cistercian Studies* 9 (1974) 36–54.

679. 'L'universo religioso di S. Colombano e di S. Giona,' *Atti del Convegno intentaz. di studi colombiani. Bobbio 28–30 agosto 1965. Colombano pioniere di civilizzazione cristiana europea* (Bobbio, 1974) 95–110.

680. 'Problèmes et orientations des contemplatives aujourd'hui,' *Vie consacrée* 46 (1974) 94–103; English in *Encounter* 11 (1976) 23–31.

681. 'Zeiterfahrung und Zeitbegriff im Spätmittelalter,' A. Zimmermann, ed. *Antiqui und Moderni. Traditionsbewusstsein und Fortschrittsbewusstsein im späten Mittelalter* Miscellanea Mediaevalia, 9 (Berlin-New York: W. de Gruyter, 1974) 1–20; English in John R. Sommerfeldt, ed., *Studies in Medieval Culture* 8–9 (Kalamazoo, MI: Medieval Institute Publications, 1976) 137–150.

682. 'Abelardo,' *Dizionario degli Istituti di Perfezione* I (Rome, 1974) 49–50.

683. 'Agiografia monastica,' *Dizionario degli Istituti di Perfezione* I (Rome, 1974) 152–153.

684. 'Amicizia nella vita religiosa,' *Dizionario degli Istituti di Perfezione* I (Rome, 1974) 516–520.

685. 'Benedettini, II. Dal sec. VI a Cîteaux,' *Dizionario degli Istituti di Perfezione* I (Rome, 1974) 1286–1290.

686. 'Bernardo di Clairvaux,' *Dizionario degli Istituti di Perfezione* I (Rome, 1974) 1394–1396.

687. 'Tradition patristique et monastique dans l'enseignement de la Somme Théologique sur la vie contemplative,' *San Tommaso. Fonti e riflessi del suo pensiero* Studi Tomistici, I (Rome, 1974) 129–153; Italian in *Monastica* 15 (1974) 20–25.

688. 'Encore Pons de Cluny et Pierre le Vénérable,' *Aevum* 48 (1974) 134–149.

1975

689. 'L'authenticité de l'épître 462 de S. Bernard *ad noviter conversos*,' *Sapientiae procerum amore. Mélanges médiévistes offerts à J.-P. Müller* OSB Studia Anselmiana, 63 (Rome, 1975) 81–96; Reprinted in Jean Leclercq, *Recueil d'études sur S. Bernard et ses écrits* 4, Storia e Letteratura, 167 (Rome: Edizioni di Storia e Letteratura, 1987) 285–299.

690. 'Textes sur la vocation et la formation des moines au moyen âge,' *Corona gratiarum. Miscellanea E. Dekkers* OSB *XII lustra complenti oblata* II (Brugge: Sint Pietersabdej, 1975) 169–194.

691. 'Spiritualité et culture à Orval au siècle de S. Bernard d'après les manuscrits,' *Aureavallis* (Orval, 1975) 74–82.

692. 'Idipsum. Les harmoniques d'un mot biblique dans S. Bernard,' *Scientia Augustiniana. Festschrift A. Zumkeller* (Würzburg, 1975) 170–183.

693. 'Psycho-history and the understanding of medieval people,' *The Hannoverian of Hanover College* (6 May 1975) 6–10; Reprinted and augmented in *Cistercian Studies* 11 (1976) 269–289.

694. 'Hugues de Fleury et nous,' *Études Ligériennes d'Histoire et d'Archéologie Médiévales* (Auxerre, 1975) 247–256.

695. 'Bernardo di Chiaravalle (1090–20 agosto 1153),' *Studi su*

S. Bernardo di Chiaravalle nell'ottavo centenario della canonizzazione (Rome: Ed. Cistercienses, 1975) 9–12.

696. 'Psicologia e vita spirituale in S. Bernardo,' *Studi su S. Bernardo di Chiaravalle nell'ottavo centenario della canonizzazione* (Rome: Ed. Cistercienses, 1975) 215–244.

697. 'Caelestis fistula,' *Verbum et signum. Beiträge zur mediävistischen Bedeutungsforschung* II (München, 1975) 59–68; Italian in *Monastica* 17 (1976) 54–60.

698. 'Der heilige Bernhard und das Weibliche,' *Erbe und Auftrag* 51 (1975) 161–179.

699. 'Literature and Psychology in Bernard of Clairvaux,' *The Downside Review* 93 (1975) 1–20.

700. 'Autour de la Règle de S. Benoît,' *Collectanea Cisterciensia* 37 (1975) 167–204; Spanish in *La regla benedictina bajo un enfoque pastoral y psicológico* (Arévalo: Seminario maestras de novicias, août 1975) 53–101; German in *Erbe und Auftrag* 52 (1976) 414–431; 53 (1977) 19–31, 115–122; Italian in *Ora et Labora* 34 (1979) 72–88, 153–165.

701. 'Experience and Interpretation of Time in the Early Middle Ages,' *Studies in Medieval Culture* 5 (Kalamazoo, MI: Medieval Institute Publications, 1975) 9–20; Italian in *Ora et Labora* 27 (1972) 49–58.

702. 'Une nouvelle puissance: le monachisme,' *Aujourd'hui l'Église* (Paris, 1975) 136–149.

703. 'Moines aujourd'hui, partout dans le monde,' *Aujourd'hui l'Église* (Paris, 1975) 170–173.

704. 'Castità,' *Dizionario degli Istituti di Perfezione* II (Rome, 1975) 662–665.

705. 'Chiesa e monachesimo,' *Dizionario degli Istituti di Perfezione* II (Rome, 1975) 1006–1113.

706. 'Clausura,' *Dizionario degli Istituti di Perfezione* II (Rome, 1975) 1166–1174; French in *Collectanea Cisterciensia* 44 (1981) 366–376.

707. 'Cluniacensi,' *Dizionario degli Istituti di Perfezione* II (Rome, 1975) 1198–1200.

708. 'Confessione (in Occidente),' *Dizionario degli Istituti di Perfezione* II (Rome, 1975) 1433–1436.

709. 'Bernard de Clairvaux (saint),' *Dictionnaire des auteurs cisterciens* II (1975) 104–108.

710. Chapel address. Recorded 21 March 1975. Southern Baptist Theological Society (On side 1 of 1 sound tape reel; analog, 3¾ ips, mono.; 7 in.).

711. 'L'ascèse comme valeur permanente dans le monachisme d'aujourd'hui,' *La vie des communautés religieuses* 33 (1975) 306–317; 34 (1976) 2–17; Spanish in *Vida religiosa* 38 (1975) 337–349.

712. Review of D. Baker, *Sanctity and Secularity. The Church and the World* (Oxford, 1973). In *The Heythrop Journal* 16 (1975) 94–95.

713. Review of *Dizionario degli Istituti di Perfezione* I (1974) and II (1975). In *La vie spirituelle* 129 (1975) 441–442, 919–920.

1976

714. 'Actualidad de la vita contemplative,' *Vida religiosa* 40 (1976) 323–349.

715. 'Psicologia moderna e interpetazione di testi medievali,' *Nuova Rivista Storica* 40 (1976) 150–168.

716. 'Liturgie et vie monastique,' *La vie des communautés religieuses* 34 (1976) 194–203; Spanish in *Vida religiosa* 41 (1976) 19–28; Italian in *Ora et Labora* 32 (1977) 155–164.

717. 'The Experience of Time and Its Interpretation in the Late Middle Ages,' John R. Sommerfeldt, ed., *Studies in Medieval Culture* 8–9 (Kalamazoo, MI: Medieval Institute Publications, 1976) 137–150.

718. 'Preface,' E. Rozanne Elder, ed. *The Spirituality of Western Christendom*, Cistercian Studies Series 30 (Kalamazoo, MI: Cistercian Publications, 1976) v-xxxiv.

719. 'Dottrine sulla Chiesa nella seconda parte del Medio Evo,' *Problemi di Storia della Chiesa. Il medioevo dei secoli XII-XV* (Milan, 1976) 133–161.

720. 'Une histoire spirituelle de l'Italie,' *Rivista di Storia della Chiesa in Italia* 30 (1976) 157–164.

721. 'Introduction,' *The Works of Bernard of Clairvaux. On the Song of Songs* 2 Cistercian Fathers Series 7 (Kalamazoo, MI: Cistercian Publications, 1976) vii-xxx.

722. 'Prologue,' J.C. Peifer, *Espiritualidad monástica* (Viaceli, 1976) 7–16.

723. 'Textes et images dans l'explication d'un symbole,' Guy Cambier *Hommages à André Boutemy* Latomus, 145 (Bruxelles, 1976) 231–243.

724. 'Economia monastica occidentale,' *Dizionario degli Istituti di Perfezione* III (Rome, 1976) 1020–1027.

725. 'Femminile (Monachesimo),' *Dizionario degli Istituti di Perfezione* III (Rome, 1976) 1445–1451.

726. 'L'hérésie d'après les écrits de S. Bernard de Clairvaux,' *The Concept of Heresy in the Middle Ages (11th–13th C.)* (Leuven-The Hague, 1976) 12–26.

727. 'Agressivité et répression chez Bernard de Clairvaux,' *Revue d'Histoire de la Spiritualité* 52 (1976) 155–172.

728. 'New Norcia et la mission bénédictine d'Australie Occidentale,' *Bulletin de l'A.I.M.* 20 (1976) 30–39; English edition, ibid., 28–37.

729. 'Le renouveau solesmien et le renouveau religieux du XIXe siècle,' *Studia Monastica* 18 (1976) 157–195; *Centenaire de Belloc 1875–1975* (Belloc, 1977) 48–84.

730. 'Imitation du Christ et sacrements chez S. Bernard,' *Collectanea Cisterciensia* 38 (1976) 263–282.

731. 'Jesus and the Oppressed,' M. Basil Pennington, ed., *Prayer and Liberation* (Alba Books, 1976) 5–27; French in *La vie des communautés religieuses* 36 (1978) 130–143.

732. 'Preface,' Sr Benedicta Ward, ed. *The Influence of Saint Bernard* (Oxford, 1976) vi-xviii; French in *Collectanea Cisterciensia* 40 (1978) 139–149.

733. 'Douze années d'études bernardines,' *Bulletin de philosophie médiévale* 28 (1976) 60–68.

734. 'Une école de spiritualité bénédictine datant du XVIIe siècle: les Bénédictines de l'Adoration Perpétuelle,' *Studia Monastica* 18 (1976) 433–452; Italian in *Ora et Labora* 32 (1977) 55–75; German in *Erbe und Auftrag* 58 (1982) 284–300.

735. 'Monasticism: Ever ancient, ever new,' *Spirit and Life* 71 (1976) 3–5.

736. 'Un amour fou,' B. Bro, ed. *Le pouvoir du mal* (Paris, 1976) 231–244.

737. 'Preface,' D. Winzen, *Pathways in Scripture. A book-by-book guide to the spiritual riches of the Bible* (Ann Arbor, MI, 1976) 1–3.

738. 'Visio Anselli,' *Enciclopedia Dantesca* 5 (1976) 1069.

739. 'Visio Eynsham,' *Enciclopedia Dantesca* 5 (1976) 1069.

740. 'Visio Sancti Pauli,' *Enciclopedia Dantesca* 5 (1976) 1069–1070.

741. 'Visio Tugdali,' *Enciclopedia Dantesca* 5 (1976) 1070.

742. Review of L. de Seilhac, *L'utilisation par saint Césaire d'Arles de la Règle de saint Augustin. Étude de terminologie et de doctrine monastiques* Studia Anselmia, 62 (Rome, 1975). In *La vie spirituelle* 130 (1976) 621–622.

743. Review of E. Gandolfo, *Esperienza umana alla luce della Biblia* (Milan, 1976). In *Collectanea Cisterciensia* 38 (1976) 103.

1977

744. 'L'ascesi come valore permanente nel monachesimo d'oggi,' *Ora et Labora* 32 (1977) 45–51, 76–90; German in *Erbe und Auftrag* 53 (1977) 337–360; Spanish in *Yermo* 18 (1980) 63–91.

745. 'The role of monasticism in the Church today,' *The Australasian Catholic Record* 54 (1977) 63–83.

746. 'Nouveaux témoins de la survie de S. Bernard,' *Homenaje a Fray Justo Pérez de Urbel* Studia Silensia IV, Silos, 2 (1977) 93–109; Reprinted in Jean Leclercq, *Recueil d'études sur S. Bernard et ses écrits* 4, Storia e Letteratura, 167 (Rome: Edizioni di Storia e Letteratura, 1987) 317–334.

747. 'Un demi-siècle de synthèse entre histoire et théologie,' *Seminarium* 17 (1977) 21–34.

748. 'L'expérience mystique d'après S. Bernard,' *Studia missionalia* 26 (1977) 59–71.

749. 'Une mystique pratique dans les sermons de S. Bernard à ses moines,' *Studia missionalia* 26 (1977) 73–86; Italian in *Monastica* 19 (1978) 32–45.

750. 'Avant-propos,' B. de Gaiffier *Recueil d'hagiographie* Subsidia hagiographica, 59 (Bruxelles, 1977) xi-xv.

751. 'Modern Psychology as an approach to the medieval psyche,' *The Indiana Social Studies Quarterly* 30 (1977) 5–26.

752. 'Les deux rédactions de la lettre de S. Bernard à Aelred de Rievaulx,' H.R. Runte, H. Niedzielski and W.L. Hendrickson, eds., *Jean Misrahi Memorial Volume. Studies in Medieval Literature* (Columbia, SC, 1977) 210–288; Reprinted in Jean Leclercq, *Recueil d'études sur S. Bernard et ses écrits* 4, Storia e Letteratura, 167 (Rome: Edizioni di Storia e Letteratura, 1987) 301–315.

753. 'The formative community according to St. Bernard of Clairvaux,' *Tjurunga* 14 (1977) 125–146; Reprinted in *Cistercian*

Studies 14 (1979) 99–119; French in *Collectanea Cisterciensia* 43 (1980) 3–21; 'St. Bernhard und die formative Kommunität,' *Cistercienser Chronik* 95 (1988) 1–15.

754. 'Études récentes sur Guillaume de Saint-Thierry,' *Bulletin de philosophie médiévale* 19 (1977) 49–55.

755. 'Formazione,' *Dizionario degli Istituti di Perfezione* IV (Rome, 1977) 131–136.

756. 'Fuggitivi,' *Dizionario degli Istituti di Perfezione* IV (Rome, 1977) 995–997.

757. 'Gesù Cristo,' *Dizionario degli Istituti di Perfezione* IV (Rome, 1977) 1032–1035.

758. 'La *Vita di S. Silvestro*, l'irraggiamento del santo e dei suoi primi discepoli,' *Studia Picena* 44 (1977) 107–127 (Atti del Congresso di studi storici VIII Centenario Nascita S. Silvestro 1177–1977, Bibliotheca Montisfani, 5).

759. Review of J. Bugge, *Virginitas: An Essay in the History of a Medieval Ideal* (The Hague, 1975). In *Medium Aevum* 43 (1977) 129–131.

760. Review of *Dizionario degli Istituti di Perfezione* III (1976). In *La vie spirituelle* 131 (1977) 150–151.

1978

761. 'Merton and the East,' *Cistercian Studies* 13 (1978) 309–317; Italian in *Vita monastica* 32 (1978) 45–56; French in *Bulletin de l'A.I.M.* 25 (1979) 44–51; English edition, ibid., 45–52.

762. 'Cultura e insegnamento (XII°–XIV° s.),' *Apogeo e crisi del Medioevo* Storia d'Italia e d'Europa, 2 (Milan: Jaca Book, 1978) 329–345.

763. 'La dynamique de la réforme liturgique: enracinement dans la tradition et élan vers l'avenir (*Sacrosanctum Concilium*),' *Éléments de Bibliographie. Bulletin de l'Association pour le Développement des Bibliothèques de Religieuses (Paris)* no. 118 (1978) [=numéro spécial: Une relecture des dossiers conciliaires] G 1 à 14; Spanish in *Liturgia* 9 (1979) 5–15.

764. 'Cerca la gioia nel Signore. San Bernardo e la sua esperienza mistica,' *Monastica* 19 (1978) 29–41.

765. 'Tendances monastiques nouvelles,' *Nouvelle revue théologique* 100 (1978) 90–102.

766. 'À propos de "La renaissance du XIIe siècle". Nouveaux témoignages sur la "théologie monastique",' *Collectanea Cisterciensia* 40 (1978) 65–72.

767. 'Il prigioniero,' *Boze '78* 1 (1978) 13–22.

768. 'Prière et louange,' *La vie des communautés religieuses* 36 (1978) 66–81; Spanish in *Liturgia* 8 (1978) 25–35; Italian in *Ora et Labora* 35 (1980) 62–76; English in *Word and Spirit* 3 (1982) 78–97.

769. 'Il monachesimo alla ricerca di un nuovo modo di presenza nella città secolare,' *Testimoni* no. 13 (15 juillet 1978) 4.

770. 'Lumières nouvelles sur Catherine de Bar,' *Studia Monastica* 20 (1978) 397–407; Italian in *Ora et Labora* 34 (1979) 96–105; English in *Vox benedictina* 2 (1985) 337–353.

771. 'La nouveauté de l'édition de saint Bernard,' *Analecta Cisterciensia* 34 (1978) 7–16; Reprinted in Jean Leclercq, *Recueil d'études sur S. Bernard et ses écrits* 4, Storia e Letteratura, 167 (Rome: Edizioni di Storia e Letteratura, 1987) 373–384.

772. 'Christliches Mönchtum in Afrika,' *Die katholische Mission* 97 (1978) 194–196; French in *Bulletin de l'A.I.M.* 24 (1978) 24–30.

773. 'Polding and Gregory in the light of monastic friendship and mission since Boniface,' *Tjurunga* 15 (1978) 47–63.

774. 'La dimension pénitente dans la vie religieuse,' *La vie des communautés religieuses* 36 (1978) 211–224; Spanish in *Cuadernos monásticos* 67 (1983) 391–400.

775. 'Jésus et les opprimés,' *La vie des communautés religieuses* 36 (1978) 130–143.

776. 'Aspects de la vie cistercienne au XIIème siècle. À propos d'un livre récent,' *Studia Monastica* 20 (1978) 221–226.

777. 'Monachisme urbain aujourd'hui: pourquoi?' *Vie consacrée* 50 (1978) 170–185; Italian in *Ora et Labora* 36 (1981) 168–181.

778. 'Lavoro dei religiosi oggi,' *Dizionario degli Istituti di Perfezione* V (Rome, 1978) 543–548.

779. 'Lectio divina. II. In Occidente,' *Dizionario degli Istituti di Perfezione* V (Rome, 1978) 562–566; Spanish in *Revista San Anselmo* 2/5 (1982–1983) 17–24.

780. 'Maddalene (3.),' *Dizionario degli Istituti di Perfezione* V (Rome, 1978) 812–813.

781. 'Monachesimo,' *Dizionario degli Istituti di Perfezione* V (Rome, 1978) 1673–1684, 1733–1742.

782. 'Una scuola di spiritualità benedettina: le Benedettine dell'

Adorazione Perpetua,' Preface to Catherine de Bar *Non date tregua a Dio. Lettere alle monache. 1641–1697* Gia e nonancora, 49 (Milan: Jaca Book, 1978) 11–24.

783. 'Preface,' Julian of Norwich, *Showings.* Edmund Colledge and James Walsh, trans. and eds. The Classics of Western Spirituality (New York-Ramsey-Toronto: Paulist Press, 1978) 1–14.

784. Review of Baudouin de Gaiffier, *Recueil d'hagiographie* (Bruxelles: Société des Bollandistes, 1977). In *Studi medievali* 19 (1978) 245–247.

1979

785. 'Consciousness of identification in 12th-century monasticism,' *Cistercian Studies* 14 (1979) 219–231; French in *Studia Monastica* 28 (1986) 51–74.

786. In collaboration with Sr Bernard Saïd, 'The Thomas Merton Commemorations,' *Cistercian Studies* 14 (1979) 307–312.

787. 'Monachisme chrétien et mission,' *Bulletin de l'A.I.M.* 26 (1979) 9–26; Reprinted in *Studia missionalia* 28 (1979) 133–152; Italian in *Vita consacrata* 16 (1980) 249–264.

788. 'Usage et abus de la Bible au temps de la réforme grégorienne,' W. Lourdaux and D. Verhelst, eds., *The Bible and Medieval Culture,* Mediaevalia Lovaniensia, 7 (Leuven, 1979) 89–108.

789. 'Les traductions de la Bible et la spiritualité médiévale,' W. Lourdaux and D. Verhelst, eds. *The Bible and Medieval Culture* Mediaevalia Lovaniensia, 7 (Leuven, 1979) 263–277.

790. 'Réflexions sur la réforme liturgique,' *La vie des communautés religieuses* 37 (1979) 278–288.

791. 'Silenzio e parola nella mistica cristiana di ieri e di oggi,' *Mistica e misticismo oggi* Settimana di studio di Lucca, 8–13 settembre 1978 (à l'occasion du 1er Centenaire de la naissance de sainte Gemma Galgani) (Rome: Passionisti-CIPI, 1979) 67–74; French in *Collectanea Cisterciensia* 45 (1983) 185–198; English in *Word and Spirit* 6 (1984) 103–122; Spanish in *Cuadernos monásticos* 20 (1985) 207–219.

792. 'Libérer ceux qui emprisonment,' *La vie spirituelle* 133 (1979) 953–963.

793. 'Pontida e la vita nei monasteri cluniacensi di Lombardia,' *Cluny in Lombardia, I* Atti del Convegno storico celebrativo del IX Centenario della fondazione del priorato cluniacense di Pontida,

22–25 aprile 1977, Italia benedettina, 1 (Cesena: Centro storico benedettino italiano, 1979) 429–445.

794. 'La figura di San Gerardo Tintore,' *Gerardo Tintore. Il santo di Monza* (Monza: Chiesa parrocchiale di S. Gerardo al Corpo, 1979) 47–55.

795. 'The image of St Bernard in the late medieval Exempla literature,' *Thought* 54 (1979) 291–302; 'Le portrait de Saint Bernard dans la littérature des *exempla* du bas Moyen Âge,' *Collectanea Cisterciensia* 50 (1988) 256–267.

796. 'Contemporary monasticism,' *Fairacres Chronicle* 12 (1979) 4–12; A summary printed in *Contemporary Monasticism* (Oxford: Fairacres, 1981) 1–10.

797. 'Sur la tradition manuscrite de deux lettres-traités de saint Bernard,' P. Cockshaw, M.-C. Garand and P. Jodogne, eds. *Miscellanea codicologica F. Masai dicata* (Ghent: Story, 1979) 265–272.

798. 'Livres et lecteurs à Saint-Thierry au XIIe siècle,' *Saint-Thierry: une abbaye du VIe au XXe siècle.* Actes du Colloque international d'Histoire monastique Reims-Saint-Thierry, 11 au 14 octobre 1976, assembled by Michel Bur (Saint-Thierry: Association des amis de l'abbaye de Saint-Thierry, 1979) 101–111.

799. 'Pour un portrait spirituel de Guillaume de Saint-Thierry,' *Saint-Thierry: une abbaye du VIe au XXe siècle.* Actes du Colloque international d'Histoire monastique Reims-Saint-Thierry, 1 au 14 octobre 1976 (Saint-Thierry, Association des amis de l'abbaye de Saint-Thierry, 1979) 413–428; English translation by Jerry Carfantan in *William, Abbot of St. Thierry* A Colloquium at the Abbey of St. Thierry, Cistercian Studies Series 94 (Kalamazooo, MI: Cistercian Publications, 1987) 204–224.

800. *Rayonnement spirituel de Cîteaux.* Conférence donnée au Centre d'Études St-Louis-de-France, Rome (27 novembre 1979) p. 7.

801. 'Merton in his Search for the Will of God,' *Cistercian Studies* 14 (1979) 42–44.

802. 'Merton and History,' Gerald Twomey, ed., *Thomas Merton, Prophet in the Belly Paradox* (New York: Paulist Press, 1979) 213–231.

803. 'L'appel contemplatif aujourd'hui,' *La vie des communautés religieuses* 37 (1979) 143–152.

804. 'Introduction,' *Mère Mectilde du Saint-Sacrement a l'écoute de saint Benoît* (Rouen: Bénédictines du Saint-Sacrement, 1979) 1–17;

Dutch in Priorij Fons Vitae, trans. (Heesch, 1980); Supplement in Italian in *Deus absconditus* 71 (1980) 72–81.

805. 'Préface,' Jean-Marie Burucoa, OSB, *La saveur de Dieu: La voie bénédictine,* Voies et étapes (Paris: DDB, 1979) 7–8.

806. 'Liturgia,' *Enciclopedia del Novecento* III (1979) 1034–1045.

1980

807. 'The tenth-century English Benedictine reform as seen from the continent,' *The Ampleforth Review* 85 (1980) 8–23; French in *Studia Monastica* 24 (1982) 105–125.

808. 'Monastic life today,' *Cistercian Studies* 15 (1980) 126–141, 239–246; French in *Collectanea Cisterciensia* 44 (1982) 131–155; Italian in *Il monachesimo nel dopo Concilio* (Parma: Monastero S. Giovanni Ev., 1981) 36–63.

809. 'Parallèles entre les vies religieuses chrétienne et non-chrétienne,' *Itinerari ecumenici. Spiritualità del nostro tempo= Quaderni Henri le Saux* 2 (Milan, 1980) 51–67.

810. 'Expérience du Christ et vie contemplative,' *Union canadienne des religieux contemplatifs* 12ème assemblée générale, 12–18 octobre 1980 (s. l., 1980) 15–28; English in *Canadian Union of Contemplative Religious,* 12th General Assembly, October 12–18 (n. p., 1980) 15–29; *Word and Spirit* 5 (1983) 75–95.

811. 'Le phénomène monastique et sa réalisation à travers les âges,' *Union canadienne des religieux contemplatifs* 12ème assemblée générale, 12–18 octobre 1980 (s. l., 1980) 29–51; English in *Canadian Union of Contemplative Religious,* 12th General Assembly, October 12–18 (n. p., 1980) 30–58.

812. 'Nuevas llaves para la interpretación de la Regla de San Benito,' *Hacia una relectura de la Regla de San Benito* Studia Silensia, VI (Silos, 1980) 35–56.

813. 'Autour de la correspondance de saint Bernard,' *Sapientiae doctrina. Mélanges de théologie et de littérature médiévales offerts à dom Hildebrand Bascour* Numéro spécial I de *Recherches de théologie ancienne et médiévale* (Leuven, 1980) 185–198; Reprinted in Jean Leclercq, *Recueil d'études sur S. Bernard et ses écrits* 4, Storia e Letteratura, 167 (Rome: Edizioni di Storia e Letteratura, 1987) 335–348.

814. 'La stabilità secondo la Regola di San Benedetto,' *Ora et Labora* 35 (1980) 10–17; Spanish in *Cuadernos monásticos* 72 (1985) 53–60.

815. 'Il monachesimo femminile nei secoli XII e XIII,' *Movimento religioso femminile e Francescanesimo nel secolo XIII* Atti del VII Convegno della Società internazionale di Studi francescani: Assisi, 11–13 ottobre 1979 (Assisi, 1980) 63–99; Partially translated into English in *The Continuing Quest for God. Monastic Spirituality in Tradition and Transition*, William Skudlarek OSB, ed. (Collegeville, MN: Liturgical Press, 1982) 114–138.

816. 'Le monachisme féminin au moyen âge. En marge d'un Congrès (= Congrès d'Assise, 1979),' *Cristianesimo nella storia* 1 (1980) 445–458.

817. 'Saint Silvestro Guzzolini était-il prêtre?' *Rivista di storia della Chiesa in Italia* 34 (1980) 75–80; Italian in *Inter fratres* 30 (1980) 147–152.

818. 'Die Spiritualität der Zisterzienser,' K. Elm, P. Joerißen and H.J. Roth, eds., *Die Zisterzienser. Ordensleben zwischen Ideal und Wirklichkeit.* Eine Ausstellung des Landschaftsverbandes Rheinland, Rheinisches Museumsamt, Brauweiler, Aachen: Krönungssaal des Rathauses, 3, Juli–28. September 1980, Schriften des Rheinischen Museumsamtes, 10 (Bonn: Rheinland-Verlag in Kommission bei Rudolf Habelt Verlag, 1980) 149–156.

819. 'Expérience et espérances du monachisme africain et malgache,' *Bulletin de l'A.I.M.* 29 (1980) 21–24; English edition, ibid.

820. 'The message of Kandy and the future of monasticism,' *Bulletin de l'A.I.M.* 29 (1980) 21–24; English edition, ibid., 38–44; French edition, ibid., 38–45.

821. 'Monachesimo cristiano e missioni,' *Vita consacrata* 16 (1980) 239–264.

822. 'Nouveaux aspects de la vie clunisienne, à propos des monastères de Lombardie,' *Studia Monastica* 22 (1980) 29–42.

823. 'Introduction,' *Thomas Merton on St Bernard,* Cistercian Studies Series 9 (Kalamazoo, MI: Cistercian Publications, 1980) 11–20.

824. 'Preface,' San Bernardo de Claraval, San Amadeo de Lausana *Homilias marianas* Padres Cistercienses, 7 (Azul: Monasterio Trapense de Nuestra Señora de los Angeles/Buenos Aires: Editorial Claretiana, 1980) 1–16.

825. 'The Making of a Masterpiece,' Preface to Bernard of Clairvaux *On the Song of Songs* 4, Cistercian Fathers Series 40, I. Edmonds, trans. (Kalamazoo, MI: Cistercian Publications, 1980) ix-xxiv; French in *Collectanea Cisterciensia* 47 (1985) 99–109.

826. 'Molldo,' *Dizionario degli Istituti di Perfezione* VI (Rome, 1980) 53–67.

827. 'Morte,' *Dizionario degli Istituti di Perfezione* VI (Rome, 1980) 162–167; French in *Studia missionalia* 31 (1982) 71–77.

828. 'Nobiltà,' *Dizionario degli Istituti di Perfezione* VI (Rome, 1980) 311–317.

829. 'Noviziato,' *Dizionario degli Istituti di Perfezione* VI (Rome, 1980) 442–448.

830. 'Pazzi per Cristo (3.),' *Dizionario degli Istituti di Perfezione* VI (Rome, 1980) 1302–1303.

831. 'Penitenza,' *Dizionario degli Istituti di Perfezione* VI (Rome, 1980) 1383–1392.

832. 'Perfezione [B)bb)],' *Dizionario degli Istituti di Perfezione* VI (Rome, 1980) 1456–1462.

833. 'Pier Damiano, santo,' *Dizionario degli Istituti di Perfezione* VI (Rome, 1980) 1686–1690; German in H.-J. Weisbender, ed. *Heilige des Regionalkalenders* I (Leipzig: St. Benno-Verlag s. d., 1980?) 107–112.

834. 'Bernhard von Clairvaux,' *Theologische Realenzyklopädie* V (Berlin-New York, 1980) 644–651.

835. 'Askese,' *Lexikon des Mittelalters* 1 (München-Zürich: Artemis Verlag, 1980) 1112–1115.

1981

836. 'The problem of social class and Christology in Saint Benedict,' *Word and Spirit* 2 (1981) 33–51; Spanish in *Cuadernos monásticos* 16 (1981) 205–218; Dutch in *Monastieke Informatie* 12 (1981) 245–263.

837. 'La concordance de saint Bernard,' *Cîteaux* 32 (1981) 357–362; Reprinted in Jean Leclercq, *Recueil d'études sur S. Bernard et ses écrits* 4, Storia e Letteratura, 167 (Rome: Edizioni di Storia e Letteratura, 1987) 401–407.

838. 'Contemporary Monasticism and the Peace Movement,' Mary Lou Kownacki OSB, *Peace is Our Calling* (n.p., 1981) 89–95.

839. 'Eucharistic Celebrations without Priests in the Middle Ages,' *Worship* 55 (1981) 160–168; R. Kevin Seasoltz, ed., *Living Bread, Saving Cup. Readings on the Eucharist* (Collegeville, MN: Liturgical Press 1982) 222–230.

840. 'Medieval Feminine Monasticism: Reality versus Romantic Images,' E. Rozanne Elder, ed., *Benedictus. Studies in Honor of St. Benedict of Nursia,* Cistercian Studies Series 67 (Kalamazoo, MI: Cistercian Publications, 1981) 53–70.

841. 'L'amour et le mariage vus pas des clercs et des religieux, spécialement au XIIe siècle,' Willy Van Hoecke and Andries Welkenhuysen, eds., *Love and Marriage in the Twelfth Century.* Mediaevalia Lovaniensia, 8 (Leuven, 1981) 101–115.

842. 'The love of beauty as a means and an expression of the love of truth,' *Mittellateinisches Jahrbuch* 16 (1981) 62–72.

843. 'San Benedetto fuori dell'Europa,' *Vita consacrata* 17 (1981) 534–548, 610–622; French in *Collectanea Cisterciensia* 44 (1982) 238–255.

844. 'Motivi dominanti del messaggio di M. Caterina Lavizzari,' *Deus absconditus* 72 (1981) 34–45.

845. 'La clôture. Points de repère historiques,' *Collectanea Cisterciensia* 43 (1981) 366–376; Spanish in *Cuadernos monásticos* 17 (1982) 187–195.

846. 'Monachisme, sacerdoce et missions au moyen âge,' *Studia Monastica* 23 (1981) 307–323.

847. 'Introduction,' Brian O'Malley, *The Animals of Saint Gregory* (Rhandirowyn: Paulinus Press, 1981) 11–15.

848. 'Preface,' Saint Bernard of Clairvaux *Les combats de Dieu* Coll. Stock Plus, Moyen Âge, Henri Rochais, ed. and trans. (Paris: Stock, 1981) 9–24.

849. Review of C.M. Vada Kkekara OSB, *Prayer and Contemplation* Studies in Christian and Hindhu Spirituality (Kumbalgud, Bangalore, India: Asirvanam Benedictine Monastery, 1980). In *Bulletin de l'A.I.M.* 30 (1981) 120.

850. Review of Maria Ignazia Angelini, *Il monaco e la parabola. Saggio sulla spiritualità della "lectio divina"* (Brescia: Morcelliana, 1981). In *Bulletin de l'A.I.M.* 30 (1981) 123–125.

851. Review of Volker Honemann, *Die 'Epistola ad fratres de Monte Dei' des Wilhelm von Saint-Thierry* (Zürich-München: Artemis Verlag, 1978). In *Mittellateinisches Jahrbuch* 16 (1981) 401–403.

1982

852. 'San Silvestro nelle Marche,' *Aspetti e problemi del monachesimo nelle Marche* Atti del Convegno tenuto a Fabriano, Monastero

di S. Silvestro abate, 4–7 guigno 1981, Bibliotheca Montisfani, 6 (Fabriano, 1982) 327–344.

853. 'L'Eucaristia, centro del mistero cristiano e della storia,' *Deus absconditus* 73 (1982) 13–22 (Seconde édition spéciale: Madre Caterina di Gesù Bambino).

854. 'Poèmes à la louange de S. Gossuin d'Anchin,' *Analecta Bollandiana* 100 [Mélanges offerts à Baudouin de Gaiffier et François Halkin] (1982) 619–635.

855. 'Dal cuore sensibile al corpo glorificato secondo San Bernardo di Chiaravalle,' R. Faricy and E. Malatesta, *Cuore del Cristo - cuore dell'uomo* (Napoli: Edizioni Dehoniane, s.d. [1982]) 75–89; French in *Mélanges à la mémoire du Père Anselme Dimier, présentés par Benoît Chauvin,* Tome 2, Vol. 3 (Pupillin: Benoît Chauvin, 1984) 341–347.

856. 'Spiritual Guidance and Counseling according to St Bernard,' John R. Sommerfeldt, ed., *Abba. Guides to Wholeness and Holiness East and West* Cistercian Studies Series, 38 (Kalamazoo, MI: Cistercian Publications, 1982) 64–87; French in *Studia Monastica* 25 (1983) 73–91.

857. 'Desiderio e intelletto: la teologia monastica,' a cura di Inos Biffi and Costante Mirabelli *Invito al Medioevo* Biblioteca di Cultura Medievale. Di fronte e attraverso, 76 (Milan: Jaca Book, 1982) 47–55.

858. 'Die Frau in der Mönchstheologie des Mittelalters,' *Communio* 7 (1982) 353–359; French edition, ibid., 64–71.

859. 'San Benedetto, San Francesco e i loro carismi nella Chiesa,' *L'Ulivo* 12 (1982) 14.

860. 'La spiritualità dei *sermones* antoniani e la sua conessione dipendente dalla spiritualità monastica-canonicale,' *Il Santo* 12 (1982) 203–216.

861. 'Office divin et *lectio divina,*' *Concilium* 179 (1982) 51–58; Italian edition, 59–68 (= 1329–1338); German edition, 635–639; Spanish edition, 341–350; English edition, 31–37; Dutch edition, 34–40.

862. In collaboration with M.C. Cymbalista, 'L'arte di invecchiare nella tradizione monastica,' *Vita consacrata* 18 (1982) 295–300; French in *Vie consacrée* 54 (1982) 366–372; English in *Aging. Spiritual Perspectives.* Opera Pia International (Lake Worth, FL: Sunday Publications, 1982) 163–169.

863. 'In praise of stability,' *Monastic Studies* 13 (1982) 89–98; French in *Collectanea Cisterciensia* 47 (1985) 259–266; Spanish in *Cuadernos monásticos* 72 (1985) 35–41; Spanish in *Revista San Anselmo* 4/15 (1985) 10–23; German in *Erbe und Auftrag* 62 (1986) 251–258; Italian in *Monastica* 27 (1986) 11–20.

864. 'Un clásico del humanismo monástico,' *Revista San Anselmo* 1 (1982) [numéro spécial] 12–18.

865. 'The Renewal of Theology,' Robert Benson and Giles Constable, eds., *Renaissance and Renewal in the Twelfth Century* (Cambridge, MA: Harvard University Press, 1982) 68–87.

866. 'Poème nuptial inspiré de saint Bernard,' Rita Lejeune and Joseph Deckers, eds., *Clio et son regard. Mélanges offerts à Jacques Stiennon* (Liège: P. Mardaga, 1982) 437–444.

867. 'La tradition littéraire de l'Église,' *Seminarium* n. s. 22 (1982) 350–364.

868. 'St Benediktus, meester in de wijsheid,' *Monastieke Informatie* 13 (1982) 5–68; French in *La vie des communautés religieuses* 45 (1987) 259–271; Italian in *Ora et Labora* 43 (1988) 118–128.

869. 'The Development of a Topic in Medieval Studies in the Eighties: An Interdisciplinary Perspective on Love and Marriage,' Patricia W. Cummins, Patrick W. Conner and Charles W. Connell, eds., *Literary and Historical Perspectives of the Middle Ages.* Proceedings of the 1981 SEMA Meeting (Morgantown: West Virginia University Press, 1982) 20–37.

870. 'La morte secondo la tradizione monastica nel medioevo,' *Studia Missionalia* 31 (1982) 71–77; *Ora et labora* 37 (1982) 155–160.

871. 'General Introduction,' *San Bernardo: I Trattati. A cura dell' abbazia di Chiaravalle, Milano* (Rome: Città Nuova, 1982) 13–63.

872. 'Introduction,' Paul VI *Discorsi ai monaci. L'uomo recuperato a se stesso* Scritti monastici n. s. 4 (Padova: Edizioni Messaggero/Abbazia di Praglia, 1982) 7–30; French in *Istituto Paolo VI. Notiziario* 6 (1983) 101–111; French in *Collectanea Cisterciensia* 48 (1986) 103–119; English in *Cistercian Studies* 20 (1985) 263–276.

873. 'Introduction,' Magdalene de Jesus OCD, *Teresa de Jesús y el Vaticano II* (Mataro, Barcelona: Carmelitas Descalzas, 1982) i–iv.

874. 'La liberté bénédictine (Conclusion),' *Atti del 7º Congresso internazionale di studi sull'Alto Medioevo. Norcia-Subiaco-Cassino-Monte-Cassino, 29 settembre–5 ottobre 1980* II (Spoleto: Centro Italiano di

studi sull'Alto Medioevo, 1982) 775–788; Italian in *Ora et Labora* 38 (1983) 20–33.

875. Review of Presentation by J. Comby, J. Gadille and C. Prudhomme, *Bibliographie d'histoire religieuse contemporaine. Acculturation du christianisme hors d'Europe* (Lyon: l'Association d'histoire religieuse contemporaine et le Centre d'échanges sur la diffusion et l'inculturation du Christianisme, avec l'aide de l'Universite Jean Moulin, 1981 [dactyl.]). In *Bulletin de l'A.I.M.* 32 (1982) 100–102; English edition, ibid.

876. Review of Emma Simi Varanelli, *'Nigra sum, sed formosa.' La problematica della luce e della forma nell'estetica bernardina. Esiti e sviluppi*= Extract from *Rivista dell'Istituto nazionale d'archeologia e storia d'arte* 2 (1979) 119–167. In *Cahiers de civilisation médiévale* 25 (1982) 307–308.

1983

877. 'Blessed Maria Gabriella Sagheddu: In Praise of Ordinariness,' *Cistercian Studies* 18 (1983) 231–239; French in *Collectanea Cisterciensia* 45 (1983) 116–123; Italian in *Vita consacrata* 19 (1983) 373–379; Spanish in *Revista San Anselmo* 3/11 (1983–1984) 89–98.

878. 'Prayer at Cluny,' *Journal of the American Academy of Religion* 51 (1983) 651–665; French in (without notes or bibliography) *Monachisme d'Orient et d'Occident: la vie monastique en Occident de st Benoît à st Bernard* Congrès de Sénanque 19–20–21 septembre 1983, Association des Amis de Sénanque (Abbaye de Lérins, n.d.) 91–115; 'Priait-on à Cluny?' *Collectanea Cisterciensia* 52 (1990) 330–342.

879. 'Lo sviluppo dell'atteggiamento critico degli allievi verso i maestri dal X al XIII secolo,' *Università e società nei secoli XII–XVI* Atti del IX Convegno internazionale di studio tenuto a Pistoia nei giorni 20–25 settembre 1979 (Pistoia: Centro italiano di studi di storia e d'arte [Editografica], 1983) 401–428.

880. 'Un jalon dans l'histoire du Vander Dochtere Van Syon,' Robrecht Lievens, Erik Van Mingroot and Werner Verbeke, eds., *Pascua Mediaevalia. Studies voor Prof. Dr. Jozef-Maria de Smet* Mediaevalia Lovaniensia, 10 (Leuven, 1983) 351–356.

881. '*Curiositas* et le retour à Dieu chez S. Bernard,' *Bivium. Homenaje a Manuel Cecilio Diaz y Diaz* (Madrid: Editorial Gredos,

1983) 133–141; '*Curiositas* and the return to God in St. Bernard of Clairvaux,' *Cistercian Studies* 25 (1990) 92–100.

882. 'De la comunión divina a la comunidad humana,' *Comunidad cristiana y comunidades monásticas,* Studia Silensia IX (Silos, 1983) 15–26; abridged in *Revista San Anselmo* 2/8 (1982–1983) 5–20.

883. 'The impact of the American Catholic experience on the Church in Europe,' *Louvain Studies* 9 (1983) 284–294.

884. 'The distinctive characteristics of Roman Catholic American spirituality,' *Louvain Studies* 9 (1983) 295–306.

885. 'Ocio contemplativo y cultura,' *Revista San Anselmo* 2/6 (1982–1983) 5–13.

886. 'Virtudes monásticas y valores humanos,' *Revista San Anselmo* 2/7 (1982–1983) 15–26.

887. 'El monje, un hombre libre,' *Revista San Anselmo* 2/8 (1982–1983) 52–56.

888. 'L'Eucaristia al centro (dagli scritti di M. Mectilde de Bar),' *Ora et Labora* 38 (1983) 33–36.

889. 'Clairvaux,' *Lexikon des Mittelalters* II (Zürich-München: Artemis Verlag, 1983) 2119–2120.

890. 'Politica,' *Dizionario degli Istituti di Perfezione* VII (Rome, 1983) 23–33.

891. 'Povertà II. L'interpretazione teologica della povertà di Cristo,' *Dizionario degli Istituti di Perfezione* VII (Rome, 1983) 251–253.

892. 'Preghiera II. Nel medioevo,' *Dizionario degli Istituti di Perfezione* VII (Rome, 1983) 606–612.

893. 'Revisione di vita,' *Dizionario degli Istituti di Perfezione* VII (Rome, 1983) 1699–1700.

894. 'Riforme II,' *Dizionario degli Istituti di Perfezione* VII (Rome, 1983) 1751–1755.

895. 'Riparazione,' *Dizionario degli Istituti di Perfezione* VII (Rome, 1983) 1801–1803.

896. 'Preface,' Regine Pernoud *Eleonora d'Aquitania* Biblioteca di Cultura Medievale. Di fronte e attraverso, 104 (Milan: Jaca Book, 1983; 1987) 7–10.

897. Review of Roger Vekemans S.J., ed., *Cristología en la perspectiva del Corazón de Jesús* (Bogotá: Instituto Internacional del Corazón de Jesús, Delegación Latinoamericana, 1982). In *Cor Christi* (International Institute of the Heart of Jesus) no. 22 (1983) 5–6.

898. Review of Roger Vekemans S.J., ed., *Cor Christi. Historia-Teología-Espiritualidad y Pastoral* (Bogotá, 1980). In *Cor Christi* (International Institute of the Heart of Jesus) no. 23 (1983) 4–5.

1984

899. 'Réparation et adoration dans la tradition monastique,' *Studia Monastica* 26 (1984) 13–42; German in *Erbe und Auftrag* 62 (1984) 169–195; Italian in *Deus absconditus* 75 (1984) 19–28.

900. 'La joie de mourir selon saint Bernard de Clairvaux,' Jane H.M. Taylor, *Dies illa. Death in the Middle Ages* (Liverpool: Francis Cairns, 1984) 195–207; 'The joy of dying according to St Bernard,' *Cistercian Studies* 25 (1990) 164–174.

901. 'Le Christ-moine,' *Studia Missionalia* 33 (1984) 403–411; Spanish in *Revista San Anselmo* 6/23 (1987) 117–121; 6/24, 176–182.

902. 'Saint Bernard a-t-il un message spécifique pour les moniales?' *Collectanea Cisterciensia* 46 (1984) 13–22; English in John A. Nichols and Lillian Thomas Shank, eds. *Distant Echoes.* Medieval Religious Women 1, Cistercian Studies Series 71 (Kalamazoo, MI: Cistercian Publications, 1984) 269–278; Italian in *Monastica* 24/3 (1984) 4–15.

903. 'Saint Bernard et la confession des péchés,' *Collectanea Cisterciensia* 46 (1984) 122–130.

904. 'Esperanza y belleza,' *Revista San Anselmo* 3/9 (1983–1984) 5–13.

905. 'San Bernardo y la guerra: ¿violento o no violento?' *Revista San Anselmo* 3/10 (1983–1984) 50–54.

906. 'Un nuevo poeta monástico (Ezequiel Bas Luna),' *Revista San Anselmo* 3/10 (1983–1984) 61–65.

907. 'Maritain and Merton: The coincidence of opposites,' *Cistercian Studies* 19 (1984) 362–370; Reprinted in Patrick Hart, ed., *The Legacy of Thomas Merton,* Cistercian Studies Series 92 (Kalamazoo, MI: Cistercian Publications, 1986) 157–170; Italian in *Contemplazione e ricerca spirituale nella società secolarizzata. La proposta di Merton e di Maritain* (Milano: Massimo, 1984) 17–29.

908. 'Mary's reading of Christ,' *Monastic Studies* 15 (1984) 105–116; French in *Collectanea Cisterciencia* 49 (1987) 107–116; Italian in *Monastica* 28/3 (1987) 35–45.

909. 'Lectio divina,' *Worship* 58 (1984) 239–248; 'Lectio divina: Jésus Livre et Jésus Lecteur,' *Collectanea Cisterciensia* 48 (1986) 207–215; Spanish in *Cuadernos monásticos* 20 (1985) 221–228; Italian in *Monastica* 28/2 (1987) 29–39.

910. 'Les nonnes et la promotion de la femme,' *La voix du nord* (mercredi 3 octobre 1984) 4.

911. 'Spiritualité abstraite et dévotion populaire à la fin du moyen âge,' *La vie spirituelle* 138 (1984) 649–658.

912. 'La SS. Trinità: Unità e diversità,' *Deus absconditus* 75 (1984) 13–19.

913. 'Otium monasticum as a Context for Artistic Creativity,' Timothy Gregory Verdon and John Dally, eds., *Monasticism and the Arts* (Syracuse: Syracuse University Press, 1984) 63–80.

914. 'Ludovico Barbo e storia dell'immaginario,' *Riforma della Chiesa, cultura e spiritualità nel Quattrocento veneto* Atti del Convegno per il VI Centenario della nascita di Ludovico Barbo: Padova, Venezia, Treviso 19–24 settembre 1982, Italia Benedettina, 6 (Cesena: Centro storico benedettino italiano, 1984) 385–399.

915. 'L'ascesi quotidiana,' Interview in *Rinascita* 22 (1984) 24.

916. 'Smaragdus,' John J. Mellerski, trans., Paul E. Szarmach, ed., *An Introduction to the Medieval Mystics of Europe* (Albany, 1984) 37–51.

917. 'Pour un portrait spirituel de sainte Françoise Romaine,' Giorgio Picasso OSB, *Una santa tutta romana.* Saggi e ricerche nel VI Centenario della nascita di Francesca Bussa dei Ponziani (1384–1984) (Siena: Monte Oliveto Maggiore, 1984) 13–23; English in *Vox benedictina* 3 (1986) 128–145.

918. 'Introduction,' E. Rozanne Elder, ed., *The Roots of the Modern Christian Tradition,* The Spirituality of Western Christendom, 2, Cistercian Studies Series, 55 (Kalamazoo, MI: Cistercian Publications, 1984) vii-xxi.

919. 'A Witness to Benedictine Spirituality in the Seventeenth Century (Catherine de Bar),' E. Rozanne Elder, ed. *The Roots of the Modern Christian Tradition,* Cistercian Studies Series, 55 (Kalamazoo, MI: Cistercian Publications, 1984) 182–199.

920. 'General introduction,' Ferruccio Gastaldelli, *Opere di San Bernardo, I, Trattati* (Milan: Scriptorium Claravallense/Rome: Città Nuova Editrice, 1984) xi-lxiv.

921. 'Preface,' Baldovino di Ford, *Il Sacramento dell'Altare. Trattato* Biblioteca di Cultura Medievale. Di fronte e attraverso, 132, a cura di Giorgio Maschio (Milan: Jaca Book, 1984) 7–26.

922. 'Preface,' *Catherine de Bar. Mère Mechtilde du Saint-Sacrenzent, 1614–1698. En Pologne avec les bénédictines de France.* Documents originaux réunis et préséntes par les bénédictines du Saint-Sacrement de Rouen (Paris: Tequi, 1984) 7–18.

923. 'Preface,' Regine Pernoud, *Eloisa e Abelardo,* Biblioteca di Cultura Medievale. Di fronte e attraverso, 129 (Milan: Jaca Book, 1984) ix–x.

924. Review of Christine Schnusenberg, *Das Verhältnis von Kirche und Theater, dargestellt an ausgewählten Schriften der Kirchenväter und liturgischen Texten bis auf Amalarius von Metz (775–852)* Europäische Hochschulschriften, Reihe 23, Theologie, 141 (Bern-Frankfurt am Main-Las Vegas, 1981). In *Benedictina* 31 (1984) 291–293.

1985

925. 'Un jalon dans l'histoire de la confession dans la vie religieuse,' *Vie consacrée* 57 (1985) 242–248; Spanish in *Cuadernos monásticos* 20 (1985) 487–491.

926. 'L'érémitisme aujourd'hui,' *Christus* 32 (1985) 249–256.

927. 'Discovering Saint Bernard,' *Monastic Studies* 16 [Special issue in Honour of Dom Jean Leclercq] (1985) 245–252.

928. 'La ricerca contemplativa, condizione di rinnovamento ecclesiale secondo San Bernardo,' *Rivista di ascetica e mistica* 54 (1985) 61–76.

929. 'Come interpretare gli scritti dei fondatori e la quotidianità,' *Deus absconditus* 76 (1985) 31–38.

930. 'Evangelizzare l'adorazione e aspetti practici dell'adorazione,' *Deus absconditus* 76 (1985) 36–43.

931. 'El humanismo de San Gregorio Magno,' *Revista San Anselmo* 4/13–14 (1985) 5–10.

932. 'San Bernardo y el deber de armar a Dios,' *Revista San Anselmo* 4/16 (1985) 97–105; 'San Bernardo e il dovere d'amare Dio,' *Parola, spirito e vita* 11 (1985) ([Amerai Dio e il prossimo tuo] Bologna: Edizioni Dehoniane) 279–287.

933. 'Saint Bede and Christian expansion,' *Word and Spirit* 7 (1985) 3–23.

934. 'Le saint Bernard de Gilson: Une théologie de la vie monastique,' *Doctor communis* 38 (1985) [Special issue: Étienne Gilson, filosofo cristiano] 227–233.

935. 'Monasticism and Asceticism II: Western Christianity,' *Christian Spirituality: Origins to the Twelfth Century.* Bernard McGinn and John Meyendorff, eds. in collaboration with Jean Leclercq. World Spirituality, 16 (New York: Crossroad, 1985; 1992) 113–131.

936. 'Learning and Fervor,' *The Distinctiveness of Pentecostal-Charismatic Theology* Society for Pentecostal Studies-Fifteenth Annual Meeting, Mother of God Community (Gaithersburg, MD, 1985) Paper F, pp. 18.

937. 'De mensen hunkeren naar spiritualiteit,' *Elseviers Magazine* (13 avril 1985) 70–81.

938. 'A homily to women about women and Jesus,' *Sisters Today* 56 (1985) 271–272.

939. 'Les vingt-cinq ans de l'A.I.M.,' *Oblats Abbaye de Clervaux* no. 2 (1985) 21–23.

940. 'Interpretazione gerbertiana della vita monastica,' a cura di Michele Tosi *Gerberto. Scienza, storia e mito* Atti del Gerberti Symposium, Bobbio: 25–27 luglio 1983, Archivum Bobiense Studia, 2 (Bobbio, 1985) 677–689.

941. 'Neue Perspektiven in der monastischen Theologie: Das Weibliche und die eheliche Liebe,' Manfred Gerwing and Godehard Ruppert, eds. *Renovatio et Reformatio. Wider das Bild vom "finsteren" Mittelalter. Festschrift für Ludwig Hödl zum 60. Geburtstag* (Münster: Aschendorff, 1985) 14–24.

942. 'Art littéraire et théologie dans les sermons de saint Bernard sur le Cantique,' *Monachisme d'Orient et d'Occident. Cîteaux, ses origines - ses fondateurs* Congrès de Sénanque 10–11–12 septembre 1985, Association des Amis de Sénanque (Abbaye de Lérins, n.d.) 105–126.

943. 'Un aspect de l'influence cistercienne sur la société: Les ordres de chevalerie,' *Monachisme d'Orient et d'Occident: Cîteaux après l'âge d'or* (n.d., 1985?) 141–163.

944. 'Introduction,' Vera Paronetto, *Gregorio Magno. Un maestro alle origini cristiane d'Europa* Nuova universale studium, 46 (Rome: Edizioni Studium, 1985) 3–7.

945. 'Preface,' J. Heuclin, *Institution Saint-Pierre 1895–1985. 90 années de présence en Avesnois* (Fournies, 1985) 5–7.

946. Review of Waltraud Timmerman, *Studien zur allegorischen Bildlichkeit in den 'Parabolae' Bernhards von Clairvaux. Mit der Erstedition einer mittelniederdeutschen Übersetzung der Parabolae 'Vom geistlichen Streit', und 'Vom Streit der vier Töchter Gottes'* Mikrokosmos, 10 (Frankfurt a.M.-Bern: Peter Lang, 1982). In *Mittellateinisches Jahrbuch* 20 (1985) 291–294.

947. Review of Peter Damian, *Book of Gomorrah. An Eleventh-century Treatise against Clerical Homosexual Practices* (Waterloo: Wilfrid Laurier University Press, 1982). In *Cahiers de civilisation médiévale* 28 (1985) 271–273.

948. Review of Brian Stock, *The Implications of Literacy. Written Language and Models of Interpretation in the Eleventh and Twelfth Centuries* (Princeton: Princeton University Press, 1983). In *Cahiers de civilisation médiévale* 28 (1985) 286–287.

949. Review of *Dizionario degli Istituti di Perfezione* VII (Rome, 1983). In *La vie spirituelle* 139 (1985) 559.

1986

950. 'Sainteté et culture. À propos de l'imaginaire de sainte Thérèse de Lisieux,' *Studia Missionalia* 35 (1986) 99–109.

951. 'Pour une hagiographie comparative,' *Studia Missionalia* 35 (1986) 111–121.

952. 'In Praise of Laughter,' *The Joyful Noiseletter (Epistle of the Fellowship of Merry Christians)* 1/4 (1986).

953. 'L'Uomo medievale tra *sapientia* e *scientia*: Bernardo e Abelardo,' *Synesis* 3 (1986) 45–61.

954. 'Nouvelles formes de vie religieuse. Histoire et actualité,' *Vie consacrée* 58 (1986) 107–112.

955. 'Gregorio VII nel nostro secolo,' *Benedictina* 33 (1986) 117–123.

956. 'La vita di San Benedetto come fonte di gioia,' *Studium* 82 (1986) 260–264.

957. 'Gleichgestaltung mit Christus in seinen Mysterien,' *Cistercienser Chronik* 93 (1986) 25–37.

958. 'La vida religiosa: Las fuentes de la doctrina de santo Tomás,' *Revista San Anselmo* 5/20 (1986) 142–147.

959. 'El puesto de la monja en la Iglesia,' *Mujeres del Absoluto* = *Studia Silensia* XII (Silos, 1986) 283–300.

960. 'Présence de saint Bernard,' *Construire* Lausanne, no. 52 (24 decembre 1986) 19.

961. 'Ecclesia *Corpus Christi* et *Sacramentum Fidei*,' *Chiesa, diritto e ordinamento della "Societas Christiana" nei secoli XI e XII* Atti della IXa Settimana internazionale di studio, Mendola: 28 agosto - 2 settembre 1983, Coll. Pubblicazioni dell'Università cattolica del Sacro Cuore. Miscellanea del Centro di studi medioevali, 11 (Milan, 1986) 11–25.

962. 'The witness of medieval monastic prayer,' *Monastic Studies* 17 (1986) 35–43.

963. 'Monastic and Scholastic Theology in the Reformers of the Fourteenth to Sixteenth Century,' E. Rozanne Elder, ed., *From Cloister to Classroom. Monastic and Scholastic Approaches to Truth*. The Spirituality of Western Christendom 3, Cistercian Studies Series, 90 (Kalamazoo, MI: Cistercian Publications, 1986) 178–201.

964. 'Baudouin de Gaiffier, Bollandiste (1897–1984),' *Cahiers de civilisation médiévale* 29 (1986) 183–184.

965. 'Introduction,' Ferruccio Gastaldelli, ed., *Opere di San Bernardo VI/1. Lettere* (Milan: Scriptorium Claravallense/Rome: Città Nuova Editrice, 1986) ix–xxxvii.

966. 'Appunti per una teologia allegra,' *30 Giorni. Mensile internazionale de Il Sabato* 4/2 (1986) 7.

967. 'Il monachesimo occidentale e la cultura europea del X secolo visti da Leclercq. Il monachesimo è la sua passione,' Interview by Massimo Borghesi and Paolo Vian *30 Giorni. Mensile internazionale de Il Sabato* 4/3 (1986) 60–65.

968. 'El monacato conservó la cultura clásica greco-latina,' Interview in *El Correo Gallego* (29 august 1986) 23.

969. 'L'Umorismo entra in monastero,' Interview by Maria Teresa Fumagalli. *Il Giornale* (14 march 1986) 3.

970. 'Introduction,' Giovanni di Fécamp, *Pregare nel medioevo. La 'Confessio theologica' e altre opere* Giorgio Maschio, notes and translation, Biblioteca di Cultura Medievale. Di fronte e attraverso, 163 (Milan: Jaca Book, 1986) 9–25.

971. 'L'identité cistercienne et ses conséquences (Conclusion),' *Cahiers de Fanjeaux. Collection d'Histoire religieuse du Languedoc au XIIIe et au début du XIVe siècle* 21 (1986) = Les Cisterciens de Languedoc (XIIIe–XIVe s.) 371–380.

972. 'Actualité de Grégoire le Grand (Épilogue),' J. Fontaine,

R. Gillet and S. Pellistrandi, eds., *Grégoire le Grand. Chantilly, Centre culturel Les Fontaines, 15–19 septembre 1982* (Paris: Éditions du C.N.R.S., 1986) 681–684.

973. Review of Ferruccio Gastaldelli, ed., *Opere di San Bernardo I. Trattati* (Milan: Scriptorium Claravallense/Rome: Città Nuova Editrice, 1984). In *Cristianesimo nella storia* 7 (1986) 187–193.

974. Review of D. L. D'Avray, *The Preaching of the Friars. Sermons diffused from Paris before 1300* (Oxford: Clarendon Press, 1985). In *Mittellateinisches Jahrbuch* 21 (1986) 299–301.

1987

975. 'Pastorale matrimoniale e amore coniugale,' *Anthropotes, Rivista di studi sulla persona e la famiglia* (Pontificio Istituto Giovanni Paolo II per studi su matrimonio e famiglia) 3 (1987) 107–117.

976. 'Traditions of Spiritual Guidance. Spiritual Direction in the Benedictine Tradition,' *The Way. Contemporary Christian Spirituality* [Heythrop College, London] (1987) 54–64.

977. 'Lettura della S. Scrittura e teologia spirituale in San Bernardo,' a cura di Salvatore A. Panimolle *Ascolto della Parola e preghiera. La "lectio divina"* Teologia sapienziale, 2 (Città del Vaticano: Libreria Editrice Vaticana, 1987) 169–174.

978. 'Le rôle civilisateur des monastères,' *Le rôle civilisateur des monastères au moyen âge* (Louvain-la-Neuve: Institut Catholique pour la Formation Continuée de professeurs des enseignements secondaire et supérieur (court et long) [ICAFOC]/Université catholique de Louvain. Faculté de philosophie et lettres. Institut de didactique. Unité de didactique en histoire. Centre de formation continuée en histoire, 1987) [stenciled].

979. 'Christian Monasticism and Its Present Encounter with Other Religious Traditions,' The Third International Buddhist-Christian Conference, Berkeley, CA, 10–15 August 1987, pp. 13; *Monastic Studies* 18 (1988) 64–78.

980. 'L'*Opera omnia* di San Bernardo di Chiaravalle promossa dallo "Scriptorium Claravallense" di Milano e dall'editrice Città Nuova. L'Immensa ricchezza della sua "scala armonica",' (Conference at the time of the presentation of the Italian edition of the works of Saint Bernard to l'Istituto dell'Enciclopedia Italiana, Rome, 26 February 1987) *L'Osservatore Romano* (1 March 1987) 3; *Rivista Cistercense* 4

(1987) 86–93 (Elogio della traduziorle); *Il Veltro. Rivista della Civiltà italiana* (Rome) 31 (1987) 327–334.

981. 'Solitude and Solidarity. Medieval Women Recluses,' Lillian Thomas Shank and John A. Nichols, eds., *Peaceweavers* Medieval Religious Women 2, Cistercian Studies Series, 72 (Kalamazoo, MI: Cistercian Publications, 1987) 67–83.

982. 'Lettres de S. Bernard trouvées depuis les Mauristes,' J. Dummer, ed. *Texte und Textkritik: Eine Aufsatzsammlung.* Texte und Untersuchungen zur Geschichte der Altchristlichen Literatur, 133 (DDR, 1987) 311–324.

983. 'L'Ordine del Tempio: Monachesimo guerriero e spiritualitá medievale,' raccolti da Giovanni Minnucci e Franca Sardi, *I Templari: Mito e storia.* Atti del Convegno internazionale Poggibonsi-Siena, 29–31 maggio 1987 (Sinalunga-Siena: Ed. A.G. Vita-Riccucci) 1–8.

984. 'Influence and Noninfluence of Dionysius in the Western Middle Ages (Introduction),' (Introductions also by J. Pelikan and K. Froelich.) Pseudo-Dionysius *The Complete Works* Colm Luibheid, trans.; Foreword, notes and translation collaboration by Paul Rorem; Preface by R. Roques (Mahwah: Paulist Press, 1987) 25–32.

985. 'Filosofia e teologia,' *Dall'eremo al cenobio. La civiltà monastica in Italia dalle origini all'età di Dante* (Milan: Libri Scheiwiller, 1987) 217–239.

986. 'John Moffit (†1987) [Nouvelles brèves],' *Bulletin de l'A.I.M.* 43 (1987) 106–107; English edition, ibid.

987. 'Saint Augustine Bishop (According to his own Memoirs),' *Word and Spirit* 9 (1987) 9–21.

988. 'Conventual Chapter and Council of the Abbot in Early Cîteaux,' *Three Studies* (Spencer, MA: Saint Joseph's Abbey, 1987) 1–10 (polycopie); *Cistercian Studies* 23 (1988) 14–24.

989. 'La circolazione della cultura (8.),' Roberto Barbieri, *Uomini e tempo medioevale.* Corso di Storia, 1 (Milan: Jaca Book, 1987) 81–84.

990. 'Introduction,' Bernard of Clairvaux, *Selected Works.* The Classics of Western Spirituality; Foreword and translation by Gillian R. Evans (New York-Mahwah: Paulist Press, 1987) 13–57.

991. 'Introduction,' to Étienne Gilson, *La teologia mistica di San Bernardo;* Claudio Stercal, trans. Biblioteca di Cultura Medievale. Di

fronte e attraverso, 201 (Milan: Jaca Book, 1987) ix–xxi (Étienne Gilson *San Bernardo e la storia della spiritualità*).

992. 'Bernard of Clairvaux (1090–1153), Saint,' *The Encyclopedia of Religions* 2 (New York, 1987) 114–115.

993. Review of Manfred Gerwing, *Malogranatum oder der dreifache Weg zur Vollkommenheit. Ein Beitrag zur Spiritualität des Spätmittelalters.* Veröffentlichungen des Collegium Carolinum, 57 (München: R. Oldenburg Verlag, 1986). In *Cîteaux* 38 (1987) 137–139.

994. Review of Julius Kirshner and Suzanne Wemple, eds., *Women of the Medieval World. Essays in Honor of John H. Mundy* (Oxford-New York, 1985); and, Review of Katarina Wilson, ed. *Medieval Women Writers* (Manchester: University Press, 1984). In *Cristianesimo nella storia* 8 (1987) 246–249.

1988

995. 'Sur la transmission d'un opuscule anselmien,' *Cultura e società nell'Italia medievale* Studi in onore di Paolo Brezzi, II (Rome, 1988) 449–455; Coll. Studi Storici, 188–192.

996. 'L'Elogio della gioia,' *Monastica* 29 (1988) 29–38.

997. 'The Queen Mother in the X–XIII centuries,' *Word and Spirit* 10 (1988) 57–77.

998. 'Le parabole nella letteratura monastica popolare. Un genere di cultura pastorale diffuso nel medioevo anche all'interno del monachesimo,' *L'Osservatore romano* (7 May 1988) 3.

999. 'Lo scrittore dotto e lo scrittore "popolare". Concluso il Convegno su S. Anselmo di Aosta,' *L'Osservatore romano* (4 March 1988) 3.

1000. Some articles contributed to Véronique Andral, OSB AP *Catherine de Bar, I: Un carisma nella tradizione ecclesiae e monastica* (Rome: Città Nuova Ed., 1988).

1001. 'Preface,' Pietro de Leo *Gioacchino da Fiore, aspetti inediti della vita e delle opere* Biblioteca di storia e cultura meridionale. Studi e testi, 1 (Soveria Manelli: Rubbettino Editore, 1988).

1002. 'Sacramenti IV. La problematica attuale,' *Dizionario degli Istituti di Perfezione* VIII (Rome, 1988) 163–164.

1003. 'Scala spirituale II. In Occidente,' *Dizionario degli Istituti di Perfezione* VIII (Rome, 1988) 1004–1005.

1004. 'Sequela IV. Il monachesimo medievale,' *Dizionario degli Istituti di Perfezione* VIII (Rome, 1988) 1307–1311.

1005. 'Silenzio,' *Dizionario degli Istituti di Perfezione* VIII (Rome, 1988) 1491–1498, 1499–1501.

1006. 'Smaragdo,' *Dizionario degli Istituti di Perfezione* VIII (Rome, 1988) 1583–1584.

1007. Review of Udo Wawrzyniak, *Philologische Untersuchungen zum 'Rithmus in laude saluatoris' des Petrus Venerabilis. Edition und Kommentar.* Coll. Lateinische Sprache und Literatur des Mittelalters 22 (Frankfurt a. Main-Bern-New York: Lang, 1985). In *Cahiers de civilisation médiévale* 31 (1988) 80–81.

1989

1008. 'Due aspetti dello stesso sant'Anselmo: Lo scrittore dotto e lo scrittore *popolare*,' I. Biffi, ed., *Anselmo d'Aosta, figura europea* (1989) 145–148.

1009. 'La sainte Radegonde de Venance Fortunat et celle de Baudovinie: essai d'hagiographie comparée,' A. Bastiaensen, *et al.*, eds., *Fructus centesimus: Mélanges offerts à Gerard J.M. Bartelink.* Instrumenta patristica, 19 (Dordrecht: Kluwer Academic Publishers, 1989) 207–216.

1010. 'Saint Bernard and El Cid: Knighthood and Two Models of Interpretation,' Patrick J. Gallagher and Helen Damico, eds., *Hermeneutics and Medieval Culture* (Albany: State University of New York Press, 1989) 71–83.

1011. 'Monasticism and the Promotion of Women,' *Women in Monasticism.* Word and Spirit, 11 (Petersham, MA: St. Bede's Publications, 1989) 3–15.

1012. 'Estudio preliminar,' *La Regla de San Benito, ordenada por materias y su vida, en el español corriente de hoy* Versión de Antonio Linage Conde (Madrid: Editorial Letamenia, 1989).

1013. 'Preface,' P. Miquel, OSB, *Le vocabulaire latin de l'experiénce spirituelle dans la tradition monastique et canoniale de 1050 à 1250.* Théologie historique, 79 (Paris: Beauchesne, 1989).

1014. 'À la recherche d'une spiritualité feminine dans la tradition cistercienne,' *Monachisme d'Orient et d'Occident: Cîteaux après l'âge d'or.* Colloque de Sénanque, 15–17 sept 1987 (Association des Amis de Sénanque, 1989) 95–139.

1015. 'Other sources and the true source: Bernard, the Early Fathers, the Bible, and Jesus Christ,' *Christian History Magazine* 8/24 (1989) 22–23.

1016. 'Friendship and friends in the monastic life,' *Cistercian Studies* 24 (1989) 293–300.

1017. 'Die intentionen der Grüder des Zisterzienserordens,' *Cistercienser Chronik* 96 (1989) 3–32.

1018. 'De l'art antique à l'art médiéval. À propos des sources du bestiaire carolingien et de ses survivances à l'époque romane,' *Gazette de Beaux-Arts* 113, no. 1441 (1989) 61–66.

1019. 'Preludio a nuovo centenario di san Bernardo,' *La Scuola Cattolica* 117 (1989) 366–377.

1020. 'La christologie clunisienne au siècle de S. Hugues,' *Studia Monastica* 31 (1989) 267–278.

1990

1021. 'Das Leben des heiligen Bernhard,' M. Sabbe, M. Lamberigts and F. Gistelinck, eds., *Bernardus en de Cisterciënzerfamilie en België. 1090–1990* (Leuven: Bibliotheek van de Faculteit der Godgeleerdheid, 1990) 1–13.

1022. 'S. Bernardo *cuciniere di Dio*,' *Bernardo cistercense.* Atti del XXVI Convegno storico internazionale, Todi, 8–11 ottobre 1989 (Spoleto: Centro italiano di studi sull'Alto Medioevo, 1990) 333–344 (Atti dei Convegni dell'Accademia Tudertina et del Centro di studi sulla spiritualità medievale. Nuova serie 3.).

1023. 'Preface,' M.-E. Montulet-Henneau, *Les cisterciennes du pays mosan. Moniales et vie contemplative à l'époque moderne* (Bruxelles: Institut Historique Belge de Rome Bibliotheque, 1990) 5–13.

1024. 'Spiritualità e cultura nel monachesimo del pieno medioevo,' G. Penco, ed. *Cultura e spiritualità nella tradizione monastica* (1990) 105–128.

1025. 'Pour l'histoire de la symbolique du Livre de Vie,' C. Augrain, ed., Κεχαριτγμενη: *Mélanges R. Laurentin* (1990) 595–602.

1026. 'Presenza di San Bernardo,' *San Bernardo nel IX centenario della nascita, 6–9 - La Scala 1990/6–9* 163–165; *San Bernardo e i Cistercensi in Puglia.* Quaderni dell'Istituto di scienze religiose, diocesi di Covano-Monopoli, 3 (Noci: Ed. La Scala 1991).

1027. 'Une doctrine spirituelle pour notre temps?' *Analecta Cisterciensia* 46 (1990) 397–410 (*La dottrina delle vita spirituale nelle opere di San Bernardo di Clairvaux*. Atti del Convegno internazionale: Rome, 11–15 settembre 1990.).

1028. 'Éloge de la rotondité,' *Collectanea Cisterciensia* 52 (1990) 86–88. [Issue no. 2, special edition: Saint Bernard neuvième centenaire 1090–1990 - Hommage à D. Jean Leclercq.]

1029. 'Saint Bernard et la tendresse,' *Collectanea Cisterciensia* 52 (1990) 1–15.

1030. 'Thomas Merton and St. Bernard of Clairvaux,' *The Merton Annual* 3 (1990) 37–44.

1031. 'Cisterciennes et filles de S. Bernard. À propos des structures variées des monastères de moniales au Moyen Âge,' *Studia Monastica* 32 (1990) 139–156.

1032. 'Saint Bernard et la vie religieuse,' *Vie consacrée* 62 (1990) 296–305.

1033. With M.-E. Lopez, 'Évolution de la clôture, théorie et pratique,' *Vie consacrée* 62 (1990) 23–29.

1991

1034. 'Faith seeking understanding through images (parables in treatises of St. Anselm),' G. Berthold, ed., *Faith Seeking Understanding* (Manchester, NH: Saint Anselm College Press, 1991) 5–21.

1035. 'Introduction,' *Ascolta, figlio. La regola di san Benedetto.* Itinerari, Collana di spiritualità (Bologna: Edizioni Dehoniane, 1991).

1036. 'Contemplation revisited (recent developments in Buddhist-Christian relations),' *Buddhist-Christian Studies* 11 (1991) 285–288.

1037. 'Temi monastici nell'opera del Petrarca,' *Lettere Italiane* 43/1 (1991) 42–54.

1038. 'Naming the Theologies of early Twelfth Century,' *Mediaeval Studies* 53 (1991) 327–336.

1992

1039. 'L'Écrivain (General Introduction),' *Bernard de Clairvaux: histoire, mentalités, spiritualité. Œuvres complètes I.* Sources chrétiennes, 380, (Paris: Cerf, 1992) 529–556.

1040. First chapter of 'Introduction,' Collette Friedlander and Gaetano Raciti, trans. and eds., *Galand de Reigny: 'Parabolaire'.* Sources chrétiennes, 378 (Paris: Cerf, 1992).

1041. '"Militare Deo" dans la tradition patristique et monastique,' *"Militia Christi" e crociata nei secola XI-XIII: Atti della undecima settimana internazionale di studio, Mendola, 28 agosto–1 sett 1989* Miscellanea del Centro di studi medioevali, 13 (Milan: Vita e pensiero, 1992) 3–18.

1042. 'Le Moi, la Compassion et la Contemplation,' *Bulletin de Littérature Ecclésiastique* 93 (1992) 39–48.

1043. 'La vie monastique, créatrice et inspiratrice de littérature,' *Collectanea Cisterciensia* 54 (1992) 333–343.

1044. 'Retour à la contemplation?' *Collectanea Cisterciensia* 54 (1992) 106–108.

1045. 'Monks and hermits in medieval love stories,' *Journal of Medieval History* (Amsterdam) 18 (1992) 341–356.

1046. 'L'Amitié et les amitiés dans la vie monastique,' *Lien des contemplatives* no. 111 (1992) pp. 7.

1047. 'Expérience du Christ et vie contemplative,' *Lien des contemplatives* no. 109 (1992) pp. 17.

1048. 'Amore e conoscenza secondo san Bernardo di Chiaravalle,' *La Scuola Cattolica* 120 (1992) 6–14.

1049. 'S. Bernard et les débuts de l'Ordre Cistercien,' *Studia Monastica* 34 (1992) 63–77.

1993

1050. 'La "paternité" de S. Bernard et les débuts de l'ordre cistercien,' *Revue bénédictine* 103 (1993) 445–481.

1051. 'Mourir et sourire dans la tradition monastique,' *Studia Monastica* 35 (1993) 55–67.

1052. 'Conversion to the Monastic Life in the Twelfth Century: Who, Why, and How?' John R. Sommerfeldt and Francis Swietek, eds., *Studiosorum Speculum: Studies in Honor of Louis J. Lekai, O.Cist.* Cistercian Studies Series 141 (Kalamazoo, MI: Cistercian Publications, 1993) 201-232.

1994

1053. 'Sainte Claire et la spiritualité nuptiale,' *Hagiographica* 1 (1994).

The compiler and the editor express their appreciation to père Henri Delhougne of the Abbaye Saint Maurice, Clervaux, for his generous help in the task of assembling this Bibliography.

Readers who become aware of *lacunae* in this Bibliography are asked to send full citations of missing references to the Editorial Director Cistercian Publications Inc. WMU Station Kalamazoo, Michigan 49009.

Contributors

David N. Bell is Professor of Comparative Religions and University Research Professor at the Memorial University of Newfoundland. A graduate of the Universities of Leeds and Oxford, Professor Bell has published on a wide range of topics in the field of monastic studies and has translated monastic sources from Coptic, Greek, and Latin. Among his works are *Image and Likeness: The Augustinian Spirituality of William of Saint Thierry*, four volumes of indexes of medieval monastic libraries, and two histories of the development of christian doctrine, a collection of animal stories from jewish, christian, and muslim sources, and a study of books and libraries in medieval English religious houses.

Constance Berman is Professor of History at the University of Iowa. After studying under David Herlihy and Maureen Mazzaoui at the University of Wisconsin, Professor Berman taught at The Catholic University of America, Georgetown University, and Bard College. In addition to numerous articles, her work in monastic economic history and women's studies includes *Medieval Agriculture: The Southern French Countryside and the Early Cistercians* (1986) and *The Worlds of Medieval Women: Creativity, Influence, Imagination* (1985) of which she is co-editor. She is currently completing two studies: one on the role of monks and nuns in reforming medieval France, and another on the endowment and administration of cistercian nuns in the ecclesiastical province of Sens.

Eoin de Bhalthraite is a Cistercian monk and priest of Bolton Abbey, near Moone, Co. Kildare, Ireland. Trained at Mount Saint Joseph Abbey, Roscrea, and San Anselmo, Rome, he has broad interests which are reflected in articles on monasticism, ecumenism, mixed marriages, and modern Ireland, and he is currently studying pre-nicene Christology while managing the abbey farm. His name reflects irish history: Eoin being Irish Gaelic for Joannes, and de Bhaldraithe Norman French for 'from Waldron', a town south of London.

E. Rozanne Elder is Editorial Director of Cistercian Publications and Associate Professor of History at Western Michigan University, as well as a member of the second Anglican-Roman Catholic International [Ecumenical] Consultation.

Gillian Rosemary Evans is University Lecturer in History at the University of Cambridge. Before accepting her present position, she taught at the University of Bristol. From 1986–1988 she was British Academy Research Reader in Theology. Her long list of publications includes studies on and translations of Alan of Lille, Anselm of Canterbury, Bernard of Clairvaux, and Gregory the Great as well as studies on the relationship of theology, philosophy and scriptural studies in the Middle Ages. She has also published in the area of modern ecumenics and is a member of the Faith and Order Advisory Group of the General Synod of the Church of England.

Hugh Feiss is a monk, priest, and librarian at Mount Angel Abbey, Saint Benedict, Oregon. In addition to his own scholarly work, Father Feiss has translated work by Peter of Celle, Achard of Saint Victor, Hildegard of Bingen, and Thomas of Cantimpré. He has published widely in the diverse areas of medieval theology and spirituality, manuscript studies, library science, and local history.

Bernard Hamilton is professor of crusading history at the University of Nottingham, and has worked on Middle Eastern as well as European sites. Among his books are *Medieval Inquisition* (1981), *The Latin Church in the Crusader States* (1980), *Latins and Greeks in the Eastern Mediterranean* (1989), and *Religion in the Medieval West* (1986).

Phyllis Jestice is Assistant Professor of History at the University of California, Davis. Her doctoral studies at Stanford University led her to concentrate her research on the monastic intellectual and social life of the ninth-eleventh centuries, particularly within the german empire and its satellites, with special attention to the compartmentalization of religious communites in that period. Her research has recently been concentrated on sources for the development of devotion to the humanity of Christ during the eleventh century.

Terryl N. Kinder combines the careers of editor of *Cîteaux: commentarii cistercienses*, archaeologist, and consultant to cistercian site work in France. Her early research on the abbey of Pontigny proved so fascinating that she has continued to study this largest of twelfth-century cistercian abbey churches while making her home in its shadow. Co-director of an ambitious exhibit of cistercian artifacts mounted by the French government to celebrate the nine-hundredth anniversary of the birth of Saint Bernard (1990), she is also co-editor of its catalogue, *Saint Bernard et le monde cistercien*, now in its second edition.

Michael Martin is a student in the graduate program of the Medieval Institute, Western Michigan University, and research assistant at Cistercian Publications.

Bernard McGinn is Naomi Shenstone Donnelley Professor at the Divinity School of the University of Chicago and a well known author in the field of medieval religious studies. Among the various subjects of his monograph studies are Isaac of Stella, Meister Eckhart, and Joachim of Fiore. His studies cover the fields of medieval spirituality, apocalypticism, and cistercian anthropology. His multi-volume History of Christian Spirituality (published in collaboration with Jean Leclercq and John Meyendorff) and his History of Christian Mysticism (two volumes to date) have opened what was until recently a specialized field to general readers and new generations of students. He is also Editor-in-Chief of the Classics of Western Spirituality series.

Brian Patrick McGuire is *lektor* in medieval history and Latin at the University of Copenhagen. A graduate of the University of California, Berkeley, and of Oxford University, where he worked under R. W. Southern, Dr McGuire is particularly well-known for his work on the theory and practice of friendship in late antiquity and the Middle Ages. Besides his work on the Cistercians in Denmark and Aelred of Rievaulx, he has written a bi-lingual *Guide to Medieval Denmark* (1994) and has worked, with his wife, Ann Pedersen, in securing the rights of asylum applicants in Denmark.

Thomas Renna is Professor of History at Saginaw Valley State University in Michigan. Long engaged in a study of the monastic, particularly cistercian, exegesis and typology of Scripture, Professor Renna has also published *Church and State in Medieval Europe* (1974) and numerous articles on medieval and patristic thought.

Dorette Sabersky practises at the Institute of Contemporary Psychoanalysis in Los Angeles. Her training in psychology followed several years of philological studies on the affective style of Bernard of Clairvaux. A native of Switzerland, she received her doctorate from the University of Zurich. Her work on the the rhetorical figure of paranomasia in the works of Bernard (Fribourg/Sw, 1979) first caught the attention of Jean Leclercq. Bringing her two disciplines together in her article, she provides new insights into Bernard's experience of grief at the death of his brother Gerard.

John R. Sommerfeldt is a professor of history at the University of Dallas. He was the founding Director of the Medieval Institute, Executive Director of the Institute of Cistercian Studies, and Director of the Centre for Contemplative Studies at Western Michigan University. He continues the work he began during his graduate studies on cistercian intellectual history in numerous articles and monograph guides to the thought of Bernard of Clairvaux, Aelred of Rievaulx, and other early cistercian theologians.

Columba Stewart is a Benedictine monk of Saint John's Abbey and Associate Professor of Theology at Saint John's University, Collegeville, Minnesota. He has studied at Harvard, Yale, and Oxford Universities, and recently spent a year in residence at the École Biblioque in Jerusalem. In addition to numerous articles, he has published two book: *Working the Earth of the Heart: The Messalian Controversy in History, Texts and Language to ad 431* (1991) and *The World of the Desert Fathers*, a translation of the Anonymous Series of the *Apophthegmata Patrum* (1986). At present he is completing a study of the monastic theology of John Cassian.

Emero Stiegman is emeritus Professor of Religious Studies at Saint Mary's University, Halifax Nova Scotia. A native of New Orleans, Professor Stiegman wrote his dissertation at Fordham University on 'The Language of Asceticism in St. Bernard of Clairvaux's *Sermones super cantica canticorum*'. In subsequent essays he has attempted to disclose the spirituality underlying the forms and formulae of classic monasticism. Attempting to facilitate dialogue between theologians and art historians, Professor Stiegman immersed himself in the study of architectural history, drawing out the theological implications of cistercian aesthetics. He has recently published a detailed commentary on Bernard's treatise *On Loving God* (1995).

Suzanne Wemple is emerita Professor of History at Columbia University and a well-known scholar in the history of the Early Middle Ages and of medieval women. Among her publications are *Atto of Vercelli: Church State and Christian Society in Tenth-century Italy* (1979) and *Women in Frankish Society: Marriage and the Cloister* (1981). Now retired, she divides her time between New York and Florida and continues her scholarly work.

Helen Zakin is Professor of Art History at the State University of New York, Oswego. Her landmark work on *French Cistercian Grisaille* Glass appeared in 1979. More recently she was been working with the American Committee of the Corpus Vitrearum in cataloguing medieval and renaissance stained glass in american collections.

CISTERCIAN PUBLICATIONS, INC.

TITLES LISTING

CISTERCIAN TEXTS

THE WORKS OF BERNARD OF CLAIRVAUX

Apologia to Abbot William
Five Books on Consideration: Advice to a Pope
Grace and Free Choice
Homilies in Praise of the Blessed Virgin Mary
The Life and Death of Saint Malachy the Irishman
Love without Measure. Extracts from the Writings of St Bernard (Paul Dimier)
On Loving God
The Parables of Saint Bernard (Michael Casey)
Sermons for the Summer Season
Sermons on the Song of Songs I - IV
The Steps of Humility and Pride

THE WORKS OF WILLIAM OF SAINT THIERRY

The Enigma of Faith
Exposition on the Epistle to the Romans
Exposition on the Song of Songs
The Golden Epistle
The Nature of Dignity of Love

THE WORKS OF AELRED OF RIEVAULX

Dialogue on the Soul
The Mirror of Charity
Spiritual Friendship
Treatises I: On Jesus at the Age of Twelve, Rule for a Recluse, The Pastoral Prayer
Walter Daniel: The Life of Aelred of Rievaulx

THE WORKS OF JOHN OF FORD

Sermons on the Final Verses of the Songs of Songs I - VII

THE WORKS OF GILBERT OF HOYLAND

Sermons on the Songs of Songs I-III
Treatises, Sermons and Epistles

OTHER EARLY CISTERCIAN WRITERS

The Letters of Adam of Perseigne I
Baldwin of Ford: Spiritual Tractates I - II
Gertrud the Great of Helfta: Spiritual Exercises
Gertrud the Great of Helfta: The Herald of God's Loving-Kindness
Guerric of Igny: Liturgical Sermons I - II
Idung of Prüfening: Cistercians and Cluniacs: The Case of Cîteaux
Isaac of Stella: Sermons on the Christian Year
The Life of Beatrice of Nazareth
Serlo of Wilton & Serlo of Savigny
Stephen of Lexington: Letters from Ireland
Stephen of Sawley: Treatises

MONASTIC TEXTS

EASTERN CHRISTIAN TRADITION

Besa: The Life of Shenoute
Cyril of Scythopolis: Lives of the Monks of Palestine
Dorotheos of Gaza: Discourses
Evagrius Ponticus:Praktikos and Chapters on Prayer
The Harlots of the Desert (Benedicta Ward)
John Moschos: The Spiritual Meadow
The Lives of the Desert Fathers
The Lives of Simeon Stylites (Robert Doran)
The Luminous Eye (Sebastian Brock)
Mena of Nikiou: Isaac of Alexandra & St Macrobius
Pachomian Koinonia I - III
Paphnutius: A Histories of the Monks of Upper Egypt
The Sayings of the Desert Fathers
Spiritual Direction in the Early Christian East (Irénée Hausherr)
Spiritually Beneficial Tales of Paul of Monembasia
Symeon the New Theologian: The Theological and Practical Treatises & The Three Theological Discourses
The Syriac Fathers on Prayer and the Spiritual Life (Sebastian Brock)

WESTERN CHRISTIAN TRADITION

Anselm of Canterbury: Letters I - III
Bede: Commentary on the Seven Catholic Epistles
Bede: Commentary on the Acts of the Apostles
Bede: Homilies on the Gospels I - II
Gregory the Great: Forty Gospel Homilies
The Meditations of Guigo I, Prior of the Charterhouse (A. Gordon Mursell)
Guigo II the Carthusian: Ladder of Monks and Twelve Meditations
Handmaids of the Lord: The Lives of Holy Women in Late Antiquity and the Early Middle Ages (Joan Petersen)
Peter of Celle: Selected Works
The Letters of Armand-Jean de Rancé I - II
The Rule of the Master
The Wound of Love: A Carthusian Miscellany

CHRISTIAN SPIRITUALITY

Abba: Guides to Wholeness & Holiness East & West
A Cloud of Witnesses: The Development of Christian Doctrine (D.N. Bell)
Athirst for God: Spiritual Desire in Bernard of Clairvaux's Sermons on the Song of Songs (M. Casey)
Cistercian Way (André Louf)
Drinking From the Hidden Fountain (Spidlék)
Eros and Allegory: Medieval Exegesis of the Song of Songs (Denys Turner)
Fathers Talking (Aelred Squire)
Friendship and Community (B. McGuire)
From Cloister to Classroom
Herald of Unity: The Life of Maria Gabrielle Sagheddu (M. Driscoll)
Life of St Mary Magdalene and of Her Sister St Martha (D. Mycoff)
The Name of Jesus (Irénée Hausherr)
No Moment Too Small (Norvene Vest)
Penthos: The Doctrine of Compunction in the Christian East (Irénée Hausherr)
Rancé and the Trappist Legacy (A.J. Krailsheimer)
The Roots of the Modern Christian Tradition
Russian Mystics (S. Bolshakoff)
The Spirituality of the Christian East (Tomas Spidlík)
Spirituality of the Medieval West (André Vauchez)
Tuning In To Grace (André Louf)
Wholly Animals: A Book of Beastly Tales (D.N. Bell)

TITLES LISTING

MONASTIC STUDIES

Community & Abbot in the Rule of St Benedict I - II (Adalbert De Vogüé)
Beatrice of Nazareth in Her Context (Roger De Ganck)
The Call of Silent Love, Carthusian Novice Conference
The Finances of the Cistercian Order in the Fourteenth Century (Peter King)
Fountains Abbey & Its Benefactors (Joan Wardrop)
A Gathering of Friends: Learning & Spirituality in John of Forde
The Hermit Monks of Grandmont (Carole A. Hutchison)
In the Unity of the Holy Spirit (Sighard Kleiner)
The Joy of Learning & the Love of God: Essays in Honor of Jean Leclercq
Monastic Practices (Charles Cummings)
The Occupation of Celtic Sites in Ireland by the Canons Regular of St Augustine and the Cistercians (Geraldine Carville)
Reading Saint Benedict (Adalbert de Vogüé)
The Rule of St Benedict: A Doctrinal and Spiritual Commentary (Adalbert de Vogüé)
The Rule of St Benedict (Br. Pinocchio)
Towards Unification with God (Beatrice of Nazareth in Her Context, II)
St Hugh of Lincoln (D.H. Farmer)
Serving God First (Sighard Kleiner)
The Way of Silent Love
With Greater Liberty: A Short History of Christian Monasticism and Religious Orders
The Wound of Love: A Carthusian Miscellany

CISTERCIAN STUDIES

A Difficult Saint (B. McGuire)
A Second Look at Saint Bernard (J. Leclercq)
Bernard of Clairvaux and the Cistercian Spirit (Jean Leclercq)
Bernard of Clairvaux: Man, Monk, Mystic (M. Casey) Tapes and readings
Bernard of Clairvaux: Studies Presented to Dom Jean Leclercq
Bernardus Magister
Christ the Way: The Christology of Guerric of Igny (John Morson)
Cistercian Sign Language
The Cistercian Spirit
The Cistercians in Denmark (Brian McGuire)
The Cistercians in Scandinavia (James France)
The Eleventh-century Background of Cîteaux (Bede K. Lackner)
Image and Likeness: The Augustinian Spirituality of William of St Thierry (D.N. Bell)
An Index of Authors & Works in Cistercian Libraries in Great Britain I (D.N. Bell)
An Index of Cistercian Authors and Works in Medieval Library Catalogues in Great Britain (D.N. Bell)
The Mystical Theology of St Bernard (Etiénne Gilson)
Nicolas Cotheret's Annals of Cîteaux (Louis J. Lekai)
The Spiritual Teachings of St Bernard of Clairvaux (J.R. Sommerfeldt)
Studiosorum Speculum
William, Abbot of St Thierry
Women and St Bernard of Clairvaux (Jean Leclercq)

MEDIEVAL RELIGIOUS WOMEN

Lillian Thomas Shank and John A. Nichols, editors

Distant Echoes
Peace Weavers
Hidden Springs: Cistercian Monastic Women, 2 Vol.
What Nuns Read: Books & Libraries in Medieval English Nunneries (D.N. Bell)

STUDIES IN CISTERCIAN ART AND ARCHITECTURE

Meredith Parsons Lillich, editor

Volumes II, III, IV now available

THOMAS MERTON

The Climate of Monastic Prayer (T. Merton)
The Legacy of Thomas Merton (P. Hart)
The Message of Thomas Merton (P. Hart)
Thomas Merton: The Monastic Journey
Thomas Merton Monk (P.Hart)
Thomas Merton Monk & Artist (Victor Kramer)
Thomas Merton on St Bernard
Toward an Integrated Humanity (M. Basil Pennington et al.)

CISTERCIAN LITURGICAL DOCUMENTS SERIES

Chrysogonus Waddell, ocso, editor

Hymn Collection of the Abbey of the Paraclete
Institutiones nostrae: The Paraclete Statutes
Molesme Summer-Season Breviary (4 volumes)
Old French Ordinary and Breviary of the Abbey of the Paraclete: Text & Commentary (2 vol.)
The Cadouin Breviary (two volumes)
The Twelfth-century Cistercian Psalter
The Twelfth-century Usages of the Cistercian Lay-brothers
Two Early *Libelli Missarum*

Cistercian Publications is a non-profit corporation. Its publishing program is restricted to monastic texts in translation and books on the monastic tradition.

North American customers may order these books through booksellers or directly from the warehouse:

Cistercian Publications (Distributor)
St Joseph's Abbey
Spencer, Massachusetts 01562
tel: (508) 885-8730 ❖ fax: (508)-885-4687

Editorial queries and advance book information should be directed to the Editorial Offices:

Cistercian Publications
Institute of Cistercian Studies
Western Michigan University
Kalamazoo, Michigan 49008
tel: (616) 387-8920 ❖ fax: (616)-387-8921

A complete catalogue of texts in translation and studies on early, medieval, and modern monasticism is available at no cost from Cistercian Publications.